ORGANIZATIONAL REALITY

Reports from the Firing Line

FOURTH EDITION

PETER J. FROST
University of British Columbia

VANCE F. MITCHELL
Embry-Riddle Aeronautical University

WALTER R. NORD
University of South Florida

 HarperCollins*Publishers*

To Nola, Fran, and Ann

Sponsoring Editor: Debra Riegert
Project Coordination and Cover Design: York Production Services
Cover Photo: © Jeff Smith 1985
Production Manager: Michael Weinstein
Compositor: York Production Services
Printer and Binder: R. R. Donnelley & Sons Company
Cover Printer: The Lehigh Press, Inc.

Organizational Reality: Reports from the Firing Line, Fourth Edition
Copyright © 1992 by HarperCollins Publishers Inc.

Library of Congress Cataloging-in-Publication Data

Organizational reality : reports from the firing line / [edited by]
    Peter J. Frost, Vance F. Mitchell, Walter R. Nord. — 4th ed.
      p. cm.
   ISBN 0-673-46173-4
   1. Organizational behavior. I. Frost, Peter J. II. Mitchell,
Vance F. III. Nord, Walter R.
HD58.7.074 1992
650—dc20   91-29085
                                             CIP

91 92 93 94 9 8 7 6 5 4 3 2 1

Contents

Preface

*T*he enthusiasm with which the previous editions of this book have been greeted by colleagues, students, and practicing managers far exceeded our initial expectations. The contrast between organizational life as presented in academic texts and the "reality" that emerges from the essentially nonacademic literature from which so many of our selections are drawn has provided a rich and flexible basis for teaching. The regularity with which students read well beyond assigned material and draw on their additional reading for class discussions attests to their reception of the book. Practitioners have also responded enthusiastically; managers frequently tell us that many of the readings describe "their" organization.

We do not believe the views presented in most academic textbooks are irrelevant. In fact, we believe that many of these normative views are both informative and potentially useful in solving organizational problems. However, it is ineffective to present them to students without complementary information about how organizations are experienced. This book attempts to fill that need for complementary information with a collection of articles, short stories, and plays about people in organizations.

The picture of organizations presented here is different from that portrayed in conventional textbooks because we draw on a wider variety of perspectives. We include ideas from organization behavior theorists, managers, service workers, blue-collar workers, poets, and short story writers. Moreover, we have intentionally placed more emphasis on the concerns of nonmanagerial employees than do conventional textbooks.

Since our objective is to convey human experiences, rather than to survey academic discourse about research and theory, this book, unlike the typical textbook, uses colloquial language and pays considerable attention to the emotional side of organizations. (We believe that emotions play a central role in organizational dynamics, a role that has not been appreciated fully by organizational theorists.) We predict, based on the experiences of ourselves and of others who have used our materials, that this book will arouse a broad set of feelings.

We pay careful attention to the sources of the articles included in this collection. Many of the selections come from what normally are considered mainstream business publications such as *Fortune,* the *Harvard Business Review,* and *The Wall Street Journal.* For example, the book includes "Environmentalism: The New Crusade" from *The Wall Street Journal* and "Managing Without Managers" from the *Harvard Business Review.* Other selections come from fictional works, academic texts and journals, and best-selling books. Still, a number of selections were written by critics of organizations and individuals who are discontented with many elements of modern life. Finally the book also includes selections from non-managerial journals such as American Sociologist and the Journal of Occupational Mental Health. We believe these selections, taken together, provide a useful picture of a number of aspects of modern organizations.

WHAT'S NEW

Over 60 percent of the selections in this edition are new. Although a number of favorites (yours and ours) remain, the fourth edition is substantially different from the third. In a number of instances, the selections we dropped were dated and have been replaced by more contemporary material. Other substitutions seemed to us more representative of the organizational reality we seek to present. A few selections that appeared in the first or second editions but were omitted from the third have been "recalled" at the request of many colleagues.

We have added a chapter (Ch. 1) dealing with entrepreneurs—those whose scale of operation is small and those who work in large corporations or on a global basis. We have created this section in response to the widespread recognition of the need for entrepreneurial behavior in our society and to illustrate that entrepreneurs do exist in many places.

While previous editions have contained a number of selections dealing with ethics, we have elected to provide a separate section (Ch. 4) highlighting this important topic since so many instances of unethical business behavior have been noted in the media. Moreover, the reader will find numerous ethical questions that surface elsewhere throughout the book.

Another new chapter (9) contains selections on secrecy in organizations. Finally, we have included a chapter on academic life in recognition of the widespread criticism of our colleges and universities.

We have reorganized the book substantially to include sections on topics of contemporary importance. Perhaps the most important of these new chapters is that concerned with the environment (Ch. 16) and the urgency with which we need to address the ill-health of our planet.

Increasing attention is being given to international business and management. Most traditional texts confine themselves to the economic and institutional aspects of international operations. The impact on individuals, however, more often than not is ignored. For this reason we have included a section (Ch. 12) devoted to the human considerations.

PEDAGOGY

The introduction to each chapter provides a rationale for our choices and a brief overview of the selections.

INSTRUCTOR'S MANUAL

We provide as a supplement to the book an Instructor's Manual, written jointly, that provides suggestions for the use of each selection either as a mini-case, as the basis for a role play or an essay, or for class discussion. Frequently we include suggested questions for discussion. We also provide suggestions for using two or more selections together and for which course topics individual selections are appropriate.

ACKNOWLEDGMENTS

This book is the product of the efforts of many people. Once again, our contributions have been distributed equally throughout the book, and the ordering of names on the title page is simply a carry-over of the random selection procedures followed in preparing the first edition. Of course, no book is solely attributable to those whose names appear on the title page, and this book is no exception.

Sincere thanks to our colleagues at the University of British Columbia—Diana Cawood, Dianne Cyr, Carolyn Egri, Paul Frost, and Larry Schetzer; to Bob Berra of Washington University, Fiona Crofton of Simon Fraser University, and Bob Quinn of the University of Michigan for material they sent our way that, in one form or another, found its way into this edition. Special thanks to Mark Maier of SUNY Binghamton for bringing to our attention "The Child and the Starfish," "The Cormorant" and poems by Natasha Josefowitz of the University of Massachusetts. We owe a debt of gratitude to the many university and professional students in our courses whose reaction to the previous editions guided this revision and served as a prod to our endeavor. We also thank the many astute and articulate students of organizations whose reports comprise this book.

We are grateful also for the valuable suggestions provided by William Haiel of George Washington University, Jay Knippen of the University of South Florida, Mark Maier of SUNY Binghamton, Mick McGill of Southern Methodist University, Glenn Pearce of Virginia Commonwealth University, B. Kay Snavely of Miami University, Peggy Snyder of the California State Polytechnic University, and Trudy Somers of Towson State University who reviewed the preliminary manuscript.

Thanks to Naslishah Alizada, Jennifer Bartolome, Renae Battaglia, Wendy

Bishop, Sharon Brooks, Karen Clark, Sarah Gaze and Kerry Sizer for technical and secretarial assistance.

Debra Riegert, our editor, has been a continuing source of support and encouragement. Finally, our deep thanks to Angela Gladfelter, project editor, who shepherded this book through with grace, good humor, and skill.

Peter J. Frost
Vance F. Mitchell
Walter R. Nord

Introduction

Suppose that you are a visitor to Earth from the distant planet Utopia. One of your assignments is to bring back printed materials to Utopian scholars who are attempting to understand what Earthlings call "formal organizations." You have limited space, so you must choose very carefully. One option is to bring back one or two of the leading textbooks on organizational behavior. Another is to bring back articles, short stories, and plays about life in organizations. Which would you choose?

If you choose the textbooks, the scholars will most likely come to view organizations as systems that are managed in a rational manner in pursuit of certain stated goals. They will likely conclude that members of organizations are usually committed to achieving these objectives, oriented towards cooperation and concerned with each other's well-being. Another possibility, depending on the particular textbook you bring back, is that the scholars will conclude that organizations do not, in fact, operate rationally and cooperatively, but that, through the application of a certain set of procedures, techniques, and philosophies, any organization could be made to do so.

By contrast, if you happen to choose this book or almost any collection of materials from nonacademic sources, the scholars will derive quite different pictures. They may conclude that members at all levels of the organization frequently pursue their own interests at the expense of the common organizational goals. The scholars may conclude that individuals experience intense stress from task demands as well as intense, often bitter, conflict with members of their own work group and with members of other work groups and of other organizations. Organizational participants may be viewed as responding aggressively against these pressures and against whatever threatens their own interests. Furthermore, it is unlikely that the scholars will discern any set of principles, techniques, and philosophies that can convert organizations into rational, cooperative systems.

Most courses in organizational behavior, introductory business, and even management policy are based on textbooks and professional journals. Many students soon learn from job experience that the organizations described in their course work are not the same as organizations in the real world. These students may reject the organizational behavior field as soft, theoretical, or irrelevant and turn to accounting, finance, economics, information systems, or marketing for useful information about organizations. Other students accept text material while in school but never find ways to translate it into action when they become managers.

We do not believe the views presented in most academic textbooks are irrelevant. In fact, we believe that many of these normative views are both informative and potentially useful in solving organizational problems. However, it is ineffective to present them to students without complementary information about how organizations are experienced. This book attempts to fill that need for complementary information with a collection of articles, short stories, and plays (or whatever) about people in organizations.

The picture of organizations presented here is different from that portrayed in conventional textbooks because we draw on a wider variety of perspectives. We include ideas from organization-behavior theorists, managers, service workers, blue-collar workers, poets, and short story writers. Moreover, we have intentionally placed more emphasis on the concerns of nonmanagerial employees than do conventional textbooks.

Since our objective is to convey human experiences, rather than to survey academic discourse about research and theory, this book, unlike the typical textbook, uses colloquial language and pays considerable attention to the emotional side of organizations. (We believe that emotions play a central role in organizational dynamics, a role that has not been appreciated fully by organizational theorists.) We predict, based on the experiences of ourselves and of others who have used our materials, that this book will arouse a broad set of feelings.

Any claim that our perspective captures the true nature of organizational life better than others would be presumptuous and impossible to support. Nevertheless, we believe there is some justification for using "reality" in our title.

Basically we are talking about social reality. We believe that a considerable portion of what is taken to be reality in the social world is created by humans themselves, from how they think, talk, and feel about their experiences. In the language of leading scholars such as Berger, Luckman, and Weick, social reality is "socially constructed."[1] Because there is a wide variety of human experiences, there are many different "social realities." We have sought to present a diverse set of thoughts, feelings, and perspectives. A more precise title for this book might be "Some Organizational Realities."

Philosophical issues aside, the reception that previous editions of this book have gotten from colleagues, their students, and our own students, including both workers and executives, leads us to believe that our approach complements traditional textbooks in exciting and informative ways. We hope that this updated collection will serve the same function.

Peter J. Frost
Vance F. Mitchell
Walter R. Nord

[1]See P. L. Berger, and T. Luckman (1967). *The Social Construction of Reality*. (Garden City, N.Y.: Doubleday, Anchor Books); K. Weick (1979). *The Social Psychology of Organizing*, 2nd ed. (Reading, Mass.: Addson-Wesley).

Chapter

1

Entrepreneurs

A number of doomsayers in recent years have decried the decline of entrepreneurship. Yet, we continue to find examples reported in the media of individuals who had an idea and made it grow into a flourishing and profitable undertaking. It seems that far from declining, entrepreneurship is alive and flourishing.

In this chapter, we include five illustrations of entrepreneurial success. In each of these selections, someone has had an idea and by following the entrepreneurial spark and working hard that idea has been transformed into a viable reality.

Our first selection, "Life in the Curb Lane," reports the experiences of a reporter who worked briefly as a bike courier, a business that sprang up following the oil crisis in the early 1970s. Bike couriers have continued to flourish as a means of providing quick deliveries not otherwise possible in the congested streets of our biggest cities.

It takes something more than routine entrepreneurial spark to found a company, establish subsidiaries in four countries, and raise the capital required before you have a product to sell. "Global Start-Up" is the story of how a French electronics engineer with little business experience did just that in the face of seemingly insurmountable obstacles. What is more, the company's first two products have revolutionized the treatment of two serious and life-threatening common ailments. The products are now sold and used world-wide.

Our next selection is the story of yet another expansion into a new and highly profitable undertaking by Walt Disney Enterprises. "Every Store Is a Stage" tells us how an innovative entry into the retail industry is paying off.

Bo Burlingham describes Anita Roddick's continuing struggle to keep The Body Shop responsive to challenges in "This Woman Has Changed Business Forever." The Body Shop is one of the most heralded and rapidly growing new organizations on the contemporary business scene. Helping such an organization to

1

stay successful over the long term is an aspect of entrepreneuring that tends to test fully the capabilities and ingenuity of a founder.

"Spotting a Golden Niche" relates a classic case of "a light going on in some-one's head" and the follow-up that translated that "light" into a million dollar busi-ness that is still growing. The niche that was spotted was to sell the vacant advertis-ing space in Yellow Pages telephone directories to national advertisers for inclusion in as many of the Yellow Page directories as possible. The story of how this idea was brought to reality is a fascinating account of entrepreneurship.

Truly, entrepreneurship can be found in many places, from the daring and insightful ideas of individuals to the continuing search for profitable innovations within large corporations.

Life in the Curb Lane

Jared Mitchell

Neither heat waves, nor rude receptionists, nor ambushes by car doors will slow a bicycle courier on his appointed rounds.
Our fearless reporter found there's plenty of pride in the trade, though not much of a living.

My short career as a bicycle courier on the streets of downtown Toronto begins as a lesson in humility. A friend assures me I'm physically unfit to work at Sunwheel Bicycle Couriers Ltd., Canada's largest bike fleet. Fred Budan, Sunwheel's opera-tions supervisor, tells me to dress properly: Shorts must be mid-thigh length and shirts must have sleeves. "You can't walk into First Canadian Place dressed like you're going to the beach," he says. Besides, a scantily dressed, sweaty man can disrupt the concentration of female workers in an office. This at least sounds like an ego boost—until I head out on my first calls. Nearly every woman I encounter studiously ignores me.

I begin to wonder what attracts people to a career in the curb lanes of Bay

"Life in the Curb Lane" by Jared Mitchell, *Report on Business Magazine*, September 1988, p. 50. Reprinted by permission of Jared Mitchell.

Street. It's not the pay; the average courier at Sunwheel collects less than $20,000 annually, and top producers make only about $25,000, all on commission. For that they endure extremes of weather all year round, perilous scrapes with motorists, sometimes hostile stares from office workers and physical exhaustion. Good couriers are hard to find—in addition to stamina, they must have the intelligence to learn the system and keep track of addresses and times, and a thick-enough skin to disregard the lowly status couriers have in the business community. You know you're not welcome when you leave sweat stains on the plush chesterfields of executive suites.

The couriers at Sunwheel are proud of their professionalism, though few believe in cycling as passionately as Sunwheel founder Hilda Tiessen. "Bikes provide so many benefits," she says, "not only exercise but also in terms of pollution and improving the urban congestion." A quiet, thoughtful woman, Tiessen and her partner Barbara Weiner have built the nine-year-old company into Canada's largest bicycle messenger fleet. Starting in 1979 with a federal make-work grant, Tiessen, a former social worker, slogged up and down Bay Street trying to persuade office managers to use her new service. The first year Sunwheel had sales of only $4,000, but even so, the competition took notice. As Sunwheel began to attract a significant customer base, larger motorized services introduced their own bicycle divisions to handle downtown deliveries.

The bicycle courier business developed in big cities such as New York and San Francisco in the early 1970s following the oil crisis, and it's now reaching its full flowering, a sign perhaps of the frenetic pace of doing business today. The only Canadian cities clogged enough to require bicycle deliveries are Vancouver, Montreal, Calgary and Toronto. Couriering as a whole is estimated to be a billion-dollar business nation-wide; the biggest chunk of the market is in Toronto, where the Yellow Pages list nearly 200 services in operation.

Sunwheel makes 1,500 deliveries a day using 55 men and women on bikes and on foot; with an estimated $1.9 million in revenues, it accounts for a third of all courier bicycles on Toronto streets. Overhead costs are low because the couriers themselves must own their own bicycles and pay for all repairs. Unlike motorized fleets that get tied up in traffic, Tiessen's nimble riders guarantee downtown deliveries in one to two hours. Prices compare favorably with the cost of sending items by taxi. A packet sent from the financial district a mile north to Bloor Street costs $3.70 for delivery in two hours, $5.55 within one hour.

After some lessons on professional comportment, filling out waybills and rules of the road, I am ready to hit the road. First there is a cheque for a scrap-metal dealer on Spadina Avenue. Sweating in 33 degree Celsius heat after only two kilometres, I arrive and find the dealer seated at the messiest desk I have ever seen. A horseshoe-shaped stack of papers rises up to his throat. Then I move across town to a Lombard Street law office to drop off mortgage papers. I am supposed to call my dispatcher for more instructions from there. I can't—the telephone in the reception area is being monopolized by a woman telling off her therapist. I head off to my third delivery: a public relations office I once wrote an unflattering article about. They recognize me and take pleasure at seeing me in my new career.

Veteran couriers are more than happy to share their tricks of the trade with me, some of which seem sly and sensible, others merely obvious. Don't, as one new courier did, change your socks in reception areas of Bay Street law offices. And unless you're sure that the doors will open from both sides, never use the stairwells in office towers. "You could be trapped in there for hours," says courier Tom Nicholson, 27. In small, older buildings that have only one doddering elevator, wedge your courier bag in its door so it can't lumber off while you're picking up a package. When passing between a streetcar and a line of parked cars, put your hand on the side of the streetcar for balance. And if a receptionist is ignoring you in favor of her switchboard, turn up the volume on your two-way radio to an obnoxious level.

I quickly learn the difference a good receptionist can make in my day. Most of the ones I encounter are cordial but neutral, and oblivious to the way I'm dressed. Some are not so charming. One of my first is a matron fronting a Bay Street law office who inadvertently reverses the pickup and delivery addresses on the waybill, then glares damningly at me when I arrive empty-handed. When I ask another in a Bloor Street office if I can use her telephone, she claps a proprietary hand on it, as though I had proposed stealing it. In a third office I lean forward to present the receptionist with the waybill and a big dollop of sweat spatters her desk: I try to wipe it away but my grubby fingers leave an oily smear. The receptionist considerately pretends not to notice.

In the sweltering heat, hard cycling exacts its physical toll. Desperate with thirst, I arrive back at Sunwheel at the end of the first day with legs that have turned to jelly. I have discovered the private luxury of pressing my sweaty backside against the cool granite walls of the Toronto Stock Exchange lobby but the relief it provides is short lived.

Even experienced bicycle couriers feel the effects of hard exercise in hostile weather. "You melt down on the job," Nicholson says. Indeed, the back room at Sunwheel is full of underweight couriers, some of whom have lost 20 pounds or more biking. Rail-thin Steve Norlock, 28, recently took a week off work expressly to gain weight. "I gained one pound," he says proudly. One obsessive former employee took up the grueling sport of triathlon—swimming, marathon running and cycling—while he was still a bike courier. He is best remembered for falling asleep against a hydro pole outside the Sunwheel offices while locking up his bike.

I sit down to total up my waybills. Another courier is seated across from me, sucking back a giant bottle of Gatorade. He has completed 28 deliveries. David Miller has been a Sunwheel courier for four years and has become its top producer; today he's done 40 deliveries. Mine add up to only 22 but after enduring unbearable heat and thundering traffic I'm pleased with my effort. Pleased until Budan totes up how much money I've earned: At a straight commission rate of 50%, it is just $40.42 for nine hours' hard biking. I am too tired, dirty and thirsty to care; I just want to go home to bed.

The next day I am determined to beat my previous record. Lunch is reduced to a cheeseburger eaten in a Spadina Avenue phone booth where I am taking down the addresses of new pickups and deliveries from the afternoon dispatcher. Seasoned couriers working with a good dispatcher can handle as many as 15 addresses at a time; novices receive only two or three. The morning dispatcher has already chewed me out for neglecting to pick up a package in the Sunwheel office bound for uptown. It was my mistake, caused by trying to hold the names and addresses of three deliveries in my head at once.

I am becoming increasingly impatient with every little incident that slows me down. On Bloor Street I enter a feverish race with two other couriers for a place to lock up. Like a pack of incontinent dogs, we all dash for the last available tree trunk, 50 metres away. The elevators in Air Canada's nearby offices prove infuriatingly slow. Later, an obese taxi driver on King Street throws open his door, making me slam to a halt. "The scariest noises come from a parked car," Tom Nicholson says of his fear of car doors opening. "It could just be settling after a drive on the highway. But still you go by and it makes a click and scares the hell out of you."

Sunwheel insists its employees behave in a professional and considerate manner, obeying traffic rules and being polite to customers. Even so, bicycle couriers are among the least-loved workers of the downtown core. Early on I encounter a group of professional cyclists known in the trade as "courier scum." Employed by other firms, they ride mountain bikes dangerously fast and wear bandannas around their heads, Aunt Jemima-style. They invariably pass me when I am stopped at red lights. But Toronto's outlaws are a bunch of Maggie Mugginses compared with New York couriers, who have earned a fearsome reputation for screaming down Fifth Avenue blowing whistles at pedestrians lawfully crossing the street. After many pedestrians were injured by cyclists, New York attempted to bar them from certain streets last year.

Though Sunwheel's owners try to distance themselves from courier scum, some of their couriers adopt the label as a matter of perverse pride. "It's a rainy day," Nicholson explains. "You've had a flat tire, so you're dirty, you're wet, you're sweaty, you're pissed off—that's a given—and you walk into an office. Everyone's dressed nice and clean in their corporate best and you realize, 'I'm scum here, I'm courier scum.' "

As much as Tiessen cherishes the business role she's built for bicycles, her company is threatened by new technology: the fax machine. Already one manufacturer boasts in ads that its machines make bicycle couriers "an endangered species." Tiessen's blood pressure rises when she considers the ad, not because it threatens her business, but because it shows packages flying off the back of a bike. "Our couriers would never be so irresponsible," she seethes. Sunwheel's owners believe there will always be a core business for bicycle couriers since much of the trade is in original legal and real estate documents and materials for graphic designers.

For many of the couriers, however, biking doesn't provide much appeal as a life-long career. Most are between other jobs; one recent recruit, for example, is a former stockbroker for Walwyn, Stodgell. Nicholson, who aspires to be a filmmaker, says, "I got this job three years ago as a two-month stopgap." Although Steve Norlock says being a courier is "the most fun I've ever had working," he admits it has a precarious future. "You start thinking about having a family and think 'one car door and you're not going to feed your kids for a month.' "

Exhausted, sweaty and plagued by a thirst that seems unquenchable, I receive the results of my last day on the road: 21 deliveries paying $44.15 for another nine hours' continuous riding. There is one final humiliation. Fred has asked the Sun-wheel dispatchers for an evaluation of my skills as a bike courier. "Not incredibly fast," writes one. "Quite slow," writes another. "Couple of weird route screw-ups." Fred kindly advises me not to take it too hard. I do show potential for improvement, he says. Courier David Miller offers career counselling: "Be more efficient and with a sense of rage, you too can be scum."

Global Start-up

Robert A. Mamis

Why Gérard Hascoët took his company international even before he had a product to sell

Maybe it hadn't been done before, but founder-to-be Gérard Hascoët saw no reason why he shouldn't give it a shot: grab the world in one fell swoop with one fell chunk of seed capital. Set up however many subsidiaries he needed to capture the major markets, cover the rest of the map with a network of company-trained distributors and agents, and do it before the competition caught on. If he had a product he could sell in any country or culture without modification, wasn't it simply a matter of allocating resources?

Yes—provided he could find enough.

The daring business plan that Hascoët unfolded in 1985 established wholly owned subsidiaries in the United States, Italy, Japan, and West Germany virtually at the same time he launched Technomed International, the parent company, in his native France. The four subsidiaries would deal in the lion's share of the high-tech medical market; the leftovers, from the Urals to La Paz, would be attended by four regional managers out of the parent office. Hascoët was so committed to his one-world, one-market concept that in his design of it, even the support staff at Paris headquarters was to be a multinational mix, from the receptionist on up.

"The advantage of *starting* international," Hascoët stressed to acquaintances with enough money and patience to hear his schemes out, "is you establish an

Reprinted with permission, *Inc.*, Magazine, August 1989. Copyright © 1989 by Gold Hirsh Group, Inc., 38 Commercial Wharf, Boston, MA 02110.

international spirit from the very beginning. Ours will not simply be a French company made over; it will be a world company." To be everywhere at once, however, would require some $5.5 million. And he was determined to get it all from individuals, rather than institutions, "because I want to have someone capable of signing a check without referring to a committee."

FIFTEEN REASONS WHY INVESTORS SHOULD HAVE DECLINED

1. There was no product.
2. No market studies had been performed for the proposed product.
3. One competitor was already in the field with an established product, and two others were about to enter.
4. No one had heard of Technomed International beyond Paris, yet its would-be founder projected sales of million-dollar machines to predictably skeptical doctors and hospitals around the world.
5. Before it could be sold in the United States—the world's largest market for medical products, at 40%—each device that Technomed might develop and manufacture would first have to earn approval from the Food and Drug Administration, a lengthy, costly, and possibly unsuccessful process.
6. For the next two largest markets, the product also would have to pass FDA-like scrutiny in Japan and meet rigorous manufacturing standards in West Germany.
7. Hascoët intended to subcontract most of the manufacturing; therefore, costs and schedules would be at the mercy of numerous suppliers in numerous countries with numerous inflation rates.
8. Currency fluctuations would play havoc with revenues.
9. Despite international patents, the machines could be reverse-engineered and duplicated in Taiwan, Singapore, Malaysia, Hong Kong, or even Japan.
10. Somebody else's technology might prove to be better in the end, somebody else's prices lower, somebody else's working capital more plentiful.
11. Attracting good people would be next to impossible; who would leave a good job to take a risk with an unproved chief executive officer?
12. There was no management besides Hascoët himself.
13. Hascoët was trained in electronic engineering, not business.
14. Hascoët saw no need for *anyone* in the company to be trained in business.
15. The French hadn't shown they were all that good at starting risky businesses, in any event.

ONE REASON WHY THEY DIDN'T

In 1985 Hascoët was unmistakably on a mission. At the age of 36, he had just resigned from a 12-year stint in the medical division of Thomson-CGR, a manufacturer and marketer that, Hascoët grew tired of complaining to deaf management ears, "was too much oriented to the French market." The field of diagnostic-imaging systems was expanding rapidly, yet his employer was hardly bothering to pursue it across the border. Not to be denied, Hascoët decided to join the management of an imaginative, farseeing, energetic company that would—his own.

"When you are not diversified with respect to product," he pleaded with the select group of investors he trusted would view it his way, "you have to be diversified with respect to geography. When one area is not generating sales, another will be. If you stick with one market and there is a recession, you're in big trouble. If you have world coverage, you avoid the fluctuation of markets."

Although the author of this worldwide enterprise had little business experience beyond haggling at the flea market, at least he recognized the folly of starting from scratch with insufficient funds. "Looking for money is not a productive activity when you're starting a business," explained Hascoët, who abhorred the thought of having to seek a loan after the seed capital was used up. "Banks don't anticipate the future; they understand only the past—the balance sheet. I have to have enough at the beginning so I won't waste my time thinking about it for at least a year."

"True, I need lots," he granted his audience, "but I promise I will not require more than what I've called for in this plan—$300,000 until the end of June, then $400,000, then a million, and so on." All agreed that Hascoët's aspirations demanded more money than French venturists were used to providing. So the venturists demanded more shares than French entrepreneurs were used to yielding. Six individuals put up most of the capital for 90% of the company; the principal threw in a few hundred thousand dollars of his own for the remaining 10%. Altogether, $5.5 million was pledged, to be disbursed as Hascoët met his business-plan schedules one by one. Technomed International was incorporated at the end of 1985 in a cramped office in downtown Paris. Hascoët has yet to go back to the backers for more capital. But he *has* moved Technomed into two sprawling floors of a new industrial complex on the outskirts of the city.

THE PRODUCT

It so happened that within France's active National Institute of Health and Medical Research (INSERM, something like our own National Institutes of Health), researchers had been pursuing a therapeutic technology that obviates the need for surgery by pulverizing kidney and gallstones from outside the patient's body. The intricate procedure, called lithotripsy (*litho* being Greek for stone, *tripsy* for who knows what), was just what the doctor ordered to get Hascoët off the mark. Devoted to pure research, the government-sponsored laboratory was seeking a commercial enterprise to develop its prototype into a marketable product. INSERM licensed Technomed to take over for a pittance in royalties. Hascoët called his machine-to-be the Sonolith and promised his investors he'd have one ready to sell within six months.

Why didn't Thomson or some other big company pick up the same emerging technology from the same labs for the same song and take the same chance on developing the same product? Because, Hascoët understood from his tour of duty in one, big companies don't think that way. "They don't like to subcontract an idea; they want to be the real father." Then they insist on spending huge amounts in R&D defending their portion of the market. But clinging to a market, Hascoët can now afford to scoff, "is like staring at your front wheel while you ride a bicycle; you observe that it is spinning properly, but you have no view of what lies ahead."

Selling the no-scalpel concept to highly skilled surgeons, whose highly billed dexterity was being replaced by computers, wasn't as tricky as Hascoët had initially feared. The winning appeal was that the machine makes everything easier and safer: you get the same professional fees, but all you have to do is push a button. Pretty soon, though, the surgeons will wise up: sure, who needs us if it can be done by technicians? And that argument is hard to counter. "In 10 years," Hascoët admits, "it *will* be all technicians. In 100 years, with our technology combined with biotechnology, there will be no surgery left."

THE SUBSIDIARIES

The United States constitutes the biggest market for Technomed's technologies, but due to rigid FDA regulations, there was no way to access it immediately. That's why Hascoët felt it was important to open several other markets while getting the FDA process under way. Until the FDA grants approval of a medical device, the manufacturer cannot sell the product to a test site at a profit (the tester is obliged to cough up the rest only after FDA approval). If Hascoët had entered the U.S. market exclusively, there would have been plenty of prestige, but pathetically little cash flow.

Lithotripsy is categorized by the FDA as a technology that is subject to the strictest degree of scrutiny. From the start of clinical trials to the receipt of permission to market the device typically takes at least two years. At first, Hascoët tried to squeeze by on a budget by hiring a specialty firm to steer the project through, but it soon became clear that internal control was needed to speed up the routine and gain on two competitors—Medstone International and Siemens—that had edged ahead in the U.S. market. Simply to meet FDA demands, Technomed has spent more than $2 million. Of the U.S. subsidiary's 37 employees, 6 have been exclusively involved in dealing with the FDA. Few companies Technomed's size fund their own regulatory affairs staff, but it has been worth every centime, Hascoët feels, merely to gain the time. And a corporate decision by anyone else to enter the U.S. marketplace, even with the technology now readily available, means the same tough two years before that company becomes a competitor.

In Italy, though, there was not even an hour's wait. While it contributes only about 7% of world sales, Italy has no health-hazard strictures whatsoever; buy a lithotripter, rent a storefront, and you're in business. Quick to snatch a first-place share there, Technomed created an Italian subsidiary because "the market had exploded in the past few years, and we wanted to be able to channel our sales most efficiently. You want Italians running an Italian business; French guys running an Italian business will not work."

CULTURAL VARIATIONS

Human body parts may be conveniently universal, but, Hascoët found, human market sectors irksomely aren't. Technomed's Japanese subsidiary, for example, cannot sell directly to the end user, as do its other three, because Japanese business protocol dictates that foreign companies deal through native intermediaries. So Technomed has a local distributor making the sales, while the subsidiary provides engineering and support. "In the States," observes Jérôme Lebon, vice-president of international sales, "once you staff your firm with Americans, there's no problem, even if the firm is a subsidiary of a European company. In Japan, however, it's a *big* problem. The perception of what is national is much stronger. The Japanese government and hospitals have to feel they are supported by Japanese people and Japanese firms, because they are far away from everything and feel we might withdraw someday."

In India, though, it's forbidden by law to deal with a distributor; only hospitals have import licenses. And in Germany a foreign product is not readily accepted from a distributorship; it does better if it comes from German speakers who directly represent the company. Even in Paris, Technomed faced conflict: when local customers sought local attention—rush delivery of machines, for example—Hascoët put them off. "I went the opposite way—speed up delivery time to *Japan*. It wasn't easy to explain that our priority had to be where our market was, not where our culture was."

Technomed's two French managers in Japan speak Japanese. "Most Japanese have difficulty with English," Lebon notes, "so knowing Japanese is important. Even though a foreigner can never hope to speak perfect Japanese and will be a foreigner for life, if he wants to have friendly commercial relationships, he'd better speak Japanese."

And if language isn't a barrier, subtle restrictions may be. Technomed has had a hard go of it selling machines in Germany, because stringent standards for electrical wiring—not for therapeutic efficacy—protect native competitors Dornier and Siemens. "Regulations like those discourage small companies like ours from doing business in some countries," Hudson admits. "It would cost thousands of dollars to pass the safety standards of Denmark and Sweden, for instance, and it's not worth the manpower and expense." Nonetheless, this June, Hascoët threw some manpower and expense into setting up his own department of international regulatory affairs, specifically to control the technical aspects of every product in every country where it is or might be sold.

WHAT, ME WORRY?

Slight and wiry, Gérard Hascoët has the coiled-spring air of a person who doesn't tolerate mistakes gladly, especially if made by himself. In any fast-growing company, however, lurks the possibility that the seemingly healthy entity actually is expanding faster than its structure and is in danger of collapsing from within. Technomed's variation on that theme seems safely to have passed. When recruitment lagged, the work force already in place became so overloaded that departments neglected to trade information not only internally, but with subsidiaries, distributors, even customers. Hascoët now has systematized intracompany communications, adapting a quality-circle approach he picked up overseas. Thus do engineers learn business.

France may be strong in basic research and garlic, but the country itself constitutes a scant 5% of the world market for high-tech medicine. Hascoët's (and his financiers') challenge in 1985, therefore, was not whether to do an instantaneous global rollout, but how. Was there, in fact, a market for lithotripters? What if the machines were too expensive, too clumsy, too unprofitable? What if there was no follow-up demand to enhance a therapy-product line? "Gut feelings were my only market study," Hascoët confesses, the logic being that if you ask consultants to do a market study for you and they are *capable of doing it,* you have arrived in that market too late.

Hence, the hurry out of the starting gate. "If I do not have the machine ready to treat patients by the end of June 1986," Hascoët had promised his investors, "you can take the rest of the money and run." The venture team barely had a chance to warm up. Less than six months passed between the day he bought Technomed's first screwdriver to the time the complex production model was plugged in at a hospital in Lyon. Close on the heels of Dornier, Technomed became the second commercial enterprise ever to treat a human with the new technique. And Technomed's was half the price. Credit Hascoët's past with his ability to cost out the product accurately, or there would likely be no Sonolith today.

But whereas in 1986 there was only one competitor in the field of noninvasive therapy, Technomed now faces several worldwide, with Siemens, the big bully, among them. As the market for the machines reveals itself globally, more giants, such as G.E. and Toshiba, undoubtedly will contend. Does Technomed care? "We *welcome* coming up against major players," senior vice-president for marketing and strategy Jean-Luc Boulnois rationalizes. "That's how you gain a market edge cheaply." It's costly for a small company to be first in a market; being slightly behind lets you position your product with features that distinguish it from the competitor's.

As of June 1, 1989, more than 100 Sonoliths had been shipped to 28 different countries, a second therapeutic system had begun selling successfully, and a promising third was in prototype. Technomed International S.A., the parent company, was scheduled to go public this fall on the Bourse in Paris. Should what its founder predicts actually come to pass—sales of $200 million by 1992—the stock will probably do *très bien, merci.*

Hascoët is here to tell us it will. "If after three years you think you can take a rest," he reflects in the language of global business—which he also is learning fast—"you make a big mistake."

Every Store Is a Stage

Christopher Knowlton

Disney outlets are popping up like magic mushrooms in shopping malls around the U.S. and dazzling retailers with their fancy numbers. While specialty stores earn an average of $250 each year for every square foot of their precious floor space, Disney stores do triple that, with a few earning as much as $1,000 a square foot. Mall owners are begging for Disney's business because the rents they charge include a percentage of a store's sales. But Disney is being choosy. Only the nation's premier malls will get a Disney outlet, and they will have to surrender prime space to win one. At the moment, 42 stores are open—sales per store average $2 million—and plans call for 100 shops by 1992 in one of the fastest expansions the trade has ever seen.

What's the big appeal? Disney is creating retail environments with entertainment as their chief motif. Step into a store and you enter a corner of the Magic Kingdom, a land of bright lights and merry sounds packed full of Mickey Mouse merchandise. From a phone at the front of each store you can order the Disney Channel or book yourself into a Disney World hotel.

Disney designers got down on their hands and knees when they laid out the stores, to be sure the sightlines would work for a 3-year-old. The back wall, normally a prime display area, is given over to a large video screen that plays continuous clips from Disney's animated movies and cartoons. Below the screen, at kid level, sit tiers of stuffed animals that toddlers are encouraged to play with. Adult apparel hangs at the front to announce that the store is for shoppers of all ages. Floor fixtures that hold the goods angle inward to steer you deeper into this flashy money trap. Managers spend six weeks in intensive preparatory classes and training before setting foot in their stores, and each sales clerk must attend the Disney University for three days, like every Disney employee.

Garnished with theatrical lighting and elaborate ceiling displays, the stores have relatively high startup and fixed costs, but once up and running they earn pretax margins of more than 15%. That's not bad for an operation that is mainly a marketing tool—stores owned by the Limited, one of the most highly regarded retailers, rarely do better than 14%. Steve Burke, who heads the Disney chain, maintains that a store's first job is promoting the theme parks and other businesses: raking in the money comes second. Says he: "Our whole strategy is making sure people walk out of the store feeling better about Walt Disney than they did when they walked in."

"Every Store Is a Stage" by Christopher Knowlton, *Fortune*, December 4, 1989, p. 132. Reprinted by permission of Fortune. Copyright © 1989 The Time Inc. Magazine Company. All rights reserved.

This Woman Has Changed Business Forever

Bo Burlingham

How Anita Roddick has customers and employees clamoring for her brand of business

Here it is, the start of another bloody *brilliant* decade, and Anita Roddick is worried. So what if *Vogue* has just anointed her a queen of the beauty industry? So what if her chain of eco-conscious cosmetics stores is the toast of England, counting the likes of Princess Diana and Sting among its boosters? So what if her company's shares continue to trade at a frigging 50 times earnings on London's stock exchange? *So bloody what?* These matters are of no interest to Roddick as she charges through the headquarters of The Body Shop International, the company she founded in a storefront 14 years ago.

What's worrying her at the moment is language. You know, *words.* Language is primary, she says, and it makes her nervous to find a whole new vocabulary creeping into her company. For the first time, people are talking about such things as three-year plans, net income, and average sale, and she doesn't like it, not one bit.

Language isn't all she's upset about, either. She's also feeling real annoyance, she says, at this obsession with meetings. "We're getting to a point where we can't fart without calling a meeting. And if I'm bored by them, and I run the bloody thing, Christ knows what other people must be thinking."

Then there's the problem of people spilling coffee on the new carpeting at headquarters, another thing that's been bugging her lately. Not that coffee stains rank high on her list of global concerns. But that's beside the point. "It's a symbol, a metaphor for a whole way of thinking. That lack of housekeeping, that lack of care. We talk about being lean and green. We deny that we have a fat-cat mentality, but I can see it creeping in. The paper that's wasted. The lights left on after a meeting. What it comes down to is arrogance. We think we're so brilliant, we're so successful that anything we do is all right, and that attitude really pisses me off."

If success is at the root of Roddick's worries, she has cause for concern. The Body Shop is already a legend in the United Kingdom, where the tale is told of a

33-year-old housewife with two young daughters, a husband yearning for adventure, and an idea for a store that would feature natural lotions and potions for the body. With a £4,000 ($6,400) bank loan, she and her husband proceeded to get the shop up and running, whereupon he took off for South America. By the time he returned 10 months later, the business had gone from one shop to two, and there was no turning back.

Nor did the pace slacken thereafter. For over a decade sales and profits continued to grow on average some 50% a year. By the end of fiscal year 1990, pretax profits had climbed to an estimated $23 million on sales of $141 million—despite the onset of a withering recession in British retailing. And here's the beauty part: in all likelihood, The Body Shop's *real* growth lies ahead.

That's because the company has barely begun to tap its potential overseas. Although it operates successfully in 37 countries, about 75% of its profits still come from its U.K. stores. The balance is shifting, however. For 13 years, The Body Shop has been acquiring experience abroad. Now, a number of the foreign operations are approaching the critical mass a retail chain needs to explode in a market. Meanwhile, after years of preparation, the company is beginning to make its big push in the United States, with Japan set to follow. And there's still room for expansion in such established markets as Canada, Germany, and the United Kingdom.

Even a professional skeptic, moreover, has trouble finding weaknesses that might keep The Body Shop from realizing these opportunities. "We're talking about a company that is capable of sustaining a growth rate of 40% to 50% per annum, not just this year or next year, but for 5 or 10 years," says John D. K. Richards, director of retail research at County NatWest Securities Ltd., one of England's leading securities firms.

What's even more extraordinary than The Body Shop's growth record, however, is the effect the company has on the people who come in contact with it. Indeed, it arouses feelings of enthusiasm, commitment, and loyalty more common to a political movement than a corporation. Customers light up when asked about the company and start pitching its products like missionaries selling Bibles. Franchisees, employees, and managers talk about the difficulty they would have going back to work in an "ordinary" company. Here in the United States, some 2,500 people had written in for franchises—before The Body Shop even got its U.S. operation off the ground. It's a kind of magnetism that even affects investment analysts. "I've never seen anything quite like it," says Richards. "The nearest comparison would be something like Flower Power in the 1960s."

The analogy is apt, particularly in the United Kingdom, where The Body Shop is almost as well known for its passionate environmentalism as for its cosmetics. The association goes back a long way. From the start Roddick has incorporated her environmental beliefs into the business—offering only biodegradable products, for example, and providing refillable containers. Today the company even has an Environmental Projects department that monitors its own internal compliance with its stated principles. Beyond that, it has used its shops as the base for a series of highly visible campaigns to save the whales, stop the burning of the rain forest, and so on.

Such activism has, if anything, enhanced The Body Shop's mystique. Once viewed as an intriguing but irrelevant remnant of the 1960s, it has increasingly come to define the mainstream. From the billboards in the London Underground to the advertising on commercial television, British companies now tout their ecological virtues. Far from a curiosity, The Body Shop is the symbol of this new business consciousness.

But environmentalism does not explain the attraction of The Body Shop, not even when coupled with a personality as dynamic as that of Anita Roddick or a manager as capable as her husband, Body Shop chairman Gordon Roddick. On the contrary, people tend to be suspicious of companies that profess devotion to social causes, and with ample reason. When altruism and business lie down together, neither one gets a good night's sleep. Indeed, it's generally expected that neither one will be alive in the morning.

What The Body Shop elicits, however, is the opposite of suspicion. Rather, it is the kind of intense commitment—Anita calls it "electricity and passion"—that companies spend fortunes trying to create, and that may yet make The Body Shop a $1-billion company by 1995. Less clear is how it actually pulls off this bit of alchemy, and Anita is not providing many clues as she races around her headquarters in Littlehampton, England, talking about language and meetings and the fat-cat mentality.

So where does that electricity come from? We are talking, after all, about a chain of stores that sells shampoo and skin lotion. Its success raises questions, not just about technique or strategy, but about some of the most fundamental aspects of business. What do customers really want from a product, and what do they want from the company that makes it? Are they motivated by forces that traditional marketing efforts ignore, and that traditional test-marketing techniques can't pick up? So, too, with employees. What do they want out of work, and what are they looking for in the organizations that provide it? Are they also motivated by forces conventional management techniques simply miss?

Those are perhaps the most important questions confronting business today. What The Body Shop's experience suggests is that it may be time to come up with some new answers.

INFORMATION, PLEASE

Appealing to the hyped-out customer

A sense of electricity and passion is not, in fact, the first thing that hits you when you walk into a Body Shop. It's the smell. A wave of exotic aromas greets you at the door and draws you in. The shop itself is bright and airy, very orderly, but with a whimsical touch. Along the walls are neat rows of products with names like Rhassoul Mud Shampoo. White Grape Skin Tonic, and Peppermint Foot Lotion. What's odd is the packaging. It is almost defiantly plain. Indeed, one whole side of the shop is covered with rows of shampoos and lotions in identical plastic bottles with black caps and green labels.

What's odder still is that no one seems to want to sell you this stuff. The salespeople are pleasant enough and quite knowledgeable about the products, but if you want advice, you have to ask for it. Nor will you find any photographs of beautiful models or promises about the miraculous benefits of using this or that cosmetic.

There is, on the other hand, plenty of information. Containers have clear, factual explanations of what's inside and what it's good for. On the shelves are notecards with stories about the products or their ingredients. There are stacks of pamphlets with such titles as "Animal Testing and Cosmetics" and "What Is Natural?" In a corner is a huge reference book called *The Product Information Manual,* providing background on everything The Body Shop sells. In some shops there's even a television set playing a video at low volume about, say, the company's manufacturing operation or one of its causes.

All of this is, of course, deliberate. In an industry built around selling fantasy, The Body Shop prides itself on selling "well-being." As a matter of stated principle, it pledges "to sell cosmetics with the minimum of hype and packaging" and "to promote health rather than glamour, reality rather than the dubious promise of instant rejuvenation." As for the shops, they are designed to be self-service, though not in the usual sense. Salespeople are expected to be able to answer any questions they might get, but they are trained *not* to be forceful with customers. In a similar spirit, the company refrains from advertising its products. Anita says she'd be embarrassed to spend a lot of money on ads for deodorant and skin lotion.

These policies reflect more than Anita's personal feelings and beliefs, however. They form the basis of the company's marketing strategy. That strategy begins with the premise that standard marketing techniques are increasingly ineffective. Consumers are hyped out. They have been overmarketed. The din of advertising and promotion has grown so loud they can no longer tell one pitch from another. Meanwhile, they are becoming more cynical about the whole process. They have heard too many half-truths, or untruths, from companies trying to move product. It doesn't matter if your particular company has wonderful products and is absolutely truthful in its marketing. Consumers have reached the point where they mistrust whatever they hear from anyone with something to sell.

All of which poses an enormous marketing challenge. How does a company cut through that cynicism and establish credibility with customers?

That's where the information comes in. The Body Shop establishes credibility with its customers by educating them. It tells them everything there is to know about its products: where they come from, how they're made, what's in them, how they're tested, and what they can be used for. It does all this, moreover, with a light touch, using anecdotes, humor, videos, and bright graphics. Few customers suspect they're in a classroom, but that doesn't keep them from learning.

Suppose, for example, that a customer is concerned about safety, as well she might be in buying a product that is applied to the skin. In this case, safety is intimately connected to product development. Most major cosmetics companies develop their products in laboratories. They must then test each product's safety by conducting extensive experiments on animals. The Body Shop, on the other hand, develops its products from ingredients that either are natural or have been used by humans for decades, if not centuries. Through brochures in the shops, it explains to customers in great detail not only what it does, but what it doesn't do—including animal testing. It reinforces the point by marking each container

"Not Tested on Animals." It thus turns a basic consumer issue—safety—into a powerful tool for differentiating its products.

Similarly, The Body Shop uses information about ingredients to differentiate its products. The label on the Rhassoul Mud Shampoo, for example, notes that it is made from "a traditional Moroccan Mud from the Atlas Mountains . . . which has astringent and toning properties." To find such ingredients, Anita travels to the ends of the earth. Several times a year she visits remote areas of Third World countries, where she observes local customs and talks with native people about their methods of skin and hair care. The ideas she gets are incorporated into Body Shop products. Not coincidentally, her trips also produce the information that is used to educate customers in the shops.

All of this information has a cumulative effect. Customers get the message that they can find out anything they care to know about the way the company does business. They can also learn about other cultures, about environmental issues, about social problems—the teaching just won't quit.

"I've just taken what every good teacher knows," says Anita, who is herself a former teacher. "You try to make your classroom an enthralling place. When I taught history, I would put brilliant graphics all around the room and play music of the period we were studying. Kids could just get up, walk around, and make notes from the presentation. It took me months to get it right, but it was stunning. Now, I'm doing the same thing. There is education in the shops. There are anecdotes right on the products, and anecdotes adhere. So I've really gone back to what I know how to do well."

As a marketing strategy, moreover, the approach is extremely effective. It cuts through the cynicism of consumers. It clearly differentiates the company from its major competitors. And it creates significant problems for would-be copycats, who can't easily duplicate the level of information that The Body Shop offers. In short, it provides all of the classic marketing benefits that conventional techniques are increasingly incapable of delivering.

More to the point, it does all that by *humanizing* the company. Customers feel that they are buying from a company whose values and business practices they *know*. The effect is to create a loyalty that goes beyond branding. Customers actively promote the company and its products to their friends, and this word of mouth fuels growth. Meanwhile, The Body Shop has yet to spend a dime (or a shilling) on advertising. Indeed, it does not even have a marketing department—in an industry that is as marketing intensive as any on the face of the earth.

So what happens to the money that would ordinarily be spent on marketing? As it turns out, a large chunk of it is used to do for employees exactly what the company does for its customers.

THE BOREDOM FACTOR

Motivating the Hyped-out Employee

The Body Shop approaches its employees with pretty much the same assumptions that it has about its customers. The operating premise is that people who work for corporations are hyped out. Companies have come up with all kinds of clever techniques for inspiring a work force: compensation and benefit plans, motivational seminars, training programs, you name it. They don't work, or at least they aren't as effective as they once were. As cynical as consumers have become, employees are even more so. It doesn't matter how much you insist that you are committed to their welfare. It doesn't even matter if you believe it. Employees simply don't buy the argument that companies are in business to make their lives better.

And, of course, they're right. Granted, a company may do other things along the way to making a profit—create jobs, for example, or make quality products—but when you come right down to it, business is about making money. The more the better. And employees know it. You can argue that this is just reality, and if employees don't like it, well, that's too damn bad. But it's hard to deny how tough it can be to get anyone very excited about generating profits for someone else.

Many companies attack the problem with equity participation or incentive programs. The Body Shop does all that, too. But such techniques almost always have a catch-22. They work by focusing employees' attention on the very thing that causes the difficulty to begin with: the goal of corporate profitability. It's not that employees don't want their company to be profitable. It's that they don't really care very much. In fact, most of them probably feel pretty much as Anita does. "The idea of business, I'd agree, is not to lose money," she says. "But to focus all the time on profits, profits, profits—I have to say I think it's deeply boring."

Therein lies the crux of the problem. To vast numbers of employees, profits are boring, even if they get a piece of the action. What's more, everything else a company does becomes boring insofar as its real purpose is to maximize profits.

So how does The Body Shop get around this one? It takes more or less the same approach that it uses with customers. It attacks cynicism with information, creating an elaborate system that deluges its employees with newsletters, videos, brochures, posters, training programs, and so on. In this case, however, The Body Shop focuses on teaching its employees that while profits may be boring, business doesn't have to be.

Consider employee training. The Body Shop's training center is its school for employees, located in London. The admissions policy is somewhat unusual in that anyone in the company, including franchisees and their employees, can attend for free. What's more unusual, however, is the school's curriculum. For all the emphasis The Body Shop places on the training, there is virtually no attention paid to making money, or even to selling. The courses for shop personnel, for example, are almost entirely devoted to instruction in the nature and uses of the products. That means everything from Herbal Hair and Problem Skin to Aromatherapy II (Advanced). It's as if McDonald's were to offer free classes in Grades of Beef and Nutrition Counseling to every kid who flips burgers throughout the chain.

The courses obviously help to improve the general level of customer service in the stores, but they are designed with the *employees* squarely in mind. "[Other cosmetics companies] train for a sale," Anita says. "We train for knowledge." And, indeed, the courses have the desired effect. They are so popular with employees that the school can't keep up with the demand.

Anita brings the same attitude to every aspect of The Body Shop's educational system, even to something as basic as the company newsletter. Aside from the format, it has almost nothing in common with other examples of the genre. For one thing, it reads like an underground newspaper. More space is devoted to the company's campaigns to save the rain forest and ban ozone-depleting chemicals than, say, the opening of a new branch or the dropping of an old product. Even the latter, moreover, are handled with humor and flair. The design is dramatic, the graphics arresting. Sprinkled throughout are quotes, bits of poetry, environmental facts, and anthropological anecdotes.

Once again, the difference is Anita. She may be the only chief executive of a $100-million business who actually invests time and energy in the company newsletter. Her brother is part of the team that puts it out, operating from a Macintosh outside her office. She herself suggests articles, checks copy, chooses illustrations, and changes design. The point is not lost on people in The Body Shop. This is not some throwaway. This is a direct line of communication from the leader to the rest of the organization, and she is telling people about all the things that make the business interesting and exciting for her.

Anita, for her part, is almost obsessive about finding new ways to get across what she calls "that real sense of excitement." To her, an empty space is an opportunity to create an atmosphere, deliver a message, make a point. Wherever you go in the company, the walls are hung with photographs, blown-up quotes, charts, and illustrations. Waiting rooms and cafeterias are lined with informational displays. The sides of the warehouse and the corridors of the factories blossom with words and images and dazzling displays of Third World art.

She uses her trips abroad the same way. When she gets back, she will burst into a managers' meeting and regale the participants with tales of her adventures. She will tap into the company grapevine, planting "rumors" (as she puts it) with the "gossips." "I mean that in a positive sense," she says. "It's actually a good way to get the word out." Meanwhile, she will work on her next video and next slide show, through which she will deliver the news to the organization worldwide.

The effect on the company is electric, though not necessarily because the news itself is so riveting. What's riveting is Anita. She is, quite consciously, creating a role model. She wants each and every employee to feel the same excitement she feels. You can learn in business, she is telling them, you can grow, you can be somebody. But to do that, you have to care. "I want them to understand that this is no dress rehearsal," she says. "You've got one life, so just lead it. And try to be remarkable."

And it works. The message gets through, and it gets through for one reason alone: Anita believes it. She is not the least bit cynical about business. Shrewd? Yes. Calculating? In a sense. Manipulative? Often. But cynicism is simply not in her repertoire. She is passionate in her belief that education matters, customer service matters, even newsletters matter—they all matter. There is no hidden agenda here. Anita really doesn't regard these as tools for boosting sales and enhancing profits. She is saying that, to have a successful company, these things have to matter *in their own right.*

More to the point, she has been able to imbue her organization with the same attitude, and the effects are apparent in the shops. Employees understand why it's important to keep a shop clean, to display products well, to treat customers courteously—in short, to take care of all the little details a retailer must get right to be successful. The point is not that these details affect sales or profits, but that they affect customers, and customer service matters for its own sake. Once again, the company is humanized, to the benefit of everyone involved.

A BANNER OF VALUES

Creating a Global Community

On a cold night in January, a ragtag group of environmentalists gathers outside the Brazilian embassy in London. There are about 20 of them, the usual suspects, from such organizations as Friends of the Earth and Survival International. They have come to draw attention to the plight of the Yanomami Indians, a Stone Age tribe that is being wiped out by diseases brought to its remote Brazilian habitat by miners looking for gold. At the moment, however, there is not much attention to be drawn. Aside from an occasional passing taxi, the only people around are the protesters. Among them is Anita Roddick, founder and managing director of The Body Shop International.

She is there, moreover, in her official capacity. Recently her company has engaged in a worldwide campaign that has drawn much attention to the plight of all the inhabitants of the Amazon rain forest. The Body Shop and its franchisees have contributed hundreds of thousands of dollars to their defense. It has mobilized employees for petition drives and fund-raising campaigns, carried out through the stores and on company time. It has produced window displays, posters, T-shirts, brochures, and videotapes to educate people about the issues. It has brought 250 employees to London for a major demonstration at this very embassy—not on a dark night, but in broad daylight, with a television crew broadcasting the event live, via satellite, to Brazil. It has even printed appeals on the side of its delivery trucks, reading: "The Indians are the custodians of the rainforest. The rainforests are the lungs of the world. If they die, we all die. The Body Shop says immediate urgent action is needed."

In the United States such corporate activism would be considered bizarre, if not dangerously radical. In the United Kingdom it draws attention, but it no longer generates much surprise. That's mainly because The Body Shop has been acting this way for years. Long before it launched its rain-forest offensive, after all, it waged similar campaigns against everything from the killing of whales to the repression of political dissidents. Almost as well known, and accepted, are its efforts to help communities in developing countries by setting them up as suppliers under a program it calls Trade Not Aid. Then there's the soap factory it has built in a poverty-stricken section of Glasgow, Scotland, with the explicit (and well-publicized) purpose of providing jobs for people who, in some cases, have been unemployed for upward of 10 years. Not to mention the community project that every shop is required to have and that every shop employee is expected to work in for at least one hour a week—a paid hour, that is, on company time.

Indeed, there is almost no end to the list of such Body Shop activities, most of which have been widely reported in the British press. This inevitably raises a question in the minds of many people, one Anita almost always hears when she appears before business groups. "They want to know, 'Isn't it all public relations? Aren't you just using these campaigns and activities to create more sales and profits?' "

She bristles at the question. "Look," she says, "if I put our poster for Colourings [a line of makeup] in the shop windows, that creates sales and profits. A poster to stop the burning of the rain forest doesn't. It creates a banner of values, it links us to the community, but it will not increase sales. What increases sales is an article in boring *Glamour* magazine saying Princess Diana uses Body Shop products. Then we'll get 7,000 bloody phone calls asking for our catalog. You can measure the effect."

It's a provocative argument, but it's a little misleading. Most of the activities are, in fact, intended to generate publicity for The Body Shop, and the company milks them for all they're worth. Even Anita would admit, moreover, that—over the long term—they do tend to increase sales and, yes, profits. What's most interesting, however, is the way that happens. Indeed, this may be the single most striking aspect of The Body Shop's entire approach to business.

The first thing you have to understand is that the primary audience for these activities is not the public: it is her own work force. The campaigns, which play a major role in her educational program, are anything but random attempts to promote goodwill. They are part of a carefully researched, designed, and executed business strategy. She regularly turns down causes that don't meet her criteria, and she won't launch any campaign until she feels confident of all the facts on the issues involved. She takes these matters far too seriously to adopt a cause that might come back to haunt the company, or to carry it out in less than a thoroughly professional manner.

More to the point, she wants causes that will generate real excitement and enthusiasm in the shops. "You educate people by their passions, especially young people," she says. "You find ways to grab their imagination. You want them to feel that they're doing something important, that they're not a lone voice, that they are the most powerful, potent people on the planet.

"I'd never get that kind of motivation if we were just selling shampoo and body lotion. I'd never get that sort of staying late, talking at McDonald's after work, bonding to customers. It's a way for people to bond to the company. They're doing what I'm doing. They're learning. Three years ago I didn't know anything about the rain forest. Five years ago I didn't know anything about the ozone layer. It's a process of learning to be a global citizen. And what it produces is a sense of passion you simply won't find in a Bloomingdale's department store."

The key word here is *bond.* For Anita is not just educating and motivating employees. She is not just selling cosmetics to customers. She is not just selecting franchisees, or establishing trade links with people in the Third World, or setting up factories to hire the unemployed. She is creating a community, a global community. The common bond, moreover, is not merely a mutual desire to save the Amazon rain forest. Rather, it is a belief that business should do more than make money, create decent jobs, or sell good products. The members of this community believe that companies should actually help solve major social problems—not by contributing a percentage of their profits to charity, but by using all their resources to come up with real answers. Business is, after all, just another form of human enterprise, as Anita argues. So why should we expect and accept *less* from it than we do from ourselves and our neighbors?

There are many people, of course, who would quiver at the prospect of companies becoming social activists. Some would contend that business ought to stick to its collective knitting and do what it does reasonably well. Others would note that, for many companies, knitting well is difficult enough without taking on society's problems in addition to their own. Still others would prefer to leave such matters to nonprofit organizations or to government, which is presumably more accountable for its actions.

But Anita doesn't buy any of those arguments. She believes that there is only one thing stopping business from solving many of the most pressing problems in the world, and it has to do with the way most of us think companies must be managed. That is precisely what she wants to change.

TRADING

Preserving the Start-up Spirit

Anita Roddick is reminiscing in her Littlehampton office. On the wall next to her are photographs of the original Body Shop in Brighton. The company no longer owns the store, she explains, but she is doing everything she can to get it back. "Then we'll put it back exactly the way it was in 1976. It's a real good reminder of the initiative and creativity that counts when you have no money."

Back then, Anita needed all the creativity and initiative she could muster, what with two children at home and her husband in South America pursuing his lifelong dream of riding from Buenos Aires to New York City on horseback. Before he had left, Gordon had run the numbers and told her she had to make £300 a week in order to stay in business. "I said, 'What happens, Gordon, if I don't?' He said, 'Give it six months and then pack it up and meet me with the kids in Peru.'"

So Anita had done all the things people do when they start a business they know nothing about, with no resources to fall back on. She worked around the clock, improvising as she went along. "We had only about 15 or 20 products," she says. "So we had the idea of offering five sizes of containers, which made it look like a bit more. And we had all handwritten labels with explanations of the products. We thought we had to explain them because they looked so bizarre. I mean, there were little black things in some of them. We had to say these were not worms. We were offering honesty of information that we didn't even know was honesty. We thought it was the only way to sell the products."

She goes on, talking about all the crazy things she did in the early days. Leaving a trail of strawberry essence on the street in hopes of luring customers with the smell. Planting a newspaper article about the morticians next door who were trying to shut her down because they thought a store called The Body Shop was bad for their business. Starting a refill service as an ecological way to reduce the need for new containers, which she couldn't afford.

It is obvious, as she talks, that she enjoys the memories. And yet, there is no trace of sentimentality in her reminiscences. She is not yearning for the good old days. Rather, she is remembering her own naïveté, and she is reminding herself how well she did *because* she was naïve. Her innocence, she is saying, led her to do the right thing.

"There was a grace we had when we started—the grace that you didn't have to bullshit and tell lies. We didn't know you could. We thought we had to be accountable. How do you establish accountability in a cosmetics business? We looked at the big companies. They put labels on the products. We thought what was printed on the label had to be truthful. I mean, we were really that naïve."

Anyone who has been involved in a successful start-up understands what she is talking about. There is terror, there is excitement. There is a sense of living by your wits, relying on your instincts, knowing that your dumb mistakes could sink you, hoping that they don't. And there is something else: a kind of simplicity, a clarity of purpose. You have a product, or a service, and everything depends on your ability to get customers to buy it. This is what Anita calls trading. "You set up a business without any understanding of business vocabulary. If you throw away all those words, you have trading going on. That's all it is. Here's a product. Here's the environment. Here's the buyer. Here's the seller."

Business on that level is exciting and rewarding. It is also very human. It is a simple activity centered on direct relationships between people. "I actually see it as ennobling," says Anita. "It's been going on for centuries. It's just buying and selling, with an added bit for me, which is the magical area where people come together—that is, the shop. It's trading. It's making your product so glorious that people don't mind buying it from you at a profit. Their reaction is, 'I love that. Can I buy that?' You want them to find what you are doing so wonderful that they are happy to pay your profit."

But businesses seldom remain on that level, not successful ones at any rate. They grow. They hire employees. They acquire assets and make commitments. Life gets complicated. Management structures are created. Responsibilities are delegated. Control becomes an issue. Reporting systems are developed. Financial discipline is introduced. And along with it comes a new language—the language of budgets and profits, of return on investment and shareholder value. In the process, business ceases to be just trading and becomes, in Anita's words, "the science of making money."

Professional management is the common term for this way of running a company. In the world of business, it is generally considered to be a good thing, not to mention an inevitable and necessary consequence of growth. Without it, we are told, a company can never reach its full potential. Sooner or later, it will be overwhelmed by chaos and die. The only way to avoid that fate—short of selling out or staying small—is to develop sophisticated, financially based management systems, to "cross the threshold" and become a full-fledged, major-league corporation.

But business is charged a steep price for this kind of "success." The bill is paid in the currency of cynicism—the cynicism of customers, of employees, of the community, even of other businesspeople. If companies are in business mainly to make money, you can't fully trust whatever else they do or say. They may create jobs, they may pay taxes and contribute to charity, they may provide an array of goods and services, but all that is incidental to their real purpose: to generate profits for shareholders.

Indeed, cynicism is so much a part of the way we view business that we don't even notice it until it is missing. No matter whether people hate business or love it, they share the same cynical assumptions about it. Then there's Anita Roddick.

Anita simply does not believe that companies need ever cross that threshold and start making decisions by the numbers. She finds it hard to understand why anyone would want to. "That whole goddamn sense of fun is lost, the whole sense of play, of derring-do, of 'Oh, God, we screwed that one up.' I see business as a renaissance concept, where the human spirit comes into play. How do you ennoble the spirit when you are selling moisture cream? It's everything we do before, during, and after we manufacture. It starts with how we look for ingredients. It's the initiative and the care and the excitement. It comes from education and breaking rules. And let me tell you, the spirit soars—God, does it soar—when you are making products that are life serving, that make people feel better and are done in an honorable way. I can even feel great about a moisture cream because of that."

Therein lies the most important lesson The Body Shop has to offer. Business does not have to be drudgery. It doesn't have to be the science of making money. It is something that people—employees, customers, suppliers, franchisees—can genuinely feel great about, but only on one condition: the company must never let itself become anything other than a human enterprise.

Oddly enough, that lesson is not a new one, as Anita often points out. There was a time when the world was filled with companies driven by a vision of improving the human condition. Many were started by Quakers and other people with deeply religious convictions. The managers who ran them were absolutely clear about their responsibilities to customers, to employees, to society as a whole. Some of these companies are still around today.

Along the way, however, something has been lost. "Businesses have forgotten that they are just buyers and sellers," says Anita. "We must never forget that. The whole value of this business lies in keeping it on the level where we know what we're trading. That's why I will never dilute the image of the shop. In our shops, we sell skin and hair care. Period. We know what the customer wants, and we fill those needs."

And that's really the point. It is trading, after all, that makes everything else possible, and yet that is precisely what she fears a traditional style of management would undermine. By establishing financial performance as the goal, it would throw the company off target. It would introduce powerful distractions. It would weaken The Body Shop's focus on the one thing that allowed it to succeed in the first place: its relationship with its customers.

In a sense, everything Anita does is designed to preserve that focus on trading. "What's imperative is the creation of a style that becomes a culture. It may be forced, it may be designed. But that real sense of change, that anarchy—I tell Gordon we need a department of surprises. Whatever we do, we have to preserve that sense of being different. Otherwise, the time will come when everyone who works for us will say The Body Shop is just like every other company. It's big. It's monolithic. It's difficult. This is going to be such a huge company in a few years. We just have to make sure we don't wind up like an ordinary company."

To be sure, her success will depend on many people, not least her husband Gordon, who oversees the operational side of the business. It is a role he has played ever since he returned from his adventure in South America, teaching himself what he needed to learn as he went along. To him, as well as Anita, belongs the credit of demonstrating that a company can be both passionately idealistic and exceptionally well managed. He himself, however, has no doubt where his inspiration comes from. "Creatively, this is Anita's company entirely," he says. "She says what she wants, and we make all her dreams come true."

Meanwhile, the pressures to conform keep growing. They come from shareholders, who want to maximize their earnings. They come from franchisees, who push the company to expand faster than its resources will allow. They even come from some employees and managers, who might be willing to sacrifice a little derring-do for the stability and security they think financial planning would allow. But mostly they come from the world in which The Body Shop operates—a world that doesn't care much about a company's social responsibility or its empowerment of employees if the benefits don't eventually show up on the bottom line.

But Anita has a vision. "I believe quite passionately that there is a better way," she says. "I think you can rewrite the book on business. I think you can trade ethically; be committed to social responsibility, global responsibility; empower your employees without being afraid of them. I think you can really rewrite the book. That is the vision, and the vision is absolutely clear."

And so she fights all the pressures. She fights them with language. She fights them with values. She fights them with education. And she fights them with her vision. "It's creating a new business paradigm," she says. "It's showing that business can have a human face, and God help us if we don't try. It's showing that empowering employees is the key to keeping them, and that you empower them by creating a better educational system. It's showing that you forsake your values at the cost of forsaking your work force. It's paying attention to the aesthetics of business. It's all that. It's trying in every way you can. You may not get there, but goddammit, you try to make the journey an honorable one."

After all, it matters. It all matters. For its own sake.

Spotting a Golden Niche

Pat Annesley

Sometimes the most brilliant ideas are the ones staring us right in the face.

Somebody takes a simple idea that has been staring us all in the face for years, and turns it into a money-making machine. That's my kind of success story.

There's something especially heartening about a couple of guys from Vancouver—*not* part of the local high-rollers scene—who have managed to break into a major U.S. industry. The industry is the Yellow Pages, conservatively worth about $8-billion a year in sales. What Yellow Spots Inc. of Vancouver has done is carve out a piece of those smashing revenues. Just a piece, mind you, but when you figure that if all the Yellow Pages filler space in the United States was sold it would be worth $140-million a year, the prospects are mouthwatering.

The concept is so simple, it's hard to believe it hasn't been tried before. The timing is perfect. And the whole thing is almost certain to make multi-millionaires of the two guys who started it, Arnie Nelson and David Horton. Both guys in their fifties who were getting a little discouraged at the way things were going for them just a few years ago.

They were fraternity brothers, back in their UBC days. Arnie went into broadcast sales, and for a while he was doing very well. David went into the money-lending business with a banking consortium and got hooked on small companies and doing deals. He went out on his own. And he did very well too, for a while. Then the recession came along in 1982 and Arnie lost his job, and David wasn't doing as many deals.

By June of 1985 Arnie had been unemployed for almost two and a half years. He was doing this little project or that little project, trying to put food on the table. He never did qualify for unemployment insurance. David was doing a little better because he still had an office and his usual assortment of irons in the fire. But even he was reduced to trotting out his MBA credentials and doing some consulting work.

On that momentous June morning three and a half years ago, Arnie was sitting in the kitchen of his rented condo in Richmond, looking up something in the Yellow Pages. His eye was caught by an ad for the Yellow Pages. Automatically his salesman's mind registered the genre: filler ad. Otherwise known as unsold space. Wasted space, from an adman's point of view. The Yellow Pages are full of them.

But the page Arnie happened to be looking at had five of them. *Five* unsold spaces? On one page? It really was, Arnie says now, "like a light going on."

That afternoon he was in the main library at Robson and Burrard, going through the U.S. Yellow Page directories. Counting, figuring, trying not to get too excited. Somebody had to have thought of the advertising potential in all that space, he thought.

Nevertheless, he had that feeling. He was onto something. He went to David. What if we could tie up all that space somehow and sell it to the big national companies looking for reinforcement advertising?

David was skeptical. But, like all doers of deals, David believes in listening to any deal that walks in the door, no matter how far-fetched it seems.

"I can supply you with an office and a phone," he said, "but no money."

It was the week before Arnie's fifty-first birthday.

Arnie's first thought was to try to interest Expo 86 in placing some spots in the directories of one of the major U.S. publishers. The timing was off, as it turned out. But the people at U.S. West Direct, a telephone company serving 13 states from Arizona to Washington, were interested in the concept. And there was at least "a glimmer" of interest in the media department at Baker Lovick, Expo's advertising agency. Next, Arnie called a couple of major Canadian advertisers, just to feel out their response to the concept. They liked it.

By January of 1986 he was ready to make his first approach to a major U.S. directory publisher, a subsidiary of Southwestern Bell. Arnie picked Southwestern because an article in *Business Week* singled them out as the most aggressive of the publishing subsidiaries of the seven "Baby Bell" telephone companies. In the intervening months he had continued to take on any selling project that would give him walking-around money. But at the same time he kept plugging away at his Yellow Pages research, along the way discovering the probable reason why nobody had yet tried to tie up unsold Yellow Pages space and turn it into a national advertising medium.

Only two years earlier a U.S. circuit judge named Harold Green had taken a look at AT&T's virtual monopoly in the telephone company business, and decreed that the territory had to be broken up. The result was the formation of the seven companies known as the Baby Bells—any two of which, incidentally, are expected to equal the old AT&T in size by 1990.

Among them the seven companies cover more than 90 per cent of the U.S. market, with a lot of small independents sharing the remainder of the pie. The Baby Bells were big business, growing fast, and so were their respective subsidiaries that were in the business of publishing directories. The subsidiaries were free to invade one another's territory and did.

Arnie went after Southwestern Bell, the apparent scrapper in the bunch.

He called. They called back, asking for more information. It was time to put something on paper. It had to go out on the old Smokebreaker stationery, and it was pretty slim at that. But eventually Southwestern Bell said: "let's meet." Arnie flew to St. Louis.

"I came back elated," he says. "Not only did they seem to want to take the next step, but they gave me names of people to contact at Bell South and NYNEX." Within a couple of months he was on his way to Atlanta to talk to the Bell South people. Their reaction was equally favourable.

"So, now we had three companies that had not said no, and some good leads on the others."

It was get serious time. Time to raise some money, put together a decent business plan, get Arnie a bit of a draw so he could keep at it. These things were David's meat. In February, 1987, they picked up a VSE shell called Stray Horse Resources, re-named it Oriole Communications and launched the operating company—Yellow Spots Inc. The seed capital came from Primary Ventures, a local venture capital firm, and after they went public there was a series of private placements. Arnie and David and Primary Ventures (principals Malcolm Burke and David Yue) are still the principal shareholders.

By the time Arnie and David flew to New York to keep their appointment with NYNEX, they had their act together. It was the fall of 1987. Earlier that year David had run into a former classmate at a University of Western Ontario reunion, a man called Bob Beauregard, who was a top advertising man in the U.S. with J. Walter Thompson and temporarily between contracts. Beauregard got involved with Yellow Spots. There was a three-day brainstorming session in Vancouver, and a lot of things started to come together. Make it into a medium, said Beauregard, develop a rate card and see if you can get Gabe Samuels on a consulting contract. Samuels was a market research whiz fresh from the top job with J. Walter Thompson in San Francisco. Like David had been, he was a skeptic, but he agreed to a short-term contract to explore the possibilities. Between them Beauregard and Samuels were able to open a lot of doors in the ad agency business.

"All of a sudden," says Arnie, still relishing the wonder of it all, "we could talk to anybody we wanted to in New York."

The NYNEX appointment was with Bernie Bloomfield, vice-president of marketing for the company's Yellow Pages subsidiary. And he went for it. Yellow Spots signed its first publishers contract with NYNEX in April, 1988.

Asked if he was immediately taken by the concept, Bloomfield says, "I was immediately taken by David and Arnie, and that had a lot to do with my willingness to listen to them."

The concept, says Bloomfield, was not new. "It had been kicked around and argued for years." But it meant a big commitment, of both time and resources. Nor is Bloomfield sure Judge Green—who is still playing out his role as regulator of the telephone industry—would have allowed the subsidiaries of the Baby Bells to act in concert and put a national media plan together.

"But what I was impressed with was their commitment, my evaluation of their ability to stay with it, the willingness to commit the necessary resources and the determination to do it on a national basis. What they brought was a willingness to sell the concept, and that's the only way the product will be successful. I'm not sure about the regulations. However, no company has done it and it's because none of us has a national sales force."

The NYNEX contract came through in the spring of 1988. It was *the* catalyst for the company, says Arnie. Yellow Spots Inc. opened a New York office that June—on Madison Avenue, where else?—with Gabe Samuels on board full time as managing director. Samuels had long since ceased to be a skeptic. Gabe and Arnie are the New York team.

"You just can't imagine," says Arnie, "the kind of gratification I'm getting now. To be able to talk to senior executives of companies like Sears and Levi and Mastercard, and have them excited about the idea . . . and it's really just since August, 1988, that we now have a business."

For Gabe Samuels, the excitement came after looking at the market research on Yellow Pages. As an old J. Walter Thompson pro, he thought he knew all the advertising media inside and out, but until now ad agencies have not tended to get involved in anything as pedestrian as the Yellow Pages. Advertisers themselves don't tend to regard Yellow Pages ads as advertising. It's a cost of doing business.

But the Yellow Pages industry had done some solid research, and Samuels found himself looking at an advertising medium—potentially a new one and a national one—that reaches almost one fifth of the adult population of the U.S. on a daily basis, on a weekly basis more than half. The demographics were good—high income, high education, the heaviest users in the all-important 18 to 49 age group, with a slight emphasis on the male user. On average people refer to the Yellow Pages three and one half times per week. It's all pretty impressive stuff.

Yellow Spots comes at a time when the Yellow Pages industry is looking for new dollars, going after the national advertiser. It's also a time when the big national advertisers are becoming distinctly disenchanted with national network television. Recent research indicates that as many as 35 to 40 per cent of the viewers of the high-rated television programs never see a commercial—they routinely click out the ads with their handy-dandy remote control gadgets.

Not only that, but as Arnie points out, exclusivity can never be guaranteed on network television, no matter how big the buy. Fuji can buy the Olympics on NBC, but there's nothing to stop Kodak from taking the local station spot that's going to run on the same show.

"Exclusivity," says Arnie, "is the foundation of our business."

Yellow Spots will come out in the first directories—those published by NYNEX, Southwestern Bell and Pacific Bell—in March, 1989. Actually Southwestern doesn't have any big directories coming out that month, so the initial buy will be substantially NYNEX and Pac Bell.

By March, 1989, according to Arnie and David, Yellow Spots will really get going. That's the target date for getting in hand the research data on the results of the charter buy. They're convinced it's going to be an enormous success, given the demographics of Yellow Pages users plus the creative approach to small spaces. "Now we have approximately 40 per cent of all the Baby Bells," said David Horton. "We'll end up dealing with 700 directories when we have all seven."

Somewhere along the line Yellow Spots acquired its own ad agency, the New York-based Ahern & Heussner. A&H has worked up some truly sparkling prototype ads for potential advertisers like Levi, Metropolitan Life, Mastercard and others. In effect, they've shown agencies how to use the space effectively, keeping in mind the reinforcement principle. Metropolitan Life uses Peanuts cartoons in its advertising—presto! A series of episodes running through the book. Levi likes the bum and the pocket—they get lots of them, up close and eyecatching. Humour. Educational stuff. Household tips. You name it. The company that promotes itself as "big ideas for small spaces" has a tailored-to-fit game plan for everybody. And as they say in their presentation, "there's no place like 100 million homes."

Yellow Spots' initial circulation when they go fully national—and it's when, say Arnie and David, not if—will be more than 123 million. Gabe Samuels has long ago worked out the cost per thousand and worked up comparisons with, say, a full page black and white buy in the top 25 national magazines.

No contest, says Samuels.

"We would be very disappointed," says David the money man, "if we didn't do $6.5-million gross this year. Based on the profit-sharing deal with the directory publishers, that's $2.6-million net. And that's only the beginning.

"Wait until the research comes out," say David and Arnie virtually in unison. "Wait until we have five directory companies signed. With only three advertisers, that's $20-million in sales."

I like it, I like it.

Chapter
2
Making It

"*M*aking it" has always been a long-standing concern. Whereas in earlier times it seems that hard work was associated with making it (i.e., succeeding), more recently the notion of making it has taken on a somewhat different connotation. As Daniel Rogers observed in his excellent book, *The History of the Work Ethic,* the notion that hard work leads to success appears increasingly to be more of a myth than a fact. As organizations have become larger and more impersonal, it appears that more than hard work and competence are required to make it. While competence and diligence are still relevant, it often appears that the appearance of competence is less strongly correlated with actual performance than managers frequently assume. So many *things* combine to determine the results of one's efforts that attributions of success or failure to individual persons, while still made, seem tenuous. Moreover, given the fact that these attributions are often difficult to support with documentation, appearances (and the manipulation of appearances) often play an important role in determining an individual's success. Under these conditions, success is a judgment call.

The contrast between this view of making it and the more traditional view is well illustrated by a story told by Karl Weick. It seems that three umpires were discussing their job of calling balls and strikes. One umpire said, "I calls them as they is." A second umpire said, "I calls them as I sees them." The third umpire observed, "They ain't nothin' till I calls them." According to this view, "making it" is seen as having strong elements of subjectivity, arbitrariness, and even invention of facts.

Furthermore, our revised view of making it suggests that many of the elements contributing to a person being judged as successful involve social, political, and personal attributes that may have little to do with the technical aspects of work but in actuality contribute a great deal to a person's ability to get things done.

Finally, as the readings in this chapter suggest, making it for many people has a more basic component than being successful: Making it often means merely surviving in the environment in which they find themselves!

Our first selection in this chapter, a poem by Samuel Foss called "The Calf Path," depicts humorously how people sometimes unwittingly fall into routines and ways of doing things that can prevent them from creating their own paths in life. The other selections in this chapter deal with how people make it in organizations. Kevin Dahill, from the book *Life and Death—The Story of a Hospital,* relates the work history and concerns associated with the job of a man who entered an organization at a very low level and as his career developed, progressed to a highly responsible position. Robert Schrank's "Furniture Factory," from his autobiographical *Ten Thousand Working Days,* is the story of his first job as a boy of fifteen and the lessons he learned from the older workers about survival in the work environment of 1932. Hugh Prather offers sound advice concerning the relationship between one's job and oneself in "Your Job Reveals Nothing About You," a selection from his book *How to Live in the World . . . and Still be Happy.* Doug Tindal argues in "Take Charge" that the first week on a new job can make you or break you. He offers a number of suggestions concerning the perils managers face on assuming a new job and some hints on how to deal with them.

Another aspect of the importance of appearances and connections is brought out in Claudia H. Deutsch's "To Get Ahead, Consider a Coach." Deutsch reinforces this same theme in the final selection, "Media Manipulation 101," where she reports how business school students at some of our leading schools are being taught the importance of appropriate media relations. The closing anonymous poem, "The Man in the Glass," reminds us of the importance of maintaining personal integrity on our organizational journeys.

The Calf Path

Samuel Foss

One day thru the primeval wood
A calf walked home, as good calves should;
But made a trail, all bent askew,
A crooked trail, as all calves do.

Since then 300 years have fled,
And I infer the calf is dead.
But still, he left behind his trail
And thereby hangs my mortal tale.

The trail was taken up next day
By a lone dog, that passed that way.
And then a wise bell weathered sheep
Pursued the trail, o'er vale and steep
And drew the flocks behind him too
As good bell weathers always do.
And from that day, o'er hill and glade
Thru those old woods, a path was made.

And many men wound in and out,
And dodged, and turned, and bent about,
And uttered words of righteous wrath
Because 'twas such a crooked path.
But still they followed, do not laugh
The first migrations of that calf.
And thru the winding woods they stalked
Because he wobbled when he walked.

This forest path became a lane
That bent, and turned, and turned again.
This crooked lane became a road
Where many a poor horse with his load
Toiled on beneath the burning sun
And traveled some three miles in one.
And thus a century and a half
They trod the footsteps of that calf.

The years passed on in swiftness fleet,
The road became a village street.
And this, before men were aware,
A city's crowded thoroughfare.
And soon the central street was this
Of a renowned metropolis.
And men, two centuries and a half
Trod the footsteps of that calf.

Each day a 100 thousand route
Followed the zig-zag calf about,
And o'er his crooked journey went
The traffic of a continent.
A 100 thousand men were led
By one calf, near three centuries dead.
They followed still his crooked way
And lost 100 years per day.

For this such reverence is lent
To well established precedent.

A moral lesson this might teach
Were I ordained, and called to preach.
For men are prone to go it blind
Along the calf paths of the mind,
And work away from sun to sun
To do what other men have done.
They follow in the beaten track,
And out, and in, and forth, and back,
And still their devious course pursue
To keep the paths that others do.

They keep the paths a sacred groove
Along which all their lives they move.
But how the wise old wood gods laugh
Who saw that first primeval calf.
Ah, many things this tale might teach,
But I am not ordained to preach.

Kevin Dahill
Director of Activation

by Ina Yalof

*The picture window in his office is less than fifty feet from the framework of the
new hospital. It is noon and the construction workers outside are just breaking for
lunch. Five men, in plaid shirts, jeans, and hard hats, sit on the steel beams eight
stories up, legs dangling, eating sandwiches.*

*His is one of the Horatio Alger stories of the hospital. A young boy starts his
career working as a part-time messenger and now, sixteen years later, he's a hospital administrator.*

"Kevin Dahill" from *Life and Death, Story of a Hospital*, by Ina Yalof, 1988, pp. 303–306. Reprinted by permission of Ballentine Books.

This hospital played a big part in my growing up. I lived in this neighborhood, and if I got hurt playing stick ball or whatever in the street, my mother brought me here to the clinic. Everyone in my family has worked here at some point in their lives. My mother was first. A little over twenty years ago she took a part-time job in the evenings in the record room. At that time, the evening shift in medical records was made up of housewives from the neighborhood. It was the famous "seven-to-eleven shift"; seven in the evening to eleven at night. These women all became very close friends. A social network developed from it.

My father, who was a Teamster official at the time, took early retirement at age sixty. So for something to do, he latched onto a job here in the cashier's office. After what he had been through—major contracts with the Teamsters and getting involved with milk strikes in New York—he thought this job was a joke. He'd walk in here in the mornings and he'd work behind the window and cash checks and set payments on bills. He'd stroll home for lunch and watch a couple of soap operas and then stroll back and do his afternoon's worth of work. He always used to tell us, "A second grader could do this job. It's so easy." But he loved it. The only reason he retired from here was because at that time, if you were sixty-five, you were out. There was no question about it.

By then I had started college and worked here as a part-time messenger. My sister worked in patient accounts, and on down the line. I have three other siblings and every one has worked here in some capacity or another. So this place has played a large part in my life. And I'm sad but in some ways I'm happy to say both my parents passed away here.

My first full-time job was in 1969. I worked evenings at the information desk. Then I became evening supervisor of admitting, and then I was the night manager of the hospital for five years. It's a strange life, working nights, but it's interesting. There are people who have done it here throughout their entire career, but it's a very strange life. Your sleeping habits, your eating habits, are totally different than the normal routine that everyone else has. People look at you strangely when you pour yourself a Scotch on the rocks before you go to sleep at nine-thirty in the morning. Or you have a hamburger and French fries at six in the morning. Things like that. In my case, as a night manager, it was even more peculiar, because we would break up the week. I would do three nights a week from midnight till eight A.M., have two days off, and do two evenings of four to twelve. The police department always complains because they go week to week and they swing shifts. They do a week of midnights and a week of four to twelves. We broke it up right in the middle of the week. So your first day off was spent mainly sleeping, just to catch up.

It was sort of like a jet lag and I began to relate to childhood friends of mine who had fathers who were cops and firemen. When you went to their houses after school, you had to be real quiet. You always got the feeling there was something wrong with someone who slept all day.

But I liked nights. And as I look back on it, I even liked the environment. It's amazing what an *esprit de corps* there is on nights—the graveyard shift, as they call it—among everyone who is on it. The doctors need the porters much more at night than they do during the daytime and they can relate to them better. There are centralized locations where everyone goes for coffee and Danish, as opposed to different places where the doctors and nurses eat during the day. At night you're all the same. There's much more of a family-type atmosphere.

Toward the end of that period, the hospital created a department of patient relations and I was put in as the director. From there, I was promoted again to the new position of director of Government and Community Affairs. Then, towards the end of '86, I got a call from Joe Corcoran, the chief operating officer. He said, "Look, we've got these buildings going up and ultimately we're going to be moving the old hospital into the new one and we need a person to be in charge of the move, and we want you to do it."

So as of January first this year, I've been the Director of Activation. It's a huge undertaking, moving a whole hospital, and it requires a large staff to look after things. Equipment has to be tested and monitored, people have to be trained to work the new equipment. There are big things and small. The furniture has to be in before the staff moves in. We even have to plan for things like wastebaskets.

It's a job just getting people to pack, asking them to make major decisions like whether or not to throw out documents from 1958. I'm thinking of staging a contest as part of the major move, for the department that discards the most hard-copy records, because I think people just hold on to things in order to hold on to them. We would have some sort of a special prize—a trip or something like that.

We're probably going to move in floor by floor, mainly because we're going to get the building turned over to us by the construction people floor by floor. When they turn it over, they're turning it over in bare-bones fashion. We've got to get the equipment operating and make sure it works and that our staff knows how to work it. We've got to clean up the place so that the state can come in and review it and make sure it meets code requirements and so on. That process takes a lot of time.

Moving the patients will be no problem. Even patients with respirators and IVs. On a given day we're going to decide this is "orthopedics' day." So we'll move all the ortho staff and their patients to the new unit. If somebody is in traction, then they'll stay in the old hospital until they can be safely moved. We'll decide in advance which patients are going to be moved that day. We'll have a schedule on that morning. We'll know that John Smith, who is now in 401, bed 3, in the old Presbyterian, is moving to Garden North, 812, bed 2. I envision a cadre of transporters and volunteers. There'll literally be a parade of patients coming across the bridges over Fort Washington Avenue. It's not difficult, when you think about it. It's like moving a patient from one room to another; it's just a longer trip.

In terms of what keeps me awake at night when I consider the move, the transfer of patients is not it. Sure, we may lose a patient temporarily, a patient may end up in the wrong room for a little while. I mean, it's realistic to expect that *somebody* will have made a wrong turn *somewhere*. But that's not what worries me. I'm concerned about the human dynamics of the staff moving to the new building. The way I see it, our entire organization has to change. Take orthopedics again. We're bringing what are now four different inpatient orthopedics units together onto one floor. We have four head nurses moving into one unit. So now who supervises the floor? Will they get along? What happens to seniority? Now maybe I'm barking up the wrong tree, but I think that these are going to be issues we'll have to contend with. I think that kind of thing is going to transcend the overall activation effort. But I also think if we do this right, we can make it a positive experience. Theoretically this should be an exciting adventure.

A lot of my outward calm is strictly for show. I'm convinced that if I, above all people, show any signs of nervousness or apprehension, then we've blown it. I've got to instill confidence in people; not just in me, but in the process. There are times, though, when I just go somewhere and scream to myself or I whack a golf ball in an effort to work it out.

A lot of people say you shouldn't stay in any organization too long, and for years I disagreed with that. I've been very lucky in this hospital. The opportunities that I've had here have been wonderful. There's been no reason to leave. But now . . . now I think maybe I should give that some thought. I think most people resist change, and it's possible that after I get them moved, they're not all going to like me a whole lot. So after the new hospital is open, maybe I'd be better off like the Lone Ranger. Maybe I should just get on my white horse and ride off into the sunset.

Furniture Factory

Robert Schrank

It was 1932 and we were in the depths of the depression. If you were lucky enough to find a job, it was usually through a friend, and that was how I got my first full-time job in a Brooklyn factory that made frames for upholstered furniture. I was fifteen years old and lived in the Bronx, traveling on the subway for an hour and fifteen minutes each way, every day, six days a week for twelve dollars. I considered myself to be the luckiest boy in the world to get that job. When Mr. Miller the owner of the Miller Parlor Frame Company, interviewed me and agreed to hire me, he made it quite clear that he was doing a favor for a mutual friend and did not really care much about giving me a job.

Like most small factory offices, Mr. Miller's was cluttered with catalogs, samples of materials, some small tools, a rolltop desk with a large blotter pad worn through the corners. The whole place was in a sawdust fog with a persistent cover of dust over everything. Mr. Miller was a short fat man who chewed cigars and sort of drooled as he talked to me. He sat on the edge of his big oak swivel chair. I had a feeling he might slip off anytime. He never looked at me as we spoke. He made it clear that he was annoyed at people asking favors, saying that he did not like people who were "always trying to get something out of me."

The sour smell of the oak sawdust comes back to fill my nose as I recall the furniture factory. It is a smell I always welcomed until I had to live in it eight hours a day. There were days, especially when it was damp or raining, when the wood smell was so strong you could not eat your lunch. Next to the smell I remember getting to the factory and back as being an awful drag. But the New York subway that I rode to and from work for many years had two marked positive effects on me. First, I felt part of a general condition that nobody seemed to like. I was part of a group and we were all in the same fix, busting our asses to get to work in the morning and home at night. While I felt unhappy, it was made easier through the traditional "misery loves company," and there was plenty of that. And second, if I had a lucky day, there was the chance of seeing or being pressed up against some sweet-smelling, young, pretty thing who would get me all excited. Sometimes I tried a pickup, but it usually did not work because the situation was too public. With each person rigidly contained, it was surprising if anyone tried to move out of his shell. Everyone in the train would be staring to see what would develop. Almost nothing did.

To be at the furniture factory in Brooklyn by 8 A.M., I would leave my house in the Bronx by 6:30 A.M. While it was always a bad trip it became less so in the long spring days of the year as contrasted with December, when I most hated getting up in the dark. It was very important to be very quiet as I would feel my way around our old frame house, so as not to wake people up who had another thirty or forty minutes to sleep. I would sleepily make a sandwich for lunch, preferably from a leftover or just bologna, grab a cup of coffee—always with one eye on the clock— and run for the station. Luckily, we lived at the end of a subway line, and in the morning I was usually able to get a corner seat in the train. The corner seat was good for sleeping because I could rest against the train wall and not have the embarrassment of falling asleep on the person sitting next to me. It meant being able to sleep the hour-long trip to Brooklyn, and it was critical to set my "inner clock" so it would wake me up at Morgan Avenue station in Brooklyn. If it failed or was a little late, which sometimes happened, panic would ensue, as I usually would wake up just as the train was pulling out of Morgan Avenue. I would make a quick, unsuccessful dash for the door, and people would try to help by grabbing at the door. Then I would burn with anger for being late and maybe losing the job. When I would end up past my stop, I would have to make a fast decision to either spend another nickel and go back or go on to a double station where I could race down the steps to the other side of the tracks and catch a train going the other way without paying an additional fare.

The trip home from work on the New York subway in the evening rush hour is an experience most difficult to describe. The train, packed full of people, hurtles into a station. The doors slide open. There is always an illusion that someone may be getting out. That never seems to happen while a mass of people begin to push their way in. All strangers, we are not packed like sardines in a can, as is often suggested; the packing of sardines is an orderly process. The rush hour subway is more like a garbage compacter that just squeezes trash and rubbish into a dense mass and then hurtles it at very high speeds through a small underground tube. Unlike the morning, at night when I was exhausted from the day's work I never was able to get a seat, and that meant standing on my dog-tired feet for more than an hour and trying not to lean on the person next to me, an almost impossible thing to do. . . .

As I walked from the subway in the morning I could smell the furniture factory a block away. It was a powerful smell; as I said, I loved that oak at first. It was a perfume from the woods: a combination of skunk, mushrooms, and honeysuckle blended to a musk, a sweet contrast to the steel-and-oil stink of the subway. Yet, by the end of a day's work, the factory, its smells, its noise, its tedium all became so terribly tiresome and exhausting that leaving every day was an act of liberation.

The factory was a five-story loft building about half a city block long. The making of furniture frames began on the bottom floor where the rough cuts were made from huge pieces of lumber. As the cut wood moved along from floor to floor, it was formed, shaped, carved, dowled, sanded, and finally assembled on the top floor into completed frames. The machines in the plant included table saws, band saws, planers, carving machines, routers, drills, hydraulic presses, all run by 125 machine operators who were almost all European immigrants. My job was to keep the operators supplied with material, moving the finished stuff to the assembly floor, a sort of human conveyor. When I wasn't moving pieces around, I was supposed to clean up, which meant bagging sawdust into burlap bags. Sometimes the foreman would come and say, "Hey, kid, how would you like to run the dowling machine?" At first I thought that was a real break, a chance to get on a machine and become an operator. I told him enthusiastically, "Yeah, that would be great." I would sit in front of this little machine, pick up a predrilled piece, hold it to the machine, which would push two glued dowels into the holes. I soon found that I preferred moving parts around the plant and cleaning up to sitting at that machine all day, picking up a piece of wood from one pile, locating the holes at the dowel feeder that pushed in two preglued dowels, then dropping it on the other side. The machine had a sort of gallump, gallump rhythm that made me sleepy and started me watching the clock, the worst thing you can do in a factory. It would begin to get to me, and I would just sit and stare at the machine, the clock, the machine, the clock.

Those first few weeks in that factory were an agony of never-ending time. The damn clock just never moved, and over and over again I became convinced that it had stopped. Gradually, life in the furniture factory boiled down to waiting for the four work breaks: coffee, lunch hour, coffee, and quitting time. When the machines stopped, it was only in their sudden silence that I became aware of their deafening whine. It was almost impossible to hear each other talk while they were running, and all we were able to do was to scream essential information at one another.

The breaks were the best times of the day, for I could become intoxicated listening to the older men talk of rough, tough things in the big world out there.

Being accepted was a slow process, and I was just happy to be allowed to listen. When I had been there for a couple of weeks, Mike the Polack said, "Hey, kid, meet in the shit house for talk." I was making it all right.

The coffee- and lunch-break talks centered around the family, sports, politics, and sex, in about that order. The immigrants from Middle Europe, and especially the Jews, were the most political. Most of them seemed to believe that politicians were crooks and that's how it is. The Jews talked the least about sex and the Italians the most. Luigi would endlessly bait Max (who would soon be my friend), saying that what he needed most was "a good woman who make you forget all dat political shit." There were a whole variety of newspapers published in New York at that time and one way workers had of figuring out each other's politics, interests, and habits was by the papers they read.

Max Teitelbaum would say to me, "See Louie over there. You can tell he's just a dummy, he reads that *Daily Mirror*. It fills his head with garbage so he can't tink about vot is *really* happening in the vorld." Arguing strongly in the defense of Franklin Roosevelt, probably too strongly, Mike the Polack told me with his finger waving close to my nose, "Listen, kid, vot I tink and vot I do is my business, and nobody, no politician or union or smart-ass kid like you is gonna butt into dat. You got it? Don't forget it!"

As people began to trust me, I was slowly making friends. Their trust was expressed in small ways, like when Luigi called me over to his workbench, held up a picture of Jean Harlow for me to look at as he shook his big head of black hair, all the time contemplating the picture together with me, and said, "Now, whaddya tink, boy?" . . . Then he said, "OK, kid, you gotta work hard and learn something. See all those poor bastards out there outa work. Watch out or you could be one of dem." Luigi was a wood-carver who made the models for the multiple-spindle carving machine and was probably the only real craftsman in the place.

One day as I distributed work in process to the operators and picked up their finished stuff, I received one of my first lessons in the fundamentals of working that I would relearn again and again in almost every job I have had: How to work less hard in order to make the task easier.

Max Teitelbaum, a band saw operator just a few years out of Krakow, Poland, a slightly built man with sort of Mickey Mouse ears, twinkling eyes, and a wry smile, would upbraid me repeatedly with such passing comments as, "You are a dummy," or "You're not stupid, so what's da matter vit you?" Finally one day he stopped his machine, turned to me, and said, "Look, come over here. I vant to talk vit you. Vy you are using your back instead your head? Max Teitelbaum's first rule is: Don't carry nuttin' you could put a veel under. It's a good ting you wasn't helpin' mit der pyramids—you vould get crushed under the stones."

I said, "But Max, if the hand truck is on the third floor and I'm on the fifth, I can't go all the way down there just for that."

"You see," he said, "you are a dummy. Vy you can't go down dere? Huh, vy not? You tell me!"

"Well," I said, "it would take a lot of time—"

He cut me off. "You see, you are vorrying about da wrong tings, like da boss. Is he vorrying about you? Like da Tzar vorried about Max Teitelbaum. Listen, kid, you vorry about you because no von else vill. Understand? You vill get nuttin' for vorking harder den more vork. Now ven you even don't understand someting, you come and ask Max. OK?" Max became my friend, adviser, and critic.

By the end of my first weeks in the factory I began to feel as if I was crushed under stones. My body helped me to understand what Max was saying. I would come home from work on Saturday afternoon and go to bed expecting to go out later that night with a girl friend. For some weeks when I lay down on Saturday I did not try, nor was I able, to move my body from bed until some time on Sunday. The whole thing just throbbed with fatigue: arms, shoulders, legs, and back were in fierce competition for which hurt the most. I began to learn what Max meant by "Always put a veel under it and don't do more than you have to."

My third or fourth week at the factory found me earnestly launched in my quest for holding the job but doing less work—or working less hard. This was immediately recognized and hailed by the men with "Now you're gettin' smart, kid. Stop bustin' your ass and only do what you have to do. You don't get any more money for bustin' your hump and you might put some other poor bastard outa job." Remember this was the depression. Most workers, while aware of the preciousness of their jobs, felt that doing more work than necessary could be putting someone else, even yourself, out of a job. "Only do what you have to" became a rule not only to save your own neck but to make sure you were not depriving some other soul like yourself from getting a job.

In the next few weeks, I was to be taught a second important lesson about working. One day while picking up sawdust, I began to "find" pieces in the sawdust or behind a woodpile or under a machine. The first few times, with great delight, I would announce to the operator, "Hey, look what I found!" I should have figured something was wrong by the lack of similar enthusiasm from the operator. Sam was a generally quiet Midwesterner who never seemed to raise his voice much, but now when I showed him my finished-work discovery behind his milling machine he shouted, "Who the fuck asked you to be a detective? Keep your silly ass out from behind my machine; I'll tell you what to pick up. So don't go being a big brown-nosing hero around here."

Wow, I sure never expected that. Confused, troubled, almost in tears, not knowing what to do or where to go, I went to the toilet to hide my hurt and just sat down on an open bowl and thought what the hell am I doing in this goddamned place anyway? I lit a cigarette and began pacing up and down in front of the three stalls, puffing away at my Camel. I thought, What the hell should I do? This job is terrible, the men are pissed off at me. I hate the place, why don't I just quit? Well, it's a job and you get paid, I said to myself, so take it easy.

While I'm pacing and puffing, Sam comes in, saying, "Lissen, kid, don't get sore. I was just trying to set you straight. Let me tell you what it's all about. The guys around, that is the machine operators, agree on how much we are gonna turn out, and that's what the boss gets, no more, no less. Now sometimes any one of us might just fall behind a little, so we always keep some finished stuff hidden away just in case." The more he talked, the more I really began to feel like the enemy. I tried to apologize, but he just went on. "Look, kid, the boss always wants more and he doesn't give a shit if we die giving it to him, so we [it was that "we" that seemed to retrieve my soul back into the community; my tears just went away] agree on how much we're going to give him—no more, no less. You see, kid, if you keep running around, moving the stuff too fast, the boss will get wise about what's going on." Sam put his arm on my shoulder. (My God! I was one of them! I love Sam and the place. I am in!) "So look," he says, "your job is to figure out how to move and work no faster than we turn the stuff out. Get it? OK? You'll get it." I said, "Yes, of course, I understand everything." I was being initiated into the secrets of a work tribe, and I loved it.

I was beginning to learn the second work lesson that would be taught me many times over in a variety of different jobs: Don't do more work than is absolutely necessary. Years later I would read about how people in the Hawthorne works of Western Electric would "bank work" and use it when they fell behind or just wanted to take it easy. I have seen a lot of work banking, especially in machine shops. In some way I have felt that banking work was the workers' response to the stopwatches of industrial engineers. It is an interesting sort of game of hide the work now, take it out later. In another plant, would you believe we banked propellor shafts for Liberty ships!

I learned most of the rules, written and unwritten, about the furniture factory, but I never got to like the job. After I had been there six or seven months, the Furniture Workers Union began an organizing drive. I hated the furniture factory, the noise, the dust, and the travel, so I, too, quickly signed a union card. I was just as quickly out on my ass. It was a good way to go, since my radical friends considered me a hero of sorts, having been victimized for the cause. The first time I ever considered suicide in my life was in that furniture factory as I would stare at the clock and think to myself, "If I have to spend my life in this hellhole, I would rather end it." Well, of course, I didn't; and as I look back, it was not the worst place I worked, but I was young and unwilling to relinquish childhood.

Your Job Reveals Nothing About You

by Hugh Prather

I don't recall how old I was when I discovered that if I answered "architect" instead of "fireman" to the question "What do you want to be when you grow up?" I got a much more satisfying reaction from adults. I still remember vague feelings of guilt about not knowing what an architect did, but at the time that did not seem to matter. Today's five- or six-year-old is likely to answer "I haven't decided between palmistry and astrophysics," although there are some kids who can be quite firm about "doing charts."

All of this is probably very harmless because children seem to enjoy this little game as much as adults do. But just a few years later the same question can become terrifying if teenagers feel pressured to set out on the impossible task of trying to second-guess what high school specialty or college major will best prepare them for the future course of their life. Most parents ought to know that the young person's distress over this is not without foundation since so few of us have ended up doing what our education supposedly prepared us for, yet some of us still persist in requiring teenagers to exercise this rather silly form of precognition. It is of course fine to choose a major, but no one should have to kid himself about its implications.

Thinking that appearances are everything, the ego naturally concludes that "you are what you do." During our middle span of life the seemingly affable question "What do you do?" really means "Are you somebody?" and most of us think far too much about how to word our answer should some stranger at a party ask us this question, even though if we just took a moment to look at our feelings we would see that we really don't care what a stranger thinks of us. It is only our ego that attempts to judge, and being quite blind, all it can see is other egos. This common social line of attack and counterattack has so very little to do with what people are at their core that you would think it would be self-evident that a person's means of earning a living reveals only the most superficial and insignificant information about what he or she is, and yet the issue of career has become a source of great unhappiness.

It is now generally assumed that anyone is capable of doing anything. "Why then," our society asks, "have you settled for work that is mediocre?" We should somehow be more creative, more humanitarian, more productive, more something. So tangled up with our job are our feelings of self-worth that businesses, if they want their fair share of good employees, must periodically spend time rewriting job titles to make the same work sound more impressive. We have actually gotten to the point of disliking people for not doing more than they do, and we ourselves cannot sidestep the disgust, however mild, we think we have managed to reserve only for others. Surely it does not have to be proved that all of this is quite insane. And yet, if you wish to be happy, you must free yourself completely from this point of view. *You are not what you do; you are how you do it.*

You will not think better of yourself by engaging in a selection of those activities currently considered to be impressive. Nor will you recognize your worth by avoiding them. You will know that you are good when you consistently bring goodness to all you do. If the job is to straighten and clean for a small family, your work is no less holy than, for instance, that of a personnel manager who hires and fires hundreds of employees for a large corporation. We have such silly ideas of what is important work! For example, what more far-reaching activity could there be than devoting oneself to helping a child be happy and unafraid and to develop into a gentle, kind adult? How many people will this one child touch within a lifetime? Is seeing to this little person's happiness really less significant than composing music, throwing pots, being socially active or "living up to one's earning potential"?

YOUR CAREER FORMS BEHIND YOU

Most people have never stopped to ask themselves exactly what it is they are seeking in place of a good life *now*. There simply is no such thing as a career. People talk about pursuing a career as if all the turns were already mapped out and their destination set there waiting for them as solid and immovable as the town civic center. Except for the straight line of automatic promotions within organizations such as the armed services, a few large corporations, and some branches of civil service, none of us advances to our goal with a predictable precision, and even within the fields where this appears to happen a closer examination shows a nest of entangling exceptions, including the employee's health and will to endure, exigencies of location, family demands, government allocations, and the goodwill of superiors. It is not realistic to think in terms of "arriving at the top of your profession." There is no perfectly defined profession and no true top.

Our trail through life can be seen only in retrospect. It *does* all add up, but not in advance of the steps taken. If each small step is guided by the present instead of by a hodgepodge of fears about the future, we can discern a lovely wake flowing from the actions we have taken, including even our mistakes. There is a beauty, a just-rightness, within the course of every life, but so often the individual is blinded to it by constant worry and second-guessing.

The only thing you can know for sure is whether you feel at ease in the present about a step that is possible to take today. No one can adequately define all the consequences, see all the people this step will affect, and accurately determine whether the ramifications will be fair to everyone eventually touched by them. You merely delude yourself if you think your vision is that free of distortion. Why then attempt to resolve interminable future implications when it is simply not possible to do so? Instead of the fantasy of a glowing future, why not settle for the very real possibility of a satisfying present?

NOTHING HAS TO BE DECIDED IN ADVANCE

When we attempt to translate a fantasy into a worldly event, the result is a different order of reality. Like most people, I have run through many such fantasies in my life. My mental pictures of what it would be like to become a sculptor, ranch hand, secondary schoolteacher, real estate broker, guidance counselor, construction worker, psychologist, circuit lecturer, and a few other false starts were so unlike the reality of the work I ended up engaged in that it is really very funny to me now that I thought I could imagine in advance what my life would be like within these various fields.

A fantasy does not give firsthand experience. That is why no matter how informed we think we are, we do not know beforehand what will make us happy. Nor is there any reason to know since it is the degree to which we have developed our capacity to enjoy the present that determines our happiness and not our job classification. This does not mean that very little care need be taken in choosing one's way of making a living, for of course care should be taken. It means only that our freedom from conflict over whether today to ask for an interview, enroll in a class, question someone within a certain line of work, or buy a book or two on a particular field is a more reliable basis for making a decision than our fantasy of an entire future course of action that will entail hundreds of separate choices. Our desire to anticipate every move we will make for broad periods of time is nothing more than our present wish to struggle, and it is simply not necessary to indulge this form of false humility. All we ever need do is take the obvious steps before us today and let our sense of direction clarify as we proceed.

There is also a strong tendency within all of us to get ourselves into a difficult situation and then think we must see it through to the bitter end. Trusting in fantasies instead of our present perception of how things are going is a major contributor to this pattern. To decide beforehand what kind of job we deserve can cause as much unhappiness as deciding what kind of child we have a right to, as many parents unconsciously do. In their mind is a constantly escalating standard of acceptable manners, the proper height, an adequate IQ, sufficient social skills, a pleasing appearance, and so forth. Inevitably the child fails in some respect and feels their disapproval. Disapproval is irrelevant to appreciating children and working with them toward their, rather than our own, feelings of well-being. And just as with a child, a job must be looked at, taken as it is, and given time.

Relax into your destiny. Giving something time is quite different from forcing yourself to see it through to the bitter end. Let each workday come to you. Watch it approach without suspicion. Expect happiness from yourself, but expect nothing from the job. Approached in this way, happiness is a possibility in any situation. Take each task as it comes and do not constantly peer over it to the next task. Don't rush to complete it, or rush toward some hour on the clock. We need not stay on guard in order to see that a job is not working out, but we do have to let down our guard to enjoy what we have pre-defined as "work." We may not be able to change the task, but we are always free to change our definition of our function within it.

FINDING A JOB

Our discussion so far may seem insensitive to the many people who sincerely want to work but cannot find employment. This is obviously an extremely complex and difficult question, and the factors within these cases can vary so dramatically that any generalizations I make here would be unfair in light of at least some people's plight. So of course there are countless exceptions, and yet I believe a few things can be said that apply to some of those who find themselves in this predicament.

Many people—far more than consciously realize it—make themselves walk a very narrow path in finding work. For instance, there are entire categories of jobs they will not consider because of a certain self-image they believe must be maintained. Other occupations go unexplored because of their conviction that society, the economy, the present controlling minority, big business, or some other generalized enemy should not be forcing this kind of choice and they must stand alone against this outrage, even if it means their family's well-being. "I won't work for a company that . . ." "I won't live in a place where . . ." "I won't take orders from a boss who . . ." and yet it does not have to be that way. Clearly we should never do what is morally intolerable, but so often this is not the real issue. We think we must be right at all costs.

Another hampering bias is directed, curiously, at ourselves. *Most people tend to look down on what they do best.* This is merely further evidence of our aversion to what is easy and simple. Our areas of greatest strength are usually the ones to be given the harshest scrutiny, and of course if you look for fault anywhere long enough you are sure to find it. Instead of doing what we know how to do (which often is also the work we can do most peacefully), we assume that the higher pursuit is to enter a new field altogether, especially one that fits the current definition of "meaningful" work. Seldom is it sufficient to simply earn a living. Better to have an erratic income and be able to give the impression that we are sacrificing ourselves to set the world straight.

Unfortunately our friends are sometimes the ones most likely to distract us from our own quiet knowing. As a general rule you will be less confused and consequently miss fewer opportunities if you will decide for yourself whether a job fits your present needs and not even open yourself up to conflict by discussing decisions you are in the middle of. Strengthen your mind by reminding yourself that *you* are in the best position to know what you should be doing. And after you have started a job save yourself the pangs of doubt by talking as little as possible about the inevitable problems that accompany a transition of this sort. Few people can resist an opportunity to sow confusion. So do not give them one. Do not be afraid to stay close to your heart, to keep your own counsel. *Do not be afraid to know.*

Another cause of defeat, although far less conscious, is the unexamined premise that the job choice one is making is permanent. Out there awaits some eternal and just-right niche, and the only real problem is locating it. And yet, *there is no right job.*

"This is right" implies "this is permanent." It shouldn't, but it does. Who could believe he had finally found the right job or, worse, was "guided" or "led" to it and still feel perfectly free to quit at the end of the first day? Given this approach, it should not be surprising that most people's major concern is to avoid making a mistake. If you believe in the existence of a right job, you will also look on all other jobs as "wrong," at least for you.

Do you see the position this puts you in? Since there is a job that is best for you, most of the work that comes to your attention is a potential mistake and your life is now like walking through a mine field. Should you already have a job, you cannot help harboring the suspicion that you chose wrongly. We think we can somehow believe in the preexistence of a right course of action in one area of our life and yet not believe in it in every other area, and because this is impossible most people also suspect that they married the wrong person (which means, of course, they have the wrong children), bought or rented the wrong place to live in (so the neighbors aren't what they should be), and probably ate the wrong cereal for breakfast this morning. I don't think any of us has managed to escape this outlook entirely.

No more absolute and awful tyranny reigns than our own fear of being wrong. We have a simple choice. We can try to avoid all mistakes or we can relax. In seeking a job it is good to drop the notion that the universe has hidden away some haloed position just for you. Now at least you will not be haunted by the vague feeling that somehow you are not going about this job-finding business in the correct way. There are a thousand correct ways because there are a thousand peaceful ways.

Do not remain in fear. Very often if someone attempting to avoid the wrong job will accept just any job, a more pleasing position will appear shortly thereafter. There is no magic to this. The elimination of fear is the beginning of vision, and to give ourselves a broad range of options permits us to see opportunities we were blind to before. It is not uncommon for an individual who is unable to find a paying job to take volunteer work or to just begin helping someone for free and suddenly have a salaried position, or sometimes several at once, become available, much like the classic example of the couple who cannot bear children, decide to adopt, and instantly become fertile.

Once again, this phenomenon is not the mystery it first seems. So often the cause of our problem, whatever it may be, is fear, and the willingness to act in a simple, direct way will begin lessening it. The precise external results are not predictable—an adoption does not automatically render a couple fertile, and volunteer work does not consistently manifest a paying job. Nevertheless, openness to starting and continuing the small steps involved in walking around a problem will eventually result in leaving the problem behind. Overt manifestations of willingness reduce inner conflict, and an unconflicted mind can step over any hindrance.

Take Charge

Doug Tindal

The first week on a new job can make you—or break you

It may not seem fair, but your first week in the new, executive job is going to make you or break you. Your first days will establish you as a strong performer who'll lead the company on to higher sales and wider profit margins than ever before. Or they'll mark you as a dud. Naturally, you won't head into the office on day one wearing your plaid sports jacket. You'll wear one of your navy blue suits—the one with the fine pinstripe would be a good choice—and, naturally, you'll wear the vest. So at least you'll look right, which certainly is a step in the right direction—but only a very, very small step, because there are so many pitfalls in a new job, so many envious skeptics waiting for you to slip, that your first days are downright perilous, to say the least.

What if you put your car in the president's parking spot? What if you get stuck in an elevator (sure, it could happen to anyone, but when it's your first day on the job . . .)? And what if Gladys from accounting is stuck in there with you? These are unlikely dangers, of course, but most of the perils of a new job are entirely real. And though they may be much more subtle, they're also much more serious.

Fortunately, there are things you can do and steps you can take (carefully) that will start you off on the right foot, as they say. There are correct moves to make— and a great many wrong ones to avoid—as you seek out the levers of power. And the key point to bear in mind, according to the experts, is that you should let the specifics of the job wait for a bit. Your first concern should be first impressions, and obviously this goes far beyond the appropriate suit or picking the right place to park.

You have to impress a lot of people. You have to impress upon your boss, and others at his level, that you're sharp and aggressive and on the move; you have to convince your peers that you're a team player, a trustworthy colleague. And the very first move, the experts say, is to make a good impression on your staff, to win their respect and trust—especially when it comes to the bright young fellow who may be all set to torpedo you because he wanted your job. The way you handle this situation will color the way the rest of the staff receives you. If you fire him, for example, you may risk a palace revolt—and lose his experience. If you let things slide, hoping that he'll soon grow to love you, you're probably deluding yourself.

Reprinted by permission of Doug Tindal

Peter Frost is a consultant and professor of organizational behavior at the University of British Columbia, and he says it's probably a good idea to assume that someone in the company has a grudge against you, even if you have no direct evidence. "It's very rare, in my experience, that a senior position is awarded without there being an internal candidate, and normally this individual feels a bit bruised when he doesn't get the job."

So what should you do? Dave Urquhart is a partner in the management consulting firm of Urquhart & Preger, Inc., in Toronto, and he recommends a very neat solution: "Chances are your subordinate was passed over because senior management figured he wasn't quite ready. So you go to him and offer to groom him—when you're ready to move on, you point out, he'll know everything he needs to know to step right into your shoes. This way, you convert a potential enemy into a valuable ally; and, you clear the way for yourself to advance, because generally, you can't move up in a company until you've prepared someone to take your place."

Urquhart says, incidentally, that when you get to the final stage of the hiring process, just before you take the job, it's quite legitimate to ask if there's an internal candidate, and if so, who. In other words, know your enemy.

There's another thing you should establish at this early stage: who will be your secretary? You may have the option of keeping the same secretary your predecessor had, and the obvious advantage of this is that she'll know all the ropes. The disadvantage is that some of them won't be *your* ropes; and if your predecessor is still with the company, your secretary may have conflicting loyalties.

So you might be better off to hire someone new. Either way, you should realize that your secretary can be much, much more than someone to answer phones and type correspondence; she (or he) can be your link to the great secretarial intelligence grid, and her perceptions of other people can be a big help.

Whenever you start a new job, you face a great many important questions that can be answered only over a period of time. You have to find out, for example, how much of your success depends on meeting performance standards such as sales targets or production quotas, and how much depends on pleasing the boss in subjective ways. If your boss is the kind of guy who likes to be at his desk by 7:45 A.M., then chances are he likes to see other people at their desks by 7:45. If you don't come in until 8:30, this may affect the way your boss perceives the quality of your work—no matter how good it is.

Frank Musten, an industrial psychologist who practices in both Ottawa and Toronto, points out that each company has its own set of norms: Should you work through the noon hour or should you take a two-hour lunch? Do you have to go to company parties? Does your spouse have to go, too? Should you join your staff in the lunchroom occasionally, to be friendly—or would they consider it an intrusion? Well, Musten says, try it: carry your bowl of tomato soup over to join the staff one day and see what happens. Nobody is likely to tell you to shove off, but if you're not welcome, you'll know it—for one thing, the conversation will dry right up.

But you don't necessarily have to obey all the norms. "If you try to become totally a company man, you'll be useless to both the company and to yourself," Musten says. "So you should decide which norms you can live with."

Peter Frost adds that when you move into a company at a senior level, usually you're expected to stir things up a bit and make some changes: "In other words, there's a degree to which you have to make the company fit you, not the other way around."

Laird Mealiea is an associate professor of organizational development at Dalhousie University in Halifax, and he points out that your new company can provide a great deal of formal information about your job. "You should make an effort to get hold of all the company's policies and procedures manuals, job descriptions, personnel files—anything that describes your position and your relationship to others. These aren't gospel, of course; you have to weigh them against the information you pick up informally and find a balance."

Urquhart suggests a number of ways to pick up informal information: "You should take the initiative to go around and meet other managers throughout the firm," he says. "Try to get to know them a bit—not just what they do, but what they value."

"It helps you to build some bridges to these guys, so they'll be more receptive to cooperating with you when you need them and it gives you a line on what kinds of people get promoted in the company. It also gives you a chance to look for potential allies, people you can use to test your thoughts about the organization."

Urquhart suggests you should find out about any key people who've recently left the company: "Call them up, tell them you'd like to take them to lunch and pick their brains about where the company is at, who the key players are, all that stuff."

Finally, he suggests you meet with your predecessor and ask him about your new subordinates: which ones are top performers, which are marginal. Naturally, you won't necessarily be guided by his perceptions, but it's valuable to hear what he thinks; and it will probably tell you something about the way he ran the department.

Pamela Ennis, an industrial psychologist who has her own company, Pamela Ennis & Associates, Industrial Psychologists, says you should also speak with subordinates: "Find out about how independent they were under your predecessor, what controls there are on their actions, how they feel about their jobs, what kind of formal communications there are in the department—you want to do something like a miniature organizational survey."

Ennis has some interesting ideas about the world of power politics and the ways it can affect your first few days on the job. "Power politics is the informal world of management," she says. "It doesn't appear on any management chart and it's not studied in any of the texts, but unless you know how to play, any success you have will be short-lived. The first thing you have to understand about power is that it's not the same thing as authority. When you go into a job on day one, you have a certain amount of authority which comes to you automatically as a result of your position, but your power is almost nil—power is the ability to influence other people and this is something you must earn."

Ennis adds that the ways to power will vary from one company to the next because the sort of thing that influences the key people in one company may cut no ice at all somewhere else. In a company that's heavily dependent on information, you might have to learn to sweet-talk the computer—if you can figure out how to get a particularly lucid kind of monthly report from the maze of data stored in its memory, you may wind up with more clout than the president. In another company, one with a heavy marketing orientation, for instance, you may have to learn how to hustle and promote yourself.

Sometimes this means you'll have to learn a whole new language. Frost says you should be alert to casual conversation and notice if people tend to talk in the language of, say, finance. If your company is planning to expand its factory, do people say the expansion will cost $3.5 million, or do they say it will trim first quarter earnings by 17 cents a share? Naturally, you should copy the corporate style on things like this. "Also," he says, "try to pick out the corporate buzzwords. Do you hear people talking about LRC (linear responsibility charting) or MBO (management by objectives)? These things may be part of what makes your company tick."

In most companies, Frost says, there's a particular story that the old hands always tell the newcomers, and you should listen for it because it can reveal a lot about the way your new colleagues see themselves: "In one company I heard of from a colleague, there's a story about a nine-day fortnight. Years ago, the company had a serious drop in sales and they had to cut back. So everyone, from the president to the janitors, took off one day without pay every two weeks. They worked nine days, instead of 10, each fortnight, and they kept this up for several months until sales picked up."

New employees of this company soon hear about "the nine-day fortnight" and, if they're alert, they realize that it's a story about how these people pulled together, toughed it out through the lean times, and went on to win. So this company may place an unusually high value on cooperation and teamwork.

"In another company, the key people like to pretend that they don't take their jobs very seriously and that they never really work hard, so they're always talking about how they take four-hour lunches. In fact, they do often take four-hour lunches, but they never talk about what happens after the lunch—they go back to the office and work until midnight." Obviously, if you want to get anywhere in this company, you should take care to project an easy-going kind of image and make it look as though you're having a good time.

Arnold Minors is an in-house consultant specializing in organizational development for Imperial Oil Ltd., in Toronto, and he points out that most companies also have corporate myths. "The corporate myth is usually in the form of a prohibition," he says. "There's something—it could be anything—which, according to everybody else in the company, you *must not do.*" For example: never make a presentation to the boss without using a flip chart. If you question this prohibition, Minors says, you'll probably find that it's not written down anywhere, that no one in living memory has tried to do it, and that, quite obviously, no one knows what will happen if you try. So the prohibition is a myth and the odds are that if you go ahead and do the thing—illustrate your presentation with an overhead projector instead of a flip chart, for instance—you may be able to pick up a reputation as a bold innovator.

Minors has just joined Imperial, and he says he spent nearly all his time during his first few days getting around to meet key people. This isn't always as easy as it sounds because, as Ennis points out, the real power points in your company may be far removed from the top positions on the organizational chart. You need to find out who actually gets things done, not who holds the title: The reason your secretary is sitting there with no typewriter could be that you sent the requisition to the head of supply services, when everybody knows nothing happens unless you send the requisition directly to Betty in the stockroom.

In your company, there are probably a couple dozen behind-the-scenes people just like Betty. These are the real movers and shakers, and it's so critically important for you to learn how to spot them that, with help from the experts—Frost, Urquhart, Mealiea, Musten, Ennis and Minors—we've put together a check list to help you:

- Whose names come up most often in conversation?
- Who do people turn to when they need information or advice?
- Who sits on the greatest number of key committees (the committees that allocate resources, money, staff, equipment, computer time and so on)?
- Who draws up the agenda for policy meetings?
- Who seems to give the most direction to these meetings (not necessarily who talks the most)?
- Who seems to have the easiest access to the president?
- Whose offices have the best view?
- Who has first call on staff time?
- When the president sends out a policy memo, who gets it?
- Whose departments got the largest budget increases last year?

The people whose names turn up most frequently on this list are the people with clout and, naturally, you should try to develop especially good relationships with them: as the experts point out, power rubs off. You can answer most of these questions by simple observation, and Laird Mealiea, the Dalhousie professor, says you should be able to complete all these observations within the first several weeks, depending on the size and complexity of both the job and the organization. But some questions, such as "Who gives the most direction to policy meetings?", require some judgment. You should check your judgments on these questions with other people and, in fact, Urquhart suggests you should try to find a mentor to help you.

Basically, he says, you should try to find someone in a senior position in the company who is willing to take you under his wing and point you in the right direction. Ideally, your boss should perform this role, but often he can't—especially at first: "Your boss has to watch you closely for the first few months to decide whether you can handle the job," Urquhart explains, "so it's often difficult for him to give you as much support as you may need. Because of this, at least one company I know of has begun to appoint a senior executive to act as a mentor for each new manager."

So you find a mentor, and you learn about all the power points and the company's language, and you hear its particular story and discover what its values are, is there anything else you ought to do? Says Mealiea: "Once you've gathered all this information, so that you know the environment, you can begin to become success-

ful at the job. You can shove your concerns about politics more into the background and get on with doing the job."

Minors, the Imperial Oil consultant, offers a good example. On his first day on
the job, Minors wore a navy blue, pinstriped suit, with vest. Minors was known as a
fairly stylish dresser on his previous job, but he says he doesn't stand out at all now
because everybody at Imperial seems to dress well. "I haven't seen polyester since
I got here."

The surprising thing is that Minors thinks this may be a problem. "As a consultant in organizational development, my job is to help people adapt to change in
the organization," he explains, "and to do this I think I have to be seen as a bit of an
individual, someone who is able to question the corporate norms. So," he says, "I
may be forced to buy a pair of jeans."

To Get Ahead, Consider a Coach

Claudia H. Deutsch

A few years ago Alix Kane, then a self-described "lowly peon" in the Guardian Life
Insurance Company of America's human resources department, was charged with
helping to set up a training program. She and her boss asked Roger Flax, a behavior coach, to hold seminars on behavioral change.

While he was there, he gave Ms. Kane a bit of private coaching. For several
days they engaged in role-playing. As a video camera whirred away, Ms. Kane
pretended that Mr. Flax was a subordinate, a boss, even the audience for a presentation. Then came the moment of truth: They watched the tapes. "I thought of
myself as assertive, but I came across as aggressive," Ms. Kane recalled. "I realized
I was putting people off."

Mr. Flax, who runs Motivational Systems Inc., of West Orange, N.J., helped
her modify that behavior. "He gave me an accurate picture of my strengths and
weaknesses, and an ability to adjust my behavior," said Ms. Kane, who now is a

senior human resources consultant at the Guardian. "I have no question that it is one reason I got ahead."

Ms. Kane is one of a growing number of mid- and high-level executives who have turned to coaches to fix personality or communications problems hindering their careers. In some cases they hired the coaches secretly, at their own expense. Far more often, bosses pay to help technically skilled subordinates develop interpersonal skills.

Many executives who work with coaches have already attended seminars in public speaking, assertiveness training or other behavior-changing areas, and found they were not enough. "Training programs and seminars are generic," said Allan L. Weisberg, vice president of human resources at Johnson & Johnson Hospital Services, who has taken coaching in communications techniques. "Coaching is customized assistance for specific problems, and that's more important."

Indeed, private coaching is on the upswing, and for good reason. During the 1980's, companies eliminated management layers, which means many executives need every tool available to compete for a dwindling number of senior jobs. Companies are also stressing teamwork, which gives people with good interpersonal skills an edge.

"For high-level people, lack of skill is not usually what gets in their way," said Bernard M. Kessler, a divisional president at Beam-Pines Inc., a New York-based human resources consulting firm. "Their styles are just inappropriate for team playing."

Not surprisingly, behavior coaching is a fundamental part of outplacement services. "We coach job hunters on how to speak to the person interviewing them in his or her style, and on how to gauge the cultural language of the organization they are applying to," said James C. Cabrera, president of the outplacement specialists Drake Beam Morin.

But increasingly, coaching is catching on with people who are employed, but just not moving ahead as fast as they—or their bosses—think they should.

One 38-year-old management consultant recently hired a coach to help him win the attention of his firm's partners. In 10 meetings, complete with videotaped role-playing sessions, he and the coach worked on making him appear more self-confident.

It worked—he recently negotiated a hefty raise and bonus. "Before I asked for it, she and I role-played it, practically scripted the conversation, put the body language together with the content," he said. "I asked for the money with a level of self-confidence that communicated that I deserved it."

The consultant, who requested anonymity, hired the coach himself, at a fee he would not disclose. Far more typically, companies will pay, often as much as $10,000 per employee.

Nancy Hutchens, a New York behavior consultant, was recently called in by a large company to work with a talented 31-year-old financial executive. She had the woman fill out psychological questionnaires, and talked to her peers, subordinates and managers. "She was such a bad people manager that they were afraid to promote her," Ms. Hutchens said. "She thought she was acting 'professional,' but others saw her as aloof."

Ms. Hutchens drew up behavior-changing steps—asking peers to lunch, discussing hobbies with subordinates. Eventually, the behavior became automatic. "Her boss says there's been a real transformation," Ms. Hutchens said. And, yes, she got the promotion.

Media Manipulation 101

Claudia H. Deutsch

Budding business grads are learning how to sell themselves in print and prime time.

The battle lines used to be clearly drawn: Reporters were the predators, executives were the prey, and public relations people ran interference between the two.

The system worked when television showed little interest in corporate news and when newspapers routinely relegated it to a few pages behind the sports section. But over the last decade, all that has changed. The internationalization of business, growing concern for the environment, the stock market crash of 1987, all have heightened the public's interest in business news—and the media's push to provide that news. The chances of an executive getting through his or her career without facing the press are growing slim indeed.

Business schools now are trying to prepare students for that new fact of business life. For at least two years, courses in media relations have been offered at Harvard, Northwestern, Dartmouth, Emory, New York University and a host of other schools. The courses, most of which are electives, are aimed at getting students to view the media as a tool that, if properly used, can enhance their companies' image and their own careers, but if improperly used, can destroy them.

The courses are attracting would-be investment bankers, manufacturing vice presidents and chief executive officers, all of whom "realize that they will be judged and graded in their careers by how well they communicate through the media," said Albert J. Tortorella, an executive vice president at the public relations firm of Burson Marsteller who is a frequent lecturer on crisis management. Added Irv Schenkler, an assistant professor of management communication who teaches media relations at N.Y.U.'s Stern School of Business: "They are people whose instincts tell them that, much as they might like to, they cannot avoid contact with the media as they climb the corporate ladder."

Those instincts are well honed. Today's typical M.B.A. candidates are in their mid-20's, and from the time they were children, they have seen business leaders both lauded and skewered in the press. Many M.B.A. candidates were working in financial firms during the 1987 crash and during the flurry of insider trading scandals, and have seen their companies' and sometimes, their colleagues', names dragged through mud.

And all have seen once-venerated companies and executives embroiled in events that made them fodder for juicy headlines—Metropolitan Edison's Three Mile Island nuclear plant meltdown, Chrysler's almost-bankruptcy, Union Carbide's Bhopal gas leak, Exxon's Alaska and Arthur Kill oil spills, to name just a few.

The students noticed that Chrysler chief Lee Iacocca and former Johnson & Johnson head James Burke, who dealt with the poisonings of the company's Tylenol, came across far more favorably during their companies' crises than did, say, Exxon's Lawrence Rawls or Carbide's Warren Anderson. And they want to be sure that, should they be faced with a public crisis, they will know how to garner the gentler treatment.

"Larry Rawls should have realized that he wouldn't have come across as so apathetic if he had flown to Alaska right away," said Kathryn M. Monahan, 26, a second-year M.B.A. student at Northwestern University's Kellogg School of Management. "That's the sort of thing these courses teach us—that the press can make or break you in a crisis, so you have to think about how you'll handle one before it hits."

Few media relations students see shunting reporters off to a public relations or legal department as an option. "If a manager can't handle the media in a crisis situation, how good can he be at managing the company?" said Christopher D. Palmer, 25, an assistant vice president at Quest Cash Management Services and a former student of Mr. Schenkler's at N.Y.U. "If there's one thing I've learned—both from the N.Y.U. course and from seeing my own reactions to businessmen in the news—it's that 'No comment' just doesn't cut it anymore."

Stacie A. Soule, a 1988 M.B.A. from Dartmouth University's Amos Tuck School who, at 28, is now production supervisor at the General Motors Corporation's Packard electric division, came to a similar conclusion after taking Tuck's media relations course.

"I used to think 'No Comment' would be the best option if a company has problems," she said. "Now I realize that executives who speak for themselves have an air of credibility, and if you play your cards right you can use the media as a tool."

Different professors use different methods to get that across. Some stress case histories. Others bring in guest speakers from the corporate and journalistic worlds, either as guest lecturers or as panelists who get to slug it out before the class. Still others use role playing, letting students act out a mock interview between reporters and executives.

Kellogg has a particularly novel twist: Its course is jointly taught by Richard C. Christian, a former public relations executive, and Newton N. Minow, a lawyer. "Generally, lawyers tell executives to shut up while public relations people tell them to communicate," Mr. Minow said. "We want to teach students to balance the conflicting advice."

Although the courses do delve into positive reasons to talk to the press, their main emphasis is on damage control.

"Managers have to learn that there is no magic pill that will transmute bad behavior into a good image, and that a good portion of their time will be taken up with external communications," said Stephen A. Greyser, who teaches the Harvard Business School's media course.

Paul Argenti, who teaches Tuck's course, is more blunt: "The press is going to tell the other side anyway, so the students might as well learn how to get their side in."

The Man in the Glass

Anonymous

When you have reached your goal
In the World of Sports,
And you have worked the Big game,
That day,
Just go to the mirror,
And look at yourself,
And see what the man has to say.
For it isn't your family or friends or coaches
Whose judgement upon you must pass;
The fellow whose verdict,
Counts in your life,
Is the one staring at you from the glass.
You may fool all the world down the avenue of years,
And get pats on your back as you pass,
But, your only reward will be remorse and regret,
If you have cheated the man in the glass.

Chapter
3

Leadership

What makes a person an effective leader? How does the leadership process work? Do leaders really make a difference to organizational outcomes and to the lives and fortunes of people in the organization? Nobody seems to have definitive answers to these questions. Indeed, many behavioral scientists, after observing or being part of the innumerable studies, debates, and theoretical formulations focused on leadership, have thrown up their hands and turned to other concepts such as organizational structure, technology, and so on in an effort to understand and to explain organizational life. Yet the fascination and indeed preoccupation with leadership remains for researchers and practitioners alike. The search for effective leaders goes on. Training courses abound that promise the development of improved leadership ability, and research money is still allocated to its study. Owners of unsuccessful organizations, such as losing sports teams, regularly blame the managers and replace them with "better leaders." People continue to attach their hopes as well as their frustrations to those chosen as leaders.

We do not have answers to the questions we are posing here. We do feel, however, that one approach to a better understanding of what leadership comprises is to examine what some students of leadership have said recently, based on their research on leaders in the field, and to take a close look at some leaders in action in their organizations. Leaders described here and in other chapters of this book appear to be dynamic, purposive, and durable individuals. Frequently leaders are manipulative, creating and interpreting realities and moving people into those realities to accomplish their goals. They often are admired and respected by their followers, but sometimes they are feared and hated by these same followers. Successful leaders typically are good listeners; sometimes they listen in order to work with those who tell them things, sometimes to take advantage of them, but always because they are relentless in their pursuit of information upon which to base their future ideas and actions.

We suspect that most people will have encountered, worked for, competed with or even acted as individuals having some or all of the leadership characteristics described in the selections in this chapter. In the article, "Managing in the '90s Like Starting Over Again," Michael Skapinker describes the challenge managers confront in helping them learn how to manage in today's environment. Next, David T. Kearns, chairman and CEO of the Xerox Corporation, recounts in "Leadership Through Quality," the steps his organization has taken to reestablish its position in the industry. Christopher Knowlton's "Imagineer Eisner on Creative Leadership," as the title implies, emphasizes the importance of creativity in leaders.

Charlotte Gray describes charisma in action in "Caucus Charisma," a description of Prime Minister Brian Mulroney's tactics with the Tory caucus of the Canadian government. While Mulroney succeeds by charming his colleagues, Warren Bennis in "Followers Make Good Leaders Good," points out the importance of thoughtful and appropriately worded dissent.

The last two selections in this chapter are both directed toward managing in a rapidly changing environment, an environment that it likely to exhibit increasingly the characteristics described and advocated in these selections. "Managing in the '90s: The Androgynous Manager," calls for a blend of traditional masculine and feminine roles and values, more expressive rather than instrumental behavior. The authors, Alice G. Sargent and Ronald J. Stupak, see this blend and the resulting managerial style as necessary both to accommodate the increasing presence of women in management and to deal with the increasing complexities of managing effectively. In "The Postheroic Leader" David L. Bradford and Allan R. Cohen emphasize the importance of a coaching style of management. This style, which is calculated to develop the capabilities of subordinates and engender teamwork, stands in contrast with the top-down management of the past.

Managing in the '90s Like Starting Over Again

Michael Skapinker

The 1990s looks like being the decade in which managers need their subordinates more than their subordinates need them.

It is not just that skill shortages have blighted many areas of industry and commerce, turning employees into a scarce resource over which companies have to squabble.

Nor is it just that companies will fail if they cannot find staff who are ready to take that extra bit of trouble, whether in raising quality, improving customer service or shortening product development times.

The more important reason why managers need their subordinates is that they can help them learn how to manage again.

As Rosabeth Moss Kanter of the Harvard Business School says, the job of being a manager has undergone such enormous change that it needs to be reinvented. The change manifests itself in many ways, but the underlying cause is the same: for organisations to succeed, employees need to become increasingly knowledgeable and skilful. The more they know, however, the less easy they are to manage.

For example, successful organisations know that they need to forge closer links with their suppliers and customers. Not all those responsible for developing and deepening those links are senior members of the corporate hierarchy. Maintaining the links requires the co-operation of middle managers, as well as salespeople, receptionists, telephonists, transport and warehouse staff. These employees often end up knowing more about customers and suppliers' needs than their superiors do.

Developments like these can be immensely threatening to senior managers. How do you know how well your staff are doing if they develop knowledge, skills and contacts which you don't have?

How can you appraise performance if your customers and suppliers know more about your staff than you do?

Kanter says that in the past, managers performed well by following set procedures. They did things by the book and ensured that their subordinates did the same. Now, however, the rule book is gone.

"In the new corporation, managers must learn to operate without the crutch of hierarchy. Position, title and authority are no longer adequate tools, not in a world

"Managing in the '90s Like Starting Over" by Michael Skapinker, (originally titled "Knowledge is an Unsettling Thing: How Managers' Will Alter in the 1990s as Old Rules No Longer Apply) *Financial Times*, December 18, 1989. Reprinted by permission of Financial Times Syndicate.

where subordinates are encouraged to think for themselves and where managers have to work with other departments and other companies."

The problem of managing knowledgeable employees has been discussed by Tom Lloyd and Karl Erik Sveiby in a book called *Managing Knowhow*. They looked particularly at the difficulties faced by companies which employ "knowledge workers", organisations like management consultants, advertising agencies, newspapers, research laboratories and computer software houses. These organisations recruit people precisely because they are creative, irreverent and able to come up with new and unconventional answers. In short, they recruit people to break the rules.

Leadership Through Quality

David T. Kearns

IN MY VIEW

Where were you 30 years ago? In March 1960, we at Xerox Corporation shipped our first 914 copiers, beginning one of the most successful new product introductions in history.

We expected to place 5,000 of the plain-paper copiers in three years, but to our surprise, 10,000 had been shipped by the end of 1962. We were backlogged with orders for many more.

For the next 15 years, we dominated the industry we had created. We were convinced that we were providing the world with high-quality machines, and our convictions were reinforced by the broad acceptance of Xerox products by our customers. Our success was so overwhelming that we became complacent.

By the mid-1970s, we found ourselves out of step with our customers and their needs. The market had changed and so had the standards for quality. This became evident when Japanese manufacturers established a position in the U.S. market with inexpensive desk-top copiers and began changing the industry.

"Leadership Through Quality" by David Kearns, *Academy of Management Executive*, 4(2), pp. 86–88. Reprinted with permission.

Initially, we dismissed the Japanese by telling ourselves that they were catering to low-volume users, a market segment of only marginal interest to us. We had always been successful, and we assumed that we would continue to be successful. Then we discovered that they were cutting into our market share by selling better, more reliable copiers at prices approximating our cost for producing comparable products.

We learned firsthand how far we had fallen behind when we began producing and marketing a copier in the United States that had been designed by our own Japanese affiliate, Fuji Xerox. To our amazement, the reject rate for the Fuji Xerox parts proved to be a fraction of the rate for American parts.

We undertook market surveys and held conversations with unhappy customers, which forced us to face up to a critical truth: Quality improvement can't be measured in a meaningful way against standards of your own internal devising. It can only be measured against the requirements of your customers.

Visits to our Japanese affiliate, Fuji Xerox, revealed another important truth: Quality in manufacturing doesn't increase real cost. It actually decreases costs by reducing rejects, eliminating excessive inspections and field service, and most importantly, by diminishing the cost of business lost to competitors.

With these hard-learned lessons in mind, Xerox entered the 1980s with a new vision. Our manufacturing organization started adopting techniques such as statistical quality control—a process that emphasizes preventing defects rather than screening them out through inspection.

With the concurrence and participation of the Amalgamated Clothing & Textile Workers Union, which represents our production employees, we organized volunteer plant workers into a small number of "quality of worklife" circles. After training the workers in interpersonal skills, group dynamics, and problem-solving techniques, we invited them to evaluate situations ranging from working conditions to production problems. We asked them to come up with recommendations for improvements.

This experiment led to training all our production workers in partnership with the union. We began a gradual transition from stand-alone, quality of work-life circles to work-family groups composed of people working together in discrete manufacturing operations. We also provided special, cross-organizational, task teams.

In 1983, we introduced what we call our Leadership Through Quality process—a management system that depends heavily on employee involvement and focuses the entire company on the achievement of total quality. We altered the role of first-line management from that of the traditional, dictatorial foreman to that of a supervisor functioning primarily as a coach and expediter.

At the time Leadership-Through-Quality was introduced, I told our employees that customer satisfaction would be our top priority and that it would change the culture of the company. We redefined quality as meeting the requirements of our customers. It may have been the most significant strategy Xerox had ever embarked on. Nearly seven years have passed, and what I said then still stands.

Our first step in implementing the Leadership-Through-Quality process was to train management with their family work groups. The training, usually conducted off-site in about three-and-a-half days, was similar to what we had already been giving our manufacturing people.

Emphasis was placed on identifying quality shortfalls and the problems that caused them, determining root causes, developing solutions, and implementing them. The family groups were taught interpersonal skills, a six-step problem-solving process, and a nine-step quality improvement process.

To assure the commitment of management at every level, Leadership-Through-Quality training began with our top-tier family work group—my direct reports and me. It then cascaded through the organizations led by senior staff, gradually spreading worldwide to some 100,000 employees.

At the same time as the training started, we intensified and institutionalized analysis of our competitive posture. In addition to conversations with customers and periodic surveys of the marketplace, we turned to benchmarking, the process of measuring ourselves against the products, services, and practices of our toughest competitors.

For example, we benchmarked L.L. Bean for distribution procedures, Deere Company for central computer operations, Procter & Gamble for marketing, and Florida Power and Light for its own quality process. This kind of benchmarking has become the responsibility of each corporate activity. Approximately 240 different functional areas of our company now benchmark against comparable areas.

Our employee-involvement teams were given considerable empowerment. Nowhere is this more dramatically demonstrated than in manufacturing, where individual assemblers have the authority to stop the assembly line when less severe problems are identified and fixed on the spot as a team by the operators. We even scrapped a multi-million-dollar assembly line because its configuration isolated the individual operators and made it impossible for them to talk to one another.

There is no magic formula to a successful quality program. The key is involvement. From the top to the bottom of our management team, we have a deep and real commitment to employee involvement. We know that if we fail to maintain this commitment, Xerox won't survive in today's global market. That's a powerful incentive.

We've also learned that it's important to have union leaders as deeply committed to the quality process as management. A strong and enlightened union leadership shared management's vision and understood that changes had to be made if there was to be a future for all Xerox employees. We shared each other's trust.

Finally, we learned that patience and discipline are necessary if a quality process is to succeed. We didn't realize results immediately from our process. There were false starts, and there were managers who perceived employee involvement as a threat. Some parts of the organization also lagged behind others. It takes time, and it takes nurturing.

At Xerox, the quality process pervades every operation. It has been invigorating and energized all of us. Now, we're reaping the rewards. For example:

- After reducing our supplier base, we achieved a 45-percent cost reduction and substantial quality improvement in purchased parts—from 92-percent defect free to 99.5-percent defect free over the past five years.

- Production-line defective parts have been reduced more than 90 percent since 1982.
- We reduced average manufacturing costs by 20 percent from 1982 to 1986, and they are continuing to come down. During the same period, we cut the time to bring a new product to market by as much as 60 percent.
- Machine performance during the first 30 days following installation has improved 40 percent in four years.

We are probably the first American company in an industry targeted by the Japanese to regain market share without the aid of tariffs, or government help.

Our achievements were recognized last year when the Business Products and Systems group of Xerox was one of only two recipients of the 1989 Malcolm Baldrige National Quality Award. The award is bestowed by the U.S. Commerce Department for "preeminent quality leadership." Within days of the Baldrige announcement, Xerox Canada Inc. won its country's first National Quality Award.

We take great satisfaction in winning these awards, but the fact is that we're far from finished with our drive to improve. We have learned that the pursuit of quality is a race with no finish line. We see an upward and neverending spiral of increased competition and heightened customer expectations.

We're out to continue improving our product reliability. We want to speed up the time it takes to bring a new product to market and continue reducing our costs. Most importantly, we want to continue making strides in satisfying our customers with our products and services. We know that success is assured only by keeping the customer satisfied.

The goals we have set are lofty, but they are also within our reach. Simply put, we expect to be the best. Our customers expect us to be the best. And we don't intend to fail them, or ourselves.

Imagineer Eisner on Creative Leadership

Christopher Knowlton

With childlike enthusiasm, Michael Eisner outlines a pet project over a bowl of frozen yogurt in the Walt Disney Studios commissary. He intends to combine a retail store selling Disney doodads with a restaurant serving healthy, low-cholesterol food. The cuisine, he gushes, will be "fun, exciting, entertaining, and wonderful!" Then he admits that the concept doesn't tie in with Disney's other businesses and that most of his associates don't see much virtue in the plan. In a resigned voice he adds, "I've been driving everybody crazy."

Eisner is a CEO who is more hands-on than Mother Teresa. His chief duty at Disney is to lead creatively, to be a thinker, inventor, and cheerleader for new ideas—in founder Walt's own words, to be an Imagineer. Says Eisner: "Every CEO has to spend an enormous amount of time shuffling papers. The question is, how much of your time can you leave free to think about ideas? To me the pursuit of ideas is the only thing that matters. You can always find capable people to do almost everything else."

He uses a number of tactics to encourage, even induce, creativity in others. To come up with the layout for Euro Disneyland he called a meeting of a dozen of the world's most respected architects and had them brainstorm in a wildly creative session that became so heated, two of the architects began shoving each other and almost came to blows. "I'll use meetings, company anniversaries, anything to create some kind of catalyst to get us all going," says Eisner. He believes he must give his people free rein if he hopes to foster an entrepreneurial spirit within such a financially disciplined corporation.

As shepherd of the Disney flock, Eisner tries to promote a family-like camaraderie among his top managers. In late September he asked each division head to perform a skit for the anniversary dinner celebrating the team's first five years at the company. The skits peppered Eisner and President Frank Wells with barbed jokes about their management styles and big paychecks. At the end of this roast, instead of giving tit for tat, Eisner, Wells, Roy Disney, and their wives danced out onto the stage and performed a raucous kick line while booming out their spoof of "We Are the World."

Befitting a former English major at Denison University in Ohio who once had a passion for writing plays, Eisner thinks in terms of story lines. He applies that thinking to all the company's activities, whether he is building a $200 million hotel or a $10 million theme park attraction. "We ask, 'What is the story we want to tell when people walk into one of our new buildings? What are they going to feel? What is going to happen next? And how will it end?' " He is using movie story-boards to create a chronology and schedule for the construction of his Colorado vacation home.

The ideas that grab him—and often he can't remember if they are his own or embellishments of someone else's—are those that surprise him and tease his imag-ination. He disdains ideas that seem too familiar. On the other hand, for an idea to succeed at Disney it can't be so avant-garde that it ceases to be commercial. The *Making of Me* attraction in Epcot Center's new Wonders of Life pavilion, which features footage of the birth of a baby, had its genesis in Eisner's own emotionally charged experiences at the delivery of his three sons. His tastes are mainstream and all-American, combined with a gut instinct for what new flavor might be pop-ular next.

Appropriately for the chief of America's leading peddler of wholesome enter-tainment, Eisner sees his family as his inspiration. He follows the tastes, interests, and activities of his children with the vigilance of a police-beat reporter. His wife, Jane, often screens his ideas. Says he: "98.5% of my ideas revolve around things that we are both involved in. With the stuff that is really on the edge, I will ask her if I'm crazy. Of course she usually thinks I am."

Caucus Charisma

Charlotte Gray

Brian Mulroney keeps his fractious Tory MPs "feeling like they've just had a snort of cocaine"

One of the perennial questions about Brian Mulroney is how does he do it? How has he kept his MPs' spirits up when his policies are in such a mess and his govern-ment is so unpopular? And can he continue to do it?

"Caucus Charisma" by Charlotte Gray, *Saturday Night*, July/August 1990, pp. 15–18. Reprinted by permission.

Until last May, after nearly six bumpy years in power, the prime minister had suffered only three defections: Robert Toupin in 1987, Alex Kindy and David Kilgour in April. Since then caucus unity has looked more fragile (Quebec MPs have begun to bolt)—but despite his lousy management of issues, Mulroney continues to be a brilliant manager of people. At noon each Wednesday, Progressive Conservative backbenchers still bound out of their weekly caucus meeting like an army of Lazaruses, ready for another onslaught of nasty letters and voters' doors slammed in their faces. The two opposition parties also hold caucus meetings every Wednesday, at which members hear from the leaders, discuss parliamentary strategy, and air grievances. But neither the Liberals nor the New Democrats emerge lubed with evangelical enthusiasm. As Tory MP John Bosley, whose family owns a large Toronto real-estate company, comments: "If I could put the prime minister in front of our salesforce once a week, we would double our business. He is one of the best motivators."

Mulroney learned from his predecessors how successfully a crabby caucus can send a leader to the cold-sweat pinnacle of paranoia. John Diefenbaker, leader from 1956 to 1967, regarded his MPs as a nest of vipers, best ignored. "I worked for Dief from 1963 to 1967," recalls Marjory LeBreton, Mulroney's deputy chief of staff, "and I can count on two hands the number of times he went to caucus. Gordon Churchill [a Manitoba MP and Diefenbaker crony] would arrive each Wednesday from the meeting to report all the rumbles of caucus discontent. But Dief just let them fester." In the end, they did Dief in.

Robert Stanfield, who took over in 1967, attended the Wednesday meeting more regularly. But as he entered the caucus room each week, he looked as cheerful as Daniel entering the lions' den. And from 1976, Joe Clark needed a bulletproof vest for caucus encounters.

Brian Mulroney, in contrast, has made caucus management a top priority. His method is a cross between corporate rah-rah (people "want desperately to be on winning teams": *In Search of Excellence* by Thomas J. Peters and Robert H. Waterman) and Amway-type inspirational zeal (Amway offers distributors "a faith to live by, a purpose to live for": *Amway* by Steve Butterfield). "The caucus is the heart of the machine," Mulroney told Graham Fraser, author of *Playing for Keeps.* The prime minister's schedule revolves round that Wednesday commitment, which he rarely misses.

Like the yuppie parent he is, Mulroney gives his MPs quality time. His predecessors often spoke early in the weekly meeting, then slipped out to face More Important Matters. But Mulroney sits attentively through the whole agenda—the brief welcome from Bob Layton, chairman of caucus; the report on the health of caucus members from old-timer Stan Darling; the reports from the whip, the House leader, the regional caucuses; comments from MPs who line up at the floor microphones. Finally, around 11:30 a.m., the prime minister rises to give a speech that is a *tour de force* of political manipulation. "He plays caucus," observes Senator Staff Barootes, "like Heifetz plays the violin."

Mulroney begins with a recap of his week in a voice close to a whisper. (Rod Steiger used the same get-them-on-the-edge-of-their-seats technique in *In the Heat of the Night.*) MPs strain forward to hear about Mila's and his exhausting trip to Dallas, his phone call from President Bush, his efforts to break the constitutional impasse. MPs love spoonfuls of secret dope: hearing things first gives them warm fuzzies about being insiders.

Turning up the volume slightly, Mulroney deals with comments he has heard from previous speakers. He deflects pleas on behalf of suffering regions (Nova Scotian Peter McCreath gave a heart-rending description of the Atlantic provinces' devastation after the budget cuts) with lavish compliments to the pleaders. They are held up to the rest of caucus as examples of "first-rate fighters for their ridings." Sitting next to the prime minister at the table facing the room, Jim Hawkes, a trained psychologist who is chief government whip, marvels at the way Mulroney "meets people's *needs*. He has the skill to hear the reality behind the grievance."

The meat of the meeting is the prime minister's unscripted comments on the government's position that week: why things are tough, what is really going on. He switches between ponderous predictions ("One point a month, colleagues, we'll climb one point in the polls a month") and self-disparaging jokes. ("I see our CBC friends decided old Mulroney's problems with the Senate were more important than the San Francisco earthquake last week. Did ya see that?")

Again and again, the Guinness-smooth voice *breaking* with conviction, he replays the same themes: how every other advanced economy has a consumption tax, or why being right is more important than being popular. He reminds MPs how often he's been right before: about the recovery from their 1987 low in the polls, about the collapse of John Turner's Liberals, about why voters would never, in the end, vote for "Mr. Perfection"—Ed Broadbent. He produces titbits of reassurance: the latest OECD chart to prove Canada's prosperity; the half-million-dollar advertisement placed in *Business Week* magazine by the Ontario government (whose premier, David Peterson, was a harsh critic of the free-trade agreement) that boasted of Ontario's absence of trade barriers thanks to the FTA. ("You wait! In three years, Don Getty will put an ad in *Business Week* for Alberta, boasting about what the GST has done for his province," he cracked.) Says Hawkes, "You get the feeling he has the blueprint for the future."

Carefully, he builds the crescendo. "Some weeks, I wonder how the hell can he find any optimism this time?" remarks Senator Finlay MacDonald. Only once, in the "Black Winter" of 1986 when his cabinet was awash in sleaze, did Mulroney take a different tack. "Colleagues, I'm a little weary of pumping you up: why don't you pump me up for a change?" he whispered. "There wasn't a dry eye in the room," MacDonald recalls.

Since then, it has been the PM doing the pumping, quoting Margaret Thatcher ("the only poll that counts is the poll on election day"), keeping MPs focused on fighting the Opposition, not each other. The appeal to self-interest is unvarnished. If there is a caucus revolt by anti-GST westerners or nationalist Quebeckers, Mulroney reminds them, they will *all* lose their jobs and leave the field wide open to the Liberals. "Your only friends in Ottawa are the people in this room."

A storm of applause explodes as he finishes (while a few old cynics at the back score him, like a figure skater, out of ten). "Everyone leaves the room on a high," marvels Senator Barootes, "feeling like they've just had a snort of cocaine."

The caucus address is a mere power cadenza in a full concerto—Mulroney's constant attention to the egos of his troop. The weekly pep talk works because Mulroney makes each backbencher feel he or she is a somebody. "Don't take any shit from my staff," he reassures MPs. "You tell me if any member of my cabinet doesn't respond to your phone calls." ("God help the minister who becomes a target in caucus," admits Mary Collins, associate defence minister.) Explicitly, Mulroney presses home the message: he's one of them.

Of course that's nonsense: the PM is about as close to his backbenchers as a galley master is to the slaves at the oars. Today's Tory caucus is an unstable brew of rednecks, Red Tories, free-enterprise crusaders, Quebec nationalists, western chauvinists, rural individualists, and urban yuppies. Philosophically, Mulroney is more sympathetic to Quebec than to most of his English-Canadian MPs, more committed to federalism than to most of his Quebec MPs, and more progressive than most members of either group. But the PM works hard to control the machine. In 1982 Clark was forced to allow his fractious caucus to choose its own chairman. Mulroney soon reversed that. The loyalty of Bob Layton, a genial Anglo-Quebec engineer whom Mulroney appointed chairman of caucus, knows no bounds. "I once led a Bible class in Montreal," Layton explains. "We talked about God as an 'infuser.' I guess that's what the prime minister is."

Conformity is rewarded with a prestige appointment (a committee chairmanship, or even a cabinet post), a new federal investment in your riding. Kilgour, the outcast, insists, "Anyone with an IQ over a hundred knows that it's fear and favours, not charm, that makes the troops buy his blarney." However, the guy who dishes out some of the inducements (parliamentary trips, invitations to official dinners) ridicules that idea. "MPs are successes where they come from," argues Jim Hawkes, the government whip. "They're not kept in line by a reward system that might work with nine-year-olds." But they *are* kept in line by activity—activity designed to make them feel like important cogs in the machine.

"When [Mulroney] took over as party leader," writes Fraser in *Playing for Keeps,* "he set up caucus committees, caucus task forces, transition teams. Titles proliferated. Everyone had a job." Today, MPs scamper between House of Commons standing committees and legislative committees. When a contentious issue such as language policy or abortion sets Tory against Tory, Mulroney prompts his MPs to form their own little committee to find a solution. "*We* wrote the abortion legislation," boasts Lise Bourgault, co-chair of the ad hoc abortion committee. "And caucus kept the committee's existence secret because it was much too important to let the press know about." The Tory caucus, once the best source of leaks in town, is now tightly caulked.

Mulroney uses caucus both to initiate policy (on issues like abortion that are marginal to his government's main agenda) and as a sounding board for policies that he knows will be difficult to sell. Usually, he is careful never to get too far ahead of caucus (unlike Stanfield, who once admitted, "I felt like a minority in my own party").

But the prime minister's most crucial skill is his understanding of human nature. Most leaders have little time, and less inclination, for the minutiae of their MPs' lives. Trudeau consistently forgot backbenchers' names; Stanfield shrank from dealing with others' personal difficulties; Clark's defensiveness was an icy barrier between him and his party; John Turner alternated between concern and careless disregard. Mulroney, however, is the reverse. He has a gut instinct for what makes individuals tick—maybe as a result of insights gained as he worked his way up from Baie-Comeau street hockey to the Mount Royal Tennis Club, maybe as a result of a career in labour negotiations and the political trenches. Mulroney knows people's fears, dreams, wormy self-doubts, silent resentments.

"He always seems to know what's on everybody's mind," says John Bosley. "And he's been up and been down himself, so when he says, 'I know what you're going through,' we know he does." MPs wallow in the sticky warmth of the leader's paternalism. "His radar is incredible," says Senator MacDonald. "He can spot discomfort a mile away. And he has a mental dossier on everyone—their business worries, their kids, their ambitions." How he works on those dossiers! Trivia about others' lives is passed to him via phone calls to LeBreton, notes from Hawkes during Question Period, a whispered word outside the House of Commons. "He wants to know everything," explains Hawkes. "Whose wife is sick, whose daughter has graduated. . . ."

The information is used to glue caucus together. Hawkes acknowledges, "My wife will never forget how he personally phoned her several times when I was in the hospital." Senator Barootes recalls how flattered his wife was when the prime minister stopped to chat with her once. (Mulroney's respect for wives is legendary: it removes the danger of an unbelieving spouse mouthing off at breakfast about the funding cuts to women's groups.) Stroke, stroke—and scribble, scribble. Personal notes and photographs signed in black felt pen whiz round the Hill. Every Tory MP's office has a large colour photo, personally inscribed. It's partly a genuine concern for colleagues. ("He's really a friendly person," insists LeBreton, who has eight signed photos of Mulroney in her office, compared to one photo of each of the other three leaders she served.) It's also a technique for building personal loyalty.

Trudeau tried to build support in his caucus by force of cold logic; Mulroney's appeals to supporters range from flattery to the insidious pressure of family guilt. "When he was warning us about scandals," says Senator Barootes, "he told us that it wasn't the embarrassment to Brian Mulroney that would count: it was the embarrassment to us, to our families, our kids—what would their friends say to them?" Only when everyone was squirming did Mulroney move on to the embarrassment to colleagues and government.

During conversations with MPs about caucus dynamics, the same comment is endlessly repeated: "If only the Canadian voters could see the prime minister that I see in caucus. . . ." But Mulroney cannot work the same magic or sign enough photos to placate a large crowd of voters hurt by his policies. Yet, the lower his credibility rating in public opinion polls, the stronger his MPs' sense of solidarity. Lise Bourgault is an outspoken Quebec nationalist. But the fragility of her commitment to Canada did not for a minute shake her blind faith in her leader last April. "I *know* the prime minister has a miracle in his back pocket. 'Count on me,' he tells us, 'the third mandate will be just as great.' "

Followers Make Good Leaders Good

Warren Bennis

The dilemma at the top

It is probably inevitable that a society as star-struck as ours should focus on leaders in analyzing why organizations succeed or fail. As a long-time student and teacher of management, I, too, have tended to look to the men and women at the top for clues on how organizations achieve and maintain institutional health. But the longer I study effective leaders, the more I am persuaded of the under-appreciated importance of effective followers.

What makes a good follower? The single most important characteristic may well be a willingness to tell the truth. In a world of growing complexity, leaders are increasingly dependent on their subordinates for good information whether the leaders want to hear it or not. Followers who tell the truth, and leaders who listen to it, are an unbeatable combination.

Movie mogul Samuel Goldwyn seems to have had a gut-level awareness of the importance of what I call "effective backtalk" from subordinates. After a string of box-office flops, Mr. Goldwyn called his staff together and told them: "I want you to tell me exactly what's wrong with me and M.G.M., even if it means losing your job."

Although Mr. Goldwyn wasn't personally ready to give up the ego-massaging presence of "yes men," in his own gloriously garbled way he acknowledged the company's greater need for a staff that speaks the truth.

Like portfolios, organizations benefit from diversity. Effective leaders resist the urge to people their staffs only with others who look or sound or think just like themselves, what I call the doppelgänger, or ghostly-double, effect. They look for good people from many molds, and then they encourage them to speak out, even to disagree. Aware of the pitfalls of institutional unanimity, some leaders wisely build dissent into the decision-making process.

Organizations that encourage thoughtful dissent gain much more than a heightened air of collegiality. They make better decisions. In a recent study, Rebecca A. Henry, a psychology professor at Purdue University, found that groups were generally more effective than individuals in making forecasts of sales and other financial data. And the greater the initial disagreement among group members, the more accurate the results. "With more disagreement, people are forced to look at a wider range of possibilities," Ms. Henry said.

Like good leaders, good followers understand the importance of speaking out. More important, they do it. Almost 30 years ago, when Nikita Khruschev came to America, he met with reporters at the Washington Press Club. The first written question he received was: "Today you talked about the hideous rule of your predecessor, Stalin. You were one of his closest aides and colleagues during those years. What were you doing all that time?" Khruschev's face grew red. "Who asked that?" he roared. No one answered. "Who asked that?" he insisted. Again, silence. "That's what I was doing," Mr. Khruschev said.

Even in democracies where the only gulag is the threat of a pink slip, it is hard to disagree with the person in charge. Several years ago TV's John Chancellor asked former Presidential aides how they behaved on those occasions when the most powerful person in the world came up with a damned fool idea. Several of the aides admitted doing nothing. Ted Sorenson revealed that John F. Kennedy could usually be brought to his senses by being told, "That sounds like the kind of idea Nixon would have."

Quietism, as a more pious age called the sin of silence, often costs organizations—and their leaders—dearly. Former President Ronald Reagan suffered far more at the hands of so-called friends who refused to tell him unattractive truths than from his ostensible enemies.

Nancy Reagan, in her recent memoir, "My Turn," recalls chiding then-Vice President George Bush when he approached her, not the President, with grave reservations about White House chief of staff Donald Regan.

"I wish you'd tell my husband," the First Lady said. "I can't be the only one who's saying this to him." According to Mrs. Reagan, Mr. Bush responded, "Nancy, that's not my role."

"That's exactly your role," she snapped.

Nancy Reagan was right. It is the good follower's obligation to share his or her best counsel with the person in charge. And silence—not dissent—is the one answer that leaders should refuse to accept. History contains dozens of cautionary tales on the subject, none more vivid than the account of the murder of Thomas A. Becket. "Will no one rid me of this meddlesome priest?" Henry II muttered, after a contest of wills with his former friend.

The four barons who then murdered Becket in his cathedral were the antithesis of the good followers they thought themselves to be. At the risk of being irreverent, the right answer to Henry's question—the one that would have served his administration best—was "No," or at least, "Let's talk about it."

Like modern-day subordinates who testify under oath that they were only doing what they thought their leader wanted them to do, the barons were guilty of remarkable chutzpah. Henry failed by not making his position clear and by creating an atmosphere in which his followers would rather kill than disagree with him. The barons failed by not making the proper case against the king's decision.

Effective leaders reward dissent, as well as encourage it. They understand that whatever momentary discomfort they experience as a result of being told from time to time that they are wrong is more than offset by the fact that reflective backtalk increases a leader's ability to make good decisions.

Executive compensation should go far toward salving the pricked ego of the leader whose followers speak their minds. But what's in it for the follower? The good follower may indeed have to put his or her job on the line in the course of speaking up. But consider the price he or she pays for silence. What job is worth the enormous psychic cost of following a leader who values loyalty in the narrowest sense?

Perhaps the ultimate irony is that the follower who is willing to speak out shows precisely the kind of initiative that leadership is made of.

Managing in the '90s: The Androgynous Manager

Alice G. Sargent and Ronald J. Stupak

We are witnessing a set of critical value shifts in American culture. The major shift affecting corporate America is from the vertical values (rugged individualism, autonomy, and independence) to the horizontal values (interdependence, mutuality, networking, and coalition building).

It is a transformation from a predominantly masculine value system to an androgynous one (*andro* is Greek for male; *gyne* is Greek for female). The new value set calls for each person to have a blend of values—competence and compassion, action and introspection. It is the style required for effective leadership in organizational America in the years ahead.

Such a blend mixes together two sets of values:

- The so-called masculine characteristics that managers will need to continue to exhibit—dominance, independence, a direct achievement style, a rever-

ence for rational, analytical problem solving, a valuing of verbal behavior, and a competitive strategic approach;
- The so-called feminine characteristics—concern for relationships, a valuing of expressive behavior, attention to nonverbal behavior, the ability to accommodate and mediate, and a vicarious achievement style (enjoying the development of others).

For contemporary role models of androgynous leadership and management, we can look to Bill Cosby, Alan Alda, Frank Furillo of "Hill Street Blues," Corazon Aquino, Marian Wright Edelman of the Children's Defense Fund, and Barbara Jordan. In a recent *Business Week* survey, Colonel Potter from television's "M.A.S.H." was selected as the manager for whom most people would prefer to work, above Lee Iacocca.

In a sense, the 1960s and 1970s were about women; the late 1980s are about men. Books about men are proliferating. At least 25 universities have begun offering courses in men's studies. Men are beginning to re-examine the male experience and the costs paid for the overuse of competition, the absence of close male friendships in adulthood, and the Lone Ranger style. Furthermore, the definition of masculinity as macho warrior, wimp, or anything not considered feminine is under intense scrutiny.

The nature of management is changing as well. Today's managers spend 50 to 90 percent of their time interacting with people—70 percent of that in groups—and 50 percent operating outside the chain of command. An androgynous blend of competencies is critical for managerial effectiveness and organizational and corporate leadership.

MANAGEMENT REALITIES

How did things get the way they are? What accounts for the shift? Let's examine the context.

Transactional Realities at the Executive Level

Frank Sherwood, a major influence in the field of public administration, says that as one progresses up the managerial ladder, horizontal skills begin to replace vertical skills as the basis for effective leadership. In other words, as a person moves up the hierarchy, with accompanying increases in formal responsibilities, problems become broader and more complex as constraints become more similar. At the highest levels of an organization, horizontal administration rather than vertical administration becomes the key to power.

That point is critical, because the vertical skills of command and control are replaced by skills that emphasize making transactions across organizational borders, brokering coalitions, and building consensus. Negotiation, bargaining, and mediation start to become more important than directing, demanding, and doing. The need to master transactional competencies determines the status, character, and effectiveness of executives in the corporate arena.

Harold Leavitt in *Beyond the Analytical Manager* and James McGregor Burns in *Leadership* say that transactional leadership skills and human-relations skills are the ones needed to master organizational realities in the American democratic, incremental context. David McClelland says the evidence points overwhelmingly to the conclusion that women are more concerned than men with both sides of interdependent relationships.

As the "female" concern for interdependence becomes an essential perspective for effectiveness at the highest levels of management, the androgynous blend needs to become an operational reality at the highest levels of organizations.

The Service Economy and the Servant Leadership Style

As we evolve from an industrial economy to one that is 60 percent service-oriented, leadership requires both masculine and feminine dimensions of power. Surely unilateral power must be blended with synergistic power. Personal dominance may be effective in small groups, but leaders who guide large groups and massive corporations in the service economy must become effective in the more subtle and socialized forms of power and influence.

In today's marketplace, where increasing numbers of followers, employees, and clients want to have a voice in the management of their organizations, a socialized leadership style must replace the autocratic, directive style of the 1930s, 1940s, and 1950s. "Servant leadership," based on a firm belief in people, generates the empowerment required to move the massive organizations of corporate America onto the new strategic stage of multinational and international competition and interdependence.

The depth and breadth of the reaction to poor service has demanded that organizations demonstrate the sensitivity and feelings necessary to get closer to customers and clients. Feedback is "the critical dimension" for those committed to an androgynous style.

Organizational Families

In *The 100 Best Companies to Work for in America*, Robert Levering, Milton Moskowitz, and Michael Katz say that the number-one factor on their list of 12 themes for successful companies is that the excellent ones "make people feel part of a team . . . or a family."

High-performing organizations demand that good managers have both the head and the heart to be effective leaders. The powerful managers who are memorable are often gracious people as well. The positive, not the negative, face of power predominates at Dana Corporation, Walt Disney, Procter and Gamble, and Hewlett Packard. Surely that suggests that the traditional masculine way of explaining the influence of a manager on his or her followers has not been entirely correct. A good manager does not use sheer, overwhelming dominance to force subordinates to submit and follow. Instead, the nurturing style of expressing power, along with the "sharing" perspective of empowerment, seems to "flame the families" toward productivity in high-performing organizations.

To paraphrase James O'Toole's *Vanguard Management,* workers can no longer be treated as bastard step-children in the corporate clan, but must be viewed as legitimate stockholders empowered to participate actively in the "family enterprise."

The 21st Century's Paradigm for Productive Performance

Generative power as opposed to imperial power (which is ruthless) appears to be essential to long-term organizational excellence. Generative power, which implies the coming together of two independent beings, has become the paradigm of productive performance in the corporate world as we shatter the traditional boundaries between black and white, men and women, public and private, and national and international.

New frameworks must be created in the multinational, multicultural corporate environment. McClelland makes it clear that men attain "generativity" more easily if they abandon some of their traditional assertiveness; women, if they abandon some of their traditional dependency. The androgynous model is relevant for leadership effectiveness in the re-created world of production, performance, and service.

Women and the Workforce

The workforce is changing. In 1984 white males became a minority in the workforce, 49.3 percent. The United States has become a two-career economy, but our social policies have not caught up with those of other two-career economies—such as Norway and Sweden—in terms of day care and parental leave. Simply stated, women are a national resource.

When the members change dramatically, it becomes critical that organizations get ahead of the power curve to create leadership styles, skills, and perspectives that allow them to leverage the workforce in the most efficient and effective manner. An androgynous blend may be one of the answers.

Soft Is Hard: "Excellence" Revisited

Tom Peters and Robert Waterman in *In Search of Excellence* forever redefined management. Peters and Waterman insist that emotions, feelings, and relationships need to be as important in the content of MBA programs as logic and quantifiable objects. They conclude that Western society needs to counteract the detrimental, rational, "masculine" one-sidedness pinpointed in their analysis of business organizations:

"We don't argue for drastically tilting the balance toward either pathfinding or implementation. Rationality is important. . . . But if America is to regain its competitive position in the world, or even hold what it has, we have to stop overdoing things on the rational side."

Peters and Waterman understand the practical need for the implementation of feeling attitudes; in their words, "the exclusively analytic approach run wild leads to an abstract, heartless philosophy."

Old-guard definitions of management harped on productivity, obedience, and control. Peters' new definition is management as concern for people—employees inside the organization and customers and consumers outside—as well as a clear concern for quality, not merely quantity. Daniel Yankelovich undergirds that new definition when he says we have shifted from control to quality as the central principle of management. Managers who focus on quality need involvement, motivation, locality, commitment, and pride from workers. That implies organizations based on trust and caring—and on a leadership blend of male and female characteristics.

The androgynous leadership blend poses a relevant style for the macro and micro relationships necessary to manage organizations in the multigender, multinational, and multisocial environments in the years ahead.

A MODEL FOR MANAGERIAL EFFECTIVENESS

The significant questions for corporations today:

- Do organizations need the values and skills that women bring—caring, cooperation, conflict resolution, good communications, and an expression of a fuller range of feelings?
- Can "female" characteristics and behaviors become a greater part of the acceptable managerial style without jettisoning the best of "male" qualities?

Surely the answer to both questions has to be yes. Progressive corporations in the United States and abroad have flattened hierarchies, encouraged employee participation, and paid more attention to employees' feelings and personal needs. They recognize that workers will perform better when they feel a sense of ownership in their jobs and organizations. Workers also do better work when they believe that the organization values their personal well-being; they see the evidence in such issues as satisfying jobs, health, and family life.

A so-called feminine approach focuses on collaboration, caring, and socialized power. The more traditional, "masculine" approach focuses on analyzing problems, exercising unilateral power, negotiating, competing, and getting credit for one's impact. The androgynous manager integrates and incorporates and employs both sets of behaviors. He or she is both dominant and flexible, and combines independence and power with nurturing and intimacy (see the figure on page 78).

When workers operate under a social contract rather than an exploitation contract, managers need skills to deal with the whole person. They need both instrumental and expressive behaviors, competence and compassion, and support and direction.

Androgynous behavior can enhance a range of managerial functions, including the following:

- Conducting performance appraisals;
- Building, developing, and maintaining team effectiveness;

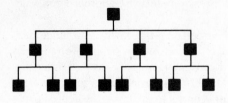

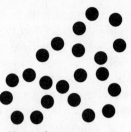

Traditional manager	*New-style manager*
Do as I say, not as I do	Models good interpersonal relationships
Rational	Rational and intuitive
Eliminates complexity; has all the answers	Comfortable with uncertainty and complexity
Compartmentalized experimentation permitted only in an R&D setting	Experiments; organization embraces errors
Standard operating procedures highly bureaucratic	Fairness; core set of values; deals with individuals
Chain of command	Networks
Conformity	Diversity

- Assisting in the career development of employees;
- Using a variety of decision-making styles;
- Dealing with conflict;
- Responding to new ideas;
- Dealing with stress.

For example, the performance of a work team depends on trust, collaboration, communication, and interdependence among team members. It also depends on competence in the technical aspects of the task. The manager cannot just tell the team members to be trustful, collaborative, and communicative. Example works much better than precept; the manager needs to model the behaviors sought in the team members. Also, how team members feel about each other is as important as how they interact with the task at hand. The androgynous manager deals with feelings and task accomplishment, with support and direction, and with productivity and morale.

Instrumental Versus Expressive Behaviors

At the core of the androgynous blend of behaviors are instrumental and expressive behaviors. The former deals with data, results, ideas, and tasks—in effect, it is role behavior. The latter deals with self-disclosure, spontaneity, authenticity, and feelings.

Such behaviors become clear to us in our relationships with family and friends. Instrumental discussions begin with such questions as "Have you paid the insurance?" "Where should we go for dinner Saturday night?" and "Who is taking the car to the mechanic?" Examples of expressive behavior include "How did it go at the office today?" and "How do you feel about your work?"

If a couple engages in too much instrumental behavior, the relationship becomes stale and routine. Communication lacks spontaneity and self-disclosure, the kinds of expressive behavior that build closeness.

Supervisor/subordinate relationships also grow dull and rigid when they become instrumental, focusing only on such questions as "Is that job finished?" and "When do you plan to take your vacation this year?" More expressive behavior is called for. Examples include "How is that project going?" and "Where would you like to be in your career five years from now?"

On the job, the absence of expressive behavior produces ineffective, stilted performance-appraisal sessions. Staff meetings become frustrating; the remarks people make informally ten minutes after the meeting are much more meaningful than opinions expressed during the meeting.

TRAINING FOR ANDROGYNY

Today, managers do not have the luxury of autocracy. Management is defined as getting things done through people—between supervisor and manager, between manager and subordinate, and between manager and peer.

Given the way managers spend their time, organizational leadership becomes an influence-peddling, coalition-visioning, and power-negotiating process. Successful management styles tend to emphasize more collaboration and less competition, and different decision-making styles in different situations. Contingency decision making and situational leadership styles are becoming more widespread; however, we really have not moved to participative management. Instead, we see a blend of the benevolent autocratic style and the consultative style.

To take a giant step toward dealing with these facts and issues, we need a three-step approach to transforming management for the future:

- We must design valid models of managerial effectiveness at the first-line, middle-management, and executive levels—models based on the androgynous paradigm.
- We must define systematic methods for performance-appraisal systems that reinforce and reward the models.
- We must develop educational and training programs to "grow" managers based on the models.

How do we train androgynous managers? Certainly not in the business schools and public-administration programs of today. Sixty-thousand MBAs are graduated every year in the United States—many of them are our future managers—but most degree programs require only nine hours of management education. As Sterling Livingston, the 72-year-old president of the Washington, D.C.,-based Sterling Training Institute, has said, "Business schools teach how to problem-solve not problem-find; how to work more with money than with people."

The inability of our business schools to teach people management and team-building skills may be the reason for the recent wave of executive disenchantment with business-school graduates, along with the return to the belief that a liberal-arts degree is better preparation for general management. Management is indeed a second career for many engineers, doctors, scientists, lawyers, and the like. They need to be educated for that career with the same commitment and intensity that went into their first career choices.

Business-school curricula and management-development programs should include work in both the theory and practice of each of the seven androgynous manager competencies:

- technical competence;
- problem-solving competence (analytical skills, left- and right-brain thinking);
- self-awareness competence (awareness of the impact of one's behavior on others—introspection);
- interpersonal competence;
- team leadership and membership effectiveness;
- entrepreneurial competence;
- leadership.

The need is for practitioner/managers capable of modeling those behaviors.

The American Management Association is trying to begin a master's degree program in management, while some business schools are trying to broaden their course offerings. For example, Harvard is taking a step in the right direction by offering a class to its second-year MBA students and their spouses called "The Executive Family." Barrie Greiff, author of *Tradeoffs in Executive and Family Life*, teaches the course. It is designed to help future leaders of U.S. businesses balance the demands of a job with the demands of a family.

A life outside the office is beginning to be recognized as an important element for managers—an element that cannot be denied or ignored. (Remember, no one on his or her deathbed ever said, "I wish I had spent more time at the office.") But much more needs to be done to teach managers how to be androgynous in the office.

A MORE POSITIVE ROLE FOR CORPORATIONS

Outside of business schools, societal trends are moving people toward androgyny: women's liberation, two-career households, couples in their late 30s starting families and becoming more home-centered, and the focus on male role expectations. The movement is slowly percolating into the workplace. But organizations need to take a more positive role in promoting the androgynous management approach.

In a *Playboy* magazine report on contemporary men's values, the priorities were as follows: health, family life, love, friends, sex, respect for others, religion, peace of mind, work, education, and money. It is clear that attitudes and behavior are not connected. Work comes ninth, according to the men who filled out the survey, but for many, it remains number one in their lives. Some men are becoming conscious of other priorities and other management models. But from consciousness to behavior change is an important step. Organizations can help by rewarding managers who display androgynous competencies, for skill not only with tasks, but also with people.

Management in the 1980s and 1990s is about people, our most precious resource. To build supportive and effective workplace climates in which people can be creative and do work of high quality, we need a blend of both masculine and feminine behaviors. Then we will have a new managerial style that combines concern for people with concern for quality. We will have a style that values interdependent as well as independent ways of doing business. We will have a style that increases options for all managers to move beyond the constraints of stereotypical sex-role expectations.

The political, social, and economic environment is crying out for those who can lead, manage, and create with dignity, sensitivity, and integrity on the local, national, and international levels. It is essential that we in the United States re-invent the corporation. And, it is a fundamental requirement that we re-invent the "American Dream" based on rational, feeling, and integrated leadership styles grounded in the androgynous paradigm.

The Postheroic Leader
David L. Bradford and
Allan R. Cohen

The enormous popularity of books on how to achieve excellence in organizations points to the unprecedented hunger that business people feel for a way to recapture the momentum of quality and innovation that was once the hallmark of U.S. business.

As valuable as these books might be, they focus almost exclusively on the total organization and speak to the chief executive officer, who makes large-scale decisions, even though the implementation of these plans falls to managers in the next levels down. The head of data processing, for example, cannot alter the organization's culture, create lifetime employment practices or invent a new corporate strategy.

Thus there lies a great gap between what is known about what organizations ought to be like and what individual managers need to do to achieve excellence. Yet it is the middle and upper-middle managers who hold the key to high performance. If they can produce, their leadership has a cascading effect on several levels of important subordinates.

Bradford and Cohen have developed an explicit leadership model to bridge the gap in attaining organizational excellence, one that suggests ways for managers to behave and influence every day. It asserts that the model of leadership used by most managers—that of the "heroic" leader who can know all, do all, solve every problem—is severely outdated and inadequate in eliciting the best performance in complex, contemporary organizations.

What do Bradford and Cohen offer in place of the John Wayne-style managerial hero? The postheroic leader: the Manager-as-Developer.

How can managers act in ways that will achieve excellence rather than block it? How can leaders act so that heroic overresponsibility doesn't prevent full use of subordinates' abilities, doesn't dampen their commitment to high performance and doesn't cause them to avoid taking initiative when problems arise?

The answer is not for the manager to renounce responsibility and abandon all control. Although some subordinates respond well to being left alone, there are too many important managerial tasks to guarantee that a no-boss-is-the-best-boss approach will work.

It is also futile to seek a magical midpoint between the extremes of too much and too little leader responsibility and control. Rather, an entirely new definition of leadership is required if a department is to be led into new and unanticipated areas.

This new definition is a fundamental reorientation away from the heroic model. Shared responsibility and control take the place of the individual hero carrying the burdens alone. For those who have staggered around trying to do it all— and have ended up forcing more burden onto their own shoulders by causing the very problems with subordinates that they wanted to avoid—the postheroic view of managing is a profound shift.

At the same time, no part of the new model is all that unfamiliar to any contemporary manager. Everyone knows about tapping subordinate talents, exciting them about the mission and building effective teams, just as astronomers in the time of Copernicus knew about the earth, sun and stars whirling in the heavens. Yet the "simple" reversal of putting the sun, rather than the earth, at the center of relationships caused a revolution in philosophy as well as science.

To achieve excellence in earthly organizations, a manager must first believe in the concept and then act in the creation of a team of key subordinates who are jointly responsible with the manager for the department's success. *At the same time that the manager works to develop management responsibility in subordinates, he or she must help develop the subordinates' abilities to share management of the unit's performance.* Only when all directly reporting subordinates are committed to joint responsibility for overall excellence—when pieces of the task are no longer conditionally delegated, but become parts of decisions—will control cease to be the sole province of the boss.

At the same time, only when subordinates become skilled in the managerial tasks required for total departmental success can the sharing of responsibility lead to excellence. Since neither willingness to accept overall responsibility nor ability to do so are automatic and instant, we have called this model the Manager-as-Developer. Skills have to be learned, common goals accepted, expectations changed and norms modified. Over time a team can be built.

This management model was created by examining leaders who achieve excellence and the images they seem to hold of managing. Rather than depending on heroic rides to the rescue—with the answers and the total responsibility—they have sought the far greater power and potential for excellence available in the commitment and abilities of their whole group. These managers have in mind a developmental, collaborative, galvanizing, but subordinate-centered image.

Unfortunately, a good, easily recognized image of this kind of leader does not exist. Flashes of description occasionally appear when leaders refer to times when "we were all in it together and we knew we could conquer the world." Certain inspirational moments display the quality of shared responsibility; the leader does not command yet is willingly joined in a pursuit where all are at risk.

Perhaps the image is most like a very demanding but supportive and inspirational coach, who works hard to bring the team along, insists on high standards and rigorous effort, but passes on all the knowledge that will help the athletes grow. This coach often works alongside the team, but delegates increasing responsibility for the game plan and especially for on-the-spot adjustments. From the sidelines the coach takes great pleasure in the centrality and achievements of the athletes.

But this coaching analogy imperfectly transfers to managing: The manager is a more involved participant in the action than a coach can ever be. Nevertheless, leaders who achieve excellence are less likely to be guided by images of the central, overresponsible and overcontrolling hero—an image that ultimately dilutes the effectiveness of technicians and conductors when they have expert subordinates doing complex and interdependent work in changing circumstances.

This new model calls for no less effort, energy, investment or imagination than does the Lone Ranger style. Since active engagement is necessary to undertake and sustain increased subordinate learning and overall responsibility, we think of the developer as postheroic rather than nonheroic. Indeed, for some managers who are used to rushing in with the answers, it takes heroic efforts not to be so heroic. Developer-managers learn to have impact without exerting total control, to be helpful without having all the answers, to get involved without demanding centrality, to be powerful without needing to dominate and to act responsible without squeezing others out.

THE CENTRAL ORIENTATION

What does it take to fulfill this tall order in management? First and foremost is a change in orientation. A whole new array of options open up when the leader's orientation becomes: "How can each problem be solved in a way that further develops my subordinates' commitment and capabilities?"

This new orientation may lead the manager to throw some problems back to subordinates ("I think you have a good handle on the difficulty, so why don't you do a first cut and come back in two days"). The manager may ask questions that help subordinates focus on the key issues, while at other times the leader can best aid development by exploring the situation jointly with a subordinate. There may also be times when it is most "developmental" for the manager to provide the answer. Whichever alternative is chosen, the underlying developmental orientation of the leader remains consistent.

What these responses have in common is achieving the dual goal of getting the job done while engaging subordinates in a way that helps them stretch. This orientation does not sacrifice task accomplishment for development (or vice versa). The leader is not saying, "I will develop today and put off solving the problem until tomorrow." Both goals are kept firmly in the forefront.

This postheroic orientation also requires that subordinate development not be restricted to off-site training functions. It occurs on the job—in real time with real issues. Fuller use is made of the already existing abilities of the subordinate while potential ones are developed.

Let's look closely at how a Manager-as-Developer would use this orientation to deal with a problem. Bob Young is faced with a problem: Increasingly, customers have been complaining about defective gaskets, a crucial component in the company's key product.[1] Concerned about this dangerous situation, Bob has called a special meeting of the operations committee. The four subordinate members of the committee have strong feelings—positive and negative—about one another and about Bob Young that make them reluctant to talk openly about the actual source of the problem: a change in supplies and inspection procedures.

This is just the sort of issue that is likely to elicit the heroic response; the organization is under severe time pressure to solve a crucial problem that subordinates are colluding to bury. Bob opened the meeting with his four subordinates as follows:

> "As you know, we are having major problems meeting our deliveries on time. Furthermore, customers are reporting that quality is not up to standard. I have heard this from several of our very important customers, and I am quite bothered, as I am sure you are. You know that we are in a highly competitive market and they can go elsewhere. We have always prided ourselves on our ability to produce gaskets that have no defects, that our customers can use without worry. Our financial future is in jeopardy unless we quickly find out what is going wrong and correct it. You are the people who best know

---

1. Adapted from Bowen, D. D. Young Manufacturing in D. T. Hall et al. *Experiences in Management and Organizational Behavior* New York: Wiley 1982

the situation; you know what causes it, and you know what the best solution looks like. Therefore, I want us in this meeting to work together and come up with the best answer."

This introduction signaled the importance of the problem, reminded subordinates of the company's identification with quality and gave an initial indication of how Bob wanted this situation to be tackled.

Yet subordinates know that words are cheap. What did Bob really mean? Was he out to find someone to blame? Did he really have an idea of how the problem should be solved and merely used a pseudoparticipative style to get them to buy into his solution?

In addition, Bob Young's statement indicated a change in the rules of the game. In trying to develop a management team with members who feel responsible for the operations of the plan and not just for individual areas, Bob Young was demanding that members change their ways of operating. No matter what objections they might have had to Bob's previous style, the subordinates had learned to live with (and around) it. Thus, they tested the waters very carefully before they jumped in and accepted at face value his statement about their enlarged responsibility.

First, they tried to revert to the previous way of operating by throwing the responsibility back to him.

"I don't know, Bob. You know the operations inside and out. What do you think the best solution is?"

Bob replied,

"This is the kind of issue we need to tackle together, because then we'll be sure not only of getting this problem solved, but we'll be able to prevent similar dilemmas in the future."

This exchange was followed by long silence; subordinates hoped they could outlast Bob and force him to take over. When it was clear that he wouldn't move in, there was another attempt to resurrect the old way of operating, in which information that might appear detrimental to any one of the four subordinates was kept from Bob while they worked out their problems on the side. The head of production, Don Blue, glanced over to the quality control manager, Roy Gray, and turned back to Bob:

"Bob, you are busy getting us major contracts. We don't have to take up valuable meeting time on this issue. Roy Gray and I will meet and come up with the solution, and I'll let you know tomorrow."

This suggestion gives the appearance of subordinates assuming responsibility, but it was actually an attempt to hide any dirty linen from Bob Young. Also, the response did nothing to build the operations committee into a mature team that could handle the major operating problems.

As a Developer, Bob Young recognized the presence of two problems: a technical one—quality products were not being delivered on time—and a managerial one—for some reason the operations group had been unable over the past several weeks to resolve the task problem. The defective gaskets problem wasn't news to any of them. Thus, Bob realized that if he delegated responsibility for solving the technical problem to two of his subordinates (or if Bob, being heroic, came up with an answer himself), he wouldn't solve the team/managerial problem even if a good technical solution was produced.

Rather than wading in to solve the problem personally, Bob decided that he had to hold his subordinates' feet to the fire while they solved the problem. He had to be sure they knew he expected them to work jointly on the solution. Bob thus responded to Don Blue's suggestion by saying:

> "Don, I'm sure you and Roy could come up with something, but I also want all of us to improve our collective ability to solve problems. To do that we need to work on it together, since everyone's involved."

After a long silence Bob turned to Fran, the most junior member of the group, and asked for possible causes of the problem. Bob wanted to be certain that Don's seniority and dominant style would not keep Fran from contributing. After Fran made a few comments suggesting that the old-timers' resistance to new methods was an issue, the others leaped in to start blaming one another. A hail of "you didn'ts" and "you should haves" filled the room. Bob showed no signs of being upset about this arguing, and after several minutes, when the accusations had died down, he said,

> "Let's see if we can keep our eyes on what happened and how to fix it. Pointing fingers only makes everyone defensive, which doesn't help quality control. What advantages did the old system have, and what were the goals in changing the system? Once we have these answers, we can determine the kind of changes we should make in purchasing practice so we get the advantages without the problems."

After Bob redirected the discussion into a problem-solving mode, the members collectively dug in to get at the basic issues. They acknowledged that they should stop playing at "It's not my fault," and instead they set up a series of procedures for solving the immediate consequences of the procurement change. They also agreed that a more thorough discussion of inventory policy was needed and set a time the next day to work out the specifics.

Bob Young worked hard to increase the team's willingness to share the responsibility for managing the plant. He recognized that one general statement would not be sufficient. He wanted the team to own not only the problem, but the solution as well.

Instead of trying to get them to disclose the information that would give him determination of the solution or manipulating them to come up with his solution, he worked at how to get the problem solved while increasing the team's commitment and capacity to solve such problems. He kept standards high by using their tradition of quality as the measure against which they could all judge what was being proposed. And by sticking to his determination to increase shared responsibility, he helped develop the team's ability to work together on future problems.

Chapter

4

Ethics

"What should I do?" The question is one of the most persistent and important ones that managers and other employees face in their day-to-day lives in organizations. Sometimes, the practical answer is clear: Simply follow the rule book or draw on established practice in the company. More often, in the modern corporation, there is a great deal of ambiguity about the way to proceed. This may be so because the individual, or the organization have not faced the situation before. The situation can be novel in any of a number of different ways. Ambiguity can occur because the interactions involved are cross-cultural, so that very different interpretations of right and wrong can exist. The decision might be biased by the potential for large corporate or personal gain or loss. The pressure then exists to maximize opportunity or minimize loss, perhaps at the expense of some other individual group, or corporation. What happens if we add the pressure of a high degree of stress to the situation—the stress of time constraints, of emotional intensity, of physical debilitation? Then the answer to the question "What should I do?"—even if given and acted on quickly—is likely to yield behavior and results that are intentionally or inadvertently unethical.

There are no simple rules for managing ethically. In many cases what is ethical must be felt as well as reasoned and the individual doing this will draw on his or her individual values and beliefs as well as the ethical context of the organization and the society in which that individual lives. What are these individual and organizational codes of ethics? The articles in this chapter reflect on this question and on the dilemmas we have raised here briefly. In "The Parable of the Sadhu," Bowen H. McCoy describes making and living with a decision that affects the life of another human being. In a poignant and dramatic story, he touches on all the critical aspects of the question "What should I do?" It is perhaps useful to walk in his shoes as the story unfolds and to ask oneself certain questions: "What would I do if I were faced with this same choice?" "How will I know if my actions are right or wrong?"

In "An Ethical Weather Report: Assessing the Organization's Ethical Climate," John B. Cullen, Bart Victor, and Carroll Stephens trace several different ethical stances that may be taken by individuals and relate them to organizations and the way they do business. The authors suggest approaches we can use to identify systematic patterns of ethical behaviour in organizations.

Making decisions one considers to be ethical may not bring with it much appreciation from other organizational members, as any whistleblower can probably attest to. Withholding liquor from a pregnant customer, in accordance with an ethical principle, cost some employees their jobs (in "Mother-to-be and Daiquiri Lead to Firings").

In "Moral Mazes: Bureaucracy and Managerial Work," Robert Jackall explores ways in which bureaucracy shapes the morality practiced in management. He compares and contrasts the original Protestant ethic with a more recent phenomenon that he calls the bureaucratic ethic.

We end this introduction with a note to the reader. Ethics in business is an important and pervasive issue for everyone who is pursuing a professional career. Many of the readings in this book have an ethical dimension. In particular, chapters on secrecy, hazards, academic life, and the environment contain material that addresses the ethical question in organizational life.

The Parable of the Sadhu

Bowen H. McCoy

Last year, as the first participant in the new six-month sabbatical program that Morgan Stanley has adopted, I enjoyed a rare opportunity to collect my thoughts as well as do some traveling. I spent the first three months in Nepal, walking 600 miles through 200 villages in the Himalayas and climbing some 120,000 vertical feet. On the trip my sole Western companion was an anthropologist who shed light on the cultural patterns of the villages we passed through.

During the Nepal hike, something occurred that has had a powerful impact on my thinking about corporate ethics. Although some might argue that the experience has no relevance to business, it was a situation in which a basic ethical dilemma suddenly intruded into the lives of a group of individuals. How the group responded I think holds a lesson for all organizations no matter how defined.

THE SADHU

The Nepal experience was more rugged and adventuresome than I had anticipated. Most commercial treks last two or three weeks and cover a quarter of the distance we traveled.

My friend Stephen, the anthropologist, and I were halfway through the 60-day Himalayan part of the trip when we reached the high point, an 18,000-foot pass over a crest that we'd have to traverse to reach to the village of Muklinath, an ancient holy place for pilgrims.

Six years earlier I had suffered pulmonary edema, an acute form of altitude sickness, at 16,500 feet in the vicinity of Everest base camp, so we were understandably concerned about what would happen at 18,000 feet. Moreover, the Himalayas were having their wettest spring in 20 years; hip-deep powder and ice had already driven us off one ridge. If we failed to cross the pass, I feared that the last half of our "once in a lifetime" trip would be ruined.

The night before we would try the pass, we camped at a hut at 14,500 feet. In the photos taken at that camp, my face appears wan. The last village we'd passed through was a sturdy two-day walk below us, and I was tired.

During the late afternoon, four back-packers from New Zealand joined us, and we spent most of the night awake, anticipating the climb. Below we could see the fires of two other parties, which turned out to be two Swiss couples and a Japanese hiking club.

To get over the steep part of the climb before the sun melted the steps cut in the ice, we departed at 3:30 A.M. The New Zealanders left first, followed by Stephen and myself, our porters and Sherpas, and then the Swiss. The Japanese lingered in their camp. The sky was clear, and we were confident that no spring storm would erupt that day to close the pass.

At 15,500 feet, it looked to me as if Stephen were shuffling and staggering a bit, which are symptoms of altitude sickness. (The initial stage of altitude sickness brings a headache and nausea. As the condition worsens, a climber may encounter difficult breathing, disorientation, aphasia, and paralysis.) I felt strong, my adrenaline was flowing, but I was very concerned about my ultimate ability to get across. A couple of our porters were also suffering from the height, and Pasang, our Sherpa sirdar (leader,) was worried.

Just after daybreak, while we rested at 15,500 feet, one of the New Zealanders, who had gone ahead, came staggering down toward us with a body slung across his shoulders. He dumped the almost naked, barefoot body of an Indian holy man—a sadhu—at my feet. He had found the pilgrim lying on the ice, shivering and suffering from hypothermia. I cradled the sadhu's head and laid him out on the rocks. The New Zealander was angry. He wanted to get across the pass before the bright sun melted the snow. He said, "Look, I've done what I can. You have porters and Sherpa guides. You care for him. We're going on!" He turned and went back up the mountain to join his friends.

I took a carotid pulse and found that the sadhu was still alive. We figured he had probably visited the holy shrines at Muklinath and was on his way home. It was fruitless to question why he had chosen this desperately high route instead of the safe, heavily traveled caravan route through the Kali Gandaki gorge. Or why he was almost naked and with no shoes, or how long he had been lying in the pass. The answers weren't going to solve our problem.

Stephen and the four Swiss began stripping off outer clothing and opening their packs. The sadhu was soon clothed from head to foot. He was not able to walk, but he was very much alive. I looked down the mountain and spotted below the Japanese climbers marching up with a horse.

Without a great deal of thought, I told Stephen and Pasang that I was concerned about withstanding the heights to come and wanted to get over the pass. I took off after several of our porters who had gone ahead.

On the steep part of the ascent where, if the ice steps had given way, I would have slid down about 3,000 feet, I felt vertigo. I stopped for a breather, allowing the Swiss to catch up with me. I inquired about the sadhu and Stephen. They said that the sadhu was fine and that Stephen was just behind. I set off again for the summit.

Stephen arrived at the summit an hour after I did. Still exhilarated by victory, I ran down the snow slope to congratulate him. He was suffering from altitude sickness, walking 15 steps, then stopping, walking 15 steps, then stopping. Pasang accompanied him all the way up. When I reached them, Stephen glared at me and said: "How do you feel about contributing to the death of a fellow man?"

I did not fully comprehend what he meant.

"Is the sadhu dead?" I inquired.

"No," replied Stephen, "but he surely will be!"

After I had gone, and the Swiss had departed not long after, Stephen had remained with the sadhu. When the Japanese had arrived, Stephen had asked to use their horse to transport the sadhu down to the hut. They had refused. He had then asked Pasang to have a group of our porters carry the sadhu. Pasang had resisted the idea, saying that the porters would have to exert all their energy to get themselves over the pass. He had thought they could not carry a man down 1,000 feet to the hut, reclimb the slope, and get across safely before the snow melted. Pasang had pressed Stephen not to delay any longer.

The Sherpas had carried the sadhu down to a rock in the sun at about 15,000 feet and had pointed out the hut another 500 feet below. The Japanese had given him food and drink. When they had last seen him he was listlessly throwing rocks at the Japanese party's dog, which had frightened him.

We do not know if the sadhu lived or died.

For many of the following days and evenings Stephen and I discussed and debated our behavior toward the sadhu. Stephen is a committed Quaker with deep moral vision. He said, "I feel that what happened with the sadhu is a good example of the breakdown between the individual ethic and the corporate ethic. No one person was willing to assume ultimate responsibility for the sadhu. Each was willing to do his bit just so long as it was not too inconvenient. When it got to be a bother, everyone just passed the buck to someone else and took off. Jesus was relevant to a more individualistic stage of society, but how do we interpret his teaching today in a world filled with large, impersonal organizations and groups?"

I defended the larger group, saying, "Look, we all cared. We all stopped and gave aid and comfort. Everyone did his bit. The New Zealander carried him down below the snow line. I took his pulse and suggested we treat him for hypothermia. You and the Swiss gave him clothing and got him warmed up. The Japanese gave him food and water. The Sherpas carried him down to the sun and pointed out the easy trail toward the hut. He was well enough to throw rocks at a dog. What more could we do?"

"You have just described the typical affluent Westerner's response to a problem. Throwing money—in this case food and sweaters—at it, but not solving the fundamentals!" Stephen retorted.

"What would satisfy you?" I said. "Here we are, a group of New Zealanders, Swiss, Americans, and Japanese who have never met before and who are at the apex of one of the most powerful experiences of our lives. Some years the pass is so bad no one gets over it. What right does an almost naked pilgrim who chooses the wrong trail have to disrupt our lives? Even the Sherpas had no interest in risking the trip to help him beyond a certain point."

Stephen calmly rebutted, "I wonder what the Sherpas would have done if the sadhu had been a well-dressed Nepali, or what the Japanese would have done if the sadhu had been a well-dressed Asian, or what you would have done, Buzz, if the sadhu had been a well-dressed Western woman?"

"Where, in your opinion," I asked instead, "is the limit of our responsibility in a situation like this? We had our own well-being to worry about. Our Sherpa guides were unwilling to jeopardize us or the porters for the sadhu. No one else on the mountain was willing to commit himself beyond certain self-imposed limits."

Stephen said, "As individual Christians or people with a Western ethical tradition, we can fulfill our obligations in such a situation only if (1) the sadhu dies in our care, (2) the sadhu demonstrates to us that he could undertake the two-day walk down to the village or (3) we carry the sadhu for two days down to the village and convince someone there to care for him."

"Leaving the sadhu in the sun with food and clothing, while he demonstrated hand-eye coordination by throwing a rock at a dog, comes close to fulfilling items one and two," I answered. "And it wouldn't have made sense to take him to the village where the people appeared to be far less caring than the Sherpas, so the third condition is impractical. Are you really saying that, no matter what the implications, we should, at the drop of a hat, have changed our entire plan?"

THE INDIVIDUAL VS. THE GROUP ETHIC

Despite my arguments, I felt and continue to feel guilt about the sadhu. I had literally walked through a classic moral dilemma without fully thinking through the consequences. My excuses for my actions include a high adrenaline flow, a superordinate goal, and a once-in-a-lifetime opportunity—factors in the usual corporate situation, especially when one is under stress.

Real moral dilemmas are ambiguous, and many of us hike right through them, unaware that they exist. When, usually after the fact, someone makes an issue of them, we tend to resent his or her bringing it up. Often, when the full import of what we have done (or not done) falls on us, we dig into a defensive position from which it is very difficult to emerge. In rare circumstances we may contemplate what we have done from inside a prison.

Had we mountaineers been free of physical and mental stress caused by the effort and the high altitude, we might have treated the sadhu differently. Yet, isn't stress the real test of personal and corporate values? The instant decisions executives make under pressure reveal the most about personal and corporate character.

Among the many questions that occur to me when pondering my experience are: What are the practical limits of moral imagination and vision? Is there a collective or institutional ethic beyond the ethics of the individual? At what level of effort or commitment can one discharge one's ethical responsibilities?

Not every ethical dilemma has a right solution. Reasonable people often disagree; otherwise there would be no dilemma. In a business context, however, it is essential that managers agree on a process for dealing with dilemmas.

The sadhu experience offers an interesting parallel to business situations. An immediate response was mandatory. Failure to act was a decision in itself. Up on the mountain we could not resign and submit our résumés to a headhunter. In contrast to philosophy, business involves action and implementation—getting things done. Managers must come up with answers to problems based on what they see and what they allow to influence their decision-making processes. On the mountain, none of us but Stephen realized the true dimensions of the situation we were facing.

One of our problems was that as a group we had no process for developing a consensus. We had no sense of purpose or plan. The difficulties of dealing with the sadhu were so complex that no one person could handle it. Because it did not have a set of preconditions that could guide its action to an acceptable resolution, the group reacted instinctively as individuals. The cross-cultural nature of the group added a further layer of complexity. We had no leader with whom we could all identify and in whose purpose we believed. Only Stephen was willing to take charge, but he could not gain adequate support to care for the sadhu.

Some organizations do have a value system that transcends the personal values of the managers. Such values, which go beyond profitability, are usually revealed when the organization is under stress. People throughout the organization generally accept its values, which, because they are not presented as a rigid list of commandments, may be somewhat ambiguous. The stories people tell, rather than printed materials, transmit these conceptions of what is proper behavior.

For 20 years I have been exposed at senior levels to a variety of corporations and organizations. It is amazing how quickly an outsider can sense the tone and style of an organization and the degree of tolerated openness and freedom to challenge management.

Organizations that do not have a heritage of mutually accepted, shared values tend to become unhinged during stress, with each individual bailing out for himself. In the great takeover battles we have witnessed during past years, companies that had strong cultures drew the wagons around them and fought it out, while other companies saw executives supported by their golden parachutes, bail out of the struggles.

Because corporations and their members are interdependent, for the corporation to be strong the members need to share a preconceived notion of what is correct behavior, a "business ethic," and think of it as a positive force, not a constraint.

As an investment banker I am continually warned by well-meaning lawyers, clients, and associates to be wary of conflicts of interest. Yet if I were to run away from every difficult situation, I wouldn't be an effective investment banker. I have to feel my way through conflicts. An effective manager can't run from risk either; he or she has to confront and deal with risk. To feel "safe" in doing this, managers need the guidelines of an agreed-on process and set of values within the organization.

After my three months in Nepal, I spent three months as an executive-in-residence at both Stanford Business School and the Center for Ethics and Social Policy at the Graduate Theological Union at Berkeley. These six months away from my job gave me time to assimilate 20 years of business experience. My thoughts turned often to the meaning of the leadership role in any large organization. Students at the seminary thought of themselves as antibusiness. But when I questioned them they agreed that they distrusted all large organizations, including the church. They perceived all large organizations as impersonal and opposed to individual values and needs. Yet we all know of organizations where peoples' values and beliefs are respected and their expressions encouraged. What makes the difference? Can we identify the difference and, as a result, manage more effectively?

The word "ethics" turns off many and confuses more. Yet the notions of shared values and an agreed-on process for dealing with adversity and change—what many people mean when they talk about corporate culture—seem to be at the heart of the ethical issue. People who are in touch with their own core beliefs and the beliefs of others and are sustained by them can be more comfortable living on the cutting edge. At times, taking a tough line or a decisive stand in a muddle of ambiguity is the only ethical thing to do. If a manager is indecisive and spends time trying to figure out the "good" thing to do, the enterprise may be lost.

Business ethics, then, has to do with the authenticity and integrity of the enterprise. To be ethical is to follow the business as well as the cultural goals of the corporation, its owners, its employees, and its customers. Those who cannot serve the corporate visions are not authentic business people and, therefore, are not ethical in the business sense.

At this stage of my own business experience I have a strong interest in organizational behavior. Sociologists are keenly studying what they call corporate stories, legends, and heroes as a way organizations have of transmitting the value system. Corporations such as Arco have even hired consultants to perform an audit of their corporate culture. In a company, the leader is the person who understands, interprets, and manages the corporate value system. Effective managers are then action-oriented people who resolve conflict, are tolerant of ambiguity, stress, and change, and have a strong sense of purpose for themselves and their organizations.

If all this is true, I wonder about the role of the professional manager who moves from company to company. How can he or she quickly absorb the values and culture of different organizations? Or is there, indeed, an art of management that is totally transportable? Assuming such fungible managers do exist, is it proper for them to manipulate the values of others?

I see the current interest in corporate culture and corporate value systems as a positive response to Stephen's pessimism about the decline of the role of the individual in large organizations. Individuals who operate from a thoughtful set of personal values provide the foundation for a corporate culture. A corporate tradition that encourages freedom of inquiry, supports personal values, and reinforces a focused sense of direction can fulfill the need for individuality along with the prosperity and success of the group. Without such corporate support, the individual is lost.

That is the lesson of the sadhu. In a complex corporate situation, the individual requires and deserves the support of the group. If people cannot find such support from their organization, they don't know how to act. If such support is forthcoming, a person has a stake in the success of the group, and can add much to the process of establishing and maintaining a corporate culture. It is management's challenge to be sensitive to individual needs, to shape them, and to direct and focus them for the benefit of the group as a whole.

For each of us the sadhu lives. Should we stop what we are doing and comfort him; or should we keep trudging up toward the high pass? Should I pause to help the derelict I pass on the street each night as I walk by the Yale Club en route to Grand Central Station? Am I his brother? What is the nature of our responsibility if we consider ourselves to be ethical persons? Perhaps it is to change the values of the group so that it can, with all its resources, take the other road.

An Ethical Weather Report: Assessing the Organization's Ethical Climate

John B. Cullen
Bart Victor
Carroll Stephens

In 1982 and again in 1986, grisly reports of poisoning by tainted Tylenol hit the newsstands. Within hours of hearing of the crisis, McNeil Laboratories, a subsidiary of Johnson & Johnson, voluntarily and completely withdrew the product from the market—and this in spite of the fact that the disaster resulted from tampering rather than manufacturing error. *The Washington Post* described the company's efforts as a textbook example of a firm's willingness to do what is right, regardless of cost. Why did McNeil make the decision that it did? The oft-cited response was, "It's the J&J way."

That simple statement expresses a somewhat more complex concept: that corporations, like individuals, have their own sets of ethics that help define their characters. And just as personal ethics guide what an individual will do when faced with moral dilemmas, corporate ethics guide what an organization will do when faced with issues of conflicting values—in the Tylenol case, the health and lives of consumers versus the short-term robustness of the balance sheet. Corporate ethics help managers and employees answer the question, "What should I do?"

There's no shortage of differing opinions about what businesses should do in various situations, and about what constitutes ethical behavior—no doubt you have seen many such opinions expressed in the news media. But information on how businesses can implement ethical practices is scant. In the wake of insider trading scandals, chemical disasters, and product liability cases such as the Tylenol episodes, the press has exhorted corporate America to behave ethically. And numerous philosophy books and academic articles give varied definitions of what constitutes ethical behavior. For example, John Rawls, author of the classic volume *A Theory of Justice* (Belknap Press, 1971), says that ethics is justice: the principles that all rational human beings would select to govern social behavior if they knew that the rules could potentially apply to themselves. In other words, if a CEO delineated one set of personnel procedures to apply to hourly workers, but he was unwilling to have those same procedures applied to top management as well—that is, to his own group—then Rawls would deem those procedures unjust and unethical.

Michael Keeley, a professor of business administration at Loyola University in Chicago, suggests that organizations are ethical to the extent that they minimize possible harm to all of their constituencies. If a manufacturer were contemplating a plant closing, for instance, it would have to consider carefully the impact of job losses on workers' families and the community at large, and take special care to protect the most vulnerable stakeholders from damaging consequences.

Furthermore, of course, virtually every executive has his or her own deeply held values about corporate morality. But how can those values be translated into action?

ETHICAL CLIMATE: A WAY TO MANAGE ETHICS

Corporate ethics drive not only the content of moral decisions—"What should I do?"—but also the process of decision making—"How shall I do it?" We wish to suggest a practical tool that executives can use to gauge the ethical climate of their companies, and, if they're not pleased with what they find, to begin to change it. The company's ethical climate helps to determine (1) which issues organization members consider to be ethically pertinent, and (2) what criteria they use to understand, weigh, and resolve these issues. Of course, the ethical climate is but one component of the organizational culture.

All organizational values that pertain to questions of right and wrong contribute to the company's ethical climate: the shared perceptions of what is correct behavior (i.e., content), and how ethical issues will be dealt with (i.e., process). Although the ethical climate is a major force driving organizational decision making, by no means are all decisions determined by the ethical climate. How information is gathered—whether by intuition or quantitative analysis —is not determined by the ethical climate. Conventions and rules whose consequences do not have an impact on morality are also excluded. And as one would expect, organizational choices that do not affect the well-being of individuals or groups are not set according to the ethical climate. Thus the ethical climate certainly pertains to the decision of whether or not to pay a kickback; but it does not have an impact on how organizational members determine whether the buyer expects a kickback—which is a question of fact—or whether the buyer should be paid in cash or merchandise—a question of convention.

Despite these exclusions, the ethical climate has a far-reaching impact on the organization. Once we know a person fairly well, we can generally describe him or her as caring, or self-interested, or principled; and we are likely to find that the person's ethics are apparent across a wide spectrum of situations. These same characteristics can apply to organizations. Johnson & Johnson, for example, describes itself as a "caring company." According to CEO Burke, the Tylenol plan for action sprang directly from the company's credo, which ranks service to consumers as its uppermost goal, followed by responsibility to workers, management, and the community; financial returns come last. (Of course, Johnson & Johnson's continuing fiscal health attests to the fact that all these goals are by no means in opposition to each other.)

UNDERSTANDING ETHICAL CLIMATE

A knowledge of both organization theory and economics is important in understanding ethical climate. Three factors determine a company's ethical climate: the environment in which the firm functions; the form of the organization (e.g., centralized, divisional, multinational); and the company's history. Johnson & Johnson, for example, had long identified itself with the medical profession. That element of corporate history may well have caused the company to be influenced by the ethos of medicine's Hippocratic oath, i.e., "First do no harm"; hence the company's swift responses to the Tylenol tamperings.

When evidence came to light that Procter & Gamble's Rely tampons were linked to the potentially fatal toxic shock syndrome, that company's response was slower than Johnson & Johnson's—for which P&G was roundly castigated by consumer groups. But P&G has an excellent reputation in the business world and people who followed the events agree that the likelihood of that company's having committed coldblooded malfeasance is very slim. In fact, J&J's Burke, who has a lively interest in corporate social responsibility, considers P&G to be one of the nation's most ethical companies. Why, then, was the firm slow to respond to the Rely problems? Part of the answer is surely due to the fact that the causal relationship between Rely and toxic shock syndrome was not nearly as clear as the causal relationship between Tylenol and poisoning.

However, a plausible explanation—which does not contradict this point—is that P&G, which is a consumer goods marketer and not a pharmaceutical firm, had no corporate history of dealing with life-or-death situations; and therefore its corporate ethics evolved along different lines than did those of Johnson & Johnson. In essence, J&J had a ready-built ethical rule which it could apply quickly and easily when the crisis occurred; P&G did not have that running start.

Although it is easy to speculate about which factors determine the company's ethical climate—environment, structure, and history—the relative impact of each of the three variables is not yet known. Before that issue can be explored further, we must have a valid and reliable measure of ethical climate against which to compare the factors.

MEASURING ETHICAL CLIMATE

Headline-grabbing incidents such as the Tylenol and Rely crises provide a rare opportunity to observe corporate ethics in action. Assessing a company's ethical climate in the absence of a particular dramatic episode is a knottier problem, and one that has not been addressed until recently. We propose a method for doing so, based upon the assumptions that (1) each company or subunit has its own moral character, (2) group members know what this character is, and (3) the group members can tell an outsider about their organization's moral character in an objective way, regardless of how they feel about it. In other words, the best way to find out about an organization's ethical climate is to ask the people who work there about it. It readily follows that in order to determine his or her own firm's ethical climate, a manager should ask the employees about it. Sample questions from a questionnaire designed for that purpose are presented in Exhibit 1.

An explanation of how we drew up the questionnaire might be helpful to the reader. As a starting point, we composed a chart showing possible ethical climates,

Exhibit 1. Ethical climate questionnaire (sample questions)

We would like to ask you some questions about the general climate in your company. Please answer the following in terms of how it really is in your company, not how you would prefer it to be. Please be as candid as possible; remember, all your responses will remain strictly anonymous.

Please indicate whether you agree or disagree with each of the following statements about your company. Please use the scale below and write the number which best represents your answer in the space next to each item.

To what extent are the following statements true about your company?

Completely False	Mostly False	Somewhat False	Somewhat True	Mostly True	Completely True
0	1	2	3	4	5

_____ 1. In this company, people are expected to follow their own personal and moral beliefs.

_____ 2. People are expected to do anything to further the company's interests.

_____ 3. In this company, people look out for each other's good.

_____ 4. It is very important here to follow strictly the company's rules and procedures.

_____ 5. In this company, people protect their own interests above other considerations.

_____ 6. The first consideration is whether a decision violates any law.

_____ 7. Everyone is expected to stick by company rules and procedures.

_____ 8. The most efficient way is always the right way in this company.

_____ 9. Our major consideration is what is best for everyone in the company.

_____10. In this company, the law or ethical code of the profession is the major consideration.

_____11. It is expected at this company that employees will always do what is right for the customer and the public.

© 1986 Victor and Cullen.

based on philosophical, sociological, and psychological theory (see Exhibit 2). The chart has two axes, representing how the ethical systems are derived and to whom they apply. As the vertical axis shows (how the systems are derived), ethical systems may be based upon self-interest, caring, or abstract principle. As the horizontal axis shows (to whom they apply), ethics may be applied to individuals, the group, or society at large.

Harvard professor of education Lawrence Kohlberg is perhaps the best-known scholar on the psychology of ethics. Although our work deals with organizations and his deals with individuals, we did use some of his concepts in drawing up the chart. Kohlberg says that as people develop morally—from early childhood to adulthood—they use different types of ethical criteria and show distinct patterns of moral reasoning. By moral reasoning, Kohlberg means reflective thinking about how ethical dilemmas ought to be solved. According to Kohlberg, moral development follows a sequence, much as does intellectual development. Moral reasoning progresses from being based on the fear of punishment, to stemming from concern for other people whom one knows or can vividly imagine, to growing out of concern for universal rights and humanity as a whole. In this progression, Kohlberg lists three types of ethical standards, which are the ones that we use on our vertical axis: self-interest, caring, and principle. These three standards, interestingly enough, correspond to philosophy's three major classes of ethical theory: egoism, utilitarianism, and deontology. Essentially, egoism is motivated by the wish to maximize one's own interests; utilitarianism by the wish to maximize the interests of oneself and significant others; and deontology is motivated by the abstract desire

Exhibit 2. Types of Organizational Ethical Climates

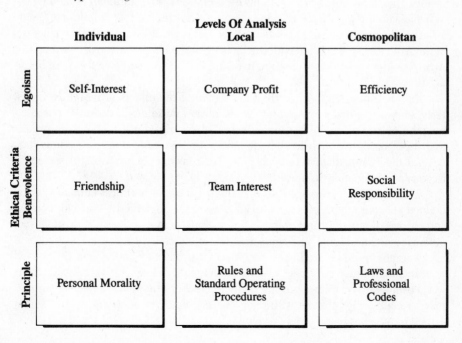

to do what is right, independent of the action's specific outcome and whose interests are particularly affected by it.

Kohlberg's theory of moral development—and much of moral philosophy in general—assume that these ethical criteria are quite distinct from each other; in fact, that they are fairly incompatible. People who are "caring" are not apt to pay a great deal of heed to laws and rules; people who are "principled" are likely to screen out the effects of a given choice on themselves, and on other individuals. Take the case of a stockbroker who is offered a hot tip from a friend based on inside information: The caring broker would probably counsel his friend to stop such harmful activities; the principled broker might well report the violation to the SEC, despite the pain that the disclosure could bring to him and his friend; and the self-interested broker would probably act on the information.

If the various ethical reasoning modes are incompatible for individuals, the same is probably true of organizations. Therefore, we place self-interested, caring, and principled cells along the horizontal axis of our typology.

Ethics and Organizational Roles

Theories of social roles in organizations and reference groups provide support for considering different levels of analysis in ethical decision making. Sociologist Robert Merton and others studying the development of social roles in organizations have identified several reference groups that help define the behavior and attitudes associated with particular organizational roles. For example, Merton makes a distinction between a local and a cosmopolitan role. In the local case, the reference groups or sources of role definition are within the organization: A worker in a steel factory, for example, might look to his or her coworkers or foreman to define how to behave on the job. In the cosmopolitan case, sources of role definition are outside the organization: An accountant might be very concerned with the standards of the AICPA, or a physician with the dictates of the Hippocratic oath. Researcher Alvin Gouldner uses this distinction to distinguish the professional from the "organization man."

Kohlberg also emphasizes the importance of the effects of moral decisions. His theory states that some people almost always make moral decisions based on how the outcomes will affect individuals. Others consider the effects on groups that they belong to, such as their family or their organization. Still others look beyond their immediate reference points to consider the interests of society at large or even humanity as a whole.

It certainly seems reasonable that the organization's ethical climate may be defined in terms of its level of ethical analysis, so we place these dimensions on the vertical axis of our chart in Exhibit 2. Some climates may be highly individualistic; others are organizational; and some are cosmopolitan in their focus. These focuses are generally mutually exclusive: Organizations that have individualistic or local ethical climates may not be as attentive to larger social concerns as organizations with cosmopolitan orientations are likely to be. For example, a tobacco company may have a "caring" climate with regard to its employees—but its caring may not extend to the consumers of its product.

Since, as the chart in Exhibit 2 illustrates, there are two dimensions on which ethical climates differ—the type of criteria and the level of analysis—and since there are three categories of each dimension, there are nine possible ethical climates. The ethical climate may focus on any one of these nine factors: self-interest, company profit, efficiency, friendship, team interest, social responsibility, personal morality, rules and standard operating procedures, or laws and professional codes.

ORGANIZATIONAL REALITIES

Of course, the fact that these categories make sense in theory does not mean that they actually occur in organizations. To test whether they do, we drew up a list of statements describing each type of ethical climate, and asked company members to choose the statements that best fit their own organizations. A sample of the statements that make up the questionnaire is shown in Exhibit 1. Our sample of respondents contained 872 people representing four organizations: a manufacturing plant, a printing company, a savings and loan institution (S&L), and a telephone company. Respondents were instructed to answer according to what the company is really like, rather than how they would like it to be. After we had collected all the responses, we used factor analysis—a statistical technique that analyzes questions that have multiple answers—to determine whether distinct ethical types emerged.

Indeed they did. Interestingly, no actual organization's ethical climate fit into the efficiency cell, but the remaining eight cells were all filled, with certain climates encompassing two or more adjacent cells. Altogether, five actual climates occurred, as compared to nine theoretical climates. An instrumental climate fell into the self-interest and company profit boxes. Statements such as, "In this company, people are only out for themselves" and "People are expected to do anything to further the company's interests" capture this ethical type. A caring climate spanned all three benevolent cells: friendship, team interest, and social responsibility. This climate is characterized by statements like, "Our major consideration is what's best for everyone in the company" and "It is expected that you'll always do what is right for the customer and the public." An independent climate emerged in the personal morality box, with descriptors including, "In this company, people are expected to follow their own personal and moral beliefs." The rules and standard operating procedures (SOP) cell had its own rules-oriented climate, characterized by statements such as, "Everyone is expected to stick by the company's rules and procedures." Finally, a laws-and-codes climate emerged in the principled-cosmopolitan cell. For this climate, organizational members selected such statements as, "The first consideration is whether a decision violates any law" and "The ethical code of the profession is very important."

Each of these actual climates represents a form of reasoning that might be used in organizational decision making. The laws-and-codes climate prevails wherever the company uses externally generated standards and principles in choosing a course of action. The rules climate is in effect when internally generated principles and guidelines are used to direct decision making. In caring climates, the company emphasizes benevolent criteria such as the interests of other employees or the welfare of the work team. Self-interest is the key criterion in organizational decision making when the firm has an instrumental climate; and individual moral judgment is of foremost importance in an independent climate.

INDUSTRY DIFFERENCES

The printing company—which has a traditional respect for craftsmanship—demonstrated the most independent climate of any organization in the study, with the least reliance on laws, rules, and codes. Contributing to this independent climate was the fact that the company had no professional manager; each worker's own judgment was thus very important.

Recall that in the questionnaire, statements about organizational ethical climate are placed on a six-point scale, ranging from 0—completely false—to 5—completely true. Respondents were asked to use this scale to say how true each of these statements is about their own organizations. At the printing company, respondents gave independence a rating of 3.0; they rated caring 3.1; they rated both laws-and-codes, and rules 2.8; and they gave instrumentalism a 2.2 rating.

The printing company not only received a higher "independence" rating than any other organization; in fact, it was the only company where independence received a rating of any significant importance: The manufacturing plant rated independence 2.4; the telephone company rated it 2.2; and the S&L rated it 2.1 in importance. Indeed, when we informed the executives of the telephone company that their employees had said that they did not use personal judgment in their ethical decision making, the executives were pleased. "That's the way we prefer it," they responded. In no organization did the respondents admit to having a predominantly instrumental climate, but the ratings showed that all the companies embodied instrumentalism to some degree: The respondents from the S&L and the manufacturer gave instrumentalism a 2.3 rating; it was rated 2.2 at the printing company; and at the telephone company it was rated 2.1. But, of course, organizations that are primarily instrumental do exist. For example, an instrumental ethical climate could be quite appropriate for a loosely controlled organization in which members—such as salespeople who work on a commission basis—function largely on their own; just as caring climates might be expected to predominate in organizations with human services missions; and firms where resources are scarce might have efficient climates.

The manufacturing plant stressed laws and codes, which received a mean importance rating of 3.6. To a lesser extent, it emphasized rules, which were rated 3.2 in importance. The mean for the importance of caring was 3.0 at this company. The relatively low emphasis on rules may have resulted from the plant's recent reorganization: Literally, the rules had changed. For most of its history, the plant had been organized according to traditional functional departments, but in the year before the survey was conducted, it had converted to a system of "business teams" organized by product. One of the explicit goals of the restructuring was to spur flexibility and innovation by reducing reliance on internal rules and standard operating procedures. In our sample, the S&L had the most emphasis on rules—they were rated 3.7—and on laws and codes, which it rated 3.8; it ranked caring at 2.9. The telephone company had an environment that was similar—rules were rated 3.3, laws-and-codes 3.3, and caring 2.8—but not as extreme as that of the S&L.

ENVIRONMENTAL CHANGE

Ethical climates, although relatively enduring, are not static. Note that two organizations in our sample—the S&L and the telephone company—function in environments that until recently were highly protected by government regulations. In this heavily regulated setting, their rules-based ethical climates made a great deal of sense. But since deregulation has resulted in both industries' becoming much more market oriented than they were, we may anticipate that the ethical climates in these industries will shift accordingly.

Indeed, an anecdote suggests that this shift in climate is already taking place. Recently, a telephone company service representative chose to cut off service to a delinquent account—a decision that, under normal circumstances, would be routine. In this case, however, the decision almost cost the company its largest commercial client. The chief executive of the commercial firm happened to be married to the target of the telephone company's action—a fact that was known and appreciated by the service representative who ordered her telephone disconnected. During a hastily called meeting to plan how to salve the chief executive's rage, the customer service rep defended his decision to cut off her service. "It was the right thing to do," he argued. "The rules are clear in this case—she didn't pay, so I cut off the line. It shouldn't matter who she is; we are the phone company!" The vice-president for marketing disagreed, saying, "We have to look out for our business, and if that means special consideration for important clients, so be it." Ethical decision making based strictly on rules was feasible when government regulations meant that customers were not free to select telephone service suppliers; in those days, no matter how angry a customer might be, he or she did not have the option of withdrawing business. Now that the market includes competition, however, the ethical decision criteria have become more utilitarian.

ALTERING THE ETHICAL CLIMATE

We hope that our readers find it interesting to learn about the ethical climates of the organizations that we surveyed using the questionnaire. But the canny executive is sure to be wondering how such descriptions apply to his or her organization, and how the information we collected might be useful. For the executive who wishes to create an environment in which issues of right and wrong are taken seriously (and we don't presume that this includes all executives), our questionnaire can be a useful tool.

The questionnaire may be administered to the employees, and analyzed either in-house or with the aid of an outside consultant. In either case, it is crucial that the employees be assured that results are reported in aggregate and that individual responses are strictly anonymous: If workers believe that top management will see their responses, they may be inhibited from giving candid answers. Another point that needs to be emphasized when the questionnaire is given to the employees is that they should respond according to what they feel the ethical climate actually is, and not according to how they think it should be. Questionnaire results are intended to provide management with an assessment of what the ethical climate of the organization is at the time that the questionnaire is administered. Management can then determine whether the firm's ethical climate fits with their personal values, and with the strategic aims of the company.

Each ethical climate poses specific hazards, which may develop either from behavior that is consistent with the climate, or from behavior that deviates from it. Since people generally behave as they are expected to, a firm faces higher risks when problems that develop stem from behavior that is consistent with its climate. For example, a rules-oriented climate that plays down the importance of the employee's individual judgment could lead to misinterpretation or conflict between various rules and regulations. A climate that is low on caring could create an environment in which employees are treated in callous and potentially illegal ways; such a climate may lower motivation and increase the turnover rate. Conversely, an employee of a caring organization, when faced with the ethical decision of offering a bribe or losing a contract, may take the illegal course; the employee may reason that he or she ought to give the bribe since the contract would help the people who work for the firm.

Flagrant types of crime, such as fraud and outright deception, may be most likely to occur in self-interested climates that stress instrumentality—that is, getting ahead—at the expense of caring and rules. On the other hand, there are sometimes important advantages to a little instrumentalism. At the savings and loan institution, the new CEO expressed dissatisfaction with the low level of instrumentalism he found in his firm. Like many S&Ls, this one was engaged in a fevered battle with the commercial banks, and the CEO believed that his employees had to change their attitudes about selling money and services in order for the firm to survive.

LEARNING FROM THE QUESTIONNAIRE

Management needs to form an impression of the particular ethical risks that the firm is likely to face, and to compare this impression with the firm's ethical climate as assessed by the questionnaire. These risks could depend on the nature of the company's environment, its industry, or the company itself. For example, a multinational firm would have more reason to be concerned about bribery than would a small, regional firm; a chemical firm might be especially attentive to ecological toxicity.

Moreover, as the market changes, so do the risks to the firm; but the firm's ethical climate may lag behind, becoming increasingly ill-suited to the new environment. At both the telephone company and the S&L we studied, the chief executives felt that the ethical climate of their firms did not match the demands of the industries' newly competitive environments. In another example, Motorola has an extensive, written code of ethics, which is appropriate for a rules or a laws-and-codes oriented climate. However, Motorola recently began implementing an aggressive, participative management program for which an independent climate would be more fitting. It is possible that the clash between these two approaches may diminish the effectiveness of both. Learning what the firm's ethical climate is can be the first step toward the implementation of change.

Once the questionnaire results are known, they must be appraised and critiqued—the second step in using the questionnaire. Management needs to consider whether the results seem valid. If they do, what are the implications of the climate for operations, missions, and goals? At the conclusion of this step, management should have accomplished the following things: identified the firm's values, priorities, and decision-making processes; made note of ethical problem areas; become aware of potential conflicts between the ethical climate and company goals; and designed a strategy for changing or strengthening the climate.

The final step is the implementation of programs based on the findings of the first two steps. Perhaps the ethical climate is found to be appropriate and effective—in that case, nothing need be done. To give one instance, an accounting firm might be revealed to have a pronounced laws-and-codes climate, which is appropriate in light of the extent to which accountants are governed by governmental regulations and professional standards. Perhaps, at another firm, the climate is fitting but requires strengthening: For example, the accounting firm could have a laws-and-codes climate, but subjects might have indicated that the company did not hold those values very firmly. At yet another accounting firm the climate might be inappropriate and need to be changed—it might, for example, have a caring climate, in which interpersonal relationships rather than abstract standards govern behavior.

Management can strengthen and change the ethical climate through education and training in ethical decision making; revision or development of a formal corporate code of ethics; changes in monitoring and supervision; and alterations in company policies, procedures, manuals, performance objectives, selection processes, and incentive structures. As in the earlier stages, these methods can be applied solely in-house, or with the assistance of outside consultants.

EFFECTIVENESS

Although the climate assessment procedure may sound prescriptive, the executive should always bear in mind that there is no one best ethical climate: Firms can be ethical in many ways. However, the *effectiveness* of an ethical climate has important implications for the ethical behavior of the organization. Effective climates may contribute to the quality and regularity of employees' ethical choices; ineffective climates may foster lapses in organizational control over employees' actions, or lead to predictable errors in the ethical decisions that employees make.

A key factor in effectiveness is a good fit between the organization's ethical climate and its strategy; moreover, the enforcing mechanisms and decision-making processes must suit the climate. For example, an extensive, written code could be quite effective in a rules-oriented climate, but might be out of place in a caring climate. Similarly, training that emphasizes utilitarian reasoning would likely be more successful in a caring than a professional climate. The decision-making process implied by a laws-and-codes climate requires obeying principles that were developed by external organizations—and thus necessitates a strong legal function within the organization. Although the rules climate in many ways resembles the laws-and-codes climate, the principles to be followed in the rules climate are centralized and internal, so in such a climate the human resources or operations management area should have a stronger voice in the management of ethics. Finally, the results of our survey indicate that a subunit's place in the total organizational structure has implications for its ethical climate: At the savings and loan association and also at the manufacturing plant, the employees at the home offices reported less emphasis on laws, codes, and rules than did the employees at the branch offices. Perhaps control by formal mechanisms becomes more necessary when direct supervision by top management is not feasible.

No matter what ethical climate is most appropriate for a given firm, consistency and clarity are crucial to its effectiveness. Management needs to decide what values it seeks to champion, and what decision-making processes it will promote in order to support those values. Employees cannot behave as management wishes them to unless they know what management expects of them, and how they can meet these expectations. As we saw in Johnson & Johnson's handling of the Tylenol case, clarity and consistency of ethical norms and processes facilitate rapid decision making that is consonant with management's espoused principles.

The existence of distinct ethical climates has clear implications for controlling ethical behavior in organizations—an activity in which firms are taking more and more interest. Learning what the current climate is constitutes the first crucial step toward making the climate as appropriate and effective as it can be.

Mother-to-be and Daiquiri Lead to Firings

Two cocktail servers were reluctant to serve alcohol to a pregnant woman. They were fired.

SEATTLE—Two cocktail servers tried to talk a pregnant woman out of having a strawberry daiquiri and ended up losing their jobs.

Danita Fitch, 21, and G. R. Heryford, 22, were fired from a Red Robin restaurant in suburban Tukwila when they tried to stop a patron Heryford described as "very pregnant" from having the drink on March 13.

A strawberry daiquiri contains two ounces of rum, and drinking alcohol during pregnancy has been linked to birth defects.

Jim Roths, Red Robin's director of operations, said Heryford and Fitch were fired because they did not treat the customer with "respect and dignity."

Heryford said he first asked the woman for age identification.

"I was hoping she didn't have it," he said. "Then I could legally refuse her service."

The woman produced ID showing her to be about 30, so he went to assistant manager Mike Buckley who ordered him to serve her.

Heryford told the *Seattle Times* he served the drink, but asked the woman twice if she wanted it without alcohol.

"She stood up and said, 'The baby's past due; it's had its chance,' " he said.

When Heryford told Fitch what happened, she peeled from a rum bottle the government warning against alcohol consumption by pregnant women, placed it on the table and told the woman, "This is in case you don't know."

The woman complained and Buckley fired Fitch on the spot. Heryford was fired the next day.

Heryford said Buckley told them their job was not to lecture customers or offer opinions on prenatal care. But Heryford said he worried the woman "could have walked out of here and had a baby born with alcohol in its blood. Would we be responsible?"

"We were just trying to use our best judgment," he said.

Doug Honig, Seattle public education director for the American Civil Liberties Union, said the ACLU supports the right of an employee to express opinions, if they don't interfere with business.

Reprinted by permission of the *St. Petersberg Times*.

"Let's say you serve high-cholesterol food," Honig said. "Do you have the right to warn customers that food could lead to heart disease?"

Honig said the employer's right to do business outweighs an employee's right to interfere, no matter how good the intentions.

Under a federal law that took effect in November 1989, alcoholic beverages must carry warnings about birth defects and other health hazards related to drinking.

Fitch and Heryford say they hope to urge the state Liquor Control Board to set a policy on serving alcohol to pregnant women.

Drinking during pregnancy can cause fetal alcohol syndrome, which is the main recognized cause of congenital defects, including mental retardation.

Thousands of babies are born each year in the United States with fetal alcohol syndrome. The risk is particularly high for women who have more than two drinks a day and for women who drink in the first trimester of pregnancy.

Studies indicate even moderate drinking in the first month or two of pregnancy—often before women realize they are pregnant—can impair the child's intellectual ability upon reaching school age.

Said James West, head of the Alcohol and Brain Research Laboratory at the University of Iowa College of Medicine: "If the data we have on alcohol and birth defects, if even a fraction of that were available for some other substance, it would be banned."

Moral Mazes: Bureaucracy and Managerial Work

Robert Jackall

With moral choices tied to personal fates, how does bureaucracy shape managerial morality?

Corporate leaders often tell their charges that hard work will lead to success. Indeed, this theory of reward being commensurate with effort has been an enduring belief in our society, one central to our self-image as a people where the "main

---

chance" is available to anyone of ability who has the gumption and the persistence to seize it. Hard work, it is also frequently asserted, builds character. This notion carries less conviction because businessmen, and our society as a whole, have little patience with those who make a habit of finishing out of the money. In the end, it is success that matters, that legitimates striving, and that makes work worthwhile.

What if, however, men and women in the big corporation no longer see success as necessarily connected to hard work? What becomes of the social morality of the corporation—I mean the everyday rules in use that people play by—when there is thought to be no "objective" standard of excellence to explain how and why winners are separated from also-rans, how and why some people succeed and others fail?

This is the puzzle that confronted me while doing a great many extensive interviews with managers and executives in several large corporations, particularly in a large chemical company and a large textile firm. I went into these corporations to study how bureaucracy—the prevailing organizational form of our society and economy—shapes moral consciousness. I came to see that managers' rules for success are at the heart of what may be called the bureaucratic ethic.

This article suggests no changes and offers no programs for reform. It is, rather, simply an interpretive sociological analysis of the moral dimensions of managers' work. Some readers may find the essay sharp-edged, others familiar. For both groups, it is important to note at the outset that my materials are managers' own descriptions of their experiences.[1] As it happens, my own research in a variety of other settings suggests that managers' experiences are by no means unique; indeed they have a deep resonance with those of other occupational groups.

WHAT HAPPENED TO THE PROTESTANT ETHIC?

To grasp managers' experiences and the more general implications they contain, one must see them against the background of the great historical transformations, both social and cultural, that produced managers as an occupational group. Since the concern here is with the moral significance of work in business, it is important to begin with an understanding of the original Protestant Ethic, the world view of the rising bourgeois class that spearheaded the emergence of capitalism.

The Protestant Ethic was a set of beliefs that counseled "secular asceticism"— the methodical, rational subjection of human impulse and desire to God's will through "restless, continuous, systematic work in a worldly calling."[2] This ethic of ceaseless work and ceaseless renunciation of the fruits of one's toil provided both the economic and the moral foundations for modern capitalism.

On one hand, secular asceticism was a ready-made prescription for building

---

1. There is a long sociological tradition of work on managers and I am, of course, indebted to that literature. I am particularly indebted to the work, both joint and separate, of Joseph Bensman and Arthur J. Vidich, two of the keenest observers of the new middle class. See especially their *The New American Society: The Revolution of the Middle Class* (Chicago: Quadrangle Books, 1971).

2. See Max Weber, *The Protestant Ethic and the Spirit of Capitalism,* translated by Talcott Parsons (New York: Charles Scribner's Sons, 1958), p. 172.

economic capital; on the other, it became for the upward-moving bourgeois class—self-made industrialists, farmers, and enterprising artisans—the ideology that justified their attention to this world, their accumulation of wealth, and indeed the social inequities that inevitably followed such accumulation. This bourgeois ethic, with its imperatives for self-reliance, hard work, frugality, and rational planning, and its clear definition of success and failure, came to dominate a whole historical epoch in the West.

But the ethic came under assault from two directions. First, the very accumulation of wealth that the old Protestant Ethic made possible gradually stripped away the religious basis of the ethic, especially among the rising middle class that benefited from it. There were, of course, periodic reassertions of the religious context of the ethic, as in the case of John D. Rockefeller and his turn toward Baptism. But on the whole, by the late 1800s the religious roots of the ethic survived principally among independent farmers and proprietors of small businesses in rural areas and towns across America.

In the mainstream of an emerging urban America, the ethic had become secularized into the "work ethic," "rugged individualism," and especially the "success ethic." By the beginning of this century, among most of the economically successful, frugality had become an aberration, conspicuous consumption the norm. And with the shaping of the mass consumer society later in this century, the sanctification of consumption became widespread, indeed crucial to the maintenance of the economic order.

Affluence and the emergence of the consumer society were responsible, however, for the demise of only aspects of the old ethic—namely, the imperatives for saving and investment. The core of the ethic, even in its later, secularized form— self-reliance, unremitting devotion to work, and a morality that postulated just rewards for work well done—was undermined by the complete transformation of the organizational form of work itself. The hallmarks of the emerging modern production and distribution systems were administrative hierarchies, standardized work procedures, regularized timetables, uniform policies, and centralized control—in a word, the bureaucratization of the economy.

This bureaucratization was heralded at first by a very small class of salaried managers, who were later joined by legions of clerks and still later by technicians and professionals of every stripe. In this century, the process spilled over from the private to the public sector and government bureaucracies came to rival those of industry. This great transformation produced the decline of the old middle class of entrepreneurs, free professionals, independent farmers, and small independent businessmen—the traditional carriers of the old Protestant Ethic—and the ascendance of a new middle class of salaried employees whose chief common characteristic was and is their dependence on the big organization.

Any understanding of what happened to the original Protestant Ethic and to the old morality and social character it embodied—and therefore any understanding of the moral significance of work today—is inextricably tied to an analysis of bureaucracy. More specifically, it is, in my view, tied to an analysis of the work and occupational cultures of managerial groups within bureaucracies. Managers are the quintessential bureaucratic work group; they not only fashion bureaucratic rules, but they are also bound by them. Typically, they are not just *in* the organization; they are *of* the organization. As such, managers represent the prototype of the white-collar salaried employee. By analyzing the kind of ethic bureaucracy produces in managers, one can begin to understand how bureaucracy shapes morality in our society as a whole.

PYRAMIDAL POLITICS

American businesses typically both centralize and decentralize authority. Power is concentrated at the top in the person of the chief executive officer and is simultaneously decentralized; that is, responsibility for decisions and profits is pushed as far down the organizational line as possible. For example, the chemical company that I studied—and its structure is typical of other organizations I examined—is one of several operating companies of a large and growing conglomerate. Like the other operating companies, the chemical concern has its own president, executive vice presidents, vice presidents, other executive officers, business area managers, entire staff divisions, and operating plants. Each company is, in effect, a self-sufficient organization, though they are all coordinated by the corporation, and each president reports directly to the corporate CEO.

Now, the key interlocking mechanism of this structure is its reporting system. Each manager gathers up the profit targets or other objectives of his or her subordinates, and with these formulates his commitments to his boss; this boss takes these commitments, and those of his other subordinates, and in turn makes a commitment to *his* boss. (Note: henceforth only "he" or "his" will be used to allow for easier reading.) At the top of the line, the president of each company makes his commitment to the CEO of the corporation, based on the stated objectives given to him by his vice presidents. There is always pressure from the top to set higher goals.

This management-by-objectives system, as it is usually called, creates a chain of commitments from the CEO down to the lowliest product manager. In practice, it also shapes a patrimonial authority arrangement which is crucial to defining both the immediate experiences and the long-run career chances of individual managers. In this world, a subordinate owes fealty principally to his immediate boss. A subordinate must not overcommit his boss; he must keep the boss from making mistakes, particularly public ones; he must not circumvent the boss. On a social level, even though an easy, breezy informality is the prevalent style of American business, the subordinate must extend to the boss a certain ritual deference: for instance, he must follow the boss's lead in conversation, he must not speak out of turn at meetings, and must laugh at the boss's jokes while not making jokes of his own.

In short, the subordinate must not exhibit any behavior which symbolizes parity. In return, he can hope to be elevated when and if the boss is elevated, although other important criteria also intervene here. He can also expect protection for mistakes made up to a point. However, that point is never exactly defined and always depends on the complicated politics of each situation.

Who Gets Credit?

It is characteristic of this authority system that details are pushed down and credit is pushed up. Superiors do not like to give detailed instructions to subordinates. The official reason for this is to maximize subordinates' autonomy; the underlying reason seems to be to get rid of tedious details and to protect the privilege of authority to declare that a mistake has been made.

It is not at all uncommon for very bald and extremely general edicts to emerge from on high. For example, "Sell the plant in St. Louis. Let me know when you've struck a deal." This pushing down of details has important consequences:

1. Because they are unfamiliar with entangling details, corporate higher echelons tend to expect highly successful results without complications. This is central to top executives' well-known aversion to bad news and to the resulting tendency to "kill the messenger" who bears that news.
2. The pushing down of detail creates great pressure on middle managers not only to transmit good news but to protect their corporations, their bosses, and themselves in the process. They become the "point men" of a given strategy and the potential "fall guys" when things go wrong.

Credit flows up in this structure and usually is appropriated by the highest ranking officer involved in a decision. This person redistributes credit as he chooses, bound essentially by a sensitivity to public perceptions of his fairness. At the middle level, credit for a particular success is always a type of refracted social honor; one cannot claim credit even if it is earned. Credit has to be given, and acceptance of the gift implicitly involves a reaffirmation and strengthening of fealty. A superior may share some credit with subordinates in order to deepen fealty relationships and induce greater future efforts on his behalf. Of course, a different system is involved in the allocation of blame, a point I shall discuss later.

Fealty to the 'King'

Because of the interlocking character of the commitment system, a CEO carries enormous influence in his corporation. If, for a moment, one thinks of the presidents of individual operating companies as barons, then the CEO of the parent company is the king. His word is law; even the CEO's wishes and whims are taken as commands by close subordinates on the corporate staff, who zealously turn them into policies and directives.

A typical example occurred in the textile company last year when the CEO, new at the time, expressed mild concern about the rising operating costs of the company's fleet of rented cars. The following day, a stringent system for monitoring mileage replaced the previous casual practice.

Great efforts are made to please the CEO. For example, when the CEO of the large conglomerate that includes the chemical company visits a plant, the most important order of business for local management is a fresh paint job, even when, as in several cases last year, the cost of the paint alone exceeds $100,000. I am told that similar anecdotes from other organizations have been in circulation since 1910; this suggests a certain historical continuity of behavior toward top bosses.

The second order of business for the plant management is to produce a complete book describing the plant and its operations, replete with photographs and illustrations, for presentation to the CEO; such a book costs about $10,000 for the single copy. By any standards of budgetary stringency, such expenditures are irrational. But by the social standards of the corporation, they make perfect sense. It is far more important to please the king today than to worry about the future economic state of one's fief, since if one does not please the king, there may not be a fief to worry about or indeed any vassals to do the worrying.

By the same token, all of this leads to an intense interest in everything the CEO does and says. In both the chemical and the textile companies, the most common topic of conversation among managers up and down the line is speculation about their respective CEO's plans, intentions, strategies, actions, styles, and public images.

Such speculation is more than idle gossip. Because he stands at the apex of the corporation's bureaucratic and patrimonial structures and locks the intricate system of commitments between bosses and subordinates into place, it is the CEO who ultimately decides whether those commitments have been satisfactorily met. Moreover, the CEO and his trusted associates determine the fate of whole business areas of a corporation.

Shake-ups and Contingency

One must appreciate the simultaneously monocratic and patrimonial character of business bureaucracies in order to grasp what we might call their contingency. One has only to read the *Wall Street Journal* or the *New York Times* to realize that, despite their carefully constructed "eternal" public image, corporations are quite unstable organizations. Mergers, buy-outs, divestitures, and especially "organizational restructuring" are commonplace aspects of business life. I shall discuss only organizational shake-ups here.

Usually, shake-ups occur because of the appointment of a new CEO and/or division president, or because of some failure that is adjusted to demand retribution; sometimes these occurrences work together. The first action of most new CEOs is some form of organizational change. On the one hand, this prevents the inheritance of blame for past mistakes; on the other, it projects an image of bareknuckled aggressiveness much appreciated on Wall Street. Perhaps most important, a shake-up rearranges the fealty structure of the corporation, placing in power those barons whose style and public image mesh closely with that of the new CEO.

A shake-up has reverberations throughout an organization. Shortly after the new CEO of the conglomerate was named, he reorganized the whole business and selected new presidents to head each of the five newly formed companies of the corporation. He mandated that the presidents carry out a thorough reorganization of their separate companies complete with extensive "census reduction"—that is, firing as many people as possible.

The new president of the chemical company, one of these five, had risen from a small but important specialty chemicals division in the former company. Upon promotion to president, he reached back into his former division, indeed back to his own past work in a particular product line, and systematically elevated many of his former colleagues, friends, and allies. Powerful managers in other divisions, particularly in a rival process chemicals division, were: (1) forced to take big demotions in the new power structure; (2) put on "special assignment"—the corporate euphemism for Siberia (the saying is: "No one ever comes back from special assignment"); (3) fired; or (4) given "early retirement," a graceful way of doing the same thing.

Up and down the chemical company, former associates of the president now hold virtually every important position. Managers in the company view all of this as an inevitable fact of life. In their view, the whole reorganization could easily have gone in a completely different direction had another CEO been named or had the one selected picked a different president for the chemical company, or had the president come from a different work group in the old organization. Similarly, there is the abiding feeling that another significant change in top management could trigger yet another sweeping reorganization.

Fealty is the mortar of the corporate hierarchy, but the removal of one well-placed stone loosens the mortar throughout the pyramid and can cause things to fall apart. And no one is ever quite sure, until after the fact, just how the pyramid will be put back together.

SUCCESS AND FAILURE

It is within this complicated and ambiguous authority structure, always subject to upheaval, that success and failure are meted out to those in the middle and upper middle managerial ranks. Managers rarely spoke to me of objective criteria for achieving success because once certain crucial points in one's career are passed, success and failure seem to have little to do with one's accomplishments. Rather, success is socially defined and distributed. Corporations do demand, of course, a basic competence and sometimes specified training and experience; hiring patterns usually ensure these. A weeding-out process takes place, however, among the lower ranks of managers during the first several years of their experience. By the time a manager reaches a certain numbered grade in the ordered hierarchy—in the chemical company this is Grade 13 out of 25, defining the top 8½% of management in the company—managerial competence as such is taken for granted and assumed not to differ greatly from one manager to the next. The focus then switches to social factors, which are determined by authority and political alignments—the fealty structure—and by the ethos and style of the corporation.

Moving to the Top

In the chemical and textile companies as well as the other concerns I studied, five criteria seem to control a person's ability to rise in middle and upper middle management. In ascending order they are:

1. **Appearance and dress.** This criterion is so familiar that I shall mention it only briefly. Managers have to look the part, and it is sufficient to say that

corporations are filled with attractive, well-groomed, and conventionally well-dressed men and women.

2. Self-control. Managers stress the need to exercise iron self-control and to have the ability to mask all emotion and intention behind bland, smiling, and agreeable public faces. They believe it is a fatal weakness to lose control of oneself, in any way, in a public forum. Similarly, to betray valuable secret knowledge (for instance, a confidential reorganization plan) or intentions through some relaxation of self-control—for example, an indiscreet comment or lack of adroitness in turning aside a query—can not only jeopardize a manager's immediate position but can undermine others' trust in him.

3. Perception as a team player. While being a team player has many meanings, one of the most important is to appear to be interchangeable with other managers near one's level. Corporations discourage narrow specialization more strongly as one goes higher. They also discourage the expression of moral or political qualms. One might object, for example, to working with chemicals used in nuclear power, and most corporations today would honor that objection. The public statement of such objections, however, would end any realistic aspirations for higher posts because one's usefulness to the organization depends on versatility. As one manager in the chemical company commented: "Well, we'd go along with his request but we'd always wonder about the guy. And in the back of our minds, we'd be thinking that he'll soon object to working in the soda ash division because he doesn't like glass."

    Another important meaning of team play is putting in long hours at the office. This requires a certain amount of sheer physical energy, even though a great deal of this time is spent not in actual work but in social rituals—like reading and discussing newspaper articles, taking coffee breaks, or having informal conversations. These rituals, readily observable in every corporation that I studied, forge the social bonds that make real managerial work—that is, group work of various sorts—possible. One must participate in the rituals to be considered effective in the work.

4. Style. Managers emphasize the importance of "being fast on your feet"; always being well organized; giving slick presentations complete with color slides; giving the appearance of knowledge even in its absence; and possessing a subtle, almost indefinable sophistication, marked especially by an urbane, witty, graceful, engaging, and friendly demeanor.

I want to pause for a moment to note that some observers have interpreted such conformity, team playing, affability, and urbanity as evidence of the decline of the individualism of the old Protestant Ethic.[3] To the extent that commentators take the public images that managers project at face value, I think they miss the main point. Managers up and down the corporate ladder adopt the public faces

---

3. See William H. Whyte, *The Organization Man* (New York: Simon & Schuster, 1956), and David Riesman, in collaboration with Reuel Denney and Nathan Glazer, *The Lonely Crowd: A Study of the Changing American Character* (New Haven: Yale University Press, 1950).

that they wear quite consciously; they are, in fact, the masks behind which the real struggles and moral issues of the corporation can be found.

Karl Mannheim's conception of self-rationalization or self-streamlining is useful in understanding what is one of the central social psychological processes of organizational life.[4] In a world where appearances—in the broadest sense—mean everything, the wise and ambitious person learns to cultivate assiduously the proper, prescribed modes of appearing. He dispassionately takes stock of himself, treating himself as an object. He analyzes his strengths and weaknesses, and decides what he needs to change in order to survive and flourish in his organization. And then he systematically undertakes a program to reconstruct his image. Self-rationalization curiously parallels the methodical subjection of self to God's will that the old Protestant Ethic counseled; the difference, of course, is that one acquires not moral virtues but a masterful ability to manipulate personae.

5.   Patron power. To advance, a manager must have a patron, also called a mentor, a sponsor, a rabbi, or a godfather. Without a powerful patron in the higher echelons of management, one's prospects are poor in most corporations. The patron might be the manager's immediate boss or someone several levels higher in the chain of command. In either case the manager is still bound by the immediate, formal authority and fealty patterns of his position; the new—although more ambiguous—fealty relationships with the patron are added.

A patron provides his "client" with opportunities to get visibility, to showcase his abilities, to make connections with those of high status. A patron cues his client to crucial political developments in the corporation, helps arrange lateral moves if the client's upward progress is thwarted by a particular job or a particular boss, applauds his presentations or suggestions at meetings, and promotes the client during an organizational shakeup. One must, of course, be lucky in one's patron. If the patron gets caught in a political crossfire, the arrows are likely to find his clients as well.

Social Definitions of Performance

Surely, one might argue, there must be more to success in the corporation than style, personality, team play, chameleonic adaptability, and fortunate connections. What about the bottom line—profits, performance?

Unquestionably, "hitting your numbers"—that is, meeting the profit commitments already discussed—is important, but only within the social context I have described. There are several rules here. First, no one in a line position—that is, with responsibility for profit and loss—who regularly "misses his numbers" will survive, let alone rise. Second, a person who always hits his numbers but who lacks some or all of the required social skills will not rise. Third, a person who sometimes misses his numbers but who has all the desirable social traits will rise.

---

4. Karl Mannheim, *Man and Society in an Age of Reconstruction* [London: Paul (Kegan), Trench, Trubner Ltd. 1940], p. 55.

Performance is thus always subject to a myriad of interpretations. Profits matter, but it is much more important in the long run to be perceived as "promotable" by belonging to central political networks. Patrons protect those already selected as rising stars from the negative judgments of others; and only the foolhardy point out even egregious errors of those in power or those destined for it.

Failure is also socially defined. The most damaging failure is, as one middle manager in the chemical company puts it, "when your boss or someone who has the power to determine your fate says: 'You failed.' " Such a godlike pronouncement means, of course, out-and-out personal ruin; one must, at any cost, arrange matters to prevent such an occurrence.

As it happens, things rarely come to such a dramatic point even in the midst of an organizational crisis. The same judgment may be made but it is usually called "nonpromotability." The difference is that those who are publicly labeled as failures normally have no choice but to leave the organization; those adjudged nonpromotable can remain, provided they are willing to accept being shelved or, more colorfully, "mushroomed"—that is, kept in a dark place, fed manure, and left to do nothing but grow fat. Usually, seniors do not tell juniors they are nonpromotable (though the verdict may be common knowledge among senior peer groups). Rather, subordinates are expected to get the message after they have been repeatedly overlooked for promotions. In fact, middle managers interpret staying in the same job for more than two or three years as evidence of a negative judgment. This leads to a mobility panic at the middle levels which, in turn, has crucial consequences for pinpointing responsibility in the organization.

Capriciousness of Success

Finally, managers think that there is a tremendous amount of plain luck involved in advancement. It is striking how often managers who pride themselves on being hardheaded rationalists explain their own career patterns and those of others in terms of luck. Various uncertainties shape this perception. One is the sense of organizational contingency. One change at the top can create profound unheaval throughout the entire corporate structure, producing startling reversals of fortune, good or bad, depending on one's connections. Another is the uncertainty of the markets that often makes managerial planning simply elaborate guesswork, causing real economic outcome to depend on factors totally beyond organizational and personal control.

It is interesting to note in this context that a line manager's credibility suffers just as much from missing his numbers on the up side (that is, achieving profits higher than predicted) as from missing them on the down side. Both outcomes undercut the ideology of managerial planning and control, perhaps the only bulwark managers have against market irrationality.

Even managers in staff positions, often quite removed from the market, face uncertainty. Occupational safety specialists, for instance, know that bad publicity from one serious accident in the workplace can jeopardize years of work and scores of safety awards. As one high-ranking executive in the chemical company says, "In the corporate world, 1,000 'Attaboys!' are wiped away by one 'Oh, shit!' "

Because of such uncertainties, managers in all the companies I studied speak continually of the great importance of being in the right place at the right time and of the catastrophe of being in the wrong place at the wrong time. My interview materials are filled with stories of people who were transferred immediately before a big shake-up and, as a result, found themselves riding the crest of a wave to power; of people in a promising business area who were terminated because top management suddenly decided that the area no longer fit the corporate image desired; of others caught in an unpredictable and fatal political battle among their patrons; of a product manager whose plant accidentally produced an odd color batch of chemicals, who sold them as a premium version of the old product, and who is now thought to be a marketing genius.

The point is that managers have a sharply defined sense of the *capriciousness* of organizational life. Luck seems to be as good an explanation as any of why, after a certain point, some people succeed and others fail. The upshot is that many managers decide that they can do little to influence external events in their favor. One can, however, shamelessly streamline oneself, learn to wear all the right masks, and get to know all the right people. And then sit tight and wait for things to happen.

'GUT DECISIONS'

Authority and advancement patterns come together in the decision-making process. The core of the managerial mystique is decision-making prowess, and the real test of such prowess is what managers call "gut decisions," that is, important decisions involving big money, public exposure, or significant effects on the organization. At all but the highest levels of the chemical and textile companies, the rules for making gut decisions are, in the words of one upper middle manager: "(1) Avoid making any decisions if at all possible; and (2) if a decision has to be made, involve as many people as you can so that, if things go south, you're able to point in as many directions as possible."

Consider the case of a large coking plant of the chemical company. Coke making requires a gigantic battery to cook the coke slowly and evenly for long periods; the battery is the most important piece of capital equipment in a coking plant. In 1975, the plant's battery showed signs of weakening and certain managers at corporate headquarters had to decide whether to invest $6 million to restore the battery to top form. Clearly, because of the amount of money involved, this was a gut decision.

No decision was made. The CEO had sent the word out to defer all unnecessary capital expenditures to give the corporation cash reserves for other investments. So the managers allocated small amounts of money to patch the battery up until 1979, when it collapsed entirely. This brought the company into a breach of contract with a steel producer and into violation of various Environmental Protection Agency pollution regulations. The total bill, including lawsuits and now federally mandated repairs to the battery, exceeded $100 million. I have heard figures as high as $150 million, but because of "creative accounting," no one is sure of the exact amount.

This simple but very typical example gets to the heart of how decision making is intertwined with a company's authority structure and advancement patterns. As the chemical company managers see it, the decisions facing them in 1975 and 1979 were crucially different. Had they acted decisively in 1975—in hindsight, the only rational course—they would have salvaged the battery and saved their corporation millions of dollars in the long run.

In the short run, however, since even seemingly rational decisions are subject to widely varying interpretations, particularly decisions which run counter to a CEO's stated objectives, they would have been taking a serious risk in restoring the battery. What is more, their political networks might have unraveled, leaving them vulnerable to attack. They chose short-term safety over long-term gain because they felt they were judged, both by higher authority and by their peers, on their short-term performances. Managers feel that if they do not survive the short run, the long run hardly matters. Even correct decisions can shorten promising careers.

By contrast, in 1979 the decision was simple and posed little risk. The corporation had to meet its legal obligations; also it had to either repair the battery the way the EPA demanded or shut down the plant and lose several hundred million dollars. Since there were no real choices, everyone could agree on a course of action because everyone could appeal to inevitability. Diffusion of responsibility, in this case by procrastinating until total crisis, is intrinsic to organizational life because the real issue in most gut decisions is: Who is going to get blamed if things go wrong?

'Blame Time'

There is no more feared hour in the corporate world than "blame time." Blame is quite different from responsibility. There is a cartoon of Richard Nixon declaring: "I accept all of the responsibility, but none of the blame." To blame someone is to injure him verbally in public; in large organizations, where one's image is crucial, this poses the most serious sort of threat. For managers, blame—like failure—has nothing to do with the merits of a case; it is a matter of social definition. As a general rule, it is those who are or who become politically vulnerable or expendable who get "set up" and become blamable. The most feared situation of all is to end up inadvertently in the wrong place at the wrong time and get blamed.

Yet this is exactly what often happens in a structure that systematically diffuses responsibility. It is because managers fear blame time that they diffuse responsibility; however, such diffusion inevitably means that someone, somewhere is going to become a scapegoat when things go wrong. Big corporations encourage this process by their complete lack of any tracking system. Whoever is currently in charge of an area is responsible—that is, potentially blamable—for whatever goes wrong in the area, even if he has inherited others' mistakes. An example from the chemical company illustrates this process.

When the CEO of the large conglomerate took office, he wanted to rid his capital accounts of all serious financial drags. The corporation had been operating a storage depot for natural gas which it bought, stored, and then resold. Some years before the energy crisis, the company had entered into a long-term contract to supply gas to a buyer—call him Jones. At the time, this was a sound deal because it provided a steady market for a stably priced commodity.

When gas prices soared, the corporation was still bound to deliver gas to Jones at 20¢ per unit instead of the going market price of $2. The CEO ordered one of his subordinates to get rid of this albatross as expeditiously as possible. This was done by selling the operation to another party—call him Brown—with the agreement that Brown would continue to meet the contractual obligations to Jones. In return for Brown's assumption of these costly contracts, the corporation agreed to buy gas from Brown at grossly inflated prices to meet some of its own energy needs.

In effect, the CEO transferred the drag on his capital accounts to the company's operating expenses. This enabled him to project an aggressive, asset-reducing image to Wall Street. Several levels down the ladder, however, a new vice president for a particular business found himself saddled with exorbitant operating costs when, during a reorganization, those plants purchasing gas from Brown at inflated prices came under his purview. The high costs helped to undercut the vice president's division earnings and thus to erode his position in the hierarchy. The origin of the situation did not matter. All that counted was that the vice president's division was steadily losing big money. In the end, he resigned to "pursue new opportunities."

One might ask why top management does not institute codes or systems for tracking responsibility. This example provides the clue. An explicit system of accountability for subordinates would probably have to apply to top executives as well and would restrict their freedom. Bureaucracy expands the freedom of those on top by giving them the power to restrict the freedom of those beneath.

On the Fast Track

Managers see what happened to the vice president as completely capricious, but completely understandable. They take for granted the absence of any tracking of responsibility. If anything, they blame the vice president for not recognizing soon enough the dangers of the situation into which he was being drawn and for not preparing a defense—even perhaps finding a substitute scapegoat. At the same time, they realize that this sort of thing could easily happen to them. They see few defenses against being caught in the wrong place at the wrong time except constant wariness, the diffusion of responsibility, and perhaps being shrewd enough to declare the ineptitude of one's predecessor on first taking a job.

What about avoiding the consequences of their own errors? Here they enjoy more control. They can "outrun" their mistakes so that when blame time arrives, the burden will fall on someone else. The ideal situation, of course, is to be in a position to fire one's successors for one's own previous mistakes.

Some managers, in fact, argue that outrunning mistakes is the real key to managerial success. One way to do this is by manipulating the numbers. Both the chemical and the textile companies place a great premium on a division's or a subsidiary's return on assets. A good way for business managers to increase their ROA is to reduce their assets while maintaining sales. Usually they will do everything they can to hold down expenditures in order to decrease the asset base, particularly at the end of the fiscal year. The most common way of doing this is by deferring capital expenditures, from maintenance to innovative investments, as long as possible. Done for a short time, this is called "starving" a plant; done over a longer period, it is called "milking" a plant.

Some managers become very adept at milking businesses and showing a consistent record of high returns. They move from one job to another in a company, always upward, rarely staying more than two years in any post. They may leave behind them deteriorating plants and unsafe working conditions, but they know that if they move quickly enough, the blame will fall on others. In this sense, bureaucracies may be thought of as vast systems of organized irresponsibility.

FLEXIBILITY AND DEXTERITY WITH SYMBOLS

The intense competition among managers takes place not only behind the agreeable public faces I have described but within an extraordinarily indirect and ambiguous linguistic framework. Except at blame time, managers do not publicly criticize or disagree with one another or with company policy. The sanction against such criticism or disagreement is so strong that it constitutes, in managers' view, a suppression of professional debate. The sanction seems to be rooted principally in their acute sense of organizational contingency; the person one criticizes or argues with today could be one's boss tomorrow.

This leads to the use of an elaborate linguistic code marked by emotional neutrality, especially in group settings. The code communicates the meaning one might wish to convey to other managers, but since it is devoid of any significant emotional sentiment, it can be reinterpreted should social relationships or attitudes change. Here, for example, are some typical phrases describing performance appraisals followed by their probable intended meanings:

Stock phrase	Probable intended meaning
Exceptionally well qualified	Has committed no major blunders to date
Tactful in dealing with superiors	Knows when to keep his mouth shut
Quick thinking	Offers plausible excuses for errors
Meticulous attention to detail	A nitpicker
Slightly below average	Stupid
Unusually loyal	Wanted by no one else

For the most part, such neutered language is not used with the intent to deceive; rather, its purpose is to communicate certain meanings within specific contexts with the implicit understanding that, should the context change, a new, more appropriate meaning can be attached to the language already used. In effect, the corporation is a setting where people are not held to their word because it is generally understood that their word is always provisional.

The higher one goes in the corporate world, the more this seems to be the case; in fact, advancement beyond the upper middle level depends greatly on one's ability to manipulate a variety of symbols without becoming tied to or identified with any of them. For example, an amazing variety of organizational improvement programs marks practically every corporation. I am referring here to the myriad ideas generated by corporate staff, business consultants, academics, and a host of others to improve corporate structure; sharpen decision making; raise morale; create a more humanistic workplace; adopt Theory X, Theory Y, or, more recently, Theory Z of management; and so on. These programs become important when they are pushed from the top.

The watchword in the large conglomerate at the moment is productivity and, since this is a pet project of the CEO himself, it is said that no one goes into his presence without wearing a blue *Productivity!* button and talking about "quality circles" and "feedback sessions." The president of another company pushes a series of managerial seminars that endlessly repeats the basic functions of management: (1) planning, (2) organizing, (3) motivating, and (4) controlling. Aspiring young managers attend these sessions and with a seemingly dutiful eagerness learn to repeat the formulas under the watchful eyes of senior officials.

Privately, managers characterize such programs as the "CEO's incantations over the assembled multitude," as "elaborate rituals with no practical effect," or as "waving a magic wand to make things wonderful again." Publicly, of course, managers on the way up adopt the programs with great enthusiasm, participate in or run them very effectively, and then quietly drop them when the time is right.

Playing the Game

Such flexibility, as it is called, can be confusing even to those in the inner circles. I was told the following by a highly placed staff member whose work requires him to interact daily with the top figures of his company:

"I get faked out all the time and I'm part of the system. I come from a very different culture. Where I come from, if you give someone your *word,* no one ever questions it. It's the old hard-work-will-lead-to-success ideology. Small community, Protestant, agrarian, small business, merchant-type values. I'm disadvantaged in a system like this."

He goes on to characterize the system more fully and what it takes to succeed within it:

"It's the ability to play this system that determines whether you will rise . . . . And part of the adeptness [required] is determined by how much it bothers people. One thing you have to be able to do is to play the game, but you can't be disturbed by the game. What's the game? It's bringing troops home from Vietnam and declaring peace with honor. It's saying one thing and meaning another.

"It's characterizing the reality of a situation with *any* description that is necessary to make that situation more palatable to some group that matters. It means that you have to come up with a culturally accepted verbalization to explain why you are *not* doing what you are doing. . . . [Or] you say that we had to do what we did because it was inevitable; or because the guys at the [regulatory] agencies were dumb; [you] say we won when we really lost; [you] say we saved money when we squandered it; [you] say something's safe when it's potentially or actually danger- ous. . . . Everyone knows it's bullshit, but it's *accepted.* This is the game."

In addition, then, to the other characteristics that I have described, it seems that a prerequisite for big success in the corporation is a certain adeptness at incon- sistency. This premium on inconsistency is particularly evident in the many areas of public controversy that face top-ranking managers. Two things come together to produce this situation. The first is managers' sense of beleaguerment from a wide array of adversaries who, it is thought, want to disrupt or impede management's attempts to further the economic interests of their companies. In every company that I studied, managers see themselves and their traditional prerogatives as being under siege, and they respond with a set of caricatures of their perceived principal adversaries.

For example, government regulators are brash, young, unkempt hippies in blue jeans who know nothing about the businesses for which they make rules; environmental activists—the bird and bunny people—are softheaded idealists who want everybody to live in tents, burn candles, ride horses, and eat berries; workers' compensation lawyers are out-and-out crooks who prey on corporations to appro- priate exorbitant fees from unwary clients; labor activists are radical troublemakers who want to disrupt harmonious industrial communities; and the news media con- sist of rabble-rousers who propagate sensational antibusiness stories to sell papers or advertising time on shows like "60 Minutes."

Second, within this context of perceived harassment, managers must address a multiplicity of audiences, some of whom are considered adversaries. These audi- ences are the internal corporate hierarchy with its intricate and shifting power and status cliques, key regulators, key local and federal legislators, special publics that vary according to the issues, and the public at large, whose goodwill and favorable opinion are considered essential for a company's free operation.

Managerial adeptness at inconsistency becomes evident in the widely discrep- ant perspectives, reasons for action, and presentations of fact that explain, excuse, or justify corporate behavior to these diverse audiences.

Adeptness at Inconsistency

The cotton dust issue in the textile industry provides a fine illustration of what I mean. Prolonged exposure to cotton dust produces in many textile workers a chronic and eventually disabling pulmonary disease called byssinosis or, colloqui- ally, brown lung. In the early 1970s, the Occupational Safety and Health Adminis- tration proposed a ruling to cut workers' exposure to cotton dust sharply by requir- ing textile companies to invest large amounts of money in cleaning up their plants. The industry fought the regulation fiercely but a final OSHA ruling was made in 1978 requiring full compliance by 1984.

The industry took the case to court. Despite an attempt by Reagan appointees in OSHA to have the case removed from judicial consideration and remanded to the agency they controlled for further cost/benefit analysis, the Supreme Court ruled in 1981 that the 1978 OSHA ruling was fully within the agency's mandate, namely, to protect workers' health and safety as the primary benefit exceeding all cost considerations.

During these proceedings, the textile company was engaged on a variety of fronts and was pursuing a number of actions. For instance, it intensively lobbied regulators and legislators and it prepared court materials for the industry's defense, arguing that the proposed standard would crush the industry and that the problem, if it existed, should be met by increasing workers' use of respirators.

The company also aimed a public relations barrage at special-interest groups as well as at the general public. It argued that there is probably no such thing as byssinosis; workers suffering from pulmonary problems are all heavy smokers and the real culprit is the government-subsidized tobacco industry. How can cotton cause brown lung when cotton is white? Further, if there is a problem, only some workers are afflicted, and therefore the solution is more careful screening of the work force to detect susceptible people and prevent them from ever reaching the workplace. Finally, the company claimed that if the regulation were imposed, most of the textile industry would move overseas where regulations are less harsh.[5]

In the meantime, the company was actually addressing the problem but in a characteristically indirect way. It invested $20 million in a few plants where it knew such an investment would make money; this investment automated the early stages of handling cotton, traditionally a very slow procedure, and greatly increased productivity. The investment had the side benefit of reducing cotton dust levels to the new standard in precisely those areas of the work process where the dust problem is greatest. Publicly, of course, the company claims that the money was spent entirely to eliminate dust, evidence of its corporate good citizenship. (Privately, executives admit that, without the productive return, they would not have spent the money and they have not done so in several other plants.)

Indeed, the productive return is the only rationale that carries weight within the corporate hierarchy. Executives also admit, somewhat ruefully and only when their office doors are closed, that OSHA's regulation on cotton dust has been the main factor in forcing technological innovation in a centuries-old and somewhat stagnant industry.

Such adeptness at inconsistency, without moral uneasiness, is essential for executive success. It means being able to say, as a very high-ranking official of the textile company said to me without batting an eye, that the industry has never caused the slightest problem in any worker's breathing capacity. It means, in the chemical company, propagating an elaborate hazard/benefit calculus for appraisal of dangerous chemicals while internally conceptualizing "hazards" as business risks. It means publicly extolling the carefulness of testing procedures on toxic chemicals while privately ridiculing animal tests as inapplicable to humans.

It means lobbying intensively in the present to shape government regulations to one's immediate advantage and, ten years later, in the event of a catastrophe,

---

5. On February 9, 1982, the Occupational Safety and Health Administration issued a notice that it was once again reviewing its 1978 standard on cotton dust for "cost-effectiveness." See *Federal Register*, vol. 47, p. 5906. As of this writing (May 1983), this review has still not been officially completed.

arguing that the company acted strictly in accordance with the standards of the time. It means claiming that the real problem of our society is its unwillingness to take risks, while in the thickets of one's bureaucracy avoiding risks at every turn; it means as well making every effort to socialize the risks of industrial activity while privatizing the benefits.

THE BUREAUCRATIC ETHIC

The bureaucratic ethic contrasts sharply with the original Protestant Ethic. The Protestant Ethic was the ideology of a self-confident and independent propertied social class. It was an ideology that extolled the virtues of accumulating wealth in a society organized around property and that accepted the stewardship responsibilities entailed by property. It was an ideology where a person's word was his bond and where the integrity of the handshake was seen as crucial to the maintenance of good business relationships. Perhaps most important, it was connected to a predictable economy of salvation—that is, hard work will lead to success, which is a sign of one's election by God—a notion also containing its own theodicy to explain the misery of those who do not make it in this world.

Bureaucracy, however, breaks apart substance from appearances, action from responsibility, and language from meaning. Most important, it breaks apart the older connection between the meaning of work and salvation. In the bureaucratic world, one's success, one's sign of election, no longer depends on one's own efforts and on an inscrutable God but on the capriciousness of one's superiors and the market; and one achieves economic salvation to the extent that one pleases and submits to one's employer and meets the exigencies of an impersonal market.

In this way, because moral choices are inextricably tied to personal fates, bureaucracy erodes internal and even external standards of morality, not only in matters of individual success and failure but also in all the issues that managers face in their daily work. Bureaucracy makes its own internal rules and social context the principal moral gauges for action. Men and women in bureaucracies turn to each other for moral cues for behavior and come to fashion specific situational moralities for specific significant people in their worlds.

As it happens, the guidance they receive from each other is profoundly ambiguous because what matters in the bureaucratic world is not what a person is but how closely his many personae mesh with the organizational ideal; not his willingness to stand by his actions but his agility in avoiding blame; not what he believes or says but how well he has mastered the ideologies that serve his corporation; not what he stands for but whom he stands with in the labyrinths of his organization.

In short, bureaucracy structures for managers an intricate series of moral mazes. Even the inviting paths out of the puzzle often turn out to be invitations to jeopardy.

Chapter
5

Being Different

*I*n times of rapid changes in values, what is rewarded and what is punished can change. People can find themselves "out of step," confused, frustrated, and unprepared during the change. On the one hand, confusion may occur because what have previously been successful attitudes and behaviors no longer work; there are no clear role models, no roadmaps for getting to a more comfortable and functional life space. On the other hand, what one brings to a situation may be well suited to what is required for effective behavior and for getting things done. Yet, frustration may be experienced because one encounters barriers created by others that can block self expression.

The condition of males and females in contemporary organizations seems fraught with intense confusion and frustration. For males, at least for many of those from white middle class America, this appears to be a time of tension, of self doubt, of searching for a new identity. In "A Gathering of Men," the first article of this chapter, poet Robert Bly argues that men in the 1990s are struggling to find a path that is not characterized by the macho, dominating "John Wayne" style of behavior common in the 1960s, nor one that is based exclusively on the sensitive male model of the 1970s and 1980s. In the conversation with Bill Moyers presented here, and in talks with men at workshops on men's issues, Bly suggests that the male model for the present and future may be one in which the male learns to balance masculine and feminine qualities and energies in his psyche, creating a male presence that is functional and healthy for men, and that allows women and men to relate to each other as equals. Bly blames the work culture of the industrial era and the demise of initiation rites in our society for many of the confusions and present-day dilemmas facing males. (For a more detailed treatment of Bly's ideas see his book *Iron John*, Addison-Wesley, 1990.)

What Bly discusses as dated and dysfunctional male behavior, Anne Wilson-

Schaef characterizes as the White Male System of functioning in organizational life. In "The Female System and the White Male System: New Ways of Looking at Our Culture," excerpted from her book *Women's Reality* (Winston Press, 1981), she compares and contrasts some of the ways females and males address such issues as defining time, experiencing relationships, exercising power, and demonstrating leadership. Her focus is on the differences between females and males. These same issues surface in a more systematic way in Jaclyn Fierman's "Why Women Still Don't Hit the Top," an analysis of a career woman's experiences in organizations.

People and the organizations they create often act as if they are threatened by sources of uncertainty. Consequently, they often find it difficult to cope with stimuli that differ in salient ways from the stimuli they assume to be normal. Some of the symptoms of these difficulties take the form of perceptual errors such as stereotypes and perceptual defenses. Prejudice still seems to be prevalent in the interactions faced by managers drawn from minority groups. Black managers, for example, appear to be second-guessed by others more often when they make decisions than are white bosses. Richard Lacayo describes this situation in "When the Boss Is Black." We still have a long way to go before we have eliminated the distortions that are associated with skin color and its impact on how an individual's organizational performance is perceived and judged.

This same observation may be made for distortions created when religion serves to disqualify certain individuals from full participation in organizational life. Drawing on memories of his own childhood experiences, Howard S. Schwartz reviews Abraham K. Korman's book *The Outsiders: Jews and Corporate America*. Schwartz describes the feelings and consequences of religious discrimination, which as he points out are not only hurtful to those who are subjected to it by "in groups," but also serve to insulate the "in group" and the organizations they run from valuable sources of vitality and innovation.

When people are labeled unfairly because of their physical characteristics, the impact on them can be very demeaning, as is shown in "Suit Accuses Airline of Sex Bias." In a case against American Airlines, management resorted to discriminatory tactics to save money. According to this suit, older women on higher pay scales in the airline are being subjected to weight checks that are not calibrated to take into account age-weight correlations. The result creates opportunities for management to get rid of well-paid employees on unfair grounds.

People sometimes use the rules of an organization to justify actions that serve their own interest, even when the logic of the application appears ridiculous, even absurd, to others. This is one of the messages in "Disabled Aussie Swimmer Sunk for Lack of an Arm."

"Why Pro-Family Policies Are Good for Business and America" looks at the positive side of dealing with differences, as corporations in America appear at least to be recognizing the benefits of progressive policies for accepting that their employees—male and female—have a life outside their professional careers. Acknowledging this reality and allowing men and women to manage their families as well as their professional careers allows for a balance that should make for healthier work organizations in the long run.

In "Institutional Bigotry" Roger Wilkins raises yet another dimension along which people are different, namely sexual preference. While the policy of the Air Force in this instance may have been extreme, Leonard Matlovich's experience of being discriminated against because he was a homosexual is by no means uncommon. Matlovich died of AIDS some years after the incident described in that article. The moving follow-up to the initial story is described in "Gay Vietnam Hero Buried with Honors."

When all is said and done, there are really more differences than similarities among organizational populations these days. It has always been important to recognize and harness differences between and among organizational participants. As we move into the twenty-first century, being different will be the norm, the reality. The challenge will be to create organizations in which this difference is celebrated and harnessed rather than being isolated and suppressed. In his lyrics for "Watching the Wheels," John Lennon captures some of the feelings that accompany the need to retain one's individuality while living out one's life.

A Gathering of Men

Bill Moyers and Robert Bly

BLY: *[at gathering]* I'll begin with a poem by Antonio Machado, the Spanish poet. There's a lot of pain and grief around men these days, and he touches on it here.

The wind one brilliant day called
to my soul with an odor of jasmine.

The wind said, "In return for the odor of my jasmine,
I'd like all the odor of your roses."

[Machado said,] "I have no roses; all the flowers
in my garden are dead . . ."

The wind said, "Then, I'll take
the withered petals, and the yellow leaves,"

Excerpt from "Bey" by Bill Moyers and Robert Bly from A Gathering of Men, (1990) pp. 3–7, reprinted by permission of Public Affairs Television Inc.

and the wind left. And I wept. And I said to myself,
"What have you done with the garden that was entrusted to you?"

Good poem, hmm? I think this feeling of the garden being blown apart doesn't happen much to you until you're 35 or so. The models we were given as men in high school, well, what were they—Eisenhower, John Wayne?—they only last till you're maybe 32 or 33. And then you notice that something's gone wrong in your business, in your private life, in your relationships; these things don't last. And so around 35, you have to find another image for what a man is, or what your man is. Is that clear, that idea?

So it takes a little bit of courage to come here. There's lots of men who feel this, and then they won't act on it. Or those in their 20s say: "I'm doing fine, Jack, I'm fine. It's true that 14 women have left me, and two beat me up, but I'm doing fine. It's true I'm bleeding from all my pores, but I'm fine."

MOYERS: Why "A Gathering of Men?" I mean, that's really rare, isn't it, to have a workshop for men only?

BLY: Maybe 20 years ago it would have been rare, but lately the men in various parts of the country have begun to gather. I think that it isn't—it isn't a reaction to the women's movement, really. I think the grief that leads to the men's movement began maybe 140 years ago, when the Industrial Revolution began, which sends the father out of the house to work.

MOYERS: What impact did that have?

BLY: Well, we receive something from our father by standing close to him.

MOYERS: Physically.

BLY: When we stand physically close to our father, something—something moves over that can't be described in material terms, that gives the son a certain confidence, an awareness, a knowledge of what it is to be male, what a man is. And in the ancient times you were always with your father; he taught you how to do things, he taught you how to farm, he taught you whatever it is that he did. You learned from him. But you had this sense of being—of receiving a food from him.

MOYERS: Food.

BLY: A food. From your father's body. Now, when the father went out of the house in the Industrial Revolution, that food ended, and I think the average American father now spends ten minutes a day with a son—I think that's what *The Minneapolis Tribune* had—and half of that time is spent in, "Clean up your room!" You know, that's a favorite phrase of mine, I know it well.

So the Industrial Revolution did not harm the mother and daughter relationship as much as it did the father and son, because the mother and daughter still stand close to each other and have stood close to each other. Maybe that'll change now when the mother is being sent out to work also, but the daughters then receive some knowledge of what it is to be a woman, or if you prefer to call it the women's—the female mode of feeling. They receive knowledge of the female mode of feeling. And the mother gets that from her grandmother, who got it from her great-grandmother, who gets it from her great-grandmother, it goes all the way down.

After the Industrial Revolution, the male does not receive any knowledge from his father of what the male mode of feeling is, and the old male initiators that used to work are not working anymore.

MOYERS: What do you mean, male initiators?

BLY: Well, the—you know, in the traditional times, you were not initiated by your father, because there's too much tension between you and your father. You are initiated by older, unrelated males, is the word that's used, older unrelated men. They may be friends of your father. They could even be uncles or grandfathers. But they are the ones who used to do it. Then they disappear. Then it falls on the father to do. Then the father is off at the office. You see the picture?

MOYERS: Yeah. In fact, in some of the traditional cultures, a night arrives, and a group of men show up at a boy's house, and they take him away from the home and they don't bring him back, then, for several days. And then when he comes back, he has ashes on his face.

BLY: Yeah. In New Guinea, where they still do it today, the men come in with spears to get the boys. The boys know nothing about the men's world. They live with their mother completely. They say, you know, "Mama, Mama, save us from these men that are coming here." Now, all over New Guinea, the women accept and the men accept one thing. A boy cannot be made into a man without the active intervention of the older men.

Now, when they all accept that, then the women's job is to be participants in this drama. So the men come and take the boys away, and the boys are saying, "Save me, Mommy," you know. Then they go across, and the men have built a tent—on this island they have built a house for the boys' initiation hut. Then they take them across the bridge, and three or four of the women, whose boys these are, get their spears and meet them on the bridge. And the old men have their spears. And the boys are saying, "Save me, Mama, save me, these are horrible men, they're taking me away," you know, and they fight and everything. And then the women are driven back. Then the women all go back and have coffee and say, "How'd I do? How'd I look?"

So that wonderful participation in it, the women are not doing the initiating, they're participating, and then, as you said, then he'll stay with the men for a year, maybe. Then they will explain to him something has to die to be born, and what will have to die is the boy. This is what isn't happening to the men in this culture.

BLY: [at gathering] I was giving a reading in Minnesota, in my little town, this year, and I gave "Rapunzel," and the cutting off of the golden hair of Rapunzel, and I said to the audience, "How many of you—do you remember when you had your golden hair cut off?" And then later a young man came up to me at the party afterwards, and he said: "I didn't dare say anything at that time, but this is what happened to me. I was about 15, and my parents wanted my long hair off. And I refused to cut it off. One day they got me and they tied me down, and they cut it off. I started to beat the ground, and I was weeping and hitting the floor. And while I had stopped hitting the floor and was still weeping, my grandfather walked in, and he saw immediately what had happened." I said, "What did your grandfather do?" They lived in Long Island. He took the boy out to the ocean and he said to the boy, "You see this ocean? Now, this is for you. This ocean is going to be here whether you have long hair or short hair."

That—only the grandfather could say that. And then that man said to me, "You know, he was right?" He said: "I went away, six years later I came back, I looked at the ocean, wham! It was incredible, like my grandfather had given it to me."

I said, "Unbelievable, unbelievable." That's the kind of thing that the older men do, that your father can't do.

BLY: *[at gathering]* When your father is away during the day and during the year, when he only comes home at five o'clock, you only get his temperament. What you used to get was his teaching and his temperament. The teaching would help you. You know how sweet it is when someone says, "Well, the way you make it is, you put your board, nail over here, you put your board over here, and you do that," and those teachings are sweet.

Even mean men are often sweet when they're teaching. And then we have that gratitude when someone has taught us something, that's so wonderful. We used to receive that from our fathers. Now he goes to work, and all we get is his temperament when he gets home at five, and he's tired. And what's more, at work he has been humiliated by older men and other men, bosses. He's been in competition with other men. He has—he has—he knows that his work—he's not going to be able to see the end of his work. It's not like making a chest of drawers. He knows that his company is probably polluting Alaska. How do you think he feels when he gets home? And that's all you're going to get.

The Female System and the White Male System: New Ways of Looking at Our Culture

Anne Wilson-Schaef

DEFINING TERMS: THE VALUE OF "WOMEN'S TALK"

My observations about the Female System and the White Male System come from women who have begun to trust their own perceptions and feel safe in expressing them. I have found that an amazing number of women with very different backgrounds and experiences tend to agree on many of these issues; this points to the existence of a clarity and commonality that are rarely observed or credited.

Far too frequently, women say only what is expected of them or acceptable in this culture. Their input generally falls into one of two categories: "women's talk" and "peacekeeping talk." Women's talk is stereotyped as useless. It is "all anyone can expect from a woman." It is allowed to exist because it does not threaten the White Male System. Peacekeeping talk does not threaten the White Male System either. In fact, it supports its concepts and ideas. It is women's way of demonstrating their understanding of the System and their reluctance to challenge its myths.

Women who have never stepped outside the pollution of the White Male System almost always communicate in one of these two modes. Even women who have begun to trust their own perceptions often fall back into one of these ways of speaking when they do not feel safe.

There is another kind of "women's talk," however. It is the kind that emerges during individual therapy, groups, and private conversations—situations in which women feel safe to explore their own evolving System. I have often been privileged to hear this meaningful and moving "women's talk." The ideas presented here were developed with the help of women who were free to voice their own perceptions. They provide us with a solid beginning as we seek to define the White Male System and our own Female System and explore other realities.

DEFINING TIME

Whenever I am comparing the White Male System with the Female System, I like to begin with a discussion of time.

In the White Male System, time is perceived as the numbers on the clock. In other words, men believe that the numbers on the clock are real and that time itself is nothing more than what those numbers measure. Five minutes equal five minutes; one hour equals one hour; one week equals one week; and so on. Time is what the clock or calendar measures. One who accepts this believes that it is possible to be early, late, or on time, and that these concepts have real meaning.

In the Female System—as well as in the other racial systems mentioned earlier—time is perceived as a process, a series of passages, or a series of interlocking cycles which may or may not have anything to do with the numbers on the clock. Frequently, the clock is irrelevant and may even be seen as interfering with the process of time. Early, late, and on time are concepts that have no real meaning.

There is an interesting correlation here between how much one buys into the White Male System and how he or she views and uses time. White women have bought into the System the most, and they are usually within fifteen minutes or so of being "on time" for an appointment. Blacks have bought in second most, and they are usually within a half hour or so of being "on time." Chicanos and Asian Americans tend to arrive within the hour. Native Americans—who have bought into the System the least—may be days or even weeks "late."

This has been one of the most difficult things for the Bureau of Indian Affairs to learn and understand. Traditionally, the white men who run it will set a meeting, and the Native American representatives may show up days later. The BIA people will angrily say something like, "What's the matter with you? You're not on time! You're late!" And the Native Americans will respond with, "What do you mean?" "We are here, and we will stay until we complete the process." That is "on time" for them!

The BIA implies that the Native Americans are sick, bad, crazy, or stupid because they are "late." They do not conform to the White Male System—the "way the world is." If they do not see time as the White Male System sees it, there must be something *wrong* with them. Neither of these approaches to time is necessarily *right,* by the way. Both can be useful. But when one is the way the world is and the other is sick, bad, crazy, or stupid, no one is free to use whichever approach is best for the situation at hand.

Let me illustrate this further with some examples from my own experience. When my son was little, I used to try to have dinner on the table by six o'clock. That meant that I usually started preparing it around five o'clock, when I got home from work. Unfortunately, this was just about the time when my son's internal time mechanism started running down. He would begin fussing and pulling at me. When I continued to go by "clock time" and focused my attention on preparing the meal, I frequently discovered that I had developed a "growth" on my leg. My son had wrapped himself around it, hanging on for dear life while I dragged him around the kitchen with me! One day I decided to treat time as a process. When I stopped what I was doing and responded to him, which only took a few minutes, he toddled off happily and kept himself amused until dinner was ready.

Neither approach to time was "right." It just happened that the process approach worked better for all concerned in this situation.

Several years ago I was an administrator in a mental health facility, where one of my assigned tasks was to run the weekly staff meetings. I soon discovered that the people who got to the meetings "on time" were not really there at all. Their bodies were there, but their beings were somewhere else. Those who came late, on the other hand, were more "present" than the others.

When I investigated further, I discovered that those who arrived "on time" had frequently stopped in the middle of something they were doing in order to arrive at the meeting on the dot. Those who "came late," however, were often late because they had taken the time to complete a task or bring it to a comfortable resting point before coming to the meeting. When they arrived at the meeting, they were ready and able to face the business at hand.

I began a quiet experiment with the group. At the beginning of each meeting, I asked the staff to sit quietly and focus on any anxieties or tensions they were feeling. I then asked them to relate each anxiety or tension to an unfinished task or process and write down what they needed to do in order to finish it. If someone felt especially tense or anxious, I would suggest that he or she take some action toward completing the interrupted task. For example, I frequently discovered that my major tension was related to the awareness that I had forgotten to take something out of the freezer for dinner. A quick telephone call home completed the process and freed me to focus on the meeting.

As we continued to do this exercise at the beginning of staff meetings, we began to use our time more efficiently. While it used to take twenty minutes for the staff to get their bodies and beings together, it now took from seven to ten minutes (a significant reduction—and a very worthwhile one, considering that most meetings were scheduled to last only an hour). We took the option of using a combination of process time and clock time, and it worked for us. Had I not suggested that option, I would have continued trying to drag the entire staff into the agenda when they were not ready for it.

Neither approach to time was necessarily "right," but the fact that we were flexible enough to explore new choices helped us to use our time better.

I once read an article in *Time* magazine about the atomic clock at the National Bureau of Standards. (I have long been fascinated by the National Bureau of Standards and believe that it is one of the citadels of the White Male System. At one point, I used to fantasize that real people did not work there. Instead, there was an elaborate hierarchy of inchworms who measured *everything!* When I finally visited it, I discovered to my amazement that it looks like any other building and that real people do in fact work there!) It seems that the atomic clock is the most accurate time-measuring instrument in the world. It sits up on a hill dividing the passage of time into equal segments. Unfortunately, it still has to be reset annually. In spite of its incredible and meticulous accuracy, the atomic clock does not know about the universe. The universe is on process time. (The universe does not know about the atomic clock either!) It is slowing down. So the atomic clock has to be set back a few seconds every year!

Which is better—process time, or clock time? Neither. Both are valid and useful. It is unfortunate, though, when our culture is denied information about process time because the White Male System insists that its way is the way the world is.

Women often find themselves in situations where process time is more efficient than clock time (for example, in childrearing and in relationships). As a result, we have learned to move back and forth between them with relative ease. Unfortunately, the White Male System often makes us feel guilty when we are "late" and implies that we are sick, bad, crazy, or stupid because we do not use time in the "right" way. It is difficult for us to communicate what we know about using time when we are constantly being made to feel insecure about ourselves and our own perceptions.

DEFINING RELATIONSHIPS

Being Peer

In the White Male System, relationships are conceived of as being either one-up or one-down. In other words, when two people come together or encounter each other, the White Male System assumption is that one of them must be superior and the other must be inferior. There are no other possibilities for interaction.

In working with men, especially business executives, I have found that many men do not necessarily want to be one-up. They just do not want to be one-down. But since those are the only two options in their System, they do their best to go one-up and put others one-down.

In the Female System, relationships are philosophically conceived of as peer until proven otherwise. (This, of course, is only true for women who feel clear and strong and have come to know and trust their own system.) In other words, each new encounter holds the promise of equality. One does not have to be one-up or one-down, superior or inferior; one can be peer.

A major difference between the two systems lies in these basic assumptions about what kinds of relationships are possible. If you can only conceptualize relationships as one-up, one-down, then you will behave in certain ways. If you can conceptualize relationships as either peer *or* one-up, one-down, you will approach them differently.

A few years ago I was living in St. Louis near Washington University and seeing a student in therapy. She was from another midwestern city where her father owned a business. When she informed him that she was seeing me, he decided to call and "check me out." He wanted to find out about my background, my credentials, my philosophy, my fees, and so on. I thought that his need to do so was both appropriate and legitimate. I was a stranger to him, I lived in a distant city, I was counseling his daughter, and he was paying the bill. If I had been in his place, I would have done the same thing.

When he called, I assumed that we would approach each other as peers. He, on the other hand, immediately approached me in a one-up manner. His tone and attitude were one of a superior addressing an inferior. Since I assumed peerness, I did not go one-down but instead offered him the opportunity to interact with me on the basis of equality. There was a slight pause, after which ensued what I call the "relationships shuffle."

When two persons are physically present in the same place, this shuffle is very obvious. For example, let's say that a man and a woman meet and begin a discussion. The man assumes that the woman will go one-down—and when she does not, he does not know quite what to do next. He shifts from one foot to the other and actually moves his body from side to side (sort of like a gamecock). It is almost possible to see in his face what he is thinking: "Oh, my goodness, she's not going one-down! She's supposed to go one-down! What do I do now? *Someone* has to go one-down!" (Pause. Gulp.) "I guess it will have to be me!" At this point, his posture visibly changes. He seems to sink and get smaller, assuming a stooping position and hating every minute of it. He also hates the person who has "made" him go one-down, and this colors their conversation from that point on.

Of course, no one "made" him go one-down. He *chose* to go one-down because that is the way he believes encounters and relationships have to be. If the woman will not go one-down, then he must—but he resents it!

This is more or less what happened during the conversation with my client's father. When I chose to stay peer and did not go one-down, he went one-down.

I happened to be talking to him on a wall telephone. My husband came into the room and started laughing. "What on earth are you doing in that funny position?" he asked. I was leaning over to the side in what must have looked like a very uncomfortable and contorted posture. In response to his question, I whispered very seriously, "Trying to stay peer with this fellow!"

When I had refused to go one-down, my client's father had shuffled and gone one-down himself. I had stooped to "stay level" with him, and he had shuffled and gone one-down again. His belief in his System prevented him from taking the opportunity to be peer with me. All he knew was that relationships had to be one-up, one-down. That was his reality; that was the way he saw the world. He could not relax into accepting a peer interaction, and trying to stay peer with him nearly gave me a backache!

The relationship shuffle is a common experience for White Male System persons. Whenever one of them meets a Black or a woman (a person who is *supposed* to go one-down) who does not go one-down, his only option is to go one-down himself—and he really resents it. Women managers often complain of this. When they do not go one-down, as expected, then the men they are dealing with go one-down, resent being there, and label the women "uppity." This entire process can take place while a woman is just standing there, giving a man the chance to have a peer relationship with her. The man's belief in the White Male System is so unshakeable that he cannot accept what she is offering him.

I think that it is very important to realize how strongly white men believe in their own System and its myths. They are thoroughly convinced that the White Male System is the only reality, that it is innately superior, and that it knows and understands everything. They are also sure that it is totally logical, rational, and objective. As a result, they are severely limited in their ability to take in new information and have new experiences.

I have a woman friend who is a well-known writer and psychotherapist. She once told me that she strongly resents the amount of time and energy she spends in trying to "stay level" with men who go one-down with her. She finds herself constantly either bending down physically or trying to "pull them up" to her level. She is now in her seventies, and it is getting more and more difficult for her to keep changing her posture in an effort to maintain equality with the men she encounters. Recently she said to me, "They will just have to think of some other way to handle this. I am too old for this stooping business!"

Center of Focus

There is another major difference in the way White Male System and Female System persons perceive relationships. In the White Male System, the center of the universe is the self and the work. Everything else must go through, relate to, and be *defined* by the self and the work. Other things in life may be important (relationships, spirituality, hobbies, and so forth), but they are never of equal importance; they always occupy positions on the periphery of the man's life, on the outside circle.

I have heard women in workshops say, "The one thing my husband and I have in common is that we both love him!"

In the Female System, however, the center of the universe is relationships. Everything else must go through, relate to, and be *defined* by relationships. This may be why women have historically not achieved as much as men. We tend to subordinate ourselves and our work to our relationships.

I used to think that men moved into the Female System during courtship. At that time, a man seems to set aside his self and his work and put the relationship at the center of his universe. He is unable to think of anything or anyone but the woman he is courting. He talks about her at work and may even miss work in order to spend time with her. He seems totally engrossed in the relationship. As a result, the woman gets very excited and starts believing that she has finally "found one"—a man who understands the Female System! She happily tells all her friends, "This one is different! He really is!" She is certain that at last she has met a man who knows how to make their relationship the focus of his life, and she is ecstatic.

As soon as the relationship is "nailed down," however—as soon as the man is sure of the woman's affections, and they are either married or have settled into some other committed arrangement—he goes back to his self and his work. She looks around at how her world has suddenly shifted and says, "I've been duped!" He begins to notice that something has gone wrong and asks, "What's the matter?" and she says, "You don't love me anymore!" He is shocked. "What do you mean I don't love you anymore?" he says. "Of course I do." (You have 180 degrees of my outside circle! What more do you want?) She responds, "Our relationship isn't the center of the universe for you anymore. And that's what love is!" And he says, "I don't know what you mean."

He really *doesn't* know what she means. She knows his System and her own System, but he does not even realize that she has a System.

Some men I have worked with have discussed this with me at length. And they really do not understand it. What I hear them saying is this: "We men don't move into the Female System during courtship. We don't even know what the Female System is. The relationship is a task (work) to be accomplished, and when it is solidified and we are sure of it we go back to our self and our work and business as usual." No wonder the women feel duped!

I once worked with a couple who came into therapy because they (mostly she) were concerned that there was no love in their relationship. Both believed that there had been earlier. When we examined the relationship more closely, it became clear that following their courtship he had gone back to his focus on his self and his work. He had added the relationship to his outside circle where it did in fact occupy a large part of the energy he did not already devote to his self and his work. The relationship was significant to him, but only as it went through, was related to, and defined by his self and his work. It was not significant in its own right.

The woman felt unloved because the relationship did not seem to be central to their lives together. He assumed that the relationship would "heal" once she understood and accepted his System and its (the) reality. Any healing to be done, however, depended on their willingness to know and value each system and then make choices as to which was appropriate at what time.

When I was first working on developing these ideas, I presented some of this material to a group of women seminary students. They in turn became furious with me. They did not like what I was saying at all! "For centuries," they said, "women have focused on primary relationships with men in order to establish identity and gain validation. We have given all of our energy to maintaining these relationships and none to taking care of our own intellectual and creative needs. We want this to stop! We want to start paying attention to our selves and our work—and we don't want to be told that we are 'selling out' to the White Male System!"

I stopped to look at this criticism. It is true that women have frequently subjugated or repressed their own creativity and ambition in the service of relationships with men. It is true that these relationships have held positions of utmost importance, since they were established to absolve women of their Original Sin of Being Born Female. And it is true that this is changing.

Over time, I have learned that women move through a number of developmental stages. We first develop primary relationships with men (or actively seek them) in order to gain our identity and absolution from the Original Sin of Being Born Female. These relationships become the center of our universe. Everything else is relegated to the outside circle. We devote our lives to maintaining our relationships with men, and our work, selves, creativity, and intellectual pursuits are all seen as secondary to these relationships and defined by them.

Then, as we become more aware of ourselves and begin to grow, we move into the White Male System. We put our selves and our work at the center of our universe. We become "selfish"—something women have a great deal of difficulty hearing—and start to put our own needs first. We devote a great deal of time, energy, and money to the process of self-discovery and the realization of our creativity. We become "workaholics." We spend more and more hours on the job. Money, power, and influence become very important to us. We want to "make it," and our criteria for "making it" are those of the White Male System.

During this phase, relationships become less important to us. Some of our relationships may survive in spite of the fact that we spend so little time maintaining them, but others may fall apart. We are beginning to discover our own capabilities, and we say things like, "I am going to make my impact on the world." "I want to make a contribution that people will remember." "I have no time for relationships. I must focus on my self and my work." Some of us become more job-centered than men!

Once we have "made it," however, we sit back and say, "So what?" We look around and wonder, "Is this all there is? It looked so good from the outside, but now that I've 'made it' I'm bored!" We then begin to move back into the Female System—but because we have changed, our concept of the Female System has also changed. It is no longer defined in terms of our relationships with men. It is no longer used *in reaction* to the White Male System. It has taken on an identity all its own.

It seems as if we must first be successful in the White Male System before we can fully and with clarity move into the Female System. During the early stages of our development when we participate in a reactive female system, in which we are not clear about ourselves and our world, we are dependent on men for our identity and absolution from the Original Sin of Being Born Female. After we move into the White Male System and become successful, we can then return to the Female System from a new perspective.

In the Female System we "come home" to, relationships are still the center of the universe. But these may or may not include primary relationships with men. They *never* include primary relationships with men that give us our identity and absolve us of our Original Sin of Being Born Female. They may include *equal* relationships with men and will almost certainly include close friendships with other women and genuine friendships with men.

This Female System includes a *relationship with the self*—something that was never present in our earlier concept of the female system. Self-awareness and focusing on the needs of the self are not the same as selfishness. We are still aware of and concerned for others. The essence of self-awareness is a tenderness toward and respect for the self which in turn allows one to be more tender and respectful toward others.

Many women never have a relationship with their selves because they have been taught that to do so is selfish. Or they never become aware of any self except as it is other-defined. Some women do acknowledge the presence of an emergent, embryonic self, but they seldom deem it worthy of a relationship.

As women become clearer and develop a sense of self, they are enthralled and amused by it and want to explore it further. Since we do not have much experience defining ourselves from within, others frequently see this process as taking something valuable away from them. This is not the case, however. We are not subtracting anything from those around us; we are simply drawing toward ourselves. By developing a relationship with our selves, we become more capable of meaningful relationships with others. This is a very different definition of "self-centeredness" than that which is experienced by the White Male System. When we make room for ourselves, we can make more room for others!

The Female System we reenter also involves a *relationship with one's work.*

Work becomes more than something one does to earn money; it becomes a "life work." It is what we need to do with our life. It means making a contribution which complements the other aspects of our life. It is not profit- and power-oriented; instead, it takes its meaning from creativity, bonding, humaneness, and service.

A woman who reaches this stage of growth—who moves out of the reactive female system, into the White Male System, and then back into the Female System again—also develops a *relationship with the universe*. She begins to have an understanding of how it all fits together and a feeling that life has true meaning. She sees herself and others in relation to the whole. She may say things like, "When I am lying on my deathbed, I think I will look back on the relationships I have had and the connections I have made. These will be the things I consider most important. It will not matter whether I have built a bridge, or written a book, or had a university named after me. I will cherish the lives I have touched and those persons whose lives have touched mine."

The essence of life in the Female System a woman comes home to is relationships—not relationships that define and validate, but relationships with the self, one's work, others, and the universe that nurture and grow. Not static relationships that are neatly categorized and packaged, but relationships that evolve and change, contract and expand. A process of relationships.

Women seem to need a two-step process to reach this stage; they move into the White Male System, and then they move back into the Female System. Men, on the other hand, have only to take one step in order to reach this level of awareness. Since they have the birthright of innate superiority, they do not have to begin by absolving themselves of any original sin or obtaining their identity through someone else. Yet they still have great difficulty taking this single step.

I believe that this is due to the fact that the position of being innately superior and having the self and the work at the center of the universe is very seductive. If one defines everything through the self and assumes that this is the way the world is, it is hard to imagine a world that is *not* self-defined. Men simply cannot conceive of any other way to be. Women, though, seem to get bored with that position after achieving success at it and seek something else. There are, however, some men who want to and do move beyond the beliefs of the White Male System.

I am not saying that either system is "right." I am merely describing a progression that many women seem to follow. It is hard for men to see and appreciate it, however, when it is labeled sick, bad, crazy, and stupid.

DEFINING POWER

In the White Male System, power is conceived of in a zero-sum fashion. In the Female System, power is seen as limitless.

The White Male System assumes that if one has, say, 20 units of power and gives 12 of them away, he (or she) only has 8 units of power left. The more one shares power or gives it up to others, the less one has for himself (or herself.) There is only so much power available, and one had better scramble for it and hoard it.

This concept of power is based on a scarcity model. I once heard a woman say, "I want to be the best-known feminist in town, and the only way for me to do that is to get rid of so-and-so" (another prominent feminist). She had bought into the White Male System model of power. She had become convinced that there was only so much influence to go around in the area of feminism, and in order to wield enough of it she would have to wrest some from the other woman.

In the Female System, power is viewed in much the same way as love. It is limitless, and when it is shared it regenerates and expands. There is no need to hoard it because it only increases when it is given away.

This difference between how men and women view love—and power—is often evident following the birth of a first child. The husband assumes that love is limited and whatever love the child gets from his wife will be taken away from what is available for him. The woman, on the other hand, finds that she has less time and energy for rituals but more capacity for love.

Similarly, as we share our power, it increases. This is also true with ideas. White Male System persons tend to hold on to, hoard, and try to "own" their ideas. Because their ideas are not allowed to move around and breathe, they stagnate. When ideas are freely given and exchanged—as in the Female System—they expand and change constantly, remaining fresh and alive.

Perhaps power, like love, is better conceived of as being infinite. Perhaps it is better used differently. In the White Male System, power is conceived of to exert domination and control over others. In the Female System, power is conceived of as *personal* power which has nothing to do with power or control over another.

Neither application is "right;" both may be appropriate, depending on the situation. Everyone needs to be free to explore alternative ways of defining and using power.

Leadership

Leadership is another symbol of power. In the White Male System, leadership means to lead. In the Female System, leadership means to facilitate—to enable others to make their contributions while simultaneously making one's own.

I have often found executive job descriptions both impressive and amusing. Many of them are written in such a way that only God could fill the position! Unfortunately, many aspiring executives are convinced that they can be God if they want to. (Many drop dead from the effort!) In their System, leading means being out front at all times, having all the answers, and presenting a strong, powerful, and all-knowing image.

In the Female System, a leader's job is to find persons who have particular knowledge and skills and then delegate responsibility to them. Leadership often means nudging people from behind rather than leading them from somewhere ahead. It also includes encouraging others to discover and develop their own capabilities. Although the White Male System does not respect the Female System's definition of leadership, it constantly makes use of it for its own purposes.

SYSTEM VS. SYSTEM: A FEW OPENING WORDS

In light of the observations I have made with the help of women who have felt "safe" enough to explain their System to me, I feel that I can begin to draw some preliminary conclusions.

The White Male System is in general an analytical, defining system. The Female System, on the other hand, is a synthesizing, emerging system.

The White Male System feels the need to analyze, understand, and explain the world. It does so by taking a whole, breaking it down into its component parts, and defining each of these parts in turn. People and things are seen as being however they are defined.

The Female System sees the world as constantly growing and changing. It cannot be defined; it can only be observed as it emerges. Understanding comes from watching, learning from, and facilitating the process of emergence. One does not need to pick something or someone apart. One does not need to control or define.

Why are the White Male System and the Female System so radically different? Because differences in and of themselves are perceived in radically opposing ways by persons in both Systems.

In the White Male System, differences are seen as threats. In the Female System, differences are seen as opportunities for growth.

When differences are labeled dangerous or harmful, it becomes essential to train everyone to think and act in similar ways. Thus, our educational system is oriented toward the "average" child. Any young person who is found to be "above" or "below" average must be made to fit the mold. Anyone who insists on her (or his) right to be different must be done away with, either literally or figuratively.

Because it refuses to see the worth and meaning inherent in differences and perceives them as threats to be overcome, the White Male System is a closed system. It stifles creativity and devours itself from within. It wastes and loses energy and is moving toward a state of entropy.

Because it perceives differences as opportunities for stimulation and growth, the Female System has been nearly eaten up by the White Male System. Women have recognized the White Male System as different from their own and sought to learn from it. But our genuine curiosity and interest—not to mention our need to survive—has backfired. We, the subordinate and inferior people, have embraced the System of the dominant and superior ones—but our own System has been ignored or undermined.

This is not intended to be an exhaustive or all-encompassing discussion of the two Systems. I see it as only a beginning, as one step in a process and progression toward understanding one another and our world.

Often, as I share my concepts and theories with other women, they beam at my descriptions of our System. Many have said to me, "This is the first time I have ever heard someone say aloud what I already know!" Women rarely hear about their System, and when they do it is usually in derogatory terms. It is important for both women *and* men to know and admit that the Female System exists and is good—not necessarily better, but good.

It is also important for women *and* men to see that the White Male System is just that—a system. It is not reality. It is not the way the world is. Reality is difficult if not impossible to change, but a system can be changed, even if it means a struggle. That gives us hope. If we can learn to recognize that there is at least one other system besides the White Male System, we can begin to see the value of still other systems and realities. We can begin to pay closer attention to the Black, Chicano, Asian-American, and Native American systems and learn from them as well. It is only then that we will begin to grow to our fullest capacity as human beings.

Why Women Still Don't Hit the Top

Jaclyn Fierman

Much of what was supposed to change hasn't. Some women leave their jobs because the sacrifices seem too great. But discrimination—however subtle—plays a part.

When will women in decent numbers finally make it into the highest ranks of corporate America? The short answer: not in this millennium. By the year 2000 women will make up nearly half the labor force. But it won't be the top half. The cool reception women once got at the door has followed them up the organizational hierarchy. For all but an exceptional few, the corner office still looks as remote as it did to Rosie the Riveter.

Just wait, was the old excuse. A decade ago even women's staunchest male advocates said time had to pass; women lacked the seasoning and seniority to run the show. Today that explanation rings increasingly hollow. Women have gained access to virtually every line of work and are bulging in the pipeline: The U.S. Department of Labor says they make up 40% of a loosely defined demographic category of managers and administrators that covers everyone from President

Bush to the person running the local Dairy Queen. But only a minuscule number of women have top jobs at America's major companies, and not many more are in the zone for promotion to those jobs anytime soon. Says Judy Mello, 46, in the early 1980s CEO of First Women's Bank in New York City: "My generation came out of graduate school 15 or 20 years ago. The men are now next in line to run major corporations. The women are not. Period."

Want proof? *Fortune* examined 1990 proxy statements of the 799 public companies on its combined lists of the 1,000 largest U.S. industrial and service companies. The cold-shower findings: Of the 4,012 people listed as the highest-paid officers and directors of their companies, we spotted 19 women—less than one-half of 1%. True, there has been progress, but it has been remarkably limited. When *Fortune* undertook a similar project in 1978, out of 6,400 officers and directors on its combined lists, which then included 1,000 industrial and 300 service companies, ten were women.

Further down the ranks the numbers are more heartening. But only slightly. To get an idea of the count—there are no authoritative studies of the number of women in upper management—*Fortune* looked through the names at the back of the annual reports of 255 major corporations. The list often goes as deep in the organization as division head and assistant vice president, and includes positions like corporate secretary that have frequently gone to women. Of the 9,293 names, 5% were women. (Admittedly, some women, especially initial users, may have escaped us, though we did pay special attention to the Leslies, Carols, and Gales. And some men may have slipped through our screen, though we did catch Mr. Shirley Beavers of First Virginia Banks.)

To once again raise a question *Fortune* posed 17 years ago when it first looked at women in the executive suite, where in blazes *are* they? Many women aren't rising to the top of large corporations because they quit or deliberately leap off the fast track. They miss their children. They miss not having *had* children. A better opportunity comes along. Or they just get tired and want out of the rat race. As comedienne Lily Tomlin quipped, "If I had known what it would be like to have it all, I might have settled for less."

For many baby-boom women, the 1980s effectively destroyed the notion that they could have it all: a full-blown career, a happy marriage, well-adjusted children, and cellulite-free thighs. Blessed with first-class educations, middle-class drive, and a sense of unlimited opportunities, these women expected a lot of themselves. They also expected equal treatment in the workplace. And they wanted to give their families—if they ever got around to having them—the same security that June Cleaver gave her children. Well-intentioned but torn asunder, many understandably failed as Supermoms.

But some women were willing to tough it out, stay the course, and make the necessary sacrifices. What they have run up against can only be called discrimination. Discrimination, you scoff, in this enlightened age? Yes, says Ralph Ablon, chairman of Ogden Corp., No. 74 on *Fortune*'s list of the 100 largest diversified service companies: "Sure there's discrimination. It's stupid to say there's not. Despite our intellectual efforts to deny it, prejudices exist and will exist until a new generation comes along that doesn't have them." That generation, it bears remembering, was supposed to be the baby boom, many of whose men have already assumed key decision-making roles at large companies.

At age 73, Ablon seems an unlikely harbinger of new thinking. But three years ago he appointed Maria Monet, now 40, as his company's chief financial officer, and he pays her more than $730,000 a year, making her one of the top-earning women in corporate America. Enlightenment, Ablon concedes, has come only with age and a lot of contemplation: "When I became CEO 29 years ago, I don't believe I could have been as liberal. And I couldn't have gotten away with appointing a woman as CFO. Today I could."

A recent poll of *Fortune* 1,000 CEOs shows that Ablon isn't alone in finding discrimination at work. Nearly 80% of 241 respondents to a survey conducted by Catalyst, a group that does research on women in the workplace, said there are identifiable barriers that keep women from reaching the top. No, they say, women do not lack the technical skills to make it. After all, they have been going to the same schools as their male counterparts and now represent over half of all college students, 37% of graduate business students, and roughly 40% of law students. The problems, said an astonishing 81% of the CEOs who acknowledged the existence of barriers, are stereotyping and preconceptions.

This is a subtle, tricky, but nonetheless pernicious form of discrimination, more apparent in the result—just look at the numbers—than in anyone's conscious intentions. Ask the typical male executive if he is prejudiced against women, and he will roundly deny it. But when it comes to choosing among several rivals for a top corporate job, he chooses a man. The next time, he does the same thing. And the next. Even Ablon, who recently retired as CEO of Ogden, chose not Monet but a man—his 40-year-old son, Richard—to succeed him.

What nonsense, you counter—if women don't get top jobs, they don't deserve them. Undoubtedly so in many cases. Besides, the volume of the uppermost quarter of any pyramid is only 1.6% of the whole, a geometric fact that automatically eliminates most women—*and men*—who aspire to the top. True also that the average CEO is in his mid-50s and most business schools began admitting women in significant numbers only in the early 1970s, which puts them around fortysomething today.

But John Reed had no trouble seeing over his desk six years ago when he was promoted to CEO of Citicorp at age 45. Nor does Cigna CEO Wilson Taylor, who is now 46. Even allowing that many women still aren't old enough or talented enough to be CEO, more should be joining their male contemporaries in the executive dining room. CEO John Mascotte of Continental Corp., a property and casualty company with $14 billion in assets, was stunned when he started counting. Two-thirds of his 15,000 employees are women, but nine out of ten senior managers are men. Says he: "It seems idiotic if we're investing in people but making it impossible for them to advance. Are we sending out signals that women need not aspire to the top?"

The signals may be no more than a slight rustling of discomfort, a bit of awkwardness in a man's body language. It may seem surprising in an era sometimes labeled postfeminist, but working closely with the opposite sex continues to make many male executives uncomfortable. Listen to Ellie Raynolds, a partner at the headhunting firm Ward Howell International: "Corporate males still don't know how to deal with women. They are afraid to yell at them or to give them negative feedback. It's as though they think they are yelling at their mothers or their wives. Men often worry women will run from the room in tears, or worse yet, yell back. They're not really sure the women will come through for them. They just don't trust them as much as the guys with whom they talk football."

Haven't we heard this before? But after ten years of supposed progress, too many of the old, uncomfortable ways persist. The offense may be as banal as the mere existence of Merrill Lynch's Chowder and Marching Society, a group of men who get together now and then for drinks and dinner. Or it may be tougher to read. "You'd hear things," says Deborah Farrington, 39, who went to Merrill Lynch after graduating from Harvard business school in 1976. "There were innuendoes. If you wore dark blue suits with floppy bow ties, there would be no talk about whether you were being flirtatious. But if you were attractive and dressed stylishly, people took you less seriously." Farrington, who spent a decade at Merrill, feels she can more easily be herself as head of corporate finance in Hong Kong for Asian Oceanic Group, a small merchant bank.

Try as women have to fit into the male business milieu, men still think they do a lousy job of it. Many believe corporate women are weak in interpersonal skills, a dimension that's largely ineffable but critical to achieving a high corporate position, where competence is assumed and chemistry often becomes key. Sometimes men see women as pushovers. More often they find women overbearing. "The most common lament of top management men is 'She's too shrill. She's too aggressive. She's too hard-edged,' " says Kenneth Brousseau, president of Decision Dynamics Corp., a human resources consulting firm in Santa Monica, California.

Women point to the persistence of precisely this attitude as the most pernicious example of discrimination in the workplace. If they are too feminine, they are viewed as softies; too masculine, and they're abrasive. "It's as if we're being asked to play a Beethoven sonata in two octaves," says Arlene Johnson, who directs work force studies for the Conference Board, a business research organization in New York. "We need the whole keyboard to show our range."

The recently decided case of Ann Hopkins, 46, formerly a management consultant at Price Waterhouse, affords a striking example of how such stereotyping works. In May a federal judge ordered the accounting firm to make Hopkins a partner and give her $370,000 in back pay because it had unfairly discriminated against her. The firm, which counts 27 women among its 876 partners, recently filed an appeal.

What happened: In 1982, Hopkins and 87 colleagues, all men, came up for consideration as partners. Though in the previous few years she had played a big part in securing some $40 million in contracts for the firm, an amount she says was more than that of any other candidate for partner in 1982, she was not among the 47 people promoted; Price Waterhouse will neither confirm nor deny Hopkins's claim. "Any woman who can be a success with her clients should qualify as partner," says Cynthia Turk, 37, who recently resigned as partner from a Price Waterhouse competitor, Deloitte & Touche, to set up her own consulting firm. "This was a clear case of discrimination."

The court, in agreeing, found particularly damning a remark made by Hopkins's mentor and chief supporter. "He told me to walk more femininely, talk more femininely, wear makeup, have my hair styled, and wear jewelry," says Hopkins, now a senior budget officer at the World Bank. Hopkins, who has two sons, 11 and 12, and a 14-year-old daughter, says the advice was largely useless: "I already wear jewelry and high heels, and I go to the beauty parlor. But I'm allergic to makeup." Even if she weren't allergic, Hopkins says applying the makeup would be difficult because she can't see without her trifocals.

Faced with this kind of prejudice, women who set their sights on top jobs and actually get them develop 20-20 vision when it comes to corporate folkways. "They understand that competence and a bus token will only get them across town," says psychologist Dee Soder, president of New York's Endymion Co., which counsels women and men who want to scale the corporate Everest. The experiences of the women on *Fortune*'s best-compensated list, plus war stories from Hopkins and other high-achieving women identified by *Fortune*, show just how tricky it is to navigate the ascent.

Go-getters who stand out in the ranks can *stick out* at the top. "When I first started out, I was extremely rough around the edges," says Lois Juliber, president of Colgate-Palmolive's Far East/Canada division. "Bully wouldn't be the right word, but I was the toughest of the tough. I didn't listen well. I had to mellow and learn to trust people."

It may help to regard the experiences of women in business as akin to infiltrating an alien world. Maria Monet of Ogden has been feeling her way and finding it since she emigrated to the U.S. from Portugal when she was 5 years old. "I grew up trying to fit in with a different culture. I didn't speak English when I went to kindergarten," she says.

Monet had her share of setbacks on the corporate climb. Twice she hit the proverbial glass ceiling, a barrier that enables women to glimpse but not grasp the corner office. A lawyer by training, she began as an associate at the Wall Street firm of Shearman & Sterling in 1974. But by 1980 it was still largely a white-shoe—no heels—firm, and Monet failed to make partner.

Investment banking, she thought, would be different. After 18 months of round-the-clock dealmaking at Lehman Brothers, she took stock: All the partners were men. So when an Ogden executive whom she met on a deal offered her a job, she leaped again. Monet quickly established herself at Ogden by reducing the time between the start and close of a deal from two years to six months. In three years she rose to chief financial officer.

If women who are puzzling over appropriate boardroom behavior feel as if their heads are spinning, so do male managers. Just what do women want, anyway? The vast majority have lobbied aggressively for special treatment. And they are getting it. Hewitt Associates, a benefits and compensation consulting firm in Chicago, found that 56% of 259 major employers offer some sort of childcare aid, 56% allow flexible scheduling, and 42% grant unpaid parental leave.

But along comes a select group of women who want no special favors—just a top job, thank you. These women figure their best shot at success is at gender-blind companies that make no concessions to their needs and require them to work the same hours as men. "There is no such thing as job sharing or part time at the top," says Phyllis Swersky, 39, executive vice president of AICorp Inc., a computer software company outside Boston. Swersky began holding meetings in her living room two days after she came home from the hospital after delivering her third child.

America's most successful businesswomen wave not the feminist banner but the corporate one. "I've never particularly thought of myself as a woman in business, so I've never let it get in my way," says Kathryn Braun, 39, senior vice president of Western Digital, a major supplier of personal computer parts in Irvine, California.

These women have interpersonal skills sufficient to finesse them through difficult situations. Edith Martin, 45, who was a Deputy Under Secretary of Defense under President Reagan and is now a vice president at Boeing, recalls the time she went on an executive outing while at Control Data. The luncheon grill was an extension of the men's locker room. Rather than sitting around with a bunch of towel-clad hearties, Martin decided to hit tennis balls while the men ate. "Yes, there are awkward moments," she says. "You can either walk off with a hot head or laugh it off. But after you have a couple of drinks and everyone laughs it off, it brings you closer." Moral: Greet the wrong gesture with the right attitude.

In breaking through stereotypes, the adage that line jobs are the straightest line to the top still holds. Women should take a lead from men and steer clear of dead ends like personnel and public relations. The most successful have typically sought out risky, thankless projects whose results become immediately apparent on the bottom line. "You have to prove you're a leader. You have to show you're willing to steal second base. Women don't project that ability well," says Mary Rudie Barneby, 38, who built from scratch a $3 billion corporate retirement plan business for Merrill Lynch. She now heads a similar division for Dreyfus Corp. in New York City.

Maria Monet stole second while working at Lehman Brothers. Her client, Ogden Corp., wanted to build a waste-to-energy plant in Oregon, but the county thought the financing it would have to provide was too burdensome. Monet calculated that if the county floated variable- rather than fixed-rate bonds to pay for construction, it could save about $5 million. "I was so new at investment banking, I didn't even realize the problems I had created," she says. "Financing a waste-to-energy project whose future revenues were predictable with bonds whose interest rates were not was unheard of." But Monet persisted, won the bankers' confidence, and caught the eye of Ogden Chairman Ablon. Her creative financing set a new industry standard and, she's convinced, clinched her career.

What Western Digital's Braun calls her acid test entailed resisting Wall Street naysayers to buy the assets of Tandon Corp.'s faltering disk drive division in 1988. Braun decided she had no choice: Without disks, she predicted, Western Digital's bread-and-butter business—computer information storage—wouldn't survive. She felt sure that the next generation of storage chips would reside directly in the disks. She guessed right. "We managed our way through the crisis," she says.

One of the explanations still cited for why women fail to get to the top is that they don't stick to it; they leave jobs more often than men do. Conclusive evidence on the point is hard to come by. But women do seem more willing than men to act on their desires for something else, perhaps because they are so acutely aware of the personal sacrifices they are making to work. When Opinion Research Corp. of Princeton, New Jersey, asked 26,500 managers in seven large companies whether they intended to quit their jobs in the next year, 17% of women said yes, compared with 11% of men.

If women would just hang in there and be patient, the thinking goes, more might reach their goals. Perhaps, allows Dreyfus Corp.'s Barneby, who in 14 years rose from clerical worker to one of the highest-ranking women at Merrill Lynch. "If I had waited, I think I would have had a shot at the top rungs," she says. "But I got tired of pushing. My shoulder started to hurt."

Don't Blame the Baby is the name Wick & Co., a Delaware consulting firm, gave its recent study of why male and female managers change jobs. The Wick research, a survey of 110 executives, found that most women quit jobs not to rock the cradle but to find greater career satisfaction somewhere else.

Nonetheless, virtually every woman interviewed for this article acknowledged the heavy—and sometimes painful—demands of juggling family or personal life and the fast track. Observes John Rosenblum, dean of the University of Virginia's Darden graduate school of business administration: "Women are discouraged about their ability to realize a vision of life that has family, career, and happiness all in the same sentence."

In choosing to make the corporate climb, Monet let some of life's other options go. She has no children and sees her husband, a general partner at Montgomery Securities in San Francisco, once a month. She reports to work every morning at seven at the New York headquarters of Ogden, which operates sports arenas, power plants, and convention centers. She eats lunch at her desk and tops off her 11-hour day with a 1½-hour workout at a nearby health club. "I used to think I could work, get married, and raise a family," she says. "I realize now it's hard enough just to do my job well. It was a rude awakening."

One very senior woman at a large consumer products company asked not to be quoted by name when she spoke of the price she had paid for success. "I would never want my mother to know how much it hurts me to be childless," she says. She is hardly alone. Nearly half the women on *Fortune*'s 1990 list of highly paid women are childless, five are divorced, and one never married. Claudia Goldin, the first tenured economics professor at Harvard, feels she might not have achieved her position had she had a family. "I'm at the top of my profession now, and it took a tremendous amount of concentration and focus in a brief period of time. If I were married and had kids, I probably wouldn't have had the energy."

Women who do try to combine traditional and fast-track lifestyles need a rock-solid infrastructure at home. Swersky of AICorp has a live-in nanny to care for her three children, ages 8, 5, and 4. She also has a live-in housekeeper and a supportive husband who runs his own accounting firm. Says Swersky: "I don't take care of the house. I don't cook. I don't do laundry. I don't market. I don't take my children to malls and museums. And I don't have close friends."

She typically leaves the house before 8 A.M. and returns around 7 P.M. "I am often gone longer, not shorter, than this," she says. "I am frequently too tired to tell my husband about my day, listen to him tell me about his, or play with the children. It was a major challenge just to figure out a simple hair style and makeup for myself."

On the question of when to bear the brood, women are often not in sync with their employers. "From an organizational point of view, the early 20s is the best time to have children," says Mary Anne Devanna, associate dean of the Columbia University graduate school of business. "Employers don't care what people do before they enter the work force." Probably so, but many women don't feel ready at that age. Says Blair Sheppard, 38, director of the human resource management center at Duke University's Fuqua graduate school of business: "The whole career ladder in the U.S. is predicated on the life cycle of a man. We tell people to prove themselves between 30 and 38. But that's when executive women tend to have babies."

The lesson: Having it all is easier if you don't insist on having it all at once. Rosetta Bailey, 55, now senior vice president at Citizens Federal Bank in Florida and a member of *Fortune*'s 1990 list, worked as a receptionist and teller in the bank for 15 years while raising two children. "By the time I got to a management level, it wasn't necessary for me to be with my children all the time," she says.

Ambitious women would do well to choose employers whose expectations are compatible with their own. Banking has always been fertile ground, perhaps because women have been paying their dues for years and now represent 91% of tellers, for instance. High-tech companies and small startup ventures too bent on survival to be exclusionary are also women-friendly. "There is no old boy network in my industry, because it's too new," says Western Digital's Braun. "So women rise more easily through the ranks."

In a business where product life cycles are as short as two years, qualified women—and men—tend to be promoted more rapidly than colleagues at mature consumer products or industrial companies. Braun headed for Southern California 17 years ago, a biology and psychology graduate fresh out of Duke University. Her first job was on the assembly line of a minicomputer manufacturer. When she realized that women weren't being promoted into sales, she quit and joined Western Digital in 1978 as a technical support person. Today she heads the company's most profitable division, which so far this year has sold $200 million of intelligent disk drives and other storage products for personal computers.

No business is as receptive as the one whose CEO feels comfortable with women at his side. "If I were working for my first employer today, I would still be a middle manager," says Ilene Beal, one of three executive vice presidents at Bay-Banks, outside Boston. Of her current boss, CEO William Crozier, she says, "He only cares about getting the job done. Maybe it's because he's married to a Ph.D. who has more degrees than he does."

Will the glass ceiling ever disappear? Yes, if history is any guide. But it won't crack and fall all at once, or even soon. For most of the first half of this century, married women were almost unemployable; they couldn't even get office jobs. When they entered the work force in large numbers during World War II, it was not so much because men wanted to hire them as because the country needed them.

The next big wave of women—mostly baby-boomers—began working in the 1970s. Men were more receptive to them, but ambivalence abounded: as recently as 1978 there were urinals in the ladies' rooms at Harvard business school. And women managers still make only 64% of what men do.

Harvard's Goldin, for one, argues that conditions for working women will gradually get better. "While there is still reason to clamor, women have made great strides, especially in the past ten years," says Goldin, author of a new book called *Understanding the Gender Gap*. She notes that in the Department of Labor's broad management category, the gap between men's and women's wages narrowed 18.5% between 1979 and 1988.

Women who look at the world not as historians but as victims may scoff at Goldin's perspective. They are also the ones least likely to survive in the corporate jungle. "Our best hope for the future are women who don't see the ceiling but the sky," says Goldin. Indeed, the best defense in a hostile world is to shed the defensive posture. "A group wants to feel that you're part of it," says Monet. "If you don't look like them, you already have something to overcome. Most men just haven't had enough experience working with women."

In the meantime, what can parents do to nudge things along? For starters, they should emphasize self-reliance in their daughters. Superachievers share a gritty, pioneering spirit, says New York psychologist Dee Soder. "I have yet to meet a truly successful woman who didn't have a courage-building experience in her childhood." Typical is Ilene Beal of BayBanks, whose mother died when she was a child. "My father brought me up to think I could do anything. If I broke a toy, he taught me to fix it. He brought out the take-charge part of me."

Another small step: Parents should encourage their daughters to take as much interest in baseball and basketball as in Barbie. Not only would the girls gain fluency in the sports-speak so common in business, but according to a 1986 survey of 2,043 adults by *Sports Illustrated*, one of *Fortune*'s sister publications, sports lovers are more successful in life than nonfans. The poll also found that sports-minded people are wealthier, and perceive themselves as wittier, more popular, smarter, and more competitive than people who don't care about keeping score.

Parents might even inspire their daughters with Dr. Seuss's current bestseller, *Oh, the Places You'll Go!* "Remember that Life's a Great Balancing Act," says the man who speaks volumes to children. He urges: "On you will go though the weather be foul. On you will go though your enemies prowl . . . Onward up many a frightening creek, though your arms may get sore and your sneakers may leak . . . And will you succeed? Yes! You will, indeed! (98 and ¾ percent guaranteed.)"

The odds for grownup women, of course, are slimmer, though demographics are on their side. Women and minorities are already the majority in the workplace, and a competitive corporate America will eventually have little choice but to include them in their leadership pool. Until then—for the next few decades, anyway—women may want to heed the following checklist for success, which itself, alas, carries no guarantee: Look like a lady; act like a man; work like a dog.

When the Boss Is Black

Richard Lacayo

As a manager at the Xerox branch office in Syracuse, N.Y., Chester Howell supervises a staff of about 20, mainly repair technicians and clerical workers. All but two
are white. Howell is black. A former copier-machine repairman who rose through
an affirmative-action promotion plan, he ran into some resistance when he first
assumed his higher job. There were fierce arguments with one of his white assistant managers. "He questioned every decision I made," says Howell. "He wanted
to double-check everything."

But was that prejudice? "Heck, no," insists his old antagonist, Vincent Venditti. "If Chet wasn't a minority person, the relationship would have been the
same. He wasn't the first black manager I worked for." Venditti says his run-ins
with Howell were not the reason he transferred to a Xerox branch office in Manhattan. But he does believe "some black managers are too sensitive."

The battle cry of the civil rights movement was equality. But in the workplace,
the bottom line is authority. As more blacks move up into higher-level jobs and
more whites find themselves working for black superiors, the two opposing principles can often collide.

Considering that it represents a reversal of centuries of black subordination,
the rise of the black manager has been accomplished with remarkably little upheaval. But not without some strain. African Americans who have risen through
affirmative-action plans can face resentment from white underlings. Some white
subordinates fret over whether black bosses will favor other blacks. And the stories
are common among black managers of white employees who ceaselessly buck their
authority or who go over their heads to complain to higher-placed whites.

As a vice president at Rockwell International in Anaheim, Calif., Earl S. Washington oversees a mostly white work force of 1,500. "I find myself under the mag-
nifying glass every day, proving that I understand how to run this business," he
says. "All bosses are second-guessed," explains Xerox vice president Gilbert H.
Scott, who heads a staff of 800 in the Southwest and California, 75% of whom are
white. "If you're a black boss, you're probably second-guessed more."

Collier W. St. Clair, a vice president for the Equitable Financial Services Co.,
was a district sales manager in North Carolina in the early 1970s. One of his responsibilities was hiring, but many white applicants balked when they saw that
their boss would be black. "A lot of them didn't come back for a second interview,"

he says. "I finally started asking people if they would have any problem working with me."

Since promotion is usually based on performance, the refusal of some whites to do business with black executives can be a source of frustration. David Grigsby is a broker at Merrill Lynch in Manhattan. When he prospects for clients over the phone, he does not always mention that he's black. That led to a surprise for at least one investor, who showed up to meet his adviser in person. He was "visibly shaken," Grigsby recalls. Not long afterward, the client asked for another broker. "It didn't take an Einstein to figure out what that meant," says Grigsby. Then he shrugs. "You have to develop a thick skin. You can't bleed to death every time something like that happens."

The American Institute for Managing Diversity, a research organization affiliated with Morehouse College in Atlanta, offers training for companies trying to manage increasing cultural mixing in the workplace. Institute director R. Roosevelt Thomas Jr. says racism is not always the explanation when a black supervisor creates discontent among white workers: "Sometimes people are not skilled at managing people who are different from themselves." As an agency manager in Atlanta a few years after his North Carolina post, Equitable's St. Clair presided over a 90-member office with just a handful of white workers. He found himself helping them cope with their minority status. Having been the only black in meetings of 300 or more people, he knew what they were going through. "Sometimes you just get lonely for somebody to relate to," he says.

Many black managers say their biggest problem is learning not to bristle at every challenge to their authority. The armed forces pioneered the elevation of blacks to supervisory ranks after President Harry Truman ordered desegregation in 1948. In 1987 Brigadier General Fred Augustus Gorden became the first black officer to serve as commandant of cadets at West Point. While he was walking across the campus one day, a white cadet failed to give the requisite salute. Gorden paused. Still no salute. He could have severely disciplined the cadet, but he chose simply to talk with him instead. "I've learned to pick and choose my battles," he explains.

But sometimes patience wears thin. If faced with a white employee who could not accept working under a black superior, says Rockwell International's Washington, he would help the recalcitrant employee find new work—at another company. "I'm not going to tolerate it," he says, "because I'm the boss."

The Outsiders: Jews and Corporate America, by Abraham K. Korman

Reviewed by Howard S. Schwartz

Having read Abraham Korman's new book, *The Outsiders: Jews and Corporate America,* I find myself with peculiarly mixed emotions. Korman claims that America's largest corporations are anti-Semitic in that they do not permit Jews to rise to executive positions. On the one hand, he marshals the available data, his own and that of others, with great finesse. I am inclined to accept his argument. On the other hand, I cannot find myself surprised. Again, I have to agree with him that there is something wrong with an anti-Semitic policy that bars Jews from high corporate levels, and I agree that Jews have as much right to be there as anyone else; but I'm inclined to paraphrase Groucho Marx in saying that I would not want to be a member of a club that would bar me because I am a Jew.

Korman argues that Jews are excluded from executive positions because they are seen as outsiders by gentiles who form the bulk of American society and occupy the executive ranks of its large corporations. These gentiles are comfortable with each other and uncomfortable with those who are outside their group, such as the Jews. Moreover, they find each other more understandable, more predictable and, hence, easier to work with than they find outsiders. Because the managerial role is inherently ambiguous and uncertain, it leads those who are hiring for it to reduce uncertainty as much as possible by hiring those with whom they will be able to empathize and those whose behavior they will be able to understand and predict. Hence, executive insiders will tend to hire other insiders for executive positions, and they will tend to shun outsiders.

But in making ease of interaction and, therefore, insider group membership into a dominant criterion for selection, Korman says, corporations have effectively insulated themselves from innovation and creativity. They have become centers of groupthink. If American corporations could acknowledge that they have selected executives on the basis of insider membership and if they could change their ways, it would be to their advantage, to the advantage of American society, and to the advantage of outsider groups such as the Jews and others. Let my people in.

The Outsiders: Jews and Corporate America by Abraham K. Korman, reviewed by Howard S. Schwartz in *AMR*, April 1989, Vol. 14, No. 2, pp. 303–305. Reprinted by permission of Prof. Howard S. Schwartz.

Here, Korman's argument is clear and persuasive. His writing is both passionate and precise, and his analysis of the tension between insider and outsider is fine phenomenology. I believe it explains much of the phenomenon of corporate anti-Semitism, but I wonder whether his exclusive reliance on the insider/outsider dynamic has not lead him to miss an element that should be considered if the full significance of corporate anti-Semitism is to be understood. Jews have not been considered just another group of outsiders. Country after European country did not systematically assault, rob, expel, and murder the Jews because they were different and because their differences made the natives uncomfortable. As Korman points out, Russia did not permit the Jews to immigrate for over 200 years; therefore, how could their presence have irritated the Russians?

When I was a kid, my family had a summer home in a community in northern New Jersey. The community, which was predominately Jewish, was located outside of a town that was, as far as we could determine, entirely gentile. One night I was walking to my friend Paul's house when a car drew alongside me and somebody asked where "Mocky Street" was. Thinking he said "Mohican," I started to give him directions. Somebody in the car grabbed my shirt, pulled me toward the car window, and began bashing my face. Somebody else began shouting, "Let's get out of here! Let's get out of here!" and my assailant gave me one last bash before the car pulled away. The geometry of the situation had worked to prevent him from hurting me very much, but he had managed to knock my glasses off, and when I found them unbroken I was very relieved. I went on to Paul's house. He wasn't there, but his mother was. I told her the story. She didn't seem surprised. After the extermination camps, who could be surprised?

To grow up Jewish, at least in my time, was to grow up with the knowledge that one's possibilities were limited. One knew that one could not be a member of certain groups, hold certain occupations, even go to certain schools. On the other hand, one also knew that there were other parts of this vast world that were entirely open. It was perhaps the grandeur of the possibilities that were open to me that permitted me to accept these limitations and to effortlessly give up the possibilities that were closed. I could be a scientist. I could be a writer. Hell, I could even be a revolutionary. Being a corporate executive was never something that I considered as an open possibility.

As I grew older I came to realize that the sense of limitation is deeply a part of the Jewish heritage. The Jewish God created people in His image, but He had not made them to be other gods. And anyone who had the *chutzpa* to think himself the equal of God would get it in the neck. The Jewish God could be talked to, bargained with, even upbraided, within limits, but it was always clear that there was a difference between the immortal and the mortal, and people were always on the short end.

Later, I came to understand that it was this belief in limitation, the frailty of man, and the tenuousness of life that was in large measure responsible for some people rejecting the Jews. Often the world of these gentiles was a world full of manic optimism, the denial of death, and the pursuit of a blissful perfection that was only possible for, and appropriate for, God. No wonder they did not want these Jews around. From their dreams, the Jews keep waking them.

Corporations puff themselves up: They become the alpha and the omega, the be-all and end-all, gods. They are built around the idea that those who become most what the corporation is, those who rise to the top, manifest this godliness the most. That's the reason behind the upward scramble to which Korman wants the Jews admitted.

When the God of the Jews spoke to Moses from the burning bush, Moses asked Him to reveal His name. He said, as near as English permits a translation, "I am Reality." Subsequently, He commanded the Jews not to take any other gods before Him. I submit that it is because the Jews have honored this commitment that the *Fortune* 500 have not embraced them. Perhaps these corporations will change. That would be very nice, but I'm not going to hold my breath.

Suit Accuses Airline of Sex Bias

American Airlines is trying to push older, better-paid women flight attendants into retirement by arbitrarily enforcing a company policy requiring weight checks for those returning from unpaid leaves, federal attorneys claimed Monday.

In a suit filed in U.S. District Court in Los Angeles, the Equal Employment Opportunity Commission said American was violating federal laws against sex and age discrimination. American is the last airline in the United States with inflexible weight rules for flight attendants.

A broader suit against American that makes similar claims on behalf of active flight attendants is scheduled to go to trial next year in Dallas.

An American Airlines spokesman declined to comment, saying that officials had yet to see a copy of the latest suit.

At issue in both suits is the airline's refusal to raise its weight limits to account for age. Government attorneys note that both United Airlines and Delta Air Lines, the nation's second- and third-largest carriers behind American, make such allowances, and that some airlines have no weight limits.

Most airlines that set weight limits, including American, use the Metropolitan Life Insurance tables of 1959, which set weight limits according to height.

"Suit Accuses Airline of Sex Bias," *St. Louis Post Dispatch,* April 10, 1990, p. 6A. Reprinted by permission of Los Angeles Times Syndicate.

At United, a 5-foot-5 flight attendant can weigh 137 pounds at age 25 and up to 146 at age 55. At American, the standard for the same woman is 129 pounds, regardless of age.

Ralph D. Fertig, supervising trial attorney in the employment commission's office in Los Angeles, said the new suit had been filed in response to a policy American adopted in 1988. The policy required flight attendants returning from leave to have their weight formally checked, as new employees are required to do.

Normally, active American flight attendants are subjected to weight checks only if a supervisor suspects that they have become too heavy, Fertig said. Unlike those returning from leave, the active attendants are permitted to keep flying while they lose weight.

Fertig, two American flight attendants in their 40s and another attendant who was fired for being too heavy, said Monday that they believed the policy on flight attendants returning from leaves was not invoked uniformly and was targeted at older women.

Disabled Aussie Swimmer Sunk for Lack of an Arm

SYDNEY (UPI)—Australian swim officials have disqualified a one-armed swimmer because he failed to touch the end of the pool with two hands.

Greg Hammond, 16, a member of Australia's Disabled Olympic team scheduled to compete in New York in June, was disqualified from second place in the open men's 100-metre breaststroke championship Sunday at Narooma, 285 kilometres south of Sydney.

The championship's referee, Pauline Gill, reluctantly disqualified Hammond following the protest of coach Paul Pike under a rule that states "the touch should be made with both hands at the same time."

The disqualification has caused an uproar. The Sydney Daily Mirror condemned the disqualification in its editorial Wednesday:

"The history of competitive swimming in this country is littered with more than enough controversial blunders caused by rules that are bad or interpretations that are even worse."

Pike, whose protest led to the disqualification, said Tuesday he had no regrets about his action. "Greg has to meet the letter of the law, which he didn't do."

Why Pro-Family Policies Are Good For Business and America

Ronni Sandroff

It's not just women who are asking for flexibility from industry. Men are, too. And unless the "Workaholic Corporation" changes its ways, it will be the big loser. Employees will join kinder, gentler companies.

When people came to work and said, 'We've got automobiles,' employers said, 'Oh, we've got to build some parking lots.' When Americans became diet-conscious, company cafeterias added salad bars. So why, asks Congresswoman Patricia Schroeder, have companies been so slow to accommodate the family needs of the two-career couples who have flooded the work force over the past 15 years?

At the heart of the delay has been the mistaken perception that child care is a women's issue. And that women managers who lobby for such "privileges" as maternity leaves, flexible work hours and subsidized day care don't have the company's finances in mind.

In the last year or so, however, this perception finally has begun to dissipate, largely because of the number of women in the work force. Close to half of all workers now are female—and about 90 percent of these women expect to have children while employed. Likewise, caring for an elderly parent increasingly is becoming a reality with demands on one's time similar to those of caring for children. Companies that don't have policies to deal with all this simply have their heads in the sand.

And it's not just female employees who are affected by family policies. Today a statement like, "I'm staying with this job because it's close to the house and I can pick up the kids from day care," is nearly as likely to come from Dad as from Mom. In 11 percent of American households, women earn more than their working husbands, and in those families the whole question of child-care responsibility takes on a different coloration. No matter how much the woman is making, her salary usually is essential for keeping the family economy afloat. So working fathers have a vested interest in making it possible for their wives to keep their jobs.

In some cases it's more than lifestyle at stake. Some family-minded men are finding that their career-conscious wives are unwilling to have children unless shared child care is agreed upon beforehand.

That's why the idea of a Mommy Track, which drew so much media attention earlier this year, seems out of step with the times. "Today both men and women are saying that they're willing to accept reduced income and slower career growth in order to be more involved with their families," says Max Messmer, chairman of the recruitment firm Robert Half International. "Employers will have to respond with a less rigid work environment. Astute managers will reexamine the 9-to-5 syndrome and experiment with creative work options, such as the Parent Track." The *Parent* Track? A corporate understanding that both sexes—not just women—need and want work flexibility that allows them to arrange their schedules so that not only does the job get done but they also are able to be involved in their children's lives for more than an hour a day. It is an especially attractive concept now, when 9 to 5 often means 8 to 7.

Since dual-income families pose a new challenge to industry, managers must find out what working parents need from their companies, take advantage of government incentives to create model programs, and help their companies move beyond ad hoc solutions to people-friendly policies that extend work flexibility to nonparents who have other personal priorities, such as going back to school or writing a book.

WHAT DO PARENTS WANT?

"When Isabel was born, I told my wife that I would always be the one who came in late or had to leave early because of the baby," says Brooks Clark, who was then a writer at *Sports Illustrated.* He figured that, because he was a man, being Mr. Mom would not have as devastating an effect on his job as the role would have on his wife's: She was a buyer for Brooks Brothers in New York. But Clark soon realized he was wrong. Writers at *Sports Illustrated* often are expected to work seven-day weeks—something he no longer could do.

So when Whittle Communications tried to convince Clark to relocate to Knoxville, Tennessee, where it's based, part of the recruiting message he heard was, "This is what you need for your family." The lure of a short commute and a family-friendly company did the trick. "My boss has a kid and also puts in some of his extra hours early in the morning rather than working late," he says.

Karen Ramsay Clark, who at press time was about to give birth to their second child, found a job in Knoxville as director of planning and distribution for Ira A. Watson Co., a department-store chain in the South. "A smaller, southern company like Watson's turned out to be more flexible than Brooks Brothers," she says. While the move to more accommodating companies has not made the Clarks' family life exactly easy, it has made it manageable. "We each do 70 percent of the child care," jokes Ramsay Clark.

The Clarks are not alone. Nearly 8 out of 10 American women *and* men prefer a job that gives them adequate time for their families, even if it means slower career advancement, according to a recent survey conducted by Robert Half International. Two-thirds of the 1,000 workers surveyed also said they would be willing to reduce work hours and salaries to gain more free time—a surprising finding in light of the get-ahead mentality supposedly driving American industry.

An increasing number of people also are interested in flexible hours. A 1988 survey at the Du Pont Company found that half of the women and a quarter of the men who use child care have considered switching to an employer that has more flexible work arrangements. "Work and family issues, including child care, parental leave and care for sick children, have become major concerns for an increasing number of male employees," says Du Pont personnel manager Benjamin D. Wilkerson.

Until very recently, the business community had to cope with the needs of two-career couples pretty much on its own. The government had failed to provide any leadership on the issue, as if unsure whether working mothers were here to stay.

"Every other industrialized country has parental-leave laws," Congresswoman Schroeder points out. "We're the only country where a woman can be fired for having a baby."

And possibly the only country where having a baby creates so much stress. When fathers and mothers in West Germany and Sweden were asked if they were overly stressed from balancing their work and family lives, they seemed surprised at the question and reported little stress, says Ellen Galinsky, co-president of the Families and Work Institute, who did the study for the National Academy of Sciences. "Even the most macho businessmen declared that people should be multi-dimensional," Galinsky says. She believes that these attitudes grow out of a culture that is supportive of working parents.

In this country the stress of balancing career and child care is legendary, set as it has been against a historic backdrop of negativism toward working couples. Almost two decades ago, President Richard Nixon vetoed a child-care bill. Opponents of the bill had claimed it would lead to the sovietization of American children. This year, at last, comprehensive child-care bills are in play in both the House and the Senate and seem likely to make it into law, setting a new tone for the 1990s. Likely provisions: grants to the states, to be earmarked for child-care centers; tax credits for low-income parents; and incentives to encourage business to take child-care initiatives.

Congressman Augustus Hawkins (D, CA) points out that the U.S. is running out of qualified individuals for the work force. "Between now and the year 2000, women and minorities will constitute 85 percent of the new entrants into the labor force," he says. "We can't afford to lose them."

Strong child-care and maternity-leave legislation could be the beginning of a new national policy that truly is profamily and probusiness.

BEYOND AD HOC SOLUTIONS

At first glance it might seem professional suicide for women managers to align themselves with family issues. An "if you can't take the heat, get out of the kitchen" approach to employees with special needs sounds very macho and, in the short run, at some companies may mark a woman as having the toughness needed for higher management.

But in the long run, ignoring the human problems of employees can only hurt the company, and a manager's career. "The entrance of masses of women in the work force cannot be treated as a little blip on the horizon," warns futurist Jeffrey J. Hallet, author of *Worklife Visions*. "We can't return to business as usual. Managers who can't learn to communicate with their staffs and be creative and flexible in helping them solve their problems will soon be obsolete."

The immediate task for managers is to get family issues on the company agenda. "The main thing I hear from corporate America is that no one is talking about family issues," says Congresswoman Schroeder. "Though some star quarterbacks of the corporate teams—like Jane Pauley—manage to negotiate individual deals, most workers are scared to death to raise the issue."

Sometimes a minor alteration in work scheduling, or permission to cut back to a four-day week for a while, is all it takes for a family to keep child-care arrangements in gear. In other cases, a change to a post that doesn't require travel, or to assignments that in an emergency can be handled from home, is needed.

But won't nonparents resent the company's flexibility? Won't everyone want to ask for novel arrangements? It's true that a bit of flexibility might make it possible for employees to fulfill other dreams—get an MBA, train for a triathlon or spend a summer volunteering in the Third World.

If people are seen as resources, not automatons, companies will encourage virtually anything employees do to develop themselves. For it takes more than long hours and competitiveness to make a valuable employee. Having children "keeps you very humble," says Congresswoman Schroeder. "You come home and you're just old Mom. You realize your job is not the center of the universe. It keeps things in perspective." Other pursuits and interests can serve the same function.

And the perspective gained may foster the wisdom needed for making the tough decisions that upper management requires, such as holding up production because the O rings on the space shuttle are not safe. Or taking a loss rather than selling sugared water as infants' apple juice. The little detours that people take on the road to success are often the biggest learning experiences of all.

One-track minds don't necessarily lead in the right direction.

Institutional Bigotry

Roger Wilkins

A Federal court in the District of Columbia recently ordered the Air Force to reinstate Leonard P. Matlovich, a former sergeant who was dismissed five years ago because he admitted that he was a homosexual. Though it is on a narrower and more technical ground than I would have liked, I am delighted by the judge's decision.

Leonard Matlovich was a superb airman. He was a decorated Vietnam veteran whose service ratings were always excellent. There was nothing in Sergeant Matlovich's behavior in the service to single him out from anybody else except that he did his job far better than most people in the Air Force did theirs. But his spirit bothered him. He wasn't being honest with the world about himself. Part of his identity as a human being was his homosexuality. But he was hiding it, pretending it didn't exist, pretending he was something other than what he was. He was behaving as if he was ashamed of what he was and that made him ashamed of himself.

So he did a courageous thing: He announced his homosexuality. And the Air Force promptly threw this distinguished airman out of the service. The Air Force had a regulation prohibiting the retention of homosexuals in the service unless "the most unusual circumstances exist." The judge said the Air Force had engaged in "perverse behavior" in being unable to explain its policy, and ordered Matlovich reinstated.

I met Matlovich and another homosexual airman back when they were both fighting their original expulsions from the Air Force. The other airman, Skip Keith, was a mechanic trained to work on C-5A engines. He loved his work and had been judged to be good at it, but when he felt he had enough of hiding part of himself from the world, he too was tossed out of the Air Force.

I am not surprised that the Air Force could not explain its position clearly. Shortly after I met Matlovich and Keith, I had lunch with a group of journalists and an Air Force lieutenant general. During the course of the lunch, I asked the general why the Air Force tossed homosexuals out on their ears. He practically choked on his food. The best I could get from him was that when he was flying he wanted a wing man he could rely on. He couldn't answer why gay airmen would be more unreliable than anybody else. He just got more incoherent.

The general was black. If I had closed my eyes and changed his words a little bit, I could have imagined that tirade coming from a white general in 1940 trying to explain why the Army couldn't be integrated. Institutional bigotry in any form stinks, and men like Len Matlovich and Skip Keith are heroes to have stood up to it.

Gay Vietnam Hero Buried with Honors

WASHINGTON (AP)—Leonard Matlovich, a Vietnam War hero whose 1975 discharge from the Air Force for his avowed homosexuality became a rallying point for gay rights activists, was buried here Saturday with full military honors.

Matlovich, 44, died June 22 in Los Angeles, from complications associated with AIDS, a fatal virus-borne disease whose chief victims have been homosexual men and intravenous drug abusers.

He was buried in Congressional Cemetery just 20 blocks from the U.S. Capitol in a ceremony that mixed the military pomp of a horse-drawn caisson and a traditional three-volley salute by seven riflemen with eulogies from gay rights activists.

"The Air Force finally did it right and on Leonard's terms today," said Frank Kameny, a Washington gay rights activist who was instrumental in counseling Matlovich on testing the military's ban on homosexuality.

"It's a pity that they didn't do it 13 years ago," Kameny said as an Air Force color guard departed the cemetery.

Matlovich, who was awarded a Purple Heart after stepping on a Viet Cong land mine and the Bronze Star for killing two Viet Cong soldiers attacking his post, first challenged the Air Force's rules on homosexuality in 1975.

At the time, he was a technical sergeant working as a drug and alcohol abuse counselor at Langley Air Force Base outside Washington with nearly 12 years of service.

"After some years of uncertainty I have arrived at the conclusion that my sexual preferences are homosexual as opposed to heterosexual," Matlovich said in a memorandum to his commanding officer. "I have also concluded that my sexual preference will in no way interfere with my Air Force duties."

Following a hearing, Matlovich was given a general discharge from the service. His challenge of the action in court put his face on the cover of Time magazine, and in 1980 the Air Force was ordered to reinstate him with back pay.

Months later, Matlovich and the Air Force reached an out-of-court settlement in which he was paid a total of $160,000 in back pay and other compensation and given an honorable discharge.

"When Leonard lived in the neighborhood, he would come over here and walk," Lee Jenny, the administrator of the cemetery where many members of the nation's first Congresses are buried, recalled Saturday.

Reprinted by permission of the Associated Press.

Ms. Jenny helped design the tombstone that Matlovich wanted for his grave as a memorial to gay and lesbian Vietnam veterans.

Matlovich's tombstone includes in the top corners pink triangles that were used by Nazis during World War II to identify homosexuals in concentration camps and that have since been adopted as a symbol in the gay rights struggle.

Under the triangles is the inscription:

"A Gay Vietnam Veteran"

"When I was in the military they gave me a medal for killing two men and a discharge for loving one."

Watching the Wheels

John Lennon

People say I'm crazy,
doin' what I'm doin'.
Well they give me all kinds of warnings,
    to save me from ruin.
When I say that I'm OK, well they look at me kind of
    strange.
"Surely, you're not happy, now: You no longer play the
    game."

People say I'm lazy.
Dreaming my life away.
Well they give me all kinds of advice.
    Designed to enlighten me.
When I tell them that I'm doing fine watching
    shadows on the wall.
"Don't you miss the big time, boy?
    You're no longer on the ball."

Chorus: I'm just sitting here
watching the wheels go round and round.
I really love to watch them roll.
No longer riding on the merry-go-round.
I just had to let it go . . .

People asking questions,
Lost in confusion.
Well, I tell them there's no problem:
Only solutions.
Well they shake their heads and look at me
   as if I've lost my mind.
I tell them there's no hurry,
   I'm just sitting here doing time.

Chorus

I just had to let it go. . . .
I just had to let it go.

Chapter
6
Images

Whether people in organizations are consciously aware of it or not, they are constantly exposed to subtle and complex influences that play a part in determining what they think, feel, and do. Many of these images are created intentionally by organizational members to bolster their positions and to maintain or enhance the power and control they have over others. Examples abound in the readings we have selected in this chapter.

Words and phrases both reflect and shape our values. They influence what we see and do, what we consider important. They also blind us to other realities. In "Language Masks Human Place in the Nature of Things," David Suzuki argues that the terms we use for the environment tell us how we view and understand nature. The forest industry uses the words "decadent" and "overmature" for primary forests. Trees are only useful when cut down and are "harvested" and "culled" to make them more "normal." Language such as this creates a strong frame for seeing forests as economic resources to be managed for human benefit. This may not be incorrect. It is, however, an incomplete, partial frame on reality. The role of language here, as elsewhere, tends to hide the fact that it is simply one view of the way things are. When profit is involved, there is a strong incentive for those seeking profit to invent and enforce language that presents their position as the legitimate or only view of what is going on. Language, particularly in times of war, is designed to hide some realities and to emphasize others. Describing war as a "conflict," hides its meaning as an arena of slaughter and carnage. So does replacing the word "bombing" with "coercive diplomacy." (In *Talking Power: The Politics of Language* Robin Lakoff documents some prevalent language games used by people and organizations.) Sometimes such jargon serves to separate the person from the event, sanitizing the violence and life and death consequences from the consciousness of soldiers and the public back home. Some commentators have likened the recent Mideast war between Iraq and the coalition of United Nations countries to a Nintendo video war game—a comparison that distances action from emotion, and hides the violence inherent in the action.

The use of space is symbolic. The office layout can influence attitudes and behaviors, suggests Suzyn Ornstein in "The Hidden Influences of Office Design." If this is so, it ought to be possible to create work space that enhances the experiences people have on the job. It may also be feasible to improve performance through better office design. Ornstein's article focuses on the issues and practices that relate to these premises.

In "To Trust Perchance to Buy," Donald J. Moine draws parallels between the intuitive techniques and styles of the successful salesperson and those of clinical hypnotists. Moine observes that effective sellers match their customer's posture, body language, and mood. He also notes that their persuasive powers are enhanced by their ability and willingness to tell stories, anecdotes, and parables and to draw on metaphors to frame their messages.

The notion that colors and color preferences create images and have an impact on how we are seen and on how we see others is the focus of "Color: A Guide to Human Response" by James Gray, Jr. While we have no information on the accuracy or validity of the predictions and prescriptions in the article, we think it is important for managers and social scientists to explore the thesis that color does play a role in the image of self as conveyed to others and as experienced by them. Readers might reflect on their own color preferences and think about the way such preferences might effect their interactions with other people at work and at home.

We return next to the initial theme of this section—that language, attitudes, and actions are closely intertwined—this time with the emphasis on sexist language. In "That's No Lady, That's My Wife," Janet Elliott describes some of the common areas of language that reinforce sex bias such as stereotyping, sexist job titles, phrases that exclude one sex ("As you look at your face each morning when you shave . . ."). She points out that use of sexist language may not be intentional, but its effect is no less degrading. (For an insightful and readable discussion of the role of language in shaping attitudes and behavior, we recommend the book *You Just Don't Understand: Women and Men in Conversation* by Deborah Tannen, New York: William Morrow, 1990.)

Some influences pervade an organization and are a part of its culture. Often these influences are so taken for granted that it becomes necessary to challenge or to contradict the culture quite dramatically to reveal its elements and interconnections. Lehan Harragan, in "Games Mother Never Taught You," argues that many of the everyday objects, arrangements, and routines we encounter in our organizational lives can have influence on us. She analyzes the symbolic meaning that can be attached to the way one is paid; the time one comes to work; where one eats; one's working location and so on. She includes in her discussion a provocative description of the immobilizing and discriminating effect on women of the clothes they wear to work.

The realities outlined in this chapter reflect a world more complex than it may seem on the surface. It is a combative world; a world in which it is wise to be wary. We think it is important for people to pay careful attention to the settings, languages, and trappings of their organizations. The precise nature of organization images and their character and impact are beginning to be carefully charted by behavioral scientists.

Language Masks Human Place in the Nature of Things

David Suzuki

As kids, we used to chant "Sticks and stones may break my bones but names can never hurt me."

Yet words can be as dangerous as sticks and stones.

We learn to "see" the world through the lenses of our value and belief systems and they in turn are expressed in language. The words we use reflect these cultural assumptions.

Feminists demanded a change in the use of words such as "chairman," "spokesman," "fireman," because the masculinity of the terms implied that women are not expected to occupy such positions. And by deliberately substituting "person" for "man," we are constantly reminded of the inequities built into our society.

Years ago, in a discussion on the environment with former federal cabinet member, Mitchell Sharp, I tried to explain why we have to abandon the belief that steady growth, especially in the economy, must be the primary goal of government and industry.

He exclaimed, "I understand what you're saying but you're talking about an end to progress."

"Progress" and "growth" have become synonymous. And since we aspire to constant progress in the future, then growth has become our goal and there will never be an end to it.

"Language Masks Human Place in the Nature of Things" by David Suzuki, *Vancouver Sun*, June 23, 1990, p.B.6. Reprinted by permission of the author.

Nowhere is the use of language more revealing than in the military where jargon is full of male sexual symbolism. Weapons are phallic, both in shape and explosive potential, while military personnel speak of various tactics as "deep penetration," "thrust," and "orgasmic release." Common terms such as "pick-up zone," "counter penetration," "rapid pursuit" and "rear penetration" have sexual connotations.

As we readjust to the rapid political changes occurring globally, we ought to get rid of the sexual terms and create a new battle language based on the "war" to save the planet. We're engaged in a global "struggle," a "fight" for survival and we have to "mobilize" people.

The forest industry is replete with words that indicate how its activity is perceived. Primary forests are described as "decadent" or "overmature" as if trees are wasted if they are not cut down. Logging is seen as a practice analogous to farming, from the "harvesting of crops" to the creation of "plantations." Foresters "cull" trees, remove "pest" species and refer to the use of pesticides, herbicides and fertilizers as "silvicultural practice."

Old growth forests that haven't been logged are called "wild" while the second growth after logging becomes a "normal" forest.

The word "management" implies we know what we are doing and can duplicate or even improve on nature.

The sign at a shopping plaza I visited said "No animals allowed" and the crowd swarming the mall obviously didn't feel those words referred to them.

Yet we learn in high school biology courses that humans occupy a position in the web of life next to our nearest relatives, the chimps and gorillas. Like all other mammals, we are warm-blooded vertebrates who have hair and feed our young with milk.

We are undeniably animals as if there is a fundamental demarcation that separates us. The word "animal" itself is a pejorative when used to refer to people and carries with it a connotation of uncontrollability and malevolence.

College students in the '50s referred to someone who would be called a nerd today as a "turkey." College women back then referred to male creeps as "lizards." A person who is a "chicken" is a coward, a "snake" is not to be trusted, an "ox" is stupid while a "mule" is stubborn.

A "wolf" is a leering flirt, a "black sheep" is a family disappointment while someone who has been made a "monkey" of or is an "ape" is not very bright.

The use of animal names to represent undesirable human traits is a denigration which also seems to elevate us.

It is the distancing and separation of humankind from the natural world, the sense of superiority to other living beings, that enables us to perpetuate the mistaken notion that we are not subject to the same laws that govern the rest of life on earth. It also seems to legitimate our treatment of wilderness and wildlife—if we are superior beings, then we can dominate the inferior and even try to improve them.

It's not easy to recognize the messages implicit in our words because the assumptions and attitudes are so deeply embedded in our culture. After a speech in which I mentioned the way we put animals down, someone pointed out that I had accused rich countries of "hogging" too much of the planet's resources. Other animals don't deserve to be downgraded by a species whose name has come to symbolize shortsightedness, destruction and greed.

The Hidden Influences of Office Design

Suzyn Ornstein

A good deal of attention has been directed at the suggestion that office design—including the arrangement of offices, furnishings, and physical objects present in the work setting—influences job performance, job attitudes, and impressions. With almost 40 million people currently working in 9 billion square feet of office space in the United States,[1] even relatively small influences of office design on performance, attitudes, and impressions could have a large impact on productivity levels and employee attitudes. Many managers are unaware of the relationship between office design and various organizational behaviors, attitudes, and impressions. In this paper, I will (1) identify and describe the ways various elements of office design influence attitudes and behaviors, (2) identify and describe symbolic messages conveyed by office design, and (3) elaborate on actions managers can take that may result in more efficient and effective work environments.

INFLUENCE OF OFFICE DESIGN

There are various elements of office design that influence attitudes, behaviors and, through symbolic messages, impressions. These elements of office design have been divided into two broad categories: office layout and office decor. Office lay-

---

1. M. Pinto, "Open Hunting Season on the Open Plan?" *Corporate Design and Realty*, May 1986, pp. 82–84.

"The Hidden Influences of Office Design" by Suzyn Ornstein, *Academy of Management Executive*, 1989, (3) 2, pp. 144–147. Reprinted by permission.

out includes the configuration of office space (who is located next to whom and where people are located), the type of office arrangement (e.g., conventional or open-office), and the arrangement of furnishings and objects within individual offices and common spaces (such as reception areas). Office decor includes style and type of furniture, decorative objects, and physical elements of the environment such as noise, lighting, and temperature. The effects of both layout and decor on attitudes, behaviors, and impressions will be discussed in turn.

Influences of Office Design on Behavior and Attitudes

"When Paul Harris, a large retailer of women's ready-to-wear clothing in Indianapolis, remodeled their corporate offices, all the buyers were moved into an open-office arrangement. This configuration—with no walls and few noise absorbing partitions—magnified the noise of the ringing telephones, talking, copying and typing equipment to such levels that the buyers were practically unable to think in their 'offices.' Decision making time dropped from a few minutes to a few days!"[2]

Office Layout   The above example illustrates the impact a poor choice of office configuration can have on employee productivity. In this case, Paul Harris subsequently removed $30,000 worth of newly purchased office components and redesigned their offices in a more conventional (i.e., individual offices) plan.

Organizational experiences have confirmed that the configuration of office space and, in particular, the choice of traditional or open-offices has a great impact on employee behavior—especially on communication. For example, when a group of product engineers were moved from traditional offices to open-offices, it was found that both the quantity and quality of their ideas increased. In this case, the open plan allowed the engineers easier access to their colleagues by placing them in physical proximity to one another. The ease of collaboration resulting from the redesign of office space allowed for improved communication, which led directly to increased productivity. Similarly, a change to an open-office layout in a manufacturing firm resulted in an improved information flow—less time was spent on the telephone, doing paperwork, and in meetings, while more time was spent in face-to-face conversations. Of course, in the Paul Harris case, an open-office office plan was ill-advised because the nature of work involved numerous phone calls and a generally hectic work pace. The open-office plan magnified all activity so that concentration and, as a result, productivity were greatly reduced. Taken together, these experiences imply that configuration of office space should be determined based on the nature of the work to be performed. For example, people who work together should be placed near one another. In addition, the choice of traditional or open-offices should be determined by the importance of privacy and the noise levels resulting from the type of work performed.

Another element of office layout—the arrangement of furnishings within individual work spaces and common areas—also has been found to have an influence

2. More information about Paul Harris' change in office design can be found in "The Trouble with Open Offices," *Newsweek*, August 7, 1978, pp. 84–86.

on employee behavior. For example, at a Southwestern Bell unit of AT&T (prior to divestiture), a change in the arrangement of desks within an open-office plan resulted in an improvement in on-time order processing from 27% to 90%, all within a one-month period. Considering that the improvement came at a time of increased workload, supervisors determined that the change in desk placement resulted in a gain in productivity equivalent to 88 weeks of worker time per year saved—or the work of approximately 1.5 full-time employees.[3]

As the placement of desks influences behavior, it has also been found that seating arrangement affects communications. People seated in chairs placed face to face are more confrontational in their behavior than are people seated at right angles. Chairs placed directly next to one another often result in rather limited communications among those seated, while chairs placed back to back generally result in no communication. Chembank discovered the power of seating arrangements when it redecorated its corporate boardroom. The original arrangement (in which the top board members sat on a dais directly facing the rest of the board members) was changed to one in which all the board members sat around a U-shaped table, with the top members seated around the base of the U. This new arrangement produced much greater participation by a majority of the board members.

The Buffalo Organization for Social and Technological Innovation (BOSTI) found that office layout was directly related to worker satisfaction or, more precisely, lack of satisfaction with their jobs. BOSTI found that the majority of employees were dissatisfied with their workplace because it was arranged in a fashion that was counterproductive to accomplishing the tasks they were required to perform.[4] The amount of space per employee has also been found to affect job satisfaction; greater space was related to increased satisfaction with work.

Office Decor   Various elements of office decor also have been found to influence individual behavior and attitude; for instance, the presence of artwork affects performance under stressful circumstances. Specifically, when people were asked to prioritize strategic decisions under time pressure, they performed much better when artwork was present in the work setting than when it was not.

The BOSTI studies found that lighting, temperature, and noise were all related to employee satisfaction. We all know that too much or too little lighting, too high or low temperatures, and a high level of noise can result in decreased job satisfaction. BOSTI also calculated the costs of turnover and absenteeism resulting from this decreased satisfaction. They found that with improvements in lighting, temperature, and noise, organizations could save from $270 to $472 per year per manager, from $162 to $282 per year per professional/technical employee, and from $85 to $148 per year per clerical employee.

---

3. The specifics of this office arrangement are discussed in R. N. Ford's "Job Enrichment Lessons from AT&T," *Harvard Business Review*, January-February 1973, pp. 96–106.

4. All information about the BOSTI studies may be found in M. Brill's *Using Office Design to Increase Productivity*, Vols. 1 and 2, Grand Rapids, MI: Westinghouse Furniture Systems, 1985.

Influences of Office Design on Impressions

"In meeting with their architects to make design decisions, Westinghouse asked that its image as a 'successful, technically superior company' be interpreted for three groups. For its industrial peers, the building should reflect strength, professionalism, and integrity. For the Orlando community, it needed to have a powerful and elegant presence without being ostentatious. Finally, for the buildings' employees, it wanted an inspirational state-of-the-art work environment."[5]

In much the same way that office design influences attitudes and behaviors, it also influences impressions through the conveyance of symbolic messages; that is, different elements of office design connote messages and images that people then use in forming impressions about the company.

Office Layout   The element of layout that has the greatest impact on impressions is the arrangement of offices themselves—the configuration. Office configuration—who is located next to whom and where—serves a symbolic function by sending messages about who and what is valued in the organization. For example, arranging offices by rank so that the highest-level executives occupy the top floor(s) and/or the largest and most nicely appointed office space (e.g., corner offices with large windows) and lower-level employees occupy successively lower floors and smaller offices conveys the message that the organization places a high value on status. Similarly, a company that arranges its offices so that the most senior managers are located together and are given the nicest offices sends a message to employees and outsiders alike about the importance the firm places on seniority. The top executives at Home Box Office chose not to move into the top floor (the fifteenth) of their new building, but rather selected the eighth floor because of its greater proximity to both the marketing and programming departments. Union Carbide serves as another case in point. When the company recently moved into its new headquarters building, all managerial-level employees were assigned offices of equal size so that employees and outsiders alike would recognize the importance the company places on equality.

Not only is office configuration important in conveying information about an organization's values, but the physical layout of the offices themselves—be they conventional private offices, open-offices, or combinations of the two—also serves to reinforce the company's values. For example, R.P.M. Carlson, chairman of the board and president of the National Bank of Georgia, chose to implement an open-office plan in the bank's new headquarters because he believed this plan would best foster a culture based on consensus and open communication. Similarly, in Procter & Gamble's new office, only open-office plans were provided so that employees would clearly recognize the importance P&G places on teamwork.

---

5. This quote appears in K. Gustafson, "Westinghouse Generates a New Corporate Culture," *Corporate Design and Realty,* November-December 1984, pp. 51–56. Many of the corporate examples are described in detail in the September 1985 and February 1986 issues of *Corporate Design and Realty.*

Office Decor   Although office decor may not connote messages about organizational values as clearly as does office layout, elements of decor have been found to serve as symbols by influencing individuals' impressions about office holders and organizations alike. Objects commonly found in reception areas influence impressions. Flags, logos, seals, and pictures of organizational leaders convey an image of an organization that provides a great deal of structure and limited autonomy for its employees. Certificates, trophies, and plaques also are perceived as suggesting a high degree of organizational structure as well as the value and rewarding of good performance. Plants and flowers have consistently been found to influence impressions of an organization's warmth and friendliness.[6]

Artwork has also been associated with perceptions of organizations, with the content of the artwork playing a crucial role. One firm that displayed an oil painting of men on horseback was perceived by women as being a cold, hostile, and unfriendly place to work. In fact, this company was having difficulty recruiting women. Further investigation revealed that the reason why many of the women formed this negative impression was they believed the painting depicted a battle between cowboys and Indians! Thus, it is not enough for managers simply to add artwork to a reception area, office, or boardroom—the content of the artwork must also be taken into account.

IMPROVING YOUR OFFICE DESIGN

Although there obviously are no simple rules to making the best decisions about office design, there are some general guidelines that can be followed so that more effective and efficient designs may be developed and employed. These guidelines are as follows:

1. When changes in office design are pending—either as a result of moving to a new building or refurbishing the present facility—managers should seek input from the employees affected by the change. Doing so has at least three tangible benefits. First, as the people "in the trenches," employees often have specific knowledge about how their jobs actually are performed. Based on this knowledge they can make suggestions about what arrangements and configurations of office space should be most beneficial to enhanced performance. Likewise, they can identify design changes that would be detrimental to performance so that these designs can be avoided. Second, employees who are given an opportunity to contribute their ideas to the design decision are likely to be more satisfied with their jobs and the ultimate design that is implemented than are employees who are not given such an opportunity. Third, by soliciting employees' participation, it is

---

6. The meanings of these and other objects are discussed in S. Ornstein, "Organizational Symbols: A Study of Their Meaning and Influences on Perceived Psychological Climate," *Organization Behavior and Human Decision Processes*, October 1986, p. 207–229.

more likely that the move to the new facility or the refurbishing will go smoothly. This will result from employees' greater psychological acceptance of the move and their increased willingness to make the necessary physical adjustments (e.g., packing their offices for relocation, using new machinery, etc.).

2. To implement more effective changes in office design, managers should thoroughly analyze the work to be performed in the space under consideration. Included in this analysis should be an assessment of the nature of the work and the physical constraints of any machinery needed to complete/augment the work. It would be appropriate for managers to focus on needs for privacy; quiet; communication among individuals, groups, and departments; and special events requiring unusual office space needs. If it is determined that privacy and/or quiet working conditions are desirable, traditional offices with floor-to-ceiling walls and doors should be selected. These choices should then be arranged according to individual, group, or department—contingent on communication needs. Those with the greatest needs for communication should be placed nearest one another. If it is necessary, or simply desirable, that groups of more than five people meet together, it is important that space be provided to accommodate these meetings. In many offices, it is also prudent to plan for machinery. Machines that make a good deal of noise or emit heat or noxious odors should be placed in a private area blocked off by doors, walls, and/or noise-absorbing partitions. Manufacturers' instructions should be followed in setting up machinery (personal computers, in particular). This often requires changes in lighting, seating, and furnishings. Ignoring these adjustments to machinery will generally result in reduced rather than improved productivity.

3. Because configuration and arrangement of offices convey specific messages to employees and outsiders about the value placed on status, productivity, and communication, managers need to consider the values, goals, and behaviors they want to reinforce by their selection of office design. Status differences may be reinforced by office placement (highest-status positions placed on highest floor in office building), size (larger offices indicate more status), appointments (more expensive and greater variety of furnishings indicate greater status), equipment (greater amounts and expense indicate greater status), and type (traditional offices indicate greater status than open-offices). Status differences can be minimized by similarly sized, placed, styled, and decorated offices.

It is also important for managers to recognize that the decor and arrangement of furnishings within individual offices serve to reinforce company values, norms, and goals. Offices that are haphazardly arranged and decorated send clear signals about the lack of importance placed on detail and planning. Offices containing Spartan furnishings and decorations suggest the value of frugality and sticking to essentials. The arrangement of seating, particularly in the offices of top management, sends information to people that they use in forming opinions about the value the company places on communication and the importance it places on authority and structure in relationships. Decorative objects such as plants, artwork, and floral arrangements generally connote images of warm and friendly office holders. If these office holders are top-level managers, often these impressions will spill over to the way in which people perceive the entire organization.

4. Managers need to consider the influence office design has on outsiders who have cause to visit the facility. The offices should be arranged to promote simple and complete customer interaction. If necessary, signs should be placed so that the customer can easily find the area in which they are to conduct business. If clients/customers spend time waiting to conduct their business, a comfortable reception area should be created. This should include comfortable seating as well as decorative objects such as plants, flowers, and artwork. The inclusion of magazines and a telephone conveys the message that the organization really cares about its clients/customers.

5. Managers should also consider how the office design may influence the impressions made by potential employees. Office design should accurately convey to potential employees the values, goals, and behaviors actually desired by the organization. To determine the messages connoted by office design, an audit of hirees' perceptions, based on office design, could be completed. This information about what messages are actually conveyed could then be compared with the desired messages and changes made accordingly.

Office layout and decor are powerful influences on employees, customer, and community attitudes, behaviors, and impressions. Managers concerned with maximizing productivity and clarity of communication should view office design as a valuable tool for the accomplishment of their goals.

To Trust, Perchance to Buy

Donald J. Moine

Maybe what Willy Loman needed was lessons from Dr. Mesmer. The best persuaders build trust by mirroring the thoughts, tone of voice, speech tempo, and mood of the customer—literally, the techniques of the clinical hypnotist.

The real-estate agent, who normally speaks quickly and loudly, is responding in a slow, soft, rhythmic voice to her slow-speaking, quiet customer. The agent opened the sales interview with a series of bland and flatly accurate remarks about the cool weather and the lack of rain. Now she is explaining her hesitation in showing her customer a particular house: "I know you want to see that house, but I don't know whether I should show it to you. It is expensive, and"—an imperceptible pause—*"just looking at it will make you want to buy it."* A bit later she repeats something that, she says, a previous customer told her about a house he'd bought: "The house has been worth every penny. My wife and I just enjoy it so much"—another pause—*"we can't understand why we took so long to buy it."*

The agent, an extremely successful saleswoman, is instinctively using weapons from the arsenal of the skilled clinical hypnotist, whose initial aim is to create in a subject a state of intensified attention and receptiveness, leading to increased suggestibility. All successful persuaders produce such an effect, probably without understanding the exact nature of the techniques that accomplish it. Our real-estate woman is lulling her customer into a mood of trust and rapport by taking on his verbal and emotional coloring, and her techniques are almost identical to those that therapists like Herbert Spiegel use with patients who come to them to be hypnotized out of, say, their fear of cats.

The conclusion that a successful sales presentation is an intuitive form of indirect hypnosis is the most provocative finding of a psycholinguistic analysis that I performed in 1981. My initial study focused on eight life-insurance salesmen, four of whom were identified as "top producers" by the presidents of their companies, and four as only average. The two groups were closely matched on such characteristics as age and experience. Taking the role of the customer, I spoke with the eight men, recorded their comments, and analyzed those comments for the 30 techniques of persuasion that Richard Bandler and John Grinder had identified in the work of the master hypnotist Milton Erickson. I next examined the work of 14 top sellers of real estate, luxury automobiles, stocks, commodities, and trust deeds. Since 1981, I have tested my findings with more than 50 other people, who sell, among other products, jets, computers, and oil and gas leases. My basic finding was confirmed: Superior sellers use the techniques of the clinical hypnotist; mediocre ones do not.

GETTING IN SYNC

The best sales people first establish a mood of trust and rapport by means of "hypnotic pacing"—statements and gestures that play back a customer's observations, experience, or behavior. Pacing is a kind of mirror-like matching, a way of suggesting: "I am like you. We are in sync. You can trust me."

The simplest form of pacing is "descriptive pacing," in which the seller formulates accurate, if banal, descriptions of the customer's experience. "It's been awfully hot these last few days, hasn't it?" "You said you were going to graduate in June." These statements serve the purpose of establishing agreement and developing an unconscious affinity between seller and customer. In clinical hypnosis, the hypnotist might make comparable pacing statements: "You are here today to see me for hypnosis." "You told me over the phone about a problem that concerns you." Sales agents with only average success tend to jump immediately into their memorized sales pitches or to hit the customer with a barrage of questions. Neglecting to pace the customer, the mediocre sales agent creates no common ground on which to build trust.

A second type of hypnotic pacing statement is the "objection pacing" comment. A customer objects or resists, and the sales agent agrees, matching his or her remarks to the remarks of the customer. A superior insurance agent might agree that "insurance is not the best investment out there," just as a clinical hypnotist might tell a difficult subject, "You are resisting going into trance. That's good. I encourage that." The customer, pushing against a wall, finds that the wall has disappeared. The agent, having confirmed the customer's objection, then leads the customer to a position that negates or undermines the objection. The insurance salesman who agreed that "insurance is not the best investment out there" went on to tell his customer, "but it does have a few uses." He then described all the benefits of life insurance. Mediocre sales people generally respond to resistance head-on, with arguments that presumably answer the customer's objection. This response often leads the customer to dig in his heels all the harder.

The most powerful forms of pacing have more to do with how something is said than with what is said. The good salesman or -woman has a chameleon-like ability to pace the language and thought of any customer. With hypnotic effect, the agent matches the voice tone, rhythm, volume, and speech rate of the customer. He matches the customer's posture, body language, and mood. He adopts the characteristic verbal language of the customer ("sound good," "rings a bell," "get a grip on"). If the customer is slightly depressed, the agent shares that feeling and acknowledges that he has been feeling "a little down" lately. In essence, the top sales producer becomes a sophisticated biofeedback mechanism, sharing and reflecting the customer's reality—even to the point of breathing in and out with the customer.

I have found only one area in which the top sales people do not regularly pace their customers' behavior and attitudes—the area of beliefs and values. For example, if a customer shows up on a car lot and explains that she is a Republican, a moderately successful salesman is likely to say that he is, too, even if he isn't. The best sales people, even if they are Republicans, are unlikely to say so, perhaps because they understand that "talk is cheap" and recognize intuitively that there are deeper, more binding ways of "getting in sync" with the customer.

THE SOFT SELL

Only after they have created a bond of trust and rapport do the top sales people begin to add the suggestions and indirect commands that they hope will lead the customer to buy. One such soft-sell technique is using their patently true pacing statements as bridges to introduce influencing statements that lead to a desired response or action. For example: "You are looking at this car and you can remember the joy of owning a new reliable car," or "You are 27 years old, and we figure that your need for life insurance is $50,000." These pacing-and-leading statements resemble the way a hypnotist leads a client into hypnosis: "You are sitting in this chair, and you are listening to my voice"—the unarguable pacing statements— "and your eyelids are getting heavy, and they are beginning to close. . . ."

There does not have to be any logical connection between the pacing statement and the leading statement. They can be totally unrelated, yet when they are connected linguistically, they form a "sales logic" that can be powerfully effective, even with such presumably analytic and thoughtful customers as doctors and college professors.

The power of these leading statements comes from the fact that they capitalize on the affirmative mental state built by the undeniably true pacing statements, with which the customer is now familiar. Customers who have agreed with sales people expect, unconsciously, further agreement, just as customers who have disagreed expect further disagreement. The "traditional" truth of these pacing statements rubs off on the leading statements, and, without knowing it, the customer begins to take more and more of what the sales agent says as both factual and personally significant. Using hypnotic language, the agent activates the customer's desire for the product.

Average sellers combine pacing and leading statements less frequently and with less skill than do their superior colleagues. They also speak in shorter, choppier sentences, and thus fail to create the emotional web of statements in which the truthful and the possible seem to merge.

One of the most subtle soft-sell techniques is to embed a command into a seemingly innocuous statement. "A smart investor knows how to *make a quick decision, Robert.*" "I'm going to show you a product that will help you, *Jim, save money.*"

Sales people insure that their embedded commands come across by changing the tone, rhythm, and volume of their speech. Typically, as they pronounce the commands, they intuitively slow their speech, look the customer directly in the eyes, and say each word forcefully. A clinical hypnotist does the same thing deliberately. "If you will *listen to the sound of my voice,* you will be able to relax."

The placement of an individual's name in a sentence seems like a trivial matter, yet the position of a name can make a significant difference in how strongly the sentence influences the listener. Placed before or after the command portion of a sentence, it gives the command an extra power.

By changing their speech rate, volume, and tone, the best sales agents are able to give certain phrases the effect of commands. "If you can *imagine yourself owning this beautiful car,* and *imagine how happy it will make you,* you will want to, *Mr. Benson, buy this car.*" The two phrases beginning with "imagine" become commands for the customer to do just that. Owning the car is linked to the leading statement of how happy it will make the customer. Finally, the statement carries the embedded command: *"Mr. Benson, buy this car."*

THE POWER OF PARABLES

A final soft-sell technique of the best sales people is the ability to tell anecdotes, parables, and stories, and to frame their comments in metaphors. For thousands of years, human beings have been influencing, guiding, and inspiring one another with stories and metaphors, so it should be no surprise that sales people routinely use them to influence customers. What is surprising is the frequency and skill with which they do so.

Some sales agents I have studied do almost nothing but tell stories. They tell them to get the customer's attention, to build trust and rapport, and even to deliver product information. A piece of information that in itself might be boring takes on a human dimension and stays in the customer's memory when placed in the context of a story. "I sold a receiver like this a week ago to a surfer from Torrance and what he liked best about it was its FM sensitivity of 1.7 microvolts."

Metaphors and stories are used to handle customers' resistance and to "close" on them without endangering rapport. A top insurance agent was attempting to close a deal for a policy with a young man who was considering signing with a smaller company. As part of his clinching argument, the salesman wove the following metaphor into his pitch: "It's like taking your family on a long voyage across the Atlantic Ocean, and you want to get from here to England, and you have the choice of either going on this tugboat or on the Queen Mary. Which one would you *feel safe* on?" Had the salesman tried to make his point with a litany of facts and figures, he might never have focused his customer's attention; the discussion could have descended into a dispute about numbers. Instead, his story spoke directly to the customer's concern about his family's safety and implied that it was now in the customer's power to decide between two choices that were clearly unequal.

Note, too, that the salesman used conjunctions to link the metaphor in one unbroken chain and give it a hypnotic cadence. Mediocre sales people who know such a story would probably tell it as several separate sentences. In addition, they probably would give no special emphasis to the phrase "feel safe" even if they had heard better sales people do so. The skill in telling it is more important than the material itself.

The same can be said about all the skills that constitute the intuitively hypnotic arsenal of the best sales agents. But obviously, these skills are not exclusive to sellers. They are common to others—politicians, lawyers, even preachers. No less than sales people, these persuaders try to influence their audiences. No less than sales people, they attempt to implant in their audiences a resolve to do something. And, like sales people, all of them use, to some extent, variations of the techniques of Mesmer, Cagliostro, and Rasputin.

Color: A Guide to Human Response

James Gray, Jr.

How does color affect the impression you make? Color preferences offer clues to personality and guide human response.

Most interesting and revealing research and theory come from color expert Faber Birren. In his book *Color and Human Response,* he looks at personal color preferences and describes how color relates to personality. The colors people select and wear consistently are a large part of their image. Look around your office. What colors do people wear? Who wears warm colors and who wears cool colors? Birren found that

> There is a major division between extroverts, who like warm colors and introverts who like cool colors. As to general response to color, it is wholly normal for human beings to

"Color: A Guide to Human Response" by James Gray, Jr. from *The Winning Image,* Ed. 3, 1982, pp. 66–71. Reprinted by permission of the author.

like any and all colors. Rejection, skepticism, or outright denial of emotional content in color probably indicates a disturbed, frustrated or unhappy mortal. Undue exuberance over color, however, may be a sign of mental confusion, a flighty soul, the person who flits from one fancy or diversion to another and has poor direction and self-poise.°

The following commentaries, adapted from Birren's book, show how color and human response are connected.

Red. There are different red types. The first comes honestly to the color, with outwardly directed interests. He or she is impulsive, possibly athletic, sexy, quick to speak the mind—whether right or wrong. The complementary red type is the meek and timid person who may choose the color because it signifies the brave qualities that are lacking. Look in this person for more hidden desires, for more sublimation of wishes than usual. Where there is dislike of red, which is fairly common, look for a person who has been frustrated, defeated in some way, bitter and angry because of unfulfilled longings.

Pink. One of Birren's studies showed that many people who liked pink were dilettantes. They lived in fairly wealthy neighborhoods and were well educated, indulged, and protected. Birren found them to be "red souls who, because of their careful guardianship, hadn't the courage to choose the color in its full intensity." A preference for pink may also signify memories of youth, gentility, or affection.

Orange. Orange is the social color, cheerful, luminous, and warm rather than hot like red. Orange personalities are friendly, have a ready smile and quick wit, and are fluent if not profound in speech. They are good natured and gregarious and do not like to be left alone. In several instances, the dislike of orange has turned out to indicate a person, once flighty, who has made a determined effort to give up superficial ways for more sober application and diligence.

Yellow. On the good side, yellow is often preferred by persons of above-average intelligence. It is, of course, associated with oriental philosophies. The yellow type likes innovation, originality, wisdom. This type tends to be introspective, discriminating, high minded, and serious about the world and the talented people in it.

Yellow in the Western world has symbolized cowardice, prejudice, persecution. Some may dislike the color for this reason.

Yellow-green. From the few cases Birren encountered, he concluded that the yellow-green type is perceptive and leads a rich inner life but resents being looked upon as a recluse. There is desire to win admiration for a fine mind and demeanor but difficulty meeting others because of innate timidity and self-consciousness.

Green. Green is perhaps the most American of colors. It is symbolic of nature, balance, normality. Those who prefer green almost invariably are socially well adjusted, civilized, conventional. Green is perhaps an expression of Freud's oral character. Because the green types are constantly on the go and savor the good

---

° Faber Birren, *Color and Human Response* (New York: Van Nostrand Reinhold, 1978)

things of life, they are often overweight. The person who dislikes the green type may resist social involvement, and lack the balance that green itself suggests.

Blue-green. Birren associated the type with narcissism, or self-love. Most people who prefer blue-green are sophisticated and discriminating, have excellent taste, are well dressed, charming, egocentric, sensitive, and refined. Where a rare dislike of blue-green is met, there is an ardent denunciation of conceit in others, the attitude: "I am as good as you are!" Or, "Who do you think you are!"

Blue. Blue is the color of conservatism, accomplishment, devotion, deliberation, introspection. It therefore goes with people who succeed through application, those who know how to earn money, make the right connections in life, and seldom do anything impulsive. They make able executives and golfers, and they usually dwell in neighborhoods where other lovers of blue are to be found. Blue types are cautious, steady, often admirable, and generally conscious of their virtues.

A dislike of blue signals revolt, guilt, a sense of failure, anger about the success of others, especially if they have not expended the effort of the hater of blue. Successful people are resented as having all the good breaks and the good luck.

Purple and violet. Those whose favorite color is purple are usually sensitive and have above-average taste. Lovers of purple carefully avoid the more sordid, vulgar aspects of life and have high ideals for themselves and for everyone else.

Those who dislike purple are enemies of pretense, vanity, and conceit and readily disparage cultural activities which to them are artificial.

Brown. Brown is a color of the earth, preferred by people who have homespun qualities. They are sturdy, reliable, shrewd, parsimonious; they look old when they are young and young when they are old. They are conservatives in the extreme.

In a distaste for brown, there may be impatience with what is seen as dull and boring.

White, gray, and black. Virtually no one ever singles out white as a first choice; it is bleak, emotionless, sterile. White, gray, and black all figure largely in the responses of disturbed human beings. On the other hand, white is the color of innocence, virtue, truth and cleanliness. White is the preferred color for weddings and for formal social events.

Black-and-white contrasts also signal upper-class status. The famous Ascot races and other social events use white and black as primary theme colors.

A preference for gray, however, usually represents a deliberate and cultivated choice. Gray's sobriety indicates an effort to keep on an even keel, to be reasonable, agreeable, useful in a restrained way. To dislike gray is less likely than to be indifferent to it. It may be that a dislike is weariness of an uneventful life, or a feeling of mediocrity.

As to black, usually only the mentally troubled are fascinated by it, though there are exceptions. Some few persons may take to the color for its sophistication, but in this preference they may be hiding their truer natures.

People who dislike black are legion. Black is death, the color of despair. Such persons often avoid the subjects of illness and death, do not acknowledge birthdays, and never admit their age.

SELECTING COLORS THAT ARE RIGHT FOR YOU

1. Respect corporate or professional standards. If top level executives most often appear in navy and gray flannel, take the hint. It's a conservative environment and you will do well to follow the standard. Gray and navy are perhaps most readily associated with conservatism; bright or new tones are more liberal and may be de rigueur for fashion and design careers.

2. Don't be afraid of color. Respect professional and corporate standards, but let your personality shine through. The gray flannel suit or blazer comes to life with a scarf in the breast pocket, but to be safe, wear complementary colors.

3. Keep the season and climate in mind. White is generally considered bad taste in winter. Black absorbs heat on a humid, muggy day, but is comfortable in an air-conditioned office.

4. Complement skin and hair tones. Light skin and blond hair combined with white is a fade-out. Red hair and a ruddy complexion over violet and orange shocks. Cosmetic counselors in respected department stores conduct free color evaluations.

5. Select several colors that both complement your skin and hair color, and express your personality and buy clothes primarily in these colors. In addition it's difficult to own too many white shirts or blouses.

6. Consider the occasion. Delivering a speech at an after-six dinner meeting calls for dark, authoritative colors. Training a group of new employees might demand an authoritative, but less-threatening, gray flannel suit.

7. In choosing accessories, match and coordinate colors. Briefcases, shoes, and pocketbooks should not blatantly contrast suit or dress colors.

The following guidelines tell how to use color to alleviate a problem with body shape and size. It's actually impossible to separate clothing and color guidelines, and you should consider both to create the most effective style.

The tall, muscular male or female. Choose softer, lighter shades in gray, beige or light blues. Avoid color contrasts and bright colors that draw attention. Choose subtle combinations of blue and gray.

The tall, thin male or female. Medium-dark tans and blues work well. Use subtle color contrasts to break a long, continuous look, a tan and cream combination, for example. Stick with solid colors; avoid bright colors and patterns.

The small, or short male or female. Stick with dark hues in blue or gray. Match colors rather than contrast them. Matched colors, especially dark colors, add power and authority. For example, a dark gray suit with a diagonally striped tie in medium to dark gray and navy is an authoritative color combination. For women, a medium-gray dress with a complementary, darker-gray jacket or blazer works well.

The hefty male or female. Wear neutral, less attention-drawing colors, gray or tan hues. Wear lighter, cooler colors, even in winter. Avoid bright colors. Wear dark colors only on occasions that demand added authority.

'That's No Lady, That's My Wife'

Janet Elliott

"Who was that lady I saw you with last night?"

"That was no lady, that was my wife." So goes Henny Youngman's old joke. Well, Henny Youngman and the supporters of changes in sexist language have something in common. They both know that language transmits values and behavioral models.

When you deliver a speech, it's important that your language be free of sexist terminology which may send values that insult or exclude some members of your audience.

Sexism was first defined in a children's dictionary published in 1972 by American Heritage Publishing Company. It referred to sexism as "any arbitrary stereotyping of males and females on the basis of their gender." Unfortunately much of our standard English is inherently sexist and reinforces inequality.

AVOID STEREOTYPES

However, by giving careful thought to your word choices, you can present fair, accurate and equal treatment of both sexes. First, be careful of words that refer to a stereotyped behavior. You don't want your careless choice of words to imply an evaluation of the sexes you don't really intend.

As that old joke of Henny Youngman's shows us, the word "lady" is associated with a certain behavior. "Lady" can be used as a parallel to "gentleman." Although it is perfectly correct to say "ladies and gentlemen," be careful not to use the term "lady," with all its behavioral connotations, when the more accurate word would be "woman."

But referring to someone as "lady" is complimentary, you say. Think again. Because the word "lady" has been overused, all sorts of connotations have developed. Do you mean bag lady, ol' lady, the fat lady or perhaps even lady of the evening?

Another stereotype practice which can be very insulting to members of your

" 'That's No Lady, That's My Wife' " by Janet Elliott, *The Toastmaster*, August 1986, p. 14. Reprinted by permission of Toastmasters International.

audience is referring to an adult female as a girl. For example, when talking about women sharing a midday meal don't refer to the event as "lunch with the girls."

A woman old enough to hold a position as a secretary should not be spoken about as "girl," as in "my girl typed the letter." Before using the words "lady" or "girl," determine if you would use "gentleman" or "boy" in a similar circumstance describing a male. If not, you should reword your statement.

Difficulties also arise from the habitual use of cliches or familiar expressions which evaluate and stereotype. For example, using the phrase "man and wife" implies differences in the activity of each. An evaluation of the roles is communicated. A use of more equal terms is "husband and wife."

Another way you may inadvertently communicate a stereotype is by describing a woman's physical attributes and a man's mental or professional attributes. If you make an introduction of Carl Smith as a great surgeon and his wife as a beautiful redhead, you have not treated each with the same dignity or seriousness.

You might say the Smiths are an attractive couple—Carl is a handsome blond and Linda is a beautiful redhead. Or you could say the Smiths are highly respected in their fields; Carl is a great surgeon and Linda is a successful lawyer.

Some adjectives, depending on whether the person you are describing is a man or woman, communicate bias. Ambitious men, but aggressive women; cautious men, but timid women are examples of adjectives that stereotype.

SEXIST JOB TITLES

A second area that can be troublesome in inadvertently presenting a sex bias in your speech is in how you state job titles. I recently attended a meeting in which nearly 80 percent of the audience was composed of young college women. The speaker was addressing the subject of career options for communications majors in business. Throughout his speech he used the term "businessman" when referring to a business executive in general. Many members of his audience were offended by the exclusion.

When a job is open to members of both sexes, describing it by a common gender term is more accurate and effective than using one job title for men and another for women. Why not use the term "reporter" rather than "newsman," "mail carrier" rather than "mailman," "member of congress" rather than "congressman" or "police officer" rather than "policeman"?

When speaking of an individual who holds a particular job or office, it offends no one to use the specific gender term, such as "newspaperman" or "congresswoman." But be careful of that term "lady" again. NBC newsman Frank Blair referred to a female head of a jury as forelady of the jury. It was specific but not entirely correct, unless he commonly speaks of a man as a jurygentleman.

You can insult members of your audience by trivializing some job titles, such as poet to poetess, director to directress or usher to usherette. The original word can be used to indicate either sex.

It is not necessary to specify gender in job titles such as woman lawyer or male nurse, unless a gender modifier is relevant; i.e. as in a course on women writers or when specifying a particular fact, such as the first female astronaut. When you specify the gender of a profession, you are implying by the label that an exception to the rule has been made.

EXCLUDING ONE SEX

The use of terminology which excludes one sex is a third area that alienates your audience. A speaker at a seminar for men and women insurance agents turned off a portion of his audience when he began by saying, "As you look at your face in the mirror each morning when you shave . . ." He did not choose his words carefully to avoid offending by exclusion all those in his audience who have never shaved their faces.

The pervasive use of "man" to represent humanity in general either excludes women when they should be included, or creates ambiguous situations; leaving the interpretation up to the individual listener.

Many publishers have developed guidelines for the use of nonsexist language in textbooks and journals. For instance, Scott, Foresman and Company suggest that, "When man invented the wheel . . ." can become, "When people invented the wheel . . ."

McGraw-Hill Book Company Publications states in their Guidelines for Equal Treatment of the Sexes, "In reference to humanity at large, language should operate to include women and girls. Terms that tend to exclude females should be avoided whenever possible."

The use of "man" to refer to both women and men is ambiguous. The best way to avoid the problem is to replace the word "man," used in the general sense, with such words as "human" or "person" or "American" or "Japanese."

Similarly, the use of masculine pronouns to refer to women and men creates the same problems. Because the English language lacks a truly generic third-person singular pronoun, avoiding ambiguity and exclusiveness is not always easy. Linguists have even attempted to coin a common gender pronoun.

In 1859 Charles Converse proposed the pronoun "thon" which he derived as a contraction of "that one." It was listed in *Funk and Wagnalls New Standard Dictionary* of 1913 with the example, "Each pupil must learn thon's lesson." It was last recognized in the 1959 edition of Webster's *Second International Dictionary*.

Other coinages have come and gone, which suggests a continuing need for an appropriate common gender pronoun.

SHARED VALUES

Language is not only a means of communication, it does indeed express values and shared assumptions about our society. Languages continually evolve to include new concepts and ideas. English is now beginning to reflect the increasing equality of women and men in our society.

Most often sexist language is not deliberate. It is usually a matter of habit or laziness. It is easier to use ready-made sexist expressions than to reword in a manner that avoids sexism.

As George Orwell said in his essay, "Politics and the English Language," "Ready-made phrases are the prefabricated strips of words and mixed metaphors that come crowding in when you do not want to take the trouble to think through what you are saying."

You are now sensitized. You have been made aware of a few of the ways our language can perpetuate sexist values. As a speaker you owe it to your audience to examine your words and choose them with greater care. Both sexes deserve equal treatment in life and in language. You can do your part in not denying your audience that right.

Games Mother Never Taught You

Betty Lehan Harragan

To awestruck sightseers in the land of the business hierarchy, the architectural grandeur is overpowering and impressive. Stately edifices dominate landscaped vistas of suburbia and mighty skyscrapers silhouette the profiles of major cities. Flowering gardens, soaring plazas, ample parking, vaulted lobbies, air conditioning, musical elevators, carpeted lounges, spacious dining rooms, and hundreds upon hundreds of linear offices bathed relentlessly in fluorescent brilliance dutifully impress gaping tourists.

But all this structural munificence does not divert the expert gamester who looks beyond the steel and concrete public visor of the corporate persona to identify the heraldic markings painted on the battle armor. Like the shields carried by knights of legend, the modern corporate building reeks with symbolism. Far from being a mere architectural wonder, every pane of glass, slab of marble, and foot of carpet performs a dual function in identifying the tournament site. The buildings are impersonal monuments to the power and wealth contained therein. Space itself, in both the exterior and interior layout, is weighted with abstract significance. Just as a heraldic seal reveals a great deal about the one using it, so spatial divisions reveal important information about the modern-day knights.

Today's business building, especially the corporate headquarters, is a physical representation of the hierarchical pyramid. It is the tangible game board. A walk through a large office, from floor to floor, is like threading a course through the hierarchy. Trappings of rank, position, and power are spread around the place like icons in a cathedral. They identify the important players and signal their positions in the game. Neophytes must grasp the design of the game board and learn the initial placement of the pieces before making any irreversible move.

Very often businesswomen approach the game of corporate gamemanship as if it were a throw of the dice which pits their future against pure chance, or luck. The real game for women more nearly resembles chess, in which one of the sixteen playing pieces is a strong female (the Queen) and the object of the game is to "check" the adverse King. Chess is an intellectual military exercise based on a combative attack against equally matched opposing fighting units. The descriptive play language of chess is indistinguishable from that of war "games" or football or business—lines of attack, defensive systems, infiltration, onslaught, sacrifice, control (territory or foes), power, weakness, strength, strategy, tactics, maneuver, surrender, challenge, conquer, win. Each pawn, rook, knight, bishop, queen, and king in the chess set is endowed with specific agility to move only in certain directions and for stipulated distances. Each piece is made clearly identifiable so that players and observers can watch the game progress and know exactly what moves have been made. Unlike cards, chess is a public game spread out for all to see.

So is corporate politics a public game. In business the so-called status symbols serve to identify the playing pieces and reveal their positions on the board. The masculine pecking system, regardless of the all-male activity, is replete with emblems and shared identity signals, many of which speak louder than words and obviate the need for verbal communication. If you've ever wondered why your boss pays inordinate attention to "silly" objects or personal privileges, very likely these are crucial business status symbols. Few of the customs and practices of business life are meaningless. They only look that way to women who have not learned the fundamentals of the game.

HOW TO TELL THE PLAYERS APART

Status symbols are two-way communications. If you can interpret them, they tell you where a coworker stands in the ranking system, and they tell others where you stand. For that reason, women cannot afford to ignore these ubiquitous symbols because each tiny accumulation of visible status is an increase in power or advancement. Indeed, as the game plays out, a woman often needs her power emblems more than a title or salary increase to effectively use any authority she acquires. It is difficult if not impossible for a pawn to behave like a bishop or queen if she doesn't have the mitre or crown that differentiates the chess pieces.

Most of the common status differentials can be perceived at even the lowest levels. As employees move up the hierarchical ladder, the emblems are gradually emblazoned with additional symbols or sophisticated refinements of the basic seal. Here are some of the categories of rank insignia which help you tell the players apart and prevent you from being bluffed by someone at your own level who tries to "pull rank" on you without justification. Conversely, a familiarity with the status symbols protects you from being duped by management if you are offered an empty promotion or promise which carries no visible authority emblem.

How You Are Paid

Not how much, *how.* Cash in a brown envelope indicates the lowest rank. A check thus becomes a status symbol, a sign of progress. If the wage is figured on an hourly basis or a weekly basis (the nonexempt jobs which are subject to overtime beyond forty hours), it has a lower status than jobs which are exempt from overtime. I remember a junior writer who tried to lord it over her friends with a claim that she had been promoted to professional ranks. She lost all respect and admiration when it was discovered that she still filled out "the little green slips" which were required for weekly time sheets. She thought she was a "writer" because she was allowed to write; her shrewd coworkers knew she was still considered an hourly clerical worker by management because that's how she was paid. An annual salary paid out in the standard semimonthly equal installments is a symbol of the supervisory and professional ranks. Very high levels of management often have options to tailor payment methods to suit their own convenience. Many executives don't get a check at all; they have it sent directly to their banks and deposited to their personal accounts. Corporate officers almost all arrange to have big portions of their high salaries "deferred," that is, not paid to them until some later date or in some other form. It pays to keep an eye on how superiors receive and cash their salary checks. Incidentally, some executives send their secretaries to the bank with their checks; these secretaries are worth wooing if you're trying to collect salary data.

What Time You Report to Work

Flexibility in choosing one's own working hours is a clear mark of distinction. The lowest degree of status is reflected in punching a time clock or being "signed in" by an overseer, the sure tag of a manual or clerical job. The time-clock insignia also extends to lunch hours and coffee breaks which are strictly regimented to the prescribed minute. As one moves upward into supervisory and professional ranks, *it is taken for granted* that you have a degree of autonomy in fixing your work hours and lunch times or breaks. Women frequently don't seem to recognize that they have this status privilege, or else they are afraid to display it, and use it. I'm often jarred when I have lunch with an apparent "executive" woman who suddenly bolts her lunch and dashes away because she'll be "late" getting back to the office within an hour. This is the time-clock thinking, lowest-level clerical insignia. If her boss is what she's afraid of (as many have told me), she is being treated as a time-clock employee and allowing herself and her job to be thus degraded. No brownie points accrue to a game player who refuses to wear her status symbols. You establish privileges simply by taking advantage of work-hour freedom according to the local department pattern.

Freedom to determine your own working hours does not mean you work shorter hours or ignore the working timetable your boss adopts. Some women consider it wise to dovetail their hours with their boss's—so they are always in the office at the same time. Others work more independently and arrive at the hour most convenient to their personal schedule and vary lunch periods to suit personal or business commitments. One woman executive I know has remained at the same job level for twenty years although a more astute gamester with her options would have progressed several steps. Her problem is low-echelon thinking; she still acts like a time-clock secretary. Even though she travels on business regularly, she schedules her trips for one-day, eighteen-hour commutes and gets home after midnight to appear in the office before nine the next morning. Bedraggled and exhausted, she complains about her terrible schedule, but neither her subordinates nor her superiors have any sympathy; they've long since chalked her off as lacking management potential. Men who progressed from a duplicate position scheduled their trips over two or three days each time; they knew better than to ignore status symbols. If you're uncertain about your status entitlement in time flexibility, watch what male colleagues and bosses do. Then go out and do likewise! Don't, for heaven's sake, complain about men who proudly display their ranking privileges and wonder why your hard work isn't appreciated after you've thrown away your own equality symbol.

Where You Eat

Not only when but where one eats is a status distinction. The lowest indication is being restricted to the premises as are many plant and factory workers. Freedom to leave the work premises (whether you do or not) is a step upward. Voluntary on-site lunching in large corporations is usually stamped with clear status distinctions. Lower-echelon workers go to the general cafeteria; middle-management dines in the executive lunchroom; and top officers eat in the private dining room. Senior executives can always drop into the general cafeteria if they want, but it takes a symbolic ID card to get into the executive dining halls. Anyone who is eligible to eat in the executive dining room but eschews the privilege to continue lunching with friends in the general cafeteria is pretty sure to be knocked out of the game very soon. If, for example, you had a boss who did that, you'd know it was time to look for a transfer or new job because you're stuck with a dead-head. See how attention to visible status emblems can tip you off?

In some companies even eating at your desk can reveal status. Did you get the food yourself from the friendly mobile vendor? Did a secretary order it from a good delicatessen and have it delivered? Was a complete hot-plate sent from the executive dining room? Or did you bring a sandwich from home in a brown paper bag?

Are you beginning to think all this is silly, like who cares? That's just it; nobody cares—if you're a woman. All your male colleagues and coworkers will ignore your eating habits as long as it keeps you out of their favorite rendezvous. They've already decided you belong with the brown-baggers (low-paid secretaries and clerks who bring their lunch), so it won't surprise them one bit to see you ally yourself with lower-status lunch groups. As an ambitious woman you have to care. It will never do for you to exclude yourself from the semisocial lunch and cocktail gatherings where more business is conducted, more information exchanged, and more contacts made than during the regular working hours. If you can't worm your way into a suitable lunch group, go to a movie or go shopping for a couple of hours, but definitely exercise your status prerogative.

The Mail You Get

Mail sorters, if they were so minded, could diagram the organizational chart by noting the incoming mail for various individuals and the routing pattern on memos. One of the first status symbols is an in-box on your desk. The next improvement is denoted by an out-box. Increasing status is determined by the style of the containers, utilitarian metal being at the lower end and hand-woven straw, hand-painted wood, or other elaborate designs being better. Perhaps because this symbol is so widely distributed, some statusy types dispense with this common denominator and have incoming correspondence neatly piled on the center of an empty desk (they probably have little of significance to do and hope their status symbols will carry them through to retirement).

More important than the box is the incoming contents. Daily deliveries of the *Wall Street Journal* and *New York Times* or regular copies of *Business Week, Fortune, Barron's, Forbes, U.S. News and World Report,* or economic newsletters are distinctive emblems. Company-paid subscriptions are status symbols in general, but the more management-oriented the publication, the higher the status rating, *Harvard Business Review* outranking the Gizmo trade journal by far.

Outgoing mail also has status value if your name is imprinted on the corporate letterhead, either by itself or as one of the partners or officers of a firm.

Your Working Location

In a factory, the operator at the end of the assembly line has more prestige than one near the beginning because the product is more valuable in its finished state. The principle of increasing value of work follows through to the top of the hierarchy where the office of the chief executive is obviously the ultimate in status and power and the choicest in location. Proximity to the power generator exudes status, with the office adjacent to the CEO being the most prestigious but the entire floor sharing in shadings of top rank. In a suburban complex with several buildings, the one with the executive offices is the power generator and a poor location there is superior to choice space in any lesser building. In short, physical locale is a status symbol, so the location of your office is one of the most telling emblems in revealing your rank in the hierarchy and your favor with the boss. It's an important piece in the game.

HOW SPACE CONFERS STATUS

The "executive floor" is known to most employees by virtue of the fact that they have never set foot on it. This is the true inner sanctum, and the power emanations are so strong that minor employees are afraid to get near. I've seen adult men literally shake in their boots at the prospect of answering a call to the executive floor. For those who are physically located "in the boondocks," "over in the bone-yard," or "out in the sticks," (i.e., distant buildings or branch offices), a move to the headquarters city or building signifies a boom in status long before anyone knows if the shift was accompanied by a change in title or a better salary. Geographic and internal physical office moves can track an executive's path through the hierarchical labyrinth more clearly than a title change. A company may have hundreds of vice-presidents or divisional managers but the really important ones are distinguished from titular peers by that prime emblem of status—the office location.

Within the physical boundaries of every corporate department or operation much the same pattern of office locale identifies the ranking of subordinates and superiors. Most department layouts are square or rectangular. The corner offices, which are larger, brighter, and most secluded, are choice spots and the highest ranking executives naturally choose them. The remainder of the outside walls are customarily divided into small offices so that each has a window or a portion of plate glass. These are known universally as the "window offices" and have much higher status value than nonwindowed offices. Size is also an emblematic factor, so a large window office is more valuable than a small window office, but a small window office is superior to a much larger "interior" office.

The internal space in a typical office floor layout can be left wide open and filled with rows upon rows of desks (generally populated with clerical women). Here employees work in the wide-open area with no privacy and where they can be easily observed by the supervisors. Another solution is to partition the vast internal space with one or more rows of "interior" offices, each of which has walls to the ceiling and doors; these are real private offices but have no windows. The third alternative, and a highly favored one, is to erect movable partitions which enclose the desks of individuals in the interior sector. These tin or plastic partitions are waist- or shoulder-high; they block the view of a person sitting at the enclosed desk but allow any passer-by to look over the top and see the occupant at work. These constructions are well known to all working women as cubicles. Status-wise, they are a step up from the wide-open clerical or secretarial pool pattern (often referred to as "paper factories"), but not as prestigious as a fully enclosed office which carries more symbolic value even if it must be shared with another. A "window" office is generally considered an "executive" or supervisory symbol.

SYMBOLIC MEANINGS OF WINDOWS AND WALLS

Since window offices can be roughly defined as officers' quarters, the position of rooms "weights" their relative values. Proximity to the corner offices carries the most weight, then comes view. An unobstructed view of the skyline or gardens is far more prestigious than a window on the ventilating shaft or one overlooking the parking lot or delivery entrance. An office located on the traffic lanes, one in the center arena of business activity, represents higher status than one hidden away in an isolated nook or placed near the non-status "public" areas, such as cloakrooms, bathrooms, lounges, elevators, or storerooms.

Offices in the middle of the outside walls, that is, those that are equidistant from either corner office, are least desirable because the occupant's connection to either corner power generator is weak, tenuous, and not immediately identifiable. Michael Korda, the best-selling folk etymologist of sophisticated male business mores, attributes this midcenter office weakness to a power dead spot. In his book *Power: How to Get It, How to Use It*, he asserts that power flows in an X-shaped pattern from each corner office to the one diagonally opposite. The center of the space (where the X-lines bisect) represents the point at which the authority of the corner person peters out. Under his theory, the center of the floor layout is equivalent to a power blackout area and outer offices parallel with the center of the room are thus located in power dead-spots.

I've seen office setups where enclaves of competing executives use the X theory to amass power. With their cronies and subordinates flanking them, they set up hostile camps in each of the corners. Newcomers or nonaligned workers invariably float to the nondescript center offices. In firms where several executives have equal rank, for instance partners in auditing, law, or brokerage firms, they can apportion the corner offices by a coin toss and the power flow runs as easily down the sides as across a diagonal. Even so, the central offices are less prestigious because ranking executives like to have their closest allies physically near them. Proximity to a superior is undoubtedly the best gauge of status within a team group. Watch carefully when offices get switched around. It means that status symbols are changing hands and the rank of the movers is being visibly altered although their titles and salaries are unchanged.

A lot of women may think this game of musical chairs with office locations is also silly and unnecessary. It may be, but the accretion of status symbols is very serious business to ambitious businessmen. They know that a display of status symbols means as much in the corporate hierarchy as a chest full of medals does to an ambitious officer in the military hierarchy. If women are to function equally in the action arena of business they must be able to decipher the code and demand the proper rank insignia for themselves as they progress haltingly up the corporate ladder. To disregard the value of preferred office location is tantamount to selecting a rhinestone ring over a diamond because the first one looked "prettier." Refusing to wear epaulets which identify your business rank because you don't appreciate the genuine value is a disastrous mistake.

DON'T GARBLE THE LOCALITY MESSAGE

Judging from my personal observations during the past five years that women have begun moving ahead in corporate jobs en masse, it seems safe to say that many have ignored the status code. Which is to say that they get a better title but they seldom get the visible emblems of rank. If you believe you are making progress on your job, count the number of times you have changed offices. A meaningful promotion almost mandates an office change; a token title and slight salary increase does not give you the necessary authority to handle the new job unless subordinates and outsiders see that you were issued the appropriate rank insignia.

By and large, women are oblivious to rank symbols because so few working women have *any* office privacy that a room of one's own is—in comparative *women's* terms—the ultimate achievement. As long as it's private and "workable," women are inclined to "accept" any office offered them and make the best of the disadvantages that inevitably appear. I know women who have sat in the same office for the past twenty years. I don't know any men in that category. In the industry circles I travel, men who are that immobile were fired or quit years ago.

If you had trouble . . . in diagramming your department's organization chart or evaluating your own advancement potential, try a different tack. Make a floor plan of the office layout and see who's sitting where. This floor plan will guide you in determining which of several people on the same job level are the more favored or powerful—they will have offices very near the top-ranked superior, or they will have established a power enclave of their own in one of the opposite corners. Then locate your own office in relation to these authority areas. You should get a pretty good idea of what your superiors think of you and your potential according to the office they assigned you. It may be more than adequate by your personal comfort standards, but if it doesn't translate into appropriate status according to the male heraldic seal, you are being symbolically downgraded or dead-ended.

ALWAYS COLLECT YOUR EARNED MEDALLIONS

Reluctance on management's part to dispense money in the form of raises is understandable because of manifest business concern but unwillingness to issue women their status insignia is propelled by pure male chauvinism. A female corporate politician must be alert to this subtle form of sex discrimination and take steps to alleviate it. Specifically, *ask* for and fight for your office emblem. Before making a final decision on a new job offer, ask to see the office that goes with the job. If you get a promotion, inquire immediately about the new office that you'll get. If you discover you have a lesser status office than your job indicates, ask for the next vacant office in the area you decide you belong in. Keep your eye on possible office vacancies and ask for a more desirable location before they put a newcomer (usually a man) in a higher status office than you have. Keep asking.

One woman I know who was an analyst in the research department of a large investment firm reacted instinctively and volubly when her company moved to elegant new offices in a beautiful skyscraper. She was the only woman in an all-male group and the covey of expensive industrial designers, office planners, and management consultants had settled her in a noisy isolated corner next to the coat room and elevator banks and off-kilter from the rest of the section. "I didn't know anything about office sites," she told me, "but I felt like I'd been slapped in the face. My intuition told me there was something seriously wrong and I refused to take the office. A young guy who had just arrived was settled in an office I liked, so I demanded that one on the basis of seniority. I loved the job, but I refused to appear at the office until I got the right accommodations. They put up a terrible fight, until I was mentally prepared to quit over the issue." Her determination paid off and she got the office space she selected. Later that year, one of the firm's partners brought his wife in to meet her, saying proudly, "I'd like you to meet the only woman in our research department." My friend pointed out that there was now another woman in research but he brushed that aside, saying, "I forget about her. I consider you our only woman because you are the only one who fought for your office!"

By contrast, a lawyer I know got a very good job in the corporate counsel's office of a huge industrial corporation. She's the only woman on the executive floor and since her first day's pro forma expense-account lunch with a few of the senior attorneys she has been totally ostracized by her colleagues. That was easily accomplished because her office (with a spectacular view from the top floor of a Manhattan skyscraper) is on a corridor on the opposite side of the building from the legal department. For all intents and purposes, she is physically as well as psychologically isolated from the counsel's team! Asked why she accepted that office she exclaimed, "Oh, it's beautiful! Carpets six inches thick, anything I request in the way of furniture and equipment, and that astronomical view. They originally apologized for it, saying nothing better was available, but I told them this was perfect. How much better could you get?" But when visiting executives from divisional offices and subsidiaries regularly take her for a temporary secretary, it's partly because she has no rank insignia, no team identification.

WATCH OUT FOR FEMALE GHETTOES

The retailing industry and fashion merchandising are typical of businesses where women predominate at lower levels and have moved upward in restricted areas to executive levels (a handful are getting close to the top). These industries are nevertheless dominated by male status symbols, and clever corporate politicians must analyze the patterns and play the game by classic standards. Many women who have "made it" through the twisted paths of historic blatant discrimination have had no opportunity to learn the game rules in entirety. They are particularly blind to status emblems or, to be more precise, they were furnished garbled emblems intended to ghetto-ize them and they now have difficulty unscrambling the hodge-podge.

I will be watching the progress of an executive friend who just began playing the corporate game in the retailing field. Helena has been floating on a relatively high plateau in specialty fashion retailing for the past several years. She's spent her entire career—close to twenty years—working with women colleagues whom she likes and admires. But once she was alerted to the broad ramifications of the corporate politics game, she recognized that her advancement opportunities were nonexistent in the retail complex where she was employed. She found a new job with a national consulting firm, using her expertise in fashion retailing as the wedge to negotiate a 50-percent salary increase. In her new firm all the employees and executives are women except for the vice-president in charge of merchandising, who is a man.

"After doing the same job for years, this offers an exciting new opportunity," she told me. "The company is dynamic, the vice-president, my boss, sounds very progressive, and the other women executives are tops in their fields, stimulating people to work with. Everything about the job seemed perfect—until I evaluated the status symbols, especially office location. I drew diagrams of the layout to analyze where my office was situated. The picture prompted me to reopen negotiations although I had accepted the job. I realized I'd be stalemated again if I didn't insist on the right office locale. I got it changed before I started."

Helena's analysis was perceptive gaming. The male vice-president had the most prestigious corner office. She had been assigned a large office next to the corner in the diagonally opposite area. All the women in that area were fashion specialists, too. Each of the corners held clusters of women experienced in various retail specialties. Helena is cognizant of the categorizing which restricts women executives to food, fashion, home furnishings, fabrics, domestics, cosmetics, accessories or whatever gave them their start. "When men start in ties, they don't end up tie specialists—they branch out to merchandising executives. When women start in dresses, they don't end up dress specialists—they're catalogued as high fashion, budget, sports, evening, lounge, or boutique. They are constricted by experience, not broadened to becoming merchandising generalists." This was the pattern she saw duplicated in the office layout at her new firm—women segregated according to narrow specialties. Since her goal was to break out of overspecialization, she perceived correctly that an office located in the midst of fashion specialists would lock her into the very trap she was escaping.

"I didn't explain *why* I wanted the particular office I chose; after all I'll be working closely with the fashion group at the beginning. But my career plan demands some proximity to the vice-president and a door on the traffic lane to his office. I'll use it for visibility and getting to know the types of merchandising clients who visit the V-P. I intend to move toward merchandising management, and my first successful game move was getting myself dissociated from all the specialty enclaves."

Office location is invested with good and poor status insignia. Office positioning has a direct relationship to job advancement. Certain office locales have high status value precisely because ambitious, aggressive people fight for them in order to get close to the central action area. Once again, watch how progressing men move closer and closer to higher superiors with every promotion. Careers and office insignia move in tandem.

WHEN STATUS EMBLEMS AND STEREOTYPES COLLIDE, MOVE!

Not much is known yet about potential boomerang effects when classic male rank symbols are acquired by women. One danger area is already evident—the office adjacent to a male senior executive. Sex, sexism, and female stereotypes can rear up to cancel out all the job benefits and rank status that traditionally accrue to men who achieve this enviable geographic site, which frequently has the invisible logo "next in line for the top job." When a woman earns that status locale, the invisible logo shifts to "she's sleeping with her boss," or "she's a glorified secretary (who's sleeping with the guy)."

Over a lunch, a female officer of a subsidiary company of a financial corporation explained how her advancement was nearly jeopardized because she occupied the office adjacent to the president. "I'm not quite sure how I got assigned to the office since I was one of several vice-presidents who were eligible for it. Probably a misguided attempt to prove they didn't discriminate against women, a laugh considering I was the only woman executive in the entire firm at the time. Take it from me, token women are more to be pitied than censured; like the first child of nervous parents we suffer from the ignorance of our elders." At any rate, she occupied what male colleagues looked upon as the most enviable office in the company, but it slowly turned into nightmare alley for her. "I had an important and demanding job but I was interrupted constantly. Executives from our own company as well as all outside visitors marched straight into my office, left messages for me to relay to the president, explained their problems to me, or dropped in for idle chats if the president got an important private phone call during their appointment."

At first she tried directing the men to the private secretaries and assistants, but each day there were other strangers who made the same automatic assumption—that the woman closest to the top executive was naturally his private secretary or assistant. "I foresaw the end of the line in my career if I remained in that close proximity to the chief executive. I was becoming identified with him and his work, not my own operating responsibilities. My authority was rapidly eroding as I was stereotyped into an 'assistant' or 'helper' to the great man. I decided I *had* to get out of there and I'm absolutely positive I'd never be where I am today, a functioning administrator and top management, if I'd allowed the implied tie-up of superior male-subservient female to continue."

The educational aspect of her story was how she made her moves to solve the problem. She assayed all the male vice-presidents who were equally eligible for the office. From the group she picked the man she disliked the most and who returned the feeling with a vengeance. He was also the one most envious of her position and most blatant about his raw ambition and his disparagement of her qualifications. When she invited him to lunch with her, he was wary and hostile. "He almost choked to death on a piece of fish when I asked him if he'd like to trade offices. He couldn't believe anybody would be so stupid as to give up the ultimate status symbol, and it took a while to convince him I was serious. Once he saw that (swallowing my story that I really *liked* his office better for its afternoon sunshine!), he joined the conspiracy with me to get the trade approved without any flak." Between the two of them they arranged the transfer smoothly and she regained her independence as a line executive. Her male accomplice gained his most cherished desire. "He was in seventh heaven in that office and the superior rank symbol pushed him steadily ahead. My freedom from that office allowed me to grow and develop on my merits and demonstrated performance; we both benefited. Best of all, he turned from an enemy into an ally. He is one of my strongest supporters and advocates."

PORCELAIN INSIGNIA THAT WON'T FLUSH AWAY

Toilets seem to be the major obstacle to women's equality. If you don't think so, you haven't heard the nuttiest arguments against the Equal Rights Amendment (i.e., the ridiculous fear that public restrooms will be coed). Or you haven't been faced with employment problems which evolve from the superior status symbolism of urinals. The good news is that women aren't entirely alone trying to revamp this physical hallmark of sexual supremacy; management is a nervous wreck as working women demand equal facilities and senior executives in many institutions expend as much energy on the dilemma of bathrooms as they do on the next quarterly earnings' prediction. Porcelain status symbols are proving to be nonbiodegradable.

Some companies try to evade the entire subject. To this day, the J. Walter Thompson Company advertising agency refuses to recognize indelicate functions. Its dozens of bathrooms hide decorously behind plain unmarked doors and nary a discriminatory word such as "Men's" or "Women's" sullies its pristine halls or executive offices. Pity the new male client or supplier whose initial contact is a woman executive (if any); the prime executive-to-executive bond has evaporated into embarrassed agony.

Some companies treat the subject like a huge, salacious joke. They are apt to be institutions that have given urinals the most visible priority status. One of the country's largest utilities (hardly the only offender in this category) left no doubt where its sympathies lay by installing men's urinals in spacious rooms off the well-lit hallways. Women's facilities (patronized by vast majorities of the working population) were jammed into dingy, cramped quarters on the unused stairway landings. Female complaints were dismissed cavalierly even though several women had been frightened or molested by rapacious public freaks who crept up the abandoned stairwell. The enraged women got together and organized a pee-in in the men's bathrooms until their class status was upgraded and the bathrooms were switched.

Some companies are just plain scared as women edge closer and closer to a highly prized male status symbol—"the key to the executive bathroom." One of the few women who arrived at this eminence insisted on her executive token and demanded her status key. She promptly ordered the sign changed from "Men" to "Executives." Every so often she pretends to use her key (of course she's the first and only woman to collect this rank emblem) just to see what male executive comes bounding out of his office to "check if it's clear." Privately she admits to gleeful friends that she'd never really use it. "I'll never give up my privilege to use the ladies' room. For one thing, I hear all the juicy gossip that doesn't get on the grapevine, or I hear things before any of the men at my level. But most of all because I'm in a position to help other women. I can get to know women from several departments and keep an eye on the progress of those I admire. Already I've pulled one promising young woman into my department simply from meetings in the bathroom. I'm anticipating the day when the women's bathroom becomes just as powerful a focal point as the men's urinals when it comes to internal political manipulation."

The Queen in the chess set (in case you don't know) can move any number of clear spaces in *any* direction, backward, forward, sideways, or diagonally. A lot of visible status symbols can be collected with that maneuverability.

WOMEN'S APPAREL IS A BADGE OF SERVITUDE

Men's clothing is not unique in assigning attributes to its wearers; women's clothing is historically symbolic, too. As far as I know, no contemporary feminist has researched the subject (no nonfeminist would care), but women who are moving into the male world of work must begin to pay attention to the symbolism of clothing.

Why are men's and women's clothes so different? Why, as a woman, do you wear what you wear? What is your conscious or subconscious motivation each morning as you dress for work? Why not just wear your bathrobe?

The phenomenon of sex differential in wearing apparel intrigued Lawrence Langner, a prodigiously successful businessman who was also an erudite scholar, a popular playwright, and a perceptive social observer. His many-faceted talents led him to the theater where he founded the Theater Guild and the Shakespeare Festival at Stratford, Connecticut. The importance of costumes to theatrical productions and the social significance of costumes impelled him to study the meaning and psychology of clothing throughout history. In 1959 he published his remarkable psycho-history of clothing through the ages, *The Importance of Wearing Clothes* (New York: Hastings House). Several years before the current wave of feminism erupted, his studies led him to the following conclusion about the marked dissimilarity between men's and women's clothes:

> Contrary to established beliefs, the differentiation in clothing between men and women arose from the male's desire to assert superiority over the female and to hold her in his service. This he accomplished through the ages by means of special clothing which hampered or handicapped the female in her movements. Then men prohibited one sex from wearing the clothing of the other, in order to maintain this differentiation.

Langner traced his hypothesis as far back as Spanish Levant rock paintings, circa 10,000 B.C. and followed the evidence through subsequent ages, civilizations, and cultures. He found the primary purpose of women's dress throughout history was to prevent them from running away from their lords and masters. The ancient Chinese bound the feet of growing girls to hopelessly deform the adult woman's feet; African tribes weighted women's legs with up to fifty pounds of "beautifying" nonremovable brass coils or protruding metal disks; in Palestine women's ankles were connected with chains and tinkling bells; Moslems swathed women in heavy, opaque shrouds from head to toe; upper-class women in Venice and Spain had to be assisted by pages when they walked in their gorgeous gowns because of the fashionable chimpanies or stilts attached to their shoes—some as much as a yard high!

The only exception to foot crippling was found among nomadic tribes where women were forced to keep up with their men during the seasonal migrations. In these groups, the women were the beasts of burden, walking with the animals and loaded almost as heavily with household goods. They could walk but could not run far.

In Western societies the ubiquitous hobbling device for women has been skirts, usually accompanied by dysfunctional stilted shoes. Although skirt styles changed over time and in various societies, skirts of all kinds served to encumber women. Skirts that consisted of long robes reaching to or below the ankles hampered movement by entangling the legs in layers of heavy textiles. In more "modern" times straight fitted skirts effectively bound the knees or ankles together to impede free stride and enforce an awkward, staggering gait. Whatever the society, skirts for females were characterized by their impracticality, inefficiency, and uncomfortable designs. Not only walking but sitting, bending, stooping, and climbing were totally enjoined via "female" dress. Utility, comfort, ornamentation, or sexual attraction has nothing to do with why females wear skirts or other distinctively "female" articles of clothing. These garments were invented thousands of years ago by men to label females as dependents and to "keep them in their place." In consequence, "female" apparel carries a universal symbolism of servitude—the badge of subservience.

In contrast the exclusive male clothing in every society where women were constricted consisted of divided garments—trousers or knickerbockers—which permitted free, unrestricted movement while protecting the wearer's extremities. Men exerted superiority over women by laying exclusive claim to clothing which gives the greatest mobility, freedom for action, and self-protection.

At all times, from earliest societies, women were prohibited from wearing the clothing of males—and vice versa. The penalties for breaking the strict laws against transvestitism ("a morbid craving to dress in garments of the opposite sex") were (and are) severe. In Deuteronomy, the Old Testament thundered the "moral" imprecations which many women feel bound by even in the twentieth century. "A woman shall not wear that which pertaineth unto a man, neither shall a man put on a woman's garment."

Despite these savage laws and vicious punishments, women have periodically rebelled against their enforced clothing shackles, especially skirts. Early American feminists of the 1850s took up the issue of women's dress reform. Amelia Bloomer is the best known of the many who took to wearing short skirts or tunics over loose trousers gathered at the ankle. "Bloomers" became the derisive term for any divided skirt or knickerbocker dress. One optimistic feminist, Helen Marie Weber, told the Women's Rights Convention of 1850 in Worcester, Massachusetts that,

"In ten years time male attire will be generally worn by women of most civilized countries." She was at least a hundred years off in her prediction; it has taken until the 1970s for women to dare to flout the age-old inventions of man to keep her inferior and immobile.

There are still corporations that issue edicts to keep women employees in their place by forbidding women to wear slacks or pants suits to work. Such a company policy is telling women employees that they are inferior beings whose only status in the corporate setup is to serve their male masters. The clothing symbolism says: "You have no mobility in this corporation." No woman who understands the significance of corporate status symbolism would be caught dead working for such a company. Displaying a blatant badge of servitude is no way to progress in the male corporate milieu, but that is exactly what "female" dress codes dictated by men set out to accomplish.

Chapter
7

The Compulsion to Perform

Much of the work of traditional organizational behaviorists has one common objective: to increase the performance of employees. Treatments of such topics as motivation, compensation, training, attitudes, leadership, and supervision, to name a few, commonly focus on how more input and hence more output can be induced (some might say squeezed) out of individual workers. More generally it appears that the institutions that socialize young people (that is, our schools, churches, and universities) are in important ways directed to the same outcomes—preparing people who are oriented to performing in modern organizations or who are at least willing to tolerate the discipline of the workplace. Given the number of people who are currently bemoaning the decline of the work ethic, it is tempting to conclude that these efforts are not succeeding.

On the other hand, we are more concerned that these efforts might be too successful. We fear that many individuals are so fully indoctrinated with work values and routines that psychologically they are not free to make reasonable choices about how much work to do, how hard to work, and how central a role to let work play in their lives. The title of this chapter—the compulsion to perform—stems from this concern. The virtues of performing work roles are so deeply ingrained in people and the costs of commitments to work and careers are so little considered, that individuals appear to play work roles compulsively without considering how they might allocate their time and energies in a more fully satisfying manner. The readings in this chapter focus on this compulsion and on some of the costs people pay as a result of the irresistible impulse to perform.

"If I can just finish *this* project/assignment/chore, *then* I will be free to do what I really want to; I can be me; I can be more balanced, and more satisfied!" This may be one of the fundamental laments and myths of the modern world of work. It would seem that the flow and variety of work we face and even seek out is endless. Yet one common assumption we seem to make is that there is relief, free-dom, serenity just over the horizon—as soon as the current overload has been overcome.

In his lyrics for the song, "Satisfied," Richard Marx captures the tension many people feel between wanting to be authentic now and delaying gratification, while working intensively at their jobs. According to Sally Solo, many CEO's seem to want the scales tipped toward working harder. They argue that North American managers have it easy, and increasing global competition will require much more intensive effort in the future, as we see in "Stop Whining and Get Back to Work."

The dilemma such leaders face, however, is that they want their managers to be more balanced in their lives, while redoubling their efforts to perform. The assumption seems to be that somehow, managers will work harder *and* smarter in the future and that they will develop breadth and depth of perspective along the way. Natasha Josefowitz, in her poem, "Can't Do It All," points out the futility of this strategy. In "The Workaholic Generation," Walter Kiechel III captures some of the elation and much of the compulsiveness of this addiction through his inter-views with men and women who discuss their work experiences. Like many others before him, Kiechel raises concerns about the narrowness of the workaholic's life perspective. On the other hand, it is important to realize how much of a sense of purpose and of enthusiasm people can gain from dedicating their lives to work. Ina Yalof describes this feeling of enjoyment and of making a difference in the work-place in "José 'Pepe' Mayorca,"a story told by a chef about his daily activities in a hospital.

One of the important issues in understanding the compulsion to perform is how little freedom we have to stop the process when it operates. Compulsion has internal as well as external sources. In "The Cormorant," we see a metaphor for workers caught in the trap of their greed and in the grip of others who manipulate that need. In "Feeling as Clue," the issue of emotion in the workplace is raised. Author Arlie Russel Hochschild discusses the way emotions can be managed by others so that organizational work can be done. Being taught to control and direct emotions in situations in which one might be provoked might help both workers and the firm. It can also create conditions where sanctions are placed on people so that they lose touch with their own true feelings and are unable to express them in ways that are healthy for them. Peter Waldman shows us that another angle on this compulsion to perform through managed feelings comes from the growing trend to inject "New Age" thinking and techniques into training programs in organiza-tions. In "Motivate or Alienate? Firms Hire Gurus to Change Their 'Cultures' " the problem is shown to lie not necessarily with the "New Age" aspect of this trend but rather in an organizational world where programs are inevitably forced rather than freely chosen. Can individuals really choose to take part in courses and expe-riences designed to *transform* their attitudes and orientations when these pro-grams are mandated by corporate policy?

People who are always busy seem to take themselves and their work very seri-ously. This typically accompanies a compulsion to perform. What such individuals might be missing in life is described rather delightfully in Benjamin Hoff's blend of Taoism and Winnie the Pooh's life published as *The Tao of Pooh*. The excerpt we have chosen is entitled Bisy Backson, which is Pooh language for "I'm busy. I'll be back soon." It captures the frenzy in the life of the overcommitted and compulsively driven workaholic.

The case for a less frantic approach to work, with accompanying positive results at work and play is made by Ann Marie Cunningham in "A Case for Inefficiency." Finally, as a mirror on the effects of compulsive performance, we have included Harry Chapin's haunting lyrics from "Cat's in the Cradle." His words suggest that how we live our work has consequences outside the workplace and that when work consumes us it can lead to irreversible regrets later in life.

Satisfied

Richard Marx

We work our bodies weary to stay alive
There must be more to livin' than nine to five

> Why should we wait for some better time
> There may not even be a tomorrow
> Ain't no sense in losing your mind
> I'm gonna make it worth the ride

Don't you know, I won't give up until
    I'm satisfied
Don't you know, why should I stop until
    I'm satisfied

Ignore the hesitation, that ties your hands
Use your imagination, and take a chance

> I won't let my moment of truth pass me by
> I've gotta make my move now or never
> And if they turn me loose on this town
> They're gonna have to hold me down

"Satisfied" by Richard Marx from *Repeat Offender* (1989) side 1 cut 2. Reprinted by permission of EMI-USA, a division of Capitol Records.

Don't you know, I won't give up until
   I'm satisfied
Don't you know, why should I stop until
   I'm satisfied Yeah

Oh, don't you know, ain't gonna stop until
   we're satisfied
Don't you know, we shouldn't stop until
   we're satisfied

Don't you know, ain't gonna stop until
   I'm satisfied
Don't you know, we won't give up until
   we're satisfied

Stop Whining and Get Back to Work

Sally Solo

You say you're toiling like a galley slave? America's top corporate chiefs think your workweek looks like a picnic compared to what's ahead in the age of global competition.

With U.S. managers working harder than ever, many have got to wonder whether relief is in sight. The answer from their bosses: Forget it. Far from easing up, CEOs overwhelmingly believe that large American companies will have to push executives *even harder* to keep up with global competition. That's the bad news. The good news is that the chiefs also understand that to get more from managers, their jobs must be made more rewarding, with more incentives and greater autonomy.

"Stop Whining and Get Back to Work" by Sally Solo, *Fortune*, March 12, 1990, p. 49. Reprinted by permission of *Fortune* Magazine.

Q Which of the following two statements comes closer to how you feel about the management of large U.S. companies?

A Large U.S. companies will have to push their managers harder if we are to compete successfully with the Japanese and other global competitors 77%
As a result of restructuring and getting leaner, large U.S. companies are pushing managers too hard..9%
Not sure 14%

Q How many hours a week, on average, do you expect a high-level executive in your company to work? How many for a middle manager?

A

	High-level executive	Middle manager
40 hours or less	2%	8%
41–49 hours	1%	21%
50–59 hours	58%	53%
60–69 hours	29%	9%
Not sure	10%	9%
Average	54 hours	49 hours

These are among the findings of the latest *Fortune* 500 CEO Poll. Clark Martire & Bartolomeo, an independent opinion research firm, conducted the survey between January 16 and 25. Some 206 CEOs of *Fortune* 500 and Service 500 companies answered our queries.

The CEOs don't doubt that their managers are already working harder than they used to. Almost two-thirds of those polled say their executive subordinates work longer hours today than ten years ago. They've had to, say the chiefs, because of restructuring and increased competition. Texaco CEO James Kinnear says heads of companies must "set objectives and monitor employee performance—and if that leads to longer hours, then so be it!"

How hard do you have to work for one of these bosses? Real hard. On average, they figure a high-level executive should work about 54 hours a week, and nearly a third of them think such an executive should work over 60 hours a week. Most of them think middle managers should work at least 50 hours a week. If that strikes you as too demanding, don't look for sympathy from these CEOs: They say they put in an average of 61 hours a week.

The chiefs don't foresee mass burnout among managers. Argues Kinnear: "It's self-correcting. People get tired and they go home." Nor does USX chief Charles A. Corry see any cause for alarm. "It always seems you operate in a crisis environment in business," he says. "The pace of management is quicker today, but the essence isn't different from what it was in the 1960s."

Q Are executives in your company working longer hours than ten years ago, shorter hours, or about the same number of hours?

A Longer hours...62%
Shorter hours 2%
About the same...35%
Not sure 1%

To be sure, a few CEOs believe that the pressure has become too intense and has to be lightened. Says David R. Carpenter, CEO of Transamerica Occidental Life Insurance: "We can't beat people into the ground anymore." San Francisco Federal Savings CEO Patrick Price adds, "We must recognize the signs when managers are being pushed too hard and help out with people, systems—whatever it takes."

Although the majority think managers are working harder than before and must work harder still, some also believe, a bit paradoxically, that an executive who spends all day and most of the evening at the office isn't necessarily a boon to the company. "I think it's absurd for business people to be divorced from the community," says John Bryan of Sara Lee. Bryan estimates that he spends 20% of his time on good works, such as serving on the board of the University of Chicago. He requires similar commitments from his executives, even giving them time off from work for community service. He believes the "political and other" skills they acquire can then be applied back at the office.

Winston Wallin, CEO of Medtronics, also encourages altruism in his executives, with a measure of corporate self-interest in mind. "People get so focused on their own business," he says. "Executives who work 80 hours a week are not likely to have the breadth of knowledge they ought to have. Managers are likely to be more creative if they have a little balance in their lives."

So how do you get executives to compete more ferociously than ever—while maintaining balanced lives, of course? There were 206 different ideas about what kind of carrot and stick a company should use as motivation. One, offered only half facetiously by Sara Lee chief Bryan: "Fear as a motivator is pretty powerful these days." Most answers fell into three broad categories: Offer more money, offer more autonomy, and offer a sense of mission.

Fully 83% of the CEOs surveyed say they already give more incentive-based compensation to their managers than they did ten years ago. Asked what they could do to get more out of those executives, a CEO was most likely to say, "Become more incentive-oriented." Corry of USX explains, "It's a stimulating device. You get the manager to believe he can influence his own compensation." USX offers bonuses that may run up to 85% of an executive's base salary. Several CEOs

Q On average, how many hours a week do you devote to your job?

A Under 50 hours 2%
50–59 hours..28%
60–69 hours..45%
70–79 hours..21%
80 hours or more 4%
Average..61 hours

Q Is the amount of incentive-based compensation in your managers' pay packages greater than it was ten years ago, less than it was, or about the same?

A Greater..83%
Less 2%
About the same..12%
Don't know 3%

touted employee stock ownership plans as a good way to give workers a stake in the company's success. "Employees as shareholders are very attractive," adds Bryan. "They have a slightly longer-term outlook."

Increasing the autonomy of managers serves two purposes in the age of the fat-free corporation. First, it means that whole layers of management, and the paperwork that goes with them, can be trimmed. Second, employees who feel trusted by the boss are freer and more willing to do what's best for the company. Says Hasbro CEO Alan G. Hassenfeld: "If you treat people well and they have responsibility and authority, they'll produce. People should be incentivized and excited about what they're doing, and they'll perform well." At PPG Industries "everyone is called a manager because each of us—engineer, truck driver, secretary, etc.—manages an asset or a function," says Chief Executive Vincent Sarni.

The same CEOs who advocate giving underlings a lot of leeway also emphasize the importance of giving them guidance and a reason to do what they do. "I call it the 'all singing the same song' theory," says U.S. Bancorp CEO Roger Breezley. Super Valu Stores CEO Michael Wright says, "People need to feel there's a purpose in their jobs. They need to know they're working for more than a paycheck." Super Valu Stores' purpose, Wright explains, is to help entrepreneurs—the store owners his company services—succeed.

The CEOs endorse another route to working better, one that's easier identified than followed: eliminating work that doesn't really need to be done. Complains Breezley of U.S. Bancorp: "We automate and automate and automate, and the paperwork still grows and grows. We are documented to death." Robert G. Sharp of Keystone Provident Life Insurance argues, "We should be putting people on the critical jobs that need to be either improved or eliminated. Managers should examine all functions on a must-have, not a nice-to-have, basis."

In Japan, when a worker dies from exhaustion, they call it *karoshi*, or "death from overwork." There may still be time to prevent the problem in the U.S. before things get bad enough to name it. But are CEOs interested in tackling the problem?

Q How should large U.S. companies better manage their executives?

A Become more incentive-oriented 27%
Encourage productivity, creativity, innovation, and risk taking 27%
Give them more autonomy and decentralize decision-making 21%
Get them to work smarter, not harder 20%
Recruit and train better-qualified people 13%
Develop a corporate culture or mission, plan for it, and communicate it 10%
Push managers to work harder... 9%
Focus on the long term.. 8%
Encourage better communication 5%

Totals more than 100% due to multiple responses.

Can't Do It All

Natasha Josefowitz

If I do this
I won't get that done
If I do that
this will slip by
If I do both
neither will be perfect.

Not everything worth doing
is worth doing well.

From *Is This Where I Was Going?* by Natasha Josefowitz, 1983. New York: Warner Books. Reprinted by permission.

The Workaholic Generation

Walter Kiechel III

They put in grueling hours, often neglecting their families. They cut
subordinates loose and compete ferociously. But does all this make them
good managers?

A new generation stands on the threshold of leadership in our society: the baby-
boomers, now a long way from babyhood. The oldest among them turn 43 this
year, the youngest, 25. They make up nearly half of America's adult population and
almost 55% of the labor force.

Given their numbers and steady march into middle age, it comes as a shock
how few of the boomers have made it across the threshold so far. Search the upper
ranks of the Bush Administration, for example, and beyond Dan Quayle, no stan-
dard-bearer for his generation, you won't find them—not in the Cabinet, not heading the big agencies. John F. Kennedy became President at 43, Theodore
Roosevelt at 42.

Nor has the torch passed in corporate America. So far fewer than a dozen from
this generation have been plucked from the executive ranks and set atop large
companies. Why not more? They're still too young, the standard response goes.
Maybe, but interviews with more than 40 of them who are corporate managers
suggest other explanations.

In many respects these people are an employer's dream. They work hard,
probably too hard, impelled by both joy and fear; their spouses and children get
short shrift compared with their jobs. As managers, and with remarkable consistency across the group, they espouse values that any progressive organization
would endorse: lots of communication, sharing of responsibility, respect for others'
autonomy. For all the talk about the "me generation," they show surprising loyalty,
though not to the company as much as to a team or project.

They are also thoroughly uncomfortable with much of what has traditionally,
and probably benightedly, been thought of as the leader's role. They don't like
telling others what to do any more than they like being told. As bosses they can be
just as controlling as prior generations—indeed, some experts think boomers are

"The Workaholic Generation" by Walter Kiechel III, *Fortune*, April 10, 1989, p. 50+. Reprinted by
permission of *Fortune* Magazine.

more control minded—but they're sneakier about it. No respecters of hierarchy, they don't want to get to the top just because it's the top. And they are a bit gunshy: Beneath their astonishing articulateness in talking about themselves, beneath their seriousness, leavened by a quick readiness to laugh, one senses at least a mild case of nerves.

In 1956 William H. Whyte, Jr., a *Fortune* writer working from articles he had prepared for the magazine, wrote *The Organization Man,* a celebrated study of the generation of managers then rising to power. The article you are reading revisits some of Whyte's themes, looking this time at today's rising managerial cadre, whose members are most clearly defined by their being part of the baby boom, that grand demographic phenomenon that has shaped their lives and set them apart.

Our sample was by no means scientific. About half the baby-boom managers we talked with were suggested by their employers, big companies such as Ford, Kodak, and Dow Chemical. Most of the others, also employed by large corporations, were proposed proudly by their colleges or business schools. In addition, we interviewed a few successful entrepreneurs—the dream of starting one's own business is ubiquitous among this generation—nearly all of whom came out of big companies. In short, if we erred it was in looking not so much at the average baby-boom manager as at those setting the pace for the rest.

The first thing you must understand about these people, for it colors every aspect of their lives, is how hard they work. Among them a 60-hour week is standard, with many—especially the younger ones, the singles, and the entrepreneurs—reporting 70, 80, even 90 hours on the job each week. The boomer's typical day: In early, at 6:30 or 7 A.M.—for this crew, 8 is latish—before what one of them calls "the normal people" arrive. Use the uninterrupted time for thinking or to catch up on paperwork. At 8:30 or 9 begins the round of meetings, phone conversations, and general managerial interaction that will occupy most of the day. When we asked them what they wanted on their tombstones, among the most common responses was some variant of "Off to another meeting," accompanied by a chuckle.

Toward late afternoon, as the interaction winds down, tackle the paperwork again. Then, if they have children, out the door by 6 or 6:30 for dinner and a spot of play with the kids. By 8:30 or so the children are asleep or off on their own, letting father, and sometimes mother, get in some memo reading or report writing before turning in for five or six hours of sleep. Such labor will also consume a few hours on the weekend. Then there's travel, of course, a couple of nights a week or more. If a manager has responsibilities abroad—more than a half dozen in our sample do, or did have earlier in their careers—he or she may be gone 70% of the time.

Experts confirm the boomers' reports of Stakhanovite schedules. Paul Leinberger, a California management consultant and product of Park Forest, Illinois, the suburb Whyte studied, is writing a book based on interviews with the original organization men and their children, many of whom went into the corporate life. He concludes that what he calls the successor generation work "much, much longer hours" than their fathers did. Sarah Hardesty, co-author of *Success and Betrayal,* a 1986 book on women in corporations, puts it another way: "Everyone I talk to seems to be so busy, rushing, and tired."

Why do they work so hard? Because they love it, they say, often using the words "fun," "creative," and "stimulating" to describe the experience. Says Harriet King, 42, a human resources manager for Dow Chemical in Midland, Michigan: "We need to have another term for it," something other than "work," with its connotations of grudging toil.

Work is also where they perform, as an athlete performs, winning the applause of the crowd. Something like four out of five of the managers we talked with, women as well as men, took part in organized sports while growing up. That experience, perhaps more than any other, shapes the way they think and talk about their work. Each is proud of being competitive. Each wants to be a winner and part of a winning team.

Cathy Jaros grew up competing as a figure skater, Sonja Henie her hero. The drive to perform subsequently propelled Jaros through a 15-year ascent up the marketing ranks at Quaker Oats, then on to the No. 2 job at Tappan Capital Partners, a Chicago firm that seeks to do leveraged buyouts of food companies. Another baby-boom manager, Edward Meagher, 42, a vice president of PepsiCo's Kentucky Fried Chicken operation, describes his motivation: "I want to be the one to carry the ball across the goal line. But if I can't do that, I want to be the coach who calls the play."

What's going on here is more subtle than the old executive locker-room rah-rah. Stanley Rosenberg, a professor of psychiatry at Dartmouth medical school who conducted a long-term study of 500 men in New England, observes: "Their fathers were looking for an occupational situation, a home in the suburbs—there was a strong feeling that those identities out there were what they wanted for themselves. Baby-boomers, by contrast, want an identity nobody ever had before, want to do something extraordinary."

Jelveh Palizban, 30, who blew through the University of Chicago business school and Harris Bank before starting her own import company, makes the point clearly: "It's funny, when the Olympics were on last year, I preferred to see them by myself. I cried through every single event—track, swimming, skiing, skating. I just wish that I could become one of them. I wish I could be a phenomenon."

Baby-boom managers work hard for less pleasant reasons too. A few mentioned a desire for security, but nobody harped on the importance of money—indeed, most seem optimistic, bordering on insouciant, about their financial prospects. But they do feel pressures born of larger economic forces. At Quaker, Jaros rose to be VP for specialty retailing. The only problem: The board decided to sell that division. Joe Robinson, 27, a budget manager at the mortgage subsidiary of First Union Corp. of North Carolina, has already seen the first two companies that employed him restructured, in the second case eliminating his job. Arthur Holden, 35, a marketing director at Baxter International, recounts what happened after the company acquired American Hospital Supply in 1985: "A number of people were let go, and the people left were asked to do a lot more." How can we compete against the Japanese, others ask, unless we work as hard as they do?

Uncertainties of another sort drive at least some in the group. Almost since birth, baby-boomers have been in the thick of major social changes—in child-rearing practices, the role of women, the nature of the family, and many others. They have seen the divorce rate in the U.S., around 150 per 1,000 marriages before

World War II, plateau first at about 250 per 1,000 through most of the Fifties and Sixties, then double to 500 per 1,000 in the mid-1970s, where it has hovered since. Half of all boomer marriages will end in divorce, the Census Bureau calculates; an estimated 60% of all children born today will spend some time growing up in single-parent households.

A few experts maintain that such statistics may understate the disequilibrium registered by the boomers. Lynne McClure, a Arizona consultant and counselor to managers, argues that only recently have we begun to understand the extent, and pervasive influence, of family dysfunction in the U.S., dysfunction in the form not just of divorce, but also of an alcoholic, or abusive, or merely absent parent. Dysfunction may even set someone on the road to the executive suite. Says McClure: "Perfectionism is a common trait among the children of these families—they think, 'If I get perfect enough, maybe Mommy or Daddy will finally help me or stop drinking.' " That perfectionism breeds a drive for achievement.

One doesn't have to carry the argument this far to assert that at least some of the boomers' immersion in work represents an attempt to escape disquietude elsewhere in their lives. If your marriage is breaking up, if you're not quite sure what's expected of you as a parent, if you find yourself living in a city a thousand miles from the small town where you grew up, where do you turn for a measure of stability and support? To your job, of course.

Boomer managers don't volunteer this, but hints come through. Concedes Larry Iwan, 42, who oversees production at five plants of Eaton Corp., a big, diversified manufacturer: "I'm a little insecure, like a number of people"—he might have said everyone—"and my wife says that I put in so much time at work because that's where I get stroked." Others, in talking about their personal lives, mention "long-term relationships" that went bust or troubles in the family as they grew up. A 28-year-old vice president of sales, on the worst thing that ever happened to him: "My father committed suicide when I was 13. I was full of self-pity and needed a lot of attention. But I made a decision that I was not going to let that break me. That's when I really turned to sports. It felt good performing."

In a time of uncertainty and upheaval, whether in the family or society, work also provides perhaps your best chance to create a world exactly as you want it to be. Dr. Wilbert Sykes, a psychiatrist whose New York City firm, TriSource Group, counsels so-called high-performance managers, observes in social scientese: "If your attempt to find structure from the environment is not really working, it becomes more important for you to create that environment. You become much more assertive about choreographing your environment. We're seeing more and more of that."

For all their variety otherwise, the men and women we talked with were remarkably uniform, tending toward boringly predictable, in their answers to one question: "How would you describe your management style, or philosophy of management?" The almost unvarying response: I make sure that my people have the training and resources they need. We sit down and talk about what has to be done, the general direction we want to go in. Then I pretty much give them free rein. If they run into trouble, they can come back to me and we'll renegotiate.

Some also talk about the importance of having the right folks on the team, in a way an echo of another standard refrain among the group: I want to work with a bunch of bright, energetic people. Most admit that you need to be more directive with a person new to the job. A few dwell on the importance of setting boundaries for subordinates. And many of the older ones, in their 40s and occupying positions of significant executive responsibility, say you have to have a vision for the organization, which you communicate to all hands.

So the day long dreamed of by some of us has finally arrived, when the great corporations of America at last embrace a more humane, democratic, and participatory brand of management. Indeed, to hear the boomer managers tell it, that day may have been years ago: Their bosses, certainly the better ones, have treated them just about the same way they treat their subordinates, whom they much prefer to call the other people on the team.

It's not quite that simple, though. Undoubtedly many of the boomers, perhaps all, manage exactly as they say they do. In this they are clearly superior to the do-it-my-way-or-else bosses of yore. But the coming of the new generation does not mean that anger or petulance or rigidity is disappearing from the managerial offices of America. They may simply have gone underground, hidden in the dark underside of the new generation's style of management. For there is an underside—not a tragic or fatal shortcoming, but a few shadows. Chief among them: what can look a lot like an unwillingness to assume responsibility for others.

Take at face value the boomers' description of how they manage and note what's going on and not going on. Nobody gives orders. Nor need the manager be particularly concerned about motivating a subordinate beyond giving him resources and latitude to do the job his way—hence the importance of having those bright, self-starting people on the team. Confides a young bank manager: "I have trouble relating to the tellers sometimes because a lot of them are there because they have to work. I have a hard time with someone who doesn't take pride in his job."

Once an assignment has been negotiated, or to use the boomers' phrase, the other member of the team has made a commitment, it's crisply clear where the blame rests if something goes awry. Says Marnie Quinn, 40, a district sales manager for Ford: "I used to do things for my people because I would try to protect them, but I realized I was doing them a disservice. I was not giving them the opportunity to fail or achieve success, which was something my bosses had always given me." This is a world of independent contractors.

Also a world where getting along with your contemporaries looms large as a value. One can see the boomers' management style as designed to play down any suggestion of obnoxious hierarchy. A common theme among the younger people we interviewed, in discussing how they got on with their bosses, often boomers themselves, was "It feels more like we're equals." Psychiatrist Sykes again: "The baby-boom generation consider their peer bonding one of the most important parts of life"—perhaps because of all the time spent in school and camp. "They feel uncomfortable in organizations hierarchically arranged, and approach things laterally. The prior generation approaches things vertically."

Other experts provide corroboration. In the late 1970s psychologists at AT&T tested a group in their mid-20s on the first rung of the management ladder there and then compared the results with those obtained when a comparable group was tested in the 1950s. The biggest difference: The boomers scored much lower on a measure social scientists call dominance, approximately the willingness to assert oneself and exert power with peers and subordinates.

The experts also note, though, that young managers today are pointedly "results oriented"—"They know they have to make their numbers," as a business school professor put it—and our interviews bore this out. But how to make sure of results while maintaining a participatory style? In part with exhortations not to let the team down, Sykes suggests, "Everybody who manages has to effect control at some point. Baby-boom managers do it by being concerned about what the group wants, by being 'good guys' themselves, and by stressing that 'We're all in this together.' But they can be as focused on making the environment what they want it to be as any authoritarian boss."

Woe betide the team member who fails to use those open lines of communication to keep his boomer boss informed. "I don't mind people going off in their own direction," says a manufacturing man. "What I can't stand is when they don't tell me about it." Or as Teri LeBeau, 39, a business director at Dow Chemical, puts it, "The thing that bothers me most is being blindsided, when somebody changes something at the last minute, goes against the confidence you put in him. I don't like playing games."

For their brand of management to work, the boomers observe, you have to know everyone on the team in considerable detail: what makes him hum, his strengths and weaknesses. They work characteristically hard at this. Dave Murphy, a 37-year-old in charge of Betty Crocker products at General Mills, periodically reviews a deck of nearly 200 photographs he keeps in his desk. They are pictures of his subordinates, with the name of each written on the back.

The participatory style takes a lot of time, another reason boomer managers put in the hours they do. But some have found ways to expedite matters while keeping the lines open. Katherine Hudson, 42, a Kodak vice president, had installed near the entrance of her office an electronic sign that reads Now SERV-ING . . . with a number in lights below, which she can change with the push of a button at her desk across the room. On Wednesday afternoon she holds Deli Day, when any of the 2,000 people in her operation can come, take a number, and wait his or her turn to talk to the boss. "Some of them just want career counseling," she says, "which you can often do in five or ten minutes."

In discussing where their own careers are headed, the boomers display what appears, in some lights, utter self-confidence, and in others an almost eerie lack of concern. Several times we heard variants on the line, "I don't much believe in planning for the future," even from people with several years at the same large company. But then, in the era of restructuring, such planning can seem bootless. Says First Union's Robinson, who was restructured out of his prior job: "I've noticed in job interviews that nobody asks what you plan to be doing five to ten years from now. They only talk about one-year plans."

Not that the boomers don't want to get ahead. They do—the younger ones, especially, will say so out loud—but many seem reluctant to equate success with moving up the ladder. This is partly because, for them, a high executive position doesn't necessarily guarantee that the incumbent is bright, capable, or in any way particularly admirable. Steven Chernys, a 27-year-old banker at Citicorp, explains why he likes to work in a decentralized organization: "I'm not confident that the people who ultimately wield the power are fully qualified to make decisions in isolation . . . I think we're all better off when more people are involved."

This lack of confidence extends to the process by which people are selected for advancement. While most of these folks have moved up steadily, rarely did anyone seem to believe this was because unalloyed merit always wins out. In describing their jobs past or present, many hold up as particularly important those posts "that gave me a lot of exposure to top management." A few of the managers also speak of higher-ups who have taken an interest in them, not as mentors, but rather as backers in a game where everybody looks a bit like an entrepreneur, with careers their enterprises. We asked: "What's the worst thing that could happen to you in business?" The most common response: "Losing my credibility."

So what, or whom, does this leave the boomer managers loyal to? Well, to the team, for starters. Many express real affection for their co-workers, talking about long days put in together or after-hours volleyball games or ski trips they've shared. Some spoke fondly of projects they worked on. And almost all were grateful, if not loyal in the traditional sense, to the provider of all that lovely work, be it the person who hired them for the job, or, yes, even the organization. But will they stay with the company? The answer of Betsy Holden, 33, a group brand manager at Kraft, is representative: "As long as I'm in an environment where I'm learning, enjoying myself, having fun, and contributing to the company, I'll stay there."

But no one voices unqualified loyalty. Ask even 20-year veterans—there are baby-boom managers with that much service with a single employer—about their ties to the company, and they will talk about how its values or management philosophy or agenda is compatible with their own. One, queried on whether he ever thought of starting his own business, said no, he was an "institution man." He conspicuously did not say "company man." No one we talked to used that phrase.

In their private lives, baby-boomers of the managerial cadre are better friends than spouses, lovers, or parents. Says one expert: "They tend to be negligent of personal relationships, except as friends." The problem, inevitably, is time. Or, more precisely, the lack of time away from work for falling in love, sitting and talking with a spouse, or answering a child's questions.

As parents, the men clearly have it easier: Their wives still shoulder most of the burden. We were surprised, frankly, at the number of male managers whose wives didn't have careers of their own. We talked to 18 married men, all but two of whom had children. The wives of only seven had regular jobs, and two of these women worked from their homes. Ozzie-and-Harriet families—he works, she stays home and takes care of the kids—may have dwindled to less than 10% of U.S. households, but not among this group, who can afford a more traditional style of life.

Except that Dad is putting in hours Ozzie never dreamed of. Chuck Boesenberg, 40, spent nine years at IBM, four at Data General, and two at Apple, before leaving recently to join MIPS Computer Systems. His longstanding regime with his wife and two children: "I try to hold from 10 P.M. Friday to 5 A.M. Monday to be home. I mean I can go to the office for a few hours but not be gone gone."

Of the 15 women we talked with, 13 were married—their husbands all had careers, in a few instances at the same company as their wives—and nine had children, all of them age 6 or younger. The mothers among this group are hard hit, putting in something close to the standard boomer-manager workweek, including travel, typically seeing their children an hour and a half in the morning, two in the evening, and on weekends, running a household on the side, and having virtually no time just to themselves. Occasionally, says Kodak's Katherine Hudson, when she and her husband have to go to work unusually early, the babysitter, a woman from down the street, will arrive in her pajamas.

These women say they couldn't work as hard as they do if they didn't feel good about the child care they had arranged. Many note that since becoming mothers they have learned to be more efficient on the job so they can leave to get home. Time is clearly precious to them. One told of taking two hours off at midday to drive her 6-year-old son and some schoolmates to a Valentine skating party. He was surprised and delighted that she brought along a pair of jeans so she could join in the fun. The woman goes on: "When I was driving them back, I told him, 'That was your Valentine present—the time.' "

However tight their schedules may be, most of these men and women, including the mothers, manage to fit in some kind of athletics—workouts at a gym during the week, weekend tennis games, even, in the Midwest, golf. Commonly this is when they get together with friends, whom they have often met through sports. Their friendships are important to them. Cathy Jaros describes the group of seven women she has been part of for a decade: "We would go to lunch every Saturday and to a fat farm in the spring. There's a lot of closeness, a lot of sincerity. We have two mothers now"—Jaros herself married a year and a half ago—"but we still try to stay close."

Many, especially the older boomers, also make time for good works. Not that anybody's out washing the feet of the poor exactly. Their activity almost always consists of service on the boards of nonprofit organizations, often at the suggestion of their employer. As they talk about it, this can sound suspiciously like yuppie networking. Most who say that organized religion plays a part in their lives also say they didn't go back to church or temple until they had children, whom they wanted "to have that experience."

In our interviews two other interests—in some instances rising to the dignity of passions—came up repeatedly. One was in literally creating the environment they wanted, in the form of their homes. Not for these people the uniform-issue suburban house that sheltered Whyte's organization man. No, they will build their own, or at least gut and redo the interior, working with an architect, poring over blueprints, sometimes doing the final detail work themselves. Joe Doody, 36, a marketing executive at Kodak, has moved three times for the company since the birth of his children, triplets, eight years ago. Each time he and his wife have had built from the ground up a new house, not the same house, mind you, but one to their liking. "You don't have to worry about the carpeting clashing with your furniture," he says. "It's just easier this way to get what you want."

Many seem to be crazy about pets too. Asked what she would like on her tombstone, Linda Rawlings, 34, president of the Otis Spunkmeyer cookie dough company, replied: "My husband says it should read 'Where's Greta?'—that's the name of my little Maltese—because I say that every day when I come home. I absolutely adore that dog." Rawlings also has two children, ages 4 and 2.

Boomer managers seem largely content with their lives, even happy about them. In our interviews they had a hard time coming up with any regrets. We asked nearly everyone, "What communities are you a part of, other than your workplace—not where do you live, but what groups do you draw strength from being part of?" The happiest of all were the few not stumped by that question. People like Jim Holmes, 37, a vice president of the Webb Cos., a nationwide real estate outfit. After telling about how he chose to change organizations rather than leave Winston-Salem, where his father and grandfather lived and worked, he talks about his community activities—on the board of his church, as a trustee of his college, and a while back in Indian Dolls, a fathers-and-daughters group. Then he volunteers: "If I found I had only six more months, I could live with it. I've done a number of things in my life."

Few of the people we talked to had done that much summing up. Retirement? The dozen or so who had thought about it mostly said they hoped never to retire completely, but to use that juncture to start up their own business, or maybe get into teaching.

One man had already had the experience. After working as a salesman for a large electronics company, he had gone off on his own as a real estate developer and made enough money to retire in his mid-30s, shortly after his marriage of 13 years broke up. "I made a list of things I was going to do—learn to speak Spanish, become a chess master—but I never did any of that. The first morning I went to the gym, lifted weights, talked to the guys. Then a lunch date, came home, petted the dog, then went out again in the evening. The next morning I went to the gym again, just the same routine all over. I did that every day for a year." He's back at work now, putting in 60-hour weeks.

Thirty years ago Whyte warned that managers could be sacrificing their individualism for a place in the organization. That isn't a threat for this generation. To take the measure of the challenge facing them, you must go back to another age when men haunted by lost certainties raised up the gospel of work. In *Culture and Anarchy*, Matthew Arnold called for less of the social ethic he termed Hebraism, with its overwhelming emphasis on the "obligation of duty, self-control, and work," and for more Hellenism, wherein "*all* the powers which make the beauty and worth of human nature" attain "harmonious expansion." It's a call the boomers could profitably heed.

José "Pepe" Mayorca

Ina Yalof

It's a tiny, overcrowded office, just inside the doorway into the kitchen. The wall of windows overlooks a huge room brought to life by the flurry of busy people in white uniforms. Two chef's hats sit in the corner of the office. A bulletin board on the wall is papered with computer printouts, schedules, and menus. As we talk, people periodically stick their heads in the door to ask him questions. "Tomorrow's fish. What kind will we have?" "Did the new icemaker arrive?" "When does the vegetable truck come?"

He's a short, pleasant man. He comes from Peru. He's been head chef for eight years, the youngest chef the hospital ever had. He's forty-two. "I live with an uncle now. We spend our weekends on a busman's holiday, trying out restaurants all over town. What I found is, my food here is just as good as any good restaurant in New York. And that's the truth."

The kitchen opens officially at three in the morning when my breakfast cooks arrive. They do all the breakfasts for the patients *and* the cafeteria, which opens at six-thirty for breakfast. They do breakfast for two thousand people or more. I used to do that before I became chef. I used to come in at one in the morning. You had to start cracking eggs then. One case of eggs contains thirty dozen eggs, and I got so good at it, I could crack eight cases in less than an hour. That's, let me see . . . two thousand eight hundred eighty eggs, or forty-eight eggs a minute. We broke them into this huge vat and then we'd beat them, strain them, and cook them. We used big paddles to stir the scrambled eggs. I used to make cereal, too. Fifty gallons of oatmeal, which you boil in huge vats. The vats, which are electrically heated, have spigots at the top, which let water in, and drains at the bottom. You fill them with water, cook in them, drain the food when you've finished, wash them, without ever moving them from their spot. You couldn't move them anyway because they're at least four feet high. When we do bacon or sausage for breakfast, you're talking about cooking one hundred pounds of bacon and sixty pounds of sausages.

As head chef, I'm responsible for ordering all the food for both the patients and the cafeteria. Eight thousand meals a day—special diets, kosher meals, you name it. When I get in, the first thing I look at is the census of the patients and see how many are in the house—this hospital can have nearly thirteen hundred pa-

---

"Jose 'Pepe' Mayorca the Chef" by Ina Yalof from *Life and Death, Story of a Hospital*, 1988, pp. 184–186. Reprinted by permission of the publisher.

tients when it's full. So we calculate the patient menus, and see what's going to be served in the cafeteria, and then I order exactly what I need. Sometimes you go a little bit over, but never under. It would cause a lot of problems to be under.

The key to being a chef, no matter where you work, is to like your trade. To like what you're doing. And, I suppose of equal importance is to produce good food. But there are many other things that either make or break it for you. A good chef knows how to motivate his people. If you don't motivate them, you don't get anywhere. I repeat this over and over: Work with your people. My job is supposed to be sitting in this office, managing my staff, and doing paper work. And I do that. But I also go out and work with my staff, usually every day. I work with them, talk to them, understand their problems. I don't just want to be called a chef and wear this tall white thing on my head.

My day is long, but varied and interesting. If I'm not cooking with my staff, I sit down with my butcher and see all the cuts of meat that we need, and the amounts we have to order. I have to discuss the groceries with my steward and storeroom manager. I have to deal with my pot washers regarding sanitation and things like that. The baker is independent. The only time he works with me is when we have a special party.

The chief dieticians propose the menus to the food service director. I get called when those menus are accepted, and then comes my part. I sit down with the new menus and I make all the calculations about how much I'm going to need. The meat is first. We have a meeting with the director and food production manager, the chief dietician, and my head butcher, and I decide how much I'm going to use, the kinds of cuts that I want to use. After I finish with the meats, I have to cover the vegetables. Say they have for lunch fillet of flounder. We produce five hundred seventy-six orders. In order to produce that amount—each portion is about six ounces of flounder—what I order is two hundred fifty pounds of fillet of flounder. The fish comes in ice and water, so you have to order more. Then you have eggplant Parmesan on the menu, too. We use about sixty pounds of eggplant cutlets. Brisket of beef? I order six hundred pounds for one meal. Mashed potatoes—I use about two hundred forty pounds of peeled potatoes.

Cooking is my life. I always make time to cook. I like Italian food, but *real* Italian food. And I like Oriental food. I've thought about opening my own restaurant. I think this is what every chef looks for. But first of all I would have to find the right place. The way that the rents are now, it's very hard. Also, you don't meet too many good cooks anymore. A lot of people get involved in the food business because of the salary and they have free meals, but not because they like it. I have a lot of friends who own restaurants. I visit them. We talk. I walk into the kitchen, and I tell you, it's not what I want.

Working in a hospital is different from working in another large institution. Here you feel you're helping people to recuperate from their illness, or whatever. A lot of people, when they hear you cook for a hospital say, "Oh, that doesn't mean anything. Anybody can cook for a hospital." But that's not true. Especially if you are a proud cook and you like what you're doing. I have a big responsibility here. I run the whole kitchen. If I don't produce, nobody eats.

The Cormorant . . .

R.G. Siu

The second piece of advice is: Observe the cormorant in the fishing fleet. You know how cormorants are used for fishing. The technique involves a man in a rowboat with about half a dozen or so cormorants, each with a ring around its neck. As the bird spots a fish, it dives into the water and unerringly comes up with it. Because of the ring, the larger fish are not swallowed but held in the throat. The fisherman picks up the bird and squeezes out the fish through the mouth. The bird then dives for another and the cycle repeats itself.

To come back to the second piece of advice from the neo-Taoist to the American worker. Observe the cormorant, he would say. Why is it that of all the different animals, the cormorant has been chosen to slave away day and night for the fisherman?

Were the bird not greedy for fish, or not efficient in catching it, or not readily trained, would society have created an industry to exploit the bird? Would the ingenious device of a ring around its neck, and the simple procedure of squeezing the bird's neck to force it to regurgitate the fish have been devised? Of course not.

Greed, talent, and capacity for learning are the basis of exploitation. The more you are able to moderate and/or hide them from society, the greater will be your chances of escaping the fate of the cormorant . . .

It is necessary to remember that the institutions of society are geared to make society prosper, not necessarily to minimize suffering on your part. It is for this reason, among others, that the schools tend to drum into your mind the high desirability of those characteristics that tend to make society prosper—namely, ambition, progress and success. These in turn are to be valued in terms of society's objectives.

All of them gradually but surely increase your greed and make a cormorant out of you.

Feeling As Clue

Arlie Rusel Hochschild

*Men are estranged from one another as each secretly tries to make an
instrument of the other, and in time a full circle is made; one makes
an instrument of himself, and is estranged from It also.*

—C. Wright Mills

One day at Delta's Stewardess Training Center an instructor scanned the twenty-five faces readied for her annual Self-Awareness Class set up by the company in tandem with a refresher course in emergency procedures required by the Federal Aviation Administration. She began: "This is a class on thought processes, actions, and feelings. I believe in it. I have to believe in it, or I couldn't get up here in front of you and be enthusiastic." What she meant was this: "Being a sincere person, I couldn't say one thing to you and believe in another. Take the fact of my sincerity and enthusiasm as testimony to the value of the techniques of emotion management that I'm going to talk about."

Yet, as it became clear, it was precisely by such techniques of emotion management that sincerity itself was achieved. And so, through this hall of mirrors, students were introduced to a topic scarcely mentioned in Initial Training but central to Recurrent Training: stress and one of its main causes—anger at obnoxious passengers.

"What happens," the instructor asked the class, in the manner of a Southern Baptist minister inviting a response from the congregation, "when you become angry?" Answers: Your body becomes tense. Your heart races. You breathe more quickly and get less oxygen. Your adrenalin gets higher.

"What do you do when you get angry?" Answers: Cuss. Want to hit a passenger. Yell in a bucket. Cry. Eat. Smoke a cigarette. Talk to myself. Since all but the last two responses carry a risk of offending passengers and thus losing sales, the discussion was directed to ways that an obnoxious person could be reconceived in an honest but useful way. The passenger demanding constant attention could be conceived as a "victim of fear of flying." A drunk could be reconceived as "just like a child." It was explained why a worker angered by a passenger would do better to avoid seeking sympathy from co-workers.

"Feeling As Clue" by Arlie Rusel Hochschild from *The Managed Heart: Commercialization of Human Feeling*, 1983, pp. 24–34. Berkeley, CA: University of California Press. Reprinted by permission of the publisher.

"How," the instructor asked the class, "do you alleviate anger at an irate?" (An "irate," a noun born of experience, is an angry person.) Answering her own question, she went on:

> I pretend something traumatic has happened in their lives. Once I had an irate that was complaining about me, cursing at me, threatening to get my name and report me to the company. I later found out his son had just died. Now when I meet an irate I think of that man. If you think about the *other* person and why they're so upset, you've taken attention off of yourself and your own frustration. And you won't feel so angry.

If anger erupts despite these preventive tactics, then deep breathing, talking to yourself, reminding yourself that "you don't have to go home with him" were offered as ways to manage emotions. Using these, the worker becomes less prone to cuss, hit, cry, or smoke.

The instructor did not focus on what might have *caused* the worker's anger. When this did come up, the book was opened to the mildest of examples (such as a passenger saying, "Come here, girl!"). Rather, the focus was kept on the worker's response and on ways to prevent an angry response through "anger-desensitization."

After about ten minutes of this lecture one flight attendant in the next to last row began tapping her index finger rapidly on her closed notebook. Her eyes were turned away from the speaker, and she crossed and recrossed her legs abruptly. Then, her elbow on the table, she turned to two workers to her left and whispered aloud, "I'm just livid!"

Recurrent Training classes are required yearly. The fact that a few fellow workers had escaped coming to this one without penalty had come to light only in the last ten minutes of informal talk before class. Flight attendants are required to come to the class from whatever city they are in at the time. The company provides travel passes to training, but it is a well-known source of resentment that after training, workers are often bumped from home-bound flights in favor of paying passengers. "Last time," the livid one said, "it took me two days to get home from Recurrent, and all just for *this*."

Addressing a rustling in the group and apparently no one in particular, the instructor said:

> Now a lot of flight attendants resent having to commute to Recurrent. It's a bother getting here and a heck of a bother getting back. And some people get angry with me because of that. And because that's not my fault and because I put work into my classes, I get angry back. But then I get tired of being angry. Do you ever get tired of being angry? Well, one time I had a flight attendant who sat in the back of my class and snickered the whole time I was teaching. But you know what I did? I thought to myself, "She has full lips, and I've always believed people with full lips are compassionate." When I thought that, I wasn't so angry.

By reminding the class that ease in using company passes, like the overall plan of Recurrent Training, was out of her hands, and by putting herself in the role of a flight attendant and her listeners in the role of an angry passenger, she hoped to show how she removed *her* anger. In fact, she also reduced the anger in the class; like the back-seat snickerer, the finger-drummer relented. The right to anger withered on the vine. There was an unfolding of legs and arms, a flowering of comments, the class relaxer came forth with a joke, and the instructor's enthusiasm rose again along the path readied for it.

FEELING AS SUSCEPTIBLE TO PREVENTIVE TACTICS

To consider just how a company or any other organization might benignly intervene in a work situation between the stimulus and the response, we had best start by rethinking what an emotion or a feeling is. Many theorists have seen emotion as a sealed biological event, something that external stimuli can bring on, as cold weather brings on a cold. Furthermore, once emotion—which the psychologist Paul Ekman calls a "biological response syndrome"—is operating, the individual passively undergoes it. Charles Darwin, William James, and the early Freud largely share this "organismic" conception. But it seems to me a limited view. For if we conceive of emotion as only this, what are we to make of the many ways in which flight attendants in Recurrent Training are taught to attend to stimuli and manage emotion, ways that can actually *change* feeling?

If we conceive of feeling not as a periodic abdication to biology but as something we *do* by attending to inner sensation in a given way, by defining situations in a given way, by managing in given ways, then it becomes plainer just how plastic and susceptible to reshaping techniques a feeling can be. The very act of managing emotion can be seen as part of what the emotion becomes. But this idea gets lost if we assume, as the organismic theorists do, that how we manage or express feeling is *extrinsic* to emotion. The organismic theorists want to explain how emotion is "motored by instinct," and so they by-pass the question of how we come to assess, label, and manage emotion. The emotion signals danger. But every emotion does signal the "me" I put into seeing "you." It signals the often unconscious perspective we apply when we go about seeing. Feeling signals that inner perspective. Thus, to suggest helpful techniques for changing feeling—in the service of avoiding stress on the worker and making life pleasanter for the passenger—is to intervene in the signal function of feeling.

This simple point is obscured whenever we apply the belief that emotion is dangerous in the first place because it distorts perception and leads people to act irrationally—which means that all ways of reducing emotion are automatically good. Of course, a person gripped by fear may make mistakes, may find reflection difficult, and may not (as we say) be able to think. But a person totally without emotion has no warning system, no guidelines to the self-relevance of a sight, a memory, or a fantasy. Like one who cannot feel and touches fire, an emotionless person suffers a sense of arbitrariness, which from the point of view of his or her self-interest is irrational. In fact, emotion is a potential avenue to "the reasonable view."° Furthermore, it can tell us about a way of seeing.†

Emotion locates the position of the viewer. It uncovers an often unconscious perspective, a comparison. "You look tall" may mean "From where I lie on the floor, you look tall." "I feel awe" may mean "compared with what I do or think I could do, he is awesome." Awe, love, anger, and envy tell of a self vis-à-vis a situation. When we reflect on feeling we reflect on this sense of "from where I am."

The word *objective,* according to the *Random House Dictionary,* means "free from personal feelings." Yet ironically, we need feeling in order to reflect on the external or "objective" world. Taking feelings into account as clues and then correcting for them may be our best shot at objectivity. Like hearing or seeing, feeling provides a useful set of clues in figuring out what is real. A show of feeling by someone else is interesting to us precisely because it may reflect a buried perspective and may offer a clue as to how that person may act.

In public life, expressions of feeling often make news. For example, a TV sports newscaster noted: "Tennis has passed the stage of trying to survive as a commercial sport. We're beyond that now. The women's tennis teams, too. The women are really serious players. They get really mad if they hit a net ball. They get even madder than the guys, I'd say." He had seen a woman tennis player miss a shot (it was a net ball), redden in the face, stamp her foot, and spank the net with her racket. From this he inferred that that woman "really wants to win." Wanting to win, she is a "serious" player—a pro. Being a pro, she can be expected to see the tennis match as something on which her professional reputation and financial future depend. Further, from the way she broke an ordinary field of calm with a brief display of anger, the commentator inferred that she really meant it—she was "serious." He also inferred what she must have wanted and expected just before the net ball and what the newly grasped reality—a miss—must have felt like. He tried to pick out what part of *her* went into seeing the *ball.* A miss, if you really want to win, is maddening.

From the commentator's words and tone, TV viewers could infer *his* point of view. He assessed the woman's anger in relation to a prior expectation about how pros in general see, feel, and act and about how women in general act. Women tennis pros, he implied, do not laugh apologetically at a miss, as a nonprofessional woman player might. They feel, he said, in a way that is *appropriate to the role* of a

---

°We may misinterpret an event, feel accordingly, and then draw false conclusions from what we feel. (We sometimes call this neurosis.) We can handle this by applying a secondary framework that corrects habits of feeling and inference, as when we say "I know I have a tendency to interpret certain gestures as rejections." But feeling is the essential clue that a certain viewpoint, even though it may need frequent adjustment, is alive and well.

†A black person may see the deprivations of the ghetto more accurately, more "rationally," through indignation and anger than through obedience or resigned "realism." He will focus clearly on the policeman's bloodied club, the landlord's Cadillac, the look of disapproval on the employment agent's white face. Outside of anger, these images become like boulders on a mountainside, minuscule parts of the landscape. Likewise, a chronically morose person who falls in love may suddenly see the world as happier people do.

professional player. In fact, as newcomers they overconform. "They get *even madder* than the guys." Thus the viewers can ferret out the sportscaster's mental set and the role of women in it.

In the same way that we infer other people's viewpoints from how they display feeling, we decide what we ourselves are really like by reflecting on how we feel about ordinary events. Consider, for example, this statement by a young man of nineteen:

> I had agreed to give a party with a young woman who was an old friend. As the time approached, it became apparent to me that, while I liked her, I didn't want the [social] identification with her that such an action [the jointly sponsored party] would bring. . . . I tried explaining this to her without success, and at first I resolved to do the socially acceptable thing—go through with it. But the day before the party, I knew I simply couldn't do it, so I canceled out. My friend didn't understand and was placed in a very embarrassing position. . . . I can't feel ashamed no matter how hard I try. All I felt then was relief, and this is still my dominant response. . . . I acted selfishly, but fully consciously. I *imagine that my friendship could not have meant that much.*

The young man reached his conclusion by *reasoning back from his absence of guilt or shame,* from the feeling of relief he experienced. (He might also have concluded: "I've shown myself to be the sort of fellow who can feel square with himself in cases of unmet obligation. I can withstand the guilt. It's enough for me that I *tried* to feel shame.")

For the sportscaster and the young man, feeling was taken as a signal. To observer and actor alike it was a clue to an underlying truth, a truth that had to be dug out or inferred, a truth about the self vis-à-vis a situation. The sportscaster took the anger of the woman tennis player as a clue to how seriously she took the game of tennis. The young man who backed out on his friend took his sense of relief and absence of guilty feelings as a clue to the absence of seriousness in his "old friendship."

Feeling can be used to give a clue to the operating truth, but in private life as well as on the job, two complications can arise. The first one lies between the clue of feeling and the interpretation of it. We are capable of disguising what we feel, of pretending to feel what we do not—of doing surface acting. The box of clues is hidden, but it is not changed. The second complication emerges in a more fundamental relation between stimulus and response, between a net ball and feeling frustration, between letting someone down and feeling guilty, between being called names by an "irate" and getting angry back. Here the clues can be dissolved by deep acting, which from one point of view involves deceiving oneself as much as deceiving others. In surface acting we deceive others about what we really feel, but we do not deceive ourselves. Diplomats and actors do this best, and very small children do it worst (it is part of their charm).

In deep acting we make feigning easy by making it unnecessary. At Delta, the techniques of deep acting are joined to the principles of social engineering. Can a flight attendant suppress her anger at a passenger who insults her? Delta Airlines can teach her how—if she is qualified for the job by a demonstrably friendly disposition to start with. She may have lost for awhile the sense of what she *would have* felt had she not been trying so hard to feel something else. By taking over the levers of feeling production, by pretending deeply, she alters herself.

Deep acting has always had the edge over simple pretending in its power to convince, as any good Recurrent Training instructor knows. In jobs that require dealing with the public, employers are wise to want workers to be sincere, to go well beyond the smile that's "just painted on." Gregg Snazelle, who directed all the commercials for Toyota's fall 1980 campaign, teaches his advertising students in the first class "to always be honest." Behind the most effective display is the feeling that fits it, and that feeling can be managed.

As workers, the more seriously social engineering affects our behavior and our feelings, the more intensely we must address a new ambiguity about who is direct- ing them (is this me or the company talking?). As customers, the greater our awareness of social engineering, the more effort we put into distinguishing be- tween gestures of real personal feeling and gestures of company policy. We have a practical knowledge of the commercial takeover of the signal function of feeling. In a routine way, we make up for it; at either end, as worker or customer, we try to correct for the social engineering of feeling.* We mentally subtract feeling with commercial purpose to it from the total pattern of display that we sense to be sincerely felt. In interpreting a smile, we try to take out what social engineering put in, pocketing only what seems meant just for us. We say, "It's her job to be friend- ly," or "They have to believe in their product like that in order to sell it."

In the end, it seems, we make up an idea of our "real self," an inner jewel that remains our unique possession no matter whose billboard is on our back or whose smile is on our face. We push this "real self" further inside, making it more inac- cessible. Subtracting credibility from the parts of our emotional machinery that are in commercial hands, we turn to what is left to find out who we "really are." And around the surface of our human character, where once we were naked, we don a cloak to protect us against the commercial elements.

---

*It is not only in the world of commerce that we automatically assume insincerity. Political reporters regularly state not only what an officeholder or candidate wants to seem to feel but also how well he or she succeeds in the effort to convey that feeling. Readers, it is assumed, demand at least this much unveiling.

Motivate or Alienate? Firms Hire Gurus to Change Their 'Cultures'

Peter Waldman

In Atlanta, clerical workers for Pacific Mutual Life Insurance Co. search their memories for a time when they felt "victimized." Trainers then ask them how they could have avoided that feeling by being more "accountable" for their actions. Later, with Dionne Warwick singing "What the World Needs Now" in the background, the trainers pass out red carnations in an expression of corporate love.

In Van Nuys, Calif., auto workers attend special retraining courses to help them gain "a greater measure of dignity, self-fulfillment and self-worth" from their labors, as one manual puts it. At one of the seminars, the General Motors Corp. employees study "Possibility Thinking"—how to overcome "cultural trances" and "flat-world barriers" that hinder performance.

Abuzz with buzzwords, corporate America has launched one of the most concerted efforts ever to change the attitudes and values of workers. Dozens of major U.S. companies—including Ford Motor Co., Procter & Gamble Co., TRW Inc., Polaroid Corp. and Pacific Telesis Group Inc.—are spending millions of dollars on so-called New Age workshops. The training is designed to foster such feelings as teamwork, company loyalty and self-esteem.

Mixed Reactions

Workers, however, have had decidedly mixed reactions to the attitudinal training, creating, in many companies, bitter conflicts between employees who embrace the new concepts and those who don't. Younger employees, especially, are more apt to praise the sessions for addressing productivity problems and for attempting to make jobs more meaningful. But many older employees say the seminars—and management—are simply paying lip service to serious concerns in the workplace.

Although the efforts to transform corporate "cultures" vary widely among companies, many of the programs draw heavily from motivational themes popularized by entrepreneurs like L. Ron Hubbard and Werner Erhard. Indeed, most of the programs share a common, simple goal: to increase productivity by converting worker apathy into corporate allegiance.

In Pacific Mutual's voluntary "Leadership Alignment" course, for example, trainers lead employees through two days of role playing and discussions to encourage them to take more responsibility for their actions. At one point, employees divide themselves according to personality types and act out roles of "promoters," "supporters" and "analysts." The exercise attempts to show how different behaviors can help or hinder productivity.

These workshops and others, consultants say, represent efforts to move away from traditional corporate structures—where managers often make decisions with little input from subordinates—toward a more collegial atmosphere. To survive, companies must emulate Japanese management styles and harness the full mental and physical talents of their workers, say these consultants.

"There's a new ideology of management emerging" at some companies, says Robert Howard, a Cambridge, Mass. based author and labor consultant. "In which the corporation is a mother-like institution that maintains family interaction and a warm home."

The attitudinal training appears to work best at companies that combine words with actions. Tektronix Inc., based in Beaverton, Ore., uses "People involvement" workshops to expose employees to new management practices already in use in some of its plants. Employees describe for their colleagues how they work in teams, schedule their own hours, evaluate each other for raises and even communicate directly with customers and suppliers when problems arise. Many Tektronix employees praise the participative system's effects on both morale and production.

At other companies, however, workers often complain that the seminars and exercises they attend are the first and last time they hear about improvements on the job; once the training ends, so does management's commitment to change. "Unfortunately, most of the so-called transformation work today is really just a substitute for giving workers real autonomy and responsibility," says Harley Shalken, professor of work and technology at the University of California at San Diego. "It's too bad because efforts at manipulation today will only create resistance to more legitimate reorganization tomorrow."

Such resistance was visible at Pacific Mutual's Atlanta claims office. Shortly after holding its "Leadership Alignment" seminar there, the company raised work quotas nearly 20%, says Edna Lee, a former claims examiner in the office. When Ms. Lee complained about the work increase, she recalls, her manager warned her that the new quotas were a "gravity issue"—a Leadership Alignment term describing uncontestable management decisions. Ms. Lee persisted in objecting until the company fired her, she says.

"Leadership Alignment was actually an attempt to blindfold us and redirect our energies away from real concerns like being overworked and having our benefits reduced," Ms. Lee maintains.

A Pacific Mutual spokesman says Ms. Lee was fired for "complex reasons" that he wouldn't discuss but which he says were validated in a National Labor Relations Board ruling in the case. Brian Seaman, the Pacific Mutual trainer who designed the Leadership Alignment course, says the training merely stresses "common-sense principles the employees can use on the job." He says the sessions helped the company save "a few million dollars" by boosting office morale and production and by helping cut worker turnover.

At GM's Chevrolet-Pontiac-Canada plant in Van Nuys, some 4,700 workers attended seven days of seminars this spring on such subjects as "Coping with Change" and "Listening Skills." The courses are part of GM's new Team Concept: a Japanese-style management system in which workers are stripped of traditional job classifications and given added responsibilities for quality and maintenance.

The training consisted of lectures and exercises meant to engender a new sense of labor-management partnership at the historically fractious plant. In one session on conflict resolution, workers learned different "strategies" for reacting to disagreements with other people. Illustrating their points, instructors mentioned the "withdrawing" turtle, the "smoothing" Teddy Bear and—wisest of all—the "problem-solving" owl. "Owls highly value their own goals and relationships," says the course's training manual.

Opening a Rift

But rather than creating a spirit of cooperation, the training seminars—and Team Concept itself—have opened a rift at the GM plant between supporters and opponents of the new program.

Some workers have taken to the new system with renewed enthusiasm for their jobs, going so far as to barrage management with daily suggestions on how to improve production. But others, many with at least 10 years seniority, charge that Team Concept is GM's attempt to break the workers' union. These critics claim that GM's instructors intentionally confused them with hours of vague advice on interpersonal relations while ducking questions about Team Concept's effect on work conditions.

"In the end, they offered Team Concept as a panacea: 'Give up your union rights and everything will be OK.' " says Paul Goldener, a 30-year veteran of the plant and a leading critic of the changes. "They're pitting brother against brother in a deliberate attempt to break the union."

Jim Gaunt, GM's director of personnel at Van Nuys, denies that GM wants to disrupt the union. In fact, he says, Team Concept may have strengthened the union; the program's inception has encouraged the company to recall a second shift of unionized workers. He adds that the training sessions weren't attempts at brainwashing but a sincere effort to refocus employees' attention on quality and cooperation.

"Our whole thrust was trying to create an attitude that change was a necessary element for our long-term viability," he says.

Similarly, Pacific Bell, in the wake of its divestiture from American Telephone & Telegraph Co., decided it needed to transform its traditional, "compliant" culture, as one spokesman describes it, into a less hierarchical, more entrepreneurial one. So the unit of San Francisco-based Pacific Telesis began a series of quarterly, two-day training seminars for its 67,000 workers to give them a common purpose and common approach to their work.

To foster greater creativity, for example, trainers discussed different "levels" of thought, energy and behavior. (In ascending order, the six levels of energy were defined as automatic, sensitive, conscious, creative, unitive and transcendent.) That session, loosely based on the teachings of G.I. Gurdjieff, an early 20th century Russian mystic, was supposed to inspire more analytical thinking among employees. In it, workers broke into groups to discuss issues like the difference between "knowledge" and "understanding."

A 'Hollow Program'

But for many employees, that session and others inspired only anger. Shortly after the program began, workers were quoted in articles about the training in local newspapers as saying that the workshops smacked of mind control, Eastern mysticism and coercion.

"Dissenters are referred to as 'roadblocks' or having 'Bell-Shaped Heads' " by supporters of the training, wrote one company employee, in response to a California Public Utilities Commission survey on the sessions. "In trying to be modern," wrote another, "I feel the company bought a hollow, intentionally cloudy program" from outside consultants.

In June, the utilities commission staff, on the basis of these and other comments, issued a sharply critical report on the program, concluding that ratepayers shouldn't bear the training's costs. The phone company suspended the workshops.

But Pacific Bell still maintains that the program is effective in providing employees with common "frameworks" and vocabulary for communicating with each other. "Having common tools and approaches saves an enormous amount of time," says Carol Westphal, a spokeswoman, "We continue to believe that the positives outweigh the negatives."

Bisy Backson*

Benjamin Hoff

Rabbit hurried on by the edge of the Hundred Acre Wood, feeling more important every minute, and soon he came to the tree where Christopher Robin lived. He knocked at the door, and he called out once or twice, and then he walked back a little way and put his paw up to keep the sun out, and called to the top of the tree, and then he turned all round and shouted "Hallo!" and "I say!" "It's Rabbit!"—but nothing happened. Then he stopped and listened, and everything stopped and listened with him, and the Forest was very lone and still and peaceful in the sunshine, until suddenly a hundred miles above him a lark began to sing.

"Bother!" said Rabbit. "He's gone out."

He went back to the green front door, just to make sure, and he was turning away, feeling that his morning had got all spoilt, when he saw a piece of paper on the ground. And there was a pin in it, as if it had fallen off the door.

"Ha!" said Rabbit, feeling quite happy again. "Another notice!"

This is what it said:

> GON OUT
> BACKSON
> BISY
> BACKSON.
> C.R.

Rabbit didn't know what a Backson was—in spite of the fact that he is one—so he went to ask Owl. Owl didn't know, either. But we think *we* know, and we think a lot of other people do, too. Chuang-tse described one quite accurately:

> There was a man who disliked seeing his footprints and his shadow. He decided to escape from them, and began to run. But as he ran along, more footprints appeared, while his shadow easily kept up with him. Thinking he was going too slowly, he ran faster and faster without stopping, until he finally collapsed from exhaustion and died.
>
> If he had stood still, there would have been no footprints. If he had rested in the shade, his shadow would have disappeared.

You see them almost everywhere you go, it seems. On practically any sunny sort of day, you can see the Backsons stampeding through the park, making all kinds of loud Breathing Noises. Perhaps you are enjoying a picnic on the grass

*Editor's note: "Bisy Backson" is Winnie the Pooh language for "I'm busy. I'll be back soon!"

From *The Tao of Pooh* by Benjamin Hoff. Copyright © 1982 by Benjamin Hoff. Used by permission of the publisher, Dutton, an imprint of New American Library, a division of Penguin Books USA Inc.

when you suddenly look up to find that one or two of them just ran over your lunch.

Generally, though, you are safe around trees and grass, as Backsons tend to avoid them. They prefer instead to struggle along on asphalt and concrete, in imitation of the short-lived transportation machines for which those hard surfaces were designed. Inhaling poisonous exhaust fumes from the vehicles that swerve to avoid hitting them, the Backsons blabber away to each other about how much better they feel now that they have gotten Outdoors. Natural living, they call it.

The Bisy Backson is almost desperately active. If you ask him what his Life Interests are, he will give you a list of Physical Activities, such as:

"Skydiving, tennis, jogging, racquet-ball, skiing, swimming, and water-skiing."

"Is that all?"

"Well, I (gasp, pant, wheeze) *think* so," says Backson.

"Have you ever tried chasing cars?"

"No, I—no, I never have."

"How about wrestling alligators?"

"No . . . I always wanted to, though."

"Roller-skating down a flight of stairs?"

"No, I never thought of it."

"But you said you were *active*."

At this point, the Backson replies, thoughtfully, "Say—do you think there's something . . . *wrong* with me? Maybe I'm losing my energy."

After a while, maybe.

The Athletic sort of Backson—one of the many common varieties—is concerned with physical fitness, he says. But for some reason, he sees it as something that has to be pounded in from the outside, rather than built up from the inside. Therefore, he confuses exercise with *work*. He works when he works, works when he exercises, and, more often than not, works when he plays. Work, work, work. All work and no play makes Backson a dull boy, Kept up for long enough, it makes him dead, too.

Where'd he go? That's how it is, you know—no rest for the Backson.

Let's put it this way: if you want to be healthy, relaxed, and contented, just watch what a Bisy Backson does and then do the opposite. There's one now, pacing back and forth, jingling the loose coins in his pocket, nervously glancing at his watch. He makes you feel tired just looking at him. The chronic Backson always seems to have to be *going* somewhere, at least on a superficial, physical level. He doesn't go out for a *walk*, though; he doesn't have time.

> "Not conversing," said Eeyore. "Not first one and then the other. You said 'Hallo' and Flashed Past. I saw your tail in the distance as I was meditating my reply. I had thought of saying 'What?'—but, of course, it was then too late."
>
> "Well, I was in a hurry."
>
> "No Give and Take," Eeyore went on. "No Exchange of Thought: 'Hallo— What'—I mean, it gets you nowhere, particularly if the other person's tail is only just in sight for the second half of the conversation."

The Bisy Backson is always On The Run, it seems, always:

GONE OUT
BACK SOON
BUSY
BACK SOON

or, more accurately:

BACK OUT
GONE SOON
BUSY
GONE SOON

The Bisy Backson is always going *somewhere,* somewhere he hasn't been. Anywhere but where he is.

"That's just it," said Rabbit, "Where?"
"Perhaps he's looking for something."
"What?" asked Rabbit.
"That's just what I was going to say," said Pooh. And then he added, "Perhaps he's looking for a—for a—"

For a Reward, perhaps. Our Bisy Backson religions, sciences, and business ethics have tried their hardest to convince us that there is a Great Reward waiting for us somewhere, and that what we have to do is spend our lives working like lunatics to catch up with it. Whether it's up in the sky, behind the next molecule, or in the executive suite, it's somehow always farther along than we are—just down the road, on the other side of the world, past the moon, beyond the stars. . . .

"Ouch!" said Pooh, landing on the floor.
"That's what happens when you go to sleep on the edge of the writing table," I said. "You fall off."
"Just as well," said Pooh.
"Why's that?" I asked.
"I was having an awful dream," he said.
"Oh?"
"Yes. I'd found a jar of honey . . .," he said, rubbing his eyes.
"What's awful about that?" I asked.
"It kept moving," said Pooh. "They're not supposed to do that. They're *supposed* to sit still."
"Yes, I know."
"But whenever I reached for it, this jar of honey would sort of go someplace else."
"A nightmare," I said.
"Lots of people have dreams like that," I added reassuringly.
"Oh," said Pooh. "About Unreachable jars of honey?"
"About the same sort of thing," I said. "That's not unusual. The odd thing, though, is that some people *live* like that."
"Why?" asked Pooh.
"I don't know," I said. "I suppose because it gives them Something to Do."
"It doesn't sound like much fun to me," said Pooh.

No, it doesn't. A way of life that keeps saying, "Around the next corner, above the next step," works against the natural order of things and makes it so difficult to be happy and good that only a few get to where they would naturally have been in the first place—Happy and Good—and the rest give up and fall by the side of the road, cursing the world, which is not to blame but which is there to help show the way.

Those who think that the rewarding things in life are somewhere beyond the rainbow—

"Burn their toast a lot," said Pooh.

"I beg your pardon?"

"They burn their toast a lot," said Pooh.

"They—well, yes. And not only that—"

"Here comes Rabbit," said Pooh.

"Oh, there you are," said Rabbit.

"Here we are," said Pooh.

"Yes, here we are," I said.

"And there *you* are," said Pooh.

"Yes, here I am," said Rabbit impatiently. "To come to the point—Roo showed me his set of blocks. They're all carved and painted with letters on them."

"Oh?" I said.

"Just the sort of thing you'd *expect* to see, actually," said Rabbit, stroking his whiskers thoughtfully. "So by process of elimination," he said, "that means *Eeyore* has it."

"But Rabbit," I said. "You see—"

"Yes," said Rabbit. "I see Eeyore and find out what he knows about it—that's clearly the next step."

"There he goes," said Pooh.

Looking back a few years, we see that the first Bisy Backsons in this part of the world, the Puritans, practically worked themselves to death in the fields without getting much of anything in return for their tremendous efforts. They were actually starving until the wiser inhabitants of the land showed them a few things about working in harmony with the earth's rhythms. Now you plant; now you relax. Now you work the soil; now you leave it alone. The Puritans never really understood the second half, never really believed in it. And so, after two or three centuries of pushing, pushing, and pushing the once-fertile earth, and a few years of depleting its energy still further with synthetic stimulants, we have apples that taste like cardboard, oranges that taste like tennis balls, and pears that taste like sweetened Styrofoam, all products of soil that is not allowed to relax. We're not supposed to complain, but There It Is.

"Say, Pooh, why aren't you busy?" I said.

"Because it's a nice day," said Pooh

"Yes, but—"

"Why ruin it?" he said.

"But you could be doing something Important," I said.

"I am," said Pooh.

"Oh? Doing what?"

"Listening," he said.

"Listening to what?"

"To the birds. And that squirrel over there."

"What are they saying?" I asked.

"That it's a nice day," said Pooh.

"But you know that already," I said.

"Yes, but it's always good to hear that somebody else thinks so, too," he replied.

"Well, you could be spending your time getting Educated by listening to the Radio, instead," I said.

"That thing?"

"Certainly. How else will you know what's going on in the world?" I said.

"By going outside," said Pooh.

"Er . . well. . . ." (Click.) "Now just listen to this, Pooh."

"Thirty thousand people were killed today when five jumbo airliners collided over downtown Los Angeles . . .," the Radio announced.

"What does that tell you about the world?" asked Pooh.

"Hmm. You're right." (Click.)

"What are the birds saying now?" I asked.

"That it's a nice day," said Pooh.

It certainly is, even if the Backsons *are* too busy to enjoy it. But to conclude our explanation of why so busy . . .

The hardheaded followers of the previously mentioned Party-Crashing Busybody religion failed to appreciate the beauty of the endless forest and clear waters that appeared before them on this fresh green continent of the New World. Instead, they saw the paradise that was here and the people who lived in harmony with it as alien and threatening, something to attack and conquer—because it all stood in the way of the Great Reward. They didn't like singing very much, either. In fact—

"What?" said Pooh. "No singing?"

"Pooh, I'm trying to finish this. That's right, though. No singing. They didn't like it."

"Well, if they didn't like singing, then what was their attitude towards Bears?"

"I don't think they liked Bears, either."

"They didn't like *Bears?*"

"No. Not very much, anyway."

"No singing, no Bears. . . . Just what *did* they like?"

"I don't think they liked *anything*, Pooh."

"No wonder things are a little Confused around here," he said.

Anyway, from the Miserable Puritan came the Restless Pioneer, and from him, the Lonely Cowboy, always riding off into the sunset, looking for something just down the trail. From this rootless, dissatisfied ancestry has come the Bisy Backson, who, like his forefathers, has never really felt at home, at peace, with this Friendly Land. Rigid, combative fanatic that he is, the tightfisted Backson is just too hard on himself, too hard on others, and too hard on the world that heroically attempts to carry on in spite of what he is doing to it.

It's not surprising, therefore, that the Backson thinks of progress in terms of fighting and overcoming. One of his little idiosyncrasies, you might say. Of course, *real* progress involves growing and developing, which involves changing inside, but that's something the inflexible Backson is unwilling to do. The urge to grow and develop, present in all forms of life, becomes perverted in the Bisy Backson's mind into a constant struggle to change everything (the Bulldozer Backson) and everyone (the Bigoted Backson) else *but* himself, and interfere with things he has no business interfering with, including practically every form of life on earth. At least to a limited extent, his behavior has been held in check by wiser people around him. But, like parents of hyperactive children, the wise find that they can't be everywhere at once. Baby-sitting the Backsons wears you out.

> "Here's Rabbit again," said Pooh. "And Eeyore."
> "Oh—Rabbit," I said.
> "*And* Eeyore," said Eeyore.
> "I asked Eeyore—," said Rabbit.
> "That's me," said Eeyore. "Eeyore."
> "Yes, I remember," I said. "I saw you just last year, out in the Swamp somewhere."
> "*Swamp?*" said Eeyore indignantly. "It's not a Swamp. It's a *Bog.*"
> "Swamp, Bog. . . ."
> "What's a Bog?" asked Pooh.
> "If your ankles get wet, that's a Bog," said Eeyore.
> "I see," said Pooh.
> "Whereas," continued Eeyore, "if you sink in up to your *neck,* that's a Swamp."
> "Swamp, indeed," he added bitterly. "Ha!"
> "Anyway, I asked Eeyore," said Rabbit, "and he said he didn't have the slightest idea what I was talking about."
> "It appears that I'm not alone in that," put in Eeyore. "You don't have the slightest idea, either. Obviously."
> "Just what *is* the Uncarved Block?" asked Rabbit.
> "It's me," said Pooh.
> "*You?*" said Eeyore. "I came all the way over here—"
> "From the Swamp," I added helpfully.
> "—from the Bog, to see *Pooh?*"
> "Why not?" asked Pooh.
> "Anything for Rabbit to keep busy over," said Eeyore sarcastically. "Anything at all, apparently."

Now, one thing that seems rather odd to us is that the Bisy Backson Society, which practically worships youthful energy, appearance, and attitudes, has developed no effective methods of retaining them, a lack testified to by an ever-increasing reliance on the unnatural False Front approach of cosmetics and plastic surgery. Instead, it has developed countless ways of breaking youthfulness down and destroying it. Those damaging activities that are not part of the search for the Great Reward seem to accumulate under the general heading of Saving Time.

For an example of the latter, let's take a classic monument to the Bisy Backson: the Hamburger Stand.

In China, there is the Teahouse. In France, there is the Sidewalk Café. Practically every civilized country in the world has some sort of equivalent—a place where people can go to eat, relax, and talk things over without worrying about what time it is, and without having to leave as soon as the food is eaten. In China, for example, the Teahouse is a real social institution. Throughout the day, families, neighbors, and friends drop in for tea and light food. They stay as long as they like. Discussions may last for hours. It would be a bit strange to call the Teahouse the nonexclusive neighborhood social club; such terms are too Western. But that can roughly describe part of the function, at least from our rather compartmentalized point of view. "You're important. Relax and enjoy yourself." That's the message of the Teahouse.

What's the message of the Hamburger Stand? Quite obviously, it's: "You don't count; hurry up."

Not only that, but as everyone knows by now, the horrible Hamburger Stand is an insult to the customer's health as well. Unfortunately, this is not the only example supported by the Saving Time mentality. We could also list the Supermarket, the Microwave Oven, the Nuclear Power Plant, the Poisonous Chemicals. . . .

Practically speaking, if timesaving devices really saved time, there would be more time available to us now than ever before in history. But, strangely enough, we seem to have less time than even a few years ago. It's really great fun to go someplace where there are no timesaving devices because, when you do, you find that you have *lots of time.* Elsewhere, you're too busy working to pay for machines to save you time so you won't have to work so hard.

The main problem with this great obsession for Saving Time is very simple: you can't *save* time. You can only spend it. But you can spend it wisely or foolishly. The Bisy Backson has practically no time at all, because he's too busy wasting it by trying to save it. And by trying to save every bit of it, he ends up wasting the whole thing.

Henry David Thoreau put it this way, in *Walden:*

> Why should we live with such hurry and waste of life? We are determined to be starved before we are hungry. Men say that a stitch in time saves nine, and so they take a thousand stitches to-day to save nine tomorrow.

For colorful contrast with the youth-destroying Bisy Backson Society, let's get back to Taoism for a moment. One of the most intriguing things about Taosim is that it not only contains respect for the old and wise, but also for the figure known as the Youthful Immortal. The Taoist tradition is filled with fascinating stories (fiction) and accounts (fact, embellished or otherwise) of those who, while still young, discovered the Secrets of Life. However the discoveries were made, the result in each case was the same: a long life of youthful appearance, outlook, and energy.

For that matter, Taoist Immortals of all age levels have traditionally been known for their young attitudes, appearances, and energies. These were hardly accidental, but resulted from Taoist practices. For centuries in China, the general life expectancy was not much more than forty years, and hardworking farmers and dissipated aristocrats often died even younger than that. Yet countless Taoists lived into their eighties and nineties, and many lived considerably longer. The following is one of our favorite examples.

In 1933, newspapers around the world announced the death of a man named Li Chung Yun. As officially and irrefutably recorded by the Chinese government, and as verified by a thorough independent investigation, Li had been born in 1677. When over the age of two hundred, he had given a series of twenty-eight, three-hour-long talks on longevity at a Chinese university. Those who saw him at that time claimed that he looked like a man in his fifties, standing straight and tall, with strong teeth and a full head of hair. When he died, he was two hundred fifty-six years old.

When Li was a child, he left home to follow some wandering herbalists. In the mountains of China, he learned from them some of the secrets of the earth's medicine. In addition to using various rejuvenative herbs daily, he practiced Taoist exercises, believing that exercise which strains and tires the mind and body shortens life. His favorite way of traveling was what he called "walking lightly." Young men who went for walks with him when he was in his later years could not match his pace, which he maintained for miles. He advised those who wanted strong health to "sit like a turtle, walk like a pigeon, and sleep like a dog." When asked for his major secret, though, he would reply, "inner quiet."

Speaking of that sort of thing, let's return to *The House at Pooh Corner*. Christopher Robin has just asked Pooh a question:

What do you like doing best in the world, Pooh?"

"Well," said Pooh, "what I like best—" and then he had to stop and think. Because although Eating Honey *was* a very good thing to do, there was a moment just before you began to eat it which was better than when you were, but he didn't know what it was called.

The honey doesn't taste so good once it is being eaten; the goal doesn't mean so much once it is reached; the reward is not so rewarding once it has been given. If we add up all the rewards in our lives, we won't have very much. But if we add up the spaces *between* the rewards, we'll come up with quite a bit. And if we add up the rewards *and* the spaces, then we'll have everything—every minute of the time that we spent. What if we could enjoy it?

The Christmas presents once opened are Not So Much Fun as they were while we were in the process of examining, lifting, shaking, thinking about, and opening them. Three hundred sixty-five days later, we try again and find that the same thing has happened. Each time the goal is reached, it becomes Not So Much Fun, and we're off to reach the next one, then the next one, then the next.

That doesn't mean that the goals we have don't count. They do, mostly because they cause us to go through the process, and it's the *process* that makes us wise, happy, or whatever. If we do things in the wrong sort of way, it makes us miserable, angry, confused, and things like that. The goal has to be right for us, and it has to be beneficial, in order to ensure a beneficial process. But aside from that, it's really the process that's important. *Enjoyment* of the process is the secret that erases the myths of the Great Reward and Saving Time. Perhaps this can help to explain the everyday significance of the word *Tao*, the Way.

What could we call that moment before we begin to eat the honey? Some would call it anticipation, but we think it's more than that. We would call it awareness. It's when we become happy and realize it, if only for an instant. By Enjoying the Process, we can stretch that awareness out so that it's no longer only a moment, but covers the whole thing. Then we can have a lot of fun. Just like Pooh.

And then he thought that being with Christopher Robin was a very good thing to do, and having Piglet near was a very friendly thing to have; and so, when he had thought it all out, he said, "What I like best in the whole world is Me and Piglet going to see You, and You saying 'What about a little something?' and Me saying, 'Well, I shouldn't mind a little something, should you, Piglet,' and it being a hummy sort of day outside, and birds singing."

When we take the time to enjoy our surroundings and appreciate being alive, we find that we have no time to be Bisy Backsons anymore. But that's all right, because being Bisy Backsons is a tremendous waste of time. As the poet Lu Yu wrote:

The clouds above us join and separate,
The breeze in the courtyard leaves and returns.
Life is like that, so why not relax?
Who can stop us from celebrating?

A Case of Inefficiency

Ann Marie Cunningham

Bertrand Russell thought that four hours of work a day was plenty for anyone. William Faulkner regretted it was possible to do more: "One of the saddest things is that the only thing a man can do for eight hours a day is work. You can't eat eight hours a day, nor drink eight hours a day, nor make love eight hours a day—all you can do is work."

Most great hunches and major breakthroughs seem to have popped into people's heads when they weren't working—when they were staring into space, goofing off or even sleeping. Stanislaw Ulam, the Polish expatriate physicist who, with Edward Teller, hit on the design for the hydrogen bomb in 1951, was considered spectacularly lazy by his colleagues at Los Alamos. While everyone else worked around the clock to win the Cold War, he never appeared at the lab before ten and was gone by four. When other scientists went hiking in the New Mexican mountains, he remained at the foot of the trail and watched through binoculars.

James D. Watson, one of the three unravelers of the structure of DNA, was too lazy a doctoral candidate to take chemistry or physics. He was drawn to science by the partying at conventions, and went to Cambridge, England, where he hooked up with Francis Crick and Maurice Wilkins, to learn biochemistry. The three were well matched: Crick girl-watched incessantly and subscribed only to *Vogue.* At the height of the race with Linus Pauling to decode DNA, Wilkins disappeared regularly for fencing lessons. Watson spent afternoons on the tennis court, showing up at the lab "for only a few minutes of minor fiddling before dashing away to have sherry with the girls at Pop's." He pondered DNA at the movies, where he spent almost every evening.

Cat's in the Cradle

Harry Chapin

My child arrived just the other day;
he came to the world in the usual way.
But there were planes to catch and bills to pay;
he learned to walk while I was away.
And he was talkin' 'fore I knew it,
and as he grew he'd say,
"I'm gonna be like you, Dad,
you know I'm gonna be like you."

And the cat's in the cradle and the silver spoon,
little boy blue and the man in the moon.
"When you comin' home Dad?"
"I don't know when, but we'll get together then,
you know we'll have a good time then."

My son turned ten just the other day;
he said, "Thanks for the ball, Dad,
come on let's play.
Can you teach me to throw?"
I said, "Not today, I got a lot to do."

He said, "That's okay."
But his smile never dimmed, it said,
"I'm gonna be like him, yeah,
you know I'm gonna be like him."

Chorus

Well he came from college just the other day;
so much like a man I just had to say,
"Son, I'm proud of you, can you sit for a while?"
He shook his head and he said with a smile,
"What I'd really like, Dad,
is to borrow the car keys;
see you later, can I have them please?"

Chorus

I've long since retired,
my son's moved away;
I called him up just the other day.
I said, "I'd like to see you if you don't mind."
He said, "I'd love to Dad, if I could find the time.
You see, my new job's a hassle and the kids have the flu,
but it's sure nice talking to you, Dad,
it's been sure nice talkin' to you."
As I hung up the phone,
it occurred to me,
he'd grown up just like me;
my boy was just like me.

Chorus

Chapter
8

Controlling and Resisting

A ll organizations face a difficult dilemma. Often, the primary concern of individuals is to satisfy their own self-interests while the concern of organizations is to induce individuals to work toward some collective end. To resolve this dilemma, organizations often go to great lengths to control what individuals do. In response, individuals try to avoid such constraints. In short, controlling and resisting are two processes that permeate organizational life.

Early in this century, Frederick Taylor tried to convince all who would listen that workers and managers had compatible interests. Since that time, students of organizations have echoed this theme. The fact that people have been motivated to write and to read so much about the possibility of such commonality suggests another fact—the commonality is not all that obvious to many. While we, too, believe that a considerable amount of organizational conflict could be avoided, we also see considerable evidence of inherent conflict. Moreover, that inherent conflict divides not only labor and management but also managers and workers. Depending on where a person stands on a particular issue, the efforts of others to assert their own interests can be perceived and labeled in quite different ways. For example, an employee's refusal to follow a supervisor's directive to use a more economical production method can be viewed as insubordination, resistance, or evidence that the employee has an "authority problem." On the other hand, the same act could be construed as principled commitment to quality work, to professional norms, or to personal ethics.

Such labels themselves are part of the process through which individuals pursue their own interests—by seeking to control others and by resisting the efforts of others to control them. These efforts to win and to resist control are some of the most interesting facets of organization reality. The selections in this chapter capture a number of ways in which these struggles occur. It is important to recognize that people at all organizational levels attempt to control and to resist. Although some of these attempts are subtle and even humorous, their earnestness should not be overlooked.

While resisting is something that is often attributed to lower level participants, sometimes it appears to be a response of managers to requests and expressions of resistance by subordinates. In "The Art of Saying No: On the Management of Refusals in Organizations," Dafna Izraeli and Todd D. Jick capture a few of these instances in describing four types of managerial refusal ceremonies for saying no. Each ceremony has the purpose of controlling employees while maintaining their commitment to the organization and shaping their expectations and actions. However, as Izraeli and Jick point out, even if subordinates accept the verdict, the manipulations may have deleterious effects on employee morale, commitment, and motivation.

In "Intimidation Rituals: Reactions to Reform," Rory O'Day describes a spectrum of behavior that those with formal authority use to control others. It is especially instructive to note how efforts at control may escalate from subtle hints to severe punishments.

Much can be learned by observing people who are successful in mobilizing the power that allows them to control and resist. For this purpose, there have been few better people to observe than Lyndon B. Johnson. The two selections by Doris Kearns provide glimpses of Johnson in action prior to his tenure as president. In "Campus Politico," we see him as a student, converting a low level post into a powerful hub. In "The Politics of Seduction," we encounter Johnson years later, building and enhancing his control as Senate majority leader. From these excerpts we can deduce a number of elements helpful in building a foundation to exercise control, including ability to read environments, people, and situations; skill at entering into the perspectives of others; and the ability to turn knowledge to one's own advantage.

In addition to learning from the behavior of those who appear to control from high levels, much can also be discovered by observing the actions of seemingly less powerful people. Although it is common to describe these individuals as "resisting" rather than "controlling," a moment's reflection reveals that both words are referring to rather similar processes through which individuals act to advance and to protect their own interests. The remainder of this chapter focuses on some of these actions.

In "Basic Victim Positions," Margaret Atwood suggests that the way in which individuals define or frame a situation is a major determinant of their willingness and ability to extricate themselves from the undesired influence of others. The importance of understanding that there are many ways to frame a given situation can be seen in the next two selections as well. "Señor Payroll," a wonderful short story by William E. Barrett, shows how a group of Mexican-American stokers foiled sustained efforts of managers to exercise bureaucratic control. Another short story, "The Catbird Seat" by the renowned James Thurber, describes a sophisticated scheme devised to fight back against a manager. While reading both stories, it is useful to identify the ways that resisters defined situations and sources of power that these definitions allowed them to call on.

So far, we have focused on control and resistance up and down the organization hierarchy. The final selection is "The Ratebuster: The Case of the Saleswoman" by Melville Dalton. This classic study reveals how people at the same level pursue and protect their interests vis-à-vis each other.

We do not want to suggest that members of organizations are always at cross-purposes. However, as this chapter makes clear, organizations cannot be understood without considering the formal and informal means that people at all levels use to try to assert their own interests.

The Art of Saying No: On the Management of Refusals in Organizations

Dafna Izraeli and Todd D. Jick

INTRODUCTION

The study of organizational culture has recently been furthered by examination of the content, function, and underlying meanings of symbols, language, stories, ideologies, rituals and myths. It has been argued that these mechanisms of culture-building convey multiple meanings. On one level, technical or instrumental information may be conveyed while, at another, one can characterize the ceremonial nature of communication in terms of its expression of values, premises, and interests embodied in the definition of the situation. This ceremonial level primarily "says things," conveys a message, rather than "does things." Thus the construction and maintenance of these common understandings or shared meanings have become increasingly subject to political analysis as to their role in sustaining and legitimating authority, in securing or preserving a semblance of order, harmony, and consensus in organizations. Wilkins (1983) noted that stories commonly told in organizations are important indicators of the social prescriptions concerning how things are to be done, the consequences of compliance or deviance, and an overall guide to what kinds of people can do what. In more subtle ways, symbols of culture convey beliefs about the use and distribution of power and privilege as reflected in rituals and myths which legitimate those distributions.

What becomes interesting is how people come to believe, accept, and legitimate power and authority. Multiple elements of everyday life in the organization serve to transmit and reaffirm the existence and legitimacy of authority and of the ability of some people to define for others who they are and what it is they are doing.

Management does not have an absolute monopoly over the definitional process. The framing of organizational problems, the interpretive schemes, and the basic definition of reality are rarely uncontroversial. Anthropological studies of life on the shopfloor are rich in their documentation of the world of workers who operate with a different cultural tool kit and whose version of "what is going on here" is frequently very different from that of management.

In the face of such tensions and conflicts, management typically seeks to build and sustain consensus while reinforcing their control. How is this done? Tools of management include selective recruitment, training, promotion, role modeling, organizational and physical design, and direct communication of desired norms and values.

But, according to Smircich and Morgan (1982), effective leadership perhaps relies most on the management of meaning to the extent that the leader's definition of the situation serves as a basis for action by others, actions oriented to the achievement of desirable ends from the leader's viewpoint. Thus, the manager's role is portrayed as "framer of contexts, a maker and shaper of interpretive schemes (who) must deal with multiple realities." This management of context and meaning is a far less visible form of control than traditional supervision in that it achieves compliance on the basis of value premises. But it is a critical ingredient in the glue which holds an organization together. Ultimately, these invisible controls powerfully influence what people do and don't do, what people say and can't say, and what people have and can't have.

THE CASE OF REFUSAL CEREMONIES AND SCARCE RESOURCES

One arena in which these mechanisms are manifest is in the distribution of incentives in organizations. For those who manage the organization, mobilizing and sustaining the willing cooperation of participants is a core dilemma. Pfeffer (1981, xi–xii) similarly observed that "one of the major tasks of managers is to make organizational participants want and feel comfortable doing what they have to do." Managers are assisted in accomplishing this by the widely accepted ideology that their authority is legitimate as well as by controlling the distribution of incentives of resources of both a material and symbolic nature.

However, the task can be especially difficult because there are always some people in the organization receiving less than they expect or less than they deem themselves entitled. Thus, the organization seeks ways to "cool out" their frustration and disappointment so as to retain the commitment and willingness of employees to give energy and loyalty to the organization's desired goals and purposes. Members must be helped to see how things are different from what they perceived and to shift their behavior accordingly. Organizations thus attempt to influence members to want less, to delay their gratification, to set policies as to who should have what, etc.

Two environmental conditions increase the prevalence with which organizations must engage in such influence rituals: a shift from economically good times to times of relative economic scarcity and an expansion of perceived entitlement. Both conditions lead to a negative shift in the ratio of those to whom the organization says "yes" to those to whom it says "no".

Consider two contemporary examples: organizational retrenchment, in which given or expected resources are typically taken away, and quality circles, in which generated requests for incremental resources may be discouraged. In both cases, a culture must be "re-worked" and power and influence exercised. In the first case, an ethos of expansiveness must give way to an ethos of frugality, restraint, and sacrifice. In the second case, beliefs in opportunity and change—stimulated by the development of quality circles—whet the appetite and encourage participants to make demands on organizational resources. Yet, the organization inevitably finds itself setting limits, defining domains, and establishing controls over resource distribution. In both cases, "reality" is brought in line with management's new definition of "what this organization needs." The result is that persons who expected to receive some benefit and may even have been initially encouraged in their expectations, must be helped to accept the new reality.

The art of saying "no" then is a process of redefining the situation and of managing meaning. The situated activity in which this is done we call a "refusal ceremony." It is through such ceremonies that we will illustrate the process by which the dominant culture is reaffirmed.

Refusal ceremonies may be classified as a specific case of breaking bad news. They are usually defined as unpleasant events by all participants involved. They are part of the dirty work of a manager's job. The task of saying no is usually assigned to the immediate superior who is expected to absorb the stings and arrows of the subordinate's disappointment. Since refusing requests is a normal part of everyday life in organizations, the immediate superior has sufficient credibility for the task.

Our presentation focuses on the negative response of a superior to an initiative taken by a subordinate. We are describing one phase in a communication process, that in which the superior's response gives meaning to the action of the subordinate. The superior's response is the definition of reality in which the subordinate is invited to share.

SAMPLE AND DATA COLLECTION

The data for this study were collected from a convenience sample of 89 respondents, 67 or whom were enrolled in graduate business courses and 22 in an undergraduate business course. Most were part-time students who were also currently employed. All have had some previous work experience and the number of organizations virtually equalled the number of respondents. Overall, though, the sample reflects individuals at relatively early stages of their careers. The great majority may be classified as lower participants. The data were collected anonymously.

Respondents were asked to describe an incident in which their request for resources was denied by someone superior to them. The specific instructions were as follows:

> You've asked for, or let it be known, you'd like something such as a budget increase, an additional secretary, larger office space, assignment of a new project, salary hike, etc. However, you found that it would not be granted.
>
> Please describe: (a) the nature of the request; (b) what was said to you regarding the refusal; (c) how it was said, (e.g., verbally, in memo form, grapevine), and, (d) your reactions and feelings.
>
> Please be as specific as possible about the chronology of events, the communications and/or dialogue between you and your supervisor(s), and the resolution.

Analysis of our data suggests four types of ceremonies are conducted to convey refusals: normative invocation, status denial, rites of attrition, and rites of benevolence.

I. NORMATIVE INVOCATION

The most prevalent ceremonial strategy to explain and legitimate a refusal is the appeal to higher order values, such as rationalism, and to their structural manifestations. Technical efficiency and functional rationality are aspects of organizational ideology which legitimate the division of labour and the system of authority. Decisions made on those grounds become legitimate and by implication, correct. "We can't afford to increase your budget this year," "It's against company policy," "It's the rule here," "The interests of the organization require that," are statements tendered as reasons for not granting a request.

Normative invocations are occasions for the superior to explicate "the organization's point of view" and in so doing, to reaffirm management's right to define what the prevailing point of view is in the situation. The following examples are taken from our data:

> Subordinate 1: "It's not in the budget."
>
> "Requested to hire an additional manager to cover afternoon shift operations. Was told could not afford to add to head count during decline in sales. Response: frustrated because I was convinced of the need and felt that the expense could be justified."
>
> Subordinate 2: "It's against corporate policy."
>
> "Requested a foreign car instead of the standard North American car (company vehicle). Was refused on grounds that corporate policy did not allow for exceptions of this nature. Response: Was only marginally disappointed—did not feel the request would be granted in any event."
>
> Subordinate 3: "You haven't the seniority."
>
> "On the part-time job requested more hours of work for the summer. The request was refused as management replied that the number of hours allotted was based on

seniority and individuals who had been with the firm longer than myself were able to obtain more hours of work. Response: I felt that work performance is a more important criterion than seniority, however, since the company places more importance on seniority, I accepted the explanation with reluctance."

Subordinate 4: "In the interest of the company."

"Requested a transfer of work classification to be retrained in a different functional area of the organization. Was told 'no'—as you are effectively performing your current job to the satisfaction and best wishes of the organization. Response: Although I understood the organization's point of view and was happy they considered me a top performer, I was bothered that they did not consider my feelings regarding the present job."

Subordinate 5: "The needs of the organization."

"Requested a subordinate be transferred for his and the Company's benefit. Was told no, not now. Needs of my boss' organization too great at this time to release him, perhaps later. Response: Felt as if I had been out of line in making the request (which I wasn't) and felt hesitant about any future requests."

Subordinate 6: "We can't afford it."

"Requested a pay raise. Was told not possible due to budget constraints. Response: Did not believe my bureau chief, I knew there was money available for raises and that it was his discretion solely that determined that distribution."

In the above cases the refusal is rationalized in terms of the rules of behaviour generally followed. In no case was the right of the superior to make the decision, and impose it upon the subordinate, questioned. The wisdom of the decision was questioned, even the wisdom of the criterion used for making the decision was criticized. Subordinate and superior, however, share an understanding of how the organization works. That understanding includes the belief that each holds about his/her relative authority and power in the situation. The ceremonies of refusal are micro-events in which these beliefs are tested against the reality and then either validated and reinforced, or weakened and perhaps transformed.

There are a number of reasons why normative invocations are the most frequently used rhetoric for conveying refusals. First, as already noted, they have high legitimacy in the organizational culture. Furthermore, reference to rational considerations impersonalize the refusal and veil the power dimension in the interaction between subordinate and superior. They are, in addition, difficult to refuse, since lower participants are usually less knowledgeable about rules and budget allocations than are their superiors. However, even when the subordinate is fully aware that the explanation is dishonest, as in the case of subordinate 6, few are ready to challenge and announce that the king has no clothes.

II. STATUS DENIAL

Organizational cultures define what kind of people are entitled to what sort of treatment. People are sorted for entitlements according to their technical skills as well as many other less formalized criteria, such as class, race, sex, age, and personal connections. The subordinate who initiates a request is frequently making a claim to being a certain kind of person or to having a certain status which entitles him/her to make the request and expect that it be granted.

A status denial ceremony is an occasion when the rejection of the claim forms the basis for the refusal. The message conveyed is that "you are not what you present yourself to be." This strategy shifts the responsibility for the refusal from the organization to the individual. If effective, the subordinate will perceive the organization as acting equitably and him/herself as inadequate. When the inadequacy is defined as remediable, and the subordinate is led to believe that s/he may become what s/he has professed to be (provided s/he completes the project, gets more experience, etc.) then fervor of effort is likely to ensue.

> Subordinate 7: "You will get what you deserve."
>
> "A better rating on my annual evaluation was requested. I was told it would not be granted because I did not 'stand out in the crowd'. I had a verbal interview. I was very angry. I requested and obtained a second verbal interview. I requested a full explanation of the evaluation process and criteria. I presented my case based on the criteria. At a third interview I was informed my rating had been improved as I had requested. I was informed that the improved rating was not due to my efforts but because my manager's superior thought I deserved the rating."

Another form of status denial is to insist that the subordinate has not met the time requirements for that which s/he requests, as in the following examples:

> Subordinate 8: "You're not here long enough."
>
> "I had requested an increase in salary from $160 to $200 per week. I had been employed a year and a half in what I considered an above average job. I was refused on the basis that no one got a raise until working two years."

> Subordinate 9: "You're not old enough."
>
> "I worked in a commercial bank. Asked to be promoted to commercial banking officer from division assistant. I was told that I was too young and not ready for the position (I was only 22 years old.)."

Merton (1982) referred to such time considerations as "socially expected durations"; namely, culturally prescribed and socially patterned expectations about the amount of time something will or should take. They are not the same as actual durations. The enactment of a socially expected duration as a justification for refusal may reflect the belief that during a specified time something will occur which is not likely to occur in less (or more) time. Time then becomes the measurable substitute for whatever process is supposed to occur.

Status denial may also take the form of discrediting the subordinate's presentation of self and accrediting him/her with a less attractive identity. The superior may select from a variety of labels (too aggressive, too impatient, uncooperative, poor team worker), any or all of which might serve to disqualify the subordinate for the very benefits being sought. Discrediting has high fear arousal potential and in that sense may belong to the category of intimidation ceremonies.

Intimidation rituals (O'Day, 1974)° aim to dissuade the subordinate from pursuing his/her claim to entitlement. The dominant emotion aroused is that of fear—of the consequences of not changing the course of action. Intimidation may be conveyed in many styles from that of direct overt threat to the light hearted manner in the following case:

> Subordinate 10: "Things could get worse."
>
> "I worked as a bricklayer this summer for a small, single owner company. The owner was my boss, he worked beside me and one other employee. I was earning $6/hr as was the other guy. After six months we both approached the owner and asked him if he could give us a 50¢ /hr. raise. The owner refused stating in a half joking, half serious way that we were lucky to have a job in the first place."

In sum, status denial represents the harshest threat to the personal identity and future role of the individual. In demeaning, threatening, or exposing the status of the individual, this tactic reinforces the sanctity and impenetrability of organizational rules, values, and stature.

III. ATTRITION

Rites of attrition are a form of "non-violent" resistance in which refusal is frequently implicit but not openly voiced. If successful, they produce motivational fatigue as the subordinate gets used to his/her condition and comes to accept it. Attrition takes two forms: avoidance and stalling.

Avoidance takes place when the subordinate's initiatives are disattended. Telephone messages are not responded to, letters are not answered. After one or two attempts, the subordinate may either get discouraged or get the message and withdraw from further initiatives.

Avoidance is more likely to take this form in large organizations where relations are relatively formalized and the person to whom the communication is directed is not the immediate superior or at least not personally known to the subordinate. These conditions make the use of informal modes of access to those in authority more difficult. Such inaccessibility may be specifically fostered for that purpose. Avoidance, however, may also occur in face to face encounters as in the following example related by a newly tenured associate professor:

> "I wrote my Dean asking for an extended leave. He didn't reply. I met him several times after that at faculty meetings but each time he avoided raising the issue. I was forced to be the one to raise it. I began to feel like a nag. Last time he walked right by me as if I weren't there. I knew I better not raise the issue there."

Avoidance is most likely to deter only the more timid and those whose position in the organization is precarious. If the subordinate persists, the superior may be persuaded to shift to another ceremonial strategy.

°O'Day (1974) describes the intimidation rituals (nullification, isolation, defamation and expulsion) performed in progression by middle level bureaucrats to control the reform initiatives of a subordinate.

"My hands are tied" or "It's not up to me" is another type of avoidance ritual in which the superior avoids dealing with the issue by pointing to other individuals, groups or organizations who may be, credibly, presented as constraining action on the part of the superior. Organizations that generate a large number of committees provide fertile ground for the use of this ritual. The superior may relate a dramatized description of the intricacies and complexities of the organization's decision making process to convince the subordinate that "It's not up to me." The superior may offer to "look into it" and thus shift from an avoidance to a stalling ceremony.

Stalling refers to tactics used to gain time, such as "I'll look into it," or "You look into it." As different from avoidance, stalling tactics convey the message that something is being done to remedy the situation. Stalling may also have an attritional effect but successful stalling rites sustain the subordinate's belief in the organization's good will toward him/her and the hope that at some time in the future the matter will be resolved to the subordinate's satisfaction, as in the following example:

> Subordinate 11: "I'll get back to you."
>
> "Requested an increase in salary. The initial response was positive with the supervisor (owner of Co.) agreeing with my request and saying he would get back to me. A few weeks passed with no response so I approached him. Again a few weeks passed and then I was told it would come in the form of a bonus and pay increase at the end of the year. It's been 6 months since my request and although they haven't said no, I haven't seen any increase or been informed of the amount."

In "I'll look into it" the manager presumably takes it upon him/herself to pursue the matter further after the subordinate leaves. This expression of intent and good will may be lent greater credibility by a jotting down of a note as an indication to the subordinate that the manager is resolved to do something, as if once recorded "I'll look into it" takes on an "as good as done" quality.

"You look into it" transfers responsibility for the next step to the subordinate. S/he is asked to do something which is presented as necessary before anything else can be done. This may require preparing a report explaining his/her position on the issue or collecting data which may be difficult to obtain:

> Subordinate 12: "Bring me proof."
>
> "I requested additional office help (1 person) for duties the junior marketing assistant had in addition to her researching and analyzing functions; since when her work load backs up, so does mine. (I am the senior marketing research assistant.) The refusal was based on the overall all-corporate freeze, in addition to the lack of long term history regarding the amount of work that such an extra person would have—in other words, I couldn't prove that there would always be 40 hours of work per week for a secretary."

Successful stalling may be extended for a relatively long time until either the superior is replaced or circumstances change so as to make the initial request no longer relevant. The following incident reveals how the first supervisor was spared the refusal while her replacement shifts responsibility for solving the problem to the subordinate, an implicit discrediting ritual:

Subordinate 13: "Wait till things settle down."

"I requested an exchange of offices, to be nearer my boss and co-workers. My boss and co-workers were clustered at the other end of the building. I wanted to be more involved in their work. My boss said to wait until 'things settled down,' then until the organizational development project was finished. I waited 12–18 months. My boss moved up to executive director, reporting to the Vice-President, and my new boss told me (2 weeks ago) that no change would be made; I was also told that it was up to me to overcome the obstacle of distance and to find ways to integrate myself into the activities of my co-workers."

Stalling ceremonies are successful when they convey a message of good will and get the manager off the hook, if only temporarily. The general cultural norm according to which it is not nice to refuse a request, makes it generally more difficult to say "no" than to say "yes". Thus, rites of attrition may reflect as much of the general culture as the local organizational values and norms.

IV. BENEVOLENCE

A refusal may take the form of a benevolence rite in which the organization affirms its concern for the subordinate as a human being. Examples of benevolence are "for your own good!!" (FYOG) and "See how fair we are." (SHFWA) In FYOG the meaning of the refusal is inverted and redefined as being in the real interest of the subordinate. In SHFWA the subordinate is offered a consolation prize.

In FYOG ceremonies the benevolence may be directed to the subordinate either as a member of the organization (the public career) or as a person and member of a family (the private career). In both, the presumption is that the superior's understanding of the subordinate's goals and the means for their achievement is greater than that of the subordinate. The primacy of the superior's concern for the subordinate's welfare is the dominant posture. In relation to the public career, typical statements are "the job is not right for you," "you think you'll like it but you won't," "a pay increase now will arouse a lot of hostility," etc. When the benevolence is strongly paternalistic scratching the surface reveals "intimidation." Statements like "If I raise this with the board, they'll think you're a trouble maker" or "I'm willing to do this for you but you will have to bear the responsibility."

"For your own good" as a private person is a tactic most likely to be used to mollify a married woman. It involves the debunking of the dominant ideology that links success with power and position and invokes an alternative value system that links success with happiness and family life: "For your own good, what do you need all that extra responsibility, it'll create tensions, at home" or "your husband might resent your having to work weekends." The manager's concern may extend beyond the woman to the welfare of her husband as in "how can we send you abroad, what will your husband do, make cocktail parties?"

"See how fair we are" is the implicit message when the subordinate is offered an alternative or consolation prize, one less costly to the organization. Consolation prizes include change in job title instead of a job, a trip to a conference, or half (quarter?) of whatever was asked for, whether time, money or some other resources. The prize may have greater symbolic than substantial value, as when the refusal is redefined as a compliment, another example of meaning inversal.

> Subordinate 14: "You're too good for a better job."
>
> "Perhaps one year ago I requested of my boss to be placed on a new project. I had been working on one project which was very large and important for a year and a half and I felt I was no longer learning what I should have been learning as a third year engineer. My boss himself explained to me that I was in a sort of catch-22 situation. In performing the responsibilities which had come to me I exhibited a consistency and reliability which caused upper management to feel confident in me handling my position. I had done so well at my job in terms of defining my role and my interrelationships with the other disciplines that I was irreplaceable. I was told that I would have to follow the project through to completion. My boss did help to bring some change into my job by getting me involved with the college recruitment effort. Although this extra responsibility only took one day every three weeks it gave me the diversification I desired. The way my boss posed the explanation was very flattering."

Being irreplaceable may also be a reflection of the lack of attractiveness of the tasks performed rather than of the special skills of the subordinate. In that case being irreplaceable would not be perceived as a consolidation.

"Cooling out" (Goffman, 1952) the subordinate is an important part of refusal ceremonies and may be done most painlessly by benevolent tactics. In Goffman's study the individual (mark) needs to be cooled out so that he does not "squawk," create a row, or be an embarrassment to the organization in some other way. Our concern has been with the refused member who needs to be "cooled out" and then "cooled in" to the culture so that his/her commitments are once again harnessed to the purpose of the organization (as defined by managers).

CULTURE-WORKING AND REFUSAL CEREMONIES: FINAL THOUGHTS

The lion and the calf shall lie down together but the calf won't get much sleep.

Woody Allen, *Without Feathers*

Refusal ceremonies have been shown to be an important part of the acculturation process. On one level, they convey explicit guidelines and information about "the way things are done around here" and they contribute to socialization. The employee, "learns," for example, the policies, priorities, and goals from the superior's viewpoint—and the rules of the game in that particular organization.

The art of saying no can also be characterized as a form of culture-working activity in so far as these ceremonies serve to define realities, who people are (e.g., their status), and what influence people can exercise. In this sense, we have indicated how culture is intertwined with structure (i.e., power and control), how defining the terms of reality can be a prominent tool in a manager's "cultural tool kit." This is what Pfeffer (1981) referred to as the institutionalization of organizational culture whereby ". . . the distribution of power, the making of certain decisions, or the following of certain rules of operation . . . become defined as part of the organization's culture." (p. 299) Similarly, Smircich and Morgan (1982) characterized this type of process as "power-based reality construction."

In a sense, it appears as if the subordinates have been "brought into" the dominant culture—i.e., accepted the legitimacy of the distribution of power and authority as shared social fact. Subordinates implicitly agree to operate according to certain rules and, to some extent, concede their autonomy. Thus, refusal ceremonies reaffirm the purposes, values, norms, beliefs (i.e., culture) of the organization as defined by managers, and sustain institutional order. Moreover, Pfeffer (1981) argues that the distribution of power ". . . is perpetuated because people come to believe that this is how things always were, always will be, and, always should be." (p. 299)

However, the reaffirmation and perpetuation of culture also arouses resentment and tensions—which may indeed test the strength of the dominant culture. Many of the refused subordinates in our study reported feeling frustrated, angry, alienated, and resentful. While part of the message of the refusal ceremony may indeed be to underscore the relative unimportance or powerlessness of the subordinates, it creates (perhaps) unintended consequences as well. In some few cases, the employee actually resigned. In others, employees tried to resist the refusal—albeit within the ground rules of "evidence" defined by management. For many, the disgruntlement resulted in demoralization, discouragement, and even some questioning of the derivation of policies, and authority positions. Thus, it was not always clear that these people were indeed appeased and discouraged from pursuing benefits denied them by the organization and willing to do what they were expected to do. (In fact, there is literature on the management of extreme cases of protest (e.g., O'Day, 1974; Ewing, 1983).)

Although the perception of the ground rules may be shared and the distribution of power generally accepted, this is not to suggest that there is complete harmony, collaboration and consensus. Accepting the cultural ground rules is different from liking them, or feeling part of them. Although the subordinates typically complied with the refusal and rarely confronted their superiors with their dissatisfaction, they clearly had not bought all the values. That is, being "in" the culture and enacting behaviour within its terms is distinct from being "of" the culture, internalizing the dominant values and definitions of reality. The subordinate is typically not an equal partner in the determination of the culture and thus the dialectic tension: the more the culture is reaffirmed, the more the potential for resentment and opposition.

In order to maximize the reaffirmation of culture and minimize the opposition, the effective management of refusal ceremonies is often a prerequisite for advancement in a managerial career. Breaking or reconfirming bad news to subordinates provides situations in which the tension between the organization's interest and human variability is most exposed. Managers are expected to attend to preserving organizational legitimacy and disattend any ethical doubt that may cause them uneasiness much as medical students acquire a look of professional cool when handling an exposed gut. Refusal ceremonies may require actions for managers that seem insincere, dishonest, or unfriendly but as Goffman (1952) observed, "certain kinds of role success require certain kinds of moral failure."

The following account reported in Margolis (1979:126–7) is by a scientist who failed the test and consequently was forced to "jump off the managerial mainline and settle for a technical sideline."

> You see, one can be very competent technically, but there are other skills. After two promotions I found that you just come up to a harsher level of reality than just doing your research.
>
> The first time you're told to go tell a lie to a bunch of people, you make speeches to your boss about fairness and everything. I did that and he looked at me and said, "Frank, this is not the Supreme Court, and don't you tell me about fair and not fair. This is it and this is the story."
>
> What happened was this. We were making some new rules about raises which were screwing some people. I had to say that you couldn't get more than one raise a year. Since I had been involved in giving some people three raises in one year, some of the people would have known that I couldn't honestly tell them that one raise was all you could get in a single year. At least I couldn't say that that was consistent with our past—the way things had always been done. So I was told to say that nobody was being hurt and that that was the way things had always been done. I said I couldn't and that we couldn't lie to our people since they'd know it and that would be like asking them to join your lie. You know, you say it and then you see who reacts and mostly people don't say anything because they don't want to get into trouble. Well, I wouldn't say it so my boss announced it. I was there though; I was listening and I didn't say anything.

The scientist in this narrative is sensitive not only to his own complicity in what he considers an unethical act, but also to the complicity of the subordinates who by their silence "join the lie" and consequently reaffirm the implicit theories which generate it. Garfinkel (1967) used the term "reflexivity" to describe the ways in which the very acceptance of the usage of a familiar term or rule, by being understood as intended, reinforces the term of rule's familiarity and further assures the actors of its reality and propriety.

Refusal ceremonies are rather routine occurrences in organizations which through their regularity and importance transmit and reaffirm the organizational culture. They are micropolitical events through which those who invoke facts and arguments, or rules of reason, not sanctioned by the culture—or contemplate the possibility of doing so—are typically brought in line and serve as examples for others. Nevertheless, it must also be suggested that further research on organizational culture should identify the conditions under which the very reaffirmation of culture hardens resistance and provokes redefinition of the underlying structure of power and control.

Intimidation Rituals: Reactions to Reform

Rory O'Day

The reaction of authority in social systems to the reform initiatives of a subordinate is viewed as a series of intimidation rituals. These rituals divide into two major phases, each involving two distinct steps. The first phase, *Indirect Intimidation,* includes the rituals of *nullification and isolation;* the second, *Direct Intimidation,* the rituals of defamation and expulsion. Why these rituals for protest-suppression in organizations are powerful tools in the hands of the middle manager is discussed. Attention is also given to various images projected by the organizational reformer and reasons for resistance to reform from within an organization.

This paper characterizes the reactions of superiors in social systems to a reform-minded subordinate as a series of intimidation rituals. Each successive "ritual of control" represents an escalation in the efforts of authority to discourage an individual (and those who may support him or her) from continuing to seek reform.

MIDDLE MANAGEMENT'S MECHANISM OF CONTROL

The rituals of intimidation satisfy the two primary concerns of authorities confronted by a subordinate who appears not only able to articulate the grievances of a significant number of other system members but also capable of proposing solutions to them. Their first concern is, of course, to control the reformer so that he does not succeed in recruiting support. Their other concern is to exercise this control in ways that absolve them of any wrongdoing in the matter. The individual in question must be controlled in such a way that he neither continues to be an effective spokesman nor becomes a martyr. When superiors are confronted with a reform-minded subordinate, they want his silence or his absence, whichever is easier to achieve. The "authorities" must also preserve their carefully managed image of reasonableness, and would prefer that the reformer leave voluntarily rather than be removed officially.

Reprinted with permission from NTL Institute, "Intimidation Rituals: Reactions to Reform," by Rory O'Day, pp. 373–386, *Journal of Applied Behavioral Science,* Vol. 10, No. 3, copyright 1974.

For purposes of illustration, this presentation will describe intimidation rituals used by various organizations in the service of protest-suppression, for organizational authorities prefer to *intimidate* a reform-minded individual rather than commit organizational energy to the structural and personnel changes required to transform a "non-conforming enclave" into a legitimate subunit.[1] It is further suggested that an organization undergoes major changes that incorporate and accommodate a group of dissidents only when the intimidation rituals do not succeed in silencing the individuals who constitute the "leading edges" of the reform movement.

In the discussion that follows, I will be concerned primarily with the reformer who emerges from the lower hierarchy in an organization and challenges the *middle hierarchy*. A reformer threatens middle management in three distinctly different ways. The first threat is a function of the validity of his accusations about the inadequacy of specific actions of middle-level members and his suggestions for correcting them. If the reformer is correct, those in the middle will fear that those at the top will punish them when they discover the truth. The second threat comes from the moral challenge presented by such a reformer, for his demand for action will reveal the strength or weakness of middle management's commitment to the organization. And thirdly, the reformer's challenge may indicate to people at the top that middle management is unable to maintain order in its own jurisdiction. To protect their interests, middle-level bureaucrats therefore feel their only defense against reform-minded subordinates is intimidation.[2]

The rituals of intimidation involve two phases: *Indirect Intimidation,* which has two steps, *nullification* and *isolation;* and *Direct Intimidation,* which also comprises two steps, *defamation* and *expulsion.*

PHASE I: INDIRECT INTIMIDATION

Step 1: Nullification

When a reformer first approaches his immediate superiors, they will assure him that his accusations or suggestions are invalid—the result of misunderstandings and misperceptions on his part. His superiors, in this phase, hope that the reformer will be so awed by authority that he will simply take their word that his initiative is based on error. If, however, the reformer insists, his superiors will often agree to conduct an "investigation." The results of such an investigation will convince the reformer that his accusations are groundless and that his suggestions for enhancing organizational effectiveness or revising organizational goals have been duly noted by the appropriate authorities.

Bureaucratic justification for this response usually rests on the argument that this method copes with the system's "crackpots" and "hot-heads," discouraging them from disturbing the smooth, routine functioning of the organization with their crazy ideas and their personal feuds. But middle management also uses these rituals of nullification to handle a potentially explosive (for them and others in the organization) situation quickly and quietly, in order to prevent unfavorable publicity, maintain the organization's state of pluralistic ignorance, and prevent the development of a sympathetic and concerned audience for the reformer's ideas. The explicit message is: "You don't know what you're talking about, but thank you anyway for telling us. We'll certainly look into the matter for you." Members of the middle hierarchy then proceed to cover up whatever embarrassing (for them) truth exists in the reformer's arguments.

The protest-absorption power of the ritual of nullification derives from an element inherent in bureaucracies: the always-attractive opportunity to avoid personal responsibility for one's actions. Thus, if people attempt reform at all, they generally do not proceed beyond the first ritual, which is a process designed to quash the reformer and allow his superiors to reaffirm the collective wisdom of the organization, while clearing their consciences of wrongdoing. Nullification even gets the would-be reformer off the hook—and he may remain grateful to the organization for this added convenience. This shedding of personal responsibility allows the reformer and the authorities alike to compromise in the belief that although it might not be a perfect organizational world, it is nevertheless a self-correcting one.

Repeated exposure to the nullification ritual (the "beating your head against the wall" phenomenon) is expected to convince any sane organizational member that a reformist voice or presence is unwelcome. He is expected to take the hint and stop pestering his superiors with his misguided opinions. Gestures of generosity on the part of the middle hierarchy are not unusual if he decides to leave the organization—and such concern is usually expressed by offering to help the individual find employment opportunities elsewhere.

Step 2: Isolation

If the reformer persists in his efforts, middle management will separate him from his peers, subordinates, and superiors, thereby softening his impact on the organization and making it extremely difficult for him to mobilize any support for his position.

Middle managers argue that these procedures represent the exercise of their rights of office in the service of protecting the organization. But these attempts to isolate the reformer can also be seen as a show of force, as a way of reassuring their own superiors (if they are paying attention), their subordinates, and perhaps themselves that they can maintain order in their own jurisdiction.

Attempts at isolating the reformer include closing his communication links, restricting his freedom of movement, and reducing his allocation of organization resources. If these do not neutralize the reformer, he will be transferred to a less visible position in the organization. In these rituals, the bureaucratic message is: "If you insist on talking about things which you do not understand, then we will have to prevent you from bothering other people with your nonsense."

Systematic unresponsiveness to a reformer's criticism and suggestions is a particularly interesting form of isolation. This lack of response is meant to convince the reformer of the invalidity of his position; but if he presses his right to be heard, it may be used to create a feeling of such impotence that the reformer overreacts in order to elicit a response from his superiors. This overreaction may then be used to demonstrate the reformer's psychological imperfections.

When subjected to organizational isolation, most people come to see the error of their ways or the handwriting on the wall. When an individual learns that there is still time to mend his ways, he usually steps back in line and becomes a silent participant in the organization. When he realizes his career in the organization is at a standstill, he may decide to leave as gracefully as possible while he can still leave under his own steam. Middle managers closest to him then often offer him assistance in finding a new job, with the assurance that "*we* only want what is best for *you.*"

Most forms of isolation are designed to persuade the reformer of the futility of trying to initiate change until such time as he is instructed by his superiors to concern himself with change. The reformer practically guarantees his defeat if he reacts to systematic organizational unresponsiveness by confronting his superiors in ways that violate policy or law. The temptation to confront administrative unresponsiveness in dramatic and often self-defeating ways stems in large part from the intense frustration induced by the reformer's belief that systematic unresponsiveness violates his basic rights of freedom of expression and carries with it the implication that he is personally ineffectual (Turner, 1973). Administrative unresponsiveness to what the reformer believes are crucial issues both for himself and for the organization may be sufficiently frustrating to compel him to act, however rashly, in order to clarify the situation. From the administration's point of view, this can be seen as "flushing the rebels out into the open," "giving them enough rope to hang themselves," or, more formally, deviance-heresy conversion (Harshbarger, 1973).

PHASE II: DIRECT INTIMIDATION

Step 3: Defamation

Should the reformer refuse to remain silent, and instead mobilizes support for his position, middle management will begin to impugn his character and his motives. "When legitimate techniques fail—the middle hierarchy might resort to illegitimate or non-legitimate ones" (Leeds, 1964, p. 126). Middle managers will often distort events or even fabricate instances of misconduct in order to intimidate not only the reformer but also those who would listen to or believe him.

Defamation attempts to cut the reformer off from a potentially sympathetic following by attributing his attempts at reform to questionable motives, underlying psychopathology, or gross incompetence. This three-pronged attack is meant to blackmail the reformer into submission and to transform a sympathetic following into a mistrustful crowd of onlookers or an angry mob that feels resentful at having been deceived by the reformer.

From the vantage point of the reformer, the Kafkaesque or Alice-in-Wonderland quality of the rituals of intimidation becomes particularly evident at this time. The reformer finds himself faced with charges which only he and his accusers know are either false or irrelevant in relation to the value of his reform initiatives. The reformer is in a double bind. His superiors will use their offices and positions of trust and responsibility to create the impression in the minds of others in the organization that their accusations of incompetence, self-interest, or psychopathology are true. If the reformer continues in the face of these accusations, he risks being viewed as power-hungry or irrational. If he allows himself to be intimidated by the threat of lies, he allows his superiors to win by default.

One tactic of the superior is to accuse the reformer of acting out his Oedipal conflicts. Such a personalization of a subordinate's reform efforts (especially a younger subordinate) permits his superior to present himself as a harassed "father" faced with a troubled "son," and blocks any examination of his conduct that might reveal provocation on his part. In this way the bureaucrat hopes to persuade others in the organization to respond to the reformer as a sick person in need of therapy or as a child in need of nurturing—a stance that allows him to take on the role of "good father" in relation to other subordinates and to the reformer, if and when the latter capitulates and admits his need for help and guidance.

Rituals of defamation are undertaken by superiors in order to focus attention away from themselves and onto the reformer. The superiors hope that by casting enough doubt on the motives, intentions, and personality of the reformer, enough people in the organization will think that "where there is smoke, there must be fire." The message of this ritual is: "Don't listen to him (his message) because you can't trust a person like him."

Like the rituals of nullification and isolation, the ritual of defamation is both an end in itself and a preliminary to the final ritual of expulsion. The superiors hope by threatening to destroy the reformer's reputation and his character, he will retreat into silence and passivity or leave the organization for greener pastures; if, however, the reformer continues his efforts, his superiors have laid the groundwork for his expulsion.

If the ritual of defamation is undertaken, its target is usually indeed a reformer and not simply a nonconformist or a deviant. His superiors would not need to engage in public tactics of intimidation if there were no substance to his challenge. It is precisely the validity of his reform initiatives that leads his superiors to attempt to destroy his credibility. If this destruction of the reformer's credibility with his peers, subordinates, and top management is effectively conducted, others in the organization will desert his cause and he can be dismissed easily as an undesirable member of the intact organizational team.

Step 4: Expulsion

When neither nullification, isolation, nor defamation can silence the reformer or force his "voluntary withdrawal" from the organization, the middle hierarchy seeks an official decision for his dismissal.

If successful, at least three aims may be achieved thereby. Obviously, by expelling the reformer, his superiors will cut him off from any actual or potential following and weaken any opposition to their authority. An official dismissal also serves as a warning to other budding reformers that middle management has the necessary power and authority to expel troublemakers. Finally, the act of expulsion—a verdict of unfitness—supports the contention that the reformer is an immoral or irrational person.

Of course, the middle hierarchy would prefer the reformer to withdraw voluntarily. Managers want to avoid the public and formal proceedings that often accompany an official request for dismissal of an employee, for the accuser (superior) can often then be scrutinized as carefully as the accused, if the accused person wishes to avail himself of the opportunity. The expulsion ritual involves the formal submission of evidence, the keeping of records, the establishment of independent investigative bodies, and the right of cross-examination, which all function to threaten the image of managers as reasonable, honest, and hardworking servants of the organization. Formal dismissal proceedings are also avoided by middle management because in some fundamental sense they imply that the organization has failed and that they, in particular, have shown themselves unable to maintain order.

THE RITUAL CYCLE ABSORBS AND DESTROYS

Indirect Intimidation attempts to absorb the accusations and suggestions of the reformer, first by depriving him of effectiveness or validity, then by treating him as if he were an "invisible person." The object here is to define the reformer as "harmless." It also attempts to absorb protest by psychologically and physically exhausting the reformer so that he comes to doubt his own experience of reality, his abilities to accomplish the task he sets for himself, and its significance. The authorities hope that the reformer will come to believe the task he has set for himself is humanly impossible and that his fatigue and confusion are the result of his inability to accept human nature for what it is. Short of this, they hope that the reformer will come to feel so inadequate that he will be grateful for continued employment by the organization, in any capacity. ("You're welcome to stay aboard as long as you don't rock the boat.")

Direct Intimidation attempts to destroy protest through destruction of the *character* of the reformer (defamation) or, if necessary, of his *position* in the organization (expulsion). Direct Intimidation represents middle management's active attempt to destroy the reformer as a source of legitimate grievances and suggestions and to terrorize, if necessary, other organizational members. Successful rituals of defamation create a "bad" person, enabling the "good" organization to close ranks once again and benefit from the curative properties of solidarity when he is cast out of the system. In this sense, the ritual destruction of the person (Garfinkel, 1956) necessarily precedes the destruction of his place in the organization.

In sum, Figure 1 portrays the specific cycles of intimidation rituals. Cycle 1 is most preferred by all organizations, while Cycle 4 is the least preferred. Cycle 2 is preferred to Cycle 3.

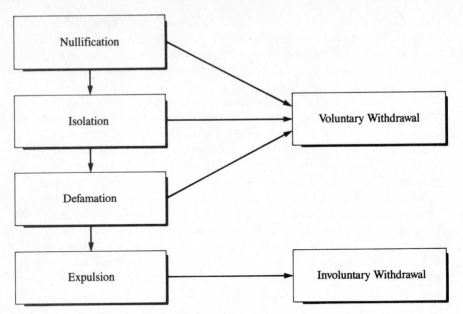

Figure 1. Cycles of Intimidation Rituals

THE REFORMER IMAGE

Throughout this discussion, the individual subjected to the rituals of intimidation has been referred to as the *reformer,* a generic term for any organizational member who resorts to voice rather than to avoidance when faced with what *he* regards as a situation of organizational deterioration or imperfection. Voice is defined as

> . . . any attempt at all to change, rather than escape from, an objectionable state of affairs, whether through individual or collective petition to the management directly in charge, through appeal to a higher authority with the intention of forcing a change in management, or through various types of actions and protests, including those that are meant to mobilize public opinion (Hirschman, 1970, p. 30).

Therefore, in the sense in which it is being used here, "reformer" includes the various meanings contained in such labels as "internal muckraker" or "pure whistle-blower" (Peters & Branch, 1972), "innovator in innovation-resisting organizations" (Shepard, 1969), "crusader for corporate responsibility" (Heilbroner, 1972), "nonconforming individual" (Etzioni, 1961; Leeds, 1964), and "heretic" (Harshbarger, 1973); but it is not intended to include the various meanings inherent in the term "organizational change agent."[3] Thus *"reformer"* refers to any member who acts, in any way and for any reason, to alter the structure and functioning of the organization, when he has *not* been formally delegated authority to institute change.

Why Intimidation Works

From this definition we can see that it is the organization which has the power to define the "reformer" as such, and attaches the stigma to many a well-meaning individual who does not see himself in a protest role. It is often the case that a potential reformer initially thinks of himself or herself only as a hard-working and loyal member of the organization who is simply trying to make things "better" and wishes to be "understood" by busy but well-meaning superiors. However, by the time authorities begin the rituals of defamation, the most naive individual usually realizes that, at least in the eyes of his superiors, he poses a threat to the established order (Herbert, 1972).

The inside reformer is vulnerable to all the intimidation rituals that his particular organization has at its disposal. The reformer outside an organization is usually vulnerable only to the rituals of nullification, isolation (in the form of systematic unresponsiveness), and defamation, unless the organization he is challenging is able to pressure the parent organization into doing the intimidating for it (McCarry, 1972).

Authorities in formal organizations are rarely directly challenged by subordinates. As in the Hans Christian Andersen tale, most individuals do not presume to stand in public judgment of their organizational superiors. Belief in the wisdom and power of the people at the top serves to keep most individuals silent about their grievances concerning the status quo and their ideas (if they have any) for enhancing organizational effectiveness or revising organizational goals. Subordinates do not generally demand, as part of their organizational contractual arrangements, the power to hold their superiors accountable for actions in direct and continuing ways. So intimidation rituals are held to be a last resort—reserved for organizational members who resist, for whatever reason, the usual mechanisms of social control (Millham, Bullock, & Cherrett, 1972).

In their discussion of the obstacles to whistle-blowing, Peters and Branch (1972) include the "loyal-member-of-the-team" trap, the feeling that "going public" is unseemly and embarrassing, and the fear of current and future job vulnerability. Thompson (1968) and Peters and Branch (1972) also refer to the subconscious accommodative device of the "effectiveness trap," an organizational argument that permits its members to avoid conflict on an immediate issue in order to ensure "effectiveness" on some more important issue, at some future time. The curator mentality and emotional detachment generated by the bureaucratic role; the tendency to resort to wishful thinking that organizational deterioration and the consequences of bad policy must soon stop simply because they cannot go on; and the fear that one disagrees with a particular exercise of power only because one is too weak to handle it further contribute to inaction on the part of most "loyal" organizational members (Thompson, 1968).

Reformer as Bad Guy

In point of fact, the protest-absorbing and protest-destroying power of intimidation rituals derives, in large measure, from their infrequent use by organizations. Conversely, if more members were willing to turn their various dissatisfactions into reformist activities, intimidation rituals would lose much of their power.

To understand the effectiveness of organizational intimidation one must examine the reasons why peers and subordinates usually fail to support the reformer, withdraw support, or even actively resist his efforts. Their passive or active resistance may indicate an increased desire or struggle for an organization's scarce resources (material benefits or status, power or prestige—or even dependency). It may also indicate that they perceive themselves as cast in an unfavorable light by the reformer's enthusiasm and heightened activities in pursuing present or changed organizational goals. Members of the organization may secretly believe that the reformer's efforts will be successful, and fear its implication for their position in the organization. If the reformer is successful in convincing top management to investigate the organizational "engine," many may fear that close scrutiny of the performance of the parts will find them wanting. On the other hand, on the outside chance that the reformer manages to seize the reins of power, peers and subordinates may fear that if they do not match his zeal in pursuing new as well as old organizational goals he will turn them out of their present positions.

It frequently seems that practically everyone except the reformer has a personal stake in preserving the complicated fantasy of the organization, even though conditions in the organization are in fact unsatisfying to all but a few elite members. Bion (1959) has described a similar situation in therapy groups where members engage in a variety of neurotic attempts to resist and discourage changing the structure and functioning of a group that is obviously less than fully satisfying. It seems likely, then, that subordinates in an organization actively or passively resist a peer's reform initiatives because the pain of the status quo is less intense than their fear of the unknown.

In general, the reformer finds himself initially with little or no support because there is an implicit acceptance of the bureaucratic order in our society (Wilcox, 1968) and because most people find it difficult and improper to question the actions of authority (Peters & Branch, 1972). There is also the well-ingrained reflex of flight in the face of crisis and change, which has characterized North American society since its colonial days (Hartz, 1955; Hirschman, 1970; Slater, 1970).

Most organizational members do not support the reformer at all, or they desert him at the first opportunity because they believe he will lose in his struggle with institutional authority—and they want to be on the winning side. Moreover, as Walzer (1969) has pointed out, most people accept nondemocratic organizational conditions on the basis of the argument of tacit consent and withhold or withdraw support from the reformer, saying that he is free to go someplace else if he does not like it where he is.

Peers and subordinates may also resist a reformer because they suspect that he is committing the unforgivable sin of pride (Slater, 1963). They may come to believe that in taking it upon himself to judge the organization and its leaders he is acting in a self-righteous manner (Peters & Branch, 1972). Those who wish to desert the reformer on this ground often use as supporting data the reformer's persistent efforts in the face of the rituals of defamation.

Since the reformer's departure is usually associated with an immediate reduction or elimination of overt conflict, which in turn relieves tension in the organization, members can wrap themselves in the organizational blanket and tell themselves that he was the source of the problem all along. When the emotional ruckus dies down, most members therefore experience a heightened commitment to the organization and return to their jobs with a renewed vigor. For those organizational members who continue to harbor some doubt about the reformer's guilt, the fear of retaliation against "sympathizers" usually dampens their enthusiasm for the reformer's cause and suppresses all but ritualistic expressions of concern for his plight.

SEIZE THE DAY

It is not possible here to do more than raise the issue of whether one should attempt to change organizations from within or whether one should create alternative organizations. Large formal organizations are going to be with us for a long time to come (Heilbroner, 1972), and their members are going to have to devise ways to make them more democratic, because there really is no place to run to anymore.

The serious reformer should be prepared to take advantage of organizational crises. He must learn how to recognize, expose, and make concrete those administratively designed arrangements that do not satisfactorily resolve critical problems. For it is in a time of crisis that an organization is open to solutions to the basic problem of survival. Organizational members will be eager to adopt new structures that promise to relieve the uncertainty and anxiety generated by a crisis (Shepard, 1969). If the organization has become weak internally, if it contains corruption and indolence at various levels, if the organization is beset by energy-consuming external pressures, and if the organizational elite lack the resources or the will to initiate changes essential for organizational survival, then the organization might well be ready for successful reform from within (Leeds, 1964). Such an organization might not be capable of successfully administering the intimidation rituals.

Internal organization reform is a difficult process. The cause of reform as well as constructive revolution cannot be served by deluding ourselves as to the ease of restructuring human society (Heilbroner, 1972; Schon, 1973). The reformer's life is not an easy one. But neither need he feel doomed from the start by the inevitability of the success of intimidation rituals mobilized against him.

NOTES

1. "Nonconforming enclave" refers to the existence of a number of organizational members who, through collective effort, ". . . could potentially divert organization resources from their current commitments, undermine organizational effectiveness, or form a front capable of capturing control of the organization" (Leeds, 1964, p. 155).
2. In a related context, Etzioni (1961, p. 241) asserts, "Once deviant charisma has manifested itself, despite . . . elaborate preventive mechanisms, counter-processes are set into motion. These are of two kinds: those which attempt to eliminate the deviant charisma; and those which seek to limit its effect."
3. It is possible, however, that an organizational change agent might find himself undergoing the rituals of intimidation if he insists that effective action be taken on his proposals for change, particularly if such action would threaten certain organizational power arrangements.

REFERENCES

Bion, W. R. *Experiences in Groups.* New York: Basic Books, 1959.

Etzioni, A. *A Comparative Analysis of Complex Organizations.* New York: The Free Press, 1961.

Garfinkel, H. "Conditions of Successful Degradation Ceremonies," *American Journal of Sociology,* 1956, *61,* 420–424.

Harshbarger, D. "The Individual and the Social Order: Notes on the Management of Heresy and Deviance in Complex Organizations," *Human Relations,* 1973, *26,* 251–269.

Hartz, L., *The Liberal Tradition in America.* New York: Harcourt, Brace and World, 1955.

Heilbroner, R. L. *In the Name of Profit.* New York: Doubleday, 1972.

Herbert, A. *Soldier.* New York: Holt, Rinehart and Winston, 1972.

Hirschman, A. O. *Exit, Voice, and Loyalty.* Cambridge, Mass.: Harvard University Press, 1970.

Leeds, R. "The Absorption of Protest: a Working Paper," in W. W. Cooper, H. J. Leavitt, and M. W. Shelly, II (Eds.), *New Perspectives in Organization Research.* New York: Wiley, 1964.

McCarry, C. *Citizen Nader.* New York: Saturday Review Press, 1972.

Millham, S., Bullock, R., and Cherrett, P. "Social Control in Organizations," *The British Journal of Sociology,* 1972, *23,* 406–421.

Peters, C., and Branch, T. *Blowing the Whistle: Dissent in the Public Interest.* New York: Praeger, 1972.

Schon, D. S. *Beyond the Stable State.* New York: Norton, 1973.

Shepard, H. A. "Innovation-resisting and Innovation-producing Organizations," in W. G. Bennis, K. D. Benne, and R. Chin (Eds.), *The Planning of Change,* Rev. ed. New York: Holt, Rinehart and Winston, 1969, pp. 519–525.

Slater, P. E. "On Social Regression," *American Sociological Review,* 1963, *29,* 339–364.

Slater, P. E. *The Pursuit of Loneliness.* Boston: Beacon Press, 1970.

Thompson, J. C. "How Could Vietnam Happen? An Autopsy," *Atlantic Monthly,* April 1968, *221* (4), 47–53.

Turner, R. H. "Unresponsiveness as a Social Sanction," *Sociometry,* 1973, *36,* 1–19.

Walzer, M. "Corporate Responsibility and Civil Disobedience," *Dissent,* Sept.–Oct., 1969, pp. 395–406.

Wilcox, H. G. "The Cultural Trait of Hierarchy in Middle Class Children," *Public Administration Review,* 1968, *28,* 222–235.

Campus Politico

Doris Kearns

From the beginning at San Marcos College (later Southwestern Texas State Teachers College), Johnson set out to win the friendship and respect of those people who would assist his rise within the community which composed San Marcos. Most obvious was the president of the college, Cecil Evans, whose favor would have a multiplier effect with the faculty and student body. But Johnson was not alone in the desire to have a special relationship with Evans. "I knew," Johnson later said, "there was only one way to get to know Evans and that was to work for him directly." He became special assistant to the president's personal secretary.

As special assistant, Johnson's assigned job was simply to carry messages from the president to the department heads and occasionally to other faculty members. Johnson saw that the rather limited function of messenger had possibilities for expansion; for example, encouraging recipients of the messages to transmit their own communications through him. He occupied a desk in the president's outer office, where he took it upon himself to announce the arrival of visitors. These added services evolved from a helpful convenience into an aspect of the normal process of presidential business. The messenger had become an appointments secretary, and, in time, faculty members came to think of Johnson as a funnel to the president. Using a technique which was later to serve him in achieving mastery over the Congress, Johnson turned a rather insubstantial service into a process through which power was exercised. By redefining the process, he had given power to himself.

Evans eventually broadened Johnson's responsibilities to include handling his political correspondence and preparing his reports for the state agencies with jurisdiction over the college and its appropriations. The student was quick to explain that his father had been a member of the state legislature (from 1905 to 1909, and from 1918 to 1925), and Lyndon had often accompanied him to Austin where he had gained some familiarity with the workings of the legislature and the personalities of its leaders. This claim might have sounded almost ludicrous had it not come from someone who already must have seemed an inordinately political creature. Soon Johnson was accompanying Evans on his trips to the state capital in Austin, and, before long, Evans came to rely upon his young apprentice for political counsel. For Johnson was clearly at home in the state legislature; whether sitting in a committee room during hearings or standing on the floor talking with representatives, he could, in later reports to Evans, capture the mood of individual legislators and the legislative body with entertaining accuracy. The older man, on whose favor Johnson depended, now relied on him, or at least found him useful.

The world of San Marcos accommodated Lyndon Johnson's gifts. If some found him tiresome, and even his friends admitted that he was difficult, they were nonetheless bedazzled by his vitality, guile, and endurance, his powers of divination, and ability to appeal to the core interests of other people. In two years, he became a campus politician, a prizewinning debater, an honors student, and the editor of the college *Star.*

The Politics of Seduction

Doris Kearns

The authority that Johnson inherited as Senate Democratic majority leader had been rendered ineffective by the Senate's inner club. Johnson set about to change all that, and before long he had transformed the instruments at hand—the steering committee, which determined committee assignments, and a hitherto unimportant Democratic Policy Committee—into mechanisms of influence and patronage in his relations with his Democratic colleagues and of control in the scheduling of legislation.

From facts, gossip, observation—a multitude of disparate elements—he shaped a composite mental portrait of every senator: his strengths and his weaknesses; his place in the political spectrum; his aspirations in the Senate, and perhaps beyond the Senate; how far he could be pushed in what direction, and by what means; how he liked his liquor; how he felt about his wife and his family; and, most important, how he felt about himself. For Johnson understood that the most important decision each senator made, often obscurely, was what kind of senator he wanted to be; whether he wanted to be a national leader in education, a regional leader in civil rights, a social magnate in Washington, an agent of the oil industry, a wheel horse of the party, a President of the United States. Yet his entrepreneurial spirit encompassed not simply the satisfaction of present needs but the development of new and expanding ones. He would, for instance, explain to a senator that "although five other senators are clamoring for this one remaining seat on the congressional delegation to Tokyo, I just might be able to swing it for you since I know how much you really want it. . . . It'll be tough but let me see what I can do." The joys of visiting Tokyo may never have occurred to the senator, but he was unlikely to deny Johnson's description of his desire—after all, it might be interesting, a relaxing change, even fun; and perhaps some of the businesses in his state had expressed concern about Japanese competition. By creating consumer needs in this fashion, and by then defining the terms of their realization, Johnson was able to expand the base of benefits upon which power could be built.

Johnson's capacities for control and domination found their consummate manifestation during his private meetings with individual senators. Face to face, behind office doors, Johnson could strike a different pose, a different form of behavior and argument. He would try to make each senator feel that his support in some particular matter was the critical element that would affect the well-being of the nation, the Senate, and the party leader; and would also serve the practical and political interests of the senator. . . .

The arrangements that preceded a private meeting were elaborate indeed. A meeting with a colleague might seem like an accidental encounter in a Senate corridor, but Johnson was not a man who roamed through halls in aimless fashion; when he began to wander he knew who it was he would find.

After the coincidental encounter and casual greetings, Johnson would remember that he had something he would like to talk about. The two men would walk down the corridor, ride the elevator, and enter an office where they would begin their conversation with small talk over Scotch. As the conversation progressed, Johnson would display an overwhelming combination of praise, scorn, rage, and friendship. His voice would rise and fall, moving from the thunder of an orator to the whisper reminiscent of a lover inviting physical touch. Transitions were abrupt. He responded to hostility with a disconcerting glance of indignation; the next minute he would evoke a smile by the warmth of his expression and a playful brush of his hand. Variations in pitch, stress, and gesture reflected the importance which he attached to certain words. His appeal would abound with illustration, anecdote, and hyperbole. He knew how to make his listeners *see* things he was describing, make them tangible to the senses. And he knew how to sustain a sense of uninterrupted flow by parallel structure and a stream of conjunctions.

From his own insistent energy, Johnson would create an illusion that the outcome, and thus the responsibility, rested on the decision of this one senator; refusing to permit any implication of the reality they both knew (but which in this office began to seem increasingly more uncertain), that the decisions of many other senators would also affect the results.

Then too, Johnson was that rare American man who felt free to display intimacy with another man, through expressions of feeling and also in physical closeness. In an empty room he would stand or sit next to a man as if all that were available was a three-foot space. He could flatter men with sentiments of love and touch their bodies with gestures of affection. The intimacy was all the more excusable because it seemed genuine and without menace. Yet it was also the product of meticulous calculation. And it worked. To the ardor and the bearing of this extraordinary man, the ordinary senator would almost invariably succumb.

Johnson was often able to use the same behavior with the press as he did with his colleagues, dividing it into separate components, and carving out a special relationship with each of the reporters.

"You learn," he said, "that Stewart Alsop cares a lot about appearing to be an intellectual and a historian—he strives to match his brother's intellectual attainments—so whenever you talk to him, play down the gold cufflinks which you play up with *Time* magazine, and to him, emphasize your relationship with FDR and your roots in Texas, so much so that even when it doesn't fit the conversation you make sure to bring in maxims from your father and stories from the Old West. You learn that Evans and Novak love to traffic in backroom politics and political intrigue, so that when you're with them you make sure to bring in lots of details and colorful descriptions of personality. You learn that Mary McGrory likes dominant personalities and Doris Fleeson cares only about issues, so that when you're with McGrory you come on strong and with Fleeson you make yourself sound like some impractical red-hot liberal."

Basic Victim Positions

Margaret Atwood

Position One: To deny the fact that you are a victim.

This uses up a lot of energy, as you must spend much time explaining away the obvious, suppressing anger, and pretending that certain visible facts do not exist. The position is usually taken by those in a Victim group who are a little better off than the others in that group. They are afraid to recognize they are victims for fear of losing the privileges they possess, and they are forced to account somehow for the disadvantages suffered by the rest of the people in the group by disparaging them. As in: "*I* made it, therefore it's obvious we aren't victims. The rest are just lazy (or neurotic, or stupid); anyway it's their own fault if they aren't happy, look at all the opportunities available for them!"

If anger is felt by Victims in Position One, it is likely to be directed against one's fellow-victims, particularly those who try to talk about their victimization.

The Basic game in Position One is "Deny your Victim-experience."

"Basic Victim Positions" by Margaret Atwood from *Survival*, (1972), pp. 36–39. Ontario: House of Anansi Press Ltd. Reprinted by permission of Stoddart Publishing Co. Limited, 34 Lesmill Rd., Don Mills, Ontario, Canada.

Position Two: To acknowledge the fact that you are a victim, but to explain this as an act of Fate, the Will of God, the dictates of Biology (in the case of women, for instance), the necessity decreed by History, or Economics, or the Unconscious, or any other large general powerful idea.

In any case, since it is the fault of this large *thing* and not your own fault, you can neither be blamed for your position nor be expected to do anything about it. You can be resigned and long-suffering, or you can kick against the pricks and make a fuss; in the latter case your rebellion will be deemed foolish or evil even by you, and you will expect to lose and be punished, for who can fight Fate (or the Will of God, or Biology)? Notice that:

1. The explanation *displaces* the cause from the real source of oppression to something else.
2. Because the fake cause is so vast, nebulous and unchangeable you are permanently excused from changing it, *and also* from deciding how much of your situation (e.g. the climate) is unchangeable, how much can be changed, and how much is caused by habit or tradition or your own need to be a victim.
3. Anger, when present—or scorn, since everyone in the category is defined as inferior—is directed against both fellow-victims and oneself.

The basic game in Position Two is Victor/Victim.

Position Three: To acknowledge the fact that you are a victim but to refuse to accept the assumption that the role is inevitable.

As in: "Look what's being done to me, and it isn't Fate, it isn't the Will of God. Therefore I can stop seeing myself as a *fated* Victim." To put it differently: you can distinguish between the *role* of Victim (which probably leads you to seek victimization even when there's no call for it), and the *objective experience* that is making you a victim. And you can probably go further and decide how much of the objective experience could be changed if you made the effort.

This is a dynamic position, rather than a static one; from it you can move on to Position Four, but if you become locked into your anger and fail to change your situation, you might well find yourself back in Position Two. Notice that:

1. In this position the real cause of oppression is for the first time identified.
2. Anger can be directed against the real source of oppression, and energy channelled into constructive action.
3. You can make real decisions about how much of your position can be changed and how much can't (you can't make it stop snowing; you can stop blaming the snow for everything that's wrong).

The basic game of Position Three is repudiating the Victim role.

Position Four: To be a creative non-victim.

Strictly speaking, Position Four is a position not for victims but for those who have never been victims at all, or for ex-victims: those who have been able to move into it from Position Three because the external and/or the internal causes of victimization have been removed. (In an oppressed society, of course, you can't become an ex-victim—insofar as you are connected with your society—until the entire society's position has been changed.)

In Position Four, creative activity of all kinds becomes possible. Energy is no longer being suppressed (as in Position One) or used up for displacement of the cause, or for passing your victimization along to others (Man kicks Child, Child kicks Dog) as in Position Two; nor is it being used for the dynamic anger of Position Three.

Señor Payroll

William E. Barrett

Larry and I were Junior Engineers in the gas plant, which means that we were clerks. Anything that could be classified as paperwork came to that flat double desk across which we faced each other. The Main Office downtown sent us a bewildering array of orders and rules that were to be put into effect.

Junior Engineers were beneath the notice of everyone except the Mexican-American laborers at the plant. To them we were the visible form of a distant, unknowable paymaster. We were Señor Payroll.

Those Mexican-Americans were great workmen: the aristocrats among them were the stokers, big men who worked Herculean eight-hour shifts in the fierce heat of the retorts. They scooped coal with huge shovels and hurled it with uncanny aim at tiny doors. The coal streamed out from the shovels like black water from a high pressure nozzle, and never missed the narrow opening. The stokers worked stripped to the waist, and there was pride and dignity in them. Few men could do such work, and they were the few.

The Company paid its men only twice a month, on the fifth and on the twentieth. To a Mexican-American, this was absurd. What man with money will make it last 15 days? If he hoarded money beyond the spending of three days, he was a miser—and when, Señor, did the blood of Spain flow in the veins of misers? Hence it was the custom for our stokers to appear every third or fourth day to draw the money due to them.

There was a certain elasticity in the Company rules, and Larry and I sent the necessary forms to the Main Office and received an "advance" against a man's paycheck. Then, one day, Downtown favored us with a memorandum:

"There have been too many abuses of the advance-against-wages privilege. Hereafter, no advance against wages will be made to any employee except in a case of genuine emergency."

We had no sooner posted the notice when in came stoker Juan Garcia. He asked for an advance. I pointed to the notice. He spelled it through slowly, then said, "What does this mean, this 'genuine emergency'?"

I explained to him patiently that the Company was kind and sympathetic, but that it was a great nuisance to have to pay wages every few days. If someone was ill or if money was urgently needed for some other good reason, then the Company would make an exception to the rule.

Juan Garcia turned his hat over and over slowly in his big hands. "I do not get my money?"

"Next payday, Juan. On the 20th."

He went out silently and I felt ashamed of myself. I looked across the desk at Larry. He avoided my eyes.

In the next hour two other stokers came in, looked at the notice, had it explained and walked solemnly out; then no more came. What we did not know was that Juan Garcia, Pete Mendoza and Francisco Gonzalez had spread the word and that every Mexican-American in the plant was explaining the order to every other Mexican-American. "To get the money now, the wife must be sick. There must be medicine for the baby."

The next morning Juan Garcia's wife was practically dying, Pete Mendoza's mother would hardly last the day, there was a veritable epidemic among children and, just for variety, there was one sick father. We always suspected that the old man was really sick; no Mexican-American would otherwise have thought of him. At any rate, nobody paid Larry and me to examine private lives; we made out our forms with an added line describing the "genuine emergency." Our people got paid.

That went on for a week. Then came a new order, curt and to the point: "Hereafter employees will be paid ONLY on the fifth and the 20th of the month. No exceptions will be made except in the cases of employees leaving the service of the Company."

The notice went up on the board and we explained its significance gravely. "No, Juan Garcia, we cannot advance your wages. It is too bad about your wife and your cousins and your aunts, but there is a new rule."

Juan Garcia went out and thought it over. He thought out loud with Mendoza and Gonzales and Ayala, then, in the morning, he was back. "I am quitting this company for different job. You pay me now?"

We argued that it was a good company and that it loved its employees like children, but in the end we paid off, because Juan Garcia quit. And so did Gonzales, Mendoza, Obregon, Ayala and Ortez, the best stokers, men who could not be replaced.

Larry and I looked at each other; we knew what was coming in about three days. One of our duties was to sit on the hiring line early each morning, engaging transient workers for the handy gangs. Any man was accepted who could walk up and ask for a job without falling down. Never before had we been called upon to hire such skilled virtuosos as stokers for handy gang work, but we were called upon to hire them now.

The day foreman was wringing his hands and asking the Almighty if he was personally supposed to shovel this condemned coal, while there in a stolid, patient line were skilled men—Garcia, Mendoza and others—waiting to be hired. We hired them, of course. There was nothing else to do.

Every day we had a line of resigning stokers, and another line of stokers seeking work. Our paperwork became very complicated. At the Main Office they were jumping up and down. The procession of forms showing Juan Garcia's resigning and being hired over and over again was too much for them. Sometimes Downtown had Garcia on the payroll twice at the same time when someone down there was slow in entering a resignation. Our phone rang early and often.

Tolerantly and patiently we explained: "There's nothing we can do if a man wants to quit, and if there are stokers available when the plant needs stokers, we hire them."

Out of chaos, Downtown issued another order. I read it and whistled. Larry looked at it and said, "It is going to be very quiet around here."

The order read: "Hereafter, no employee who resigns may be rehired within a period of 30 days."

Juan Garcia was due for another resignation, and when he came in we showed him the order and explained that standing in line the next day would do him no good if he resigned today. "Thirty days is a long time, Juan."

It was a grave matter and he took time to reflect on it. So did Gonzales, Mendoza, Ayala and Ortez. Ultimately, however, they were all back—and all resigned.

We did our best to dissuade them and we were sad about the parting. This time it was for keeps and they shook hands with us solemnly. It was very nice knowing us. Larry and I looked at each other when they were gone and we both knew that neither of us had been pulling for Downtown to win this duel. It was a blue day.

In the morning, however, they were all back in line. With the utmost gravity, Juan Garcia informed me that he was a stoker looking for a job.

"No dice, Juan" I said. "Come back in 30 days. I warned you."

His eyes looked straight into mine without a flicker. "There is some mistake, Señor," he said. "I am Manuel Hernandez. I work as the stoker in Pueblo, in Santa Fe, in many places."

I stared back at him, remembering the sick wife and the babies without medicine, the mother-in-law in the hospital, the many resignations and the rehirings. I knew that there was a gas plant in Pueblo, and that there wasn't any in Santa Fe; but who was I to argue with a man about his own name? A stoker is a stoker.

So I hired him. I hired Gonzalez, too, who swore that his name was Carrera, and Ayala, who had shamelessy become Smith.

Three days later, the resigning started.

Within a week our payroll read like a history of Latin America. Everyone was on it: Lopez and Obregon, Villa, Diaz, Batista, Gomez, and even San Martin and Bolivar. Finally Larry and I, growing weary of staring at familiar faces and writing unfamiliar names, went to the Superintendent and told him the whole story. He tried not to grin, and said, "Damned nonsense!"

The next day the orders were taken down. We called our most prominent stokers into the office and pointed to the board. No rules any more.

"The next time we hire you *hombres*," Larry said grimly, "come in under the names you like best, because that's the way you are going to stay on the books."

They looked at us and they looked at the board; then for the first time in the long duel, their teeth flashed white. "*Si, Señores,*" they said.

And so it was.

The Catbird Seat

James Thurber

Mr. Martin bought the pack of Camels on Monday night in the most crowded cigar store on Broadway. It was theater time and seven or eight men were buying cigarettes. The clerk didn't even glance at Mr. Martin, who put the pack in his overcoat pocket and went out. If any of the staff at F & S has seen him buy the cigarettes, they would have been astonished, for it was generally known that Mr. Martin did not smoke, and never had. No one saw him.

It was just a week to the day since Mr. Martin had decided to rub out Mrs. Ulgine Barrows. The term "rub out" pleased him because it suggested nothing more than the correction of an error—in this case an error of Mr. Fitweiler. Mr. Martin had spent each night of the past week working out his plan and examining it. As he walked home now he went over it again. For the hundredth time he resented the element of imprecision, the margin of guesswork that entered into the business. The project as he had worked it out was casual and bold, the risks were considerable. Something might go wrong anywhere along the line. And therein lay the cunning of his scheme. No one would ever see in it the cautious, painstaking hand of Erwin Martin, head of the filing department of F & S, of whom Mr. Fitweiler had once said, "Man is fallible but Martin isn't." No one would see his hand, that is, unless it were caught in the act.

Sitting in his apartment, drinking a glass of milk, Mr. Martin reviewed his case against Mrs. Ulgine Barrows, as he had every night for seven nights. He began at the beginning. Her quacking voice and braying laugh had first profaned the halls of F & S on March 7, 1941 (Mr. Martin had a head for dates). Old Roberts, the personnel chief, had introduced her as the newly appointed special adviser to the president of the firm, Mr. Fitweiler. The woman had appalled Mr. Martin instantly, but he hadn't shown it. He had given her his dry hand, a look of studious concentration, and a faint smile. "Well," she had said, looking at the papers on his desk, "are you lifting the oxcart out of the ditch?" As Mr. Martin recalled that moment, over his milk, he squirmed slightly. He must keep his mind on her crimes as a special adviser, not on her peccadillos as a personality. This he found difficult to do, in spite of entering an objection and sustaining it. The faults of the woman as a woman kept chattering on in his mind like an unruly witness. She had, for almost two years now, baited him. In the halls, in the elevator, even in his own office, into which she romped now and then like a circus horse, she was constantly shouting these silly questions at him. "Are you lifting the oxcart out of that ditch? Are you tearing up the pea patch? Are you hollering down the rain barrel? Are you scraping around the bottom of the pickle barrel? Are you sitting in the catbird seat?"

It was Joey Hart, one of Mr. Martin's two assistants, who had explained what the gibberish meant. "She must be a Dodger fan," he had said. "Red Barber announces the Dodger games over the radio and he uses those expressions—picked 'em up down South." Joey had gone on to explain one or two. "Tearing up the pea patch" meant going on a rampage; "sitting in the catbird seat" meant sitting pretty, like a batter with three balls and no strikes on him. Mr. Martin dismissed all this with an effort. It had been annoying, it had driven him near to distraction, but he was too solid a man to be moved to murder by anything so childish. It was fortunate, he reflected as he passed on to the important charges against Mrs. Barrows, that he had stood up under it so well. He had maintained always an outward appearance of polite tolerance. "Why, I even believe you like the woman," Miss Paird, his other assistant, had once said to him. He had simply smiled.

A gavel rapped in Mr. Martin's mind and the case proper was resumed. Mrs. Ulgine Barrows stood charged with willful, blatant, and persistent attempts to destroy the efficiency and system of F & S. It was competent, material, and relevant to review her advent and rise to power. Mr. Martin had got the story from Miss Paird, who seemed always able to find things out. According to her, Mrs. Barrows had met Mr. Fitweiler at a party, where she had rescued him from the embraces of a powerfully built drunken man who had mistaken the president of F & S for a famous retired Middle Western football coach. She had led him to a sofa and somehow worked upon him a monstrous magic. The aging gentleman had jumped to the conclusion there and then that this was a woman of singular attainments, equipped to bring out the best in him and in the firm. A week later he had introduced her into F & S as his special adviser. On that day confusion got its foot in the door. After Miss Tyson, Mr. Brundage, and Mr. Bartlett had been fired and Mr. Munson had taken his hat and stalked out, mailing in his resignation later, old Roberts had been emboldened to speak to Mr. Fitweiler. He mentioned that Mr. Munson's department had been a "little disrupted" and hadn't they perhaps better resume the old system there? Mr. Fitweiler had said certainly not. He had the greatest faith in Mrs. Barrows' ideas. "They require a little seasoning, a little seasoning, is all," he had added. Mr. Roberts had given it up. Mr. Martin reviewed in detail all the changes wrought by Mrs. Barrows. She had begun chipping at the cornices of the firm's edifice and now she was swinging at the foundation stones with a pickaxe.

Mr. Martin came now, in his summing up, to the afternoon of Monday, November 2, 1942—just one week ago. On that day, at 3 P.M., Mrs. Barrows had bounced into his office. "Boo!" she had yelled. "Are you scraping around the bottom of the pickle barrel?" Mr. Martin had looked at her from under his green eyeshade, saying nothing. She had begun to wander about the office, taking it in with her great, popping eyes. "Do you really need *all* these filing cabinets?" she had demanded suddenly. Mr. Martin's heart had jumped. "Each of these files," he had said, keeping his voice even, "plays an indispensable part in the system of F & S." She had brayed at him, "Well, don't tear up the pea patch!" and gone to the door. From there she had bawled, "But you sure have got a lot of fine scrap here!" Mr. Martin could no longer doubt that the finger was on his beloved department. Her pickaxe was on the upswing, poised for the first blow. It had not come yet; he had received no blue memo from the enchanted Mr. Fitweiler bearing nonsensical instructions deriving from the obscene woman. But there was no doubt in Mr. Martin's mind that one would be forthcoming. He must act quickly. Already a precious week had gone by. Mr. Martin stood up in his living room, still holding his milk glass. "Gentlemen of the jury," he said to himself, "I demand the death penalty for this horrible person."

The next day Mr. Martin followed his routine, as usual. He polished his glasses more often and once sharpened an already sharp pencil, but not even Miss Paird noticed. Only once did he catch sight of his victim; she swept past him in the hall with a patronizing "Hi!" At five-thirty he walked home, as usual, and had a glass of milk, as usual. He had never drunk anything stronger in his life—unless you could count ginger ale. The late Sam Schlosser, the S of F & S, had praised Mr. Martin at a staff meeting several years before for his temperate habits. "Our most efficient worker neither drinks nor smokes," he had said. "The results speak for themselves." Mr. Fitweiler had sat by, nodding approval.

Mr. Martin was still thinking about that red-letter day as he walked over to the Schrafft's on Fifth Avenue near Forty-sixth Street. He got there, as he always did, at eight o'clock. He finished his dinner and the financial page of the *Sun* at a quarter to nine, as he always did. It was his custom after dinner to take a walk. This time he walked down Fifth Avenue at a casual pace. His gloved hands felt moist and warm, his forehead cold. He transferred the Camels from his overcoat to a jacket pocket. He wondered, as he did so, if they did not represent an unnecessary note of strain. Mrs. Barrows smoked only Luckies. It was his idea to puff a few puffs on a Camel (after the rubbing-out), stub it out in the ashtray holding her lipstick-stained Luckies, and thus drag a small red herring across the trail. Perhaps it was not a good idea. It would take time. He might even choke, too loudly.

Mr. Martin had never seen the house on West Twelfth Street where Mrs. Barrows lived, but he had a clear enough picture of it. Fortunately, she had bragged to everybody about her ducky first-floor apartment in the perfectly darling three-story red-brick. There would be no doorman or other attendants; just the tenants of the second and third floors. As he walked along, Mr. Martin realized that he would get there before nine-thirty. He had considered walking north on Fifth

Avenue from Schrafft's to a point from which it would take him until ten o'clock to reach the house. At that hour people were less likely to be coming in or going out. But the procedure would have made an awkward loop in the straight thread of his casualness, and he had abandoned it. It was impossible to figure when people would be entering or leaving the house, anyway. There was a great risk at any hour. If he ran into anybody, he would simply have to place the rubbing-out of Ulgine Barrows in the inactive file forever. The same thing would hold true if there were someone in her apartment. In that case he would just say that he had been passing by, recognized her charming house and thought to drop in.

It was eighteen minutes after nine when Mr. Martin turned into Twelfth Street. A man passed him, and a man and a woman talking. There was no one within fifty paces when he came to the house, halfway down the block. He was up the steps and in the small vestibule in no time, pressing the bell under the card that said "Mrs. Ulgine Barrows." When the clicking in the lock started, he jumped forward against the door. He got inside fast, closing the door behind him. A bulb in a lantern hung from the hall ceiling on a chain seemed to give a monstrously bright light. There was nobody on the stair, which went up ahead of him along the left wall. A door opened down the hall in the wall on the right. He went toward it swiftly, on tiptoe.

"Well, for God's sake, look who's here!" bawled Mrs. Barrows, and her braying laugh rang out like the report of a shotgun. He rushed past her like a football tackle, bumping her. "Hey, quit shoving!" she said, closing the door behind them. They were in her living room, which seemed to Mr. Martin to be lighted by a hundred lamps. "What's after you?" she said. "You're as jumpy as a goat." He found he was unable to speak. His heart was wheezing in his throat. "I—yes," he finally brought out. She was jabbering and laughing as she started to help him off with his coat. "No, no," he said. "I'll put it here." He took it off and put it on a chair near the door. "Your hat and gloves, too," she said. "You're in a lady's house." He put his hat on top of the coat. Mrs. Barrows seemed larger than he had thought. He kept his gloves on. "I was passing by," he said. "I recognized—is there anyone here?" She laughed louder than ever. "No," she said, "we're all alone. You're as white as a sheet, you funny man. Whatever *has* come over you? I'll mix you a toddy." She started toward a door across the room. "Scotch-and-soda be all right? But say, you don't drink, do you?" She turned and gave him her amused look. Mr. Martin pulled himself together. "Scotch-and-soda will be all right," he heard himself say. He could hear her laughing in the kitchen.

Mr. Martin looked quickly around the living room for the weapon. He had counted on finding one there. There were andirons and a poker and something in a corner that looked like an Indian club. None of them would do. It couldn't be that way. He began to pace around. He came to a desk. On it lay a metal paper knife with an ornate handle. Would it be sharp enough? He reached for it and knocked over a small brass jar. Stamps spilled out of it and it fell to the floor with a clatter. "Hey," Mrs. Barrows yelled from the kitchen, "are you tearing up the pea patch?" Mr. Martin gave a strange laugh. Picking up the knife, he tried its point against his left wrist. It was blunt. It wouldn't do.

When Mrs. Barrows reappeared, carrying two highballs, Mr. Martin, standing there with his gloves on, became acutely conscious of the fantasy he had wrought. Cigarettes in his pocket, a drink prepared for him—it was all too grossly improbable. It was more than that; it was impossible. Somewhere in the back of his mind a vague idea stirred, sprouted. "For heaven's sake, take off those gloves," said Mrs. Barrows. "I always wear them in the house," said Mr. Martin. The idea began to bloom, strange and wonderful. She put the glasses on a coffee table in front of a sofa and sat on the sofa. "Come over here, you odd little man," she said. Mr. Martin went over and sat beside her. It was difficult getting a cigarette out of the pack of Camels, but he managed it. She held a match for him, laughing. "Well," she said, handing him his drink, "this is perfectly marvelous. You with a drink and a cigarette."

Mr. Martin puffed, not too awkwardly, and took a gulp of the highball. "I drink and smoke all the time," he said. He clinked his glass against hers. "Here's nuts to that old windbag, Fitweiler," he said, and gulped again. The stuff tasted awful, but he made no grimace. "Really, Mr. Martin," she said, her voice and posture changing, "you are insulting our employer." Mrs. Barrows was now all special adviser to the president. "I am preparing a bomb," said Mr. Martin, "which will blow the old goat higher than hell." He had only had a little of the drink, which was not strong. It couldn't be that. "Do you take dope or something?" Mrs. Barrows asked coldly. "Heroin," said Mr. Martin. "I'll be coked to the gills when I bump that old buzzard off." "Mr. Martin!" she shouted, getting to her feet. "That will be all of that. You must go at once." Mr. Martin took another swallow of his drink. He tapped his cigarette out in the ashtray and put the pack of Camels on the coffee table. Then he got up. She stood glaring at him. He walked over and put on his hat and coat. "Not a word about this," he said, and laid an index finger against his lips. All Mrs. Barrows could bring out was "Really!" Mr. Martin put his hand on the doorknob. "I'm sitting in the catbird seat," he said. He stuck his tongue out at her and left. Nobody saw him go.

Mr. Martin got to his apartment, walking, well before eleven. No one saw him go in. He had two glasses of milk after brushing his teeth, and he felt elated. It wasn't tipsiness, because he hadn't been tipsy. Anyway, the walk had worn off all effects of the whisky. He got in bed and read a magazine for a while. He was asleep before midnight.

Mr. Martin got to the office at eight-thirty the next morning, as usual. At a quarter to nine, Ulgine Barrows, who had never before arrived at work before ten, swept into his office. "I'm reporting to Mr. Fitweiler now!" she shouted. "If he turns you over to the police, it's no more than you deserve!" Mr. Martin gave her a look of shocked surprise. "I beg your pardon?" he said. Mrs. Barrows snorted and bounced out of the room, leaving Miss Paird and Joey Hart staring after her. "What's the matter with that old devil now?" asked Miss Paird. "I have no idea," said Mr. Martin, resuming his work. The other two looked at him and then at each other. Miss Paird got up and went out. She walked slowly past the closed door of Mr. Fitweiler's office. Mrs. Barrows was yelling inside, but she was not braying. Miss Paird could not hear what the woman was saying. She went back to her desk.

Forty-five minutes later, Mrs. Barrows left the president's office and went into her own, shutting the door. It wasn't until half an hour later that Mr. Fitweiler sent for Mr. Martin. The head of the filing department, neat, quiet, attentive, stood in front of the old man's desk. Mr. Fitweiler was pale and nervous. He took his glasses off and twiddled them. He made a small, bruffing sound in his throat. "Martin," he said, "you have been with us more than twenty years." "Twenty-two, sir," said Mr. Martin. "In that time," pursued the president, "your work and your—uh—manner have been exemplary." "I trust so, sir," said Mr. Martin. "I have understood, Martin," said Mr. Fitweiler, "that you have never taken a drink or smoked." "That is correct, sir," said Mr. Martin. "Ah, yes." Mr. Fitweiler polished his glasses. "You may describe what you did after leaving the office yesterday, Martin," he said. Mr. Martin allowed less than a second for his bewildered pause. "Certainly sir," he said. "I walked home. Then I went to Schrafft's for dinner. Afterward I walked home again. I went to bed early, sir, and read a magazine for a while. I was asleep before eleven." "Ah, yes," said Mr. Fitweiler again. He was silent for a moment, searching for the proper words to say to the head of the filing department. "Mrs. Barrows," he said finally, "Mrs. Barrows has worked hard, Martin, very hard. It grieves me to report that she has suffered a severe breakdown. It has taken the form of a persecution complex accompanied by distressing hallucinations." "I am very sorry, sir," said Mr. Martin. "Mrs. Barrows is under the delusion," continued Mr. Fitweiler, "that you visited her last evening and behaved yourself in an—uh—unseemly manner." He raised his hand to silence Mr. Martin's little pained outcry. "It is the nature of these psychological diseases," Mr. Fitweiler said, "to fix upon the least likely and most innocent party as the—uh—source of persecution. These matters are not for the lay mind to grasp, Martin. I've just had my psychiatrist, Dr. Fitch, on the phone. He would not, of course, commit himself, but he made enough generalizations to substantiate my suspicions. I suggested to Mrs. Barrows when she had completed her—uh—story to me this morning, that she visit Dr. Fitch, for I suspected a condition at once. She flew, I regret to say, into a rage, and demanded—uh—requested that I call you on the carpet. You may not know, Martin, but Mrs. Barrows had planned a reorganization of your department—subject to my approval, of course, subject to my approval. This brought you, rather than anyone else, to her mind—but again that is a phenomenon for Dr. Fitch and not for us. So, Martin, I am afraid Mrs. Barrows' usefulness here is at an end." "I am dreadfully sorry, sir," said Mr. Martin.

It was at this point that the door to the office blew open with the suddenness of a gas-main explosion and Mrs. Barrows catapulted through it. "Is the little rat denying it?" she screamed. "He can't get away with that!" Mr. Martin got up and moved discreetly to a point beside Mr. Fitweiler's chair. "You drank and smoked at my apartment," she bawled at Mr. Martin, "and you know it! You called Mr. Fitweiler an old windbag and said you were going to blow him up when you got coked to the gills on your heroin!" She stopped yelling to catch her breath and a new glint came into her popping eyes. "If you weren't such a drab, ordinary little man," she said, "I'd think you'd planned it all. Sticking your tongue out, saying you were sitting in the catbird seat, because you thought no one would believe me when I told it! My God, it's really too perfect!" She brayed loudly and hysterically, and the fury was on her again. She glared at Mr. Fitweiler. "Can't you see how he has tricked us, you old fool? Can't you see his little game?" But Mr. Fitweiler had been

surreptitiously pressing all the buttons under the top of his desk and employees of
F & S began pouring into the room. "Stockton," said Mr. Fitweiler, "you and Fishbein will take Mrs. Barrows to her home. Mrs. Powell, you will go with them."
Stockton, who had played a little football in high school, blocked Mrs. Barrows as
she made for Mr. Martin. It took him and Fishbein together to force her out of the
door into the hall, crowded with stenographers and office boys. She was still
screaming imprecations at Mr. Martin, tangled and contradictory imprecations.
The hubbub finally died out down the corridor.

"I regret that this has happened," said Mr. Fitweiler. "I shall ask you to dismiss
it from your mind, Martin." "Yes, sir," said Mr. Martin, anticipating his chief's
"That will be all" by moving to the door. "I will dismiss it." He went out and shut
the door, and his step was light and quick in the hall. When he entered his department he had slowed down to his customary gait, and he walked quietly across the
room to the W20 file, wearing a look of studious concentration.

The Ratebuster: The Case of the Saleswoman*

Melville Dalton

THE SALESWOMEN

Of the six people in the boys' department only the head was male, and he made
sales only occasionally. Two of the women were high sellers—Mrs. White and Mrs.
Brown. Mrs. White was fifty-nine years old, large physically and somewhat taci-

---

*The names of the individuals in this case and the department store (Lassiters) are fictional. The inci-
dents described took place in the boys' department of Lassiters. The saleswomen in the department
were all on commission.

As Dalton observed in a portion of this article which was omitted here, it is common for members of
work groups who are on a commission or other system of incentive payments to avoid showing each
other up. In other words, there are informal standards about what members of the group perceive to be
a reasonable amount of work. Individuals who produce significantly above this level are often called
"ratebusters" or "grabbers" by social scientists. Members of the work group often apply less complimentary labels and even sanctions to individuals who violate the output norms. At Lassiters, ratebusters
were called "saleshogs" by their peers—*Ed. note.*

turn. She had worked at Lassiters for fourteen years. Mrs. Brown was a small active person, thirty-two and had been with the store for eight years. Masters told me that when she started in the store she was much taken with Mrs. White and copied and improved upon Mrs. White's selling techniques. Then, too, Mrs. Brown had the insights that came from close personal experience in outfitting her son. Over a period of several months they developed a rivalry. For the last six years or so, according to Masters [Mike Masters, head of the boys' department], they were coldly polite to each other when it was necessary to speak. Masters regarded existence of this hostility as one of his major problems. His professed ideal was that the women should all be circulating among the customers, busy all the time and cordial to each other.

The other three salesgirls were Mrs. Bonomo, thirty-five, a quiet amenable person, in the department for four years; Mrs. Selby, forty-eight, an employee for five years, who took things as they came without being much disturbed—though judging from her behavior and remarks she made, she disliked Mrs. White much more than she did Mrs. Brown. Mrs. Dawson, at twenty-two, was the youngest member of the department. She had dubbed Mrs. Brown and Mrs. White "saleshogs." She had worked there less than two years. She liked Mrs. Brown despite the epithet she had given her. Mrs. Dawson had two years of college, the most schooling in the department.

The saleswomen received from $1.75 to $2.25 per hour, depending on how long they had been in the department. Records of sales (dollar-volume) for the department were kept for the past year and varied from month to month. These records established the quota for the current year. Once this was equaled, the women started drawing commission pay at the rate of five percent. Commission was paid separately once a month.

Before describing the selling tactics of Mrs. Brown and Mrs. White, the ratebuster types, it is instructive to note the average daily sales established over a six month period[1] by the five saleswomen. Mrs. Brown with $227 average daily sales is over twice as much as Mrs. Dawson and Mrs. Selby, nearly twice as much as Mrs. Bonomo, and $74 more than the second ratebuster, Mrs. White. Masters assured me that Mrs. White had slowed up noticeably in her selling over the last two years, but in terms of dollar sales and her constant challenge to Mrs. Brown she should still be classified as a ratebuster, or a ratebuster in decline.

Lassiters had an employee credit union. Masters had access to the complete membership which was seventy-six. He gave me *rank only* of the five saleswomen

Saleswomen	Average Daily Dollar Sales
Mrs. Brown	227
Mrs. White	153
Mrs. Bonomo	119
Mrs. Selby	110
Mrs. Dawson	101

based on the individual amounts deposited in the credit union. (He was so shocked when I requested the total savings of each of the saleswomen that I gladly accepted the partial data.) Mrs. White stood third in the store, and Mrs. Brown was fourth. Mrs. Selby ranked forty-ninth and Mrs. Bonomo was sixty-sixth. Mrs. Dawson was not a member. These data alone do not tell much, but they do indicate that Mrs. White and Mrs. Brown were among the top investors, and that commission was important in their behavior.

RATEBUSTER TACTICS

Mrs. Brown apparently had more personal relations with customers than anyone in the boys' department. She learned from Masters when specially-priced merchandise was coming in. She telephoned customers she knew well and made arrangements to lay away items of given size and style that were scheduled to go on sale. When she had filled these private orders there was little of the merchandise left for the general public when the official sale day arrived. These sales by telephone constituted about fifteen percent of her total sales. Relatively new customers who bought heavily a time or two she filed in her retentive memory and took steps to acquaint them with her special services.

Among her repeat buyers was a working woman with four sons who treated their clothing roughly. Every six weeks this woman came in to buy nearly complete outfits for the boys. This included shirts, underwear, socks and blue jeans, which amounted to what the sales force called a "big ticket" of about $120.

Mrs. Brown had another woman customer who did not believe in having the younger boys of her five sons wear the older boys' outgrown clothing. She did not come in much oftener than once a year to buy complete outfits, usually just before Easter, which could run to two hundred dollars or more. Mrs. Brown acted as though she had an exclusive right[2] to these customers, and several others that she knew who had only two sons. When Mrs. Brown expected these people, she would skip her lunch hour for fear she might miss them, or ask Masters to make the sale and ring it up on her cash drawer in case the woman came when she was out to lunch. He was glad to do this. When business was very good, whether she expected specific customers or not, she ignored the coffee breaks (ten minutes each morning and afternoon) and the lunch hour, leaving the selling floor only long enough to eat a sandwich in the dressing room.

She also had a practical monopoly on sales for boys on welfare. These boys had to be presented by an agent on the welfare organization the first time they did business with the store. Masters turned the welfare customer over to Mrs. Brown and forever afterwards[3] she made the sales. In some cases the welfare officer brought the boy, or boys, with their only clothes on their backs, to buy a complete outfit with extra socks, handkerchiefs and underwear. (Shoes were not sold in the boys' department.) In any case, Mrs. Brown took care of the sales then and afterwards.

Mrs. Brown's housekeeping area was just inside the entrance from the parking lot. She watched this approach closely. When she was not busy, or was talking to the other members of the department, she could break off instantly—even when she was telling a joke—and move toward the door. If she did not recognize the person she formed some judgment on him based on the affluence of his dress and his bearing. If the customer had a boy along, she judged whether he would be hard to fit. In her own words, she had a theory that "the kids who are tall and skinny or short and fat are hard to fit."[4] Thus she made quick appraisals of everybody who moved toward the department. If she approached a customer and learned that he was not as promising as he looked, she often brought the person to one of the other saleswomen and presented him with a statement of what he wanted as though—according to the women—she was giving them an assured sale. She made no revealing comment on the matter, but she seemed at the same time to be putting a restraint on her rivals.

Mrs. Brown's most galling behavior to the group was her practice of getting sale claims on as many prospective buyers as possible. She thus deprived the other saleswomen of a chance at the buyers. For instance, as she was serving one person, she would see another coming through the door—which she nearly always faced even when busiest. Quickly she would lay a number of items before the first person with the promise to be back in a moment, then hurry to capture the second customer. If the situation were right, she might get her claim on three or four buyers while two or more of the saleswomen were reduced to maintaining the show cases, and setting things in order so as not to appear idle. Mrs. Brown was able to do this because her own housekeeping and stocking area (assigned by Masters) lay between the entrance to the store and the other sections of the boys' department. Only Mrs. White would challenge her by intercepting a patron. The rivalry between them never came to a visible break. As noted earlier some of the other saleswomen resented Mrs. Brown's behavior and privately called her a "sales hog." She was not called that by Mrs. Bonomo and Mrs. Selby who thought—as they said—that Mrs. Brown in action was a "show in itself."

A standard device was used by Mrs. Brown, for ends not intended, with the understanding and collaboration of Masters. On very slack days she frequently left the store shortly after one or two o'clock to do "comparative shopping," that is, to compare the selling prices of items that Lassiters sold with the prices that other local stores charged for the same or similar items. Sometimes Mrs. Brown actually did this, but often she would attend a matinee, or go home to catch up with her housework, or just take a nap. (Her time card was punched out by Masters at the official quitting time.) In any case, to the favorable implications of "comparative shopping," the further obvious inference was made that her absence from the store allowed the other salesgirls to make more commission. (Actually, business was so slow on some days, because of weather, etc., that it was not possible for any of the saleswomen to earn bonus pay.)

Mrs. Brown's conduct may suggest total indifference to the group. But possibly because she was a female in our society, she was not as nonconformist as the grim ratebusters in industry. Some of these could work for years without exchange of words with people, only a few feet away, that they knew hated them. To a degree Mrs. Brown was concerned about her group. Every week or so she would buy a two pound box of choice chocolates from a candy store near Lassiters and bring it in to share with the group. She could have bought a less expensive grade of candy at Lassiters. Sharing of the candy was almost certainly calculated (she ate little of it herself) but it appeared spontaneous and was received without hesitation. The saleswomen could not direct an unqualified hostility toward her.

She had another uncommon practice which made her stand apart from all of Lassiters' employees. Despite her determined assault on the commission system she did not use her right to a discount on items that she might buy for herself or members of her family. She took her fifteen-year-old son to a local independent department store to buy his clothes. She vigorously declared that "I don't want anything that [Lassiters] has." She was emphatic to the group—and implicitly condemned them—that she did not want to participate in the common practice of getting legal price reductions in addition to the regular employee discount by buying items at the end of a season. For example, an assortment of women's purses would be delivered to the selling floor. This was the "beginning of the season" for that batch of purses. The saleswomen with friends in the purse department would look at the display and select ones that appealed to them. These were laid away until the "end of the season" when they could be bought at the sale price which was further reduced by the regular discount. Mrs. Brown would have nothing to do with such items. She clearly did not want it said that she was taking advantage of her job.

A likely interpretation is that she sensed she was rejected and widely criticized for her methods and high bonus pay. She feared that some envious salesperson would report any borderline activity on her part to top management. Her own explanation implied that her esthetic taste could not be satisfied by the merchandise at Lassiters. In effect she downgraded the status of the store. As part of this complex she also implied that she was morally somewhat above the group. Also she may have been posing to hide her possible guilt feelings about her treatment of the group.

Although the aim of this paper is not to deal with morale problems, it was glaringly clear that Masters damaged group feeling by routing welfare customers to Mrs. Brown, and by ringing up some of his sales on her cash drawer. His tacit approval of her behavior discouraged the other saleswomen from attempting to control her.

NOTES

1. Masters gave me these figures based on an average of 44 hours a week and including the back-to-school buying months of August and September 1969.
2. Probably she was encouraged by the customers to think that way; certainly some customers waited for her to be free to serve them.
3. The other saleswomen knew about this and resented it. Grateful to Masters for allowing me to observe and talk with the saleswomen, I naturally did not ask him why there was no sharing of such sales among his force. I inquired, but there was no voiced conception of a "day's work" among the saleswomen. This general practice of informal rewarding is not

uncommon in industry where it is sometimes done even with the knowledge and coop-eration of individual officers of the union. (Lassiters was not unionized.)

4. Alteration of coats and trousers was done free by the store's tailor. But measuring and marking and the extra trying on were time-consuming. In the extreme cases this was futile. In any case Mrs. Brown avoided customers with "odd size" boys unless she knew them to be liberal buyers and worth her time.

Chapter
9
Secrecy

T here appears to be a curious inconsistency in the thinking of many students of organization. On the one hand, when they write about communication, they emphasize the importance of openness and sharing information widely. Their major concern seems to be with trying to help managers open up communication channels. This position seems to assume that managers and other organizational participants want to share information. On the other hand, many of these same students acknowledge that "information is power."

If information is power, or, as we believe an important source of power, then there will be times when people want to keep it to themselves. The selections in this chapter reveal that, in fact, secrecy is a major concern of people throughout organizations. Issues over secrecy are related to individual privacy, corporate technological advantage, and the competitive positions of nations as well as corporations.

"Is Your Boss Spying on You?" is one of many articles written recently concerning how organizations use new technologies to gain information about employees. As a person interviewed for the article observed, this topic appears likely to become one of the most controversial organizational issues of the current decade.

In the next selection, "Politicians Should Never Forget Cardinal Telephone Rule," Ken MacQueen looks at privacy beyond the workplace. Although the episode described concerns government officials, it should warn all managers that their conversations are not as private as they often assume.

"At Apple, Proper Business Attire May Someday Include a Muzzle" reveals the importance of secrecy to modern organizations and how difficult it can be to maintain. Even people who have no intention of communicating company secrets can inadvertently do so with a casual remark over lunch.

In "CIA Leader Wants Agency Active in Industrial Spying," James McCartney looks at the secrecy issue in national policy and international competitiveness. Is it possible that the economic viability of the United States and other modern nations could depend on their willingness and ability to engage in industrial espionage? Should our government, through such units as the CIA, become involved?

Since these selections describe events of the last few years, they emphasize the role of relatively new technologies. Consequently, it may appear that concerns about privacy and secrecy in organizations are of recent origin. Few things could be further from the truth. While new technologies have added tools, spying on workers and attempting to obtain illicit information about competitors have been a part of organizational reality for a long time. In light of the role of new technologies, the attention currently focused on these issues should not be surprising. In our view, it is also noteworthy how little attention students of organizations have devoted to them until now.

Is Your Boss Spying on You?

Jeffrey Rothfeder, Michele Galen, and Lisa Driscoll

High-tech snooping in "the electronic sweatshop"

"*True or false:*

- *I am very strongly attracted to members of my own sex.*
- *I believe in the second coming of Christ.*
- *I have no difficulty starting or holding my urine.*"

It isn't information that most people volunteer. But applicants for security guard at Minneapolis-based Target Stores must answer those and 701 similar questions.

Reprinted from January 15, 1990 issue of *Business Week* by special permission. Copyright © 1990 by McGraw-Hill, Inc.

Last April, Sibi Soroka passed the test and snagged a job. Afterward, though, he felt "humiliated" and "embarrassed" at having to reveal "my innermost beliefs and feelings." So in a class action filed last September, he has accused Target of illegal prying.

That dispute over workplace privacy highlights what will be "the hottest employment-law topic of the 1990s," predicts Eric H. Joss, a corporate lawyer in Santa Monica, Calif. More than employees imagine, federal and state laws always have given private employers wide latitude for prying. Bosses could rifle through desks or listen in on calls, though they may not have done so often.

But now, new snooping technology is leading to more frequent and foolproof spying. Employers are bugging and tapping workers, monitoring them at their computers, even using special chairs to measure wiggling (wigglers aren't working). "The electronic sweatshop is here," says Sanford Sherizen, president of Data Security Systems Inc. in Natick, Mass., a computer-security consultant. And getting new attention. Last year, Congress outlawed the use of lie detectors at work. This year, it may go further.

The Big Time   No one knows exactly how much workplace spying goes on. But it's spreading, says William P. Callahan, president of United Intelligence Inc. in New York, which does everything from installing bugs to tailing workers. Some examples: General Electric Co. says it uses tiny, fish-eye lenses installed behind pinholes in walls and ceilings to watch employees suspected of crimes. Du Pont Co. says it uses hidden, long-distance cameras to monitor its loading docks around the clock. At airlines such as Delta, computers track who writes the most reservations. And Management Recruiters Inc. in Chicago says its bosses surreptitiously watch computerized schedules to see who interviews the most job candidates.

There are lots of good reasons for checking up on workers. Court cases have led to the so-called negligent hiring theory, which holds a boss liable for a worker's crimes or negligence on the job if the employer fails to screen for personality quirks or past misdeeds. "If *Encyclopaedia Britannica* sends a convicted rapist door-to-door, the company will pay mightily in court if something goes wrong," says Lawrence Z. Lorber, attorney for the American Society for Personnel Administration.

Another goal is preventing theft. Holy Cross Hospital in Silver Spring, Md., says it was trying to track disappearing narcotics in 1987 when nurses discovered by chance that the silver box with red lights hanging on their locker-room wall was a camera. Trouble was, the images it captured were broadcast over the hospital's closed-circuit TV network. Holy Cross said only the security chief should have seen them, which upset the nurses even more, since that person was a man.

More Careful   Monitoring can create friction even when employees know about it. Safeway Stores Inc. in Oakland, Calif., has dashboard computers on its 782 trucks. The boxes record driving speed, oil pressure, engine RPMS, idling time, and when and how long a truck is stopped. If anything is abnormal, the driver is questioned. Safeway says this helps hold down maintenance and fuel costs; monitored drivers are more careful, knowing that the data can help build a disciplinary case.

George Sveum, secretary of Teamsters Local 350 in Martinez, Calif., says Safeway tries to suspend or discharge up to 20 drivers a year using the computer data—prompting grievance filings. "If a trucker is just two minutes late, he can be brought up on charges," says Sveum.

Electronic snooping can get employers in trouble if it isn't done right. In an internal investigation last year, a high-tech company found that an executive had a checkered past and was sharing confidential marketing plans with competitors. With the manager nearing dismissal, his attorney, August Bequai, says he "did a reverse investigation to find out how they discovered the truth about my client." Bequai found that the company—he won't name it—had improperly gotten copies of the executive's credit reports, used a law-enforcement source to look at confidential arrest records, and may have tapped the executive's office phone without a warrant or his permission. Bequai got the company to let his client resign—with a settlement in the high six figures.

Oblivious For the most part, a company must be sloppy to get cornered. Federal and state laws let employers intercept phone and electronic communications with a court order or the consent of at least one party to the call. They also permit monitoring of business-related conversations. In 1987, some 14,000 employers eavesdropped on the telephone conversations of close to 1.5 million workers—most of whom had no idea they were being monitored, says Representative Don Edwards (D-Calif.).

Employees can sue for invasion of privacy. But to win damages, judges have said, workers must prove that their "reasonable expectations of privacy" outweigh the company's reasons for spying. Employers can get around even this rule by informing workers of surveillance policies. Some have applicants sign privacy waivers as a condition for hiring.

And despite their loss last year on polygraphs, employers usually have fended off attempts to stiffen the rules on privacy. In 1987, the telemarketing industry helped kill a bill that would have required an audible beep when employers eavesdrop on worker phone calls. A year earlier, American Telephone & Telegraph Co. says, it helped repeal a similar law in West Virginia by threatening to locate a proposed credit management center elsewhere.

Still, privacy advocates have gotten new life from a recent police scandal. Last November, a special governor's committee in Connecticut found that for 15 years the state police had illegally bugged incoming and outgoing calls at its barracks—including privileged discussions between defendants and lawyers. Within weeks, unauthorized phone tapping also was uncovered at police departments in Rhode Island, West Virginia, and Utah.

Now, two proposed federal laws, once considered dead, may have a better chance. Last June, Representative Ronald V. Dellums (D-Calif.) introduced a bill that would ban phone bugging without a warrant, unless all parties to the call consent. The Dellums bill also would require that voice-activated tape recorders be equipped with beep tones. The other bill, introduced by Representative William L. Clay (D-Mo.), goes further. Employers would have to notify workers with a visual or aural signal when they're being monitored with computers, cameras, or taping machines. It also would give employees access to records collected on them electronically—and bar job-performance decisions based solely on such data. While chances of passage this year seem slim, growing public awareness of abuses "is strengthening the drive for remedial legislation," says Janlori Goldman, the American Civil Liberties Union's privacy expert.

Such measures wouldn't be foolproof. Polygraphs have been replaced with so-called honesty tests, such as the one at Target. A Target spokesperson says the test is required only for security guards, about 1,200 of its 85,000 employees, and helps assess suitability for "high stress" positions. Now, the Congressional Office of Technology Assessment is studying whether such tests can predict behavior relevant to job performance. Its findings are expected in February.

Privacy advocates aren't looking for a ban on surveillance, just better controls. But even that isn't likely soon. So workers may just have to live with the idea that bosses can learn more about them than they would tell their best friends.

SPY VS. SPY: THE WORKERS ARE SNOOPING, TOO

Not just employers are snoops. Employees do it, too—"to get ahead," says Larry V. Rigdon, a security consultant in Atlanta.

And to protect themselves. In 1986, a new regime took control at Cincinnati-based Baylis Bros. Company Inc., which makes girls' dresses. Design manager Stephanie Ludwig wanted to know her fate. So she and her husband hired a private eye, David W. Reifsteck, who installed three bugs to listen in on reorganization discussions. Reifsteck got six months in jail for conspiracy after Ludwig changed her mind, removed the devices, and fessed up to a U.S. Attorney. But prosecutors didn't go after the Ludwigs because they didn't profit illegally.

Another case seems to protect employee prying. On Dec. 6, a federal appeals court in New York ruled that "surreptitious tape-recording" by a former compensation director at Champion International Corp. in Stamford, Conn., might represent "a kind of disloyalty to the company" but isn't automatic grounds for dismissal. That case involves Irwin Heller, who in 1982 feared that he would be demoted because of his age—then 52. After checking with a lawyer, Heller taped his supervisor when he got demoted. Fired for that, he sued Champion for age discrimination, among other things.

A jury gave Heller $350,000. The judge threw it out, only to be reversed by the U.S. Court of Appeals for the Second Circuit. "Every disgruntled employee-. . . will feel free to report to work with a tape recorder hidden on his person," wrote the lone dissenter.

Maybe not: Champion could still win a new trial. But for now, it seems, all's fair when it comes to snooping.

Politicians Should Never Forget Cardinal Telephone Rule

Ken MacQueen

Former B.C. attorney-general Bud Smith lost his cabinet portfolio for violating a cardinal rule of modern politics: Don't say anything into a telephone that you wouldn't want to see on the front page of tomorrow's newspaper.

It is a rule Prime Minister Brian Mulroney and his cabinet follow religiously and one that Manitoba Premier Gary Filmon has learned, to his disgust.

Thanks to cellular and car telephones—which broadcast with radio waves rather than through telephone lines—eavesdropping is almost as popular now as during the days of the rural party line.

No one group has embraced this sad lapse in ethics more ardently than political junkies—as Smith learned too well.

He was angered and disgusted Wednesday when a New Democratic Party MLA released tape recordings of two embarrassing telephone calls Smith had made, apparently on his car telephone.

The calls—one to a senior bureaucrat, one to a reporter—recorded attempts by Smith to discredit a Victoria lawyer hired by the NDP to privately prosecute a former cabinet colleague of Smith's.

The incident has quickly degenerated into one of the ugliest slugging matches in recent B.C. political history—no small feat.

Politicians and the public seem at a loss to decide who committed the most disgusting deed.

Was it Smith for apparently attempting to meddle in a private prosecution even though, as attorney-general, he has a legislated responsibility to be the impartial chief law officer of the Crown?

Or was it NDP justice critic Moe Sihota, who sifted through tapes of many of Smith's private telephone calls and released recordings of the two conversations.

"There are some serious questions about the ethics of that," Sihota admitted.

Sihota said he was given the recordings by a person not connected to the NDP. Suppressing knowledge of what Sihota calls Smith's "tampering with the administration of justice" would have been a greater wrong, he insists.

At any rate, Smith did find his conversations on the front page of Thursday's papers.

Reprinted by permission of *Southam News*.

Indeed, by accident or design, the Vancouver Province ran the entire transcript of his conversation opposite a full-page advertisement for cellular telephones. "CELLULAR LEADERS STRIKE AGAIN," said the ad's headline.

Debate rages over whether acting on information gathered by monitoring cellular and other radio-telephone frequencies may violate privacy laws. It is illegal to tap telephone lines without court authorization. But cellular calls can be monitored by using commercially available radio scanners in much the way that hobbyists, most news organizations and some criminals can monitor police, fire and ambulance radio broadcasts.

"No question, it's an area that's been a problem for a while," said Sgt. Val King, head of the RCMP computer crime section in Ottawa.

"The problem is . . . is it a private communication if it's sent out over public airwaves? Is the scanning of that considered illegal? Those are some of the questions that are still to be answered by the courts."

But while monitoring the airwaves for cellular calls may fall into a legal grey zone, there is little doubt that it is common practice in the world of hardball business and politics.

Just last month, Filmon accused federal officials of eavesdropping on private cellular telephone conversations between members of his delegation during the Meech Lake constitutional discussions.

"There was a couple of instances in which calls we made by cellular to people for specific information were known by federal people within 20 minutes of the call," Manitoba's premier said.

The charge was flatly denied by the prime minister. In fact, Mulroney said he warned the premiers against using cellular telephones, noting that ministers in his cabinet have found that conversations on their car telephones have been monitored.

Indeed, the offices of many senior cabinet ministers are equipped with at least one secure telephone, designed to thwart either telephone taps or radio monitoring.

"That's generally known, that you shouldn't be saying too much into any phone, including your car phone . . . or even your regular office phone," said Tom Van Dusen, press secretary to Deputy Prime Minister Don Mazankowski.

Sunni Locatelli, a spokesman for the prime minister's office, said there is no cabinet directive, but "cabinet ministers are reminded that cellular telephones are not a secure means of communication."

The federal Liberal party, not wishing to air its backroom dealings, banned radio scanners from last month's leadership convention in Calgary.

In Victoria, the Social Credit government is rushing to limit further damage.

An electronic sweep of all areas of the legislature, from ministerial offices to the press gallery, has been ordered.

At Apple, Proper Business Attire May Someday Include a Muzzle

G. Pascal Zachary

John Sculley is in the throes of a nightmare. Clad in white pajamas, Apple Computer Inc.'s chief executive officer dreams that careless employees have leaked confidential information, causing his company's demise. "Apple Suffers Information Hemorrhage," a tabloid headline screams. Mobs of angry customers storm the company's offices, dubbed "the leaky palace." Apple was "too free, too open," a television newscaster intones.

Mr. Sculley never actually had this nightmare. Last December, he and others acted out the drama for an in-house video crew. Since then, Apple has shown the six-minute video to every new hire and hundreds of veteran workers as part of a big internal campaign aimed at educating employees on the perils of loose lips.

Apple has always had a problem keeping secrets. Gossip about its latest developments is valuable currency in the social milieu of Silicon Valley. It suggests you are hip, "an insider," says independent software developer Heidi Roizen. But recently leaks have become more frequent and more unsettling. Now Apple is determined to plug them.

In March, Apple hired a manager of information security who promptly launched a war against leaks. Among the weapons are buttons for the workforce of 13,000 ("I know a lot but I can keep a secret") and brochures on the importance of secrecy. "Information protection coordinators"—staffers who volunteer to help spread the word—patrol their work groups.

Apple also has plastered its office walls with posters on the dangers of spilling inside information. One shows Albert Eisenstat, Apple's senior vice president and former chief legal counsel, wearing sunglasses and a white British barrister's wig. He warns: "The law says that Apple can dismiss any employee who discloses confidential or proprietary information. . . . But we'd rather not. Honestly."

Another features Delbert Yocam, president of Apple's Pacific division, gagged by a table napkin and holding aloft his utensils. The message: beware of gabbing about the company in restaurants. A third pictures Christopher and Sue Espinosa, two employees who are married. They caution that "there are some things that are so confidential they shouldn't be revealed even to your closest relatives, friends and significant others."

Apple's campaign may win awards for cuteness, but probably not for effectiveness. Some suspect the program may even be backfiring. "It almost seems as if the more Apple tries to do, the worse the leaks get," says Daniel Ruby, editor of MacWeek, a trade magazine devoted to news about Apple's Macintosh computer. Sensitive information has been leaked in at least three incidents since the campaign began. Apple refuses to discuss the incidents.

The most alarming leak involved a mysterious group of software pirates called the New Prometheus League. The group, which surfaced in early June, mailed floppy disks containing some of the Macintosh's secret software code to an undetermined number of people, including a computer-industry analyst on Wall Street.

The group, named after a Greek god who stole fire from the gods and gave it to man, said in a letter that accompanied the disks that it wanted to make it easier to make copies of the Macintosh. Apple has never licensed the computer's code to anyone and has successfully defended in court its copyrights, barring competitors from making compatible but less expensive versions of the machine. The disclosure apparently wasn't damaging, but it highlighted Apple's vulnerability. The New Prometheus League hasn't been heard from since that incident.

Apple has proven that it intends to do more than plead with employees to button up. Three months ago, Apple fired a software engineer who had disclosed plans for some future products on a computer bulletin board. David Ramsey, the engineer, claims he didn't think the information was confidential because Mr. Sculley had disclosed similar information to a trade journal late last year. "There's one set of rules for executives and another for everybody else," says Mr. Ramsey, who has since joined another electronics firm.

Stolen Thunder

In July, there was yet another leak. MacWeek managed to get its hands on the still-secret Macintosh IIci—two months before the new machine was to be introduced. MacWeek says its coup was courtesy of an outside firm that had been loaned the machine by Apple.

The magazine's editors pored over the computer, testing its capabilities and photographing its innards. A detailed account of the machine and a picture were splashed on the cover of the magazine's July 25th issue. Apple has assigned several former Federal Bureau of Investigation agents now on staff to try to identify the leaker.

The incident wasn't highly damaging to Apple. At the most, it robbed the company of some suspense in its introduction of the computer. But it illustrated the difficulties the company faces in trying to put a lid on inside information.

Silencing the Multitudes

At one time or another, some 11,000 outside developers are privy to various secrets about products in development. The firms, which make software or accessories for Apple computers, often get prototypes of new products months before they are announced publicly. Apple swears the developers to silence by requiring them to sign a pledge of secrecy. Prototypes are also "marked differently in very subtle ways, so if there's a picture or description in the press we can track down the source," says Kirk Loevner, director of Apple's developer group.

More recently, however, Apple has stepped up efforts to enforce secrecy among outside developers. Staff detectives drop in without warning more frequently to check for security violations. Apple has punished some developers in the past by denying them access to important technical data and the opportunity to get new products before they hit the market.

Apple's anti-leak campaign has sparked some concern within the company. Some workers think the effort conjures up a sense of working under an Orwellian Big Brother, ironically an image Apple used in a famous 1984 television commercial attacking rival International Business Machines Corp. "People are working scared," says one worker who asks not to be named. In particular, Mr. Ramsey's firing raises "a lot of fear about job security," the worker adds.

Jane Paradise, Apple's manager of corporate information security, says the company isn't spying on workers. "We're not a police state—far from it," she says. The drive to tighten security has a lot of support among workers, she insists. "Employees have been outraged by the leaks," she says. "Awareness is up. We're making progress."

She may be right. Employees seem to be embracing the campaign. After Mr. Ramsey was fired, for instance, he was treated as a pariah by former co-workers. "It was though I had some dread communicable disease," Mr. Ramsey recalls.

In any case, Apple's campaign isn't likely to put Mr. Sculley's nightmares entirely to rest. That's partly because of people like Charles Farnham. Mr. Farnham, a San Jose engineer and a passionate Apple fan, has made a hobby of collecting and doling Apple secrets out to other devotees.

"The universe is divided into three types of people," he says. "Those who sleep with the machine, those who use the machine and the business people. Guess which category I'm in?"

Selling a Scoop

Mr. Farnham recently rummaged through several of Apple's dumpsters while a cohort recorded the escapade on videotape for posterity. Mr. Farnham says his foraging turned up scores of technical reports and 20 discarded computer monitors. He combed the company's garbage, he says, to highlight the lax security.

On another occasion, Mr. Farnham persuaded an Apple employee to give him copies of the company's plans for a portable computer. Mr. Farnham sold a story about the plans to a computer weekly. Documents he found during another foray in the corporate garbage can went to a computer users group in Kansas City; the group gave them away as a door prize at a meeting in June.

Mr. Farnham says he is skeptical that Apple will succeed in protecting its secrets. "It all comes down to how many people like me are floating around," says Mr. Farnham. "If there's zero, they don't have a problem. If there are 100, Apple's in big trouble."

CIA Leader Wants Agency Active in Industrial Spying

James McCartney

The United States has become "a victim" of worldwide industrial espionage, according to CIA Director William Webster.

Because of this, the nation must vastly increase its intelligence capabilities in business and economics if it is to remain competitive in the post–Cold War world, Webster argued in an interview.

"It is certainly our role to detect and identify that type of activity and to assist our policy-makers in confronting it," said the CIA chief.

"High technology is no longer our private campground," Webster said, and the United States must learn what its competitors are doing if there is to be "a level playing field."

Webster's proposal to increase economic spying, destined to be controversial, would represent a major shift in emphasis for the CIA intelligence efforts, which for 40 years have concentrated on the military power struggle with the Soviet Union.

It was immediately questioned by Sen. Arlen Specter, R-Pa., a member of the Senate Intelligence committee, and was questioned by a former CIA chief.

"I do not think it is a healthy thing to start eavesdropping on our economic competitors," Specter said. "I don't think the American taxpayers expect us to do that unless it is defensive."

In a separate interview, former CIA Director William Colby warned that "there are limits" to what the CIA should do in economic intelligence because of the nation's free economy.

"What if we discover the Japanese have found a great new electronic gizmo?" Colby asked. "If you gave the information to General Electric, TRW would go up in smoke."

Webster discussed his economic spying proposal in detail in a wide-ranging interview in which he predictably argued for increased spending on intelligence activities despite abatement of tensions between the world superpowers.

The CIA, he said, faces pressing new challenges in combating terrorism and drug trafficking, monitoring arms control agreements and following power struggles in an increasingly unstable Third World.

Webster conceded, however, that over the next five years the CIA "will be sharing in some of the reductions that Defense is experiencing," a view increasingly shared among lawmakers on Capitol Hill.

Webster granted the rare interview in the wake of several sharp attacks on the CIA in recent weeks, in which questions have been raised about whether the agency is ready to adapt to a world without a Cold War.

A former National Security Council staff member, Roger Morris, described the agency as "a rusting relic of the Cold War . . . with often no apparent vision save conflict." A recent Newsweek story attacked the agency for what it described as a series of intelligence failures, including failure to foresee the collapse of communism in Eastern Europe.

The intelligence budget; now highly classified, is believed to amount to about $30 billion for 1991—an all-time high. The CIA has about 14,000 employees, worldwide, also a peak.

In the interview, Webster, a soft-spoken former appeals judge from St. Louis and former FBI director, also asserted that:

- Many countries in the Middle East are obtaining fast-flying, relatively long-range missiles capable of carrying both chemical and biological weapons, threatening a new era of instability.
- New arms control treaties, involving both strategic and conventional arms, will require extensive verification facilities.
- The Soviet military threat has not disappeared, even though it has receded, and will require continued monitoring for many years to come.
- Covert action by the CIA, its most controversial area of operations, will continue to be necessary to encourage democratic movements around the world.
- CIA agents on the ground, so-called "human intelligence," should be expanded to improve the quality of the agency's analysis.

Regarding his campaign for improved business intelligence, Webster said national security in the future is likely to depend far more heavily on economic factors than on military, as in the last 40 years.

At this point, he hastened to add, the CIA has not embarked on a specific program of direct business spying, declaring that "these are policy judgments for the future," but adding that "we have done major things to improve our capabilities."

Webster indicated that an internal debate on exactly how far the United States might go in spying is still under discussion in the intelligence community.

"I don't want to say, 'Don't worry fellows, we're not doing anything,' " he said, smiling. "We want to know what they are able to do and what they will be able to do in the future.

"We want to track their technical progress, but that is different than trying to steal their technology."

He singled out for special attention "new centers of economic strength—the European Community, a powerful reunified Germany and "an increasingly strong Japan."

Chapter
10

Rises and Falls

C onventional textbooks on management and organizational work concentrate for the most part on upward mobility and how to achieve it. Comparatively little recognition is given to the frequency with which hitherto successful managers "fall from grace." The economic disasters associated with recession have led to increased recognition of this aspect of organizational life in the popular press and business-oriented media. The selections in this chapter describe various types of "falls." We see some of the reasons for these falls, as well as their impact on the individuals concerned.

"Hotel Queen's Behavior May Be Rather Common" echoes the glee many former employees felt when Leona Helmsley was convicted of tax fraud but suggests that her behavior that alienated so many is really quite common among bosses. Unfortunately, too many bosses retain the pattern of overbearing behavior that has been the stereotype of "the big boss" for many years. Like Helmsley, they either do not realize or do not care about the impact such behavior has on the emotions and productivity of their employees.

David Kirkpatrick looks at the "rises" side in "Is Your Career on Track?" Kirkpatrick uses illustrations drawn from several large corporations to show that the trend for upward mobility in organizations is coming much more slowly. This change in organizational life has been noted elsewhere by Judith Garwood as "plateauing." One consequence that Kirkpatrick notes is that managers really get to know their jobs, which did not happen in the days when promotions came every few years. Lateral assignments, once greeted as a sign of failure, are increasingly coming to be viewed as a fresh challenge.

"Managers Under Pressure" illustrates that the demand for performance by chief executive officers is reflected in a high rate of turnover in these positions. It is interesting to speculate just what effects the pressure for inspired leadership will have on the managerial style of chief executive officers.

Failure to accurately assess the situation with which a rising star is confronted can damage the individual, as Sally Quinn discovered in her brief struggle with CBS in "We're Going to Make You a Star." In this case the struggle took on Kafkaesque proportions as neither side appeared to know which reality they were inhabiting. The emotional, psychological, and physical costs to individuals and, at times, the costs to organizations, may be very high if a system is either too loose or too programmed and depersonalized.

"Howyadoon? Fuller Brush Calling" by Cathryn Donohoe describes the experiences of a long-time Fuller Brush sales representative. We see the decline of what once was an American institution and the dedication of one employee to his vanishing craft as a door-to-door salesman. The selection that follows is from Arthur Miller's *Death of a Salesman*. A theme that has received far too little attention is examined here: obsolescence. This process is often more brutal than retirement because it has few of the humane, social institutions that make retirement a somewhat dignified process. Retirement is an expected event that organizations can handle through routine procedures such as gifts, parties, and speeches, thus submerging any sense of personal failure. However, there are few such procedures for handling an individual such as Willy Loman, whom the organization defines as obsolete.

In "CIO Is Starting to Stand for 'Career Is Over' " Jeffrey Rothfeder and Lisa Driscoll show us how promising careers growing out of advanced technology can run into snags. Problems can arise both from resistance to change by older, established departments in the organization or the failure of the new technology to show a rapid improvement in the bottom line. Likewise, premature decisions to dump the advocate of a new technology can later prove to have been unwise, as was the case with Bank of America.

Hotel Queen's Behavior May Be Rather Common

Jolie Solomon

Many people gleefully watched the recent tax fraud trial of Leona Helmsley. But for workers with dictatorial bosses, management experts say, her conviction proved especially gratifying.

"Sure people love to see the rich go down," says Bea Harris, of Harris Rothenberg Associates, a Wall Street psychological consulting firm. "But this has to do with another kind of powerlessness people feel—people who feel victimized [by bosses] and helpless to do anything about it."

Many witnesses testifying against Mrs. Helmsley, the self-proclaimed hotel queen, were former employees describing her cold and abusive behavior as a boss. While Mrs. Helmsley's case may look extreme, some consultants say it isn't. "There are many employers who act just like that," says Ms. Harris.

What is rare is that Mrs. Helmsley's excesses were exposed. In most cases of such bosses, says Jim Oher, a New York consultant, employees don't call them on it, fearing they'll be "fired . . . or humiliated."

Fear below ranks is matched by tolerance and denial above. "If someone's really running operations well, meeting [the] bottom line, who's going to hold that person accountable?" says Ms. Harris. She's called in for advice on such cases, she says, only if the boss's behavior causes valued subordinates to defect.

Some companies are starting to tackle the problem of difficult bosses. John Reed, Citicorp's chairman, recently circulated a videotape telling managers the company won't tolerate those who treat people badly.

Is Your Career on Track?

David Kirkpatrick

Forget the old rules. Promotions are coming more slowly. Lateral moves are in. But if you're trying for the very top, you still need to stick close to the P&L.

Gauging your career progress has always been more art than science, but what on earth are you supposed to make of the signals you're getting now? You haven't been promoted in quite a while, but then neither have many of your peers—at least not *really* promoted, though some have been shuffled into completely new areas. Out in the job market there's that clomping herd of baby-boomers behind you, or around you, or ahead of you. And as you fight your way up the corporate slope, you start to wonder if it's worth the effort. Maybe you should think about quitting, about becoming an entrepreneur like some of your former colleagues.

If you're confused, take heart. You are not alone. Figuring out where your career stands has never been harder. Says David Rhodes, 38, of the consulting firm Towers Perrin: "The rules are changing, but we don't know what they are yet." Palo Alto consultant Paul Leinberger, 42, echoes the thought: "What it means to be on the fast track today is quite unclear." And yet, from all the confusion, from the tumult of restructuring, globalization, mommy tracks, empowerment, and work teams, new wisdom is emerging to enlighten today's aspiring executives on what's really happening with their careers.

The most striking change in the rules of career progress: You may go years between promotions and still be doing just fine. Many managers are sitting in jobs longer regardless of their age, talents, or skills. Explains Rhodes: "When companies flatten organizations, that limits the number of rungs on the ladder, which lengthens the time between promotions." Susan Doten, 31, is director of marketing in Quaker Oats' pet food division, and she has moved quickly through six jobs in nine years. But the managerial pyramid has flattened so markedly that, she says, "I will hang out at this level for a lot longer than I hung out at the lower levels. There are about 13 marketing directors in U.S. grocery products, then only four vice presidents of marketing at the next level." Consultant Rhodes predicts that by 2000 the typical large corporation will have half the management levels and one-third the managers that it has today.

Promotions are slowing for another reason. Many companies that once moved the best and brightest on a fast track to a new job every 12 to 18 months are wondering if that isn't *too* fast. Says Blair Sheppard, 37, director of the human resource management research center at Duke's Fuqua business school: "American firms after restructuring are much closer to meritocracies than they used to be." And that means they want people to stay in place longer so it's clearer whether they succeeded or failed. David Hogberg, 37, a pet food marketing manager at Quaker, encountered this phenomenon early. In 1982 he was working his way up the ladder in the company's manufacturing operations, getting promoted roughly every year. Then he became manager of manufacturing for Kibbles 'n Bits dog food, and his boss decided to keep him there three years. He looks back: "It seemed like an eternity, but this was a big job, with 70 people working for me. I trusted that in the long term it wouldn't be a career setback."

It wasn't, and he thinks no other path would have taught him what he learned: "I got to see the effects of changes I made and work through their implications. It helped me learn to approach every job as a long-term opportunity, to stand back and ask what changes we need to make in this whole picture, even if it has been done one way for the last 15 years."

If you can't move up right away, you can sometimes move across, and this may be a smart idea. As Doten of Quaker Oats puts it, "I may eventually have to move to another area to grow myself." Growing yourself makes sense because the future corporate honcho will be a generalist—not a production or finance or marketing person, but a people person, more a leader than a master of any one discipline. Says recruiter Henry de Montebello, 44, of executive search firm Russell Reynolds

Associates: "In the future everybody will have strategic alliances with everybody else, and the executives who thrive will be well-rounded. You can't be a specialist at senior levels anymore."

Anne Pol, 42, of Pitney Bowes buys that message. Five years ago, after a career spent mostly in human resources, she left a senior position in that function to run a plant that makes parts for mailing machines. She considered herself a candidate for the company's highest jobs but knew she needed solid operating experience to have a reasonable shot. Then she came back to the top personnel job and a position on Pitney Bowes's 11-person corporate management committee, but only on condition she could go back to operations later. This spring she returned to the heart of the company, as vice president for manufacturing operations in the mailing systems group. Her conclusion: "It's very obvious that lateral moves are necessary if you want to progress up the corporate ladder."

If assessing your accumulation of job titles is more complicated than it used to be, surely you can still get a quick read on your status by checking your salary—can't you? Not so fast. For the organization men of the Fifties and Sixties, the longstanding rule of thumb was that you were doing okay if you earned your age times $1,000. Today you can't go by such simple rules—even adjusted for inflation. For one thing, people prefer compensation in different forms than they used to. They are more likely to want a piece of the business, or profit sharing. "It's give me money or give me equity," says de Montebello. "People will take extraordinary risks in their careers for equity."

By contrast, the perks so cherished by organization men no longer carry as much weight. In typical boomer voice, a 30-year-old middle manager at a big Manhattan public relations firm says, "All those executive dining rooms and bathrooms generally just satisfy somebody's ego. I'd rather have cash in hand than spend it to take a limo from point A to point B."

In general, after accounting for inflation, rising managers today make about as much as or perhaps a bit more than they did two decades ago. But headhunter de Montebello states an opinion advanced frequently by human resources experts: "There's no formula for how much you should make. The test is, Where are your peers? If your classmates, the people you started with, are all group VPs and you're an assistant controller, there's a discrepancy. But then you may be a serious tennis player and having more fun."

Comparing your achievements with those of your peers is harder than it used to be because the number and nature of your cohorts may vary enormously, depending on your age. Managers of all vintages worry about the career impact of 78 million baby-boomers surging through the work force. But whether *you* have reason to worry depends on how old you are and with which group of baby-boomers you are competing.

Just because boomers all grew up listening to the Beatles and Rolling Stones, that doesn't mean they all sing the same song today, especially when it comes to career attitudes. After all, they were born over a 19-year period. Edith Weiner, 41, of the Manhattan trend analysis firm Weiner Edrich Brown, credibly argues that boomers should be divided into three subgroups.

The leading edge is the so-called Woodstock generation, who were roughly 18 to 23 in 1969 and are 39 to 44 today. This group pioneered emancipated styles of life in their youth, helped initiate the women's movement, and fought against—or in—the Vietnam war. When they entered the job market the economy was, aptly, booming. There were ample entry-level slots for them, and their attitude reflected a certain cockiness because they felt they had changed society. When it came time to buy a house, by today's standards it was easy to afford.

The second group, today about 33 to 38, didn't test social barriers nearly so hard. Yet they were affected enough by the freewheeling Sixties to have felt considerable confusion about career goals, and typically they didn't decide until relatively late what they wanted to do. They took their first stab at the job market during or after the recession of the mid-Seventies and began to feel a competitive squeeze for jobs and housing.

By the time the third wave of boomers, now 26 to 32, emerged from school, competition was so keen in both job and housing markets that economic success became the consuming goal in their lives. This is the tough group that helped define the word yuppie and that unashamedly sought megabucks at a tender age on Wall Street.

While no objective evidence demonstrates that these last are stealing promotions from older boomers, the first two groups are definitely hearing footsteps behind them. And they don't like it. A successful 43-year-old who runs two business units and manages 150 people at a major money center bank is leaving her job, partly, she says, because of the competitive pressure she feels from young MBAs. The woman, who started 22 years ago as a secretary to a branch manager, complains: "These 1980s graduates we call yuppies are incredibly aggressive. They will lick your shoes to get you to do something for them. And once you do they'll forget your name. These little twits are coming in and eating our lunch."

For all the pressure they feel, the early boomers still have a demographic advantage over the legions that trail them. Thanks to the birth dearth of the Depression and World War II, relatively few older managers stand in the way of boomer promotions to the high-level jobs that survive. In addition, many older executives are bailing out well before age 65, lured by entrepreneurship and fat retirement packages, or are being restructured out. Guess who will fill their positions? In some reviving industries the older generation of managers was so decimated by cutbacks in the Eighties that boomers face truly extraordinary opportunities. At companies like Bethlehem Steel, Caterpillar, and Navistar International, their careers could thrive.

Younger boomers who haven't yet received the promotions they feel they deserve may also benefit as their more successful comrades, who got the early promotions, move further up in the hierarchy. That's because of the birth dearth that followed the boom. Says Sylvester Schieber, 43, the optimistic director of research for the Wyatt consulting firm: "The people at the back end of the baby boom will be more likely to get these fill-in promotions. You only dead-end if you go to sleep at your desk." In short, the youngest and oldest boomers find a career advantage in being adjacent to a birth dearth. Those stuck in the middle, with masses of peers above and below them, face a tough slog the rest of their lives.

One of the most important changes in the career picture, affecting not just baby-boomers but all ages, is occurring not around today's managers but inside them. Personal fulfillment and the flexibility to do more of what one wants are becoming top-rank career goals. Says Pitney Bowes's Anne Pol: "The key issue for people today is getting satisfaction in your work and feeling that you are making a contribution." It's a feeling people have always sought. But earlier generations were more willing to suppress this desire in return for other rewards, primarily job security. For all their careerism, many baby-boomers, steeped in the heritage of the Sixties, are decidedly ambivalent about compromising personal goals in pursuit of a job somewhere up there in the corporate empyrean. Consultant Leinberger observes: "The baby-boom generation places creativity and self-expression at the center of their being. They view themselves as walking works of art." This ethos has extended to managers of all ages. As one navigates corporate America, one can almost hear the voices crying, "Don't fence me in!"

If independence, control, stimulation, and a feeling of satisfaction are what people increasingly crave, few profess to care about their title. Says Burke Stinson, 48, a public relations manager for AT&T: "Folks are less concerned about the trappings than if the job itself is rewarding, the company progressive, and the environment comfortable—does it nurture me as a guy or gal on the way up?"

Janet Cooper, 36, relishes her job as Quaker's assistant treasurer because she finds the changing capital markets exciting. "I could take another job and make more money," she says. "But it would be a trade-off for doing something less interesting each day." George Foyo, 43, a sales vice president for AT&T's national accounts who just returned from a four-year general management assignment in Spain, feels the same way: "I'm very strongly motivated by change and challenge. Compensation and title are less important."

This resistance to categorization also expresses itself in a sense, sometimes disquieting, of being endlessly in motion. "People today consider themselves to be in a constant state of change," says Edith Weiner. Are you married? Currently. Do you have children? Not yet. Consider the highly satisfied Peggy Clarkson, a cheery 38-year-old who, thick appointment book always at her elbow, manages a staff of six marketers for IBM in Norwalk, Connecticut. How does this 16-year Big Blue veteran and mother of two feel about her career? "Right now I'm very happy in my job," she says. "I love it. It allows me to balance career and home very well." Right now.

Managers are seeking deeper satisfaction just when many employers are less likely to give them the wider and more rewarding responsibilities that come with a promotion. Something's got to give, and it may take the form of managers bailing out, or of companies changing policies in an effort to keep them. Says a 32-year-old man who left IBM in 1988 after eight years to join a small software company: "In a big company you're always trying to avoid the brick wall. Now my status depends on how I perform. I don't care about my title. I'm looking for a challenge."

Smart companies trying to retain such people are finding ways to create more challenge and satisfaction for managers who otherwise might feel stuck. AT&T senior vice president of human resources Harold Burlingame says, "We are starting to have broader bands for people. Instead of getting a $10,000 raise and moving on, they can earn much more within a job as they grow in and grow their business." At IBM, where restructuring eliminated 6,200 of 34,000 management jobs in the U.S. between 1986 and 1989, those that remain have more autonomy, at least according to higher-ups. Says Dick Hallock, director of employee relations for IBM: "We're driving responsibility down so that within each job there's more room for growth and development. In some areas we use the slogan, Make it your business."

But companies aren't attacking the problem sufficiently. Indeed, employees often complain that when they learn more and broaden themselves, the company doesn't notice. Quaker human resources vice president Robert Montgomery, 43, says that "plateaued" managers are bailing out, and his company, like others, isn't yet doing enough to keep them.

Career-conscious women face a whole additional set of considerations. No independent career expert interviewed for this article denies that a glass ceiling curtails corporate advancement for women, and most volunteer it as one of the most important factors shaping the future of today's managers. Yet a substantial number of experts also believe that women's careers may thrive in the corporate environment of the future. Neil Yeager, 37, who recently wrote *Career Map: What You Want, Getting It, and Keeping It,* says, "Women know how to network in a less politicized way. They know how to nurture relationships and empower other people. They manage groups better than men. And they have a greater appreciation of motivations other than money." Those are just the qualities companies will need in the Nineties.

With the struggle up the ladder especially trying and confusing for today's managers, it's little wonder that many seem particularly interested in an ancient question: Just what, finally, is career success anyway? Judith Bardwick, 57, a La Jolla, California, consultant, insists that there are other ways to cope with nonpromotion than to feel that you've failed. "Don't sit in the corner and suck your thumb," counsels a stern Bardwick, who proffers similar advice in seminars to employees at companies like BellSouth, Kraft General Foods, and Pacific Gas & Electric. To address those feelings without quitting, she suggests, "take your ambition to another area of life. Get involved with your local school board, for example. Or go get the education to increase your flexibility on the job."

While corporate backwaters still exist—often in human resources, public relations, and legal, among others—even fast-trackers will occasionally find themselves spending a brief time in one. "Both line and staff jobs will be expected for the CEO of the future," says IBM's Hallock. International experience will surely be a plus as well, he says.

But staying close to profit and loss responsibility remains the most important talisman for those with their eyes on top management. Says author Yeager: "For getting to the top, the bottom line is still the bottom line." Seek such responsibility early, and try to ensure that the results you produce for the company can be measured in dollars and cents.

Beyond that, IBM's Hallock offers this advice: "Take the initiative in your own development. Learn new things. Read widely. Absorb as much as you can, whether or not it's related to your current job, so you can put it into context. You've got to understand the mission objectives of your employer and relate your own efforts to the company's overall goals."

Managers Under Pressure

American companies, looking for ways to enhance profits, are replacing more chief executive officers and general managers, a Korn/Ferry International survey reported last week.

"Replacement management will be the watchword for 1990," said Lester Korn, chairman of the executive search company. "As business conditions get tougher, there will be intense pressure on senior managers to perform."

"Companies will have little tolerance for mediocrity and executive shifts will be made much faster than in the past."

The demand for chief executive officers during the current quarter totalled 15 per cent of all executive hiring, up from 11 per cent for the year-ago quarter, according to the survey by Korn/Ferry of Los Angeles.

The demand for general managers during the current quarter reached 45 per cent of all executive hirings, up from 42 per cent for the current quarter, the survey said.

The survey, called the National Index of Executive Vacancies, was based on responses from 750 clients of Korn/Ferry, which calls itself the nation's largest executive search company with 1989 revenues of about $100 million.

"Whether expanding, downsizing or reorganizing, U.S. companies are going to require inspired leaders who can gain competitive advantage and maintain profitability," said Richard Ferry, president of Korn/Ferry.

"Managers Under Pressure" reprinted by permission of United Press International. The Province, January 2, 1990, p. 49.

We're Going to Make You a Star

Sally Quinn

The countdown: Dick Salant, president of CBS News, was beaming. Hughes Rudd was chuckling to himself and Sally Quinn was fending off questions about her sudden rise in TV news. The setting was a luncheon at "21" in New York and the guests included members of the press, who were given an opportunity to meet and chat with the CBS correspondents who will go on the air next Monday. Salant was saying he'd love to switch the time of the *CBS Morning News* show from 7 A.M. to 8 A.M. but he'd run into opposition from the fans of *Captain Kangaroo*. "I know because I raised all my children on *Captain Kangaroo*." If the new team is a success, Salant said naturally he'd take credit for the show, but if the show bombs he said he's going to find someone to point the finger at. Who dreamed up Rudd and Quinn? he was asked. "That was Lee Townsend." Townsend, the executive producer, however, modestly disclaimed credit. "It was a group effort," he told Eye, *Women's Wear Daily*, Tuesday, July 21, 1973 . . .

When Gordon and I first discussed the job I told him I had grave reservations about his choice. I reminded him that I was controversial, opinionated, flip, open and had no intention of changing. Was he sure this was what he wanted on television? Did they really want me to say what came to my mind during the ad libs, and would they not try to turn me into a bland, opinionless, dull-but-safe marshmallow? And I wondered aloud whether, if we were supposed to be journalists, we could maintain any kind of objectivity and still express controversial opinions—or any opinions, for that matter.

"Paley wants controversy," Gordon had said. "And so does Salant. You can get away with much, much more at that hour than you ever could on the *Evening News*."

I had doubts and so did a lot of people I talked to, but I figured CBS knew what it wanted.

I also pointed out to Gordon that I had a rather unconventional life style. I had been living on weekends with Warren, I explained, and if I moved to New York I would move in with him. I would also be talking about him openly and freely in interviews. I saw nothing wrong with it, and I had no intention of hiding the fact.

I think Gordon gulped a little at that one, but he gamely said that was just fine,

I could say anything I wanted to. After all, CBS was not hiring me because or in spite of my personal life.

On Friday morning, June 22nd, the first piece about me appeared in *The Washington Post*. The head ran "SHOWDOWN AT SUNRISE," and it carried pictures of me and Barbara opposite each other. I wasn't too crazy about that. It created an atmosphere of rivalry I would have preferred to avoid. But my editors laughingly pointed out that I was now a public personality and had no say in the matter. They also pointed out that it was clearly the right angle for the story. They were right.

TV critic John Carmody had written, "Although a number of her candid interviews had attracted CBS's attention, it was, ironically enough, her appearance on Miss Walters' *Not for Women Only* TV program that whetted the network's interest." He quoted Salant as saying that the format of the revamped show would "have no relationship to the *Today* Show" and would "retain the integrity of the basic news show." But also as predicting that "*Today* is ripe to be taken."

Stuart Shulberg, the producer of the *Today* Show, was quoted: "We welcome fresh competition. *Today* has led the morning field for so long that we could run the risk of growing too fat, smug, and sassy. This will speed up the pace, sharpen our competitive spirit, and provide the kind of honest competition we need and relish. May the best program win."

Barbara Walters was quoted: "The only thing I can say as a woman in broadcasting is that I welcome any new member to the fold. . . . I have respect and friendship for Sally. I know her very well. And I applaud both her and CBS for a very smart choice."

And Sally Quinn said: "Barbara is a great friend of mine and one of the most professional people I've ever known. As far as competing with each other, we covered the Shah's celebration in the desert of Iran together last year and stayed in the same dormitory. That's like being in combat together, and I imagine this will be a somewhat similar situation."

And we were off. . . .

Monday, rehearsals began. Thank God. Now they were going to roll it all out for us, lay it on, let us in on all the fabulous plans for the first week of shows. And it was about time. I had begun to have doubts, but I knew that they would disappear as soon as we got to the studio and saw what they had for us.

We were to arrive at 6 A.M. to start getting the feel of getting up early. We would watch the *Morning News,* then go into a simulation of what our anchor booth was going to look like (it wasn't nearly ready) and tape a news broadcast. We were to write it from the same wires and newspapers that John Hart had used earlier.

Lee Townsend was jittery. Townsend, the most even-tempered man I know, was also as irritated as I had ever seen him. He had been against the promo tour (though he didn't object violently enough) because he felt we could have better used our time rehearsing. His objections had been overridden by Blackrock, which—who? I never got the pronoun straight—had insisted that it was necessary. So Townsend was nervous and angry because we had been away and virtually co-opted by the PR department, and because it was then clear to him that we didn't have a super-duper razzle-dazzle show to put on the air in a week's time. And no real studio to rehearse in.

He had reason to be more than nervous, and we did exactly what we had done for the pilot except at greater length. We wrote a little news and a few lead-ins to film pieces, and Hughes wrote an essay. I couldn't think of anything that morning, and besides, I'm not an essayist. I'm a reporter and interviewer. Hughes would do essays, which he did marvelously, and I would do what I did best.

In front of the camera, they outfitted me with an ear-piece on a wire, called a Telex, which enables them to talk to you from the control room. They handed us mikes, rolled our copy onto the TelePromTers, and away we went. It was a disaster. There were two cameras and I didn't know which one to look at. The stage manager waved his hands around, but I hadn't a clue what he was trying to tell me. I was fumbling my words and couldn't read the prompters. They were shouting in my ear through the Telex to do this and do that, and three minutes here and twenty seconds there, and ad lib here. The ad libs were always by surprise, and I would fumble around trying to think of something clever to say about a film piece we had just seen. It might have been a bloody plane crash or a dairy farm. It BOMBED, and I was shell-shocked by the time it was over. Suddenly I *knew* this was the way it was going to be. There was nothing I could do about it. It was too late to get out of it.

I was even more upset when everyone came out of the control booth and said it was just fine and all it needed was a little smoothing out and we would be just great by the end of the week. No mention of any guests for interviews, no mention of any special film pieces that would lend themselves to interesting, informative ad libs and, most frightening of all, no mention of anything I should do to improve myself. I realized fully for the first time that I didn't know anything, and I panicked.

As we were filing down the stairs to the *Morning News* section, Jim Ganser, one of the producers, caught up with me. He was to be the only one at CBS who really tried to help me.

"Try to punch your words a little more," he sort of whispered out of the side of his mouth, as though he didn't want anyone to hear.

I fell on him. "What? How? What do you mean?" I said desperately. "Tell me, for God's sake. Tell me what I'm doing wrong."

And he told me. "You're wrong to expect anyone to give any help or guidance of any kind. You're a big star now, and people figure if you're a big star you must know what you're doing. Nobody's going to stick his neck out to help you."

I went to the ladies' room and threw up. But I had to hurry. Hughes and I were the "big stars" of a large press luncheon at the "21" Club, and we were late. . . .

We finally got into our own studio on Friday, and we rehearsed there Friday and Saturday. Nothing went right. Friday morning after John Hart's last show someone came into the Cronkites, where we were working, and said that the staff of the *Morning News* was having a farewell party for John and the old producer. I hadn't really seen John to talk to him. I like and respect him a great deal, but we had been so busy working the lobster shift (that's the night shift in newspapers) that we just hadn't had a chance to see each other.

"Oh, great, I'll go up and tell John goodbye," I said, jumping up from my chair.

"I wouldn't if I were you," someone said. "There's a great deal of hostility up there toward the new team. And the atmosphere upstairs is more like a wake than a party. I think you had better forget it."

That was the first I had heard of resentment or hostility on the home team front. It worried me because, except for Townsend, Hughes and me, the "team" was the same. There had been no staff changes. I had found that curious. If they had really wanted a whole new format, with more entertainment and a lighter mood, I thought that they would surely have tried to bring in some people who were more in the show-biz line. The *Morning News* staff was very good. But they were hard-news oriented, and Gordon had said the idea was to take on the *Today* Show.

That morning when I went in to get my makeup done for the rehearsals my hair was a mess. While I was upstairs, the woman who was doing my makeup said her friend Edith, the hairdresser for *Edge of Night,* was right down the hall and maybe she would roll my hair up on the hot rollers for me. She called Edith, and a round-faced woman in her late fifties, with reddish hair, big, wide innocent eyes, a very strong New York accent, and dyed-to-match pants, vest, blouse, and shoes, came rushing in. Edith said she would be delighted. She had the lightest, most soothing touch, and the whole time she did my hair she told me how great I looked and how terrific I was going to be on the air and that she was honored to do my hair. Then she asked who my official hairdresser was.

"Hairdresser? I don't have a hairdresser." Both women were stunned. "You have to have a hairdresser," they chimed. "Every woman on television has one. You can't just go on with your hair like this every morning."

Edith asked me if she could be my hairdresser and said she was sure that if I asked they would let me have one. I told Lee and Sandy Socolow about it and they both went blank. Nobody had given my hair a thought. They okayed it right away, but it indicates how little thought went into the planning for the first woman network anchor. Edith was a godsend. She not only took care of my hair, she took care of my ego.

After the rehearsal on Saturday, I was about to leave. No interviews were lined up for me for the following week. The big interview for Monday was with Patrick Buchanan, the President's speech writer, and that would be out of Washington. I had no idea what film pieces were going to be used. They weren't sure.

I was so depressed and scared that I didn't really care. I wanted to go somewhere and hide. As we were leaving (Sunday was a free day) Lee Townsend gave me a big smile and said, in a way I couldn't decide was joking or not, "Let me know if you have any good ideas tomorrow for the show."

Sunday was the worst day of my life. I thought about ways to disappear where no one would hear from me for years and would think I had been kidnapped by some freak. I considered the possibility of having plastic surgery so I would never be recognized as Sally Quinn. I fantasized about going on the broadcast and saying, "Good morning, I'm Sally Quinn and we are not prepared to do this show and I don't know what I'm doing up here." I thought seriously about calling Salant and Manning and telling them. I came close to quitting.

The water pipes broke in our apartment and I had to go to a friend's place on West End Avenue to wash my hair.

When I got out of the shower, I put on a large white robe that was hanging on the door. I came out of the bathroom draped in that robe and I said to Warren, who had been babysitting me all day, "I really feel like one of those ancient Aztec virgins who has been chosen to be sacrificed on top of the temple of the gods. All the other virgins are wildly jealous of her because she has this fabulous honor bestowed on her. What they don't know is that she doesn't want her heart cut out with a knife anytime by anyone. It hurts."

I went to bed at 5 P.M. It was bright and sunny outside, and I could hear the children playing on Riverside Drive and happy couples walking and chatting and laughing as they strolled in Riverside Park.

"I will never be happy again," I thought. "My life is over."

I never went to sleep. We had been coming in around 4 or 5 in the morning that week, but it wasn't proper preparation for coming in at 1:30. The alarm went off at 1:00 A.M. Warren was waiting to walk me to my limousine, which arrived promptly at 1:30 A.M. It was like being escorted in a golden carriage to the guillotine.

I didn't feel too hot. I figured it must be because I hadn't slept. I slipped into the gloamings of the enormous black car and we glided over to Hughes' apartment, the Apthorpe, a few blocks away on West End Avenue. He hadn't slept either. We didn't say a word. A few minutes later we arrived at the studio and went directly back to the *Morning News* area and into the Bullpen.

In front of each of us was a pile of news wire stories, the first edition of *The New York Times* and the *Daily News*. Bob Siller, the copy editor, was there and so was Dave Horowitz, one of the assistant producers. They would make up the "line-up." The line-up was a sheet on which the show was blocked out minute-by-minute. Taking all the film pieces and counting their time, they would, along with Hughes and me and Lee Townsend, decide what the top news stories were and allot a certain amount of time to each, from forty-five seconds to a minute, and then block out time for commercials (we had only network commercials for the first six weeks) and station breaks. They would leave about a minute and a half for Hughes' essay, and what was left—roughly five minutes—would be allotted for "ad libs."

While this was going on, Hughes and I read the papers and the wires to get an idea of what stories we wanted to use. When we had finished, about 3 or 3:30, Bob and Dave came back with the line-up designating which one of us would write which stories and which lead-ins to film pieces. If the film piece was ready, Hughes and I would try to take a look at it so that we could write a clearer lead-in; if not, there was generally some kind of script. Often the film piece wasn't ready. Horowitz and Siller, with our advice or without, would figure out which film piece seemed like the best topic for conversation and block in a certain amount of time for ad libs after those pieces. There was some freedom to move around, but not much. Everything we were to say we typed out on our enormous typewriters.

We had two writers who were to do the weather, sports and late-breaking news. Hughes was to read all the sports. We had tried to divide it, but I didn't understand sports and kept fumbling and breaking up in the middle of the report. Hughes hated it too, but it wasn't quite as ridiculous when he did it.

By the time Hughes and I would have read everything thoroughly, discussed camera angles with Bob Quinn, our director, who came in about 4, written all our news items, lead-ins and station and commercial breaks, had something to eat at our desks (it was called "lunch" and usually came from the CBS cafeteria, known appropriately and without affection as "the Bay of Pigs"), it would be about 6 A.M.—time for Edith and Rickey, the makeup person, to arrive and get us ready.

At around 3:30 I had started to break out in a cold sweat and I became weak and dizzy and slightly nauseated. I couldn't concentrate on what I was writing. Finally I went into Townsend's office and passed out. I tried to get up about 4 A.M. and write, but I stayed at my typewriter for about twenty minutes and then went back to Townsend's office and passed out again. I thought it was probably because I was tired and nervous, but by then my throat was so sore and I was coughing so badly that I could barely talk. I had shivers and had to be wrapped up in a blanket.

Everyone piled into Townsend's office and stared at me in horror. "Do you think you can do it?" Lee asked, terrified.

"I just don't know, Lee." I didn't.

I think at that point I was more scared not to go on than to go on.

"I'll try. I'll really try. But I can't talk. And I'm so dizzy. Is there any way I could get a vitamin B shot or something to give me quick energy?"

By then it was 5:30 in the morning and I was so sick I couldn't breathe. I kept trying to sit up and I would just fall right down. I couldn't tell whether the beads of perspiration on my head were from temperature or desperation. Finally Townsend said that they had to get me to a hospital. Somebody had a car and they carried me out to the front of the building, stuffed me in the car, and drove two blocks away to Roosevelt Hospital to the emergency room. A young doctor took me back to examine me and take my temperature. I had a temperature of 102 and he said he thought I might have pneumonia. I was coughing so badly that my body was racked. "You don't understand," I practically screamed. "I'm making my television debut in an hour."

"So I've heard," he smirked.

"Well, I can't possibly go on like this. Can't you give me a vitamin B shot or something? Anything."

He said that in my condition a vitamin B shot wouldn't do any good. The only thing he could do for me was to give me a throat spray that would stop me from coughing for a few hours. But he suggested that I get to a doctor immediately afterward for proper medication.

"Anything else I could give you now," he said, "would knock you out." Oh, how I wished . . .

He left the room and came back a few minutes later with the most enormous syringe I have ever seen, with a needle a mile long.

"Forget it," I said, backing away from him.

"Don't get hysterical," he said, laughing, "This is a throat spray. I'm not going to stick the needle in you."

He stuck the needle in my mouth and sprayed a gooey liquid, which coated the inside of my throat.

Lee grabbed me, back we went into the car, and we screeched off around the corner and back to CBS as though we were bank robbers getting away.

It was a little before 6:30. Edith and Rickey were frantic, and Hughes looked as though all his blood had drained out of him. Edith rolled my hair while Rickey sponged some makeup on me. I lay down while all this was going on. The hot rollers stayed in too long and I looked like Shirley Temple when my hair was combed out. There was nothing we could do about the frizz. At about ten minutes to seven they finished on me. I was still so weak and dizzy that I could barely move, and all I can remember is a large fuzz of Warren leaning over me asking me if I was all right, Townsend in a frenzy, and Hughes pulling himself together as he walked into my dressing room. "Hughes—" I tried to smile—"get me off this horse immediately." Hughes tried to smile, too, but he wasn't very convincing. "Don't worry," he growled, "you'll make it, kid."

I tried to say thank you, but the throat spray had a numbing effect, like Novocain, and I couldn't feel whether my tongue was touching the roof of my mouth or whether I was forming my words properly.

"You look beautiful, darling, just beautiful. You'll be wonderful, I know you will," Edith was murmuring.

I looked in the mirror. I was hideous. My hair was frizzy, the granny glasses looked wrong, and the only thing I owned that wasn't blue (I hadn't had time to shop that week) was a yellow battle jacket that made me look like a dyke.

"Well," I thought, "there's no way anybody is going to accuse me of being a sex bomb this morning."

Somebody shoved a pile of telegrams in my face and I tried to read. They were all amiable, from close friends and family, but it was upsetting me. "Oh, God," I thought, "if only they knew how terrible I'm going to be."

They were screaming for me to get into the studio and I ran in, got behind the desk, had my mike adjusted, and somebody handed me my Telex, which I stuck in my ear.

"One minute," yelled the floor manager.

My mouth was dry. No possibility of talking. I looked at Hughes. He was looking at me as though we were copilots and I had just been shot. He tried to smile. I tried to smile back.

"Thirty seconds," said the floor manager.

I looked straight outside the glass partition to the newsroom and saw everyone staring.

"Five seconds," the floor manager said.

For a fleeting moment I thought maybe I would wake up and find out this wasn't happening.

An arm went out to me and a finger pointed. I gazed at the TelePromTer.

"Good morning," I read, "I'm Sally Quinn. . . ."

I don't remember much else about that hour. I was propped up with several pillows because I was so weak and dizzy that I couldn't sit up by myself.

I coughed a lot. I remember a swirl of sweltering bright lights, moving cameras, different noises and shouts in my ear through the Telex—"Turn to Camera 2, thirty seconds to ad-lib, five seconds till commercial, ten seconds more of interview"—hand signals, desperate and self-delirious mumblings . . . and then it was over. And when it was over I felt completely numb. Nothing. . . .

When I walked back into my office there were three bouquets. One was from Charlotte Curtis, then editor of *The New York Times'* Family, Food, Fashions and Furnishings, now editor of the op-ed page of *The Times* and probably the woman I admire most in journalism. One from Vic Gold, former press secretary of former Vice President Spiro T. Agnew and now a columnist. And one from Connie Tremulis of "Flowers by Connie," Rockford, Illinois.

I still have their cards.

Everybody was talking at once and saying what a great show it had been and how did I ever get through it, and, boy, what a terrific start we had gotten off to, and how terrible the *Today* Show was outdoors in front of Rockefeller Center. I don't remember seeing Hughes. I remember Lee Townsend taking me by the hand and leading me outside to a taxi. I put my head back on the seat and stared out the window as we went whizzing up Central Park West. It was a beautiful day. I thought about all the people walking along the street and bicycling in the park and about how happy they looked. I thought how odd it was that my work day was over and it was only 8, and that that was going to be my life from now on. And how depressing it was. I did not think about the show. It had not happened. Nor did Lee mention it. . . .

During the first week, I had not seen or heard from Gordon. I debated whether or not to call him or leave a message, but then I figured if he wanted to see me he would have come back or sent a note. I will never understand why, after the first show, he didn't come screaming back to the *Morning News* and fire everybody, or put Hughes on with straight news, tell the world I had terminal pneumonia, and send me away to some hideaway studio in Connecticut with his trustiest producers and cameramen to work me over.

As far as I knew, nobody had seen or heard from Gordon. I waited each day for him to ask me into his office and explain gently that I needed some kind of training; that they were going to change the format, get a new set and a jazzy producer, set me up with taped interviews, get me out of reading the news, get me voice lessons, make me put on contact lenses, and demand that I grow my hair longer and cut out the ad libs.

Nothing.

The broadcast Monday was uneventful, including my first live television interview. It was—I still have a hard time believing this was the best person CBS could think of for my TV interview debut—the designer Emilio Pucci. I discovered that he was branching out from lingerie into sheets and men's wear.

Hughes did not participate. He wasn't all that anxious to, didn't particularly like to do interviews, and I'm sure he didn't have all that much to talk to Pucci about anyway, except the fact that they were both World War II pilots.

I called Gordon and left a message after the show. I was told he was out. Gordon soon became for me a Major Major Major figure from *Catch-22*. Hard to reach. . . .

My health all along had not been good. I still felt dizzy and nauseated in the early mornings, and I was constantly exhausted though there wasn't anything wrong with me as far as anyone could see.

There was, however, a major cosmetic problem.

For the first time since I was seventeen years old, I was developing acne. And it was getting bad. Rickey switched to an allergenic makeup, but it didn't help. The makeup and the bright lights must be doing it, I decided. I should have my face cleaned.

I remembered that a classmate of mine from Smith had a mother who ran an Institute of Cosmetology on East 62nd Street, which I occasionally read about in *Vogue* or *Harper's Bazaar.* Her name was Vera Falvy, and she was a Hungarian with the most beautiful complexion I had ever seen.

Mme. Falvy examined my face carefully and asked about my eating habits, health, and life style. She knew I was on TV but had no idea of the hours or the pressure. She felt the breakout was caused by emotional tension. I would need regular treatment. We made another appointment and she gave me a special lotion which I was to use under, or preferably instead of, makeup.

Altogether I visited Madame six times, and the bills ran close to $300. She did her best, but the tensions kept building and my face got worse. My complexion has never been the same. I have scars on my face to show for those horrible months. . . .

That week I got a call from Barbara Howar. We chatted for a bit and Barbara, who had had her own TV shows, gave me a few pointers. She told me that I was coming along really well and shouldn't worry. Then she said, "Why don't you look at the right camera when the show is closing each day? Half the time the camera zooms out to the newsroom while you're looking straight ahead into the camera in the studio, and whenever the camera is in the studio you're looking across at the newsroom. You've got to keep your eye on the red light."

"Red light?"

"For God's sake," she screamed, "hasn't anyone told you about the red light?"

"No," I said. "What about it?"

"There's a light on the side of the camera," she said, "and when it goes on red it means that camera is on you and that's where you're supposed to look."

"Oh, no," I moaned. "No wonder. I saw that light flash on and off but I didn't know what it meant.". . .

Thanksgiving was the next day, and we never had holidays off. It was the tenth anniversary of Kennedy's assassination. When I looked at the line-up that morning, I saw that the only scheduled interview was one I had done several weeks earlier with a woman who had written a diabetic cookbook.

I couldn't believe it. Hughes complained to no avail. That seemed like the final straw. On the tenth anniversary of a president's death we were to do a mediocre (at best) taped interview with a diabetic-cookbook writer. There was no hope for any of us, or that broadcast.

Without staff meetings, there was still no coordination. Things hadn't gotten better. Usually, we didn't know who the guest was to be until we came on the program, and half the time it was someone neither of us was interested in or wanted to interview. We wrote lists of suggestions and notes, but nothing ever came of them. It is not that the people on the staff were incompetent, but just that there was zero direction, that morale was low, and that there was no coordination.

We had a rule about not accepting guests if they'd already been on the *Today* Show, and they had the same rule about our show. What that meant was that we hardly ever got any of the good people because the *Today* Show had a much larger audience and no publisher would allow his author on our show unless he couldn't get him or her on the *Today* Show.

I thought that was dumb. I thought we should take people who'd been on the other show, then try to do a better, or a different kind of interview. We were in a no-win situation.

Another problem I kept hearing about third-hand from my friends was that some of them had talked their publishers into letting them go on our program because they were friends, and then for some odd reason they were rejected. This happened to Art Buchwald and Teddy White. There would be some vague explanation; but usually there were about three people involved in setting up the interviews, and often they weren't there when I was, so I couldn't find out. It was a mini-example of the total method of functioning at CBS. It was exasperating and, in the end, useless to try to do anything about anything.

The broadcast was beginning to take on a slight death smell. I had to get out. . . .

I've often asked myself how CBS could have made so many mistakes, how they could have let me go on the air with no experience.

Part of my despair during that terrible time had stemmed from trying to fathom where I had gone wrong. The thing is, nobody really yet understands the medium. Television isn't even fifty years old. Shows go on and off every month, people are hired and fired ruthlessly, because nobody knows what will work and what won't. They don't know what terrible vibes a great-looking or -talking person may give out over the air or what good vibes a clod may transmit. So they don't want to make decisions—especially long-term ones. Therefore nobody does. It's what Sander Vanocur calls the "how-about?" school. Somebody said, "How-about-Sally-Quinn?" and there was a generalized mumble, and that was it. They hired me and nobody ever did anything about it again. Mainly because they didn't know what to do.

So much money is at stake—millions and millions of dollars in advertisements—that those who make mistakes cost their company a lot of money. If they do that too often they lose their jobs. On newspapers everything doesn't ride on one story or one series but on the long run. Everyone in television is basically motivated by fear.

And television news is run by the network. It is not really autonomous. Those in charge of entertainment have ultimate charge over the news programs. CBS News has a buffer between the management and the news division: Richard Salant. In fact, that is his primary function. He is a lawyer, not a newsman, and he is able to negotiate the vast differences of approach between the news side and Blackrock and to work out acceptable compromises. . . .

Thursday of the first week, Small asked me to come down to his office. Gordon was sitting there. I was surprised, to say the least. He hadn't told me he was coming down. He asked where I would be later in the day. He said he would call.

He called around 3:30 and asked if I could have a drink with him. I suggested he have a drink with Ben [Bradlee, *Washington Post*] and me, since they were old friends.

He hedged. Then he said he could get a hotel room and stay over if I wanted him to. We could have dinner. I suggested we all have dinner. He hesitated. I couldn't figure out what he wanted. "Well, Gordon," I said finally, "what do you want?"

He mumbled something about dinner for the two of us and how he could get a hotel room. I said I thought it would be more fun with the three of us. He blew up. . . .

"Gordon," I said quietly, "I'm going to quit CBS. I'll try to be out in about six weeks. But I've got to find a job first. Just get Small to let me stay in Washington until then. I can't—won't go back to the anchor job. But I don't want to just quit and have it look like I was a total loss. I want to have a great job to go to. Will you do that much for me? Just hold them off for a while?"

He looked relieved. "I'll do it," he promised.

We walked in silence to the Watergate Terrace Restaurant and made polite conversation through dinner. Nobody ate anything. I ordered gazpacho but I couldn't swallow it. As we were leaving I asked Gordon what I had been longing to ask him since we went on the air.

"Gordon, why did you do it? Why did you hire me and then throw me on the air like that with no training? Why did you do it to me?"

"What if I had told you we wanted to make you the anchor on the *Morning News* but that you'd have to have about three to six months' training on one of our local stations first. Would you have done it?"

"Of course not."

"That's why." . . .

The morning after I quit, Hughes signed me off: "Sally Quinn is leaving CBS News for *The New York Times*—not necessarily sadder, but certainly wiser. And we hope she's happier there than she was here. For one thing, the help over there don't have to get up as early as they do here."

I thought it was touching and funny in Hughes' own gruff way.

Later that morning Richard called to say that Don Hamilton, Director of Business Affairs, wanted that day to be my last day. I pointed out that I had two film pieces to finish and that I intended to work two more weeks, that I had two further weeks of vacation coming to me, and that therefore they could count me on the payroll for another month. I wasn't to start at *The Times* until March 18.

Richard said Hamilton wouldn't buy that. I told Richard that I would call Salant or Bill Paley if I had to, and give interviews about what a cheap crumby outfit CBS was if I heard another word on the subject. Just get me the four weeks' pay. I didn't care how he did it.

Richard understood that I meant it. A half hour later he called back and said, "It's all set."

It still made me chuckle, though, that such a huge corporation would be so unbelievably cheap, especially under the circumstances. But I don't know why I was surprised, after what I had been through.

Saturday, I got a letter from Dick Salant.

Dear Sally,

In case you missed the AP story, I am attaching it. It quotes me absolutely correctly.

I am terribly sorry that things did not work out as we all expected and hoped. The fault, I honestly believe, was ours—mine.

In any event, best wishes for every sort of satisfaction and happiness. And if you can bear it, do drop in so I can say goodbye and good luck.

All the best,

Dick Salant

The AP story was enclosed. It said: "CBS News President Richard Salant said Thursday that CBS would not hold her to her contract. Asked if he considered Miss Quinn's move a slap at CBS, Salant said, 'No, not at all. She doesn't owe us a thing. We owe her a lot. And we damn near ruined her by making a mistake and pushing her too far too fast.' "

On February 7 Gordon Manning was fired from his job as news director. He was given a job as "vice president and assistant to the president of CBS News."

Gordon had been news director for nine years. His ten years were up in June and he was to receive a pension. That's why he was given that job, to hold him over so he could get his pension. He was fifty-seven in June, 1974. Somehow Gordon managed to redeem himself, partly by landing Solzhenitsyn for Walter Cronkite to interview. He stayed on after June and became a producer for the public affairs division of CBS News.

Bill Small was given Gordon's job. Sandy Socolow was given the Washington bureau. The day the change was announced Small was in Gordon's office.

Reached there, he said he was completely surprised by the promotion. "I've only been at this desk for six hours," he said. "I'm just trying to find out where the men's room is and where they keep the key to the liquor cabinet."

On February 28 Lee Townsend was fired. They had no ready title for him to assume. He was later assigned to the investigative unit. The new *Morning News* producer was the Rome bureau manager, Joseph Dembo.

Howyadoon? Fuller Brush Calling

Cathryn Donohoe

Nothing stops the Fuller Brush man. Not snow, not rain, not heat—and certainly not the little lady at her kitchen door who tells him there's nothing she needs today.

"Invariably, the one that says that is the one that buys the most," David Schenerman explains.

Schenerman is 58. He has been a Fuller Brush man for 30 years. He is one of the last of the shoe-leather door-to-door salesmen, the kind who will walk any street, ring any bell, dodge any dog to conjure up a sale and close on it. He works, after all, on commission alone.

Every three weeks he wears out the heels on his support shoes, every two months the soles. He works when he's tired, when he's sick and when he's injured. When laryngitis steals his voice, he talks with his hands. One day when he couldn't speak he simply pointed to the products in his sample case and to his sales brochure. That, he says, was one of the best sales days he ever had.

And this morning, as he looks for a place to park and start his rounds in Stevenson—an upper-middle-income development of about 1,000 lawns northwest of Baltimore—he drives his white Chevy Nova with one hand. The left, held up to keep the blood from flowing toward it, wears oozing gauze around the ring finger, which was nearly lopped off below the nail in a camping accident two days before. For the pain he takes nothing. He needs a clear head to drive and to sell.

What he sells is an 84-year-old name. For years it was part of the American weave, one celebrated not just in hundreds of farmer's daughter jokes in the 1930s but in the movies and the glossy magazines as the epitome of door-to-door sales as well. To anyone over 40 these days—as most of the Schenerman customers are—the name can be an open sesame.

"Hi! Fuller Brush! Howyadoon? I got the mops on sale, and the brooms!"

Open sesame! He's in the kitchen. But that doesn't mean he'll make the sale.

"Here are the moth deodorant blocks for the closets. Keeps the closets smelling fresh. The moths are coming. And our sponge mops are on sale, and the feather dusters. And now, this is great: the over-the-door rack. We do a great job with that. For lingerie. It even handles heavy winter coats."

The lady of the house, a regular customer, resists by indirection: "I wish my kids would use them."

"Howyadoon? Fuller Brush Calling," by Cathryn Donohoe, *Insight* Magazine, May 28, 1990, p. 42. Reprinted by permission of *Washington Times*.

"This they will. It's real sturdy. Because it's steel, and it's vinyl-coated. Notice the way everything is beveled, so you don't have any sharp edges. You can put towels, lingerie, necklaces, heavy winter coats on there. And I got the good, super, mini carpet sweeper."

More indirection: "People don't use carpet sweepers like they used to."

"But this is great. This uses no electricity, works by friction. And by the way, you can adjust it to different heights for rugs or wood. And it picks up dog hairs and cat hairs better than a vacuum cleaner."

"I think I have everything," the lady says.

"Right. You got the mops and brooms last time. Scissors? Oh, and I got a good sale on the knives, the professional knives—"

"I have knives."

"—and a super sale on household shears. Ironing board cover?"

"I just bought one. Look, my husband told me I could not spend any more money this week. If I buy anything today, it's divorce, OK? So why don't you come by in a couple of weeks, and maybe I can buy something then, OK?"

"Good enough. Catch you next month."

And he's out.

He sprints down the driveway, listing to starboard with his brochure, his sample case and a brown sack of gifts—white plastic funnels, mesh scrub squares, plastic rain bonnets and the traditional Fuller vegetable brushes—in his good hand.

He is an independent contractor, a man with his own business, working full-time and exclusively for Fuller Brush. And in 12 years in this neighborhood he has built up a bevy of repeat customers whose buying patterns he reviews each morning before he leaves home. Sometimes they buy, sometimes they don't. When they don't, he knows they will buy next time.

"I'm not trying to convert anybody. It's not a pressure thing," he says. "I'm looking for people who are interested. If there's no interest, I'm gone."

He drives past 200 houses every day, checking driveways and garages for cars that tell him someone is behind the door. Once he parks, he will talk to 20 people—regulars as well as those he canvasses cold—and close, on the average, 10 sales.

That comes to $40,000 to $50,000 worth of Fuller products sold each year at a commission rate he refuses to reveal, though he says he will not quarrel with 35 percent to 50 percent. (Who knows? It might be higher.) It puts him among the company's top 100 salesmen.

"I do well," he says.

Not bad for a high school grad from Newark who pushed planes on the USS Coral Sea, then sold shoes and insurance when the Korean War ended. Schenerman and his wife, Toby, a high school teacher, have put three children through college, one as far as a doctorate and another to a master's.

The secret to all this, he says, is "the ABC of selling: Always Be Closing." That and the knowledge, picked up over 30 years, of how to negotiate the major obstacles.

First come the Dogs. "Even if they know you, you gotta be careful," he says, staring at a chain leash snaked across a front porch. In spite of it all, they got to him twice, and now he takes tetanus shots every five years.

Then comes the Door. "First of all, a good percentage of doorbells don't work. So you don't trust the doorbell. You knock too. If you don't get any answer, you get out fast. You don't make money talking to a door," he says.

"You go to the kitchen door if you can. You like to get them relaxed, and generally they're in the kitchen. If you go to the front door and they have to run in from the kitchen, they won't be relaxed."

The rest is ABC.

"Hi! Fuller Brush! Howyadoon?"

It's the kitchen door again and the lady of the house in a bathrobe.

"I don't have the pants hangers that you like on sale. But I got the deodorant moth protection for the closets. And this is great: the barbecue brush. It's a new item. You can scrape the grill with it. This is the last one. Take it. Take it."

"I'll give you a kiss," says the lady. "What happened to your hand?"

"I put it in the wrong place. Look, here's something you're gonna love. This is the best bathroom cleaner to ever hit the market. You squeeze a little bit of that on, and scrub, and it gets off all the stains in the bathroom. Lime, scale, rust, hard-water buildup. $6.98 for two. They're on an introductory special."

"I've got so much of that crap, it's unbelievable," says the lady of the house.

"I got the prelaundry. Takes out grass stains, grease stains, chocolate, mustard, catsup, perspiration. You buy two, you get the third one free on the sale. It's three times stronger than Spray 'n' Wash. Let me show you the can. Look, there's the can. It'll take out any stain. Grass stains, grease stains, chocolate, mustard, catsup, perspiration. We do a fantastic job with it."

"Naah."

"This is the new brush that gets your refrigerator coils clean."

"That's it. I want that."

"OK. A dozen? I'm kidding. You want one for your daughter? And I got a fantastic sale on scissors. And this is the new upholstery brush. That gets all the lint off the chairs and couches."

"It does?"

"Yeah. It's excellent. It gets lint off your chairs, your upholstery, your couches. It's the old-fashioned upholstery brush. We brought it back. See the way the tip is made? It picks everything up nicely. It has a wooden handle. And you know Fuller. It'll never wear out."

"I think that's a good idea."

"One will be enough? If you're going to get one for your daughter, you might as well get it on sale."

"She's getting a new sofa."

"There you go."

"It's going to be leather."

"Well, then she won't need it."

"So much of this junk I buy and I have," says the lady of the house. "Here, save your hand! You want me to write it up for you?"

Total this sale: $15.21.

When Schenerman takes time to reflect on his work, he talks first about selling, then about listening. To him, in some ways, they are one and the same.

"When you're selling, you always have to be selling. Get in, get the business and go," he says. "But sometimes you're like a bartender. People tell you things they probably wouldn't even tell their husbands. You let it go in one ear and out the other; you never repeat anything. You might not get a sale that day, but you gotta listen if they want to talk."

For more than 30 years he has been more than a bartender. He has rushed an injured boy to the hospital. He has played ambulance to five women in labor. One thing he has missed out on: "I've never been propositioned in 30 years. I don't know what's wrong with me."

In fact, he prefers to see husbands around. "When the woman's alone, she's afraid her husband will think she's spending too much. But when he's there, she'll say, 'Dear, can I buy this?' And he'll say, 'Sure, go ahead.' So I end up with a bigger sale."

To most people under 40, according to Fuller's own studies, the name that Dave Schenerman sells means either nothing or something their parents bought.

"Younger people will say, 'When I was a little kid, I remember the Fuller Brush man coming around,' " says Russ Imler, nine years with the company and a member of the board of directors of Fuller Industries in Great Bend, Kan.

Observers of the industry say the company's studies turned up even more. "There was absolutely no recognition of whether the company is still in business and, if so, how you bought one of their products," says George Hescock, an executive vice president of the Direct Selling Association, a Washington-based trade group.

Twenty-five years ago Fuller Brush had about 100,000 field representatives, by Imler's estimate. Today it has 13,000—80 percent of them women, most of them part-timers who sell by telephone to friends and neighbors, and none of them pledged exclusively to Fuller unless, like Dave Schenerman, they choose to be.

But even more, the Fuller story is the tale of a small company gobbled up by a corporate giant that, according to Imler, was geared toward retail and mail-order sales and "did not understand" the direct-sales tradition.

So when Sara Lee Corp. (which, as Continental Foods of Chicago, bought Fuller 22 years ago) last year offered to sell Fuller to Imler and a small investor group he heads, he jumped at the chance. It meant taking private again the business Alfred C. Fuller began in his sister's basement in Boston in 1906.

The brand-new, old-fashioned Fuller Brush is heading down a bumpy road. Under Sara Lee it had begun selling through mail-order catalogs and in discount stores. Company officials expect that to continue. Yet even as the deal became final last month, Imler resigned as Fuller Industries' president—in a conflict, according to one employee, over the new company's direction.

To Schenerman, one of the few old-timers left, it's just good news that the company is back. He disdained Sara Lee's focus on recruiting part-timers. "I'm a professional," he says, "and I don't consider the part-timers professionals. They just don't have the product knowledge I have."

"Hi! Fuller Brush! Howyadoon?"

The lady of the house, a gray-haired woman in a white T-shirt, hangs up the kitchen phone. "My friend says, 'Don't start an affair with the Fuller Brush man, because everybody tells jokes about it.' "

"Look, I got the new microwave oven cleaner and the microwave sponge. You get both of them for $3.99. And this is great: the new upholstery brush. Detergent OK? You should need another one. You want me to put you down for one? Good. These are the new skirt hangers. I got the 10-year light bulbs and a super sale on the knives. How about the degreaser and the steel sponges?"

"I have a self-cleaning oven," says the lady. "There isn't much I don't have."

"How about the can opener? Egg slicer? Jar opener? Those are great."

"Somebody said the jar opener was pretty good."

"OK, I've got two kinds. This one you mount under the cabinet and this one you hold in your hand. Both are good. It's just a matter of taste. This one you stick in the drawer. See, the inside ring is for small jars and the outside ring is for big jars. You put it on there, and it opens the jars instantaneously. $9.99. You want two? Or three? It's good for somebody who has trouble opening things. They make nice presents. How many do you want me to put down?"

"I don't know if I want any. Don't get excited."

"OK. You know me. I don't get excited. How about a window brush? You don't have to climb a ladder. Push broom? Ironing board cover? Let me look. You need an ironing board cover, hon, and the pad too. The whole set."

"I don't want the jar opener."

"They're really good. The only trouble is, once you try that jar opener, you'll want more for gifts. You'd order a whole bunch of them. They are just real helpers. They are really good."

"I know. I've heard people talking about them. How thick is it?"

"It's real easy to handle. They're nice. And they come in a box in case you want to use them as gifts. You know, if you have an aunt or somebody who has a hard time opening jars."

"I think I'll take that."

"One or two?"

"I want one for myself. It's for jars, right?"

"Yes. It'll open a jar. And you know what else I've got that you're gonna love? One of my favorites. The kitchen scissor."

"No. Finished."

"The toilet bowl swab?"

"Finished," says the lady of the house. "They used to say, 'If you don't go out, you won't spend any money.' Now it's not true."

Total for detergent, pad, cover, jar opener: $46.16.

Dave Schenerman finished his day at noon because of the throbbing pain in his left hand. By then he had racked up $249 in sales. This in spite of the women who assured him there was nothing they needed or wanted to buy.

But for the Fuller Brush man, this is the world as it was meant to be. "The more noes you get," Schenerman says, "the closer you are to a yes."

Death of a Salesman

Arthur Miller

From the right, Willy Loman, the Salesman, enters, carrying two large sample cases. The flute plays on. He hears but is not aware of it. He is past sixty years of age, dressed quietly. Even as he crosses the stage to the doorway of the house, his exhaustion is apparent. He unlocks the door, comes into the kitchen, and thankfully lets his burden down, feeling the soreness of his palms. A word-sigh escapes his lips—it might be "Oh, boy, oh, boy." He closes the door, then carries his case out into the living room, through the draped kitchen doorway.

Linda, his wife, has stirred in her bed at the right. She gets out and puts on a robe, listening. Most often jovial, she has developed an iron repression of her exceptions to Willy's behavior—she more than loves him, she admires him, as though his mercurial nature, his temper, his massive dreams and little cruelties, served her only as sharp reminders of the turbulent longings within him, longings which she shares but lacks the temperament to utter and follow to their end.

LINDA, *hearing Willy outside the bedroom, calls with some trepidation:* Willy!

WILLY: It's all right. I came back.

LINDA: Why? What happened? *Slight pause.* Did something happen, Willy?

WILLY: No, nothing happened.

LINDA: You didn't smash the car, did you?

WILLY: *with casual irritation:* I said nothing happened. Didn't you hear me?

LINDA: Don't you feel well?

WILLY: I'm tired to death. *The flute has faded away. He sits on the bed beside her, a little numb.* I couldn't make it. I just couldn't make it, Linda.

LINDA, *very carefully, delicately:* Where were you all day? You look terrible.

WILLY: I got as far as a little above Yonkers. I stopped for a cup of coffee. Maybe it was the coffee.

LINDA: What?

WILLY, *after a pause:* I suddenly couldn't drive any more. The car kept going off onto the shoulder, y'know?

LINDA, *helpfully:* Oh. Maybe it was the steering again. I don't think Angelo knows the Studebaker.

WILLY: No, it's me, it's me. Suddenly I realize I'm goin' sixty miles an hour and I don't remember the last five minutes. I'm—I can't seem to—keep my mind to it.

LINDA: Maybe it's your glasses. You never went for your new glasses.

WILLY: No, I see everything. I came back ten miles an hour. It took me nearly four hours from Yonkers.

LINDA, *resigned:* Well, you'll just have to take a rest, Willy, you can't continue this way.

WILLY: I just got back from Florida.

LINDA: But you didn't rest your mind. Your mind is overactive, and the mind is what counts, dear.

WILLY: I'll start out in the morning. Maybe I'll feel better in the morning. *She is taking off his shoes.* These goddam arch supports are killing me.

LINDA: Take an aspirin. Should I get you an aspirin? It'll soothe you.

WILLY, *with wonder:* I was driving along, you understand? And I was fine. I was even observing the scenery. You can imagine, me looking at scenery, on the road every week of my life. But it's so beautiful up there, Linda, the trees are so thick, and the sun is warm. I opened the windshield and just let the warm air bathe over me. And then all of a sudden I'm goin' off the road! I'm tellin' ya, I absolutely forgot I was driving. If I'd've gone the other way over the white line I might've killed somebody. So I went on again—and five minutes later I'm dreamin' again, and I nearly—*He presses two fingers against his eyes.* I have such thoughts, I have such strange thoughts.

LINDA: Willy, dear. Talk to them again. There's no reason why you can't work in New York.

WILLY: They don't need me in New York, I'm the New England man. I'm vital in New England.

LINDA: But you're sixty years old. They can't expect you to keep traveling every week.

WILLY: I'll have to send a wire to Portland. I'm supposed to see Brown and Morrison tomorrow morning at ten o'clock to show the line. Goddammit, I could sell them! *He starts putting on his jacket.*

LINDA, *taking the jacket from him:* Why don't you go down to the place tomorrow and tell Howard you've simply got to work in New York? You're too accommodating, dear.

WILLY: If old man Wagner was alive I'd a been in charge of New York now! That man was a prince; he was a masterful man. But that boy of his, that Howard, he don't appreciate. When I went north the first time, the Wagner Company didn't know where New England was!

LINDA: Why didn't you tell those things to Howard, dear?

WILLY, *encouraged:* I will, I definitely will. Is there any cheese?

LINDA: I'll make you a sandwich.

WILLY: No, go to sleep. I'll take some milk. I'll be up right away. . . .

[*Editor's note:* The scene shifts to Howard Wagner's office the
following day.]

WILLY: Pst! Pst!

HOWARD: Hello, Willy, come in.

WILLY: Like to have a little talk with you, Howard.

HOWARD: Sorry to keep you waiting. I'll be with you in a minute.

WILLY: What's that, Howard?

HOWARD: Didn't you ever see one of these? Wire recorder.

WILLY: Oh. Can we talk a minute?

HOWARD: Records things. Just got delivery yesterday. Been driving me
crazy, the most terrific machine I ever saw in my life. I was up
all night with it.

WILLY: What do you do with it?

HOWARD: I bought it for dictation, but you can do anything with it. Listen
to this. I had it home last night. Listen to what I picked up. The
first one is my daughter. Get this. *He flicks the switch and
"Roll out the Barrel" is heard being whistled.* Listen to that kid
whistle.

WILLY: That is lifelike, isn't it?

HOWARD: Seven years old. Get that tone.

WILLY: Ts, ts. Like to ask a little favor if you . . .

The whistling breaks off, and the voice of Howard's daughter is heard.

HIS DAUGHTER: "Now you, Daddy."

HOWARD: She's crazy for me! *Again the same song is whistled.* That's me!
Ha! *He winks.*

WILLY: You're very good!

The whistling breaks off again. The machine runs silent for a moment.

HOWARD: Sh! Get this now, this is my son.

HIS SON: "The capital of Alabama is Montgomery; the capital of Arizona
is Phoenix; the capital of Arkansas is Little Rock; the capital of
California is Sacramento . . ." *and on, and on.*

HOWARD, *holding up five fingers:* Five years old, Willy!

WILLY: He'll make an announcer some day!

HIS SON, *continuing:* "The capital . . ."

HOWARD: Get that—alphabetical order! *The machine breaks off suddenly.* Wait a minute. The maid kicked the plug out.

WILLY: It certainly is a—

HOWARD: Sh, for God's sake!

HIS SON: "It's nine o'clock, Bulova watch time. So I have to go to sleep."

WILLY: That really is—

HOWARD: Wait a minute! The next is my wife.

They wait.

HOWARD'S VOICE: "Go on, say something." *Pause.* "Well, you gonna talk?"

HIS WIFE: "I can't think of anything."

HOWARD'S VOICE: "Well, talk—it's turning."

HIS WIFE, *shyly beaten:* "Hello." *Silence.* "Oh, Howard, I can't talk into
this . . ."

HOWARD, *snapping the machine off:* That was my wife.

WILLY: That is a wonderful machine. Can we—

HOWARD: I tell you, Willy, I'm gonna take my camera, and my bandsaw, and all my hobbies, and out they go. This is the most fascinating relaxation I ever found.

WILLY: I think I'll get one myself.

HOWARD: Sure, they're only a hundred and a half. You can't do without it. Supposing you wanna hear Jack Benny, see? But you can't be home at that hour. So you tell the maid to turn the radio on when Jack Benny comes on, and this automatically goes on with the radio . . .

WILLY: And when you come home you . . .

HOWARD: You can come home twelve o'clock, one o'clock, any time you like, and you get yourself a Coke and sit yourself down, throw the switch, and there's Jack Benny's program in the middle of the night!

WILLY: I'm definitely going to get one. Because lots of time I'm on the road, and I think to myself, what I must be missing on the radio!

HOWARD: Don't you have a radio in the car?

WILLY: Well, yeah, but who ever thinks of turning it on?

HOWARD: Say, aren't you supposed to be in Boston?

WILLY: That's what I want to talk to you about, Howard. You got a minute? *He draws a chair in from the wing.*

HOWARD: What happened? What're you doing here?

WILLY: Well . . .

HOWARD: You didn't crack up again, did you?

WILLY: Oh, no. No . . .

HOWARD: Geez, you had me worried there for a minute. What's the trouble?

WILLY: Well, tell you the truth, Howard. I've come to the decision that I'd rather not travel any more.

HOWARD: Not travel! Well, what'll you do?

WILLY: Remember, Christmas time, when you had the party here? You said you'd try to think of some spot for me here in town.

HOWARD: With us?

WILLY: Well, sure,

HOWARD: Oh, yeah, yeah. I remember. Well, I couldn't think of anything for you, Willy.

WILLY: I tell ya, Howard. The kids are all grown up, y'know. I don't need much any more. If I could take home—well, sixty-five dollars a week, I could swing it.

HOWARD: Yeah, but Willy, see I—

WILLY: I tell ya why, Howard. Speaking frankly and between the two of us, y'know—I'm just a little tired.

HOWARD: Oh, I could understand that, Willy. But you're a road man,

Willy, and we do a road business. We've only got a half-dozen salesmen on the floor here.

WILLY: God knows, Howard, I never asked a favor of any man. But I was with the firm when your father used to carry you in here in his arms.

HOWARD: I know that, Willy, but—

WILLY: Your father came to me the day you were born and asked me what I thought of the name of Howard, may he rest in peace.

HOWARD: I appreciate that, Willy, but there just is no spot here for you. If I had a spot I'd slam you right in, but I just don't have a single solitary spot.

He looks for his lighter. Willy has picked it up and gives it to him. Pause.

WILLY, *with increasing anger:* Howard, all I need to set my table is fifty dollars a week.

HOWARD: But where am I going to put you, kid?

WILLY: Look, it isn't a question of whether I can sell merchandise, is it?

HOWARD: No, but it's a business, kid, and everybody's gotta pull his own weight.

WILLY, *desperately:* Just let me tell you a story, Howard—

HOWARD: 'Cause you gotta admit, business is business.

WILLY, *angrily:* Business is definitely business, but just listen for a minute. You don't understand this. When I was a boy—eighteen, nineteen—I was already on the road. And there was a question in my mind as to whether selling had a future for me. Because in those days I had a yearning to go to Alaska. See, there were three gold strikes in one month in Alaska, and I felt like going out. Just for the ride, you might say.

HOWARD, *barely interested:* Don't say.

WILLY: Oh, yeah, my father lived many years in Alaska. He was an adventurous man. We've got quite a little streak of self-reliance in our family. I thought I'd go out with my older brother and try to locate him, and maybe settle in the North with the old man. And I was almost decided to go, when I met a salesman in the Parker House. His name was Dave Singleman. And he was eighty-four years old, and he'd drummed merchandise in thirty-one states. And old Dave, he'd go up to his room, y'understand, put on his green velvet slippers—I'll never forget—and pick up his phone and call the buyers, and without ever leaving his room, at the age of eighty-four, he made his living. And when I saw that, I realized that selling was the greatest career a man could want. 'Cause what could be more satisfying than to be able to go, at the age of eighty-four, into twenty or thirty different cities, and pick up a phone, and be remembered and loved and helped by so many different people? Do you know? when he died—and by the way he died the death of a salesman, in his green velvet slippers in the smoker of the New York, New Haven and Hartford, going into Boston—when he died, hundreds of salesmen and buyers were at his funeral. Things were sad on a lotta trains for months after that. *He stands up. Howard has not looked at him.* In those days there was personality in it, Howard. There was respect, and comradeship, and gratitude in it. Today, it's all cut and dried, and there's no chance for bringing friendship to bear—or personality. You see what I mean? They don't know me any more.

HOWARD, *moving away, to the right:* That's just the thing, Willy.

WILLY: If I had forty dollars a week—that's all I'd need. Forty dollars, Howard.

HOWARD: Kid, I can't take blood from a stone, I—

WILLY, *desperation is on him now:* Howard, the year Al Smith was nominated, your father came to me and—

HOWARD, *starting to go off:* I've got to see some people, kid.

WILLY, *stopping him:* I'm talking about your father! There were promises made across this desk! You mustn't tell me you've got people to see—I put thirty-four years into this firm, Howard, and now I can't pay my insurance! You can't eat the orange and throw the peel away—a man is not a piece of fruit! *After a pause:* Now pay attention. Your father—in 1928 I had a big year. I averaged a hundred and seventy dollars a week in commissions.

HOWARD, *impatiently:* Now, Willy, you never averaged—

WILLY, *banging his hand on the desk:* I averaged a hundred and seventy dollars a week in the year of 1928! And your father came to me—or rather, I was in the office here—it was right over this desk—and he put his hand on my shoulder—

HOWARD, *getting up:* You'll have to excuse me, Willy, I gotta see some people. Pull yourself together. *Going out:* I'll be back in a little while. *On Howard's exit, the light on his chair grows very bright and strange.*

WILLY: Pull myself together! What the hell did I say to him! My God, I was yelling at him! How could I! *Willy breaks off, staring at the light, which occupies the chair, animating it. He approaches this chair, standing across the desk from it.* Frank, Frank, don't you remember what you told me that time? How you put your hand on my shoulder, and Frank . . . *He leans on the desk and as he speaks the dead man's name he accidentally switches on the recorder, and instantly*

HOWARD'S SON: ". . . of New York is Albany. The capital of Ohio is Cincinnati, the capital of Rhode Island is . . ." *The recitation continues.*

WILLY, *leaping away with fright, shouting:* Ha! Howard! Howard! Howard!

HOWARD, *rushing in:* What happened?

WILLY, *pointing at the machine, which continues nasally, childishly, with the capital cities:* Shut it off! Shut it off!

HOWARD, *pulling the plug out:* Look, Willy. . . .

WILLY, *pressing his hands to his eyes:* I gotta get myself some coffee. I'll get some coffee . . .

Willy starts to walk out. Howard stops him.

HOWARD, *rolling up the cord:* Willy, look . . .

WILLY: I'll go to Boston.

HOWARD: Willy, you can't go to Boston for us.

WILLY: Why can't I go?

HOWARD: I don't want you to represent us. I've been meaning to tell you for a long time now.

WILLY: Howard, are you firing me?

HOWARD: I think you need a good long rest, Willy.

WILLY: Howard—

HOWARD: And when you feel better, come back, and we'll see if we can work something out.

WILLY: But I gotta earn money, Howard. I'm in no position to—

HOWARD: Where are your sons? Why don't your sons give you a hand?

WILLY: They're working on a very big deal.

HOWARD: This is no time for false pride, Willy. You go to your sons and you tell them that you're tired. You've got two great boys, haven't you?

WILLY: Oh, no question, no question, but in the meantime . . .

HOWARD: Then that's that, heh?

WILLY: All right, I'll go to Boston tomorrow.

HOWARD: No, no.

WILLY: I can't throw myself on my sons. I'm not a cripple!

HOWARD: Look, kid, I'm busy this morning.

WILLY, *grasping Howard's arm:* Howard, you've got to let me go to Boston!

HOWARD, *hard, keeping himself under control:* I've got a line of people to see this morning. Sit down, take five minutes, and pull yourself together, and then go home, will ya? I need the office, Willy. *He starts to go, turns, remembering the recorder, starts to push off the table holding the recorder.* Oh, yeah. Whenever you can this week, stop by and drop off the samples. You'll feel better, Willy, and then come back and we'll talk. Pull yourself together, kid, there's people outside. . . .

REQUIEM

[*Editor's note:* Biff & Happy are Willy's sons. Charley is a neighbor.]

CHARLEY: It's getting dark, Linda.

Linda doesn't react. She stares at the grave.

BIFF: How about it, Mom? Better get some rest, heh? They'll be closing the gate soon.

Linda makes no move. Pause.

HAPPY, *deeply angered:* He had no right to do that. There was no necessity for it. We would've helped him.

CHARLEY, *grunting:* Hmmm.

BIFF: Come along, Mom.

LINDA: Why didn't anybody come?

CHARLEY: It was a very nice funeral.

LINDA: But where are all the people he knew? Maybe they blame him.

CHARLEY: Naa. It's a rough world, Linda. They wouldn't blame him.

LINDA: I can't understand it. At this time especially. First time in thirty-five years we were just about free and clear. He only needed a little salary. He was even finished with the dentist.

CHARLEY: No man only needs a little salary.

LINDA: I can't understand it.

BIFF: There were a lot of nice days. When he'd come home from a trip; or on Sundays, making the stoop; finishing the cellar; putting on the new porch; when he built the extra bathroom; and put up the garage. You know something, Charley, there's more of him in that front stoop than in all the sales he ever made.

CHARLEY: Yeah. He was a happy man with a batch of cement.

LINDA: He was so wonderful with his hands.

BIFF: He had the wrong dreams. All, all, wrong.

HAPPY, *almost ready to fight Biff:* Don't say that!

BIFF: He never knew who he was.

CHARLEY, *stopping Happy's movement and reply. To Biff:* Nobody dast blame this man. You don't understand: Willy was a salesman. And for a salesman, there is no rock bottom to the life. He don't put a bolt to a nut, he don't tell you the law or give you medicine. He's a man way out there in the blue, riding on a smile and a shoeshine. And when they start not smiling back—that's an earthquake. And then you got yourself a couple of spots on your hat, and you're finished. Nobody dast blame this man. A salesman is got to dream, boy. It comes with the territory.

BIFF: Charley, the man didn't know who he was.

HAPPY, *infuriated:* Don't say that!

BIFF: Why don't you come with me, Happy?

HAPPY: I'm not licked that easily. I'm staying right in this city, and I'm gonna beat this racket! *He looks at Biff, his chin set.* The Loman Brothers!

BIFF: I know who I am, kid.

HAPPY: All right, boy. I'm gonna show you and everybody else that Willy Loman did not die in vain. He had a good dream. It's the only dream you can have—to come out number one man. He fought it out here, and this is where I'm gonna win it for him.

BIFF, *with a hopeless glance at Happy, bends toward his mother:* Let's go, Mom.

LINDA: I'll be with you in a minute. Go on, Charley. *He hesitates.* I want to, just for a minute. I never had a chance to say good-by.

Charley moves away, followed by Happy. Biff remains a slight distance up and left of Linda. She sits there, summoning herself. The flute begins, not far away, playing behind her speech.

LINDA: Forgive me, dear. I can't cry. I don't know what it is, but I can't cry. I don't understand it. Why did you ever do that? Help me, Willy, I can't cry. It seems to me that you're just on another trip. I keep expecting you. Willy, dear, I can't cry. Why did you do it? I search and search and I search, and I can't understand it, Willy. I made the last payment on the house today. Today, dear. And there'll be nobody home. *A sob rises in her throat.* We're free and clear. *Sobbing more fully, released:* We're free. *Biff comes slowly toward her.* We're free . . . We're free . . .

Biff lifts her to her feet and moves out up right with her in his arms. Linda sobs quietly. Bernard and Charley come together and follow them, followed by Happy. Only the music of the flute is left on the darkening stage as over the house the hard towers of the apartment buildings rise into sharp focus, and The Curtain Falls.

CIO Is Starting to Stand for "Career Is Over"

Jeffrey Rothfeder and Lisa Driscoll

Once deemed indispensable, the chief information officer has become an endangered species

---

Ronald Brzezinski thought he had finally arrived. When Quaker Oats Co. hired him in 1983 as its chief information officer, top management gave him carte blanche to overhaul the foodmaker's antiquated information system. During the next five years, as Brzezinski's technicians networked personal computers through-out the company, Quaker's computer budget rose by 400%. The company pros-pered, but by 1988, Brzezinski no longer seemed critical to that success and was out of a job—a mutual decision, he says. "I represented change," says Brzezinski, now a partner in charge of information technology planning and strategy at Coo-pers & Lybrand, "and Quaker didn't want that anymore."

Brzezinski is not alone. These days, being a CIO—in title or in function—is perilous. A decade ago, CIOs were the up-and-coming darlings of the executive suite, hired to turn computers into strategic weapons. Now, many like Brzezinski are finding they're no longer wanted. According to Touche Ross & Co., the CIO dismissal rate doubled last year, to 13%. That compares with around 9% for all top executives. Facing heavy debt or lean times, many corporations are paring technol-ogy budgets. And CIOs, some of whom earn seven-figure incomes, are getting the ax. Others are hanging on, but with diminished power. The CIO title may sound impressive, but "it can be a hollow shell," says Thomas R. Madison, vice-president for information technology at consultants United Research Co.

It's a surprising turnabout. When William R. Synott coined the term "CIO" in his 1981 book, *Information Resource Management: Opportunities & Strategies for the 1980s,* his timing seemed perfect. Information technology was bursting beyond back-office accounting jobs and being used creatively. Managers were tapping into market information on corporate data bases; clerks were using farflung networks to complete transactions.

More than just a technology whiz, the CIO was expected to think up strategi-cally important information systems—and then lead the hardware and software development. CIOs sprouted all over. By 1989, 40% of *Business Week* Top 1000 companies had a CIO, according to Synott, now banking technology director at consultants Nolan Norton & Co.

But despite this early rush to hire them, only a handful have ever gained real power. "The CIO is usually the odd man out among the executives," says Thomas A. Cooper, a former BankAmerica Corp. chief operating officer and now chief executive officer at Goldome, a Buffalo-based bank holding company. Indeed, a half-dozen recent surveys say that less than 10% of CIOs take part in strategic planning sessions, and even fewer report to the CEO or president (see table on page 338). Without influence at the top, "it's impossible to make a difference," says R. W. Eaton, CIO at Levi Strauss & Co. Eaton says that because he reports to Levi's chief operating officer, he developed in only 18 months the huge Levi-Link network that ties the apparel maker's computers to those at its retailers, suppliers, factories, and warehouses.

Thin Ice   And without a secure power base, even a visionary CIO is likely to lose the political struggle with other executives. Take BankAmerica. In the 1980s, it hired a series of high-profile CIOs, including Max D. Hopper, now senior vice-president for information systems at American Airlines Inc. Each time, other executives clashed with the CIO. Old-liners had little interest in refining the bank's internal systems and developing consumer services such as home electronic banking. "There were shouting matches in the halls," says a former BankAmerica vice-president.

Another occupational hazard for CIOs is overblown expectations. When new information systems don't produce instant results, management tends to "blame the CIO," says Herbert Z. Halbrecht, president of executive search firm Halbrecht & Associates, which places CIOs. That seems to be the case at Merrill Lynch & Co. In 1986, Merrill chose DuWayne J. Peterson to be its CIO. At the time, Peterson was a CIO superstar because of pioneering work at Security Pacific Corp. There he set up a profitable unit that sells high-tech banking systems and computer expertise to the parent bank and to other banks as well. Merrill wanted advanced technology to handle vast numbers of new customers in global and domestic services.

Peterson has been modernizing Merrill by decentralizing computer systems and hiring MCI Telecommunications, American Telephone & Telegraph, and IBM to rig new networks. But he hasn't created a breakthrough service, such as the Cash Management Account system, which helped Merrill win new customers in the early 1980s. "He hasn't hit any home runs," says a computer consultant. Now, sources close to Merrill say that top management is upset that Peterson hasn't helped the bottom line. During a recent reorganization, three technology groups were taken from Peterson and turned over to Merrill business units. Peterson's associates say the 56-year-old CIO may leave when his contract ends next year. Merrill and Peterson refused to comment.

For some companies, CIO-bashing could be costly, analysts say. In the next few years, CIO expertise will be a must for, among other things, forging electronic links for exchanging money and documents with customers and suppliers and building sophisticated data banks for marketing, sales, and decision support. Companies ignoring these technologies "are going to find themselves playing an expensive game of catch-up," warns Fred Forman, executive vice-president at computer consultants American Management Systems Inc.

Tough Lesson   Indeed, BankAmerica discovered why it needed a CIO—the hard way. In 1984, when massive problems in its loan portfolio surfaced, BankAmerica "lacked a computer system for getting a handle on how bad the situation was," says Charlie H. Rand, a former BankAmerica vice-president and now executive vice-president of consumer services at Crestar Financial Corp. in Richmond, Va. BankAmerica learned its lesson. The current CIO, Michael Simmons, and the bankers are cooperating. BankAmerica is turning a profit again, and Simmons has played a role. He has installed the largest network of ATMs in California, helping the bank cut costs by shutting 320 branches.

Still, embattled CIOs get little sympathy from their colleagues at other companies. Frequently, they say, chief information officers have been guilty of empire building—measuring their influence by the number of computers and networks they control, not by whether they have helped to improve the company's competitiveness. "Equipment is a commodity," says Gary J. Biddle, corporate vice-president for information and systems technology at American Standard Inc. "A CIO has to prove that he can use it strategically."

No Growth   Biddle, in fact, has largely dismantled American Standard's internal computer empire. In 1988, he shut its data center and hired Genix Enterprises Inc. to do the industrial supplier's computing operations. This "outsourcing" cut Biddle's staff from 200 to only 5 and allowed him to slash his budget by $2 million a year. Now, he says, he can focus on building an information system to "reduce the customer order-to-delivery cycle from 16 weeks to 48 hours." It helps, Biddle says, that he has a good working relationship with CEO Emmanuel Kampouris, who backs him.

That's promising, analysts say, but the proof that CIOs are taken seriously will be when one becomes CEO or president. So far, the CIO has been mostly a dead-end job. Despite his success, Levi's Eaton has no illusions of obtaining the corner office: "CEO's come from marketing, and that's not likely to change soon." There are exceptions. Frank E. Glover at Owens-Corning Fiberglass Corp. moved from CIO to become a vice-president for marketing—but he had spent most of his career in sales and accounting before becoming CIO.

The CIO may yet make a mark on Corporate America. The current crop of mostly computer-illiterate CEOs will soon give way to a new generation of computer-wise executives. Moreover, as companies see competitors use information systems to gain an advantage, CIOs will be prized again. According to Thomas Friel, managing partner for information technology at headhunters Heidrick & Struggles Inc., in five years, virtually every major company will have a CIO who's a peer to the CEO. CIOs welcome such optimism. They just hope this time it's for real.

WHERE DO CIOs STAND?
A Survey of 300 Chief Information Officers

	Yes	No
On the corporate board?	2%	98%
Report to the CEO and/or president?	7.7%	92.3%
On a senior management committee?	40%	60%

DATA: Heidrick & Struggles, Inc.

Chapter

11

Hazards

*B*efore you read this chapter, we'd like you to record your answers to the following statements:

1. The typical work week of almost all "full-time" nonmanagerial employees is forty hours.

1   2   3   4   5   6   7

Strongly agree   Strongly disagree

2. Physical safety is seldom a problem in the modern workplace.

1   2   3   4   5   6   7

Strongly agree   Strongly disagree

3. While affirmative action programs have created some discontent among white employees, they have proved extremely satisfactory to black employees.

1   2   3   4   5   6   7

Strongly agree   Strongly disagree

4. Any child would be better off if the primary breadwinner in his or her family held an executive position rather than a blue-collar job.

1   2   3   4   5   6   7

Strongly agree   Strongly disagree

5. Modern executives show a strong concern with the physical well-being of their employees.

1   2   3   4   5   6   7

Strongly agree   Strongly disagree

6. Modern executives show a strong concern with the physical well-being of members of their communities.

1   2   3   4   5   6   7

Strongly agree   Strongly disagree

7. Generally speaking, government actions have been helpful in reducing the hazards of work.

1   2   3   4   5   6   7

Strongly agree   Strongly disagree

These questions explore a few of the issues treated in this chapter. After you read the chapter, we suggest that you answer the questions again, using a different colored pencil or pen, to see if your ideas have changed. We suggest keeping in mind as you read, the changes in the workplace that have occurred with the development of technology. An observer may fail to notice the hazards introduced by new technology and conclude erroneously that the workplace has become safer.

In "Automation: Pain Replaces the Old Drudgery" Peter T. Kilborn describes the cumulative-trauma disorders workers in business and industry are experiencing as a result of new technology coupled with pressure to get the work out.

We have included several articles that highlight hazards that exist because of the products made by organizations and the processes used to create them. E. S. Evans reports the impact of one in "Ailing Workers Tell of Long Years Amid Asbestos Dust." "Crisis in Bhopal" by Paul Shrivastava is the story of the Bhopal Chemical spill disaster. Philip Jalsevac tells of a frequently overlooked danger in "Fourth Firefighter Dies after '87 Blaze" as a result of hazardous materials stored at the site of fires.

Well intentioned governments efforts can backfire as described by Bob Baker in "Overtime Takes Toll on American Workers," by Don Wycliff in "Blacks Debate the Costs of Affirmative Action," and in "The Right to Privacy: There's More Loophole than Law," by Michele Galen and Jeffrey Rothfeder.

Both the federal government and its major contractors have deliberately exposed employees to life threatening conditions. Kenneth Schneider relates one such case in "Nuclear Tests' Legacy of Anger: Workers See a Betrayal on Peril." Another is described by Russell Mokhiber in "Crime in the Suites."

A hazard brought on by social rather than physical processes is described in "Humiliating Times for a Boss Who Smokes" by Deirdre Fanning. Finally, the impact on family life and particularly children is described by Brian O'Reilly in "Why Grade 'A' Execs Get an 'F' as Parents."

Automation: Pain Replaces the Old Drudgery

Peter T. Kilborn

For nine years, Paula Tydryszewski has operated a video display terminal in New Jersey's tax collection office. She types numbers and names from tax returns at woodpecker speeds into a keyboard that is tied to a big computer in the center of the room.

Ms. Tydryszewski and the 111 other full-time data entry clerks do white-collar work with blue-collar rhythms and discipline. They are tethered to their tasks by machines that let them do vastly more work than they could have done 15 or 20 years ago with paper and ledgers and typewriters.

Like Ms. Tydryszewski, an increasing number of workers around the country say they are suffering from ailments caused by the repetitive motion of their jobs. These potentially disabling ailments include cysts, inflammation of tendons, nerve damage that can lead to a loss of feeling in the fingers, and arm or shoulder pain.

Shift in Values a Factor

Occupational health specialists, labor unions and the Federal Government say tens of millions of workers, like the keyboard operators here, are at risk of these cumulative-trauma or repetitive-motion disorders. The Bureau of Labor Statistics said the disorders accounted for 48 percent of the 240,900 workplace illnesses in private business in 1988, up from 18 percent of 126,100 illnesses in 1981. The problem showed up first in factories and is now spreading through the growing office sector of the economy.

Experts attribute some growth in injuries reported to more awareness of a relationship between the ailments and work. Another factor is a shift in values: in the late 20th century, safeguarding the environment and protecting one's health are probably cherished as much as keeping the economy going and keeping one's job.

Experts say the actual numbers of injuries are proliferating because people are being pressed to work hard—in private industry to keep up with foreign competition, in government to hold down spending.

Automation has done away with heavy lifting by humans and replaced it with light lifting at rat-a-tat-tat speeds.

"We're really asking people to do more," said Don Chaffin, director of the University of Michigan's Center for Ergonomics, which studies ways to adapt working conditions to suit workers. "That has a cost."

Vern Putz-Anderson, who leads a group of professors at the university who are studying the disorders, said, "More than half the nation's workers now have jobs with the potential for cumulative-trauma disorders."

Among the jobs are those in the automobile and textile industries, and in meatpacking, where carcasses are turned into steaks and chops by a sort of assembly line in reverse.

With better workplace and equipment design, and with more breaks for relaxing, occupational health specialists say most problems can be avoided. But many employers have been slow to acknowledge a link between work and the disorders. And some workers, including Ms. Tydryszewski, are reluctant to report injuries, out of fear that employers will let them go or shift them to lower-paying jobs.

Nor can workers' problems be easily linked to cruel bosses. "New Jersey is fighting a budget deficit, and putting tax receipts into the bank promptly means the state can collect that much more interest before it pays its bills," said Barbara Jo Crea, assistant chief of the New Jersey Division of Taxation. "The mission of this branch is to deposit the money."

ONE WOMAN'S STORY: SCARS ON ARMS TELL OF PAIN

Ms. Tydryszewski's problems are showing up in her work. Her union, Local 1033 of the Communications Workers of America, points to two two-year-old incisions on her left wrist, one across the base to remove a ganglionic cyst, a formation of syrupy fluid on sheaths surrounding the tendons; the other incision running lengthwise, from the palm about two inches up the arm, to relieve a more serious condition known as carpal tunnel syndrome.

The cyst, a grape-sized lump, appeared first. "I kept pushing it back inside for two years," Ms. Tydryszewski said. "One morning it wouldn't stay down, so I went to the doctor. I had surgery and did exercises. Then I dropped a milk bottle. I had no feeling in three fingers. So I had surgery for that."

Now at the end of each day, Ms. Tydryszewski said, muscles near the back of her neck tighten into a knot, and her right arm has begun to hurt. But she said she would not complain; she is afraid of losing her $18,000-a-year job.

In early May, her supervisor sent her a memorandum. "My records indicate that you received a written warning for excessive errors on Nov. 8, 1989," it said in part. "As of today, you have not made any improvement in this area. On April 26, 1990, as documented by computer compiled statistics, you entered 189 documents with 264 errors."

Management repeatedly advises Ms. Tydryszewski to take more time, but taking more time means falling below its requirement that she make 8,000 keystrokes an hour. Working faster, on the other hand, could mean more visits with the surgeon.

WORKPLACE CHANGES:
COMPUTERS SPREAD; SO DO PROBLEMS

In the past, most reported cumulative trauma disorders arose in heavier work, especially in meat and poultry-packing plants and in automobile assembly. The Federal Occupational Safety and Health Administration has won agreement from several leading meatpackers to correct working conditions that contribute to the disorders, and in February it cited a 2,000-employee General Motors parts plant in Trenton for 40 cases of workers who needed surgery to correct repetitive-motion injuries.

But the disorders are now showing up widely in computer work. Supermarket checkout clerks appear to be getting them as a result of the twisting motions they make in sweeping people's purchases over the little windows through which laser beams record the product and the price. And they are proliferating among millions of office workers, who also have other concerns stemming from the use of computers, including exposure to radiation.

Sixty-one percent of 645 Associated Press news employees who participated in a recent Newspaper Guild survey said they had neck and back pains, said the union's research director, David J. Eisen. And a study by the National Institute of Occupational Safety and Health and the University of Michigan said 38 percent of the reporters and editors at the Long Island-based newspaper Newsday had similar complaints arising mostly from the speed and the time that reporters spend using their terminals.

The Los Angeles Times surveyed 1,200 news employees and found more than 17 percent, mostly reporters, complaining of symptoms of various types of disorders. "Two or three have needed surgery, and six or seven have been diagnosed with carpal tunnel syndrome," said Michael G. Manfro, the newspaper's safety and environmental affairs manager. He said the company now provides better working equipment that requires less strain to operate, along with special glasses.

OSHA'S VIEW:
LAWS MAY TAKE YEARS TO ENACT

Gerald F. Scannell, the head of the Occupational Safety and Health Administration, said that in view of the rising injuries, the agency would soon issue voluntary guidelines for meatpacking companies to use in preventing the disorders. Later, perhaps in August, he said it would issue guidelines for all other industries. The guidelines, he said, could be followed by regulations that would have the force of law, but that could take years. Until then, OSHA can go after employers over repetitive-motion injuries by charging them for unsafe working environments.

Mr. Scannell said he also supported a proposal of Senator Frank R. Lautenberg, Democrat of New Jersey, to triple, to $30,000, the amount OSHA can fine employers for each worker found to be working in violation of health and safety laws, but he said he opposed the Senator's proposal that OSHA raise the limit unilaterally every five years to keep pace with inflation.

Roger L. Stephens, OSHA's top specialist in the science of adapting the things people use to avoid pain or injury, said workers had always done awkward repetitive tasks, but infrequently enough or slowly enough that their tissues and tendons restored themselves. "Today," he said, "we see a lot of production demands."

Repetitive-motion ailments, like writer's cramp and tennis elbow, have plagued people for ages, but their connection to the workplace is fairly new. Among the most common are ganglionic cysts; tendinitis, an inflammation of the tendons; tenosynovitis, another form of tendon-sheath inflammation; peritendinitis, an inflammation of the area around the tendons; bursitis, an inflammation of a sac of fluid over bones that allow movement of the tendons, and carpal tunnel syndrome.

Carpal tunnel syndrome seems to arouse the most concern because of the involvement of the vital median nerve. The nerve runs down the arm and through a tunnel at the wrist, about an inch in diameter, into the hand, where it services most of the palm, the base of the thumb and the other fingers except the last. Ten tendons, enveloped in sheaths and running parallel with the nerve, protect the nerve and control the fingers. A ligament forms a belt across the tendons and binds the wrist bones, adding more protection.

Doctors say frequent and awkward maneuvers of the hand and wrist irritate the tendons over months and years. This can cause the tendons to inflame, and to squeeze and rub the median nerve, ultimately damaging it.

Proper posture can help prevent carpal tunnel syndrome. This means sitting in an upright "piano" position at the keyboard. Ideally, one's arms are parallel to the floor and there is some support for the wrists.

Symptoms of carpal tunnel syndrome are numb and tingling fingers, usually at night, and loss of feeling. Early on, it can be treated with rest, a job change, wrist splints that avert unnatural movements, and cortisone.

As symptoms worsen, the last—and usually effective—resort is cutting the ligament at the base of the wrist. As Dr. Putz-Anderson wrote in a book, "Cumulative Trauma Disorders," after recovery "it is important that the worker is not returned to the same job or task that precipitated" a disorder.

Even so, some of the victims of the disorders who work for the State of New Jersey return to their old jobs after they are cured.

AT THE KEYBOARD: THE WORKER'S BODY DOES THE ADJUSTING

Trenton's tax collection office, similar to other data entry centers in the state government, uses two large rooms, one for smokers and one for non-smokers. The clerks sit at tables, each about a yard wide, with white formica tops. Chairs can be adjusted for height and to rock but nothing else. Some people bring in pillows.

On the tables in the data processing offices are 16-year-old terminals, about half the size of conventional desk-top computers. Neither the keyboards nor the screens can be tilted, turned, raised or lowered. Because they cannot adjust the equipment, the clerks adjust their bodies.

During the peak of the tax season, from February until June, the office hires about 200 temporary clerks at $7.53 an hour. In the most intensive six weeks, the temporary clerks get an incentive: 10 cents an hour more for every 500 keystrokes an hour above 8,000.

In a tacit acknowledgement of a connection between the injuries and computer work, the New Jersey Department of Health has issued guidelines for the safer use of video display terminals. Among other things, they urge installation of more adjustable chairs, work tables and computers.

Ms. Crea said she and the Division of Taxation supported such changes. But in view of budget problems, she said, new equipment "is not in the cards."

Some state clerks like the work. Robin Sabol, 32 years old, who works in a Labor Department data-entry office, said that her required keystroke rate was 10,000 an hour but that her actual rate was 18,000 to 21,000. "I like to push myself," she said. "Ten thousand is boring and monotonous." As for aches and pains, she said: "Sometimes it gets to you. But if you like the job, you're going to do your best."

But complaint and discomfort seem more the norm. In a survey of 118 clerks at the tax office completed two weeks ago by Local 1033, 81 percent said they had had hand or wrist pain, 47 percent experienced numbness or tingling in their fingers, and 82 percent had had arm or shoulder pain. In addition, 15 percent said a doctor had found them to have tendinitis, 8 percent said they had cysts on the hands or wrists and 7 percent—eight workers—had carpal tunnel syndrome.

Terri Croushore, who is 35 and sits near Ms. Tydryszewski, has not had maladies as acute as her colleague's in her four years on the job. But Ms. Croushore, who does 14,000 keystrokes an hour when the work is heavy, says she is beginning to get a burning sensation in her elbows, a tingling in her wrists and numbing in her fingers. She doesn't complain. "They would just tell me to slow down," she said.

FLOOD AWAITED:
MANY MORE CLAIMS ARE EXPECTED

New Jersey officials say they accommodate injury cases when employees can bring persuasive evidence from doctors that an injury is job-related. The worker receives full pay and benefits without losing any of the 10-day-per-year sick leave. Ms. Tydryszewski, who was out for six months in 1988, said she had never heard of the policy, but even if she had she might have had a tough time proving her case.

Ms. Crea said she had had only two requests for sick-leave benefits related to cumulative trauma disorders, one involving carpal tunnel syndrome and the other tendinitis. The requests were denied, she said, because they were deemed "preexisting conditions."

New Jersey officials, like many employers, say they have to be tough about granting benefits to people who allege work-related disorders, partly because of budgetary constraints, partly because the ailments are often hard to trace to any single cause.

For those reasons, and others like fear of demotion, disability claims for treatment of the disorders are low. Stover H. Snook, ergonomics director at the Liberty Mutual Insurance Company in Boston, said repetitive-motion injuries accounted for 1 percent of his company's claims and 1.5 percent of the cost of the claims.

"But it's a major health problem," he said. "In the past, workers would tolerate it just so they could get work. Now they're less tolerant of pain and discomfort. Any employer that has large numbers of employees doing these tasks has got to worry about the floodgates."

Ailing Ex-Workers Tell of Long Years amid Asbestos Dust

E. S. Evans

"When I walked up the steps into the courthouse," Bernard J. Schaefer told a federal jury. "I had to stop and rest before I could make it."

Schaefer, 80, of Florissant, had come to U.S. District Court in St. Louis to tell the jury that he was suffering from asbestosis and how he got the often disabling lung ailment. He had worked 32 years in an asbestos-products plant in St. Louis County.

He and four other longtime employees of the plant, their wives and the widows of two others are suing eight American, Canadian and British suppliers of raw asbestos fiber. They allege that they were not warned that breathing asbestos dust could cause lung ailments and cancer.

The multimillion-dollar suit here is one of about 20,000 that have been filed in courts across the country.

The civil trial resumed today in Judge William L. Hungate's courtroom. It began last week and was expected to last at least two more weeks.

Schaefer and other plaintiffs testified last week that they suffered from shortness of breath. They described the asbestos shingle-and-pipe plant where they worked as constantly clouded with asbestos dust. Dust collection machinery often failed, they said, and respirators were seldom used because workers had not been advised of the health hazards until the 1970s.

Coughing as he spoke, Schaefer said shortwindedness stopped him from continuing the odd-job work he did after retiring in 1966 from the Certain-Teed Corp. plant. Formerly the Keasbey and Mattison Co. plant at 600 St. Cyr Road in Bellefontaine Neighbors, it was closed in May 1980.

The defendant companies contended in opening statements that it was the users' responsibility to take precautions, rather than the producers'.

"I cough a lot at night," Schaefer said. "Because I don't want to disturb my wife too much, I go to the bathroom. In the mornings when I get up, I do a lot of coughing and spitting."

He and others said they sleep poorly at night, frequently having to sit up to get any rest. They have to avoid stairs and cannot do household chores like mowing the lawn or shoveling snow.

They said that they had crushed and mixed asbestos fiber with cement, had cut shingles and pipe made from the material and had unloaded porous burlap bags of raw asbestos from boxcars, but that they had never seen any markings on the bags warning of health hazards. Clouds of dust rose when the asbestos was tossed onto wagons, shoveled into the crusher and dumped into mixing vats, they recalled.

When James E. Hullverson, the plaintiff's attorney, asked Schaefer whether such a warning would have made any difference to him, the battery of defense attorneys objected. Hullverson argued that his clients would testify that they would have quit their jobs, and he prevailed.

"I'd have tried to get out of there, one way or another," Schaefer answered. On cross-examination, he admitted that he was aware that there might be a health hazard, "but I didn't think it would affect me."

He said the plant always had asbestos in the air. "You could see it fall off the joists up above when the mechanisms shook the building a little bit," he noted.

Albert Wiese, also of Florissant, worked at the plant 45 years and testified that when the dust collectors broke down, "the dust would get so thick you couldn't walk through it."

His breath was shortened after nearly 30 years on the job. "If I walked the length of the plant, I would be puffing," he said.

Later, a company doctor told him he had asbestosis, but he continued work until retiring when the plant was shut down. However, being a foreman, he spent as much of his last working years as he could in the office.

"I became known as a guy who didn't do very much, I guess, because I got away from the stuff," Wiese said.

Lorraine Wiese, his wife, told the jury that he used to bring the dust home on his clothes. About his lung condition, Mrs. Wiese said, "When he goes to bed, his breathing is so heavy that I have to go to another room to sleep."

Vera Dile testified that her husband, Eugene, died in 1979 of cancer, 16 years after contracting asbestosis. He had retired at age 65 with 40 years' service at the plant and died at 68, she said.

Medical authorities have forecast that 200,000 cancer deaths would be attributed to asbestos exposure in the next 20 years.

Since 1900, research has accumulated evidence that inhalation of asbestos, microscopic stone fibers valued in construction materials for their resistance to heat and fire, can cause some kinds of cancer tumors and asbestosis. The dust impregnates the walls of the lungs many years after initial exposure. The asbestos industry contends that the extent of the danger was not understood until the mid-1960s, when protective measures were begun.

A deposition was read to the jury from Robert R. Porter, retired president of the old Keasbey and Mattison Co. He said that he could recall no warnings to workers of the danger nor management concern for their health during his 1955–62 tenure. He said he had seen photographic evidence of lung damage from asbestos impregnation, which the company's owner ordered destroyed, but had known little about asbestosis.

"If you inhale a lot of water, you can't breathe," Porter stated. "If you breathe enough asbestos, you're going to smother. That's about all I knew about it."

Porter said that during a 1955–56 tour of asbestos plants in England, he noticed that workers were wearing masks to prevent inhalation of the dust. Porter said he was told that sanitation laws were much more stringent in the United Kingdom than in the United States.

His company was owned at that time by Turner & Newall Ltd. of Great Britain, one of the defendants in the suit. Other defendants include Bell Asbestos Mines Ltd. and Asbestos Corp. Ltd., both controlled by a Quebec government agency, and Johns-Manville Corp. of Denver, which once owned Bell Asbestos.

Certain-Teed was not a defendant in the suit when it was filed two years ago, but has been named in a cross-claim brought by defendants.

Overtime Takes Toll on American Workers

Bob Baker

Some workers desperate for money, others miss leisure

Facing furious deadlines, Margaret Nix worked 34 out of every 35 days on the Boeing Co.'s aircraft assembly line. Mandatory overtime, 12-hour days. She gained a pile of money. She lost a disgruntled husband. Then her teenaged daughter suffered an unrelated psychological breakdown.

One day Nix, who asked that her real name not be used, tried to coax the withdrawn girl to recall some of the family's good times.

"Mom," her daughter said, "you were never home."

Such stories, drenched in guilt and anger, contributed to a 48-day strike last fall by 57,000 Boeing machinists. Some of the strikers carried picket signs demanding stricter limits on overtime with slogans such as, "Do your children know what you look like?"

Life at Boeing, where the company now promises to limit overtime to a mere 144 hours every three months, is an extreme example of the pressure overtime work can generate. Yet late in the afternoon each day in many offices and factories, the same kind of tension gurgles in the stomachs of hundreds of thousands of employees who pray that they won't be asked or ordered to work overtime—and those who are equally hopeful that they will.

America's workforce has a love-hate relationship with overtime. On one side are people desperate for more money. On the other are people desperate for more personal time.

For every Margaret Nix at Boeing there is a co-worker like Charles Anderson, a generation younger, who came to the Everett plant last year badly in debt and volunteered to work far beyond maximum mandatory overtime to pull his bank balance up. Figure it. If you work 20 hours a week overtime on a $14-an-hour machinist job—and Anderson has worked as many as 40 extra hours some weeks—your pay shoots from $560 to $980.

Some Boeing workers are relieved that the company is cutting back on OT in the wake of the strike. But Anderson, who is married and the father of a 2-year-old

"Overtime Takes Toll on American Workers" by Bob Baker of the LA Times, *Vancouver Sun,* January 20, 1990, p. D4. Reprinted by permission of the Vancouver Sun.

daughter he barely knew until the strike, is going crazy. He was planning on buying a house this spring. Now he is uncertain if he will make enough money to do it.

More than 10 million Americans who work for hourly wages supplement their pay cheques by $40 billion to $50 billion a year by working an average of nine extra hours a week at time-and-a-half. The money pays for things as discretionary as vacations and as crucial as mortgages and cars.

Overtime can mean limitless potential for some workers, such as the Los Angeles County fireman who worked so many consecutive 24-hour shifts a few years ago that he made $98,000—more than the county fire chief.

It can mean countless headaches for others, such as the working mothers who make frantic telephone calls to day-care centres to say they will be late.

It generates arguments with supervisors over uncomfortable questions—who should get first dibs on OT, who should volunteer or who should be volunteered on days when nobody wants to work the extra hours.

Overtime is the grease that allows many companies to pare their workforces in this era of so-called "lean and mean" business. It is the friction that drives many of today's demands for flexible schedules and childcare facilities at businesses for the convenience of working parents.

All told, 34 million people, or nearly one-third of the U.S. workforce, work more than 40 hours a week. Most do not get paid for their extra hours because they are either self-employed or are salaried supervisors or "professionals" exempt from the federal Fair Labor Standards Act, which requires time-and-a-half for work beyond eight hours a day or 40 hours a week.

The federal bureau of labor statistics has not separately surveyed paid overtime workers since 1985. Its current surveys, which lump together those who labor with and without overtime pay, show that 12.6 million Americans work 49 to 59 hours a week and another 9.3 million work 60 or more hours.

These numbers are soaring twice as fast as the size of the workforce.

While the total number of employed persons rose 19 per cent in the past decade, the number working 49 to 59 hours rose 46 per cent. The number working 60 or more hours rose 38 per cent.

These increases have contributed to today's portrait of a sometimes strained American family life.

Median weekly hours worked by Americans increased 20 per cent between 1973 and 1985, from 40.6 a week to 48.8, while the leisure time plummeted 32 per cent, from 26.2 hours to 17.7 hours, according to polls taken by Louis Harris and Associates.

Americans are working harder because earnings by hourly workers have lagged 15 per cent behind consumer price increases since the late 1970s, labor economists say. Not only do the number of two-income households continue to rise, but more than 7 million people now work two jobs—the highest level in more than 30 years.

In the United States, the overtime premium created by the Fair Labor Standards Act, passed in 1938, was intended as a penalty to coerce employers into hiring more people rather than using longer shifts. But it lost most of its force long ago.

Because of the soaring costs of company-paid health insurance and other benefits, which now make up 25 per cent to 35 per cent of the cost of compensation, employers find it far cheaper to scale back the number of permanent employees and get the job done by paying overtime.

Crisis in Bhopal

Paul Shrivastava

At about 12:40 A.M. on December 3, 1984, Suman Dey looked at the gauges on the control panel in total disbelief. Dey was the control-room operator at the Union Carbide pesticide plant in Bhopal, India, and what he saw was so far out of the ordinary that it terrified him. Inside a storage tank containing the dangerous chemical methyl isocyanate gas (MIC), which was supposed to be refrigerated, the temperature had risen to 77°F. Pressure in the tank, which ordinarily ranged between 2 and 25 pounds per square inch (psi), had risen to 55 psi.

Bewildered by the readings, Dey ran to the storage tank area to investigate the problem. He heard a loud rumbling sound and saw a plume of gas gushing out of the stack in front of him. Dey, along with the MIC supervisor on duty, Shakil Qureshi, and several operators, attempted to control the gas leak by turning on safety devices. Together they tried switching on the refrigeration system to cool the storage tank. They started the scrubber through which the gases were passing and sprayed water on escaping gases, hoping to neutralize them. When all these efforts failed, they fled the plant in panic.

Across the street in a slum hut, a twenty-eight-year-old woman named Ganga Bai was awakened by incoherent shouting. She felt a burning sensation in her eyes and rubbed them, hoping to soothe them. Outside, she saw terror-stricken neighbors running through the narrow gullies between the huts, shouting single words: "Run!" "Gas!" "Death!" She woke up her husband, picked up her two-year-old daughter, and ran out of the hut.

Ganga Bai bypassed the crowd by running on the muddy ledge between a row of huts and the main road. As she ran, she saw death in its most bizarre forms. People were choking and gasping for breath. Some fell as they ran, and some lay on the roadside, vomiting and defecating. Others, too weak to run, tried to clutch onto people passing them in the hope of being carried forward.

After running for several miles, Ganga Bai stopped to catch her breath. The crowd had thinned out, and she was far away from her neighborhood. She thought she had escaped death. But actually she had been carrying it in her arms all along. She looked down into the glazed, open eyes of her still daughter and fell unconscious.

The Bhopal district collector, Moti Singh, and the superintendent of police, Swaraj Puri, were awakened in the middle of the night by the insistent ringing of their telephones. Singh and Puri were in charge of district administration, the local police department, and civil defense efforts. They rushed at once to the police control room to coordinate emergency relief efforts. But they, along with hundreds of other governmental officials and Union Carbide plant managers, were caught sleeping in more ways than one. Nobody seemed to know what gas had leaked, how toxic it was, or how to deal with the ensuing emergency. The police and the army tried to evacuate affected neighborhoods. They were too slow, and instead of being told to lie on the ground with their faces covered with wet cloths, people were urged to run; 200,000 residents fled in panic into the night.

Morning found death strewn over a stunned city. Bodies and animal carcasses lay on sidewalks, streets, and railway platforms, and in slum huts, bus stands and waiting halls. Thousands of injured victims streamed into the city's hospitals. Doctors and other medical personnel struggled to cope with the chaotic rush, knowing neither the cause of the disaster nor how to treat the victims. Groping for anything that might help, they treated immediate symptoms. They washed the eyes of their patients with water and then soothed the burning with eye drops. They gave the victims aspirin, inhalers, muscle relaxants, and stomach remedies to relieve their symptoms.

Before the week was over, nearly 3,000 people had died. More than 300,000 others had been affected by exposure to the deadly poison. About 2,000 animals had died, and 7,000 more were severely injured. The worst industrial accident in history was over.

But the industrial *crisis* that made the city of Bhopal international news had just begun. Its ramifications were both local and global. As time went on, victims suffering from the long-term health effects of exposure to MIC died. There were continuing controversies over how many people had actually perished and which treatments might be helpful to surviving victims. Family life in Bhopal was radically disrupted, as wives and children with no preparation for life outside the home were forced to go to work and manage the family's financial affairs. The victims sued the government of India and Union Carbide. The government, seeking to protect its own legitimacy, sued Union Carbide in the United States on behalf of the victims. Governments in other countries took steps to stop Union Carbide and other chemical companies from establishing similar plants in their communities.

Union Carbide's top executives were arrested upon their arrival in Bhopal, and the corporate prestige and financial health of the thirty-seventh-largest company in the world—a strong and proud corporation with a long history—was dealt a heavy blow.

In one sense, the Bhopal crisis was simply an industrial accident—a failure of technology. But the real story behind the accident goes much deeper than mere technology. It extends to the organizational and socio-political environment in which the accident occurred.

Organizational pressures within Union Carbide contributed to both the accident and the ensuing crisis. The Bhopal plant was an unprofitable operation, for the most part ignored by top Union Carbide officials. With several of Union Carbide's traditionally profitable divisions in the United States faltering, the Bhopal plant was a prime candidate for divestiture. The Indian subsidiary that owned the plant, Union Carbide (India) Ltd. (UCIL), was primarily a battery company that had made an unsuccessful foray into the pesticides market. At the time of the accident, the Bhopal plant operated at only about 30 to 40 percent of capacity and was under constant pressure to cut its costs and reduce its losses.

But it was more than Union Carbide's financial difficulties that set the stage for the crisis. The economic, political, and social environment of Bhopal also played a contributing role. At the time of the accident, Bhopal was a peculiar combination of new technology and ancient tradition sitting in somewhat uncomfortable relation to each other.

Though the city is nearly 1,000 years old, its industrial capacity, until recently, was primitive. In the last thirty years industrial growth was encouraged in Bhopal, but the necessary infrastructure needed to support industry was lacking. There were severe shortcomings in the physical infrastructure, such as supplies of water and energy and housing, transportation and communications facilities, as well as in the social infrastructure, including public health services, civil defense systems, community awareness of technological hazards, and an effective regulatory system.

Nor was industrial growth accompanied by rural development, which might have slowed the migration of people from the hinterlands. The city's population grew at three times the overall rate for the state and the nation in the 1970s. This heavy in-migration, coupled with high land and construction costs, caused a severe housing shortage in the city. For shelter, migrants built makeshift housing, which in turn became slums and shantytowns. By 1984, more than 130,000 people, about 20 percent of the city's population, lived in these slums. Two of these large slum colonies were located across the street from the Union Carbide plant.

Thus, at the time of the accident, several thousand, for the most part illiterate, people were living in shantytowns literally across the street from a pesticide plant. They had no idea how hazardous the materials inside the plant were, or how much pressure the plant was under to cut losses. Indeed, most of them believed it produced "plant medicine" to keep plants healthy and free from insects.

Not all industrial accidents become crises. They trigger crises only when technological problems occur in economic, social, and political environments that cannot cope with them. The Bhopal accident became a crisis not because of technological problems alone but also because of environmental conditions outside the plant. The plant was operated by a company under pressure to make profits and/or cut losses; it was sanctioned by a government under pressure to industrialize, even though the appropriate industrial infrastructure and support systems were missing; and it was located in a city completely unprepared to cope with any major accident. It was these factors, combined with the technological failures that actually caused the accident, that expanded the initial event into a crisis.

Although it was the worst industrial crisis in history, Bhopal-like crises are hardly unusual. All over the world—and, increasingly, in developing countries—industrial crises have become more frequent and devastating. For this reason they deserve close attention. For example, the dioxin poisoning in Seveso, Italy, and the Three Mile Island and Chernobyl nuclear power plant accidents represent industrial crises. These crises present a novel and challenging set of problems for corporations, government agencies, and communities. The causes of crises—in particular, the causes of the secondary effects that turn an accident into a crisis—are difficult to ascertain and remedy because they are so deeply rooted in the various social and economic systems of the countries involved. But failure to meet the challenge will result in more deaths, continued environmental destruction, and a severe downgrading of quality of life.

While it is probably not useful to think about dealing with industrial crises in terms of "solutions"—there is no single solution applicable to all conditions—we can build a greater understanding of who the *stakeholders* are in industrial crises and how their actions can exacerbate or minimize these crises. Bhopal provides a textbook case study for building this kind of understanding.

Fourth Firefighter Dies After '87 Blaze

Philip Jalsevac

Lawmakers must ensure that firefighters know what hazardous products are involved in a blaze, Kitchener's fire chief said Thursday after the funeral of a fourth colleague who fought a 1987 chemical fire.

"Fourth Firefighter Dies After '87 Blaze" by Philip Jalsevac, *Vancouver Sun*, July 13, 1990, p. A8. Reprinted by permission of Kitchener Waterloo Record.

"This is the kind of incident which helps focus attention on the need for that kind of change," Chief James Hancock said after the service for Capt. Edward Stahley, who died of cancer Sunday.

"It's much too important an issue to stay in neutral. And Kitchener (Ontario) knows it better than anyone."

Hancock said industries must be forced by law to register information about their hazardous substances, "not just what chemicals, but quantities and where they're stored."

About 250 firefighters from across Ontario attended the funeral of Stahley, 57. Two other firefighters and one policeman who fought the March 1987 blaze at Horticultural Technologies Inc. here have died of cancer in the last year.

As well, the Kitchener Professional Fire Fighters' Association says 13 others who attended the fire have developed various ailments, including one case each of skin cancer and Parkinson's disease and kidney and liver dysfunctions. And association president Harry Kalau said Thursday that two children have been born with birth defects, one with a facial deformity and the other with Down's syndrome.

There are concerns that the fathers, a policeman and a firefighter who were also at the fire, may have suffered genetic damage, Kalau said. And, in at least one case, the physician said the defect could be related to the fathers' exposure to a hazardous chemical.

Although Ontario's labor ministry has launched an investigation, nobody knows for sure if the deaths—three firemen and one police officer—and the illnesses are linked to the 1987 fire.

But if not, "it's one hell of a coincidence," said Kitchener Ald. Geoff Lorentz.

Hancock conceded "there's a number of schools of thought" on the cause of the rash of deaths and illness. Normally, cancer is not contracted so soon after exposure to hazardous chemicals. But the chief said "it might have been a lifelong exposure (to various contaminants on the job), and this fire may have been a triggering mechanism."

Whatever the case, Kalau said, when firefighters first arrived at the scene at Horticultural Technologies on that cold March night in 1987, "the sky was every color of the rainbow. This was something out of the ordinary."

Hancock said the Ontario Association of Fire Chiefs has not backed his call for legislation because many chiefs believe the volume of detail and paperwork required would be too cumbersome to make any information system workable.

Atom Tests' Legacy of Anger: Workers See a Betrayal on Peril

Keith Schneider

High radiation exposure at Nevada site is issue

Workers at the Nevada Test Site, the desert proving ground for American nuclear weapons, were repeatedly exposed to dangerous levels of radiation from underground and atmospheric atomic blasts over three decades, according to Government records made public in a court case here.

The records show that miners were ordered soon after nuclear blasts to recover instruments from tunnels filled with radioactive dust and strewn with contaminated debris. During the era of atmospheric nuclear tests in the 1950's, workers cleaned up rubble at ground zero without respirators that would have guarded their lungs from atomic particles.

Health officers and commissioners of the Atomic Energy Commission, the Department of Energy's predecessor, often discussed the large number of overexposures and the danger to workers at the Nevada Test Site, according to the records. But the commissioners ultimately decided not to reduce the exposures or to inform the workers of the threat because doing so would have meant changes in procedures and equipment that would have halted nuclear testing.

The papers were made available to the *New York Times* by two Las Vegas lawyers, Alan R. Johns and Larry C. Johns, who have filed a lawsuit against the Government alleging that radiation from bomb tests caused the cancer deaths of 200 employees and caused cancer illnesses in 18 others who worked at the Nevada Test Site from 1951 to 1981. The Government would not comment specifically on the case, but an official at the test site said no one had been exposed deliberately to large doses of radiation.

The once-secret documents open a new chapter in the emerging story of working conditions at the nation's nuclear weapons plants and laboratories. Some documents disclose events not previously known, and most of the others provide new details of incidents that received scant attention when they occurred.

New Light on Old Events

The declassification of the documents began in 1978 and 1979. Some were declassified as a result of legally enforceable requests filed under the Freedom of Information Act by veterans and former workers, and some were declassified at the request of Congressional committees then holding hearings on the effects of the nuclear weapons program.

"I know now that I got an awful big dose from some of those tests," said Keith L. Prescott, a disabled 63-year-old miner who worked at the test site for eight years in the 1960's and is now a plaintiff in the lawsuit.

Mr. Prescott has been sick since 1969 with multiple myeloma, a cancer of the bone marrow that scientists have linked to exposure to high levels of radiation. Mr. Prescott said in an interview at his home in Kamas, Utah: "We were told that it was safe. What did we know? We believed it was safe. They even told us we could take our clothes home, with all that stuff on it, so my wife could wash them with the family clothes."

THE ISSUES:
WAS WORKERS' TRUST BETRAYED?

At issue in the Federal Court suit, which was filed in 1980 and has been expanded to include 218 civilian workers at the test site, is whether the Government failed to protect workers from levels of radiation it knew could cause harm. The Department of Energy, the owner of the Nevada Test Site, and the Department of Justice declined to discuss any aspect of the case. But Bruce W. Church, the assistant manager of environment, safety and health at the test site, said, "I am confident that Nevada Test Site workers were never deliberately exposed to high levels of radiation."

Federal scientists have argued for years that radiation from the atomic weapons program has not caused cancer among workers, military veterans, or American citizens who worked at the test site or lived downwind of it. Their assurances are based largely on Government studies of the effect of low levels of radiation on human health, an issue that has been a source of conflict among scientists for half a century. Critics assert that the studies are tainted by their Government sponsorship and that the dangers are real and evident.

The workers represented by the Nevada lawsuit belong to one of three groups that have asserted that radiation from bomb tests in Nevada caused thousands to fall ill or die. In 1988, Congress enacted legislation to enable 62,000 military veterans who participated in atmospheric testing at the Nevada Test Site from 1951 to 1962 to be eligible for disability benefits if they had any of 13 types of cancer. The Congressional action followed a lawsuit brought by the veterans in the early 1980's that failed because courts ruled that the Government could not be sued for carrying out its own policies.

Residents File Suit

The second group, more than 1,100 residents of northern Arizona, eastern Nevada and southern Utah, sued the Government for illnesses and injuries they believed resulted from radioactive fallout from atmospheric tests. Those plaintiffs are among an estimated 25,000 residents of the three states that were exposed to fallout.

In 1984, a Federal District Judge in Salt Lake City, Bruce S. Jenkins, ruled that the tests caused cancer deaths and that the Government was liable for them. But three years later, the Court of Appeals for the 10th Circuit overturned the ruling, saying, as in the earlier case, that the Government was immune from liability. Utah's Senator Orrin G. Hatch, a Republican, and Representative Wayne Owens, a Democrat, have proposed legislation to establish a $100 million trust fund to compensate those residents.

In those cases, the Government prevailed by arguing that under a provision of the 1946 Federal Tort Claims Act, Federal officials had the "discretionary authority" to pursue the atomic weapons program without fear of future liability.

The Government sought the same immunity in the case brought by the civilian workers at the Nevada Test Site case, but a Federal District Judge in Las Vegas, Roger D. Foley, turned aside the Government's pretrial motions because of two developments that cleared the way for a trial, which will be the first since 1979 to focus on the effects of radiation on workers at a nuclear weapons plant.

A Secret Arrangement

The first was the disclosure of a secret agreement between the Government and the Nevada Industrial Commission that enabled the Atomic Energy Commission to supersede the state in considering workmen's compensation claims for radiation-related injuries. The agreement, ruled illegal and invalid by Judge Foley in 1981, meant that Reynolds Electrical and Engineering, the company that managed the test site for the Government, did not need to maintain workmen's compensation insurance coverage for radiation injuries.

The pact, signed in 1956 and discovered by Alan Johns in 1980, effectively barred Nevada Test Site workers from gaining benefits if they asserted that their injuries were caused by radiation. But an unintended result was that Keith Prescott and the other plaintiffs in the lawsuit had no forum other than Federal court to argue their claims.

The second development was a Supreme Court opinion. In 1988, the High Court, in an unrelated case, ruled that although the Federal Tort Claims Act protected those who developed Federal policies, it did not protect officials who may have been negligent in carrying out the programs. On Oct. 27 Judge Foley ruled that a jury should decide whether there was a "failure of Federal officers and employees to observe objective standards of care for the protection of the health and safety of human beings" that would amount to "actionable negligence" under Federal law.

THE TEST SITE:
PERILS THAT SPREAD FROM GROUND ZERO

"Neither Larry nor I fall into the anti-nuke category," said Alan Johns, the plaintiff's lawyer who has lived in Las Vegas for most of his 51 years. "We watched the test shots from here in the 1950's. We've never had a resentment of the Government's development of nuclear weaponry."

"But when people are being negligently exposed and then dying, you can't close your eyes," added Larry Johns, the 44-year-old younger brother. "People can accept the truth if you tell them. The Government never told them. And they didn't protect them."

No other place on earth has been battered more often by nuclear weapons than the Nevada Test Site, a haunting 1,350-square-mile stretch of flat mesas and forbidding desert whose eastern boundary is 70 miles northwest of Las Vegas. Since the first test on Jan. 27, 1951, more than 700 atomic bombs have ripped the atmosphere and shaken the earth from shafts and tunnels hundreds of feet below the surface. Radioactive contaminants blanketed the desert, and countless yawning craters opened amid the sagebrush and Joshua trees.

Like the 16 other plants and laboratories that make up the core of the American nuclear weapons industry, the Nevada Test Site has been plagued for decades by accidents and mishaps. The most recent occurred on Oct. 31, when Richard W. Mascarenas, a 28-year-old laborer, was killed when a pipe crushed his chest during an operation to clear debris from a deep tunnel following a nuclear blast. It was the first death from operations at the test site since Feb. 15, 1984, when one man was killed and 13 workers were injured after a crater opened beneath them three hours after a blast.

Concern at the Start

Yet it is the threat to the health of workers from radiation that has been shown to be a more enduring concern than industrial accidents. The concern about radiation appeared at the top levels of the Atomic Energy Commission soon after the test site opened. According to minutes of their weekly meeting in Washington on Sept. 23, 1952, "The commissioners expressed concern that workers might be exposed to radiation hazards for too long a time." Two weeks later, the commissioners were told that the program for determining the amount of radiation hundreds of workers were being exposed to "was not always as reliable as might be desired."

By May 13, 1953, some commissioners were calling on Nevada Test Site officials to reduce worker exposures by sharply lowering the Government's safety limit, which stood then at 12 rems a year, more than twice the 5-rem safety limit in effect today. A rem is a unit of measurement for determining a radiation dose. One rem is the rough equivalent of seven or eight X-rays. A 500-rem dose is usually fatal.

Dr. John C. Bugher, the director of the division of biology and medicine and the Atomic Energy Commission's chief health officer at the time, counseled against changing the standard. Reducing the safety limit, said Dr. Bugher, "would make it impossible to conduct operations at the test site without major changes in present procedures."

THE INCIDENTS:
MISSTEPS MARK A SOMBER TRAIL

Resulting from the policy that put production ahead of safety was a series of blunders, mishaps, and accidents that exposed workers to levels of radiation far in excess of safety limits.

On March 1, 1955, Eugene D. Haynes, a security guard who had never been trained in radiation safety, received a dose of at least 39 rems, more than three times the annual limit in effect at the time, when he wandered to within a quarter-mile of where a nuclear bomb had been tested hours before.

A report on the incident from scientists at Los Alamos National Laboratory said Mr. Haynes had been ordered to accompany two radiation specialists to the blast site and stand guard while highly radioactive plutonium parts were recovered. At some point, Mr. Haynes lost track of the specialists and while trying to locate them blundered into the contaminated zone near ground zero. Mr. Haynes died in 1985 of lung cancer at the age of 66. His widow is a plaintiff in the lawsuit.

At least four workers received radiation doses far in excess of the safety limit during a series of experiments in November 1955, and January 1956. In the experiments, atomic bombs were destroyed by conventional explosives to simulate how warheads would behave if they were involved in airplane crashes or other transportation accidents. According to a declassified teletype report from the Atomic Energy Commission's office in Albuquerque, N.M., to headquarters in Washington, one worker received 28 rems of radiation during the tests, another received 18 rems, a third received 13 rems, and the fourth received nearly 8 rems.

A 1956 Death is Recalled

One of the workers, Oral B. Epley, died on Feb. 1, 1956, of a brain hemorrhage at the age of 57. At the time, Government and private physicians in Las Vegas said radiation was not related to Mr. Epley's death. Another of the workers, Joe Carter, died of brain cancer in 1980. The families of Mr. Epley and Mr. Carter are plaintiffs in the lawsuit.

On Nov. 24, 1961, 108 miners were pulled out of two tunnels deep beneath the mesas in the far northern sector of the Nevada Test Site after radiation safety monitors determined that all had absorbed doses that exceeded safety limits. A report by the Atomic Energy Commission, prepared four days after the incident, said that problems in containing radioactive gases produced by atomic blasts in the tunnels caused the overexposures. The miners were offered as much beer as they could drink for a week to flush the contaminants from their bodies.

The report on the incident by Brig. Gen. A. W. Betts, the director of military application for the Atomic Energy Commission, also said officials were considering raising the safety limit in order to provide the legal and medical justification for ordering the miners back into the tunnels. There was concern, said the report, that unless the miners went back to work, a new series of atomic blasts would be delayed.

Before dawn on June 6, 1963, 13 miners who had been clearing rubble from a deep tunnel on the night shift were discovered to have been contaminated by radioactive iodine produced by an atomic test in the same tunnel the previous day. Several miners became weak and dizzy in the tunnels, though it is not known if radiation caused the sicknesses. The miners were rushed to the Donner Laboratory in Berkeley, Calif., where they were decontaminated and evaluated.

Meanwhile, Atomic Energy Commission officials ordered miners on the next shift to continue operations in the contaminated tunnel despite their knowledge of the danger. One of the miners who worked that morning in the tunnel was Keith Prescott, the disabled miner who now lives in Utah. "I remember a few hours after we started, they pulled us out to check us with monitors," said Mr. Prescott. "Then they put us back in after a Government guy came by to see what was going on."

Big Improvement Is Seen

Bruce Church, the environment safety and health official at the Nevada Test Site, said in an interview that radiation safety and training programs have been sharply improved since the 1960's. "Nobody is receiving any radiation to speak of at the Nevada Test Site now," he said.

Mr. Church also said there is no indication that a cancer epidemic has developed at the Nevada Test Site, but he acknowledges that this has not been tested scientifically. The Energy Department, which has been studying the health of workers at atomic weapons plants since 1964, has never conducted a survey of Nevada Test Site employees. One reason, said Mr. Church, is that the radiation record-keeping at the test site was poor in the 1950's and 1960's. As a result, the Energy Department is unable to determine precisely how many people have ever worked at the Nevada Test Site.

One group of test site workers that is under evaluation by Energy Department epidemiologists are those who have received the highest doses of radiation. Mr. Church said the study, being conducted by Energy Department epidemiologists in Tennessee, is due to be completed in 1991.

Humiliating Times For a Boss Who Smokes

Deirdre Fanning

In business corridors, smoking has become the great new equalizer, at least in the minds of some chief executives who are unable to quit. Cigarettes are no longer a symbol of strength, machismo and style, and smoky rooms, no longer synonymous with serious business. Executives who smoke these days tend to feel weak, embarrassed and ashamed. Smoking makes them feel less in control. It can shake their self-confidence.

"I'm responsible for overseeing about $1 billion a year, and sometimes I think maybe the fact that I am ruled by this one little thing—cigarettes—means the wrong person is sitting in this chair," said one health care executive, who asked not to be named for fear of being further harassed by colleagues for his smoking. "Sometimes I think the kid in the stockroom who doesn't smoke is brighter than I am."

No smoker of any stripe commands social respect today. But many executive smokers are harder on themselves than on others in their organizations who smoke. By virtue of their education and professional stature, they believe they should know better than to sign their own death warrants. And the fact that they don't can leave a deep seam of humiliation for subordinates to mine.

"My employees make jokes about my smoking habit," the health care executive said. "And that hurts. I've had some very uncomfortable days at work because I can't stop smoking, and I've had about as much of that as I can handle."

Indeed, with the country increasingly divided into smoking and no-smoking zones—in restaurants, airplanes and office buildings—one might expect the executive battle line to be drawn between those who smoke and those who don't. But the struggle "is really within the smokers themselves," said Robert Rosner, executive director of the Seattle-based Smoking Policy Institute, which helps companies set up no-smoking policies. "These executives are control people. As smokers, they feel out of control."

That is why some executives go to extraordinary lengths to avoid being discovered. And even those who are out of the closet don't want their colleagues to know the level of their dependence. "I'm Mr. Clean until you smell my breath," said the health care industry executive, who says he often pops breath mints to disguise the problem.

Other executives refrain from smoking at any meeting where nonsmokers may be in attendance. "Generally, if you feel you have to ask permission, you don't smoke," said John F. Kirby, a senior vice president at the Continental Corporation who is one of the only remaining smokers among senior managers at the insurance company. "I have gone out of my way to avoid controversy."

The stress of the job, of course, makes quitting cigarettes a tough assignment. Ask Steven Smith, another top executive at Continental, who tried to quit for years. A smoker for 20 years, Mr. Smith would kick the habit every weekend only to resume it on Monday. "I'd come back into work every Monday morning and see how long it took me to start again," said the executive vice president. "Usually it was around 10 A.M., but I think twice I made it until Tuesday."

He finally managed to quit three years ago. (And none too soon, as the insurer goes smoke-free on July 1.) "Smoking made me feel inferior, less worthy, weak in some way," he recalled.

But perhaps the hardest personal struggle comes for those executive smokers who, for whatever reason, institute companywide no-smoking policies and are supposed to obey and enforce rules that they dread themselves. Since 1984, Paul O'Brien, the president and chief executive of New England Telephone and Telegraph, has been steadily tightening the restrictions on smoking at the office. And last week, the company announced that on July 1, smoking would be completely banned at all offices. What of his own pack-a-day habit? "Well, I haven't quite made up my mind about quitting," he admitted. "But I realize that as president, the one overriding thing you can do is to give a sense of example. I am prepared for some difficult times ahead with this."

New England Telephone vice president of human resources, Peter Bertschmann, another smoker, is less sanguine. "We haven't quite figured out how to handle it," he said. "I know there'll be bad days when cigarettes are very important and I don't see myself going down 17 flights to smoke outside. We just ended a long strike with some of our workers and I can tell you, there was some pretty heavy smoking going on around these offices during those months."

Some executives even complain that no-smoking policies cause their productivity to fall by adding to their tension levels. "Smoking relaxes me," said Paul Russell, a senior vice president at National Medical Enterprises Inc. in Santa Monica, Calif.

Even tobacco companies, the stalwart upholders of smokers' rights, have stumbled in the changing tide. According to the best-selling "Barbarians at the Gate," when George Roberts, a partner at Kohlberg Kravis Roberts & Company, entered a meeting in 1988 at the headquarters of RJR-Nabisco to discuss the buyout firm's proposed purchase of the company, he immediately became irritated by the cigar and cigarette smoke hanging heavy in the conference-room air. Waving away the fumes, he asked Peter Cohen, then the chief executive of Shearson Lehman Hutton Inc., which had submitted a competing offer, to extinguish his cigar. Eyebrows were raised. Had Mr. Roberts forgotten he was trying to take over a cigarette manufacturer? Surely not. Kohlberg is the new owner.

Blacks Debate the Costs of Affirmative Action

Don Wycliff

Two years ago, at a seminar on higher education sponsored by the Congressional Black Caucus, a young man who obviously didn't know better breached etiquette by posing a discomfiting question.

Citing his own experience as a black student in a predominantly white college, he wondered whether affirmative action hadn't had an inadvertent negative effect, since he suspected he wasn't held to the same level of performance and achievement as some of his white fellow students. Had his educational experience—and his personal achievement—perhaps been compromised by the policy of racial preference?

A member of the seminar panel, Dr. Reginald Wilson of the American Council on Education, quickly set the young man straight. In stern, almost reproving tones, Dr. Wilson recited the historical-legal rationales for affirmative action, after which the panel moved on to other matters. But the student's question hung in the air.

It hangs there still, and increasingly is posed in more sophisticated form. Most recently and prominently, Shelby Steele, the essayist and English professor at San Jose State University, posed it in the May 13 issue of the *New York Times Magazine*.

Thomas Sowell, the conservative economist and longtime critic of affirmative action, has mounted a fresh assault with his new book, "Preferential Policies: An International Perspective." He finds that such policies are, virtually without exception, more hurtful than helpful.

And from the opposite ideological perspective, William Julius Wilson, the University of Chicago sociologist, expressed serious doubts about the practice in an article in the inaugural issue of the new quarterly "The American Prospect."

To be sure, opposition to affirmative action remains a minority view among blacks. And the nation's quarter century of experience with the practice must be set against three and a half centuries of negative action. Nevertheless, misgivings about affirmative action are common, and the fact that three such prominent black scholars have gone public with their concerns is significant. All the more so since two of them—Mr. Steele and Mr. Wilson—couch theirs as concerns over a policy that once may have been useful, or at least hopeful.

Mr. Sowell, who expressed opposition as long ago as 1970 (also in the *New York Times Magazine*), says the new skepticism is "from my point of view a heartening development," but takes no particular delight in saying "I told you so."

He contends that affirmative action programs on college campuses have failed to benefit poor blacks, in whose interest they were ostensibly created, and are responsible in great measure for the current atmosphere of racial antagonism.

"I predicted back then that when these programs failed, the conclusion would be not that they are half-baked programs, but that blacks just don't have it," he said. Now, he added, that prediction is being borne out.

Mr. Wilson's argument is political and strategic: "Race-specific" plans to overcome the educational, employment and other deficits created by slavery and segregation have benefited mainly the best prepared and least disadvantaged. More important, he says, such policies have alienated some whites from the Democratic Party and become an obstacle to the political coalitions needed to enact "race-neutral" social programs—job training, educational aid and so forth—that would benefit all low-income people.

Mr. Steele's is a psychological argument. "Under affirmative action," he wrote in the *Times Magazine*, "the quality that earns us preferential treatment is an implied inferiority." And its ultimate effect is to put blacks "at war with an expanded realm of debilitating doubt, so that the doubt itself becomes an unrecognized preoccupation that undermines their ability to perform, especially in integrated situations."

Mr. Wilson's position is familiar as part of a standard analysis of the decline of the Democrats in Presidential elections. He takes pains to distinguish it from "the neo-conservative critique of affirmative action that attacks both racial preference and activist social welfare policies." Even so, however, he gently reminds his fellow liberals that "a society without racial preference has, of course, always been the long-term goal of the civil rights movement."

Mr. Steele's argument is newer, and seems to cause more heartburn to those who support policies of preference. Some call him naïve; some call him worse. The most thoughtful concede that he is on to something but worry about how he treats it.

"My sense is that he tells part of the story very well," said Drew S. Days, a law professor at Yale who was assistant attorney general for civil rights in the Carter Administration. "But he leaves out a whole lot that would enrich his and his readers' understanding of affirmative action."

That affirmative action has a "corrosive effect" on some of its intended beneficiaries is obvious, said Professor Days. But what Mr. Steele leaves out, he said, is the dreadful history of racist oppression and exclusion that initially was the justification for affirmative action remedies: "It's as though he were writing about Mars."

Mr. Steele does not neglect history, however; he only says that in the day-to-day situations in which blacks have to deal with the implication that they need special treatment, the history doesn't matter. "There are explanations and then there is the fact," he wrote in the *Times*. "And the fact must be borne by the individual as a condition apart from the explanation."

Julius Chambers, director-counsel of the NAACP Legal Defense and Educational Fund Inc., contends that Mr. Steele and others who share his views are naïve about the tenacity of racist resistance. Part of the purpose of affirmative action, he says, is to "change the climate in which decisions are made" about hiring, college admissions and so forth. Once the gatekeepers see competent blacks, their judgments may change. Better still, once blacks are in decisionmaking positions, they can enforce fairness.

Mr. Steele seems to bristle at the charge of naïveté. "Only two days ago I was called 'nigger' from a passing car," he said in a recent interview. "I think racism is tenacious, that's it is a human instinct. But we can't continue to blame all our troubles on racism."

In a Harvard Law Review article last year, Randall Kennedy, a black professor of law at Harvard, digressed briefly on the issue of "race-conscious affirmative action." While there might sometimes be "compelling reasons" to support it, he said, "I simply do not want race-conscious decision-making to be naturalized into our general pattern of academic evaluation. I do not want race-conscious decision-making to lose its status as a deviant mode of judging people or the work they produce."

Those comments echo similar ones made by Mr. Days in a January 1987 article in The Yale Law Journal. Clearly no opponent of affirmative action, Mr. Days nevertheless wondered whether a certain carelessness had not crept into the use of race-conscious programs.

"Our national sensitivity to racial classifications requires that they be used only when they represent a focused effort to remedy the effects of racial discrimination and to prevent its recurrence," he said. And for all their departures from the principle of a "color-blind Constitution"—either as violations or as remedies—that principle, embodied in a "society in which government avoids using race to allocate benefits and burdens among its citizenry," remains an ultimate goal for Americans.

The Right to Privacy: There's More Loophole Than Law

Michele Galen and Jeffrey Rothfeder

His bank cost Theodore Cizik his job. In 1983, the former controller at a New Jersey company sided with his employer in a dispute with Midlantic National Bank/North—just after he applied for his own loan there. When Cizik wouldn't budge, he claims, the bank got even. It told Cizik's boss that he had a Rolls-Royce and Mercedes—assets he had wanted kept secret but had listed on his loan application—and the bank suggested that he had been moonlighting. Fired from his $45,000 job on that pretext, he says, Cizik sued the bank, and ultimately settled out of court.

Cizik's case highlights a startling fact: Almost no information is private. Only rarely, moreover, can individuals find out that information on them is being used. With about 10 privacy laws on the books, how can that be? The laws are narrow, and full of holes.

'Bork Bill'   The Fair Credit Reporting Act of 1970 is a case in point. It sounds good. It gives individuals the right to see and correct their credit reports and limits the rights of others to look at them. But it has five exceptions, including a big one: Anyone with a "legitimate business need" can peek. Legitimate isn't defined.

Then there's the Right to Financial Privacy Act of 1978. It forbids the government to rummage through bank-account records without following set procedures. But it excludes state agencies, including law enforcement officials, as well as private employers. And more exceptions are tacked on every year. Says John Byrne, the federal legislative counsel for the American Bankers Assn.: "There's not a lot to this act anymore."

The best protection, in fact, is for customers of video stores. In 1987, a Washington (D.C.) weekly, *The City Paper*, published a list of videotape titles borrowed by Robert H. Bork, then a U.S. Supreme Court nominee. Outraged, lawmakers passed the Video Privacy Protection Act of 1988. Called the Bork Bill, it bars retailers from selling or disclosing video rental records without a customer's permission or a court order. While this is a breakthrough of sorts, privacy advocates say it's silly to pass such laws when medical and insurance records remain unprotected. Others find it ironic that the government itself continues to reveal more than anyone else.

For instance, the Privacy Act of 1974 was supposed to bar federal agencies from sharing information on U.S. citizens, a practice called matching. But it's O.K. to share information if the disclosure is consistent with the purpose for which the stuff was collected. That's called the routine use exception. In 1977, Health, Education & Welfare Secretary Joseph A. Califano Jr. crafted the exception to help root out welfare cheats by letting HEW review federal payroll records. His reasoning: Efficiency is a goal of all federal agencies. So they can share data to ensure it.

Watching Watchers   Today, matching remains alive and well. When Congress passed last year's Computer Matching & Privacy Protection Act, which regulates the way federal agencies verify eligibility for benefits or recoup delinquent debts, it gave the government explicit permission to perform frequent matches. It tossed a bone to the subjects of matches. Before their benefits can be cut off, an agency needs two pieces of proof for its findings. And it has to notify individuals who are under suspicion.

Every bit helps, of course, but reformers want more. George B. Trubow, the former general counsel to the White House Right to Privacy Committee, wants a federal data protection agency to "watch the watchers." David F. Linowes goes further. The former chairman of the U.S. Privacy Protection Commission, which was set up by the Privacy Act, is in favor of rules without exceptions. And he would give individuals $10,000 in punitive damages every time an abuse occurs. An interesting idea. But not one that Congress is likely to buy soon—at least not outside of video stores.

Why Grade 'A' Execs Get an 'F' As Parents

Brian O'Reilly

The qualities that make for corporate success are often not what are needed to be an effective mom or dad. Some parents show how to avoid the worst mistakes.

You can solve that thorny problem in Jakarta with a few crisp commands to your underlings, but ask your teenage son why he got in late last night and you're reduced to impotent fury in seconds. For all their brains and competence, powerful, successful executives and professionals often have more trouble raising kids than all but the very poor. Alas, the intensity and single-mindedness that make for corporate achievement are often the opposite of the qualities needed to be an effective parent.

Six years ago when AT&T was in the throes of divesting its operating companies, Ma Bell conducted a survey of its managers and top executives and discovered that their kids caused these employees more stress and worry than anything else, including their careers. Says attorney Robert Weinbaum, head of antitrust and marketing law at General Motors: "I think it's real tough for kids growing up in families where the parents are highly successful." Weinbaum went through years of turmoil with his own son before they resolved their difficulties.

Many parenting problems are common to everyone: paralyzing uncertainties about how strict or lenient to be, a sense of powerlessness in the face of peer pressure, preoccupation with professional problems, or just plain forgetting what a kid needs from mom or dad. But raising happy, successful children is not a hopeless task or just dumb luck. Interviews with scores of educators, psychologists, drug experts, executives, and troubled teens reveal some consistent differences between kids who turn out "good" and those who go "bad," and provide some suggestions on how to avoid the most colossal blunders.

The most important thing a parent can do for a child is to encourage a high sense of self-esteem. Easier said than done, of course. The tricky part is helping children set appropriate, satisfying goals and then providing an environment that lets them reach the goals on their own. Building your child's self-esteem is an inconvenient, time-consuming, and maddeningly imprecise occupation, and don't be amazed if you mess up. Intuition and good intentions often don't seem to be much help, and you need skills that rival a pilot's ability to land a jet at night on an aircraft carrier. But kids who have a sense of self-worth flourish. Kids who don't are vulnerable to drug and alcohol abuse, unwanted pregnancy, anxiety, depression, and suicide. Even worse, they may not get into Harvard.

In case your long-range plans include working triple time at the office until the brats turn 17, then deftly steering them into the Ivy League, listen up. Serious emotional problems usually start when children are in sixth to eighth grade, and hit crisis proportions by the sophomore year of high school. Says Sheila Ribordy, a clinical psychologist at De Paul University: "By junior year they're on track or in serious trouble."

Don't think your brains, money, or success will pave the way to parenting glory. In a survey of large corporations providing extensive insurance coverage, Medstat Systems, an Ann Arbor, Michigan, health care information firm, discovered that some 36% of the children of executives undergo outpatient treatment for psychiatric or drug abuse problems every year, vs. 15% of the children of nonexecutives in the same companies.

Top executives have special problems as parents. Many are highly educated, driven personalities who routinely put in 12 to 15 hours a day on the job—workaholics, in other words. Says Susan Davies-Bloom, a Connecticut family therapist who treats senior managers: "They are so accustomed to functioning at a high level of control at the office that when they get home, they try to exert the same kind of control."

The milieu that executives attempt to establish at home can be highly stressful for children. The attributes a manager must develop to succeed include perfectionism, impatience, and efficiency. Says Andrée Brooks, author of *Children of Fast Track Parents:* "Contrast those traits with what it takes to meet the needs of a growing child—tolerance, patience, and acceptance of chaos."

During their teens, kids assert their own individuality, rebelling against whatever their parents value most. Unfortunately for the kids of driven executives, what mom and dad often value most is achievement. Says Davies-Bloom: "I find many workaholic executives felt they were mediocre in popularity, grades, and athletics." Frequently the parent tries to create a child who was everything he was not, or thinks he can steer the kid around every pitfall. Sparks fly, and the youngster refuses to perform.

Worse, some parents are so absorbed with their own careers that they scarcely notice their children, who respond by behaving in increasingly bizarre and dangerous ways to attract attention. "My father worried about me from his desk," says the son of an IBM executive. The kid started stealing from his parents—trinkets, at first. But when he took his father's gun and began disappearing at night, family therapy finally began.

Given 70-hour workweeks, divorce, or a spouse with a career or demanding social schedule, and complications set in fast. You thought buying a big home in a wealthy suburb would bestow bliss on your offspring? Too often it has the opposite effect. Thousands of business people who were No. 1 somewhere else move to towns where everyone else is successful too. All the other kids in school are very bright and also under pressure to achieve.

Soon the parents wonder why their kid isn't at the top of the class. Says Constance McCreery, formerly a public school guidance counselor in Darien, Connecticut: "In wealthy towns you get what I call the Big Apple syndrome. It's the problem of keeping all the children full of enough confidence that they *can* succeed."

Mom and a tightknit community used to be able to keep child rearing running smoothly even if dad was putting in overtime. But most younger mothers work nowadays, and wives of senior executives often have commitments that keep them out of the home, even if they don't have paying jobs. Suzanne Gelber, a benefits consultant, was on the board of a day care center in Chappaqua, New York, where most of the mothers who dropped off their kids did not work. "They have so many philanthropic and social responsibilities that they are very busy women," she says. "They are not home baking brownies."

Nobody can prove that children with nannies wind up in reform school more often than those who don't, but some kid watchers are concerned. Says Tom Collins, executive director of Fairview Deaconess Hospital, an adolescent drug treatment center in Minneapolis: "Every move you make away from kids in pursuit of your own happiness and career increases their chance of getting into trouble. Lending kids out to babysitters and day care makes it a crap shoot."

Ask a bunch of educators how life for well-to-do kids has changed over the years and you get a surprising answer: The children are under far greater strain than their parents ever were to perform well academically and win acceptance to high-prestige colleges. At New Trier Township High School near Chicago, principal Dianna M. Lindsay says, "The pressure to get into a name-brand college is monumental. I see kids buckle under it."

Part of the stress is classic pushy-parent stuff. Says Carol Perry, director of counseling at the exclusive Trinity School in Manhattan: "This is an era of designer children. No parent wants an average child." Adds Lindsay: "Parents want their kids to go to a school whose name is recognized at the country club."

Much of the mounting anxiety springs not from overt parental pressure, however, but from the students themselves, whose values have been not so subtly affected by mom and dad's affluence. Many well-off kids have grown up using a financial yardstick to evaluate themselves and others. But the prospects for these wealthy kids to improve on or at least maintain their current lifestyles are frighteningly slim. "Successful moms and dads come here because the environment breeds success," New Trier's Lindsay observes, "but the kids say, 'I can never match this. This is the best my life will ever be.'"

Students at New Trier are encouraged to do social service, such as working in soup kitchens, and once a year they are asked to fast for a day in recognition of world hunger and donate lunch money to the poor. Says Lindsay: "We have to teach the kids there are other standards besides material possessions. It's a real, serious problem."

The predictable consequences of all the stress on kids: alcohol, drugs, and suicide, the ultimate parental nightmare. Teenage suicide rates doubled between

1968 and 1987, to 16.2 per 100,000 boys and 4.2 per 100,000 girls. Suicide now ranks as the second cause of death, after accidents, among 15- to 19-year-olds. Some factors that prompt suicide, such as depression caused by the death of a loved one, are not the result of demanding parents. But pressure to do well in school and athletics is a contributor to suicide, and children in a close-knit family are less likely to kill themselves than kids without strong family ties.

Though drug use appears to have peaked in the early 1980s, it is still very high. According to the University of Michigan's Institute for Social Research, more than half of all high school seniors have reported using an illicit drug at some time in their lives—usually marijuana—and a third have tried something stronger. Virtually all seniors—92%—have experimented with beer or hard liquor, and in the two weeks before the institute's survey was taken, 35% had been drunk at least once although every state now bans drinking under age 21.

Rare is the parent who cannot recall sneaking more than a few beers in his or her youth, but the prevalence of teenage drinking has many people worried. Donald R. Geddis, the principal at Summit High School in New Jersey, is more concerned about the use of alcohol among his students than he is about any other substance. "Its use is so widespread it outstrips all others," he says.

Drinking is starting early—the average age for that first surreptitious sip is 13—before many children have developed better methods of coping with stress. Youngsters are aping the attitude of adults: "I've had a tough week and I'm entitled to blow off a little steam." Worse, drunk kids are also more likely to experiment with other drugs they would shun while sober.

Since practically every kid drinks and most experiment with drugs, what distinguishes those who tinker with the stuff from those who develop a serious dependency is "the degree of anxiety for which they are seeking surcease," says Virginia Kramer Stein, a clinical psychologist in New Jersey. Although no kid is as supremely self-confident as many try to appear, youngsters who think of themselves as losers or unwanted by their busy parents, or who have trouble making friends, are at a higher risk of abusing alcohol and drugs than other kids.

When they drink or take drugs, many kids feel transformed for the first time from awkward geeks into cool and appealing characters. "Addiction has a lot to do with self-esteem," says Jeri, 16, the daughter of a Minneapolis-area businesswoman. Jeri started drinking at 11; then her sister introduced her to marijuana, which she smoked every day through much of her first year of high school. By the time she was in tenth grade, she was caught selling grass, and sent to a rehabilitation program at Fairview Deaconess.

How do parents reduce the stress on their kids, boost their self-esteem, and keep them off drugs? Says Summit High's Geddis: "If I've learned one thing, it is that the main priority for parents is to help their kids find something that makes them feel good about themselves. That's the greatest deterrent to drugs and alcohol."

An important first step is to ease up on relentless pressure to make the youngster perform well in school. Focus only on grades and you're handing the kid a weapon to punish you with. If the child appears "only average" but is attending one of the toughest high schools in the country, find out where he or she ranks among peers on standardized achievement tests. That will help you know whether a B or C average is reasonable.

Do not greet your children every evening with an ostensibly cheery "How'd you do in school today?" It is a very threatening question and often elicits no more than a mumbled "Okay." Good grades help get you into a top college but don't predict a happy, successful life, says Robert Klitgaard, former faculty head of admissions at Harvard's Kennedy school.

In case you forgot, success in high school is not achieved the same way as success in a corporation. You get ahead in a company by climbing the ladder and paying your dues, concentrating on things you're good at, and delegating or avoiding areas where you are not competent. You may be a whiz at corporate finance in part because the job does not require you to decline French verbs or find the area of an isosceles triangle. But your sophomore does not have the luxury of hiring a Harvard MBA to do her homework.

Don't ignore the possibility that the apple of your eye simply is not as smart as you are. Children have roughly the same IQ as the average of their parents', but there are plenty of deviations. About 7% of the time, a child will be 15 points higher or lower than the parents' average, and one time in a thousand, a 30-point difference will pop up.

The average college graduate has an IQ of 115 and Ph.D.s typically score 130, according to John E. Hunter, a professor of psychology at Michigan State University. "It doesn't take much of a slip, and the child of parents who struggled to get through college will not be able to make it," he adds. (Of course, there's an equal chance your daughter is justified when she calls you stupid.) Though you may be a genius yourself, if you married a good-looking but dim bulb, you can't expect your progeny to send rockets to Mars. If your kid has been a whiz all along, however, and his grades collapse in high school, emotional or drug problems are the likely culprits—not his IQ.

Spend time with the family. Ordering your secretary to book 50 minutes of "quality time" into your schedule is better than nothing, but quality time has a habit of fitting your routine, not the kids'. Del Yocam, 45, former chief operating officer at Apple, religiously went home for dinner at 7 P.M. at least twice during the week, and avoided business commitments on weekends. "The children have come to expect it," says Yocam. In November he retired from Apple. His devotion to his family didn't hurt his career there, Yocam says, but "it's time to move on to other things."

Hugh McColl, chairman of NCNB, the big Southern regional bank, cut out weekend golf and reduced entertaining at night years ago to have more time with his three children. But he still has some regrets about the time he spent away from home. He was coaching his son's YMCA basketball team in the early 1970s, and a league championship game was looming. Instead McColl went to a banking convention, and the team lost by two points. "My son still blames me," says McColl with a laugh. "He figures if I'd been at the game he would have won."

Robert Butler, a senior engineer at Chevron in San Francisco, is also determined not to let his job overwhelm his family. He schedules time for his children, leaving for the office at dawn on days he has to depart early to coach his son's soccer team. Says he: "You can always put things off for the future, but you can't get back the years with your kids."

Use the time you spend with the children to listen sympathetically to them. That skill is particularly difficult for men to acquire, according to Ronald Levant, a Rutgers University psychologist and author of *Between Father and Child.* "Men are not trained to be empathetic listeners," he says. "We're taught to listen to our opponents to discover their weaknesses." Men see themselves as problem solvers, not as shoulders to cry on.

Thus, the father who comes home and sees that his 15-year-old daughter has just eaten a whole box of Oreos will probably want to warn her about pimples and weight. Resist the urge. Just let her pour her heart out. Don't be hurt or angry if she doesn't respond the first dozen times you try to be understanding. If you've been a clod for the past 15 years, she may be confused or think you're trying to trick her.

You may learn from all that listening that your son really doesn't want to go to Stanford, is the laughingstock of Kenilworth when you force him to practice drop-kicking at the country club, and dreads following your footsteps into the brake shoe business because he can't figure out what a brake shoe *is*. Fight the desire to dis-own him, and he may confess that he is fabulous at lawn bowling and likely to get a scholarship from East Cowflop University to study French cooking.

Go lawn bowling with him and let him whip up some frog legs Provençale for you. You won't enhance your bragging rights with the board of directors, but you will do wonders for his self-esteem. And you could be pleasantly surprised: You may find that a newly energized youngster has replaced the sullen adolescent of just a few weeks before. "There are no lazy teenagers," says Carol Perry. "More likely they're turned off or depressed."

Some parents conclude that boarding schools can do a better job of teaching and raising their children than mom or dad will. For example, a single parent who has to travel on the job might want the youngster in a stable environment that provides a sense of security for both child and parent. Such places range from exclusive prep schools such as Groton, Exeter, and Lawrenceville, which rival Ivy League colleges in admission requirements and costs; to less well-known but highly regarded private institutions such as the Webb Schools in Claremont, California, St. Stephen's Episcopal School in Austin, Texas, and Wayland Academy in Beaver Dam, Wisconsin; to military academies like Valley Forge in Pennsylvania that boast of instilling "conservative Christian values" in their charges.

Then there are boarding schools where many of the kids have serious behav-ioral and emotional problems, among them drug abuse, petty theft, truancy, or depression. Among these academies are Cedu in Running Springs, California, Franklin Academy in Sabbatus, Maine, and the Brown Schools in Texas. Bob Weinbaum, the GM attorney, sent his son John to the DeSisto School, a prep school in Stockbridge, Massachusetts. With the Broadway producer Joseph Papp among the first board members, Mike DeSisto, a rumpled Catholic ex-seminarian who once ran a private school on Long Island, started the school in 1978. The annual tuition of $19,000 is more than the cost of a year at Yale.

In addition to a rigorous academic schedule, DeSisto students undergo multi-ple private and group therapy sessions each week. But an important part of their

development occurs as the kids learn to be accepting of each other and affection-
ate. Most conversations seem to begin and end with vigorous bear hugs. DeSisto
himself is both warm and demanding. He lets kids pile onto his living room sofa
and fall asleep on his lap until the 10 P.M. curfew. But kids don't "graduate" until
they complete the course requirements, perform well at increasingly difficult and
responsible campus jobs from washing dishes to assigning dorm rooms, and demonstrate they can be effective "parents" for newer arrivals.

If you're committed to winning the Dad or Mom of the Year Award, one of the
biggest and most common mistakes you can make awaits you: being a wimpy and
overprotective parent. Says Gary McKay, co-author of *The Parent's Handbook* (see
box): "One of the greatest handicaps a child can suffer is to be raised by a 'good'
parent."

These well-meaning types try to do everything for the kids, rushing upstairs
five times to wake them for school, exhorting them to eat breakfast faster, and
driving them to school when they miss the bus. All this service winds up depriving
the kid of self-confidence and independence, says McKay. Far better to be a "responsible" parent. Buy the youngster an alarm clock, explain that breakfast ends at
7:30, and if he misses the bus let him walk to school. Don't scold, don't say, "I told
you so," don't debate, don't give in.

Bob Weinbaum fell into a good-parent trap, trying so hard to be a "fair and
reasonable" father that he was coming across as overprotective, vague, and indecisive to his son John. "In retrospect, I wish I had remembered that *I* was the father—that *I* was the one in charge," says Weinbaum, whose credits include winning federal approval for the GM-Toyota deal in Fremont, California, and
managing his son's baseball team. John grew up with a lot of love and attention, but
Weinbaum now admits he tried to do too much for his son, even his homework.
"John told me once I was so involved, I made him feel incompetent."

By the time John was a sophomore in high school, their relationship was in
tatters, and both parents were worried. "I remember his violent outrages and kicking the door apart," says Weinbaum. "He was in a lot of pain." Schoolwork deteriorated, and the parents began finding marijuana butts on the floor. When the son
started going to parties and not coming home at night, Weinbaum was frazzled. An
adolescent treatment center in Detroit determined John's problems were not
drug-related, so Weinbaum wound up sending John to the DeSisto School. He
graduated in three years and is now at a college near Baltimore.

For all three years Weinbaum and his wife attended monthly group support
meetings with other DeSisto parents in the Detroit area and gradually learned how
to improve relations with John. "He is a spectacular, wonderful son," says Weinbaum today.

If you plan to run out and start putting your foot down, do not mistake harsh-
ness or violence for firmness. Says one tall 17-year-old student at DeSisto: "My
father used to throw me up against a wall, demanding that I get better grades. But
there was never any follow-through." The boy wanted his parents to talk to him
about why he was having trouble in school and offer some help, but they did not.
Says he: "Parents often think if they've yelled and sent you to your room that their
job is done."

Since so much experimentation with drugs and alcohol begins in the preteen years, start long before they're in sixth or seventh grade to communicate with your children, and practice being assertive. Says Bruce Thompson, superintendent of the middle school in Woodside, a San Francisco suburb: "This is the best time to catch them. They're still little kids, on the way to adults."

How strict is strict enough when dealing with kids on the verge of becoming teenagers? "You ask kids where they're going when they go out," says Thompson. "They do their homework and you check their homework. They show up for dinner, they don't go out on school nights, and when they say they're sleeping over at Johnny's, you call up Johnny's parents and ask if they will be home that evening. Will the child complain? Yes."

When kids in middle school and high school do go out at night, parents should be up and awake to greet them when they return. Says Tom Collins, head of Fairview Deaconess, the drug rehab center in Minneapolis: "Sit down and talk with your kids when they come in. You should be able to say to them, 'You look weird. Have you been doing drugs?' "

If you take time to observe a teen, you can soon tell whether he's drunk or stoned. Do kids want to be stopped? Absolutely. "If you don't see it soon enough," Collins warns, "your child will go through lying, stealing, cheating. It gets rolling and you can't stop it until the kid is in so much pain he wants treatment."

Many parents don't even suspect a problem until they find drugs or get a call from police or school officials. Warning signs that a kid is becoming an abuser include suddenly erratic grades, skipping school, dropping out of extracurricular activities, avoiding the family, swings in mood, violence, depression, no savings from a part-time job, and a crop of unfamiliar and unimpressive new friends.

Most parents will never have to deal with anything more serious than their own chronic sense of clumsiness and frustration. In case you think you are hopelessly inept and suspect your kids secretly fired you a long time ago, be assured that you are far more influential than you suspect. "The best manipulation parents have is their attention. It is an extraordinary power that most of them neglect to use," says David, 17, the troubled son of a high-ranking Ford executive. "Parents are very important to kids—more than they will ever let on."

A REPAIR MANUAL FOR FIXING RELATIONSHIPS WITH YOUR KIDS

If you spend most of your workday racing through terse memos to prepare for that presentation on expansion strategies for the 1990s, you're going to find it tough to absorb homey suggestions on child rearing. Touchy-feely stuff like "Help your children feel useful by identifying their talents and suggesting ways they can contribute to the family" may make your flesh crawl.

Giving goose bumps to executives hasn't hurt psychologists Don Dinkmeyer and Gary D. McKay, authors of *The Parent's Handbook* (American Guidance Service). The $9.95 paperback has sold nearly two million copies, making it one of the most successful publications ever on raising kids. Among its virtues is practicality. The book is short—only 127 pages including cartoons—and reads more like a repair manual than a scholarly treatise.

When McKay and Dinkmeyer were guidance counselors in the Midwest two decades ago, they were bombarded with questions from parents who, says McKay, "with the best of intentions, didn't know how to help their kids learn responsibility." The two men put together course material to help teachers, clergy, and school counselors, among others, lead group training sessions for frustrated parents. The *Handbook* is part of the course but useful on its own and available in most bookstores. Herewith some of the book's advice for moms and dads:

- Don't give a child attention on demand, even for positive acts, because you will foster an inappropriate desire for the spotlight. Youngsters can easily come to believe that if you are not focused on them 100% of the time, you don't care about them.
- Tell your children you love them, especially when they are not anticipating such a comment. Nonverbal signs such as pats, hugs, kisses, and tousling their hair are also extremely important.
- Encourage kids rather than praise them. Praise is a reward given for winning and being the best. Encouragement, by contrast, is a reward for effort or improvement, however slight. It makes a child feel worthy, as in "I have confidence in your judgment" or "You seem to like that activity." Some praise is appropriate, of course. If the child hits a home run, go ahead and shout, "*Wow*, what a hit! That was great." Just don't restrict your pride in the child to his or her accomplishments.
- Listen to your kid. Think of a feeling that describes the emotions a child is expressing—bored, guilty, vengeful, or happy, accepted, respected. When your son says, "That teacher is unfair. I'll never do well," don't respond with, "Of course you will. What's the matter with you?" Try: "You're angry and disappointed and you're thinking of giving up." The second response shows acceptance and concern so the child will be encouraged to tell you more.
- Avoid blaming and criticizing your children. They will correct misbehavior faster if you dispassionately describe how that lapse interferes with your needs or rights. Instead of screaming "You came home three hours late last night, you idiot!" try "When you don't call or come home at the time we've agreed on, I worry that something might have happened to you because I don't know where you are."
- Let your youngsters experience the consequences of their behavior once they know enough to make informed decisions. Children who won't eat go hungry; those who dress inappropriately get cold or get razzed by their peers. Buy good food that they like, but don't force them to eat it. The difference between dishing out punishment and letting them experience consequences is often in your tone of voice. If your son loses dad's hammer, you don't have to yell or threaten. The child should simply buy a new one. Dad is also justified in coolly explaining that junior apparently isn't ready to use Dad's tools.
- Treat your children with the courtesy and sensitivity you reserve for your friends. With luck, they may turn out to be some of your very closest friends.

Crime in the Suites

Russell Mokhiber

On June 6, 70 federal agents raided the Rocky Flats Nuclear Weapons Facility in Colorado. The decision to invade the bomb plant came on the heels of a lengthy investigation described in FBI agent Jon S. Lipsky's 116-page affidavit, which convinced a federal judge to unleash the agents. In his report, Lipsky accused Rockwell International and the U.S. Department of Energy (DOE) of "knowingly and falsely" stating that the plutonium-processing plant complied with this country's environmental laws. In doing so, the contractor and its government client concealed "serious contamination" at the site. Lipsky charged that Rockwell and DOE secretly dumped hazardous waste into public drinking water and surreptitiously operated an incinerator they said had been shut down.

While scandal at nuclear weapons plants seems almost a regular news feature of late, the capacity demonstrated by the Justice Department in Colorado to deploy an environmental police force—replete with FBI agents, investigators, prosecutors, wiretaps and aerial surveillance—is in fact an unusual thing. The government rarely flexes its legal muscle to prosecute major environmental crimes or, for that matter, corporate crimes generally. For every Rocky Flats, there are dozens of corporate environmental crimes that go undetected, unprosecuted and unpunished.

"Crime is a sociopolitcal artifact, not a natural phenomenon," writes legal scholar Herbert Packer in *The Limits of the Criminal Law*. "We can have as much or as little crime as we please, depending on what we choose to count as criminal." In this country, we have chosen to have very little corporate crime. Most corporate wrongs against humans and the environment are not considered criminal in the traditional sense—that is, activity that is prohibited by the state and prosecuted to conviction. While corporations like Rockwell International can be criminally prosecuted for serious violations of environmental laws, they usually face less demanding and less visible civil procedures.

On the face of it, this leniency is grossly out of proportion to the effects of the corporate crime wave. Every year, roughly 28,000 deaths and 130,000 serious injuries are caused by dangerous products. At least 100,000 workers die from exposure to deadly chemicals and other safety hazards. Workplace carcinogens are estimated to cause between 23 and 38 percent of all cancer deaths. More than 45,000 Americans die in automobile crashes every year. Many of those deaths either are caused by defects or are easily preventable by a simple redesign.

"Crime in the Suites" by Russell Mokhiber, *Greenpeace*, September/October 1989, p. 14. Reprinted by permission of Greenpeace.

The financial cost to society is staggering. The National Association of Attorneys General reports that fraud costs the nation's businesses and individuals upwards of $100 billion each year. The Senate Judiciary Committee has estimated that faulty goods, monopolistic practices and other such violations annually cost consumers $174 to $231 billion. Added to this is the $10 to $20 billion a year the Justice Department says taxpayers lose when corporations violate federal regulations. As a rule of thumb, the Bureau of National Affairs estimates that the dollar cost of corporate crime in the United States is more than 10 times greater than the combined total from larcenies, robberies, burglaries and auto thefts committed by individuals.

The full extent of the corporate crime wave is hidden. Although the federal government tracks street crime month by month, city by city through the FBI's Uniform Crime Reports, it does not track corporate crime. So the government can tell the public whether burglary is up or down in Los Angeles for any given month, but it cannot say the same about insider trading, midnight dumping, consumer defrauding or illegal polluting.

Still, we do know that corporate crime is pervasive. A 1979 Justice Department study "Illegal Corporate Behavior," found that 582 corporations surveyed racked up a total of 1,554 law violations in just two years. A 1980 *Fortune* magazine survey revealed that 11 percent of 1,043 large companies had been convicted on criminal charges or consent decrees for five offenses: bribery, criminal fraud, illegal political contributions, tax evasion and criminal antitrust. A *U.S. News & World Report* study of the 500 largest corporations found that "115 have been convicted in the last decade of at least one major crime or have paid civil penalties for serious misbehavior" in excess of $50,000. And in 1985, George Washington University Professor Amitai Etzioni found that roughly two-thirds of America's 500 largest companies were involved to some extent in illegal behavior over the preceding 10 years.

By the mid-1930s, evidence was mounting that exposure to asbestos was a threat to human health. In 1982, the Manville Corporation (previously Johns Manville), the nation's largest manufacturer of asbestos, filed for bankruptcy to shelter its assets from 16,500 personal injury lawsuits. In the intervening 50 years, the corporation actively suppressed asbestos studies and hid information from its employees on the dangers of working with asbestos. They even cut workers off from their own health records. "As long as [the employee] is not disabled," rationalized the company's medical director in 1963, "it is felt that he should not be told of his condition so that he can live and work in peace, and the company can benefit from his many years of experience."

Over the next 30 years, 240,000 people—8,000 per year, almost one every hour on average—will die from asbestos-related cancer. The company will pay some $2.5 billion to its victims, a hefty civil penalty. But no asbestos executive has ever been prosecuted for reckless homicide.

Likewise, it was not a "crime," in the traditional sense of the word, for Union Carbide's Bhopal, India, subsidiary to operate a pesticide manufacturing plant so incompetently that in 1984, clouds of deadly methyl isocyanate gas escaped, killing 2,000 to 5,000 persons and injuring 200,000.

And it is not a "crime" for the tobacco companies knowingly to market a highly addictive drug that kills more than 365,000 Americans a year, 1,000 every day. This toll is higher than the number of Americans killed annually by AIDS, heroin, crack, alcohol, car accidents, fire and murder combined.

And it is not a "crime" to market known cancer-causing pesticides such as Alar. Nor is it a "crime" to dump toxins into the air and water. General Motors (GM), among others, has been campaigning actively against public health for decades. In 1949, the company was convicted of conspiracy to destroy the nation's mass transit systems by buying up and then dismantling electrical transit systems in urban areas around the country.

The environmental consequences of this crime are still felt today. Los Angeles, which in the 1930s boasted an efficient system of electrified public transit that served 56 cities, saw the system destroyed and replaced with diesel buses and a freeway network for GM's cars. The city now has one of the worst air pollution problems in the country, and the Bush administration has proposed exempting it from some provisions of the Clean Air Act.

"What is good for General Motors is not necessarily good for the country," former San Francisco Mayor Joe Alioto told senators in a hearing about the destruction of the electric transit system in the Bay Area. "In the field of transportation, what has been good for General Motors has, in fact, been very, very bad for the country."

With the enormous resources available to them, companies like General Motors can ensure that the laws protecting us from them remain weak. During the last decade, for example, General Motors has successfully opposed amendments that would strengthen federal clean air and federal fuel-efficiency standards. GM has spent more than $1.8 billion lobbying Congress against clean air amendments since 1981, the year the Clean Air Act came due for reauthorization. In addition, GM's political action committee made more than $750,000 in campaign contributions, much of it to legislators who sit on committees with jurisdiction over clean air issues.

Lack of accountability is deeply embedded in the concept of the corporation. Shareholders' liability is limited to the amount of money they invest. Managers' liability is limited to what they choose to know about the operations of the company. And the corporation's liability is limited by Congress (the Price-Anderson Act, for example, caps the liability of nuclear power companies in the aftermath of a nuclear disaster), by insurance and by laws allowing corporations to duck liability by altering their corporate structure (the Manville bankruptcy dodge, for example).

In addition, since the turn of the century, most laws governing corporate behavior give regulators the option of avoiding criminal charges and proceeding with less burdensome and less noticeable civil enforcement. In this way, corporations avoid either admitting or denying that they violated the law and are let off with slap-on-the-wrist fines and consent decrees. For environmental, labor, securities, energy, and food and drug violations, the civil injunction is today the primary method of enforcing the law against big business.

Fines, dismissed by criminologists as "license fees to violate the law," are the customary civil penalty for corporate wrongdoing. "One jail sentence is worth 100 consent decrees," said one federal judge. "Fines are meaningless because the defendant in the end is always reimbursed by the proceeds of his wrongdoing or by his company."

Under civil enforcement, the executives of criminal corporations are freed from the stigma of prosecution and possible jail sentences. "The violations of these laws are crimes," wrote Edwin Sutherland in his 1949 classic, *White-Collar Crime*, "but they are treated as though they are not crimes, with the effect and probably the intention of eliminating the stigma of crime."

Sanctions for egregious corporate crimes rarely match the gravity of the offense, nor do they compare well with the punishment meted out for common street crimes. Not one corporate executive went to jail for marketing thalidomide, a drug that caused severe birth defects in 8,000 babies during the 1960s, but Wallace Richard Stewart of Kentucky was sentenced in July 1983 to 10 years in prison for stealing a pizza. Not one Hooker Chemical manager went to jail, nor was Hooker charged with a criminal offense after the company exposed its workers and Love Canal neighbors to toxics, but under a Texas habitual offenders statute, William Rummel was sentenced to life in prison for stealing a total of $229.11 over a period of nine years. And General Motors was fined a mere $5,000 for its mass transit conspiracy, which set back the country's environmental standards for decades.

"No amount of money paid out of corporate assets can address the wrongful acts of the individuals responsible within the organization," says Kenneth Oden, a District Attorney in Austin who has prosecuted a number of occupational homicide cases. "Sometimes the boss needs to be placed in handcuffs and taken to jail." While incarceration of street criminals may have a limited deterrent effect, jail time for corporate executives has a markedly different impact. "I would starve before I would do it again," said one General Electric official, convicted and jailed in a price-fixing scandal.

In February 1983, a worker at Film Recovery Systems' silver extraction plant became nauseated while working in a room with open vats of hydrogen cyanide. He staggered outside the plant, collapsed and died. The medical examiner reported that he died of "acute cyanide toxicity." A month later the state attorney for Cook County, Chicago, charged three executives of Film Recovery Systems with homicide.

Prosecutors argued that plant employees were forced to work in the equivalent of a huge gas chamber, that the company hired mostly illegal aliens who spoke little English, that the company had scraped skull and crossbones warnings off the side of the cyanide drums, and that ventilation was so inadequate that a thick yellow haze hung inside the plant.

After a two-month trial, each of the three executives was found guilty of murder and reckless conduct, fined $10,000 and sentenced to 25 years in prison for murder and 364 days for reckless conduct. Two operating corporations were found guilty of reckless conduct and involuntary manslaughter and fined $11,000 each.

The Film Recovery Systems case represents the first time a corporate executive has been found guilty of murder in an occupational death case, and public

CORPORATE CRIME-BUSTING:
SOME LEGAL AND SOCIAL REMEDIES

Congress should pass an executive responsibility statute making it a criminal offense for a corporate supervisor willfully or recklessly to fail to oversee an assigned activity that results in criminal conduct. The globe-trotting chief executive, like Exxon's Lawrence G. Rawl, would have a new incentive to monitor the safe conduct of his corporation.

Corporate managers should be required to report to federal authorities a product or process that may cause death or serious injury. This would ensure that R&D departments keep worker health and safety in mind. A bill to this effect, introduced by Representative George Miller (D-CA) in 1979, was defeated thanks in part to corporate lobbying.

Congress should require publicly held corporations to report their litigation records—indictments, convictions, sentences, fines and product-liability lawsuits—to the FBI. This corporate crime database could then be used by communities and prosecutors to inform their fights against criminally inclined companies.

At the local level, corporate crime-watch committees should be formed to keep an eye on the activities of neighboring corporations and to keep police and prosecutors on their toes. Victims of corporate crime, such as those who have been injured by the Dalkon Shield, Agent Orange and asbestos, have formed organizations to lobby for just compensation, strong laws and, where applicable, effective prosecution and strict sentences.

Creative penalties should be devised, such as court-ordered adverse publicity. As a condition of probation, for example, a judge could order a company to take out network television advertisements telling viewers about its long criminal record.

More than anything else, corporate criminals should do time. They should be jailed alongside the mugger and drug dealer, not in the posh "Club Feds" usually reserved for white-collar crooks.

---

sentiment seems to be calling for more such legal actions. Earlier this year in Torrance, California, the city attorney, citing the fear of a "disaster of Bhopal-like proportions," filed an unusual lawsuit against Mobil Oil. He sought to have Mobil's giant Torrance refinery declared a public nuisance, thus giving the city the authority to regulate it. The lawsuit cites the plant's appalling safety record—127 accidents at the refinery since December 1979, including the fiery deaths of three persons, among them a passing motorist, in an explosion and fire at the tank farm.

The district attorney (DA) for Los Angeles County requires prosecutors to investigate the circumstances of every occupational death or serious injury on the job. In the past four years, the DA has investigated more than 100 such cases and has brought criminal charges in more than two dozen cases. And in Austin, Milwaukee and New York City, activist prosecutors are hitting employers with homicide charges for death on the job.

In early 1989, the Commonwealth of Massachusetts announced the creation of a statewide Environmental Crimes Task Force that will use prosecutors, scientists, investigators and police officers to target high-priority threats to public health and natural resources. The 34-member strike force will specialize in major cases involving threats to drinking water supplies, harm to wetlands, illegal dumping and toxic discharges into sewage systems.

"This should send a clear message to everyone across the state: If you pollute, we're going to catch you and you'll pay the price," said Massachusetts Environmental Affairs Secretary John DeVillars. "Poisoning someone's water supply or illegally dumping material isn't a victimless crime. It's a costly crime that has a major impact on individuals whose health may suffer. It damages our quality of life."

At the federal level, the Justice Department's Environmental Crimes Section, which was created in 1983, has recorded 520 indictments and more than 400 convictions, bringing in $22 million in fines and more than 240 years of actual jail time. Earlier this year, Ashland Oil was found guilty of violating federal environmental laws in connection with the collapse of an Ashland storage tank that spilled more than 500,000 gallons of oil into the Monongahela River outside of Pittsburgh on January 2, 1988.

The developments described above point to a new willingness on the part of the public and the judicial system to see corporate crime punished fairly. Until now, the law has taught that if you are strong, rich and corporate, you can inflict the most egregious wrongs on society and continue business as usual. There is no reason why this cannot change. In a just society, the criminal law should also teach that those who poison the air, water and land, injure and kill others, or inflict cancer and birth defects are criminals and should be justly punished.

Chapter
12

Personal Alignments and Realignments

*T*his chapter focuses on relationships between several sets of processes that take place constantly in organizations. These processes are critical to both the success of organizations and the well-being of their members.

The first set of processes is well known. It includes such things as job descriptions, expectations of supervisors, peers, customers and subordinates; rules and laws; and professional norms. These processes exert pressures on organizational members to behave in certain ways. The second set occurs within the individual and involves the internal standards of conduct that influence beliefs about certain things: what an individual should and should not do, what is meaningful and worth doing and what is not, and what constitutes success and failure. These processes often conflict with the demands advanced by the organization.

The third set of processes involves what is referred to as "alignment," as individuals attempt to seek some congruency between internal and external demands. According to Culbert and McDonough, alignment involves "what an individual goes through in attempting to relate his or her subjective and self-centered interests to what he or she perceives as the objective requirements of the job."[1] Many psychologists and our own experiences tell us that when people achieve effective alignments (i.e. synergistic relationships between internal and external demands), they are happier, more energized, and more productive.

In the final set of processes alignment goes on continuously. Both internal and external standards change over time and previous alignments can become ineffective very quickly. Thus we need to talk about alignments and realignments. As the

---

[1]S. A. Culbert, and J. J. McDonough (1985). *Radical Management: Power Politics and the Pursuit of Trust* (New York: Free Press).

selections that follow reveal, achieving effective alignments and realignments can be very difficult to do and may require a great deal of introspection.

In "The Invisible War: Pursuing Self-Interest at Work," Samuel A. Culbert and John J. McDonough explain and illustrate the alignment process. The next two selections ("I Have Arrived" and "The Tragedy of Tragedies: The Story of Hugh") call attention to some of the most frustrating of human experiences involving individuals who (1) can achieve everything they sought and then wonder if what they sought was worthwhile and (2) never obtain an authentic image of who they are.

"The Hero's Journey," excerpted from Carol S. Pearson's *The Hero Within*, encourages us to examine some dysfunctional aspects of some longstanding and pervasive cultural standards. Pearson then outlines a new image that may be more fulfilling. "Annmarie Feci—Page Operator" is the story of an individual who appears to be well-aligned in her job.

Barbara E. Kovach's "Successful Derailment: What Fast-Trackers Can Learn While They're Off the Track" reveals that the issues discussed in the previous selections are directly relevant to some of the most talented managers in modern organizations. Managers' understanding of themselves turns out to be a major variable that determines their abilities to achieve successful realignments as they move through their careers.

In "The Day at the Beach" Arthur Gordon provides some ideas for the type of self-reflection that may help a person achieve successful alignments and realignments. It is far from a panacea but in our view points in some very useful directions.

The Invisible War: Pursuing Self-Interest at Work

*Samuel A. Culbert and
John J. McDonough*

Each time people enter a new work situation they engage in the implicit process of *aligning* personal values, interests, and skills with what they perceive to be the task requirements of their job. They seek an orientation that maximizes self-pursuits and organizational contribution. *Alignment* is our term for the orientation that results from such an effort, however implicitly this takes place. Once such an orientation has been evolved, it becomes a self-convenient lens through which all organizational happenings are viewed. That is, once people hit on an alignment—an orientation that lines self-interests up with the task-requirements of their jobs—this alignment serves to alert them to meanings they can use in promoting and supporting their personal and organizational endeavors, and to meanings put forth by others which threaten the credibility and relevance of what they are pursuing.

Not all alignments are effective. That is, the orientation some people use is too far removed either from the needs and obligations of their jobs or from expressing the inner themes that can make their jobs personally meaningful. We say an individual possesses an "effective" alignment when the orientation directing that person's actions and view of reality allows him or her to represent important self-interests while making a contribution to the organization. We say an individual lacks an effective alignment when important discrepancies exist between what that person inwardly values, endeavors to express, does well, and needs to do in order to satisfy what he or she perceives to be the task requirements of the job.

Now we can return to the questions raised at the beginning of this chapter. [in original—eds.]

Why do people with the same job perform their assignments so differently?

Easy, they have unique interests, values, and competencies to bootleg into their jobs at every opportunity.

Why do people with comparable organizational goals see the same situation differently and fight unyieldingly over which interpretation is correct?

From *The Invisible War: Pursuing Self-Interest at Work* by Samuel A. Culbert and John J. McDonough, 1980, pp. 60–71, 219–222. New York: John Wiley & Sons, Inc. © 1980. Reprinted by permission of John Wiley & Sons, Inc.

Easy, while they may be striving to attain comparable organizational objectives, what they are striving to attain in their lives and careers is very different. This causes them to attend differently to each of the elements in a given situation. Finally,

What determines the specific way individuals decide to perform their jobs and how they interpret each situation?

Easy again, it's what we've termed alignment. People proceed with a job orientation that spontaneously spins out interpretations and meanings that serve the unique way they need reality constructed in order to be a "success." How individuals do a job and what they see are influenced by what they find personally interesting, by the concepts they can master and the skills they can perform with excellence, by the self-ideals and values they seek to attain, by their unique ideas of what constitutes career advancement, by what they believe will score on the checklist that others will use in evaluating their performance, and by what they genuinely believe the organization needs from someone in their role.

Few people are all that aware of their alignment. Even fewer are conscious of the fact that systematic biases permeate their view of the organizational world. And, almost no one understands that such biases play a major role in making organizations effective. All this is because most people work their alignment out implicitly and take its presence for granted until a change in the external scene, in other people's views of their effectiveness, or in their own sense of satisfaction show it to be obsolete. Then they can appreciate what they lost and strive for a new alignment that will again allow them to satisfy self-interests and personal pride while getting acclaim for doing a good job. For example, consider what happened to a middle manager named Pete who had a marvelous alignment until he got promoted and suddenly found himself faced with a serious gap between his own and the organization's definition of success.

Pete was one of twenty in his corporation who, some five years ago, agreed to take on a newly created mission, that of improving communications and managerial competence within his company. This function seemed right up Pete's alley. He'd attended sensitivity training sessions, had a reputation of being genuinely concerned with people, and was respected up and down the ranks for his leadership ability even though he had not burned up the track with his progress.

Pete saw the new assignment as a chance to bolster a lagging career. He had never been overly concerned with rising in the hierarchy, but his failure to take a fast track to the top was presenting him with daily redundancies that left him feeling somewhat stale. At forty-five he needed another challenge and this assignment held the potential to revitalize his career. Eagerly he accepted.

Pete threw himself into the new position. He enrolled in outside courses and hired skilled consultants to design training programs for the corporation's managers. Whenever possible he assisted the consultants and within a short time he understood their technology and was able to play a role in tailoring their inputs to the specific needs of his corporation. His learning continued and soon he was running programs on his own, involving personnel from each divisional level. Almost immediately his reputation as a man who genuinely cared was enhanced by widespread recognition of his competence in the management development technologies. And he was no soft touch either. He aggressively challenged managers on their "self-sealing" logics and constructed boat-rocking experiments to confront higher-ups with the demotivating and profit-eroding consequences of their autocratic styles.

Pete's involvements took an exciting turn with the advent of minority and women's consciousness. If the corporation's managers weren't racist, their de facto hiring and promotion policies were. This meant a greater volume of work and warranted an increase in the size of his staff. From a resource base that started with himself and a secretary, his department increased to two professionals, an administrative assistant, and two secretaries. Their operation hummed. They did career development counseling with secretaries. They got involved with the corporation's recruiters, both to encourage the hiring of blacks and females and to create programs that would support the new employees' progress in an essentially all white male management structure. They hired racial-awareness consultants to get managers in touch with their prejudices and help them work these out. And with this heightened workload, Pete even found time to continue his efforts in getting managers to identify areas in which their style intruded on the effectiveness of others.

Pete also had marvelous latitude in job definition which he exploited to match his interests and values. He enrolled in personal growth courses, attended conventions, joined professional associations, and on occasion even used the company plane. Because Pete identified both with the welfare of people and the productivity of the corporation and was concerned that his work produce tangible outcomes, his indulgences were hardly noticed—rather they were seen as part of his power. The people on his staff looked up to him and nondefensively brought him their toughest problems for coaching and support. His credibility with people lower in the hierarchy provided him a position of influence with those at the highest corporate levels. And, delightfully for Pete, his reputation among blacks and women was impeccable.

Within a couple of years Pete had worked out an ideal *alignment*. He had a way of engaging each constituency that allowed them to see how his actions related to results they valued. There seemed to be a 99 percent overlap between his personal definition of success and the missions and responsibilities assigned to him, and no one in the company could perform them better.

The other nineteen managers receiving the same charter as Pete, but working elsewhere in the corporation, didn't fare nearly as well. Perhaps lack of know-how, perhaps enculturation in the corporation's way of doing things, or perhaps a different tolerance for conflict had made them reluctant to aggressively challenge higher-ups. With time, to a greater or lesser degree, their roles degenerated to those of commiserator and management "go-for." They always seemed to be on the defensive, trying to prove themselves rather than challenging others to be more excellent. Their weakness and low-keyed tactics made Pete's strength and accomplishments look all the more potent.

Eventually those sitting in upper corporate echelons took notice of the overall situation and decided that Pete was the role model of what they were trying to achieve. They approached Pete with an offer of a promotion if he would agree to supervise and train the other nineteen managers. Pete's first reaction was to accept, but something held him back. At the time, he didn't understand his hesitancy, so he merely used it to negotiate a sweeter deal. He would not take responsibility for the others, there were too many bad habits to overcome. But he would step up a level in his current territory and accept overall responsibility for recruitment, career planning, minority advancement, and improved managerial functioning.

Pete's promotion put him on the same level with other line managers. He became a regular member of the management team and now directly supervised three managers who were responsible for about forty professional employees and oversaw the hiring of outside consultants.

Unfortunately, at this point, his alignment fell apart and his work life became filled with aggravation. *First,* his former associates began treating him like their boss, which he was, and this severely undermined his ability to coach and openly suggest. Now his suggestions were heard as orders and his inadvertent questions were received as well-thought-out criticisms.

Next, his relationships with blacks and women went to pot. His elevation in the hierarchy caused him to be seen as manager rather than human rights worker and he was treated to rounds of Mau-Mauing and confrontations, as what formerly had been received as his in-group remarks were interpreted as racial and sexist slurs.

Next, Pete found that the added amount of time his new job required for supervision, staff meetings, and report writing reduced the time available for the internal consulting role he prized.

On top of everything else, a "screw-up" in another division involving a racial-awareness consultant set off a reactionary wave up to an executive vice-president who responded by ordering sharp cutbacks in the use of outside consultants. For Pete, this had the personal effect of cutting off sources of his support and learning and the task effect of withdrawing the quality resources needed to keep his operation competently stationed and challenging to the status quo.

To top these disappointments, after about three months in the new job, Pete's boss called him in for a coaching session where he received word that his new peers were concerned that he was hurting his career by appearing to be such a deviant and advocate for minorities. Pete returned to his office screaming, "What the hell is going on here, these are the same jokers who wanted me promoted because I *was* such a deviant?!"

This was the last straw. Not only were his former constituents treating him like one of the "other guys" but the "other guys" were claiming that he was too much of a deviant for them.

From our perspective Pete was caught without either a personally effective or an organizationally successful alignment. His personal viewpoint wasn't registering anywhere. Nowhere was he actively shaping reality. His alignment had become obsolete. He was in the same position his nineteen former counterparts had found themselves in when they were charged with a mission to which they could not personally relate and thus could not confidently assert an articulate point of view.

Incidentally, and no pun intended, this is not a case of the "Peter Principle."

We know Pete and he's anything but a person who had been promoted above his level of competence. We believe it is just a matter of time before Pete constructs a new alignment, one that allows him to use his new job for personal expression and to further the missions he values. But until he gets realigned, the self-deliberations entailed in trying to match self-interests with what seems to be required by his job will provide him with many lonely hours of unhappiness and frustration.

Pete's story was chosen because it illustrates the active dimension of the orienting process we call alignment. It shows the importance of an individual's commitment to inner values. That Pete could succeed, both inwardly and outwardly, where nineteen others could not is a tribute to his success in finding a good match between his personal needs and interests and what he saw as needed by the job. He had an effective alignment. The nineteen others lacked an effective alignment and most of them became either *cynics* or *careerists*. The cynics converged on alignments that subordinated the organization's needs to their own interests and values. They saw management's view as constraints to be navigated around, not perspectives to be joined and possibly learned from. Conversely, the careerists adopted alignments that subordinated their personal interests and values to what they thought would score on the organization checklist. They ground out workshop after workshop, training event after training event, but without the conversations and conflicts that could budge the status quo.

The concept of alignment, and Pete's story, provides support for most people's contention that repackaging themselves to fit a particular job or role does not constitute a sell-out to the job, although to an outsider their compromises frequently appear fatal. As Pete's situation illustrates, people need to shift alignments when they change jobs or experience a new set of external demands, even though their interests, skills and values remain the same. While self-interests remain relatively constant, the form in which they are pursued and expressed must shift. How often we've seen people criticize the way their boss operates only to themselves embody much of the same behavior as they shift alignments upon moving up to the boss's level in the organization.

In summary, we see the concept of alignment as a key addition to how people should be thinking about organizations. There's a level of organization residing within each individual that explains how that person does his or her job and views external organization events. If there's an external organization that determines how groups of people relate in doing work together then there's an *internal organization,* far more encompassing than an individual's personality, that determines how individuals within groups transact their business and work for the greater institutional good. Moreover, despite their lack of prominence in how people present themselves, self-interests are a dominant factor in determining what gets produced in the name of organizationally required product and how what is produced is received. And you don't need the skills of a psychoanalyst to understand these self-interests. You merely need to comprehend what an individual is trying to express personally and achieve in his or her career, and what he or she perceives as making a valuable contribution to the job. At every point personal needs and organization goals impact on one another, and it's always up in the air whether the needs of the job or the interests of the individual will swamp the other or whether a synergy of interests will evolve.

Thus *alignment* is our term for the highly personal orientation one takes to the job that must be known before we can comprehend the meaning and intent of someone's actions. Sometimes people do different things for the same reason. Sometimes people do the same things for different reasons. Without knowing people's alignment, taking their actions on face value—even those with a direct connection to bottom-line product—leads to erroneous conclusions. The only way to comprehend what people are about is to know what they are trying to express and achieve personally and what assumptions they are making about the organizational avenues for doing so.

At this point we provide a guide to comprehending the personal side of an individual's orientation to the job. It's a set of questions which, when thoughtfully answered, provide a new perspective on why an individual does his or her job the way he or she does it, and why that person views organization events in a particular way. Add in the task requisites of the job, as the individual sees them, and you've got that person's alignment. Incidentally, we've had marvelous results using an abbreviated list of these questions as preparation for team-building meetings at which a boss and his or her subordinates get together for a long session to discuss opportunities for improving their work-group's effectiveness. Twenty to forty minutes each, around the group, and the edge comes off many premeeting criticisms. Instead of being programmed to fault one another for inadequacy, the discussion takes a constructive turn as participants contrast the fit between an individual's needs and talents with what participants see as the task requisites of that person's job.

The questions we use in seeking to understand the self-interest side of an individual's alignment fall into three categories: personal, career, and organizational. Specifically we ask questions drawn from, but not limited to, the following list.

SELF-INTEREST QUESTIONS

Personal

What are you trying to prove to yourself and, very importantly, why?

What are you trying to prove to others? Give an instance that illustrates why and how.

What style of life are you trying to maintain or achieve? (Does this entail a change in income? geography? family size? etc.)

Name the people who have played significant roles in your life and say what those roles were.

What dimensions would you like to add to your personal life and why?

What motto would you like to have carved on your tombstone and how do you want to be remembered by the people who are close to you?

Career

What profession do you want to wind up in? (If you are an engineer and you say "management," tell why. If you are not in that profession, say how you plan to get into it.)

How did you, or will you, develop competency in that profession?

What do you want to accomplish in that profession?

What honor or monument would you like to have symbolize your success in that profession? Say why it would constitute a personal hallmark.

Organizational

What has been your image in your organization and what would you like it to be?

Describe a bum-rap or overly simplistic category others have used in describing you and tell either why you are different now or why their statement was simplistic or too categorical.

What is the next lesson you need to learn and what are your plans for doing so?

What would you like to be doing two to five years out? °

What would you like to be doing ten years out? °

While we encourage people to share perspectives generated by these questions with work associates whom they trust, we do not recommend that they reveal specific instances in which self-interests played a role in determining one of their organizational actions. We don't because we fear that others, however well-intentioned, will inadvertently misuse such candor later on. What we advocate is that each individual simply provide associates a more valid context for viewing his or her goals and accomplishments. . . .

CONCLUSION

It's appropriate that we've saved our favorite story for the end. It's a story about a manager who embodies the best of both the subjective and the rational approaches to leadership and for us is a symbol that it can be done. This manager is able to go toe to toe with hard-boiled characters like Charlie and at the same time remain sensitive to the contributions made by leaders like Fred. °° He's a manager who searches for ways of relating to the uniqueness of those reporting to him while he

---

°Think of "doing" in terms of a specific assignment (job, position, status) and specify it in terms of a specific role (player, coach, expert) and how you would like to be performing it.

°°Charlie and Fred are characters introduced earlier in the book from which this excerpt is taken—*Ed. note.*

shuns calling "objective" that which he sees as arbitrary and a matter of personal convenience.

The manager we have in mind demonstrated the effectiveness of much that we are advocating in three distinct settings: industry, education, and public service. First, he fought his way through the highly competitive world of consumer products where he became chairman of the board of one of the nation's largest and most successful conglomerates. Next, in the educational field, he became the dean of a large and prestigious professional school, instituting changes that brought national recognition to that institution. And most recently he was the President's choice to head a world-renowned agency and this appointment brought instant acclamation from the Senate Hearings Committee. All this took place before his forty-seventh birthday!

In our view the key to this manager's success lies in his ability to see the connection between personal effectiveness and organizational efficiency. To him, these are highly related issues. He believes that organizations exist to serve people, not the other way around, and he constantly searches to understand what people are trying to achieve in the way of personal meaning and career success. Nevertheless, his style is one which frequently gets misinterpreted as soft and permissive leadership and does not produce an easy route to universal love and appreciation. His understanding of personal projects allows him to penetrate many of the facades people construct, and this makes him the target of behind-the-scenes ambivalence and face-to-face suspicion. Let's examine his impact more closely.

In the first place, he resists spending the bulk of his energies responding to problems defined by others as "crises." This orientation allows him to take tough stands with respect to the succession of "crises" any top administrator faces, and which, if passed down through the organization, can make it impossible for anyone to align self-interests with the task requirements of their job in a way that's constructive for the institution. In the short run his "nonresponsiveness" makes him vulnerable to the charge that he is not on top of a situation. In the long run, however, he frees himself and the people in his organization from the oppressive burden of always responding to someone else's fire drill.

We certainly don't want to mislead you into thinking that our hero, or any other leader, could emerge from each of these settings totally unscarred. To the contrary, on his way to the board chairmanship he spent more than three years going eyeball to eyeball with a manager whose style was the antithesis of his own and whose subordinates consider him to be "the biggest prick you're ever going to find in a chief executive's office." When our leader realized that he was going to be locked in mortal combat for as long as he stayed with the conglomerate, he began to look around. That's when he got into education. Some say things got too hot for him to handle. In our minds his decision revealed that he saw more to life than surviving corporate death struggles.

It's interesting to contrast the subordinates who value his leadership style with those who don't. Those who see flexibility in the construction of their own alignments generally appreciate his style. But he causes fits among those with careerist and martyr mentalities. These people are confused by his respect for the personal side of their alignments. They mistake his sensitivity to what is personally meaningful to them as agreement with their self-beneficial formulations of what the organization needs to do. Consequently they experience small betrayals when learning of a decision he takes after surveying their perspective. What they don't understand is that our hero seriously considers competing perspectives prior to making a decision and that his integration is almost always original, with even the people who influenced him the most finding themselves unable to identify their input in what he prints out. But for those with open-ended questions, his print-outs are almost always educational. By factoring out what he added, they deduce what this leader sees as the limitations in their formulations.

For almost everyone, his style is disarming. His searching respect for the subjective side of an individual's participation is responded to as a warm and irresistible invitation to tell all. This makes it quite difficult to fragment. Knowing that he knows their subjective interests causes most people to tell their whole story— either out of a fear of looking stupid or one of getting caught telling a half-truth. In subtle ways this leader conveys the message that he's not there simply to serve the self-indulgent needs of individuals but to provide another perspective on what the organization needs and to challenge people to find a more synergistic means of relating their needs to organization product. And he's been able to do this and still score on the traditional checklist.

In many ways this leader is bigger than life; certainly his accomplishments surpass what most of us are externally striving to achieve. Today's society seems to worship external success, yet each of us knows that we're up to so much more. Our hero often strikes us as a very lonely man and we can't help but think that a major part of what appears to be a self-imposed solitude derives from an understanding that, in today's world, his accomplishments are valued for reasons which bear little resemblance to what he sets out to do. But help should be on the way. We believe the evaluation categories which convey illusions of objectivity and overemphasize externals will gradually change. And as more people demonstrate an enhanced appreciation for the subjective involvements that everyone brings to organization life, this leader, together with the rest of us, will have an easier time being himself and gaining recognition for just that.

I Have Arrived

Natasha Josefowitz

I have not seen the plays in town
  only the computer printouts
I have not read the latest books
  only *The Wall Street Journal*
I have not heard birds sing this year
  only the ringing of phones
I have not taken a walk anywhere
  but from the parking lot to my office
I have not shared a feeling in years
  but my thoughts are known to all
I have not listened to my own needs
  but what I want I get
I have not shed a tear in ages
  I have arrived
Is *this* where I was going?

From Natasha Josefowitz, *Is This Where I Was Going?*, 1983. New York: Warner Books. Reprinted by permission.

The Tragedy of Tragedies:
The Story of Hugh

John Bradshaw

Once upon a time a Royal person was born.* His name was Hugh. Although I'll refer to Hugh as "he", no one actually knew what his sex really was and it didn't really matter. Hugh was unlike anyone who had ever lived before or who would ever live again. Hugh was precious, unrepeatable, incomparable, a trillion-dollar diamond in the rough.

For the first 15 months of life, Hugh only knew himself from the reflections he saw in the eyes of his caretakers. Hugh was terribly unfortunate. His caretakers, although not blind, had glasses over their eyes. Each set of glasses already had an *image* on it. So that each caretaker only saw Hugh according to the image on his glasses. Thus, even though Hugh's caretakers were physically present, not one of them *ever actually saw him.* By the time Hugh was grown, he was a mosaic of other people's images of him, none of which was who he really was. No one had really ever seen him, so no one had ever mirrored back to him what he really looked like. Consequently, Hugh thought he was the mosaic of images. He really did not know who he was.

Sometimes in the dark of the night when he was all alone, Hugh knew that something of profound importance was missing. He experienced this as a gnawing sense of emptiness—a deep void.

Hugh tried to fill the emptiness and void with many things: power, worldly fame, money, possessions, chemical highs, food, sex, excitement, entertainment, relationships, children, work—even exercise. But no matter what he *did,* he never felt the gnawing emptiness go away. In the quiet of the night when all the distractions were gone, he heard a still quiet voice that said: "Don't forget; please don't forget me!" But alas! Hugh did forget and went to his death never knowing who he was!

---

*For grammatical consistency and clarity, the pronouns "he," "his" and "him" have been used throughout instead of "she or he," "his or her" and "her and him." No sexual bias or insensitivity is meant.

The Hero's Journey

Carol S. Pearson

Heroes take journeys, confront dragons, and discover the treasure of their true selves. Although they may feel very alone during the quest, at its end their reward is a sense of community: with themselves, with other people, and with the earth. Every time we confront death-in-life we confront a dragon, and every time we choose life over nonlife and move deeper into the ongoing discovery of who we are, we vanquish the dragon; we bring new life to ourselves and to our culture. We change the world. The need to take the journey is innate in the species. If we do not risk, if we play prescribed social roles instead of taking our journeys, we feel numb; we experience a sense of alienation, a void, an emptiness inside. People who are discouraged from slaying dragons internalize the urge and slay themselves by declaring war on their fat, their selfishness, or some other attribute they think does not please. Or they become ill and have to struggle to get well. In shying away from the quest, we experience nonlife and, accordingly, we call forth less life in the culture.

The primary subject of modern literature is this experience of alienation and despair. The antihero has replaced the hero as the central figure in literature precisely because the myth of the hero that dominates our culture's view of what it means to take our journeys has become anachronistic. What we imagine immediately when we think of the hero really is only one heroic archetype: the Warrior. The Warrior typically takes a long, usually solitary journey, saves the day, and rescues the damsel-in-distress by slaying a dragon or in some other way defeating the enemy.

GENDER AND THE REDEFINITION OF HEROISM

In our culture, the heroic ideal of the Warrior has been reserved for men—usually only white men at that. Women in this plot are cast as damsels-in-distress to be rescued, as witches to be slain, or as princesses who, with half the kingdom, serve as the hero's reward. Minority men, at least in American literature, typically are cast as the loyal sidekick (think of Huck and Jim in Mark Twain's *Huck Finn* [sic] or the Lone Ranger and Tonto).

In *The Hero with a Thousand Faces* Joseph Campbell wrote that the hero is "master of the world."[1] And it is the masters of the world—the kings, the princes, and their poets—who have defined for us *what* the heroic ideal is and *whose* it is. Of course, they designed it in their own image and saw heroism as the province of the few. With the rise of democracy and the development of the ideal of an equalitarian society, first working-class white men and then women and minority men began claiming the heroic archetype as their own.

Ironically, just as women, working-class men, and minority men are embracing the Warrior archetype, many white middle- and upper-class men are expressing great alienation from it. In part, I think that is so because, although this archetype is a myth that presides over a healthy capacity for assertion and mastery, it also, in its usual form, is based upon separation—upon cutting oneself off from other people and the earth. Many men have discovered that, however satisfying it is in the short run, the urge to be better than, to dominate and control, brings only emptiness and despair.

The Warrior archetype is also an elitist myth, which at its base embodies the notion that some people take their heroic journeys while others simply serve and sacrifice. Yet we are all really one; as long as we are not all taking our journeys, finding our voices, our talents, and making our unique contributions to the world, we start feeling less and less alive—even the most privileged among us. No one can truly profit for long at another's expense.

When I first began to examine this myth, I thought virtually all of modern malaise was due to the prevalence of the Warrior archetype. Surely, having a "slaying-the-dragon" paradigm for problem solving was not going to bring us world peace or eliminate world hunger. Later I came to realize that the Warrior archetype is not the problem per se, for it is developmentally critical to the evolution of human consciousness. Certainly it is as critical for women and minority men as it is for white men, even though the archetype gets redefined somewhat when everyone gets into the act instead of only a privileged few. The problem is that focusing on *only* this heroic archetype limits everyone's options. Many white men, for example, feel ennui because they need to grow beyond the Warrior modality, yet they find themselves stuck there because it not only is defined as *the* heroic ideal but is also equated with masculinity. Men consciously or unconsciously believe they cannot give up that definition of themselves without also giving up their sense of superiority to others—especially to women.

In doing research for *Who Am I This Time?* and later for *The Female Hero in American and British Literature*,[2] I realized that the belief that there are no true heroines in modern literature simply is not accurate. Women, for example, as Katherine Pope and I showed in *The Female Hero,* often are portrayed heroically. Encouraged by feminism, many women enact the Warrior archetype. But that is not the whole story. They also are exploring patterns of heroism that, at first, seemed to me to be specific to women. This mode, which is different from men's, is based upon integrity rather than on slaying dragons. Female heroes often even flee dragons! While male heroes like Owen Wister's Virginian (in *The Virginian*) would leave even their bride on the wedding day to fight a duel (for honor's sake), women tend to assume that it simply is good sense to run from danger. Further, they do not see slaying dragons as very practical, since the people who often entrap women are husbands, mothers, fathers, children, friends—people who insist that good women forgo their own journeys to serve others. That is why there often are no true villains in stories about female heroes. Or at least it does not occur to the hero to slay them.

I was pleased to discover that women had developed an alternative to the hero-kills-the-villain-and-rescues-the-victim plot, one with no real villains or victims—just heroes. This mode of heroism seemed to offer hope that there is a form of heroism that can not only bring new life to us all, but do it in an equalitarian way. However, this mode of heroism could never fully blossom if only one sex seemed to know about it. While I observed all around me women optimistically playing out a hero/hero/hero script, most men I knew were acting out the old hero/villain/victim one. Men who could not be the hero in that old definition found the only other role available to them was the victim, or antihero. But then I noticed some men and some male characters in literature who had also discovered the hero/hero/hero plot and were feeling fully alive, joyous, and heroic in acting it out.

I began to recognize that men and women go through—albeit in somewhat different forms and sometimes in a slightly different order—the same basic stages of growth in claiming their heroism. And ultimately for both, heroism is a matter of integrity, of becoming more and more themselves at each stage in their development. Paradoxically, there are archetypal patterns that govern the process each of us goes through to discover our uniqueness, so we are always both very particularly ourselves and very much like one another in the stages of our journeys. In fact, there is a rather predictable sequence of human development presided over respectively by the archetypes of the Innocent, the Orphan, the Wanderer, the Warrior, the Martyr, and the Magician, even though our culture has encouraged men and women to identify with them differently.

THE ARCHETYPES AND HUMAN DEVELOPMENT

The Innocent and the Orphan set the stage: The Innocent lives in the prefallen state of grace; the Orphan confronts the reality of the Fall. The next few stages are strategies for living in a fallen world: The Wanderer begins the task of finding oneself apart from others; the Warrior learns to fight to defend oneself and to change the world in one's own image; and the Martyr learns to give, to commit, and to sacrifice for others. The progression, then, is from suffering, to self-definition, to struggle, to love.

It was clear to me that the heroism of the Wanderer is not defined by fighting. It is the very act of leaving an oppressive situation and going out alone to face the unknown that is the Wanderer's heroic act—for men or women.

But at first I missed the heroism of the Martyr, since more modern literature celebrates liberation from the older ideal of sacrifice. The antimartyr feeling is particularly strong in literature about women, because female socialization and cultural norms have reinforced martyrdom and sacrifice for women well into the twentieth century. Women have been cramped by the Martyr role even more than white men have been by the Warrior-only role. Looking again at the archetype of the Martyr, I began to respect its power and to see why, for example, Christianity, with the centrality of the image of Christ martyred on the cross, so appealed to women and minorities, and also why suffering and martyrdom have been so important in Judaism, especially in the many times and places marked by anti-Semitism.

I discovered the emergence of an ancient archetype heretofore reserved for even fewer people than the Warrior and that now is being redefined as a mode of heroism available to everyone. In this mode, the hero is a Magician or Shaman. After learning to change one's environment by great discipline, will, and struggle, the Magician learns to move with the energy of the universe and to attract what is needed by laws of synchronicity, so that the ease of the Magician's interaction with the universe seems like magic. Having learned to trust the self, the Magician comes full circle and, like the Innocent, finds that it is safe to trust.

Each of the archetypes carries with it a worldview, and with that different life goals and theories about what gives life meaning. Orphans seek safety and fear exploitation and abandonment. Martyrs want to be good, and see the world as a conflict between good (care and responsibility) and bad (selfishness and exploitation). Wanderers want independence and fear conformity. Warriors strive to be strong, to have an impact upon the world, and to avoid ineffectiveness and passivity. Magicians aim to be true to their inner wisdom and to be in balance with the energies of the universe. Conversely, they try to avoid the inauthentic and the superficial.

Each archetype projects its own learning task onto the world. People governed by an archetype will see its goal as ennobling and its worst fear as the root of all the world's problems. They complain about other people's ruthlessness, conformism, weakness, selfishness, or shallowness. Many misunderstandings arise from this. The Wanderer's independence often looks to the Martyr like the selfishness Martyrs abhor. The Warrior's assertiveness may appear to the Orphan like ruthlessness. And when the Magician proclaims that if the response is genuine, it is perfectly fine to act in any way, including all the ways you formerly feared and rejected (selfish, lazy, etc.), it sounds to almost everyone else like the worst kind of license!

At the Magician's level, however, dualities begin to break down. The Orphan's fear of pain and suffering is seen as the inevitable underside of a definition of safety that assumes that life should be only pleasurable and easy. Magicians believe that in fact we are safe even though we often experience pain and suffering. They are part of life, and ultimately we all are held in God's hand. Similarly, Magicians see that it is an unbalanced focus on giving that creates selfishness. The task is not to be caring of others *instead* of thinking about oneself, but to learn how to love and care for ourselves *as well as* our neighbor.

Magicians see beyond the notion of individualism versus conformity to the knowledge that we each are unique *and* we all are one. Beyond strength versus weakness, they come to understand that assertion and receptivity are yang and yin—a life rhythm, not a dualism. Finally, they know that it is not even possible to be inauthentic, for we can be only who we are. Inevitably, we do take our rightful place in the universe.

Each archetype moves us through duality into paradox. Within each is a continuum from a primitive to a more sophisticated and complex expression of its essential energy. The chapters that follow [in the original—eds.] describe the archetypes and the stages of awareness the hero encounters in exploring each one. The pattern described is schematic, however, so it is important to recognize while reading it that people do not go through these stages lockstep. Individuals chart their own unique courses through these "stages," and there are predictable differences in the ways people encounter them. This holds true in general for many cultural groups—different ethnic or racial groups, people from different countries or regions—but in this work, because of my own background and experience, I will focus on differences between men and women.

For example, male and female modes of heroism seem different because men linger longer in some stages and women in others. Because women are socialized to nurture and serve, and perhaps also because women give birth, their lives tend to be overly dominated by the Martyr archetype even before they have had the opportunity to explore the possibilities embodied by the Wanderer and the Warrior. Men, on the other hand, are pushed into having control over their lives and power over others, into being Warriors, before they know who they are. They get to the Warrior stage quickly but then get stuck there—and not only *there*, but often at its more primitive levels. They often have little or no encouragement and few male role models for developing their capacities for sensitivity, care, and commitment.

Women often do not like the Warrior stage and, hence, either refuse that journey or, if they embark upon it, whiz right on through it to become Magicians. That's why, I think, the changes I describe as the Wandering and Warrioring stages appear in Carol Gilligan's pioneering work, *In a Different Voice: Psychological Theory and Women's Development,* as a mere "transition" stage between a morality based on care of others (sacrifice) and, at a higher level, one in which the self is filtered back into the picture (interdependence).[3]

Women seem to linger in the stages that emphasize affiliation (Martyr and Magician) and men in those that emphasize separateness and opposition (Wanderer and Warrior). As Gilligan has shown, women are more likely to see the world in terms of nets and webs of connectedness; men see it in terms of ladders and hierarchies, where people compete for power. When we look at where most women or men are, without seeing the overall developmental pattern, it may look as if there are distinct and different male and female paths. Or, if one looks just at the paths and not at the different time and intensity of commitment to each archetype, it appears that men and women are developmentally the same. Neither is true. Men and women are developmentally the same; *and* they are different.

The typical male pattern of development in this culture is to go directly from the Orphan to the Warrior stage and stay there. Movement occurs, if at all, during the mid-life crisis, when a man is forced into confronting identity issues. Often the result is a more compelling concern with issues of intimacy, care, and commitment than he has known before. His typical progression looks something like this:

Orphan   Warrior   Wanderer   Martyr   Magician

The traditional female, on the other hand, moves from the Orphan into the Martyr stage, where she may stay the rest of her life, unless something propels her to grow. Sometimes when the children leave, the husband strays, her self-esteem sinks, or she encounters liberated ideas, the resulting identity crisis forces her to ask herself who she is, after which she learns to be more assertive. Here is her pattern:

| Orphan | Martyr | Wanderer | Warrior | Magician |

A career woman who strives to be independent early in life may work on war-rioring and martyring simultaneously, being tough at the office and all-giving at home. Many men also organize their lives this way as well. Whether male or female, the pattern reduces to this:

```
        ┌─► Martyr ─┐
Orphan ─┤           ▼─► Wanderer ──────────────────────────► Magician
        └─► Warrior ─┘
```

In this case, identity issues are forced when the split seems untenable and the conflicting values of the Martyr and the Warrior find enough integration that we feel whole again.

It is important to recognize that men and women, however, do not always and inevitably experience these stages in different orders. Individual differences are great. Moreover, there is a variation on the pattern described here by personality type. In Jung's type theory, some people are governed by their analytical, thinking process, and others by their empathic, feeling modes. Feeling types have a greater affinity with the Martyr archetype and thinking types with the Warrior mode. What we like we often develop first, waiting to explore our less preferred attributes at a later time. Therefore, both women with a preference for thinking and men with a preference for feeling are likely to work on martyring and warrioring simultaneously because one urge is reinforced by sex role conditioning and the other by their personality type.[4]

But some generalizations about gender seem to hold up. At this particular time, most men's values are very much defined by the Warrior ethic. The way of contemporary women, however, is split. Most women either are Martyrs or they have moved quickly through the Wanderer and Warrior stages and are beginning to experiment with being Magicians. Depending on which group of women you notice, you can argue that the Martyr archetype is distinctly female in contrast to the Warrior mode, which is distinctly male, *or* that the Magician mode is the new emerging female system in contrast to the old patriarchal Warrior way of being in the world. The first position has been adopted by conservatives and the second by many feminists. Neither is wrong, but neither gives us the whole story, either.

In the cultural mind, feminists generally are associated with the archetype of the Amazon, but truly liberated women seem to have a particular affinity for the Magician's way of operating and are leading the way into exploring the archetype that presides over the current transformation of human consciousness—a transformation as important as when men led the way in exploring the possibilities for positive (yang) action and aggressiveness as a means to improve the world. The discovery that the Magician's wand and staff are appropriate tools for today's world is a profoundly hopeful one for both men and women, promising a restoration of peace and loving energy between them and between humankind and the earth.

A NEW HEROIC PARADIGM

The Warrior's life, with its focus on power over other people and the earth, is lonely and ultimately tragic. We may complete our journeys, be rewarded by being made king or queen, but we all know that the story goes on. We will, we know, lose power, be replaced by the new hero, and die. And our last moments on this earth will be marked by the least control over ourselves, other people, the future, and even our bodily functions of any time in life—except perhaps birth. And it is the end of the story that traditionally determines whether the plot is comic or tragic. No wonder modern literature and philosophy are so despairing!

But what if we simply shift our expectations a bit? What if the goal of life is not to prevail, but simply to learn? Then the end of the story can seem very different; and so can what happens in between birth and death. Heroism is redefined as not only *moving* mountains but *knowing* mountains: being fully oneself and seeing, without denial, what is, and being open to learning the lessons life offers us.

Box-Car Bertha's autobiography, *Sister of the Road,* ends with Bertha looking back over a life that has included abandonment by her mother at a very young age; a dehumanizing stint as a prostitute (culminating in a case of syphilis); and the experience of looking on helplessly when one lover was hanged and another run over by a train. She declares: "Everything I had ever struggled to learn I found I had already survived. . . . I had achieved my purpose—everything I had set out in life to do, I had accomplished. I had wanted to know how it felt to be a hobo, a radical, a prostitute, a thief, a reformer, a social worker and a revolutionist. Now I knew. I shuddered. Yes, it was all worthwhile to me. There were no tragedies in my life. Yes, my prayers had been answered."[5] Bertha sees herself as neither a suffering Martyr nor a Warrior, but as a Magician who received everything she asked for. She both takes responsibility for her choices and is thankful for the gift of her life.

Similarly, Annie Dillard in *Pilgrim at Tinker Creek* surmises that life "is often cruel, but always beautiful . . . the least we can do is try to be there," to be fully in life. She imagines that "the dying pray at the last not 'please,' but 'thank you' as a guest thanks his host at the door. . . . The universe," she explains, "was not made in jest but in solemn, incomprehensible earnest. By a power that is unfathomably secret, and holy, and fleet. There is nothing to be done about it, but ignore it, or see."[6]

Magicians view life as a gift. Our job here is to give our own gift and to engage fully with life and other people, letting in and receiving some gifts and, of course, taking responsibility to decline others. Tragedy, in this view, is a loss of the knowledge of who you are, with the result that you do not contribute what you are here to do.

For example, Gertie, in Harriette Arnow's *The Dollmaker,*[7] is a six-foot-tall hillbilly who is extremely wise, but she habitually discounts her wisdom. Because she does so, she slowly loses almost everything she loves: She loses the Tipton Place (a farm she had planned to buy) because she listens to her mother, who says a woman's duty is to be with her husband, and forgoes the farm to join her husband in Detroit; she loses her favorite daughter because she listens to a neighbor who tells her she must not let Cassie play with the doll that is her imaginary friend (Cassie sneaks off to play with the doll and is run over by a train); she does not take her vocation as a sculptor seriously, calling it "whittlin' foolishness," and her ultimate act of self-disrespect is chopping up a block of fine cherry wood, out of which she has been carving a "laughing Christ," to make cheap figurines and crucifixes. The "laughing Christ" is a visual image of her life-affirming philosophy in contrast to the deathly Puritanism she had been taught by her mother. To chop up that block of wood is equivalent to killing or maiming herself. Lest we miss this, earlier in the novel Cassie enjoins her to finish the statue and "let *her* out." "Her," of course, is Gertie.

The moment in which she chops up the cherry block is genuinely tragic, because in doing so she has denied herself and her own vision, yet even then it is not without hope. We all have moments of cowardice, when we deny our wisdom, our integrity, and our divinity. Although the novel ends here, we do find that Gertie's self-destructive act has forced her into a new level of understanding. Her excuse to chop up the cherry block when her family needed money was that she could not find the right face for Christ. At the novel's close, she says, "They's millions an millions a faces plenty fine enough . . . some a my neighbors down there in th alley—they would ha done."

From the vantage point of the Martyr, Gertie may have been seen as admirable, because she does almost nothing except sacrifice for her husband and children or to please her mother. What makes this novel different from conventional stories about women is that Arnow portrays her sacrifices as unnecessary and destructive. However, even though Gertie often does not claim either her own wisdom or the power to change her life, Arnow does not cast her as an antihero, either. Gertie is still a hero. While it is clear in the novel how many forces—external and internal—acted on her to reinforce her inability to trust herself, she is not portrayed as a helpless victim but as someone with responsibility for the choices she has made. Her life is tragic because she cannot act more fully on her heroism. This is, of course, similar to Shakespeare's portrayal of Hamlet or Lear. A major difference is that Gertie does not die in the end, so we have a sense of life as a process that continues.

From the Warrior's perspective, Gertie's story is tragic. But what of the Magician? What if we assumed, as Shirley Luthman does in *Energy and Personal Power,* that our beings attract to us the things we need, that we all are working out exactly what we need to learn in this life for our growth and development?[8] From this point of view, we would posit that Gertie propelled herself into situations from which she could learn to trust herself. In doing so, she had first to learn—with all the attendant pain—what happens when she does not do so.

The point is not for her to prove her heroism, as it is for the Warrior, but to claim it. The idea of proving heroism is tied up in the notion that it is a scarce commodity and that there is a hierarchy of people. When we come to understand that the real task is not to work hard to prove ourselves but to allow ourselves to be who we are, things seem very different. Throughout the novel, Gertie always is trying hard to *do* the right thing or sometimes just to learn what the right thing is. She comes to understand at the end that had she simply allowed herself to be herself and to go for what she honestly wanted, her dreams could have come true. Most likely she would have been the owner of the Tipton Place, surrounded by her family, completing her sculpture. She realizes in retrospect that she even had plenty of support for staying on that farm, but in her self-distrust she listened to those voices that undercut her. Even her husband explains that he would have supported her had she only trusted him enough to tell him what she was doing.

In the initial stages the Martyr assumes that suffering is simply what is. It must be endured by someone, so the Martyr suffers either so that others might be happier or to purchase happiness for another time. The Warrior discovers that with courage and hard work people can take a stand and can make changes—for themselves and for others. The Magician learns that neither suffering nor struggle is the ground of life. Joy is also our birthright. We can attract joy as easily as we attract pain, and we need neither martyr ourselves nor struggle unduly to make abundant life for ourselves or those we love.

It is this new mode—embodied in the journey of the Magician—that is the cutting edge of consciousness in contemporary culture, and it is the awareness that the Magician's archetype is now an appropriate, available, and powerful model for ordinary human life that motivates me to write this book. I also write it out of a need to honor the Martyr, the Wanderer, and the Warrior. We learn key lessons from each—lessons we never outgrow.

GROWTH AS SPIRAL TOWARD WHOLENESS

These heroic modes are developmental, but they actually are not experienced in linear, ever-advancing steps. I would illustrate the typical hero's progression as a cone or three-dimensional spiral, in which it is possible to move forward while frequently circling back. Each stage has its own lesson to teach us, and we reencounter situations that throw us back into prior stages so that we may learn and relearn the lessons at new levels of intellectual and emotional complexity and subtlety. In our first tries at warrioring, for example, we may come on like Attila the Hun, but later we may learn to assert our own wishes so appropriately and gently that we are able to negotiate for what we want without any noticeable conflict. And it is not so much that the spiral gets higher, but that it gets wider as we are capable of a larger range of responses to life and, hence, able to have more life. We take in more and have more choices.

The chart on page 406 summarizes the stages within each archetype. The first time around the wheel, many people move through the center circle twice until they can move out by mastering the second and third levels of learning. While this schematic is helpful conceptually, human development is rarely that neat and tidy. The point is, however, that the archetypes are interrelated, and often one cannot resolve the psychological or cognitive dilemma embedded in one without working through another. Warrior and Martyr are two sides of a dualistic formulation about life in which you either take or you give. *Until you can do both, you can do neither freely.* Therefore, we go to school with each archetype many times in our lives. Further, events in our lives influence the order and intensity of our learning. Any massive change or crisis requires a reconsideration of identity issues. Any new

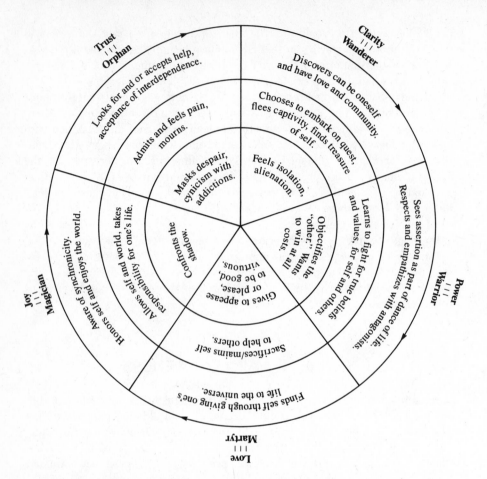

commitment raises questions about sacrifice. Each time we encounter the same archetype, we have the opportunity to do so at a deeper level of understanding.

The virtues that the hero learns in each guise are never lost or outgrown. They just become more subtle. As Innocent, the hero learns to trust; as Orphan, to mourn. As Wanderer, the hero learns to find and name one's own truth; as Warrior, to assert that truth so that it affects and changes the world; and as Martyr, to love, to commit, and to let go.

These virtues all involve some degree of pain or struggle. The virtue the Magician adds to these is the ability to recognize and receive the abundance of the universe. As the circle widens, the Magician gains what the Orphan longed for, the return to the lost Eden, first on the microcosmic, personal level, and later on the most cosmic level; but instead of experiencing plenty from a childlike, dependent position, the Magician enters the garden on the basis of interdependence—with other people, with nature, and with God. The last lesson the hero learns, then, is happiness.

We carry with us the lesson of each stage into the next, and when we do so, its meaning is transformed, but the lesson itself is not lost or outgrown. For example, at the first level of martyrdom, heroes sacrifice to propitiate the gods or some authority figure. Later, they do so simply to help other people. In becoming a Warrior, the hero transforms sacrifice into discipline: Some things are sacrificed so that other things can be achieved. As Magicians, heroes understand that nothing essential ever is lost: Sacrifice becomes the organic and gentle letting go of the old to make way for new growth, new life.

To people who move into a stage when it is appropriate for them, the myth brings life. When those who are at an earlier stage of development jump prematurely into a role, the same archetype makes for deadness, for it is not where their true growth lies. Men or women who are developmentally ready to move out of the Warrior stage, for example, may not be able to do so because they do not know there is anything else. They will feel deadened, claustrophobic, trapped, just as women who have been trapped in the Martyr role may get stuck because they have been told that the archetypes of the Wanderer and the Warrior are roles reserved only for men. Many women have expressed their excitement about *The Female Hero in American and British Literature* because the book reclaimed heroism— especially the Wanderer's and the Warrior's journeys—as an appropriate aspiration for women, and thus helped them move along on their journeys. I now hope that by reclaiming what is valuable in the Martyr archetype and by describing the archetype of the Magician I can help make the journey easier and less painful for both women and men.

I also believe that we all have access to every mode all the time. What "stage" we are in has to do with where we "hang out" the most, where we spend the greatest percentage of our time. The most oppressed victim will have moments of transcendence. And none of us gets so advanced that we stop feeling, every once in awhile, like a motherless child. In fact, each stage has a gift for us, something critical to teach us about being human.

SUGGESTIONS TO THE READER

Because I have indicated that there is a kind of predictable order in which people address certain developmental tasks, I hasten to emphasize again that *we do not leave one behind in a linear fashion and go on to another.* The deeper levels of understanding and performance associated with any of the archetypes are dependent upon also deepening our investment in the others. We continually are sharpening and refining skills in each category, for this journey is truly a matter of high-level skill development. Ultimately, we gain a repertoire of possible responses to life, so we have incrementally more choices about how we will respond in any given situation.

Actually, encountering these archetypes is a bit like redecorating a house. We begin by moving into a house furnished in part by attitudes, beliefs, and habits passed on to us by our families and by our culture. Some people never make the house their own and so do not develop a distinct identity or style. Those who do take their journeys and (to continue the metaphor) furnish their own houses do so at different paces and in different orders.

Some people do one room at a time, finish that, and go on to the next. Others may do a bit in each room, paint the whole house, then put up all the drapes, etc. Some people hurry and finish quickly and others are more leisurely in their work. Of course, this psychological house is a bit different from most homes because there are some rooms that cannot quite be finished until you have worked a bit on the adjacent one(s). While people do explore their learning tasks in many different orders, the archetypes are related and interdependent. Ultimately, we do not finish any of them completely until we finish them all. Like a house, moreover, the task is never quite done. Inevitably, whenever you think you have completed decorating it, you notice that the couch you bought first is worn or the wallpaper is torn, and there you go again!

Most people, then, work on all the learning tasks all their lives. But, like interior decorating, it is easier to work on, say, the Martyr room when you already have put some sustained effort into it over time and have made it yours. You begin to get the hang of it. So, too, when you learn the lessons offered by each archetype, you can "do" that archetype elegantly. Whether you are in Martyr, Wanderer, Warrior, etc., your reactions will be graceful and appropriate to the situation. If you have learned discretion, the responses you choose will fit who you are in the moment and the situation at hand. You will know you are on target because you feel centered and clear. When you feel awful and off-center, it is appropriate to take some time to focus on what response would have been more authentic or might have acknowledged more fully the other's realities as well as your own.

You might find that the theories in this book can help you get moving when you are feeling stuck. For instance, it sometimes is useful to remember that when you feel powerless and Orphan-like, it is time to look for help. When you feel alienated and cut off from people, you probably are dealing with wandering issues. Instead of worrying about how to be more intimate, attend to your identity issues. When you work them out so that you can be more fully authentic, relationships often fall into place. Similarly, if you feel martyred and can see that you are giving and giving, hoping to make a situation turn out right, then *let go* of your image of what "right" means and pay attention to taking your journey.

If you feel compulsive about remaking the world or getting another person to agree with you, the issue is always fear that if your environment does not change, you cannot be or have what you want. Your survival feels threatened, but the issue is not getting others to change, it is your own courage. This is the time to take a leap of faith, act authentically *now*, and contribute your own truth to the world without insisting that others agree with you. When you do that, change almost always happens (although you cannot control the outcome of that change).

Trusting yourself and your own process means believing that your task is to be fully yourself and that if you are, you will have everything you genuinely need for your soul's growth. If you find you are too attached to a particular outcome, that you are trying to force it to happen the way you want it to, and that you are suffering with lack of success in doing so, this is the time to cultivate the Magician's faith in the universe, in mystery, in the capacity of the unknown to provide you with what you need. Recognize that what you want and what you need often are not the same and that it is quite rational to trust the universe, God, or your higher self and let go.

Using these theories requires an awareness that we are multidimensional creatures. Most people work with different archetypes in different arenas of their life. For example, some are highly influenced by the Magician's consciousness when they think about spiritual issues but not when they think about their health. Exploring possibilities inherent in each archetype in different parts of your life may be a way of broadening your skills, or it may be stultifying. You may find that you are just stuck in roles that are defined by the context, and your responses do not, or no longer, reflect your true feelings.

You may fear that people will be thrown off if, say, you experiment with some of your Warrior skills at home or your Martyr ways of proceeding at work. Or you might fear a loss of power as you put aside highly developed skills to try out ones you may be awkward and unsure with at first. Yet you might find it interesting, challenging, and even fun to vary your repertoire and experiment with new approaches to old situations. Being assertive in your private life is different in style and in substance from what it is in public life, for instance. You learn new aspects of each archetype according to the context you are in.

Also note that the more primitive versions of any of the stages are jarring to people, simply because they are blunt, not yet refined. Remember that in their more refined and subtle forms none of the approaches are difficult for most other people to deal with. If people do have difficulty, it may be that they are just disoriented by change of any kind. Or, as you change and grow, a few people may always drift away, but your compensation is that gradually you will attract to you people who have mastered more of the skills you have and hence there can be more appreciation and reciprocity between you.

The chart that follows summarizes the various ways of approaching life characteristic of the most typical worldview associated with each archetype. Notice how in any month—or week—you may have all the responses listed. It is useful in thinking about these archetypes to recognize that we all really know about all of them. When I am feeling like an Orphan, I want the world to be handed to me on a silver platter, and I am annoyed that it is not. When I feel like a Wanderer, I really distrust association and need to do things alone.

After reading the book, use the following chart and take the test in the Appendix [in the original, Eds.] to refresh your memory. You will see which approach you take most often and therefore get some indication about what your primary lessons are at this point in your life. Being conscious of where you are can help you move on, if you wish to. For instance, if you feel rather practiced in a certain approach to life, try moving on to another level and try out some new responses to see how they feel. Note that the chart gives the more typical characteristics of each archetype rather than its most highly developed aspect. However, the most advanced stages of all the modalities, taken together, give a prescription for good mental health.

We are all so practiced in thinking linearly (and this chart is so linear) that I hasten to remind you that it is not necessarily better to be a Magician than an Orphan. Both the Magician and the Warrior run the risk of pride when, as a result of their real increase in power and self-confidence, they forget how dependent we all ultimately are on each other and the earth for our very survival. Not too long ago, I was feeling particularly proud of my (Warrior) achievements and competence; but I found myself waking up one morning, asking, "Why me?" when a series of challenges, inconveniences, and catastrophes hit me all at once. I experienced all the classic Orphan responses: victimization, the wish to be rescued, self-blame, and the urge to scapegoat others. Ultimately, however, the gift was the reminder of my real vulnerability and interdependence, as I was forced to ask my friends, family, and colleagues for help. Having a tendency toward too much self-reliance, I needed the reminder through their loving help that I was not alone.

The point is to be more complete, whole, and to have a wider repertoire of choices—not to be higher up a developmental ladder. (Imagine tearing out the chart and pasting the top and bottom together to make a circle.) Indeed, the Innocent is simply a Magician who has not yet encountered the other archetypes and learned their lessons. If you decide that being a Magician is better than being a Warrior or a Martyr and you try to limit your ways of responding to the world to those of this one archetype, you will be as one-sided and incomplete as the Orphan who has not yet gained skill in any other modality.

We do not outgrow any lessons. A nice example of this is in politics. Each archetype has its own contribution to make. Orphans want to follow a great leader who will rescue them. Wanderers identify as outsiders and see little or no hope, especially in conventional politics. (That is why people seem so apolitical these days.) Many of the kinds of people who used to be engaged in politics are now responding to major cultural change by removing themselves and addressing identity and values issues that help make a new politics possible. Warriors get involved in conventional politics and causes and try to make change happen. Magicians are more likely to emphasize the creation of new alternative communities, institutions, and ways of relating to one another without trying to get people to change who are not ready to do so.

The point is that none of these responses by themselves are adequate and none are bad. There are times for recognizing that someone else knows more or is a better leader and following them. There are times for removing yourself from the action to be sure of your values. There are times for political engagement, and there are times to focus on what you can create right where you are.

However, we do not always feel so tolerant and appreciative. Sometimes when we first move into a stage, we are a bit dogmatic about it and see it as the only way to be. When we leave that position, we usually flip-flop and reject where we have been.

For people just moving out of the early-stage Martyr mode, any positive statement about the value of sacrifice is likely to seem masochistic. And, of course, the point is that they are right—for them. If we are just moving from Martyr into being a Wanderer, the temptation to stop the journey and give to others is an ever-present and real threat. It is like leaving a love affair. Few of us can just say to our partner that we are ready to move on and leave with a simple thank you for what has been. Instead, we spend a great deal of time chronicling the faults of our former lover and how bad the relationship was. Often we create high drama this way to divert ourselves from our fear of the unknown, or because we do not believe we have a right to leave anything unless it is positively awful.

We also may reject stages we are not ready to move into yet, the ones we have had little or no experience with. Instead, we may redefine them in terms we know, and thus completely misunderstand the point. That is all right, too, because at that point the truth that we do not understand is not yet relevant to us developmentally. For instance, to a person just confronting the fall from Eden, just learning some rudimentary sense of realism, the Magician's claim that the universe is safe will sound like the worst possible example of denial![9]

I recently shared these ideas with a class, and it became clear to me that many students wanted to skip to Magician without paying their dues to the other arche-types. I do not believe that can be done—or if it can be done, it cannot be sus-tained over time. We do have to pay our dues by spending some time in each stage. What I hope, in such cases, is that knowing where we likely are going will free us up somewhat from the fear that often paralyzes us as we confront our dragons.

There is a paradigm shift that occurs when people move from being Warriors to being Magicians: their perception of reality actually changes. They come to realize that seeing the world as a place full of danger, pain, and isolation is not how the world is, but only their perception of it during the formative parts of their journey. This new knowledge can be very freeing.

While most people are concentrating on the news reported in the media—news that focuses primarily on disasters, wars, and contests—something transfor-mative is happening in the culture that you do not see until you begin to change. Learning about this change is like learning a new word that you never knew before; suddenly, to your surprise, you hear it everywhere you go. Probably it was always there somewhere in your environment, but you did not notice it. When you learn a new way of being and relating in the world, all of a sudden you start meeting people like yourself, and pretty soon you are living in a new society, a new world, that operates on principles different from the old. The fact that you are reading this book suggests that it is time for you at least to know that world exists—if you are not living in it already.

People who must have power over others in order to feel safe themselves sometimes are threatened by others' moves into the Magician's domain, because Magicians cannot be controlled and manipulated very easily. "Power over" is de-pendent upon fear and a belief in scarcity—that there is not enough, so we all must compete for it. This fear keeps people docile, dependent, conformist, hoping to stay in the good graces of those in power, and/or jostling for power themselves. In the most affluent country in the world, people are motivated to work by their fear of poverty. Surrounded by others, people are motivated to buy this and that prod-uct in order to be loved. As Philip Slater explains in *The Pursuit of Loneliness,* in our society advertising augments the cultural belief in scarcity by creating artificial needs.[10] Instead of fearing poverty per se, people may fear that they will not be able to buy a fancy car or designer jeans.

People in power reinforce artificial scarcity because it sells products and keeps the work force compliant. The rest of us do not reject or dismiss the belief that resources and talent are scarce because we need to believe they are. We all need to go on our perilous journeys, and we must believe our fears are real. Unless we fear hunger, want, isolation, and despair, how will we ever learn to confront our fears? We are not ready for abundance, for a safe universe, until we have proven our-selves—to ourselves—by taking our journeys. It does not matter how many people love us, how much wealth we have at our disposal; we will attract problems and we will feel alone and poor as long as we need to. Have you ever known someone rich who, like Dickens's Scrooge, lived in terror of losing money, and as a result became a veritable slave to making and hoarding it? Similarly, no matter how much we are loved, until we are ready to let it in, we will feel lonely.

Ultimately, there is no way to avoid the hero's quest. It comes and finds us if we do not move out bravely to meet it. And while we may strive to avoid the pain, hardship, and struggle it inevitably brings, life takes us eventually to the promised land, where we can be genuinely prosperous, loving, and happy. The only way out is through.

NOTES

1. Joseph Campbell, *The Hero with a Thousand Faces* (New York: World Publishing Co., 1970), p. 136.
2. Carol S. Pearson and Katherine Pope, eds., *Who Am I This Time? Female Portraits in American and British Literature* (New York: McGraw-Hill Book Co., 1976) and Pearson and Pope, *The Female Hero in American and British Literature* (New York: R. R. Bowker and Co., 1981).
3. Carol Gilligan, *In a Different Voice: Psychological Theory and Women's Development* (Cambridge, Mass.: Harvard University Press, 1982), passim.
4. See Isabel Briggs Myers, *Gifts Differing* (Palo Alto, Calif.: Consulting Psychologists Press, 1980) for a full discussion of differences by type.
5. Box-Car Bertha, *Sister of the Road: The Autobiography of Box-Car Bertha,* as told to Dr. Ben L. Reitman (New York: Harper & Row, 1937), p. 280.
6. Annie Dillard, *Pilgrim at Tinker Creek* (New York: Bantam Books, 1975), p. 278.
7. Harriette Arnow, *The Dollmaker* (New York: Avon Books, 1972).
8. Shirley Gehrke Luthman, *Energy and Personal Power* (San Rafael, Calif.: Mehetabel and Co., 1982), pp. 56–69.
9. See Anne Wilson Schaef, *Women's Reality: An Emerging Female System in the White Male Society* (Minneapolis, Minn.: Winston Press, 1981), pp. 146–160, for a complete discussion of the concept of "levels of truth."
10. Philip Slater, *The Pursuit of Loneliness: American Culture and the Breaking Point* (New York: Beacon Press, 1976), pp. 105–123.

Annmarie Feci—Page Operator

Ina Yalef

She has worked in the phone room for twelve years. It's a small room, adequate for five operators, located on the fourth floor of the service building. "They've given us the name 'Telecommunications.' Real fancy. To us, though, it's still the Phone Room."

The main number of this hospital is 305–2500. That's what people calling Presbyterian Hospital dial to reach us. During the day there are six girls here at one time. Three or four girls on the switchboard, plus one girl on page and one girl on patient information. On evenings and nights we have less.

They all do different things. The patient information girl tells the caller if a person is here, what room he's in, and the status of the patient. We're very careful about what information we give out, though. You'll get lots and lots of nosy neighbors who call and ask, "Can you tell me what the patient died of? Did he have AIDS? Did he have this? Did he have that?" They want to know things which are not anybody's business except the patient's immediate family. You have to be careful what you say and who you're saying it to because you really never know who's on the other end. And at all times you have to hold your patience, which often is not easy to do, sitting there all day, listening to some of these people.

I don't get ruffled easily . . . my personality runs basically the same all the time. To really get me riled somebody on the other end has to be so obnoxious that I can't deal with them. People get really annoyed when it takes too long to get through to the hospital. I understand that. Say a call comes in to 2500, the main number, and the caller asks to be connected to a patient named Smith. We transfer her to patient information to get Mr. Smith's room number. Those girls have a rack of index cards with patients' room numbers on them. Well, if they haven't gotten the information from admitting yet, they don't know where the patient is. So we have to transfer the call to admitting. So the caller has now waited to get through to 2500, they've gotten transferred to 3101—patient information—now we're connecting them down to 2536—admitting. In the interim they've gotten disconnected so you'll get them back on 2500 and now they're *really* riled. But we're doing our best. Really we are.

"Annmarie Feci—Page Operator" by Ina Yalef from *Life and Death, Story of a Hospital*, 1988, pp. 187–190. Reprinted by permission of the publisher.

Sometimes we get calls from non–English-speaking people. You try and understand their broken English, if they even *speak* English. If the caller is speaking a language other than English or Spanish, we'll connect the call to Patient Relations. If they think it's something that's really important, they get an interpreter to come to the phone and try and speak to the person. Patient Relations is able to find people who speak languages I never heard of. I guess maybe when you come in to be interviewed for a job they ask if you speak a second language. That way they're able to keep track of people who speak various languages. If someone calls and asks for a person who we know has died, we tell them to get in contact with the family. If they get too upset or say they don't know the family—we connect them to our AOD [administrator on duty].

There are times when every one of our console positions is covered, and people are still waiting to get through to the hospital. We probably spend twenty seconds on an average call, assuming of course that it's not an old lady whose hearing aid isn't working, or somebody who doesn't speak English. Those are some of the things that hold you up. But barring unforeseen circumstances, we can easily handle three or four calls a minute. Then you have to figure if there are four girls sitting on four consoles, you've answered maybe twelve calls in a minute, at least, and that's not saying how many people are waiting during that time also to get in.

People say, "Telephone operator, eh? What an easy job." But it's a lot of work. Patient information girls have all those cards to file. They have all the ICUs to check to see how patients are. In the morning they have to get admissions from the emergency room from the night before. They write up all those cards from all those midnight people that have come in and file them, plus they're answering the calls that they're getting in on 3101, Patient Information.

The paging girl does the overhead paging that's heard throughout the hospital. Most of the doctors are on beepers now, though. They have a computerized system where you dial a number in the hospital and a computerized woman's voice speaks to you—everybody calls her "Patti Page"—but there are still reasons to use the overhead, like arrest calls and calls to staff without beepers.

A lot of things can happen just sitting up here in the service building. But I think the most devastating experience I ever had was the night that John Wood died. What happened was, we got a call from EMS that they were bringing in a gunshot. If it's a gunshot or a stabbing, EMS usually calls from the road—and you connect them to the emergency room. The next thing we get a call from the nurse in the ER to put Dr. John Wood on page. See, he was the resident on call that night in the ER, and he was on arrest duty too, so he was carrying the arrest beeper. But he wanted to go home to see his wife, who wasn't feeling well. So before he left, he gave the beeper to another doctor. We didn't know that at the time, though. So there we are paging "Dr. John Wood. Dr. John Wood." No answer. Next thing, maybe a minute later, the ER nurse calls back again and she says to us, "My God, my God," she says, "John Wood is the *patient!*"

We were all crying. He was special to everyone who knew him. To me, he was the pediatrician who took care of my kids and now all of a sudden you're paging an arrest for somebody only to find out that it's somebody who's probably the nicest person that God ever put on the face of the earth. I mean, he was an absolute sweetheart.

When you're on Patient Information, you begin to get familiar with names of people who come in for lots of admissions. Just the names. You have the patient information index so you're filing the cards and you say, "Oh, my God, that poor child, he's back in again." A lot of times you really don't know what's wrong with the child but you see that ticket and you know that child is in. Then all of a sudden you get notified of an expiration and it's him. And your heart drops; you never met the child, didn't know his mother or father, but yet you feel just as bad. Probably because it was a kid. Or even sometimes adults who come in that we know are oncology patients because they're on Harkness One. You never met the person but you say, "Oh, my God, So-and-so, they died." It's like one of the family passed away. You never met them but you feel awful about it.

I was raised on 169th Street. My mother worked in Presbyterian for thirty years. She retired in 1980. She worked in accounting. I feel like I have been raised in this place. When I graduated from high school I couldn't wait to work at Presbyterian. It was taken for granted; if you lived in the neighborhood, you had to work at Presbyterian. You weren't one of the "in" crowd if you didn't work here. But I put nine thousand applications in and never, never got hired. I was downstairs in personnel every time they turned around, trying to get a job. Nothing. Finally I came in one day and the fella down in personnel said, "Listen, I've got a job in the phone room." We weren't called telecommunications then. I said, "I can answer phones. That I can do."

In thirteen years, I've really seen this place grow. I've seen Babies' add the addition on and Eye add its addition and Atchley Pavilion go up. I watched them tear Maxwell Hall down. I watched them tear down Harkness Hall. My bridal shower was in Harkness Hall. Yes, that was a nice place. It was a shame that they tore it down. But that's what modernization is. You've got to keep moving.

Telecommunications is the main access point of this hospital. We're the central unit. When people call up for conditions on patients, that comes through us. When doctors need to be paged, that comes through us. When they need to put an arrest on, that's through us. When there's a fire, we put the fire brigade on. Those beepers are through us also. So we're touching kind of all bases: medical, maintenance . . . you name it.

Think about it. We're saving lives! You figure EMS calls us, they need to get the ER to let Alice know that they've got a gunshot coming in. If somebody is calling Dr. Rose because they have a heart in another state, we get the call. We give it to Dr. Rose. He gets the heart. But it came through us first. So, we're it! We're really where it starts from. The central unit that makes this place go. I'm telling you. People might not think of us that way, but it's true. We're the heart of this hospital.

Successful Derailment: What Fast-Trackers Can Learn While They're Off the Track

Barbara E. Kovach

Executives who get derailed from the fast track typically view themselves as failures. But the author suggests that a career slowdown or derailment can provide an opportunity for personal growth and development.

While speaking to a group of corporate executives recently, I was challenged about the cooperative attitude manifested by the senior executives who took part in my initial study, *Survival on the Fast Track* (Dodd, Mead, 1988), which considered corporate fast-trackers on the way to the top in major U.S. corporations. Two assumptions underlay the challenge: (1) that one has to move upward, and (2) that one has to compete against one's peers in order to move to the senior level. The second assumption could be put aside more easily than the first: There are other studies demonstrating that cooperation—not competition—is the key to moving up to the executive ranks.

The first assumption, however, is embedded in the American culture, and because this assumption had not been examined, it had shaped the context of the previous study. The implication of the study was, in fact, that upward mobility is a good thing and that derailment is something to be avoided if at all possible. If derailment proved inevitable, went the logic, certain approaches could turn this state of affairs into a plus, putting the individual once again on the road to the top. It is time to examine this assumption—and several related ones—and to use the resulting conclusions to form the context in which to examine the follow-up stories of fast-trackers two years after the completion of the initial study.

Reprinted by permission of the publisher, from *Organizational Dynamics*, Autumn 1989. © 1989. American Management Association, New York. All rights reserved.

SPECIFIC ASSUMPTIONS ABOUT UPWARD MOBILITY

There appear to be several secondary, underlying assumptions that taken together add up to the first main assumption, i.e., that moving upward is good. Even though there is no real evidence that these secondary assumptions are true, they underlie casual conversations among many talented people and are subjects of humor and satire in many popular works. If we were to work backward from the general assumption about upward mobility, we might find that the following secondary assumptions make up the general one:

(1) Everyone is suited for the next-level position.
(2) The odds of moving up continuously are sufficient to justify keeping upward mobility as a primary career goal.
(3) Individuals have enough control of the situation that going after the next job may have a significant impact on whether or not they get that job.
(4) When they arrive at that job, they will experience a sense of accomplishment and satisfaction that justifies the struggle to attain it.

Let us examine each underlying assumption in turn. First, the idea that one should always seek the next-level position (and this idea's attendant assumption that the seeker can handle the job and wants to do it) is at the heart of the accepted American tradition that guides those who are on a high-achievement track. But does this idea stand up under further analysis?

Many experts, for example, have agreed with the Peter Principle, which says that people are promoted to their level of incompetence. In many cases, however, incompetence is not the issue. Instead, people are often promoted until they don't "fit" with the system at a particular level, and then ways are found to remove them. In fact, there is no reason to believe that, just because someone likes one job, he or she will necessarily like the next, higher job as much; for not everyone is suited for a higher job. But the American corporate belief system has not taken this into account.

Second, in any hierarchical, pyramidal organization, the number of jobs decreases sharply on the way up the pyramid. Thus not everyone can move up. In fact, most people can't move up. The odds are that any given individual will not make it all the way to the top. Let's look at those odds. In a given company there are 30,000 employees. Let us assume that 15%, or 4,500, are managers. In the career lifetime of any of these employees there are likely to be about 4.5 chairmen of the board. Thus the odds are a thousand to one that any given manager who enters the company will eventually become its chairman. Would we take bets on those odds? Would we put money on a horse running at a thousand to one against the odds? Not likely. Given their assumptions about the general importance of upward mobility, this means that in a career history of about 45 years, 4,445.5 people are going to view themselves as losers. Some will feel that they lost at lower levels and some at higher levels, but if they accept the American mythology about moving ahead, they will all see themselves as losers.

Third, the degree of control that individuals exercise over whether they will be promoted diminishes markedly after they have climbed the first few rungs of any organizational ladder. For example, a very senior chairman was discussing the possibility that either of two senior statesmen (see below) in his previous company might, in fact, become chairman. He remarked, "It's unlikely, because they are both the wrong age; the appointment of someone either five years younger or older is much more likely." The judgment of this chairman was realistic: He foresaw that the company (the board, in fact) would choose someone already accomplished enough to carry out the scenario formed by the board and then retire without further ado; or else the board would select someone less senior who could be groomed for the position and then hold it for at least a decade. The two people being discussed at the time fell in between these two categories. They were likely to lose in the final round only because they were *the wrong age* for the company's needs. And their age was clearly not a factor under their control.

Yet such characteristics as age greatly affect one's possibilities of promotion. The higher one goes in the organization, the more one's chances of promotion depend on a variety of factors other than one's abilities and achievements—including the state of the economy as it affects the organization. Most of these factors are not within the purview of individual control.

Moreover, individuals on the promotion ladder do not operate in a vacuum; they are part of a network made up of many members, each of whose perceptions and actions affect the final outcome of any situation. Events throughout this network affect the "promotability" of a given person at a given time, and this too is not under an individual's control.

Fourth, the expectation that one will experience profound satisfaction by reaching higher and higher levels in the company is probably not justified, for two reasons. First, there is no final resting place—not even the virtually unattainable chairmanship—at which one can say, "I have arrived." Instead, with each promotion, individuals adopt a new frame of reference suitable to that level. The new position may have appeared to be at the top of the heap when it was viewed from below. But when the individual reaches that level, it may appear unsatisfactorily low when compared with the position above it—and the one above that.

For example, one of the fast-trackers in the original study has just been promoted to the president's chair in his company. This move, in most frames of reference, would appear to put him on the top of the heap—or so close that any further moves would appear inconsequential. However, this man must share this chair with another man and report, along with his counterpart, to the chairman of the company. When this move was announced, a Wall Street observer casually commented that this president-to-be "must not be pleased to be in this one-down position." Given this new frame of reference, even a newly promoted chairman might perceive him- or herself as being beneath those who are chairmen of bigger companies. Almost inevitably, people find themselves close to the bottom in whatever is their current frame of reference both in the perception of others and, more important, in their own.

Moreover, moving up the ladder increases the visibility of the individual and the likelihood of both praise and severe criticism from a vastly increased sector of the world at large. If all goes well, the company and its chairman may profit from the increased attention and publicity, as in the case of Jim Burke of Johnson & Johnson during the Tylenol crisis of 1984. Burke showed great tact and responsibility, and he and the company alike emerged from the crisis with the respect and admiration of the public. However, the affection of the press and the public for a given leader may change dramatically during a short period of time, as in the case of Roger Smith of General Motors. Smith was widely praised for his financial astuteness during the 1984–1985 years, during which he acquired new companies and poured money into technology for the large auto company. But when profits turned down and Ford soared ahead of GM, Smith and his company received a severe press-bashing that may just now be coming to an end. Smith may have enjoyed the challenge of heading up a major corporation, and he may even have experienced a thrill at being a public figure. However, one wonders just how satisfying it was for him to be perceived by the public as a bumbling or even a malevolent leader.

Abiding by the assumption that success entails moving up the career ladder virtually guarantees winding up a loser at one time or another. Perhaps what matters most in one's career history is how one deals with the necessary fact of *not* moving into a higher position—an experience which, according to our commonly held beliefs and traditional script, is defined as losing at whatever level upward progress comes to a halt.

We might say, in fact, that all of the fast-trackers written about in the earlier study are probably headed down the road to derailment. The question is not whether they will be derailed, but when—and how—they will cope with their derailment. Will they accept it easily, or will they react with anger, bitterness, or world-weary resignation? Will they allow the experience of being stopped on the "ladder to success" to stop them in other areas of their lives as well? Or will derailment provide the incentive to become more fully involved in their families, their communities, or their present jobs? Will it spur them to engage in another business venture?

Many fast-trackers are asking these questions of themselves as they move along on what they hope will be the track to the top. Perhaps it's time to examine these assumptions about upward mobility and to write a new script which emphasizes the importance of doing work that is challenging, the value of accepting responsibility for others and for the stability of our institutions, and the satisfaction that comes from working wholeheartedly in the environment in which we find ourselves—and which puts less stress on how fast we are moving toward the top.

THE FAST-TRACKERS: 1986

A bit of background about my study of fast-trackers: From April to July of 1986, I interviewed 17 people in five major corporations who were perceived by their peers and direct reports to be "doing better" than others at the same rank. These 17 fast-trackers—15 men and two women—held positions at various levels of their companies; their ages ranged from 30 to 52 in 1986. Their points of view about success were clearly delineated by age; these delineations allowed me to develop a hypothesis about three career stages that many fast-trackers pass through.

Junior Stars

The youngest fast-trackers were in their early 30s, and all their answers to my questions were alike in important ways: They were universally enthusiastic, convinced that they were the best, and eager to know how far and how fast they would move up.

Mid-Careerists

Those fast-trackers who were only a few years senior to the junior stars—within five years of age 40—spoke differently about their work. Their enthusiasm was less constant and more tempered. They rarely described themselves as the best, and they were more reflective than their juniors were about a broad reach of personal and professional issues in their lives. In many cases, their recent experience had taught them that asking how far and how fast would not lead to any satisfactory answers. This group of mid-careerists was passing through what I call the "executive transition."

Senior Statesmen

Finally, those fast-trackers who were older than 45 spoke differently yet about their work. These people displayed neither the continuous enthusiasm of the junior stars nor the reflective wonderings of the mid-careerists. These senior statesmen spoke of the bad and the good in the same breath, saw their career as less important than the organization's performance, and were concerned with their future status primarily in terms of finding a place that offered the same degree of challenge and intensity to which they had grown accustomed.

Of the 17 subjects, five were termed senior statesmen, eight were mid-careerists, and four were junior stars.

Characteristics of All Fast-Trackers

Regardless of personal style and family/career history, all the fast-trackers shared certain characteristics. In general, they *loved* their work; put in long hours; had good relationships with people at work and with their families; demonstrated an almost startling degree of clarity about themselves, their strengths, and their weaknesses; and believed in helping and being helped by others. It was clear from the interviews and follow-up talks with these 17 people that doing well at work was, for them, a result of throwing themselves into their work without reserve.

Derailment Among the Fast-Trackers

In the initial study, two fast-trackers discussed having been derailed during the executive transition. Fast-tracker Hank was not given an official change of status. Nonetheless, he was removed from his current position, was not given the expected promotion, and was given a position with virtually no responsibilities for a period of more than six months. During this time he was ignored by the company's hierarchy, his telephone calls were not returned, and various allegations were made about his wife's inability to adapt to new situations. Hank's response during this period was to "sit tight and wait it out."

When a shift occurred in the roles of those above him, Hank received a substantial promotion to a job with significant responsibilities. He said in his initial interview with me that he was cautious in taking his new place on the ladder and careful not to be angry at those who had abandoned him or plotted his derailment. Hank has since been promoted twice, has a secure place on the succession ladder, and is excited and enthusiastic about both his current position and his future prospects.

The other fast-tracker, Larry, discussed his derailment more briefly. While on his way through the executive transition, Larry was shuttled off to a job out of the mainstream and off the succession track. Angry at first, he said that he turned this position into "the learningest job he ever had," greatly broadening his own knowledge of the company and helping to increase company profits. From this position, he was then promoted to a significant new position as head of his own venture within the company.

Other fast-trackers commented less on their journey through the executive transition, but they did speak briefly of difficulties they had encountered along the way. The log of their promotions reveals a clear slowdown for many during the executive transition. For one fast-tracker, the distance between promotions was 15 years. It seems unlikely that during this period he could have perceived himself as being on his way to the top. There were periods of seven to nine years between promotions for other fast-trackers. Many of them, in short, have had times in their careers when they might easily have perceived themselves as failures.

Derailment, then, has already been a part of life for several of the fast-trackers. And, in fact, derailment at one time or another is part of life for all of them—and for all of us. How can we reconcile the enthusiasm and full-hearted involvement in work of these fast-trackers with the prospect of ultimate derailment in their journey up the corporate ladder? Could it be that full-hearted involvement in the work at hand is one of the best forms of insurance against an emotional and professional downturn at the first signs of derailment?

The initial study suggests that the fast-trackers' attitudes toward derailment were critical in determining whether they returned to the fast track. The potential for derailment exists for all. Did they all demonstrate the attitudes toward potential slowdowns and life off the track that could bring them back on at some later point? Was rejoining others on the fast track necessarily the most productive or most satisfying option? Let us see what we can learn from the fast-trackers as we describe the results of recent interviews with these junior stars, mid-careerists, and senior statesmen, all of whom have aspirations for reaching the top of their particular pyramids.

THE FAST-TRACKERS: 1988

My initial interviews with the fast-trackers led me to believe that they would hold certain attitudes about their work, depending upon their age group, which would be reflected in their comments during the follow-up interviews. Specifically, I expected that the junior stars would respond enthusiastically to the opportunity to discuss their careers, would either have been promoted within the last year, and/or would expect to receive promotions in the immediate future, and still would have their sights set on achieving major vice-presidencies within their companies. (I expected those junior stars who were approaching or passing the age of 35 to show characteristics more like those of the fast-trackers in mid-career).

I expected that the mid-careerists would be less enthusiastic about their positions, would be more uncertain about further upward mobility, and might, in fact, be responding to a slowdown in their career movement by looking at other opportunities.

Finally, I expected that the senior statesmen would be as forthcoming as the junior stars were about their career possibilities, but that (a) they would emphasize not only the positive but the positive and negative aspects intertwined with each other; (b) they would dwell not on the virtues of self but on the virtues of the organization; and (c) they would describe their expectations about the future not in terms of career moves but in terms of challenges, responsibilities, and contributions. Let us see if my expectations were correct.

Junior Stars

Among the five junior stars, two had been promoted twice in the past year, a third had been promoted once, a fourth had remained in his former position, and a fifth (the oldest, at 38 now classifiable as a mid-careerist) had moved laterally in the company. In other words, three of the four who were still younger than 35 had been promoted within the past year.

The two men who had received double promotions were enthusiastic about their work. One, more effusive and forthcoming than the other, responded that this had been an extraordinarily productive year—a great time—and that his work relationships were outstanding. The other, in a more task-focused manner, spoke about the specific challenges of his current position and the fact that he was starting to make significant progress. The one woman in this group, who had been promoted once, responded that this year had been spectacular. She declared, "I am doing extraordinarily well" and "I'm in charge of my own career."

The individual who had remained in the same position spoke of the challenges of that year and of his learning about the importance of finances and budgets. (He is in a division that is likely to be taken over by another firm, and chances of getting an immediate promotion are thus slim.) The fifth junior star (now actually a mid-careerist) spoke enthusiastically of his recent lateral move and said that he had had a good year.

In some ways, the best clues to what these fast-trackers felt about their professional growth in the past year lay hidden in their remarks about other issues. All but one of the junior stars mentioned being more concerned with family matters now than they had been in the past. This group included two of the junior stars who had been promoted: One man, who had received a double promotion, is expecting his third child and trying to find a better balance between work and family; and the group's only woman described herself as being more supportive on the home front now than she had been in the recent past. The individual who stayed in the same position was even more specific than the others were in describing his new concerns about the home front. "This was the first year ever," he said, "when I've been persuaded by my two little girls to take a family vacation." He also is spending more time at home, and talked about the importance of spending quality time with his children. He interpreted his new attitude toward his children in terms of the phraseology of the manufacturing plant where he works: "You know, with kids you have to supply first-time-through quality—there's no rework. So I have to be there now."

The individual who had passed into the mid-career stage and received a lateral promotion also spoke about family concerns. Although he prefers his new position to the one he held before, he is still concerned that his wife is not happy in this part of the country. His primary concern in the next career move he makes will be finding a geographic location that meets his family's needs.

Mid-Careerists

The seven mid-careerists, ages 37 to 41 in 1986, were now between 39 and 43 years old. Of the seven in this group, one had received a double promotion, one had gotten a single promotion, four were in the same positions, and one had been moved laterally. Two of the seven had received promotions, by contrast with three of the five in the junior star group.

Part of this lowered rate of promotion is inevitable because of the narrowing of job possibilities as one moves up the corporate ladder. In their book *Habits of the Heart* (Harper & Row, 1986), Robert Bellah, Richard Madsen, William M. Sullivan, Ann Swidler, and Steven M. Tipton make this point quite clear: "The grade grows steeper at the peak of a professional field, the ledges narrower at the top of a corporate pyramid." Yet just a few years ago, these mid-careerists were junior stars, all expecting to stop no lower than the senior vice-president level. How are they responding to the reality of inevitable slowdown for many, even as a few continue to move upward? Is the change in the probabilities for promotion reflected in the comments of both those moving up and those standing still?

The mid-careerist who had received a single promotion described his move with enthusiasm akin to that of the junior stars. He said this was an "exciting time," that the new job was "enlightening," and that he "loved it." However, this was his first promotion in nine years, and it was greeted with more delight than many of his earlier, more expected promotions. He reflected too that his new job greatly increased his scope and responsibility within the division. The other mid-careerist who had been promoted, a woman who moved up two levels, was quieter in her response but stated clearly that these two moves had fulfilled her expectations completely. She, too, elaborated on the scope of her new responsibilities and the overwhelming amount of learning that was necessary in order for her to handle this job well. These comments were similar to those made by Hank, who was derailed earlier but promoted just before this follow-up year began. Hank initially spoke of his promotion in a manner like that of a junior star ("I have done an outstanding job"), but he immediately went on to talk about the scope of his responsibilities and learning. He was still learning about how to motivate the workforce in a large organization where the sheer number of employees makes developing personal relationships with each of them impossible.

The three unpromoted individuals were more reflective in their evaluations of their positions than were those who had been promoted. One, who had recently remarried, placed the most emphasis of all the fast-trackers on the need to seek balance in his life and to learn how to share goals with a partner. He said this was a year of reflection and broadening awareness. A second focused on his day-to-day work experience to a much greater extent, and said that the work had proceeded much as expected. He said, though, that as in the past, he was still bucking the tide, questioning the organization, and fighting the same dragons. Much like those who had been promoted, however, he was concerned about the scope of his responsibilities, which he identified as "moving forward, keeping the water calm, and dealing with the ambiguities for both myself and my people."

The third unpromoted mid-careerist focused on the unsettling nature of this past year in company terms, describing the likelihood that his division would be sold to another company. In many ways, his responses displayed the good/bad integration heard most clearly in the comments of the senior statesmen and less often in those of the mid-careerists. He talked about the changes within his unit as it met global challenges. In the face of such challenges, he explained, the immediate leadership had little control over the events most affecting the business. He said this was a tremendous challenge for the leadership of the unit but that the learning coming from this was positive: People at all levels of the unit were more involved in the decision-making processes and, consequently, morale in the unit was up, not down. On a personal note, he said that he had learned to delegate more effectively, increasingly recognizing the limits and abilities of his people and, therefore, providing them with the best possible balance of structure and responsibility.

By contrast, the remaining mid-careerist, who had moved laterally in the past year, reflected on his personal disappointment more than the other fast-trackers did; he believed that there would be no further upward mobility for him within this company. He had grown, he said, in his knowledge of the business, but his prospects for advancement in this job had not, and would not, materialize. "I have become more reflective," he said, "and more tolerant this year." This was the only fast-tracker who perceived himself as definitely having been derailed.

Senior Statesmen

Among the five senior statesmen, there had been one lateral move—or what appears to have been a lateral move—to a job that involves significantly increased responsibilities. There was also one announced promotion, which is scheduled to take place within the next year. The other three senior statesmen remained in the same positions. Yet each one, in his own way, described this as having been a "great" year in which significant goals were accomplished.

The senior fast-tracker with a new position spoke primarily in terms of growth and change within the company in the past year. He said, "I have an expanding and continuing awareness of both competition and threat. In terms of specific decisions," he continued, "it has been necessary to take hard action in order to remain competitive." What he is most pleased about is his new awareness of "the receptivity to change of people all the way down the line. Change is uneven but I am impressed with the people who are making the changes." He is more optimistic about his company's prospects this year than last, and concluded that "adversity is still the best teacher."

The senior fast-tracker with a major promotion in the offing emphasized his optimism about the company's future and said his primary concern was learning how to manage growth. He displayed enthusiasm as he recounted specific examples of how this learning was already taking place. His comments about himself emphasized his confirmation of previously held beliefs, an increased degree of self-confidence, and an equally increased willingness to listen. "My job is to listen," he said. "These other people have the information. My job is to draw it out, and to help them make the most of it." He also spoke spontaneously and warmly about his family—his wife and two very young children—summarizing his comments by saying, "We are very connected now."

Two senior statesmen who had remained in their previous positions also spoke with enthusiasm—akin to that of the junior stars—about the events of the last year. One said that the direction of his work was the same but that it had taken on greater intensity; he summed up his perceptions by exclaiming, "It has been a great year! Unbelievable!" The second placed his personal and organizational life in counterpoint to each other, saying that the first had led to greater reflection and the second, to greater achievement than he had anticipated. This year he was very ill for the first time, an experience which provided both motivation and time to reflect on his life, to talk more with his wife, and to seek a better balance between work and personal life. At work he said he "had one of the most significant years of my career, in which all the plans of the past are coming into being!" He continued to speak of his fascination with the process of change and commented that both inside and outside his particular company, "The change going on now is mind-boggling!"

The last senior statesman—who is also still at the helm of the same ship—said that he had learned a great deal this year about the "politics of leadership—a skill that I've avoided in the past." He elaborated on this by saying, "I'm trying to understand people, to present them with a political solution and not a problem." He feels that he is growing in leadership abilities and consolidating his philosophy and skills. Unlike the other two senior men, who are now viewing the realization of plans, this senior statesman had led his company through the formulation of such plans—which are about to be implemented. In short, he said, "We've been planning our climb to Mount Everest and now we're at the base camp looking up." The next few years will see how far and how well he and his people climb the mountain.

What do these stories say about the complex of factors that lead to promotions, and about the attitudes which one might most profitably adopt to view the slowdowns or derailments that take one off the track? In each of the next two sections, we shall examine these stories in terms of what they can teach us about upward movements *and* derailment.

On Being Promoted:
The Influence of Work Relationships

Five of the 17 fast-trackers in the study were promoted in the past year: three of the junior stars and two of the mid-careerists. In three of these five cases, including both mid-careerists, the fast-trackers' descriptions of their promotions showed that they clearly recognized that they were working in a network of relationships that were critical in determining their career progress. The two who did not mention these relationships were both junior stars and both under age 35; both had been promoted twice in the past year. Their promotions may or may not have been affected by work relationships. In the other three cases, work relationships were clearly the predominant factor that led to the promotions.

The three recently promoted individuals who mentioned the importance of relationships—the two women (a junior star and a mid-careerist) and a man in mid-career—emphasized the importance of having a new boss. The junior woman attributed her new and surprising success (she had previously been at the same level for about eight years) to the new boss who became her mentor, strengthened her confidence in herself, and extended much more responsibility to her than her former boss had done. Similarly, the other woman, whose double promotion this year fulfilled all her expectations, attributed the promotions to the new president's recognizing her talent and giving her the responsibilities that would allow her to develop that talent. She is very pleased—but also somewhat overwhelmed by the amount of learning that lies before her. She said, "I am focusing on learning to do this job well, and not looking any further." Speaking about her personal growth and learning, she commented, "Last year I said that patience was a virtue; now I know it is an absolute necessity."

Don, the mid-careerist who was promoted after nine years at the same level, was even more explicit about the role of relationships. The new president of the division, who assumed that position one year ago, had in the past been separated from this particular fast-tracker by a layer of management. This layer had now been removed so that Don reported directly to the president. Shortly after this change was implemented, the president recognized Don's talent and promoted him in short order to a vice-presidency in the division. Don believed that having a new boss who was able to recognize his potential was almost the sole factor in his promotion.

Don said, for example, that his work record had been outstanding for four years: The only difference was the arrival of a new boss. He described this change as follows:

> It took a change of leadership for me to be promoted. I lost the guy between me and my current boss, Alan. Alan is a mentor, the closest I've had in a long time. This reaffirms the notion that if you've got anybody strong enough in your corner, anything can happen. My results had been great for four years. This did not change. One person's opinion made a change.

He also talked about the years between promotions, when at various times he considered opening his own small business and leaving the company. He said:

> This [promotion] really has confirmed what I believe. You have to keep going. I kept going even when I was not rewarded. Never did I give up or slow down. My numbers were good—the numbers had to be there. It's not *just* a personality thing.

Yet Don sees the "personality thing" as critical—and increasingly important as one moves up the ladder. He made an analogy between work and sports: When one first starts out in any sport, he remarked, the gains are easy. There are lots of gains for not too much effort. But after one becomes pretty good, every gain is much harder. When one is going for world-class status there's lots of effort needed for just a bit of gain.

And so it is with the mid-careerists. Even the one who received two promotions spoke of the necessity of patience: of waiting for one's number to come up. For all these individuals, there is a sense that work sometimes provides little personal gain, or that the gain comes only after one endures trials and tribulations that build character and strengthen resolve. At the mid-career level, there is little of the easy exuberance of the junior stars, just a few years younger, whose promotions appear to be influenced by individual merit as often as by work relationships. For those at mid-career, it seems, the relationships have taken precedence.

On Not Being Promoted: A Tendency to Reflect

The reflectiveness that characterized the comments of the mid-careerists who were promoted—about themselves and their careers—is much more emphasized in the responses of those who were not promoted this year. It is clear that any slowdown in the career, regardless of the eventual outcome, prompts a period of questioning oneself and one's relationship to others. This finding suggests, in fact, that some period of perceived derailment may have prompted the inner reflections that now appear to be at the core of the philosophic world-view which is held by all three of the senior statesmen.

The junior stars expected to be promoted. The two junior stars who were not promoted responded to their lack of promotions with a new emphasis on self-reflection; this, in turn, led to a new involvement in family matters—after a previous concentration on work to the exclusion of most other concerns. This was true for the older junior star (or junior mid-careerist), who remained concerned that his wife is not fully supportive of his career, and who would consider taking a job outside the company in order to meet his wife's wishes that the family relocate.

This was also true for fast-tracker Pete, who is now willing for the first time to take vacations with his wife and their two little girls.

Pete stayed in the same job this year, but he clearly attributes his lack of promotion to the difficulties facing his division. His response to the tightening of financial accountability within his facility was twofold. On one hand, he learned a great deal from his situation—it was the first time his unit had been in the red—and earned himself a quick education in budgeting, finance, and accounting. On the other hand, at the same time, he turned more of his attention than he had before homeward. His career goals, however, remain as they were before—albeit the timetable has been slowed down. He plans to stay with the company, and expects to be promoted more than once, until he is in charge of a sizable part of one of the company's divisions. He regards this year as a delay—a time to get to know himself and his family—and not as a derailment.

Among the mid-careerists there is more disappointment—and more reflection. All three who received no promotions, or what appear to be only lateral moves in the past year, emphasized that they have grown in awareness, and spend more time in reflection on life and partnerships. In terms of their career goals, one mid-careerist spoke of reevaluating his goals, and another contemplated leaving the company within five years. A third discussed the possibility of being permanently stalled within the company, and all spoke of job searches begun on the outside. In speaking of the past year, however, all acknowledged that they had learned much and grown personally as a result of their experience.

Lessons to Be Learned

There are several lessons to be learned from the experiences and the comments of the fast-trackers who were derailed.

1. First, these fast-trackers are passing through the perilous executive transition, during which most derailments occur. The pyramid in each case has narrowed considerably and there are fewer places at the top. Thus it is inevitable that many people in mid-career are going to move no farther upward in the company. Yet all or almost all of those at this level are highly skilled and very talented. Thus skill and talent can no longer be the primary criteria for upward movement. Other factors, such as personal relationships in the workplace, are going to affect this movement. And if one holds onto the notion that upward mobility is necessarily essential—and desirable—then one must conclude that many who are able and talented are going to lose out at this point. Thus instead of asking the usual question—"How can an individual avoid a derailment or slowdown?"—it may be more constructive for us to ask, "What can the individual learn from a derailment or slowdown that can help him or her to become more tolerant, understanding, and productive?"

2. However, examining individual cases, as we have done, shows us that derailment is not necessarily a permanent condition. Being moved off the track may provide the time for reflection and the broadening of viewpoint that can take one back onto the track again. Indeed, even being stalled as long as 10 years or more in between promotions does not mean that one's upward mobility is over.

3. Finally, the soul-searching and reflectiveness that appear to accompany derailment are critical parts of the senior statesmen's approaches to the world. The senior fast-trackers are reflective as well as active, accepting of the bad along with the good, and willing to go to battle against the awesome forces that stand in the way of essential change. How did they reach the point at which reflection on themselves and on the world at large becomes a critical but natural component of their way of thinking? It seems likely that career derailments or slowdowns (as well as crises in their personal lives) may have provided one learning ground for this mature orientation to the self and others. Derailment, as one example of perceived adversity, is certainly an important educational setting for the fast-trackers.

In short, some, or perhaps even most, of the fast-trackers in this study will not make it through the executive transition to achieve the status of senior statesmen within their companies. However, whether or not one has been derailed or slowed down appears not to be a reliable indicator of the later success of any particular individual. Rather, the attitude with which one meets these difficulties is significant in determining one's future success.

But even one's attitude is not the major determinant of upward movement in the latter half of one's career. Rather, how one's company is faring in the overall economic picture, what qualities (including age) the company requires at a given time in its most senior people, what mentoring relationships one is able to develop with a boss—and the personality and skills of the boss him- or herself, and the nature of relationships in the workplace in general may have an overriding impact on which individuals—out of a selection of talented, skilled, and experienced mid-careerists—will be selected to move further up the corporate ladder. Whether one makes it to the top, therefore, is largely beyond one's control. What is within one's control, however, and what determines one's true success is how one copes with adversity and turns it into an opportunity for growth and learning. Learning is ultimately the key to success—and being faced with disappointment, whether through derailment or otherwise, can provide an important chance to learn.

Learning and Derailment: Necessarily Intertwined?

The importance of following a continuous learning curve in order to achieve both personal satisfaction and career success has been propounded by many psychologists and observers of the human scene. In *The Transformational Leader* (John Wiley, 1986), researcher Noel Tichy identifies the primary characteristic of his transformational leaders (people who are unusually influential and successful) as being that "they are lifelong learners." He continues, "Perhaps one of the most intriguing parts of our protagonists is their continuous commitment to learning. Their heads have not become hard-wired." Morgan McCall, Jr., Michael M. Lombardo, and Ann M. Morrison make the same point in *Lessons of Experience* (Lexington Books, 1988). Successful executives, they found, are "ready to grab or create opportunities for growth, *wise enough not to believe that there's nothing more to learn,* and courageous enough to look inside themselves and grapple with their frailties." (Italics mine.)

Learning is thus the hallmark of leaders and successful executives and, indeed, of all those who continue to grow and develop throughout their lives. And for many, adversity provides the best opportunity for learning. Derailment, or a career slowdown that may become derailment, provides one such opportunity for reflection and learning. It is at such times that individuals learn most about themselves, about others, and about their organizations. They are challenged to establish their priorities, to seek out what matters, and to put what matters most first in their own lives.

The predictable slowdown at mid-career is thus an opportunity for individuals to enter into a state of reflection and learn new ways of looking at themselves and others; out of this reflection they can create a solid hierarchy of priorities and values to guide them during the next stage of their lives. This strong set of values may become the foundation for the philosophy or world-view that guides the individual in the senior statesman stage; or it may be the base of a philosophical outlook that leads fast-trackers to reaffirm their commitment to their family lives, or to enter a new business or a new vocation altogether. Clearly, a slowdown or a derailment need not be viewed as a failure: Instead it should be seen as an opportunity to work toward achieving success—not only in one's career, but in all aspects of one's life. Perhaps people should hope, in fact, that they have more such periods, during which the pace of life slows sufficiently for them to become more fully conscious of their priorities and values.

It is time for us to rid ourselves of the false assumptions that we have held for too long: (1) that moving upward on a career ladder is necessarily desirable and better than staying where we are or moving onto another ladder altogether, and (2) that competitiveness rather than cooperation is the key to success. We need to realize that any stoppage or slowdown on a particular track is—at least in part—out of our hands; such a slowdown, moreover, can be a step in an educational process which can sustain us on any path we take—whether that path leads to the company president's chair or to a closer relationship with our family. How we respond to life—particularly in difficult times—is a choice that is ours. How high we rise on the corporate ladder is a choice that others make. The fast-trackers who learn and accept this lesson are most likely to achieve true success.

Selected Bibliography

This study follows up on many of the themes first suggested in my theoretical article, "The Derailment of Fast-Track Managers" (*Organizational Dynamics*, Autumn 1986) and my book *Survival on the Fast Track* (Dodd, Mead, 1988), which draws lessons from interviews with managers and executives in major corporations.

Numerous other works question or reject commonly held assumptions about career success. Emphasizing the importance of cooperation over competition, Robert Waterman states in *The Renewal Factor* (Bantam, 1987), "Recent findings from the behavioral sciences suggest that cooperation is much more effective than competition. In the literature about competition and cooperation, virtually every experiment about cooperation yielded much better results than competition." John Kotter's *The Leadership Factor* (Free Press, 1988) acknowledges the need for competition but also emphasizes the need to cooperate in order to function effectively in complex organizations. Kotter also writes about the individual's lack of control over his or her upward mobility in *Power and Influence* (Free Press, 1983).

Many other writers have also discussed the American assumption that moving up and getting ahead are the best or only options. One of the best books on this subject is *Habits of the Heart,* by Robert Bellah, Richard Madsen, William M. Sullivan, Ann Swidler, and Steven M. Tipton (Harper & Row, 1986), which speaks of the "inordinate rewards of ambition in our culture," and traces the development of the managerial ethos in our time. Morgan McCall, Jr., Michael M. Lombardo, and Ann M. Morrison from the Center for Creative Leadership in North Carolina reveal these assumptions as well, by taking them for granted in their discussions of difficulties and derailments in *Lessons from Experience* (Lexington Books, 1988). These authors assume, as did the executives in my study, that derailment is necessarily a problem. Yet as Arnold Mitchell points out in *Nine American Lifestyles* (Warner, 1983), continuous upward mobility is not possible for all Americans, but only for a small group of achieving, competent, and talented individuals.

Yet these assumptions are endemic in our society. Thus Lawrence Peter's works, *The Peter Principle* (Bantam, 1969) and *Why Things Go Wrong* (Bantam, 1984), which satirize our belief that up is always better—with the result that people are promoted to their level of incompetence—touched a nerve in Americans and became bestsellers.

Finally, several other works have emphasized the idea that personal and professional growth of managers is derived from hardship. These works include Noel Tichy's *The Transformational Leader* (John Wiley, 1986), and John Kotter's *General Managers* (Free Press, 1981). The best exposition of this point of view, however, is perhaps Abraham Zaleznik's article, "The Management of Disappointment," included in *Executive Success: Making It In Business* (Harvard Business School, 1983).

The Day at the Beach

Arthur Gordon

Not long ago I came to one of those bleak periods that many of us encounter from time to time, a sudden drastic dip in the graph of living when everything goes stale and flat, energy wanes, enthusiasm dies. The effect on my work was frightening. Every morning I would clench my teeth and mutter: "Today life will take on some of its old meaning. You've got to break through this thing. You've got to!"

But the barren days went by, and the paralysis grew worse. The time came when I knew I had to have help.

The man I turned to was a doctor. Not a psychiatrist, just a doctor. He was older than I, and under his surface gruffness lay great wisdom and compassion. "I don't know what's wrong," I told him miserably, "but I just seem to have come to a dead end. Can you help me?"

"I don't know," he said slowly. He made a tent of his fingers and gazed at me thoughtfully for a long while. Then, abruptly, he asked, "Where were you happiest as a child?"

"As a child?" I echoed. "Why, at the beach, I suppose. We had a summer cottage there. We all loved it."

He looked out the window and watched the October leaves sifting down. "Are you capable of following instructions for a single day?"

"I think so," I said, ready to try anything.

"All right. Here's what I want you to do."

He told me to drive to the beach alone the following morning, arriving not later than nine o'clock. I could take some lunch; but I was not to read, write, listen to the radio or talk to anyone. "In addition," he said, "I'll give you a prescription to be taken every three hours."

He tore off four prescription blanks, wrote a few words on each, folded them, numbered them and handed them to me. "Take these at nine, twelve, three and six."

"Are you serious?" I asked.

He gave me a short bark of laughter.

"You won't think I'm joking when you get my bill!"

The next morning, with little faith, I drove to the beach. It was lonely, all right. A northeaster was blowing; the sea looked gray and angry. I sat in the car, the whole day stretching emptily before me. Then I took out the first of the folded slips of paper. On it was written: LISTEN CAREFULLY.

Source: Arthur Gordon. "The Day at the Beach." *Reader's Digest* (1960), 76, 79–83. Reprinted with permission from the January 1960 *Reader's Digest*.

I stared at the two words. Why, I thought, the man must be mad. He had ruled out music and newscasts and human conversation. What else was there?

I raised my head and I did listen. There were no sounds but the steady roar of the sea, the croaking cry of a gull, the drone of some aircraft high overhead. All these sounds were familiar.

I got out of the car. A gust of wind slammed the door with a sudden clap of sound. Was I supposed, I asked myself, to listen carefully to things like that?

I climbed a dune and looked out over the deserted beach. Here the sea bellowed so loudly that all other sounds were lost. And yet, I thought suddenly, there must be sounds beneath sounds—the soft rasp of drifting sand, the tiny wind-whisperings in the dune grasses—if the listener got close enough to hear them.

On an impulse I ducked down and, feeling fairly ridiculous, thrust my head into a clump of seaweed. Here I made a discovery: if you listen intently, there is a fractional moment in which everything seems to pause, wait. In that instant of stillness, the racing thoughts halt. For a moment, when you truly listen for something outside yourself, you have to silence the clamorous voices within. The mind rests.

I went back to the car and slid behind the wheel. LISTEN CAREFULLY. As I listened again to the deep growl of the sea, I found myself thinking about the white-fanged fury of its storms.

I thought of the lessons it had taught as children. A certain amount of patience: you can't hurry the tides. A great deal of respect: the sea does not suffer fools gladly. An awareness of the vast and mysterious interdependence of things: wind and tide and current, calm and squall and hurricane, all combining to determine the paths of the birds above and the fish below. And the cleanness of it all, with every beach swept twice a day by the great broom of the sea.

Sitting there, I realized I was thinking of things bigger than myself—and there was relief in that.

Even so, the morning passed slowly. The habit of hurling myself at a problem was so strong that I felt lost without it. Once when I was wistfully eyeing the car radio a phrase from Carlyle jumped into my head. "Silence is the element in which great things fashion themselves. . . ."

By noon the wind had polished the clouds out of the sky; and the sea had a hard, polished, and merry sparkle. I unfolded the second "prescription." And again I sat there, half amused and half exasperated. Three words this time: TRY REACHING BACK.

Back to what? To the past, obviously. But why, when all my worries concerned the present or the future?

I left the car and started tramping reflectively along the dunes. The doctor had sent me to the beach because it was a place of happy memories. Maybe that was what I was supposed to reach for: the wealth of happiness that lay half-forgotten behind me.

I decided to experiment: to work on these vague impressions as a painter would retouching the colors, strengthening the outlines. I would choose specific incidents and recapture as many details as possible. I would visualize people complete with dress and gestures. I would listen (carefully) for the exact sound of their voices, the echo of their laughter.

The tide was going out now, but there was still thunder in the surf. So I chose to go back 20 years to the last fishing trip I made with my younger brother. (He died in the Pacific during World War II and was buried in the Philippines.) I found that if I closed my eyes and really tried, I could see him with amazing vividness, even the humor and eagerness in his eyes that far-off morning.

In fact, I could see it all: the ivory scimitar of beach where we were fishing; the eastern sky smeared with sunrise; the great rollers creaming in, stately and slow. I could feel the backwash swirl warm around my knees, see the sudden arc of my brother's rod as he struck a fish, hear his exultant yell. Piece by piece I rebuilt it, clear and unchanged under the transparent varnish of time. Then it was gone.

I sat up slowly, TRY REACHING BACK. Happy people were usually assured, confident people. If, then, you deliberately reached back and touched happiness, might there not be released little flashes of power, tiny sources of strength?

This second period of the day went more quickly. As the sun began its long slant down the sky, my mind ranged eagerly through the past, reliving some episodes, uncovering others that had been completely forgotten. For example, when I was around 13 and my brother 10, Father had promised to take us to the circus. But at lunch there was a phone call: some urgent business required his attention downtown. We braced ourselves for disappointment. Then we heard him say, "No, I won't be down. It'll have to wait."

When he came back to the table, Mother smiled. "The circus keeps coming back, you know."

"I know," said Father. "But childhood doesn't."

Across all the years I remembered this and knew from the sudden glow of warmth that no kindness is ever wasted or ever completely lost.

By three o'clock the tide was out and the sound of the waves was only a rhythmic whisper, like a giant breathing. I stayed in my sandy nest, feeling relaxed and content—and a little complacent. The doctor's prescriptions, I thought, were easy to take.

But I was not prepared for the next one. This time the three words were not a gentle suggestion. They sounded more like a command. REEXAMINE YOUR MOTIVES.

My first reaction was purely defensive. There's nothing wrong with my motives, I said to myself. I want to be successful—who doesn't? I want to have a certain amount of recognition—but so does everybody. I want more security than I've got—and why not?

Maybe, said a small voice somewhere inside my head, those motives aren't good enough. Maybe that's the reason the wheels have stopped going around.

I picked up a handful of sand and let it stream between my fingers. In the past, whenever my work went well, there had always been something spontaneous about it, something uncontrived, something free. Lately it had been calculated, competent—and dead. Why? Because I had been looking past the job itself to the rewards I hoped it would bring. The work had ceased to be an end in itself, it had been merely a means to make money, pay bills. The sense of giving something, of helping people, of making a contribution, had been lost in a frantic clutch at security.

In a flash of certainty, I saw that if one's motives are wrong, nothing can be right. It makes no difference whether you are a mailman, a hairdresser, an insurance salesman, a housewife—whatever. As long as you feel you are serving others, you do the job well. When you are concerned only with helping yourself, you do it less well. This is a law as inexorable as gravity.

For a long time I sat there. Far out on the bar I heard the murmur of the surf change to a hollow roar as the tide turned. Behind me the spears of light were almost horizontal. My time at the beach had almost run out, and I felt a grudging admiration for the doctor and the "prescriptions" he had so casually and cunningly devised. I saw, now, that in them was a therapeutic progression that might well be of value to anyone facing any difficulty.

LISTEN CAREFULLY: To calm a frantic mind, slow it down, shift the focus from inner problems to outer things.

TRY REACHING BACK: Since the human mind can hold but one idea at a time, you blot out present worry when you touch the happinesses of the past.

REEXAMINE YOUR MOTIVES: This was the hard core of the "treatment," this challenge to reappraise, to bring one's motives into alignment with one's capabilities and conscience. But the mind must be clear and receptive to do this—hence the six hours of quiet that went before.

The western sky was a blaze of crimson as I took out the last slip of paper. Six words this time. I walked slowly out on the beach. A few yards below the high water mark I stopped and read the words again: WRITE YOUR TROUBLES ON THE SAND.

I let the paper blow away, reached down and picked up a fragment of shell. Kneeling there under the vault of sky, I wrote several words on the sand, one above the other. Then I walked away, and I did not look back. I had written my troubles on the sand. And the tide was coming in.

Chapter

13

Organizational Realignments

C onstant pressure to change is a reality for many modern organizations. Because of new technology, market demands, and variations in political and social environments, some (though certainly not all) organizations feel pressures that conflict both with their previous ways of operating and with traditional organizational models.

Often these pressures call for changes in conceptual frameworks as well as in organizational procedures and structures. We use the term "realignment" to refer to a pattern of organizational changes in concepts, procedures and/or structure in response to changing circumstances. In this chapter, we look at some organizational realignments and some refusals to realign, in response to pressures to change.

The first few readings deal with some ideas about some contemporary organizations that are recognized for their abilities to come up with and implement new products and services. In a sense these ideas are a sort of conventional wisdom about what it takes for large organizations to be innovative. However, many of the ideas are in conflict with ingrained beliefs about how organizations should be designed. As Russell Mitchell points out in "Nurturing Those Ideas," the ingrained ideas may hinder the ability of U. S. organizations to compete effectively. In the next two selections, "Ability to Innovate" and "Creating a New Company Culture," Brian Dumaine describes some of the ways that organizations may need to be redesigned in order to realign themselves and some of the actions that executives may find helpful.

In the next article, Peter Frost and Carolyn Egri indicate and demonstrate that many of the barriers to organization realignment are political rather than structural and that political strategy rather than simply "good ideas" may be critical to successful innovation.

The concluding three selections introduce some less than glamorous realignments still facing organizations. Due to failures of the American education system, many of today's workers are deficient in basic skills such as reading and writing. In "Business Shares the Blame for Workers' Low Skills" John Hoerr outlines some of the dimensions of the problem and indicates that business is apt to face increasing pressures to do something about it. In " 'Change-or-Else' Warning to Business" Joan Beck calls attention to another type of realignment facing many organizations. Although we have dealt with the problems of discrimination at other points in the book, Beck's article is useful here in calling attention to how at least some organizations may need to alter some of their longstanding ways of doing business to respond to pressing social concerns. The final paper ("Cost Cutting: How to Do It Right") deals with one of the least glamorous of all realignments—that required by cutbacks in response to declining performance. These last three selections share a theme with several earlier selections in this chapter—the importance of developing and empowering lower level participants.

Nurturing Those Ideas

Russell Mitchell

The hierarchy in U.S. companies has often meant that brainstorms from the troops languished. But now that's changing

Why can't more American companies keep up with overseas competitors? Industry after industry is being slammed in the world marketplace by foreign rivals who have proved more adept at translating great ideas into great products—or into better ways of making them. True, corporate profits have been strong in the U.S., and the trade gap is shrinking. But profit growth has already slowed, and the recent resurgence of the dollar could be painful for American manufacturers, particularly in fields where foreign rivals have managed to keep pace.

Examples aren't hard to find. Despite dramatic changes at the Big Three auto makers, Japanese cars still account for a record 24% of domestic sales. And the steel industry, after shuttering one unprofitable mill after another, says it still needs protection from imports to prosper. "Look at the leading (U.S.) company in almost any industry five or ten years ago," says Andrall E. Pearson, a professor at Harvard business school and former PepsiCo Inc. president. "Today you'll find that company will be floundering around."

American managers have drawn up a long list of excuses for their lack of competitiveness. Overseas rivals have lower labor costs. They rely on unfair trade practices. They can raise capital more cheaply. U.S. managers have their homegrown complaints, too: Wall Street is too quick to abandon a company at the first sign of softness in quarterly earnings. Compounding that pressure, many companies have to contend with raiders or takeovers—hostile or friendly. But while there may be some truth in all these complaints, there's no escaping one fundamental fact: U.S. companies are being outmanaged by their toughest competitors.

The main reason may be structural. Most American companies are organized around hierarchical, almost military, models, with the CEO as general. That means ideas from the troops are often ignored—if they can fight their way up the chain of command at all. This kind of vertical structure also discourages communication between different disciplines such as research and manufacturing. The result: missed opportunities for new products and sluggish reactions to changing markets. "We manage innovation out of the system rather than into it," says consultant Robert H. Waterman Jr. author of *The Renewal Factor* and co-author of *In Search of Excellence*.

Despite that grim assessment, some of the nation's best-managed companies have found ways to weave an innovative spirit back into their organizations. One talent top innovators share is a heightened ability to cross organizational lines to tap employees' creativity. To nurture sprouting ideas that might otherwise get trampled by the bureaucracy, they are encouraging cooperation between executives at different levels. To hone product development, innovative companies are assembling teams that bring marketing, manufacturing, and R&D together at a project's earliest stages. To make sure employees are doing the job most suited to them, they are creating separate career paths for researchers and are making sure top research executives command more respect. And more than ever, companies are willing to scrounge for useful ideas wherever they can be found.

The easiest step managers can take may be simply encouraging executives to break ranks and fraternize with coworkers from other departments within the company. At General Electric Co, for example, the heads of all major businesses meet regularly to discuss projects they're working on. Similarly, Monsanto Co. has established what it calls a technology council, comprising top researchers from each of the company's divisions. The council helps scientists swap ideas and avoid duplicating costly research efforts.

Other methods of encouraging innovation require more fundamental management shifts. The most important of those techniques may be using teamwork. Many laggards have clung to a product development process derisively dubbed the "bucket brigade." Someone in a research lab comes up with an idea. Then it is passed on to the engineering department, which converts it into a design. Next, manufacturing gets specifications from engineering and figures out how to make the thing. At last, responsibility for the finished product is dumped on marketing.

While it may be easy to keep track of, the bucket brigade is slow and inefficient. Too often, engineers design products that are too expensive or too complex to manufacture profitably. Plans are constantly pushed back down the chain to fix problems that could have been avoided. After all that, marketing experts are frequently handed products that aren't what customers want most. The outcome: slow response times, high costs, and shoddy quality.

Compare that to the system most Japanese companies use. They take what's called a "fast cycle" approach to development—whipping out new products and reacting in a flash to shifts in consumer preference. To accomplish that, managers make communication a top priority at the earliest stages of a project. They pull together a team of experts from each business function to anticipate glitches and to guide the project through the organization from start to finish.

The system can work wonders. Consider cars: It routinely takes U.S. auto makers up to five years to bring a new car to market, while Japanese competitors do it in only three years. The upshot: Fresh Japanese models hit the showroom faster, and they are often better made.

Simple as it sounds, the team concept doesn't fit easily into traditionally organized U.S. companies. "Senior management's success is ingrained with 30 to 40 years of hierarchy and control," says Daniel J. Valentino, president of consultant United Research in Morristown, N.J. But building teamwork requires shifting some authority to team members—which may alienate the managers traditionally responsible for those tasks. What's more, the team concept often faces resistance from the accounting department. That's because accountants usually keep budgets for each vertical department in a corporation. Using teams that cross traditional financial boundaries forces companies to find new ways to track spending.

But where U.S. companies have bridged those barriers, the results are impressive. At Perkin-Elmer Corp., bringing in pros from different disciplines helped cut by half the number of engineering changes required to produce a product. Speeding up the process isn't the only benefit—it has also helped cut manufacturing costs as much as 55%. One example: By collaborating early, designers developing a new instrument for chemical analysis scrapped their plan to include a metal fan attached by bolts. Manufacturing experts suggested a plastic version that snapped into place and required fewer parts.

This kind of cooperation often requires team members to develop skills outside their own field. That's especially true for R&D directors, who are usually called upon to lead the teams. But it demands management skills as well as technical prowess—a combination rarely emphasized in the past. "It used to be the bigger the nerd you were, the better the researcher you were," says François P. van Remoortere, president of W. R. Grace & Co.'s research division. "That's changed now."

To smooth the transition, some companies are providing R&D personnel with a choice of career paths: management or pure research. Companies used to promote top researchers automatically into management ranks, regardless of managerial aptitude. Now, more corporations are looking to hire researchers with good communication and people skills that they can tap later for leading teams. Meanwhile, they're providing better pay and more responsibility to employees who choose to stay in the lab.

Contact-lens maker Bausch & Lomb Inc. has developed a system for doing just that. New lab employees can choose between management and research routes after two to five years with the company. To make sure researchers don't feel slighted, the company has created vice-president-level spots for them, bringing bigger salaries, stock bonuses, and other perks. "The fact that financial rewards will be equal provides a clear sign that we're serious," says Terry Dolak, research vice-president for personal products. So far, only about 5% of Bausch & Lomb's R&D staff have taken the research track, but the company expects that figure to stabilize at 10%. In the past, nearly all of the company's brightest technicians were channeled into management.

Not every company has been so successful. At Rolls-Royce Motor Cars Inc., for example, the dual ladder "works only for the few," says Kenneth W. Bushell, vice-president for engineering. "It only works if you're a genius, or should I say genius squared?" Worse, at some companies research is perceived as a sidetrack for managers past their prime. That kind of half-hearted commitment can backfire by hurting morale and actually slowing product development.

Despite such setbacks, plenty of other companies are searching for new ways to take care of their technical staff. At GE, that has meant creating the post of Chief Technical Officer, to be filled by the company's top R&D executive. The new post is meant as a signal to employees outside the lab that GE considers research and development critical to the company's success. "If a division head finds a technical person in with the CEO, he gets the idea," says Roland W. Schmitt, president of Rensselaer Polytechnic Institute and former head of R&D at GE.

Learning new communication skills is hardly the biggest challenge researchers face. Even the largest and most successful companies have trouble keeping track of all the latest scientific developments. In addition, the soaring cost of research often makes relying solely on homegrown ideas impractical. As a result, more companies are engaging in what they call hunting and gathering—searching for new ideas outside their own labs. That often means developing costly technologies by working closely with university researchers or forming joint ventures—even overseas. "We [U.S. managers] probably looked with unwarranted arrogance at some of our competitors around the world and felt we had little to learn," says Gordon F. Brunner, senior vice-president at Procter & Gamble Co.

No more. In industries that require heavy research spending or demand a global marketing presence—such as computers, telecommunications, and pharmaceuticals—joint ventures have already become routine. In addition to spreading development costs, forming joint ventures can also speed the introduction of new products by avoiding duplication of research efforts.

In addition to seeking partners, companies now routinely search outside the U.S. for technical breakthroughs. To keep tabs on developments abroad, they're setting up satellite labs. That helps them get closer to international markets and lets them spot ideas that could result in new products at home. W. R. Grace, for example, has set up an operation in Japan specifically to transfer suitable technology back to the corporate labs in the U.S.

The hunting and gathering approach raises new challenges to management skills. Some companies that have linked up with tiny, leading-edge research firms have been badly burned—especially when they used the joint venture to enter an unfamiliar market. Consider Du Pont Co.'s abortive joint venture with HEM Research Inc., a tiny Philadelphia outfit that needed cash to develop a drug to treat AIDS patients. Hot to build a presence in pharmaceuticals, Du Pont was dazzled by HEM's early research on the drug Ampligen. But soon after the giant chemical maker signed on and started pouring millions into a two-year research project, it became clear the remedy was not effective. While plenty of research projects fizzle, even Du Pont officials now admit they didn't investigate HEM carefully enough: It had been passed over as a venture partner by several other companies with longer histories in drug development.

Like most changes, getting managers to encourage innovation can be painful. But plenty of companies are already showing that the rewards are worth it. Witness the 20 companies selected by *Business Week*'s editors as examples of the most innovative companies in America. And while methods vary, one common theme emerges: Managing for innovation enables them to keep up with the competition.

Ability to Innovate

Brian Dumaine

Ever since those long afternoons spent tinkering with his junior chemistry set in the basement of his parents' Sioux City, Iowa, home, Allen "Jake" Jacobson has had a hankering for innovation. It shows. During his four years as CEO, the 3M corporation has pumped out new products at a rate of about 200 a year. Many are modest variations of such ordinary but ubiquitous industrial and consumer items as masking tape or sandpaper. But 3M is also a leading maker of high-tech medical diagnostic equipment and computer imaging systems.

Among U.S. companies only Merck is rated as more innovative than 3M in this year's survey. Naturally, being inventive earns the company something beyond praise. Since last January, 3M's stock has risen 29%.

3M functions as a kind of corporate petri dish that fosters the spirit of innovation in its scientists and engineers. Technical people are encouraged to swap information and ideas in the halls. Once a year the company holds its own private trade show. Each of its more than 115 research labs sets up a booth displaying the latest

"Ability to Innovate" by Brian Dumaine, *Fortune,* January 29, 1990, p. 43, 46. Reprinted by permission of Fortune Magazine.

technologies, and for three days scientists, like hucksters at a fair, try to "sell" their work to each other.

A corporate committee of 3M scientists oversees all research, making sure there is no duplication and cross-pollinating new ideas among divisions. Jacobson gives technical people all the resources they need. In 1988, 3M spent 6.5% of sales, or $689 million, on R&D, twice the average of U.S. industry.

Jacobson believes that top managers go astray if they try to impose too much of their own thinking. Says he: "You've got to sponsor your people's ideas. You've got to help them along." At 3M researchers are encouraged to spend 15% of their time pursuing projects that will pay off only far down the road. But that carrot hides a stick: Jacobson also insists that 25% of each division's annual sales come from products developed in the prior five years.

The company holds scientists and engineers in particularly high esteem. The lab-coat crowd accounts for half of 3M's 135 general managers. A two-tier promotion system allows inventors who don't want to manage to rise to the equivalent of vice president—pay, perks, and all.

Jacobson, 63, a chemical engineer, pushes his researchers to put customers first. "Innovation works from understanding consumer needs," he says. A few notable failures overseas—one was a tape gun that the Japanese wouldn't use because it was shaped like a weapon—have taught him to pay more attention to those who are closest to local markets. That's why he's glad that in the past decade 3M has doubled the number of scientists and researchers working abroad to 2,000.

He believes that if 3M and other American corporations are to keep their innovative edge, the country will have to produce more engineers. Says the father of three: "It has to start in the second grade. Unless you make a home environment where a child can get interested in math and science, you'll never get anywhere."

Creating a New Company Culture

Brian Dumaine

More managers are doing just that to boost their competitiveness. A few have found some common keys to success—notably that change begins at the bottom.

So it has come to this: You've automated the factory, decimated the inventory, eliminated the unnecessary from the organization chart, and the company still isn't hitting on all cylinders—and you've got an awful feeling you know why. It's the culture. It's the values, heroes, myths, symbols that have been in the organization forever, the attitudes that say, Don't disagree with the boss, or Don't make waves, or Just do enough to get by, or For God's sake, don't take chances. And how on earth are you going to change all *that?*

If your company is like a great many others, it will have to step up to this challenge. The changes businesses are being forced to make merely to stay competitive—improving quality, increasing speed, adopting a customer orientation—are so fundamental that they must take root in a company's very essence, which means in its culture. This news depresses those who remember corporate culture as the trendy concern of the mid-Eighties, when consultants ranging from the super-sober to the wacky tried to change companies' cultures and almost always found they couldn't. But take heart. An increasing number of enterprises are at last figuring out how to alter their cultures, and more than ever are doing it.

The basic lesson sounds like a Confucian principle: Cultural change must come from the bottom, and the CEO must guide it. Despite the apparent contradiction, Du Pont, Tandem Computers, and many others are making that idea work. Says Du Pont CEO Edgar Woolard: "Employees have been underestimated. You have to start with the premise that people at all levels want to contribute and make the business a success."

The CEO must show the direction of the change to make sure it happens coherently. But a cultural transformation is a change in the hearts and minds of the workers, and it won't happen if the CEO just talks. David Nadler, the president of Delta Consulting Group, warns of the plexiglass CEO syndrome: "CEOs encase

"Creating a New Company Culture" by Brian Bumaine, *Fortune,* January 15, 1990, pp. 127–131.

their mission statement in plexiglass, hand it out, and people laugh. You have to change the way the person who assembles the machine or designs the product acts." This means the CEO must live the new culture, become the walking embodiment of it. He must also spot and celebrate managers and employees who exemplify the values he wants to inculcate.

No cultural change happens easily or quickly. Figure five to ten years for a significant improvement—but since the alternative may be extinction, it's worth a try. Here's how the most successful companies are changing their cultures today:

Beyond Vision   Yes, a CEO must promulgate a vision, but the most brilliant vision statement this side of Paraguay won't budge a culture unless it's backed up by action. At a major manufacturer, a manager who preached quality found that a part in the tractors coming off his assembly line was defective and would burn out after 300 hours of use rather than the specified 1,000 hours—a problem the customer wouldn't notice for quite a while. The manager could ship the tractors and make his quarterly numbers, or he could fix the flaw. He decided to fix the flaw. His people now know he's serious about quality.

Du Pont CEO Woolard, who preaches that "nothing is worthwhile unless it touches the customer," understands that communicating isn't enough. At a number of his plants he has a program called Adopt a Customer, which encourages blue-collar workers to visit a customer once a month, learn his needs, and be his representative on the factory floor. As quality or delivery problems arise, the worker is more likely to see them from the customer's point of view and help make a decision that will keep his "adopted child" happy.

Management at Florida Power & Light is changing its culture from that of a bureaucratic backwater to one that worships quality and service. The company shows it is serious by giving even the lowliest employees extraordinary freedom to practice that religion. Example: The utility discovered that its meter readers suffered more on-the-job injuries than any other type of employee, and they were nasty ones—dog bites. The meter readers in Boca Raton wanted to form a team to study the problem. Under the old culture, management would have scoffed at such a notion as a waste of time. Says executive vice president Wayne Brunetti: "It would have been so easy for us to reject this kind of idea." But the new ethos allowed the meter readers to take the initiative. They formed a team of ten who surveyed households, found out which ones had fierce Fidos, and then programmed hand-held computers to beep just before a visit to a dangerous address. Dog bites (and absenteeism) are down, and morale (and service) is up.

Alter History   A company with the wrong history and myths can get itself in big trouble. For years after Walt Disney's death his ghost stalked the halls of the company's studios in Burbank, California, causing executives to freeze in their tracks and wonder, "What would Walt have done?"

These hero worshipers were driving the studio into the ground with an outdated line of family flicks. Realizing that sometimes history can't be changed without changing the players, CEO Michael Eisner came aboard and cleared the deck, bringing in new managers, most of whom had never met Disney. The new crew,

KEYS TO CHANGE

- Understand your old culture first. You can't chart a course until you know where you are.
- Encourage those employees who are bucking the old culture and have ideas for a better one.
- Find the best subculture in your organization, and hold it up as an example from which others can learn.
- Don't attack culture head on. Help employees find their own new ways to accomplish their tasks, and a better culture will follow.
- Don't count on a vision to work miracles. At best it acts as a guiding principle for change.
- Figure on five to ten years for significant, organization-wide improvement.
- Live the culture you want. As always, actions speak louder than words.

freed of the spectral overseer, began to create a culture that was more sophisticated than stodgy, more adventurous than cautious, more ambitious than content. They have turned the company around by (among other moves) daring to make grown-up films like *The Color of Money* and *Ruthless People,* which would have irked old Walt.

Can something as amorphous as history be changed without spilling blood? Consider what a Fortune 500 manufacturer did with a factory that had a history of poor quality, hostile labor relations, and terrible productivity. The company hired a consultant who started out by talking with the employees. They eagerly told him about Sam, the plant manager who was a 300-pound gorilla with a disposition that made King Kong look like Bonzo the chimp.

One time Sam examined a transmission, didn't like the work he saw, picked up a sledgehammer, and smashed it to pieces. A worker summoned to Sam's office threw up on the way. Another time Sam drove his car into the plant, got up on the roof, and started screaming at his workers. One worker, fed up, poured a line of gasoline to the car and lit it.

The stunned consultant made an appointment to see the plant manager. When he walked into the office he saw a slim, pleasant-looking man behind the desk; his name was Paul. "Where's Sam?" asked the consultant. Paul, looking puzzled, replied, "Sam has been dead for nine years."

From then on Paul and the consultant realized they had a serious problem. For years Paul had been trying to instill a sense of fairness and participation, but the plant's nightmarish history was so strong his efforts had failed. To cope, Paul and his supervisors sat down with groups of eight or ten assembly workers to discuss the plant's *history*—300-pound Sam and all. Just discussing it helped clear the air.

Paul also tried hard not to do anything Sam would have done. Once, while on the noisy shop floor, he abruptly pointed at a worker, commanding him to throw away a coffee cup left near a machine. Paul merely thought he was taking care of a safety hazard. The workers on the floor, mindful of the hateful Sam, thought something like, "Ah, he's just another militaristic S.O.B. who loves spit and polish." Better for Paul to have tossed the cup away himself—a small gesture, yet that and a thousand other subtle messages will eventually help transform a culture. After four years of effort, Paul's plant this fall won his company's top award for quality.

Symbols, Symbols, Symbols   As Paul learned, executives often underestimate the power symbolic gestures have on workers. Taking the corporate jet to a Hawaiian retreat to discuss cost cutting isn't exactly going to send the right message to the troops.

At Tandem, the computer company in Cupertino, California, a general manager once told CEO Jimmy Treybig that he wanted to fire an employee. Treybig said OK, but first find out why the person wasn't performing. The general manager discovered the employee had serious family problems and decided to give him another chance, sending a signal to everyone else in the company that we treat people around here with consideration. Says Treybig: "You have to keep remembering what your company is. All your work is done by your people."

Something as simple as an award can help make a culture more innovative. In Japan, Sharp rewards top performers by putting them on a "gold badge" project team that reports directly to the company president. The privilege instills pride and gets other employees scrambling for new ideas and products in the hope that they too may make the team.

Awards can also encourage risk taking. About a year ago, the people in Du Pont's relocation department—who help move executives to new cities—thought they could boost productivity by installing a new computer system. The experiment failed, but rather than chastise those who suggested it, the company in November presented them with a plaque that told them: We're proud of your effort and hope you try again as hard in years to come.

Create Universities   Michael Beer, a Harvard business school professor, urges CEOs to identify models within the corporation. Scour the company to find some maverick manager who has figured out how to do it right—achieving high quality, good morale, innovative products. Then hold up this department or factory as a kind of university where employees can learn how others have succeeded. It's important not to force managers to adopt everything the university offers. Let them choose what works best for them.

In a study of six Fortune 500 companies that wanted to change their cultures, Beer found the only one that truly succeeded used the model approach. "With this one," says Beer, "the change began way before the CEO became fully aware of it. It was started in a small plant by some innovative managers. The top learned about it from the lowest level and spread the best practices around the company."

A caveat: The model concept works only when top management believes that *all* its employees have the ability to learn and grow. Too often a company stereotypes its blue-collar workers as dumb, inarticulate, and mindlessly loyal to archaic values like macho exhibitionism and anti-intellectualism. Shake it. Says Du Pont group vice president Mark Suwyn: "These people manage their lives well outside the factory. They sit on school boards or coach Little League. We have to create a culture where we can bring that creative energy into the work force."

Du Pont considers its plant in Towanda, Pennsylvania, which makes materials for printed circuitboards and other products, a model of the kind Beer is talking about. The plant, organized in self-directed work teams, lets employees find their own solutions to problems, set their own schedules, and even have a say in hiring. Managers call themselves facilitators, not bosses. Their main job is to coach workers and help them understand the tough, external market forces that demand a dedication to quality, teamwork, and speed. Over the past four years productivity at Towanda is up 35%.

Last spring Du Pont surveyed 6,600 of its people, including some at Towanda, and found that flexible work hours were a top priority. Working mothers and single parents said it was hard to cope with the kids while keeping to a rigid plant schedule. A team at Towanda got together and devised a novel solution: Take vacation time by the hour. During slack times when three of the four team members could easily handle the job, one could take off a few hours in the afternoon to go to a school play or bring a sick kid to the doctor. Today other Du Pont workers and managers visit Towanda to learn about flextime. A few have already borrowed it for their own plants.

Getting the most out of the university idea, CEO Woolard has found it helps to assign different goals of excellence to various Du Pont factories. He may tell the manager of one plant to be the best in team building, another the best in employee benefits, and a third the safety leader. As they improve, he holds up their accomplishments as examples to others. Says he: "It's win-win. You don't have to say one plant is a dog."

Trust Starts From Within   After a decade of restructuring, layoffs, and astronomical CEO salaries, worker trust has taken it on the chin. One of the biggest cultural challenges is to persuade workers to get religion again. It won't be easy. Making an angry, distrustful worker a believer requires fiddling with deep-rooted values. As almost any psychiatrist will tell you, it's a Herculean task to change a single individual. So imagine what it takes to change the beliefs of thousands.

Stephen Covey, a consultant to IBM, Hewlett-Packard, and other major companies, and author of *The 7 Habits of Highly Effective People,* believes every individual from the CEO down must realize that trust starts from within himself. Says he: "It's ludicrous to think that you can build trust unless people view you as trustworthy." In his seminars Covey gets managers to examine their deepest motives and to realize the importance of integrity and openness. And it's not all touchy-feely. Says Covey: "The best way our clients save money is to increase the span of control. When people trust you, you don't have to ride them, and that means fewer managers can oversee more people."

A manager can destroy a lot of trust by acting as if he's better than the people who work for him. Tandem CEO Treybig remembers suggesting that a couple of visiting managers spend a half day on the assembly line. They balked, thinking it a waste of time to mingle with blue-collar workers. "It was like you offered them syphilis," Treybig says.

He thought the idea made sense because much of Tandem's long-term success, he believes, comes from treating people as equals. For the past 15 years Tandem every Friday afternoon has put on its legendary get-togethers, once known as beer busts but now called popcorn parties (the Tandemites don't drink like they used to). Here Treybig and his top managers mix with the troops and exchange ideas about what's bad, what's good, and what can be done better in the company. As a bonus, employees from different parts of the business share ideas about the latest technologies. Four times a year Treybig spends five days in different resorts around the country with a couple of hundred people from all levels of the corporation. They talk business, play, drink beer until 2 A.M., and generally learn to trust each other. Says Treybig: "They'll go back and tell fellow employees that you care about people."

Du Pont CEO Woolard argues that the best way to create a more trusting environment is to reward the right people. "The first thing people watch," says he, "is the kind of people you promote. Are you promoting team builders who spend time on relationships, or those who are autocratic?"

Covey agrees, adding that managers should tailor reward systems to recognize team effort rather than individual accomplishment. As the wrong way to do it, he cites a CEO who would call his managers into his office each week to talk about team spirit. At the end of the meeting he'd point to a large painting of racehorses with photos of the managers' faces pasted over the thoroughbreds' heads. Then he'd announce, "So and so is ahead in the race to win the trip to Bermuda." Says Covey: "It nullified everything he said earlier."

Trying to change an institution's culture is certain to be frustrating. Most people resist change, and when the change goes to the basic character of the place where they earn a living, many people will get upset. Says the University of Pittsburgh's Kilmann: "If you talk about real change and people aren't getting uptight and anxious, they don't believe you." Some will fight. After months of working on cultural change with employees of a company, Kilmann asked the group to write down what they were doing differently. One manager wrote: "I wore a different color tie."

Managers seeking a way to think about the process might reflect that a company trying to improve its culture is like a person trying to improve his or her character. The process is long, difficult, often agonizing. The only reason people put themselves through it is that it's correspondingly satisfying and valuable.

The Political Nature of Innovation

Peter J. Frost and Carolyn P. Egri

The innovator makes enemies of all those who prospered under the old order, and only lukewarm support is forthcoming from those who would prosper under the new . . . because men are generally incredulous, never really trusting new things unless they have tested them by experience.

Niccolo Machiavelli, *The Prince*

As observed long ago by Machiavelli, the introduction of an innovation or change continues to induce and become the focus of political activity in modern society and its organizations. It is in these disputes over the ambiguous means and ends of an envisioned change that the process of innovation becomes political. How then, does an innovation emerge and survive whatever conflict it engenders? Under what conditions and when does organizational politics flourish in the innovation process? Research evidence indicates that political gamesmanship is most likely to be positively linked with the degree of originality, with the degree of perceived risk, and with the complexity of the situation. Perhaps the most vulnerable time of the innovation process is during the implementation stage when the dysfunctional nature of organizational politics is most often highlighted. It is responsible for, among other things, unnecessary delays, excessive conflict, compromised outcomes, and sometimes, ultimate failure.

The main theme throughout studies in which these results are observed is on the "problem" of the social and political dynamics engendered by innovation. Consistent with the general pro-innovation bias found in society, these resistances to innovation are generally regarded by managers as threats rather than opportunities. For those managers who are more entrenched in an organization (either by virtue of age, seniority or through the benefits accorded them by the status quo) the messiness, disorder and "muddling through" required of the innovation process can be particularly distasteful, thereby resulting in avoidance or resistance.

To illustrate the tangle and complexity of the innovation process and its polit-

Peter J. Frost and Carolyn P. Egri "The Political Process of Innovation" in *Research in Organizational Behavior, 13*, eds. L.L. Cummings and B.M. Staw (Greenwich, Conn.: JAI Press, 1991), 229–295. Adapted with permission from JAI Press.

ical nature, we present several case studies which describe the process in some detail. There do not appear to be as many studies of innovation which deal with the politics of innovation. Most common treatments of innovation either do not address process or gloss over or truncate its detail in the interest of limited space or because the authors are addressing other questions.

THE TRIALS OF PRODUCT CHAMPIONS AND SPONSORS—NASA MOONLANDER MONITOR

The case of the development of the NASA Moonlander Monitor is one which illustrates the integral role an innovation champion and his/her managerial sponsors can play in the development of a new product. It is also an example of how innovators can successfully be mavericks within an organizational culture which, while posing at the surface level a number of obstacles to such initiatives, is supportive of innovation and change in its deep structure.

As a young engineer at Hewlett-Packard, Chuck House proved to be instrumental in the development and application of oscilloscope technology for new venues (Pinchot, 1985). Initial impetus for the project was provided by the Federal Aviation Administration, which identified the need for an improved airport control tower monitor. Although the Hewlett-Packard monitor did not meet the FAA's specification for a high resolution picture and subsequently lost out to competitors, there were features of their prototype which struck House as worthy of further investigation. House believed that the size (smaller and lighter than other models), speed (20 times as fast), energy efficiency and brighter (but fuzzier) picture of his group's monitor was a significant technological breakthrough—although one which had yet to find its niche in the marketplace.

In the course of his efforts to demonstrate the merits of his team's model, House proved to be a political gamesman who operated as a maverick by violating a number of organizational rules and boundaries. His first foray into the political arena involved conducting his own market research on potential applications. To gather such information, House personally showed the monitor prototype to 40 computer manufacturers and potential customers in an organizationally unsanctioned trip from Colorado to California. In doing so, not only was he violating functional organizational boundaries by circumventing the marketing department but he was also violating a cardinal Hewlett-Packard security rule which forbade the showing of prototypes to customers. However, based on the marketing information collected during his trip, House was able to gain a temporary reprieve from senior management for his project. During the next 18 months, the project team continued development work in the lab and on-site with customers.

The next obstacle to the continuation of the project came during the annual division review by senior management. This review was influenced to a large degree by a marketing department telephone survey which projected that there was only a total demand for 32 monitors. The resistance and lack of creative initiative of the marketing group (perhaps motivated by House's previous incursion into their territory) was evident in the manner in which the survey was conducted. As Pinchot (1985: 26–27) reports: "Chuck argued that marketing had failed to understand his strategy for marketing the product. They had called only upon oscilloscope customers, the only customers they knew. New applications required new customers, Chuck explained. Besides, the device was difficult to describe: Because it was new, only demonstrations could uncover its saleability." Marketing's forecast of demand for the monitor prevailed over House's group's projections which were based on direct operating feedback from customers (and were, to some extent, obtained through organizationally illegitimate means). Not only was House's project threatened by the lack of administrative innovation by the marketing group, his project did not have the support of the chief corporate engineer who favored an alternate technology.

The conclusion of the divisional review was that, in light of the apparent lack of market demand and technological support from others in the organization, the only rational action was to abort the project. In corporate founder David Packard's words: "When I come back next year I don't want to see that project in the lab!" (Pinchot, 1985: 27).

It is at this point that House's political gamesmanship was put to the test. Unwilling to accept this decision, House "chose" to reinterpret Packard's pronouncement to mean that the project would be out of the lab in one year's time but in production, not on the scrapheap. With the covert support of his boss Dar Howard, the tactic of covering up development costs of the project from budget restrictions started in earnest as House's team raced to complete the project in one year when the normal length of time would be two. In the face of continuing opposition from the marketing department, House gained additional support by convincing interested potential customers to personally call on his superiors and argue for the project.

Fortunately for House and his team, they made their deadline and when Packard returned one year later, the monitor was indeed in the marketplace. Packard was reported to be both amused and impatient with this obvious re-interpretation of his order but perhaps indicative of his own maverick origins, he now supported the obviously successful project. Rather than being punished for their insubordination, House and his team were now given permission to continue to develop additional applications, among them the eventual use of the oscilloscope monitor for the NASA Moon Mission, the medical monitor used in the first artificial heart transplant, and a large-screen oscilloscope which was used as part of an Emmy-award–winning special effects system. Without the committed championship of House and the sponsorship of his immediate superiors, these landmark innovations could have easily been the victims of opposing political forces.

DESIGNING POLITICAL BATTLES TO BUILD A NEW COMPUTER

In his Pulitzer-prize–winning book, *The Soul of a New Machine*, Tracy Kidder (1981) treats us to a detailed account of the trials of the design engineer in the highly competitive computer industry. He also gives us an inside look at how competitive political contests can be surreptitiously orchestrated by senior managers to promote innovation.

Data General prided itself on its maverick culture—a culture which could be directly traced back to its founding members, three young computer engineers who left DEC in 1968 to set up shop in a former beauty parlour. Within ten years, Data General was on the Fortune 500 list and had carved out its niche in the minicomputer market. However, by 1976, Data General was also sorely in need of a new product, namely, a 32-bit minicomputer which was comparable, but better, than those recently introduced by their competitors.

The political stage was set by senior executives headed by CEO Ed de Castro when they announced that Data General would build a new research and development facility in North Carolina. It was here, they publicly announced, that major research would be conducted to develop the needed 32-bit minicomputer. The important Fountainhead Project (FHP) was transferred to the new location along with 50 of the most talented DG engineers and technicians. Meanwhile, among those who remained behind in Westborough, Massachusetts, were Tom West and his small Eclipse group. Their previous project had been cancelled in favor of the FHP—Data General could not afford to fund two major competing projects. Instead, West was assigned to revamp the lower priority 16-bit Eclipse. Although de Castro never put it in writing, West received tentative approval to transform the Eclipse into a 32-bit minicomputer as the rechristened Eagle project. Technically, the Eclipse group was not to do any groundbreaking developments—that was the territory of North Carolina's FHP. How West and his managers were able to do just that in record time is a testament to skillful team building and political acumen.

The first priority was to keep a low profile so as not to appear to be in competition with FHP. This political strategy was justified by West as follows:

> You gotta distinguish between the internal promotion to the actual workers and the promoting we did externally to other parts of the company. Outside the group I tried to low-key the thing. I tried to dull the impression that this was a competing product with North Carolina. I tried to sell it externally as not much of a threat . . . It was just gonna be a fast, Eclipse-like machine. This was the only way it was gonna live. We had to get the resources quietly, without creating a big brouhaha, and it's difficult to get a lot of external cooperation under those circumstances." (Kidder, 1981: 47)

Part of this low profile strategy was physical. The Eclipse group was located in the cramped basement quarters of Westborough headquarters where even the air conditioning didn't work properly. This resulted in both physical and social isolation from the rest of the company, all the better to facilitate covering up their real agenda for the Eagle project. The Eclipse group's low profile was also facilitated by the type of engineers recruited for the project. West and his lieutenant Carl Alsing hired recent engineering graduates not only for their excellent academic credentials but also for their willingness to work long hours and their unbridled enthusiasm for computer design work. By doing so, the group was ensured a low profile in that there were few who would see them as competition for the higher priced and proven talent in North Carolina.

One example of the lengths to which Eclipse group members went to avoid appearing to be in competition with FHP or encroaching on their territory is how computer architect Steve Wallach got his job done. If there was a computer instruction which deviated from the approved parameters of the Eagle project and might be construed as infringing on the FHP project, Wallach would work with his friends in System Software on the item. When finished, he would then ask his friends to write a memo requesting inclusion of the controversial instruction into the Eagle—thus avoiding any charges that the Eclipse group was going outside of approved project parameters.

Throughout the project, team members were constantly negotiating with support groups for their assistance. The competition for resources was difficult for the Eclipse group as Kidder (1981: 112) relates: "The game was fixed for North Carolina and all the support groups knew it." Through personal contacts and persuasive skills they were able to gain the needed resources.

What is particularly interesting in this case is that many of the engineers on the Eclipse team were unaware of the full extent of West's role in ensuring survival of the project. It was all part of his managerial style which was to stay separate from the team and to run interference with other corporate bodies in order that his engineering team could be creatively free. West also benefitted from having a management sponsor in Vice-President of Engineering Carl Carman who authorized the project and the money to recruit staff. Fortuitously, the FHP reported to a different Vice-President so there was no internal organizational conflict for Carman.

Finally, in a classic David vs. Goliath scenario, the small Eclipse group overcame all organizational and technical obstacles to deliver the 32-bit minicomputer ahead of North Carolina. This was a tale of a maverick group operating effectively within a maverick culture. For de Castro, it was a relatively low cost exercise in creative insurance so that Data General would have the desired product.

AN OUTSIDER DOING BATTLE WITH THE DEEP STRUCTURE: THE DVORAK SIMPLIFIED KEYBOARD

The case of the Dvorak Simplified Keyboard (DSK) is one which clearly demonstrates how self-interested political actors can effectively forestall a demonstrably beneficial technological change. When invented in 1873, the current universal "QWERTY" typewriter keyboard was designed to prevent typists from striking two adjoining keys in quick succession. Otherwise, the keys would "jam" together in the basket of a machine which relied on the forces of gravity to pull the keys back to their original positions. Technological improvements to the typewriter (the introduction of spring-loaded keys at the turn of the century and later, the invention of electric typewriters) overcame the jamming problem but the original keyboard remained. Enter Dr. August Dvorak, education professor, who through scientific time and motion studies developed a new keyboard configuration which would enable typists to work faster, more accurately (50% fewer mistakes) and with less physical strain to gain productivity improvements ranging from 35% to 100%

(Dvorak, Merrick, Dealey, & Ford, 1936). Additionally, Dvorak proved that typists could learn their skill in one-third of the time it took to learn on the QWERTY keyboard. Why then, aren't we all (present authors included) typing on this technologically superior invention?

Perhaps the chief culprits in resisting this technological innovation were the typewriter manufacturers who had considerable financial interests in retaining the traditional keyboard. During the 1930s when Dvorak introduced his invention, there was little incentive for typewriter manufacturers to convert over to a keyboard which would increase typist productivity thereby conceivably resulting in fewer sales. Furthermore, they would be required to pay royalties on Dvorak's patented invention.

Rejected by the manufacturers, Dvorak then reasoned that publicity at the World Typewriting Championships would help generate public demand for his invention. From 1934 to 1941, DSK-trained typists did indeed win the top typing awards at these competitions. However, the championships were sponsored by the manufacturers who, faced with these embarrassing outcomes, worked to deny Dvorak the publicity he sought. When publishing contest results, they only listed the names of the winning typists, not the machines they used in competition. An attempt by contest officials to ban DSK typists from competition was aborted when Dvorak threatened to advise the newspapers. Dvorak was even forced to hire security guards to protect his machines during the contests when it was discovered that they had been sabotaged.

The manufacturers were also skillful in networking with the American National Standards Institute. As members of the ANSI Keyboard Committee, they were able to prevent inclusion of the DSK into the national standards manual. Dvorak's attempts to gain a government contract for his typewriters were also unsuccessful. Despite the demonstrated superiority of the DSK in experimental tests conducted in the U.S. Navy and the General Services Administration, both rejected the possibility of a conversion. The rationale was that the measurable costs of replacing obsolete equipment and retraining typists outweighed the intangible future benefits of productivity improvements. This was a surprising conclusion since the trial results showed an average productivity increase of 74% with retraining costs being amortized over 10 days. Then in the ultimate covering up political tactic, the U.S. Navy assigned the DSK test results a security classification.

It is no wonder that, after 30 years of political battles to fulfil his dream, a frustrated Dr. Dvorak told Parkinson: "I'm tired of trying to do something worthwhile for the human race. They simply don't want to change!" (Parkinson, 1972: 18)

But as this account of innovation politics suggests, it is not all humans who resist change but rather those interest groups who stand to lose their financial stake if the innovation is implemented.

THE POWER OF VESTED INTERESTS TO FRUSTRATE NEW IDEAS: HELPING AUTISTIC CHILDREN

As related by Graziano (1969) in his account of a mental health innovation, the realm of interorganizational innovation is often the scene for political action at the deep structural level. Set in the 1960s, this account shows how the entrenched interests of a medical establishment (expert in the psychoanalytic treatment of such patients) actively resisted acknowledging or experimenting with a new technique (behavioral modification) to treat autistic children. The power of the professional elite is demonstrated by their ability to effectively maintain the status quo of local mental health services while circumventing efforts of an opposing group to gain local funding for an alternative treatment.

At a fundamental level, the two opposing interest groups were aligned into one which was supported by the medical profession versus one which was community-based. On the side of the entrenched power elite in the mental health community were the private-practice psychiatrists who operated the local clinics and dominated the local Mental Health Association. How they were able to parlay their position to influence other institutional actors (the local university and the "United Agency" fund-raising organization) is particularly interesting in this drama of innovation. In opposition to this coalition for the status quo was the Association for Mentally Ill Children (ASMIC), which was a lay group comprised of the parents of those autistic children who had not been helped by the psychoanalytic methodology (either because they had not responded to this course of treatment or had parents who could not afford the expensive private clinics). The ASMIC had employed a psychologist skilled in this new approach (remember that the time was the early 1960s when behavior modification was still a relatively radical new theory) to assist them in their attempt to change the system. However the integral role in which organizational politics plays in the course of innovation is highlighted by Graziano's (1969: 10) comment that: "The *conception* of innovative ideas in mental health depends upon creative humanitarian and scientific forces, while their *implementation* depends, not on science or humanitarianism, but on a broad spectrum of professional or social politics."

Although both groups initially worked together for four years in a local clinic offering both methodologies, the subsequent struggles over the resources to be allocated to each program and evaluation of the therapeutic effectiveness of each led to their separation.

Operating independently, the ASMIC tried repeatedly to gain financial support for their alternative approach. Once outside the mainstream of the medical establishment though, they encountered political resistance orchestrated by the local private clinics at both the surface and deep structure levels. An ASMIC proposal to the local university to try an experimental pilot project testing the merits of the behavioral modification methodology was rejected on two counts—it was too radical and it was not supported by the local mental health community.

Attempts to gain independent funding for their project from the local community funding agency ("United Agency") were first delayed and finally rejected after three years of efforts by the ASMIC to comply with the agency's demands. The influence of the established clinics (which were also funded by the United Agency) could be surmised to have played a role in the construction of these obstacles to implementation. Even though the ASMIC had garnered enough funds (from the parents of the autistic children and latterly from the State Department of Mental Health) to operate at a minimal level of service, the United Agency's rationale for withholding funds proved to be innovative in their own right. First there was the criticism that the program was first only a "paper proposal"; then after six months of operation, the United Agency contended that the program had been in operation "too brief a time on which to base a decision." After another year, the funding application was rejected because it had not been "professionally evaluated"; with a positive State Department of Mental Health evaluation in hand, the ASMIC program was then deemed to be a "duplication of services"; with state endorsement that it was a nonduplicated service, the United Agency declared that state financial support was required; and finally, with a state grant in hand, the United Agency rejected the application outright because the ASMIC had been "uncooperative" by not providing confidential information on clients' names, addresses, and fathers' places of employment.

AUTOMATICALLY CONTROLLED MACHINE TOOLS— AN OBJECT OF DEEP STRUCTURE POLITICS

That class conflict and the ideology of progress inform the institutions, ideas, and social groups which determine the design and use of a particular technology is the basic thesis of Noble's (1984) analysis of machine tool automation in manufacturing production. This case illustrates how deep structure politics were used to preserve and extend the control and power of the sectional interests of the owner/ managerial, scientific technical and military communities at the expense of those of workers. The capacity of a societal ideology to influence not only the choice of a technology but also to frame (in a pre-emptive manner) that decision in terms of the criteria and assumptions which are used, demonstrates the covert and subtle nature of deep structure power games.

Following WW II, there were two viable avenues by which machine tool automation could proceed. The first was Record Playback (R/P) which built on the skills and knowledge of machinist craftsmen thereby enhancing their traditional power base in the production process. In R/P, automatic control of a machine tool was achieved via a taped program which recorded the movements of the machine operator. It required a skilled machinist to make the initial program and any subsequent changes and adjustments to it. The second option was Numerical Control (N/C) technology in which the tape was programmed not by repeating a machinist's movements but by using scientific engineering methods. This in turn resulted in the assignment of machine programming responsibilities to staff engineers and technicians.

At a fundamental level, what did each technological approach represent? By removing the critical programming function from the shopfloor, N/C extended managerial control over production start-up, pace, and maintenance. In contrast, the R/P approach would be a continuation of the current sharing of production control with the skilled workers on the shopfloor. The overwhelming choice of industrial management was to pursue the N/C technological approach. The primary motive for this managerial decision was that it enabled management to regain control over production.

This impetus for the assertion of managerial control was only reinforced by the growing unionization of the American blue-collar workforce during the 1950s which (when coupled with the union movement's ideological alliance with Communist ideals) served to elevate managerial perceptions of threat. Support for this observation can be found in the fate of R/P systems which were developed in a number of large firms such as General Electric and the Ford Motor Company. Despite positive preliminary test results (based on production efficiency and cost criteria) corporate management consistently cancelled these experiments in favor of more complex engineer controlled N/C systems. Significantly, the decision at GE was made during a period of labor union unrest.

Managerial interests were also influenced and supported by the actions of other societal interest groups which preferred the N/C technology. The power of the scientific and military communities in channeling the course of machine tool automation should not be underestimated. The military underwrote much of the research and development costs of N/C projects in the university labs. MIT, at the forefront of computer microelectronic research, was an early advocate of N/C technology. Not only did N/C research provide MIT with a promising venue for applications of their new-found computer technology, but it also was consistent with an ideological bias for the superiority of formal educational expertise (needed to program N/C tapes) over layman experience (the basis of R/P technology).

SOME LESSONS FROM THE TRENCHES

Very briefly, we can draw some inferences from the experiences of innovators in these organizations. These propositions need to be tested in other settings and under conditions in which their effects can be carefully identified and analyzed. For the time being, we think it is useful for managers and others to consider the following lessons.

Lesson 1: Product innovation success within organizational settings requires a combination of both product *and* administrative innovation.

A good idea or product is simply not enough to guarantee successful implementation and diffusion within and outside an organization. For example, Hewlett-Packard's NASA Moonlander Monitor was a technological innovation which was almost terminated by a lack of administrative innovation. The information House gained from hands-on development with customers enabled him to modify the monitor to meet their needs while generating demand for the end-product. In this case and others, reliance on standard operating procedures are often insufficient to meet the unique requirements of new products or ideas.

Lesson 2(a): When a proposed innovation is congruent with the organizational and societal deep structure, political activity remains primarily on the surface, is benign or at a low level. Consequently, the probability of the acceptance and diffusion of such an innovation is enhanced with the support of the deep structure.

Lesson 2(b): A proposed innovation which threatens power relationships at the deep structure level evokes the full breadth and depth of opposing political forces, strategies and tactics. Consequently, the probability of acceptance and diffusion of such an innovation is significantly reduced.

These propositions focus on the type and range of political tactics which emerge or are elicited when a proposed innovation either confirms or threatens existing power relationships. As evidenced in the cases of the Dvorak Simplified Keyboard, the mental health innovation and those areas of ICI which resisted OD initiatives, when those interests which benefit from maintaining the status quo perceive an innovation to be a threat, the politics of change are both numerous and powerful. What results is a mismatched contest where the deep structure frames the rules of the game and to a large extent preordains the outcome. The metaphor of a "corporate immune system" is a useful one in understanding the dynamics of this response. As Pinchot (1985, p. 189) relates:

> When you start something new, the system naturally resists it. It is almost as if the corporation had an immune system which detects anything that is not part of the status quo and surrounds it. If you are to survive, you will have to lull this immune system into ignoring you. You will have to appear to be part of the corporate self, rather than identified as a foreign body.

Although Pinchot focuses on the intraorganizational arena, we believe that the same "immune system" can be activated in the interorganizational and societal realms. As outsiders or newcomers to the arenas in which they were trying to introduce their changes, Dvorak and the ASMIC were easily allocated the role of unwanted invaders by a system which perceived few, if any, benefits to influential system members through effecting a change to the status quo.

At ICI, the OD change agents were also perceived to be outsiders to the production process. However the success of Ripley and Bridge's program in the Agricultural Division could be traced to their strategy of first developing a strong, coherent program for change independent of the corporate system before attempting to enter it and then, to work within the system in a nonthreatening manner. They started low in the organizational structure and built support in an incremental way. In contrast, the OD programs in the other areas were more visible and did not have the strength of unity in either philosophy or personnel to withstand the opposition.

When the proposed innovation or change is consistent and/or supports existing power relationships, the politics remain at the more manageable surface level. The contests at Hewlett-Packard and at Data General were against a backdrop of a unity of interests between innovators and the corporate ethic. These innovators were secure in the knowledge that the organizational mission was to be at the forefront of their technology—a deep structure which desired technological change for competitive purposes. They also benefitted from cultures with a deep structure mythology of hero-founders who were mavericks in their own right. By acting as mavericks themselves, they were only continuing the organizational tradition and could count on a degree of understanding of their actions at the highest corporate levels. Opposition to these product innovations were of a more traditional and restricted nature in terms of internal power plays, managing line vs. staff territories and gaining the necessary resources for development. As corporate insiders, these innovators could draw on their past experience and that of others in the organization to gauge how best to proceed—which political tactics had succeeded in the past, which had failed, the relative risks involved, who were the power players and who were not.

For administrative innovations, political gamesmanship played a major role in the eventual success or failure of the proposed change. Success often hinged on the innovator's ability to marshall a wide range of supportive political tactics at both the surface and deep structure levels. Ripley and Bridge at ICI's Agricultural Division proved to be politically adept at numerous influence tactics. Review of these successful administrative innovations reveals that there was a minimal number of opposing political games, either at the surface or deep structure levels.

Administrative failures at ICI present a contrasting picture. The tactics of appealing to higher authority and appealing to reason proved to be ineffective against the deep structure games of a resistant organization. These OD change agents were effectively pre-empted by divisional managements which denied that any change to the status quo was needed and rejected the claim that these staff persons had a right to be involved in any change process.

> *Lesson 3:* Within organizations, the political strategy of "asking for forgiveness" is limited to only the initial phases of the conception and development of a product innovation. For the adoption and diffusion of a new product, the innovator must "seek and secure permission" of the organization.

We note in these case studies of innovation there are two distinct types of political strategies—that of "asking for forgiveness" and that of "seeking and securing permission." "Asking for forgiveness" occurs when an innovator proceeds to the point of adoption without official organizational knowledge and/or sanction. It is an independent course of action often marked by secrecy and the furtive seconding or transfer of corporate resources. Alternatively, the strategy of "seeking and securing permission" usually encompasses the political strategies of developing champions and sponsors and of building networks and coalitions. Neglecting to do so may threaten the long term viability of an innovation.

In our view, asking for forgiveness is a viable strategy when pursuing product innovation. Seeking and securing permission is a more viable strategy when pursuing administrative innovations. It is possible to hide a product innovation from potential naysayers in the important fragile early phases of that innovation. Social and administrative innovations, on the other hand, depend more immediately on corporate interdependencies for their successful implementation. Thus it becomes important for the innovator to both seek *and* secure permission from organizational actors in a variety of positions and levels to ensure success. In the long run, product innovations move from the laboratory to implementation and thus to integration with other organizational routines and procedures. This entails a shift to a greater emphasis on the permission rather than the forgiveness strategy.

These accounts of innovation demonstrate the integral role political strategy plays in both promoting and suppressing innovation. If the proposed change threatens the self-interests of a powerful dominant coalition (as in the mental health innovation, the Dvorak keyboard, and machine tool automation), we find that the emergence of a technological innovation is a tenuous one. In these cases, the full breadth of deep structure and surface politics is elicited to preserve prevailing power relationships. Apparently, rationality is subsumed in these high stakes interorganizational and societal level battles for survival of the fittest. On the other hand, if there is no perceived fundamental threat, the political activity remains on the surface and can be more readily managed by prospective innovators.

REFERENCES

Dvorak, A.; Merrick, N.L.; Dealey, W.L.; and Ford, G.C. (1936). *Typewriting Behavior: Psychology Applied to Teaching and Learning Typewriting.* New York: American Book Company.

Graziano, A.M. (1969). "Clinical Innovation and the Mental Health Power Structure: A Social Case History," *American Psychologist 24*(1), 10–18.

Kidder, T. (1981). *The Soul of a New Machine.* New York: Avon Books.

Noble, D.F. (1984). *Forces of Production.* New York: Knopf.

Parkinson, R. (1972). "The Dvorak Simplified Keyboard: Forty Years of Frustration," *Computers and Automation 21*(11), 18–25.

Pinchot, J. III (1985). *Intrapreneuring.* New York: Harper and Row.

Business Shares the Blame for Workers' Low Skills

John Hoerr

America, once the home of the world's most skilled labor force, now may be throwing it all away. Schools continue to turn out poorly educated young people. Employers continue to reject the idea of spending large amounts of money to train workers and upgrade skills. The easiest—but most damaging—way to remain competitive is to downgrade skills and cut wages. Indeed, the U.S. is on a de-skilling binge for the sake of short-term productivity growth that could prove disastrous for business and the economy in the long run.

So concludes a major new study by a group called the Commission on the Skills of the American Workforce. Most companies, it finds, accept the idea that they must live with a low-skilled work force. Less than 10% of employers surveyed

Reprinted from June 25, 1990 issue of *Business Week* by special permission. Copyright © 1990 by McGraw-Hill, Inc.

are creating jobs that call for workers with broad-based skills and the ability to adapt to fast-changing technology and markets. In other words, business by and large is not demanding—and the society is not delivering—the large-scale improvements in education and training that American industry needs.

The commission's study, titled "America's Choice: High Skills or Low Wages," will be issued on June 18. Established by the nonprofit National Center on Education & the Economy, the 32-member commission is a bipartisan group of business, academic, and labor representatives chaired by Ira C. Magaziner, a business strategy consultant who is president of SJS Inc. The commission co-chairmen are Ray Marshall and William E. Brock, who served as Labor Secretaries in the Carter and Reagan Administrations, respectively. The report is funded by the Carnegie Corp. of New York, New York State, Towers Perrin, and the German Marshall Fund.

"The Worst"   The commission conducted in-depth studies of workplaces and education-training systems in the U.S., Germany, Sweden, Denmark, Japan, Ireland, and Singapore. It concludes that, except for Ireland, the foreign countries provide far better schooling and job training for noncollege-bound youth than the U.S. As a result, American youth rank near the bottom in comparisons of school performance. The other nations also have well-organized national systems for moving high school graduates into industry. The transition from school to work in the U.S. is described as "the worst of any industrialized country."

The study focuses on some 82 million jobs in the U.S. that do not require a four-year college education. These include skilled employees, such as nurses and construction workers, as well as line workers such as machine operators, assemblers, retail clerks, and health service employees. According to projections, most recruits for these jobs will be deficient in such basic skills as reading and writing. Even so, the skills commission found, relatively few employers plan to sharpen their employees' skills through remedial training. Although all the U.S. companies surveyed complained about a lack of skills, most were concerned more about workers' attitudes and personalities than educational skills.

In contrast, America's competitors tend to upgrade line workers' jobs and fill them with well-educated young people. Most important, a high percentage of foreign companies is achieving large productivity gains by reorganizing work to eliminate tiers of managers and give workers more of a say. The resulting "high-performance" workplace calls for multiskilled line workers who have good reading, math, science, and problem-solving skills. These workers can readily absorb new skills as technology and production requirements change. With workers who adapt quickly to new conditions, manufacturers can introduce new products on short cycle times and frequently switch production runs.

High Road   In the U.S., however, the commission discovered that fewer than 10% of the 400-plus companies interviewed are reorganizing work in this fashion. Instead of investing in workers, most companies are pursuing other strategies to remain competitive: cutting wages, exporting production jobs to low-wage countries, or de-skilling jobs through automation. All of these methods are based on what Magaziner calls a "high-turnover, low-wage model." Many employers, he says, assume that the U.S. will have a large pool of uneducated, unskilled people. That being the case, the companies are using automation to create very simple work tasks—jobs described by some critics as "idiot-proof"—with low wages and no employment security.

Companies that take this path may be successful, but only in the short term, the commission says. The nation faces a choice. "We can choose forms of work organization which achieve cost competitiveness in the short run based upon low skills, low wages, and ultimately a society with a low living standard," Magaziner says. "Or we can choose forms of work organization which require more investment but which result in cost competitiveness based upon higher skills, higher wages, and a higher living standard."

The commission wants the U.S. to take the high-wage path. It recommends fundamental changes in the way the U.S. educates and trains the 70% of young people who will not graduate from four-year colleges. It urges the government to encourage companies to adopt high-performance work systems. Employers would be required to invest 1% of payroll in either their own training programs or a national fund to upgrade worker skills. These are controversial proposals, but the U.S. needs strong action to upgrade its work force to world-class standards.

"Change-or-Else" Warning to Business

Joan Beck

CHICAGO—OK, Ann B. Hopkins won a significant victory for the cause of women's rights and equal opportunity in the higher levels of corporate America.

It should knock another hole in the glass ceiling that so subtly and effectively keeps hard-working, successful women from making it all the way to the top executive offices and prestigious partnerships.

And it should write an indelible "change or else" warning on the walls of corporate suites and clubby old-boy networks trying to barricade themselves from women and minorities by means of partnership rules, tenure committees and other exclusionary strategies.

Even so, it is troubling that the courts are getting involved in dictating personnel decisions at management level to private employers, however justified the reasons.

Many feminists are concerned that the ruling will simply remind corporate sexists to camouflage their prejudices more cleverly and hide their biases better behind code words that sound sexually neutral if legally challenged.

Hopkins, 46, won a major—perhaps final—round in her six-year sex discrimination case against Price Waterhouse last week.

A District of Columbia federal district judge ordered the big accounting firm to give Hopkins the partnership she was denied in 1983, plus back pay of about $400,000.

The long case has already been to the Supreme Court to settle the question of what the standard of proof should be in such lawsuits. The high court said last year that plaintiffs must initially show some evidence of discrimination.

But in their defense, employers need not present "clear and convincing evidence" that they acted in a nondiscriminatory way but only the less stringent "preponderance of evidence" to justify their actions. The Supreme Court then sent the case back to the lower court.

The high court ruled in 1984 that a law firm could be sued by a woman associate who was rejected for a partnership. That case was finally settled out of court. But the woman did not rejoin the firm.

Hopkins apparently does want to be a Price Waterhouse partner, however difficult her working relationship will be with colleagues who are forced to make her an equal.

The judge ordered the accounting firm to take her back on July 1 and pay her what management consultants who made partner in 1983 are earning now.

Law firms, accounting firms and other companies organized as partnerships have long found it easy to keep women and minorities in subordinate positions. Partners were considered a collegial group of business peers who just happened to be white and male and if they chose other white males to join their tight professional circle, they had to account to no one but each other for their decisions.

College faculties, too, have managed quite skillfully to exclude women and minorities from tenured jobs except in token numbers. Here, too, intangibles—teaching abilities, quality of research, prestige of publications on a resume—can easily be interpreted to favor the candidates the selection committees want: more white males.

Criteria for promotion become harder to quantify, too, the higher up the career ladder people climb. Leadership abilities, skills with people, vision, the image a person projects all become valid qualities to consider—and partners, senior faculty and corporate boards tend to see them most readily in those most like themselves—white males.

This is changing, as the promotion ladders, organization charts and associateships fill up with highly qualified, nontraditional professionals—women and minorities who work so hard and are so effective their employers can't risk their loss.

But there are still great discrepancies between the number of well-qualified women and minority professionals at entry and middle-management levels and the number who are partners, senior faculty, CEOs and corporate board members.

Too few women have yet cracked through the glass ceiling. Price Waterhouse, after all, has 900 partners, only 27 of them female.

"Price Waterhouse intentionally maintained a partnership evaluation system that permitted negative, sexually stereotyped comments to influence partnership decisions," wrote the judge in this case.

Evidence was presented at the trial which showed Hopkins had been told she would have a better shot at a partnership if she walked and talked more femininely, had her hair styled and wore more jewelry and makeup.

Had not some Price Waterhouse partners been so indiscreet, Hopkins would not have had such a strong legal case, however real the discrimination that kept her from being promoted.

It's not likely professional firms or corporate employers will make blatant mistakes like that again.

But there are still other ways to discriminate against women—and minorities—in partnerships and promotions, other ways of making decisions on the basis of "not like us" that won't add up to sufficient evidence of discrimination in court.

Women are still a long way from equality.

Cost Cutting: How to Do It Right

Ronald Henkoff

So far, downsizing just hasn't delivered. Companies are sometimes leaner but rarely meaner. Lessons for the Nineties: Eliminate work, not necessarily workers.

Downsizing, cost cutting, restructuring—will they ever end? It seems not. After nearly a decade of slashing overhead and slicing jobs, corporate America has entered the Nineties ready to slash and slice some more. The list of companies that announced work force reductions in the past six months alone would fill this page.

A few of them: Apple Computer, AT&T, Bank of New England, Boeing, Business-land, Caterpillar, Chrysler, Eastman Kodak, Gillette, Grumman, Honeywell, Hughes Aircraft, Levi Strauss, Merrill Lynch, McGraw-Hill, US West Communications.

If there is an apt, semicomic image for the past decade, it would be a harried, still-in-shock chief executive who returns from the office and exclaims to his wife: "Honey, I shrunk the company! What do I do now?" With alarming frequency, the answer appears to be: *Shrink it some more.* In each of the past three years, according to surveys by the American Management Association, roughly a third of American companies have cut their payrolls.

As executives prepare for yet another round of downsizing, many have come to a staggering realization: They've been doing it wrong. They have lost some of their best employees, and those who remain are overburdened and disgruntled. Learning from their mistakes, managers at some companies have begun to adopt a new approach to downsizing for the Nineties—cut the workload, not just the work force. In some quarters, this idea has even acquired a name, "right-sizing." Today's cost cutting goes beyond changing the size of your company to require that you also change the way you manufacture, report, count, supervise, inspect, evaluate, and sell.

Clearly, a new approach is needed. Downsizing has become an opiate for many companies. Administered in repeated doses, it can hurt product quality, alienate customers, and actually cut productivity growth. It can foster an organization so preoccupied with bean counting, so anxious about where the ax will fall next, that employees become narrow-minded, self-absorbed, and risk-averse.

Worse, downsizing begets more downsizing. Says Eric Greenberg, editor of the American Management Association's research reports: "The best indication of whether a company will downsize next year is whether it has downsized in the past." Eastman Kodak, for example, is shrinking for the third time in six years, Honeywell for the second time in four years.

Cost cutting wasn't supposed to work this way. Yes, corporate America had to slim down; it had grown bureaucratic—overstaffed and overmanaged. But companies have been laboring to become "lean and mean" for nearly a decade. Shouldn't they be honed, toned, and sinewy, ready to face the world by now? The Fortune 500 industrial companies sweated off 3.2 million jobs in the Eighties. Isn't that enough?

Not by a long shot. Says Daniel Valentino, president of United Research, a management consulting firm that helps companies restructure: "The Eighties were just the tip of the iceberg, and we're going to see dramatic reductions in the Nineties. Corporate America is still as much as 25% overstaffed."

What went wrong? Simply stated, cost cutting, as it has usually been practiced, hasn't delivered the goods. Despite all those layoffs, all that automation and just-in-time inventory management, all those speeches about leanness and meanness, U.S. nonfarm productivity crept up by a scant 1.2% a year on average in the Eighties. That's virtually no improvement from the rate in the Seventies.

If that number doesn't tell the tale, try this one: More than half the 1,468 restructured companies surveyed by the Society for Human Resource Management reported that employee productivity either stayed the same or deteriorated after the layoffs. In another poll, conducted by Right Associates, a Philadelphia outplacement firm, 74% of senior managers at recently downsized companies said that their workers had low morale, feared future cutbacks, and distrusted management.

Contrary to the duchess of Windsor's famous dictum, you *can* be too thin. You can also be lean in the wrong places. Look at corporate spending on R&D. After growing at an average real rate of 8.2% annually in the first half of the Eighties, it inched up 1.3% a year between 1985 and 1988, according to the National Science Foundation. Last year it fell by an estimated 0.9%, the first decrease in 15 years.

Downsizing, when poorly implemented, can also make a mockery of other corporate goals. The wrong way begins with an edict from on high: All departments shall cut their budgets by 10% this year. That 10% usually comes from what is euphemistically called "head count" or "human assets." You take a one-time charge to earnings, your operating margins improve, and Wall Street cheers.

But the folks still on the payroll become frustrated and confused: The same amount of work has just been loaded on the backs of fewer workers. The survivors groan, *I can't possibly do all this stuff. What's the most important?* Either some of the tasks don't get done, or the organization finds new ways of doing them. Consultants—often recently terminated employees—will be hired, temps will be added, the budget will creep up again. "Costs exist for a reason," says William Fowble, general manager of photographic products at Kodak. "If you don't take the reasons away, the costs will return." Then it will be time for another round of cutting, as Kodak and other companies know only too well.

Want your workers to assume more responsibility, take more risks, become more accountable? Want them to love their customers, to focus on quality, to make decisions faster? Downsizing imposed by executive fiat can have precisely the opposite effects. Wary of losing their heads, workers become reluctant to stick their necks out. Says consultant Gary Neilson of Booz Allen & Hamilton in Chicago: "The whole quality of decision-making suffers. Employees are always looking over their shoulders. Managers are afraid to take risks."

Budget-conscious executives defer maintenance, skimp on training, delay new-product introductions, and shy away from potential but unproven new businesses. Says Robert Gunn, a management consultant at A. T. Kearney: "You get a bottom-line benefit from the payroll cut, but then all these other things have gone wrong. The net change is zero."

There doesn't have to be such a devastating downside to downsizing. It is possible to be both lean and *fit*. Executives at companies as diverse as Oryx Energy, US West, Colgate-Palmolive, and H.J. Heinz have made this discovery. Says Gary Ames, CEO of US West Communications, a subsidiary of the Baby Bell regional operating company headquartered in Denver: "At some point in your dieting process you come to the realization that if you really want to keep the weight off you have to change your habits." Sadder but wiser managers propose some new habits to replace the old inefficient ones and to transform downsizing into right-sizing:

SIX RULES OF RIGHT-SIZING YOUR DOWNSIZING

- Cut unnecessary work.
- Put quality first.
- Bust your paradigms.
- Empower people.
- Communicate.
- Take care of the survivors.

Cut Unnecessary Work   Oryx, a Dallas-based oil and gas producer, will save $70 million in operating costs this year—no small matter for a company that earned $139 million in 1989. How? By eliminating rules, procedures, reviews, reports, and approvals that had little to do with finding more hydrocarbons.

As the price of crude softened in the early Eighties, Oryx, a subsidiary of Sun Oil until it was spun off to shareholders in 1988, began trimming. From 1982 to 1986 the company cut 1,500 of its 6,000 jobs in a process that Harold Ashby, vice president for human resources, calls "incremental twitches, tightenings, and squeezings." By 1987, says Ashby, "we thought we were at minimum staffing levels."

They thought wrong. With a barrel of oil hovering around $14, Oryx's costs were still too high. Says Ashby, drawing a subtle distinction: "We were more efficient. We just weren't more effective." The company hired an opinion research firm to survey its remaining employees. It discovered that they were overworked, overly fixated on meeting budget targets, and insufficiently focused on discovering more oil.

With help from consultants at United Research, Oryx set up teams with representatives from various departments to identify work that didn't need to be done. At the recommendation of the teams, the company junked 25% of all internal reports, reduced from 20 to four the number of signatures required on requests for capital expenditures, and compressed from seven months to six weeks the time it took to produce the annual budget. Between 1987 and 1989, Oryx also eliminated another 1,500 jobs, but this time the cuts included many middle managers whose work had largely been eliminated.

Thanks in part to liberating its employees to adopt new drilling technology, make new discoveries, and acquire new reserves, Oryx is now the largest independent oil and gas producer in the world. In the past four years the company has doubled the rate at which it replaces its depleted reserves and has cut in half the average cost of finding that new oil and gas.

Colgate-Palmolive also tried across-the-board head count reductions in the Eighties when it set out to reduce spending at its technology group. But the cuts didn't prove permanent. "The business added back what it needed," says William Cooling, executive vice president and chief technological officer.

So three years ago Cooling, who oversees a staff of 1,100, including 600 scien-

REDUCING THE BILE FACTOR AT HEINZ

Anthony J.F. O'Reilly, chief executive of Heinz since 1979, realizes that a company, much like a plastic bottle of ketchup, can be squeezed only so much. Even at Heinz, one of industry's most successful cost cutters, downsizing has its limits.

In the Eighties, O'Reilly closed factories, laid off workers, and revved up production lines with enviable results. Gross profit margins swelled from 33% to 39% of sales, and Heinz posted average earnings increases of 15% per year in a decade when the processed-food industry was bedeviled by sluggish growth, merciless competition, and bitter takeover battles.

But O'Reilly now realizes that his sharp pencil, while financially successful, alienated workers, interfered with the quality of the products, and left the company still wasting millions of dollars a year on unnecessary work. His solution: Stop squeezing and start changing. Concentrate on quality, not cost.

Under the company's total quality management (TQM) effort, introduced two years ago, teams of workers are reexamining virtually everything Heinz does—from the way it packages French fries to the way it conducts market research. O'Reilly figures that TQM can save the company $250 million over the next three years, mostly by eliminating waste and rework.

The Dublin-born O'Reilly, 53, is a former star rugby player who owns six provincial newspapers in England, an outdoor advertising agency in France, and a recently acquired stake in Waterford Wedgwood, the crystal and china maker. He spoke about Heinz's cost and quality control with *Fortune*'s Ronald Henkoff:

The Cost-Cutting Imperative We feel the spear of the marketplace in our back. We are extremely conscious of the vulnerability of even our greatest brands. All it takes is a modest shortfall in volume or a modest hiccup in cost control and we become exposed to earnings loss very quickly. We are in a business where, in most sectors, the volume increase is 1% per year. That's pretty chilling.

The Emphasis on Quality We want to secure our cost reductions from something we never concentrated on before—the price of nonconformance. That is, the need to get things right the first time. So we've begun to question our entire system, our entire manufacturing processes right across the spectrum. The thing I like about TQM is that it's more Socratic than surgical.

The Removal of Waste There is an enormous amount of redundancy in every corporation. For example, we've reduced from five to one the number of market research services we use. Market research is an area of exotica, where everyone has a set of numbers that flatters his particular perceptions. We just said: One bible is called for in this case.

The Focus on Service We've realized that Weight Watchers, which we own, is not based on cost structures. It's based on service satisfaction. That's an enormous shift for us. When people decide to come to a Weight Watchers class, cost is not their primary concern. The question is how can we, for example, harness the power of the computer to provide them with a complete statement of their goals, their weight loss, and their caloric intake over the last week?

The Bile Factor   Over the years the relentless pressure of cost cutting had created within Heinz a mounting feeling of bile. The notion that when people on high exhort you to cut costs they're talking about cutting your costs, not theirs, bred distaste. There was an ever-increasing feeling of hostility among the employees. Fewer people do more work. Layoffs create a degree of insecurity because workers wonder if 50 people were cut last year and 100 this year, how many will go next year?

The Empowering of Workers   Working in teams creates a great sense of interdependence. Jobs are now substantially more sophisticated, interesting, and exciting. Instead of staring mindlessly at a moving belt of peas or carrots or bottles or whatever, workers are now able, for example, to work the computerized photo-imaging machinery that controls the labeling line.

   The advent of TQM has greatly elevated the dignity of the worker at Heinz. In the past there was very little consultation with employees. That led to a natural sense of human irritation, a sense that "at least they could have bloody well asked me about that. After all, I've done this particular job for 20 years."

The Future   If we are going to make this company grow to match the expectations of the stock market—that is 10% to 12% growth a year—we have to do it by doing better what we do best. Henry J. Heinz, our founder, had a marvelous phrase that I think exactly describes TQM: "doing common things uncommonly well." One hundred twenty years later, I couldn't put it any better myself.

---

tists, had all his technology group managers fill out a questionnaire devised by Temple Barker & Sloane, a management consulting firm based in Lexington, Massachusetts. The TBS survey asked the managers how they and their subordinates spent their time. The results were illuminating: Instead of concentrating on how to make teeth whiter or clothes brighter, scientists were expending too much energy on supervising and reporting. Researchers at different locations and in different departments were duplicating one another's efforts. They were also preoccupied with designing new factories, a task that had little to do with the tech group's responsibility for inventing and improving products.

   After the survey, Cooling cut two layers of management and farmed out factory design to consultants. To free the scientists from activities such as purchasing and budgeting, Cooling increased support services. The tech group shut down two of its four major labs around the world and cut the total number of research projects by 40% after managers agreed on which ones were important.

   To improve the efficiency of his workers, Cooling scrubbed old functional divisions like basic research, processing, and packaging, and grouped people into teams in product areas such as oral care, pet food, and household cleansers. He also took the radical step of putting basic researchers directly in touch with consumers, so the once cloistered lab scientists could see exactly what the Jones family expected from a dishwashing liquid or a can of dog food.

Since the reorganization, the tech group has come up with a string of new products, including a toothpaste that Colgate claims greatly reduces plaque and gingivitis. (Having launched it in Europe, the company is currently seeking FDA approval for the dentifrice in the U.S.) The bottom line? Cooling calculates that he's saved $40 million in the past three years.

At US West Communications, Gary Ames is just beginning to find out how his troops spend their time. Like all the Baby Bells, US West was born bulbous—freighted with too many managers, analysts, technicians, and clerical workers—and has been trying to downsize for more than six years. Since 1984 the communications subsidiary, which is the company's biggest, has cut its work force by 8,000 to 58,000. This year alone, Ames, whose 52nd-floor office affords a commanding view of the Rocky Mountains and Mile-High Stadium, has cut an additional 3,800 managers.

But he isn't slashing blindly. He seconded 17 top executives to a special task force that spent three months asking 7,000 middle managers what they and their underlings did every hour of every day. One early shocker: Some 350 people are involved in drawing up the annual budget. Ames wants to cut that number down to 100: "We don't need our people to work harder, we need them to work smarter." He reckons he has to spend at least $250 million annually for the next five years on new technology while keeping costs flat on an absolute basis. The only way to accomplish both those goals is to cut out useless work.

MANAGING

Put Quality First   If any company has earned the right to crow about cost cutting, it is Pittsburgh-based H.J. Heinz, the king of ketchup. This penny-pinching monarch has increased its operating margins every year since 1977, a feat virtually unrivaled in American industry. Chief Executive Anthony O'Reilly, renowned for his relentless attention to costs, has closed factories, laid off workers, and speeded up production lines (see preceding box). Then Heinz discovered that overzealous cost cutting can injure product quality. Says J. Wray Connolly, a senior vice president: "I won't sit here and tell you that we allowed our quality to erode, but the focus was not on quality." It is now.

Two years ago, with some Heinz products losing market share, O'Reilly and his team began a round of soul-searching that resulted in shifting their sights from cost cutting to quality—for both their products and their production processes. The Heinz executives became acolytes of consultant Philip Crosby, whose slender tome, *Quality Is Free,* is their bible. Crosby's thesis—make things right the first time and you will save money on inspection, wastage, and rework—debunks the axiom that improving quality means spending more money.

By emphasizing quality, Heinz managers have learned to stand conventional cost-cutting logic on its head. Among their apostatic discoveries: *Adding* workers can boost effectiveness. So can *slowing down* a production line. With these and other measures, Connolly estimates, Heinz can save at least $250 million a year by the mid-1990s. He makes his case with a few stunning examples.

Under its low-cost operator programs, Heinz had cut the work force at its StarKist tuna canning factories in Puerto Rico and American Samoa by 5%. With tough competition coming from low-wage rivals in Thailand, keeping a lid on labor costs seemed to make sense. But the fish cleaners were so overworked that they were leaving literally tons of meat on the bone every day. Says Connolly, who heads the company's total quality management effort: "We discovered that we had to add people, not subtract them. In the past, we just wouldn't have done that."

StarKist managers slowed down the production lines, hired 400 hourly workers and 15 supervisors, and retrained the entire work force. They installed four more lines to take some of the load off each worker and to expand volume. All told, StarKist increased labor costs by $5 million but cut out $15 million in wastage. Net saving: $10 million annually.

At Heinz's Ore-Ida potato processing plants, managers realized that years of take-no-prisoners cost cutting had actually changed the taste and texture of the company's popular Tater Tots, contributing to a decline in sales. New high-speed slicing machines were whizzing the spuds through the plant, but they were also dicing some of the potatoes too fine, making the Tots mushy instead of chunky.

Like their colleagues at StarKist, the Ore-Ida managers slowed down the production lines, allowing the machines to churn out more uniform morsels. Efficiency went down, but effectiveness went up—there's that dichotomy again. Tater Tots now taste the way they used to, and the increased sales volume—up 8.8% in the past year—has more than paid for the cost of going slow.

Bust Your Paradigms   As Heinz has discovered, speed and automation, two totems of modern management, do not necessarily reduce costs, whereas prosaically low-tech innovations can sometimes work wonders. The trick is to question long-held assumptions about the way things work, a process Heinz managers call "paradigm busting."

For years engineers at the Ore-Ida factory in Plover, Wisconsin, were puzzled by the frequent breakage of frozen French fries that were being skimmed along the conveyor belt prior to being plunked into packages. Last year they examined every step of the production process, starting from the point where trucks laden with whole potatoes pulled into the unloading bays. The Ore-Ida engineers assumed that the uncooked spuds were tough tubers that could withstand routine three-foot to 14-foot drops as they tumbled along the production line.

That was the paradigm, but it was only half right. The spuds weren't breaking or bruising, but they were developing microscopic fault lines causing the finished French fries to fracture much farther down the line. The solution: eliminate potato free fall by installing a few metal slides. The annual savings: $300,000.

When workers at the space and communications group of Hughes Aircraft, part of GM Hughes Electronics, set out to build satellites more cost-effectively, they mapped out every step that went into building each bird—from design to delivery. Says Joe Sanders, group vice president for operations: "When you stretch it out on the wall like that, things leap out at you. You say, 'What the hell am I doing that for?' "

Working in multidisciplinary teams composed of workers from design, manufacturing, purchasing, and marketing, the Hughes employees identified 131 steps that were candidates for "major improvements," and then they focused on 30 of the most urgent. By making a series of seemingly small changes, such as moving a hole a quarter of an inch so an inspector could more easily insert a testing probe, Hughes cut the time it took to build a satellite control processor—the brains of the machine—from 45 weeks to 22 weeks, saving millions of dollars.

Empower People   The latest trendy slogan? Yes. But even hierarchical Kodak has boosted productivity by grouping workers into teams, teaching them how to inspect their own work, and then listening to their suggestions. Once so paternalistic that it was known as "Great Yellow Father," the Rochester, New York, company has struggled for six years to cut costs—with mixed results. Operating margins actually shrank last year, and the company wrote off $875 million pretax in divestments, plant closures, consolidations, and work force cuts. Some 4,500 employees have left the company in the past six months.

But deep within the confines of Kodak Park, a 2,200-acre jumble of turn-of-the-century red-brick factories, a revolution has occurred at the precision components manufacturing division. Assembly workers who make X-ray cassettes and spools, canisters, and cartons for Kodak film now arrange their own hours, keep track of their productivity, and fix their machines.

Three years ago, for example, Daniel Cardinale did nothing but operate a punch press eight hours a day. Now he coaches fellow team members in statistical process control, meets with suppliers, interviews prospective recruits, and helps manage just-in-time inventory. What's the connection with cost cutting? More effective use of manpower and brainpower has enabled Cardinale's unit to do nearly the same amount of work in one shift that used to require three. Says Richard Wilkinson, a supervising engineer: "We realized that there was a tremendous resource that was not being tapped." He means people.

Communicate   When a company is shrinking, its reason for being in business often gets lost in the wash. When Booz Allen, the consulting firm, surveyed 170 Fortune 500 companies, half the executives admitted that their middle managers—never mind the poor hourly workers—had no understanding of corporate objectives or only a partial grasp of them. The problem reflects content clutter, the clangor of conflicting executive directives to cut costs, improve quality, serve the customer, boost productivity, slash the work force, and empower the remaining work force.

At Square D, a leading manufacturer of electrical equipment, Chief Executive Jerre Stead has set up an in-house academy called Vision College. His aim is to slice through the content clutter and get everyone in the company speaking the same language. By 1991 all 19,200 employees of this Palatine, Illinois, company will have been through a two-day program of lectures and seminars that stress the primacy of quality and customer service.

Stead, a trim, athletic manager who never closes his office door, has also installed an outsize scoreboard at corporate headquarters. Up on the board are the quarterly results broken down by profit per employee, sales per employee, and return on equity for Square D and its competitors, among them Emerson Electric, General Electric, and Westinghouse. Square D workers know exactly what they're up against.

These tactics sound simplistic, but simplicity has its virtues. When Stead joined Square D from Honeywell as president in 1987, a lieutenant cheerfully presented his new boss with four thick manuals of official corporate policies and procedures. There were some 760 rules in all, many concerning who could talk to whom within the company and several dealing with who could talk to customers and under what circumstances. Stead has dumped the rule books in favor of 11 policy statements.

He has also tried to bring some sanity to Square D's cost cutting. Even as Stead has divested businesses, closed plants, and laid off employees, he has increased spending on travel for salesmen and on training for everyone. "We had frozen our field sales organization," he says. "We hadn't had a sales conference in ten years. We were turning the screws short term to try to keep artificial profit coming." So far, Stead's mix of talking, training, and trimming seems to be working. Since 1984 Square D has cut its work force by 17% and increased its sales from continuing operations by 37%.

Take Care of the Survivors   Having gone to extreme lengths to assist the people they laid off, companies are only now realizing that workers who are still aboard need support. At Colgate's tech group, Bill Cooling has upgraded the human resources department, bringing in experienced counselors to advise his scientists on career opportunities.

Managers are also wondering if early retirement, once seen as a relatively painless way of cutting the work force, is so benign after all. Inducing experienced middle-aged employees to leave makes little sense when incoming generations of workers are poorly educated. At Square D, Jerre Stead shut down a program that had encouraged veteran workers in their middle and late 50s to quit. Says he: "We were losing some of our best assets."

In an age of progressively stiffer global competition, rapidly developing new technologies, and increasingly complex jobs, the success of any company's rightsizing will depend ultimately on the quality of its workers. "The fewer people you have, the better they have to be," says Colgate's Cooling. Like many managerial insights this one seems painfully obvious, but it is a breakthrough. Gary Neilson of Booz Allen points out that "Eighties cost cutting underestimated the value of the employee. Now managers are discovering that the human element can make a great deal of difference in organizations."

Those "human elements" will have to be trained, sometimes in the basic skills that they failed to learn in school. And they will require coaching in the art of working in a leaner, smarter, and more flexible company. "Every time we sell a box of Kodak film, there's a bit of training investment in it that maybe the Japanese didn't have to make," concedes Richard Neubauer, the manager of Kodak's components division. In short, some costs just can't be cut. But most companies still manufacture a great deal of redundancy and waste every day. Take a look around. Listen to your employees. Spare the work. Spoil the worker.

Chapter
14

Academic Life

*I*n 1908, F. W. Cornford gave the following warning to young aspiring college professors about their academic colleagues. "You think (do you not?) that you have only to state a reasonable case, and people must listen to reason and act upon it at once. It is just this conviction that makes you so unpleasant . . . Are you not aware that conviction has never yet been produced by appeal to reason, which only makes people feel uncomfortable? If you want to move them, you must address your arguments to prejudice and the political motive." (p. 2) Could such advice possibly be sound for someone entering today's esteemed centers of higher learning?

It is still possible for a person to graduate from college (perhaps even complete a doctoral degree) and yet be ignorant of the realities of life in colleges and universities. Stereotypes of the "halls of ivy" are strong and are supported by the components of academic life (e.g., lecture halls, libraries, laboratories, professors' offices) that are most visible to students. While many students are victims of considerable thoughtlessness and arbitrary treatment (e.g., long lines and indifferent responses from staff members during typical registrations), these slights may not be interpreted by them as indicators of a pervasive lack of humanity. After the immediate frustration has waned, students may even come to support the traditional view that universities are poorly run because professors, due to preoccupation with highly prestigious scholarly endeavors, "understandably neglect" administrative details. Universities are forgiven for being inefficient and inhumane because they are "different" from other organizations.

Is academic life really that different from corporate life? Are universities as organized arenas of action susceptible to the same realities as other organizations? In many ways, universities are, in fact, different from other organizations. Leading scholars such as Cohen and March (1986) have even suggested that universities require new theories of decision making to understand them and new theories of management to guide them. However, like all the other organizations we have been considering, universities also have their dark sides. Some administrators lie and break commitments to faculty members. Similarly, some faculty members pursue their own interests in ways that harass students and staff and that conflict with widely held professional codes. Staff members may pursue their own agendas in ways that are grossly inconsistent with even the broadest interpretation of the organization's mission. Then too, by their own admission, a large number of students cheat.

In all probability, the people who manage and work in universities are neither more nor less noble than their counterparts in other organizations. Certain features of universities may, however, make it particularly difficult to detect and control transgressions. For one thing, when goals (e.g., advancing knowledge) are very broad and vague, it is difficult to assess performance. Further, since much of the actual work is carried out by experts in a specialized field of knowledge, few administrators have the competence to evaluate the experts' work further. Autonomy is highly prized and protected by academic traditions and practices. Mintzberg (1983) described some of the dynamics of these organizations well:

> First, because the output or performance of expert work is not easily measured, goals imposed from above are easily deflected. Second, because the experts are committed to their own skills, they have a notable tendency to invert means and ends, to focus on the skills they provide rather than the mission for which these skills are intended. Third, because professionals identify strongly with their own professional societies . . . groups form as factions and conflicts arise between them. (p. 401)

Because efforts to cope with conflicts behind the ivy-covered walls often take on the appearance of scholarly discourse, to the outsider it may appear that conflicts are less self-serving and more apt to be resolved objectively than in other organizations. Perhaps, sometimes this is true. However, in our experience, Cornford's emphasis on prejudice and politics reflects considerable insight into the realities of university life.

The selections in this chapter deal with a diverse set of topics. Each is intended to show that one or more of the themes developed elsewhere in the book is manifested on campus. The first selection, "The Indictment" is excerpted from Charles J. Sykes' widely discussed book *ProfScam*. To put it bluntly, Sykes suggests that modern universities are corrupt and that the self-interested pursuits of their professors are the primary corrupting agents. Some readers are likely to view Sykes as irrational in his criticisms of academic life and as having something of an axe to grind. We do not believe that the way he depicts academics is a definitive perspective. Nor do we believe it is totally off the mark. As in every profession and in most organizations, there is much that goes on that is constructive and leads to positive outcomes. Nevertheless, we invite the reader to read the articles in this chapter to see whether they confirm Sykes' indictment.

The next article, "Glass Ceiling Closes in at Business Schools," suggests that the problems women have in making it to the top in "the real world" are at least equally common on campus. In "Ex-Colleagues Turn Combatants," John Noble

Wilford reveals how the quest for money can corrupt the scientific process and the institutions devoted to it.

The following two selections reveal that universities, like other organizations, often deal with their "warts" by trying to hide them. Sykes, in "The Fate of Critics" shows how one major college dealt with student criticisms. The next selection about the demise of the sociology department at Washington University requires a few words of background. Washington University is a private, medium-sized university located in St. Louis. In the late 1960s and early 1970s, it was known as one of the foremost sociology departments in the U.S. The department also had a reputation for being politically radical. Over time, the department's stature declined dramatically. By 1989, the university's administration (who many accused of having starved the department for years) formally abolished the department. Robert L. Hamblin, the author of the selection included here, is a leading sociologist who was chairperson of the department at a key point in its history. Alvin Gouldner, the faculty member who figures so prominently in the account, was one of the world's most highly regarded sociologists. The impression management, personal attacks, retaliation, hint of cover up, potential criminal charges, and even violence, reveal that the metaphor of war, used elsewhere in this book to describe life in business organizations, captures some of the reality of university life as well.

The following selection, "Business Group Uses Professors, Not Cash, to Influence Congress" reveals the role that some professors now play in advancing parochial rather than scholarly interests. While there is nothing illegal or even necessarily unprofessional about lobbying, the piece supports key elements of Sykes' thesis.

In "Hero in Exposing Science Hoax Paid Dearly," we see, as in other organizations, the importance and the costs of the exercise of individual conscience in the service of honest practice. The search for a job in academia can be a turbulent, stressful experience, as Anne Matthews observes in "Deciphering Victorian Underwear and Other Seminars." The article also captures some of the excitement and energy people feel who work in the world of ideas.

REFERENCES

Cohen, M. D. and March, J. G. (1986). *Leadership and Ambiguity*, 2nd ed. Boston, Mass.: Harvard Business School Press.

Cornford, F. M. (1908). *Microcosmographia Academia. Being a Guide for the Young Academic Politician.* London: Bowes and Bowes.

Mintzberg, H. (1983). *Power in and Around Organizations.* Englewood Cliffs, N.J.: Prentice-Hall.

Sykes, Charles J. (1988). *ProfScam: Professors and the Demise of Higher Education.* New York: St. Martin's Press.

The Indictment

Charles J. Sykes

H. L. Mencken had a simple plan for reforming American higher education. He suggested that anyone who really wanted to improve the universities should start by burning the buildings and hanging the professors.[1]

It's easy, of course, to dismiss Mencken's prescription as frivolous, lacking the ponderous gravity that afflicts debates about higher education. And surely stringing up a few professors of sociology, chemistry, and French, along with the stray expert in Chaucerian verse, is hardly a serious or humane reform program, entertaining as it might be for the undergraduates.

But Mencken's plan did something the hosts of critics and would-be reformers before and after him have failed to do: It went directly to the rot at the heart of the university. In recent years, dozens of commissions, foundations, and free-lance pathologists have conducted endless post-mortems on higher education: the decline of humanities, the fragmentation of the curriculum, the pathetic state of teaching, and the boggling price tag on the universities' tapestry of failure.

And predictably, they have rounded up the usual suspects: the students themselves, television, the federal government, capitalism, public grade schools and high schools, teenage sex, German philosophers Nietzsche and Heidegger, and, for good measure, the Walkman radio. So far they all have missed the mark.

Mencken, writing more than 80 years ago, with his usual directness, identified the real villain of the piece: the American university professor.

Mencken caught the flavor of the New Academic when he wrote: "The professor must be an obscurantist or he is nothing. He has a special unmatchable talent for dullness; his central aim is not to expose the truth clearly but to exhibit his profundity—in brief, to stagger the sophomores and other professors."[2]

With only minor updating (the modern professors would rather have root-canal work than spend time with any undergraduates), Mencken's analysis remains on target. The professoriate has multiplied in the years since Mencken's analysis even beyond his grimmest nightmares. The result is a modern university distinguished by costs that are zooming out of control; curriculums that look like they were designed by a game show host; nonexistent advising programs; lectures of

---

[1]Cited in Mitchell, Richard, *The Graves of Academe,* New York, Simon & Schuster, p. 69

[2]Mencken, H. L., *Prejudices: A Selection,* New York, Vintage Books, 1958, p. 149

droning, mind-numbing dullness often to 1,000 or more semi-anonymous undergraduates herded into dilapidated, ill-lighted lecture halls; teaching assistants who can't speak understandable English; and the product of this all, a generation of expensively credentialed college graduates who might not be able to locate England on a map.

In the midst of this wasteland stands the professor.

Almost single-handedly, the professors—working steadily and systematically—have destroyed the university as a center of learning and have desolated higher education, which no longer is higher or much of an education.

The story of the collapse of American higher education is the story of the rise of the professoriate. No understanding of the academic disease is possible without an understanding of the Academic Man, this strange mutation of 20th-century academia who has the pretensions of an ecclesiastic, the artfulness of a witch doctor, and the soul of a bureaucrat.

His greatest triumph has been the creation of an academic culture that is one of society's most outrageous and elaborate frauds. It is replete with the pieties, arcane rituals, rites of passage, and dogmas of a secular faith. It also has an intimidating and mysterious argot (best described as "profspeak") and a system of perks and privileges that would put the most hidebound bureaucrat to shame. Ultimately, the academic culture represents a sort of modern-day alchemy in which mumbo-jumbo is transformed into gold, or, in this case, into research grants, consulting contracts, sabbaticals, and inflated salaries.

Professors have convinced society that this culture is essential for higher learning, and have thus been able to protect their own status and independence while cheating students, parents, taxpayers, and employers, and polluting the intellectual inheritance of society. Over the last 50 years, this academic culture has secured professors almost ironclad job security and the freedom to do whatever they like—and to do it well or poorly—or to do nothing at all.

A bill of indictment for the professors' crimes against higher education would be lengthy. Here is a partial one:

- They are overpaid, grotesquely underworked, and the architects of academia's vast empires of waste.
- They have abandoned their teaching responsibilities and their students. To the average undergraduate, the professoriate is unapproachable, uncommunicative, and unavailable.
- In pursuit of their own interests—research, academic politicking, cushier grants—they have left the nation's students in the care of an ill-trained, ill-paid, and bitter academic underclass.
- They have distorted university curriculums to accommodate their own narrow and selfish interests rather than the interests of their students.
- They have created a culture in which bad teaching goes unnoticed and unsanctioned and good teaching is penalized.
- They insist that their obligations to research justify their flight from the college classroom despite the fact that fewer than one in ten ever makes any significant contribution to their field. Too many—maybe even a vast major-

ity—spend their time belaboring tiny slivers of knowledge, utterly without redeeming social value except as items on their resumes.

- They have cloaked their scholarship in stupefying, inscrutable jargon. This conceals the fact that much of what passes for research is trivial and inane.
- In tens of thousands of books and hundreds of thousands of journal articles, they have perverted the system of academic publishing into a scheme that serves only to advance academic careers and bloat libraries with masses of unread, unreadable, and worthless pablum.
- They have twisted the ideals of academic freedom into a system in which they are accountable to no one, while they employ their own rigid methods of thought control to stamp out original thinkers and dissenters.
- In the liberal arts, the professors' obsession with trendy theory—which is financially rewarding—has transformed the humanities into models of inhumanity and literature departments into departments of illiteracy.
- In the social sciences, professors have created cults of pseudo-science packed with what one critic calls "sorcerers clad in the paraphernalia of science . . . wooly-minded lost souls yearning for gurus,"[3] more concerned with methodology and mindless quantification than with addressing any significant social questions.
- In the sciences, professors have mortgaged the nation's scientific future and its economic competitiveness to their own self-interest by ignoring undergraduates and an epidemic of academic fraud.
- In schools of education, their disdain for teaching and the arrogance with which they treat their students has turned the universities into the home office of educational mediocrity, poisoning the entire educational system from top to bottom.
- They have constructed machinery that so far has frustrated or sabotaged every effort at meaningful reform that might interfere with their boondoggle.
- Finally, it has been the professors' relentless drive for advancement that has turned American universities into vast factories of junkthink, the byproduct of academe's endless capacity to take even the richest elements of civilization and disfigure them into an image of itself.

The extent of the professors' success in imposing their culture on the university should really not be surprising. Professors, after all, control everything that matters in the universities.

"Their authority in academic matters is absolute," declared the U.S. Supreme Court in a 1980 case.[4] "They decide what courses will be offered, when they will be scheduled, and to whom they will be taught. They debate and determine teaching methods, grading policies, and matriculation standards. They effectively decide which students will be admitted, retained, and graduated. On occasion their views

---

[3] Andreski, Stanislav, *Social Sciences as Sorcery,* New York, St. Martin's Press, 1972, p. 16

[4] *NLRB v. Yeshiva University,* 100 S. Ct. 856 (1980)

have determined the size of the student body, the tuition to be charged, and the location of a school. . . . To the extent the industrial analogy applies, *the faculty determines within each school the product to be produced, the terms upon which it will be offered, and the customers who will be served.*"

The modern university—insatiable, opportunistic, and implacably anti-intellectual—is created in the image of the *Professorus Americanus*. Today, the professor is the university.

The modern professoriate bears little resemblance to the rumpled, forgetful, impractical academics of popular imagination. In the years since World War II, the profession has changed radically. The modern academic is mobile, self-interested, and without loyalty to institutions or the values of liberal education. The rogue professors of today are not merely obscurantists. They are politicians and entrepreneurs who fiercely protect their turf and shrewdly hustle research cash while they peddle their talents to rival universities, businesses, foundations, or government.

But when it comes to the decline of American higher education, they have been remarkably successful in diverting attention from themselves and assigning blame elsewhere. Yet the impact of their scam on their customers has been devastating.

- For students, it has meant watered-down courses; unqualified instructors; a bachelor's degree of dubious value; and an outrageous bill for spending four or five years in a ghetto of appalling intellectual squalor and mediocrity.
- For parents who pay college costs (especially those who chose a school because they thought their children would actually study at the feet of its highly touted faculty), it has meant one of the biggest cons in history.
- For American business, it has meant hiring a generation of college graduates who are often unable to write a coherent sentence, analyze even simple problems, or understand why their elders keep talking about a *Second* World War (was there a First?).
- And for American society—which has picked up the tab for hundreds of thousands of literary scholars, social workers, sociologists, economists, political scientists, psychologists, anthropologists, and educationists—it has meant the realization that we are not discernibly more literate, more competent, more economically secure, safer, wiser, or saner than we were before spending untold billions on this embarrassment of academic riches.

Glass Ceiling Closes in at Business Schools

The resignation of Elizabeth Bailey as dean of Carnegie Mellon University's business school, effective next month, leaves only four female deans at accredited business schools, and none at top-ranked schools. A few years ago, there were as many as eight women deans at the 272 accredited schools, says a spokesman at the American Assembly of Collegiate Schools of Business.

Dean Bailey, who declined to be interviewed, said through a spokeswoman that women's issues weren't involved in her resignation.

Others, however, say women's issues can't help but be involved. "Women business school deans are still an endangered species," says Lynda Phillips-Madson, an associate dean at Vanderbilt University's Owen School of Management. "Regardless of the individual circumstances, I do see it as a loss for women," she says, because the appointments are critical for visibility.

Eugene Rackley, a recruiter at Heidrick & Struggles Inc., says the dean scarcity isn't for want of trying. "Every search committee tries to go out of its way to generate as many names [of women] as possible," he says, adding that the pool of qualified candidates is "pretty small."

Nonsense, retorts Anne Jardim, co-dean of Simmons College's Graduate School of Management. "This is part of the still-bigger problem of the situation of women in society."

Other women cite school jitters. "Search committees just don't want to take a chance on women," says Laurie Larwood, business school dean at the State University of New York at Albany. "They see it as a risk."

Ex-Colleagues Turn Combatants

John Noble Wilford

Two respected medical researchers, once close colleagues, are now locked in a bitter legal fight that raises new concerns about how scientific institutions handle cases of alleged misconduct in research and how they treat "whistle-blowers" who bring charges of such practices.

Over a decade, their working relationship had been productive, seemingly harmonious and fairly typical in science. Dr. Leonard M. Freeman, chief of nuclear medicine at Yeshiva University's Albert Einstein College of Medicine and the Montefiore Medical Center in New York City, was the mentor. Dr. Heidi S. Weissmann was his enterprising junior associate and a rising star.

Beginning in 1977, in her fourth year as a resident at the hospital, Dr. Freeman and Dr. Weissmann collaborated on several dozen reports, primarily radiological diagnostic techniques for liver and gall bladder disorders. The two became recognized internationally.

"I doubt that many other 30-year-old investigators could match her first-class productivity," wrote Dr. Freeman in 1984 in recommending Dr. Weissmann for an award by the Society of Nuclear Medicine.

That was before the circumstances that led to charges brought by Dr. Weissmann in 1987 of copyright infringement and sex discrimination. She contended that Dr. Freeman gave his name as the author of an article that she had written. In a separate complaint, she accused Dr. Freeman, the medical college and the hospital of improperly denying her a promotion and of paying her less than men in comparable positions.

The ensuing lawsuits set off reverberations among other scientists, major donors to Yeshiva University and Congressional investigators.

CONGRESSIONAL REPORT DUE

The House Subcommittee on Human Resources and Intergovernmental Relations, headed by Representative Ted Weiss, Democrat of Manhattan, is expected to include the dispute in a report next month on its investigation of fraud, conflicts of interest and other cases of alleged misconduct by scientists and their institutions. Dr. Diana M. Zuckerman, a subcommittee investigator, wrote recently of "outrageous examples" of possible misconduct, including "one medical school that fired an individual who made allegations and then promoted the person accused of wrongdoing and paid the accused's legal fees." Dr. Weissmann has, in fact, left the medical school, and Dr. Freeman was subsequently promoted.

But Dr. Freeman, Einstein College of Medicine and Montefiore deny that they have done anything wrong. They also dispute Dr. Weissmann's contention that she was dismissed from the staff of the hospital.

In taking up Dr. Weissmann's cause, the National Coalition for Universities in the Public Interest, a small Washington organization founded by Ralph Nader, contends that the medical school and hospital may be "protecting" Dr. Freeman because his research brings in money from pharmaceutical companies.

But Dr. Freeman said in an interview that he had received less than $25,000 for his research over the last 10 years. And Nadia Adler, general counsel at Montefiore, said, "Dr. Freeman's not a big producer of grant money."

Further pressure is being brought by Rita Kaplan, secretary of the Rita J. and Stanley H. Kaplan Foundation, a major contributor to Jewish institutions in New York, who complained that the university, medical college and hospital continued "to treat Dr. Weissmann as someone to be humiliated and silenced" rather than an "ethical whistle-blower."

Einstein College of Medicine said last week that it and Montefiore Hospital had initiated separate inquiries into the issues raised by Dr. Weissmann.

LOWER COURT IS REVERSED

One of the two suits, the copyright infringement case, was resolved in Dr. Weissmann's favor in February 1989. After a Federal district court ruled for Dr. Freeman, an appeals court decided by a 2-to-1 vote that the lower court had been wrong, that the disputed article was "solely" Dr. Weissmann's and that Dr. Freeman "actually attempted to pass off the work as his own."

Dr. Freeman had been invited to speak at a seminar on nuclear medicine at Mount Sinai Hospital and School of Medicine in August 1987. As is routine, Dr. Freeman was asked to submit a survey paper on his subject for distribution to participants.

Dr. Weissmann charged—and Dr. Freeman acknowledged at the trial—that he took a photocopy of an article that carried her byline and submitted it under his own name.

"I generated the ideas, carried through and did the research and writing," Dr. Weissmann said last week.

Dr. Freeman said he had been "dumbfounded" by Dr. Weissmann's reaction. "I feel she had no right to take credit for the entire paper based on our joint work," he said."

He described the article as an "evolving paper," which was added to by each researcher to reflect developments. Much of the work, he said, represented his findings and writings.

Dr. Stanley Goldsmith, a radiologist at Mount Sinai, said he believed that "hostility behind the scenes" contributed to the falling-out.

On the day she filed suit, Dr. Weissmann said, she went to her office at Montefiore and was met by two security officers, who advised her she could not remove any documents and would have to surrender her keys. She said she concluded she had been dismissed in retaliation for her lawsuit.

But Dr. M. Donald Blaufox, chairman of the department of nuclear medicine at the medical college and hospital, wrote Dr. Weissmann that her "failure to return to work constitutes a resignation of employment." Simultaneously, he announced Dr. Freeman's promotion to vice chairman of the nuclear medicine department.

"The whole thing has been very disillusioning," said Dr. Weissmann, who has yet to find a new job in medical research and has spent $500,000 in legal fees.

Dr. Freeman, who now faces an inquiry by the medical school and the hospital, said he was "quite confident that the peer review process would show I did nothing out of the ordinary."

Sidebar: The Fate of Critics

Charles J. Sykes

As critics of academia quickly learn, there is a paradox at the heart of the academic culture. Although the professors insist on absolute freedom for themselves, they accord no such tolerance to anyone who challenges their own privileges and status.

"The only thing that we can't criticize or investigate is ourselves," notes David Berkman, himself a dissident academic.[1] When national figures such as Secretary of Education William J. Bennett critique the pretensions of the universities, they are accused of being ignorant, racist, elitist, and hostile to higher learning. Robert Isoue, the president of York College, quickly discovered the limits of academia's tolerance of dissent when he broke ranks to chide his fellow academics for their avoidance of teaching and to declare that as a result of academia's distorted priorities, "students are getting ripped off."

"The mere mention of Isoue's name," noted *The Chronicle of Higher Education*, "draws groans from his colleagues. . . ."[2]

When students rebel against the vagaries of the professoriate, the university faculty and administration often respond with arrogance and hostility verging on hysteria.

The case of *The Dartmouth Review* is illustrative. Published by conservative students at Dartmouth College in New Hampshire, *The Review* is a controversial, irreverent newspaper that has vigorously championed quality teaching, traditional educational values, and high academic standards. Unfortunately, its spirited young editors have also been given to a certain amount of sophomoric excess, including an incident in which some of them tore down a shanty town erected by anti-apartheid protestors on the Dartmouth campus. Subtlety is not their forte. *The Review's* staffers sometimes find themselves writing excruciatingly close to the far-edges of good taste and, on occasion, have crossed over.

But it is not necessary to unconditionally endorse *The Review's* tactics to recognize the full-flowering hypocrisy of Dartmouth College's treatment of the youthful muckrakers.

The Review's cardinal sin was its frontal assault on Dartmouth's academic pretensions. Taking note of the $18,000-a-year Ivy League school's *au courant* low-calorie curriculum, the paper administered E. D. Hirsch's basic cultural literacy test to 349 Dartmouth students. Only half could identify Charles de Gaulle as the leader of the French government-in-exile in World War II or name any three of the liberties protected by the First Amendment.[3] This was provocative enough. But the paper went further by publishing trenchant critiques of the teaching styles of some of Dartmouth's celebrated faculty.

In January of 1983, Laura Ingraham, then a Dartmouth sophomore, was assigned by the paper to sit in on a music class taught by Professor William Cole. In her subsequent article, she said that while Cole was a competent musician, his classroom demeanor was characterized by a sloppy handling of the subject matter, politically charged rambles, and occasional racial asides. Much of her article was composed of direct quotes from Cole.

Her report was published in *The Review* on a Thursday. Two days later, early on Saturday morning, Ingraham's dorm roommate was awakened by a loud banging on the door. According to Ingraham, Cole stood outside of her dorm room shouting that he was going to have her thrown out of Dartmouth if she didn't come to his class to apologize to him. "I was in New York, but he woke up the entire dormitory," Ingraham says. "It was really unprofessional behavior." But it only marked the beginning of a bizarre chain of events involving *The Review* and Cole.

Cole announced that he was suspending his class indefinitely until Ingraham apologized and then made attendance at the class optional, thus, says Ingraham,

---

[2]*The Chronicle of Higher Education*, October 14, 1987

[3]"Dartmouth Teaches . . . Censorship," *Wall Street Journal*, March 8, 1988

"illustrating Professor Cole's dedication to learning."[4] Cole also filed a libel suit against *The Review*. (He dropped it two years later.)

Cole was reprimanded by his dean for pounding on Ingraham's door,[5] but otherwise Dartmouth stood loyally behind its faculty member. One of his colleagues was even quoted in print as saying that if Ingraham ever showed up in one of his classes he would have "busted her kneecaps."[6] The refusal of Dartmouth officials to take any effective action did little to defuse the increasingly tense atmosphere.

In the summer of 1985, another editor of *The Review*, Debbie Stone, was walking across the campus with a classmate and an alumnus when Professor Cole reportedly began shouting at her. According to Stone, he pointed at her and yelled: "I'm going to fucking blow you up!" When she reported the incident to the local police, they told Stone to change her walking patterns and to avoid walking alone on campus. "My parents were definitely concerned," she says. But when she reported the incident to Dartmouth authorities, Cole denied her allegations and college officials decided to take no action. Instead, she says, they told her not to file any further complaints about the incident or tell anyone else about it.[7]

The Review editors were not, however, deterred. In February of 1988, the paper again published a critique of Cole's teaching style. Like the 1983 piece, the article was largely based on a transcript from one of Cole's classes—an indictment of Cole using Cole's own words. The story said that Cole's class "does not meet Dartmouth standards," and labelled it one of the school's "most academically deficient courses." Following standard journalistic practice, the paper's staffers made several efforts to get a response from Cole. When they reached him by phone, however, he hung up.[8] On the advice of counsel, the paper's editor also wrote to Cole to solicit his point of view.[9] Finally, four *Review* staffers went to Cole's classroom to get his comments. Specifically, they wanted to present Cole with the paper's written policy, giving him the right to submit a response of up to 1,500 words "as long as it contained no obscenities."[10]

According to the students, Cole reacted angrily, shouting obscenities and racial epithets. Somehow in the exchange, the student photographer's flash device was broken.[11] The students say that Cole not only broke the camera, but also threatened them.[12]

---

[4]Interview with author, June 24, 1988

[5]Raspberry, William, "The Beautification of Dartmouth, Phase II," *Washington Post,* March 7, 1988

[6]Interview with Laura Ingraham, June 24, 1988

[7]Interview with author, June 24, 1988

[8]"Blackmail," *National Review,* April 1, 1988

[9]"Dartmouth Teaches . . . Censorship," op. cit.

[10]"Four college journalists suspended for harassment," *Editor & Publisher,* March 19, 1988

[11]"Blackmail," op. cit.

[12]"Dartmouth Teaches . . . Censorship," op. cit.

What followed was a combination of academic farce and tragedy. The incident took a genuinely Kafkaesque quality when Dartmouth President James Freedman moved to discipline, not Cole, *but the four student journalists.* The school's Afro-American Society called rallies to attack *The Review* as racist (Cole is black). Freedman addressed one of the rallies, saying: "I feel dreadful about the attack on Professor Cole."[13] It was in this climate that the school's disciplinary committee met in private and refused to hear the students' countercharges against Cole for assault and damage to property. In April of 1988, three of the student journalists were suspended and a fourth was put on probation for allegedly "harassing" Cole, violating his privacy, and disorderly conduct.[14]

President Freedman waxed Orwellian in explaining the sanctions against the student reporters. *The Review* staffers, he said, should not be protected by First Amendment free press rights, because they were merely "ideological provocateurs posing as journalists." The administration stepped up its attack on the student paper by issuing a news release that labelled the newspaper "sexist, racist and homophobic."[15] (Notes one former editor: "It's interesting to note that *The Review* has more blacks on its staff than Dartmouth has tenured black professors." In addition, two of the paper's seven editors have been women.)[16]

But even Dartmouth College's full-court smear campaign against the student paper and the racial and political overtones of the case cannot obscure the fundamental issues at stake.

"We suspect," the *Wall Street Journal* commented aptly, *"the students' true crime was presuming to assess scholarship at their college."*[17]

In other words, they had dared to attack the academic culture. The treatment of the four students—contrasted with the school's indulgence of Cole's conduct—was an obvious travesty of justice. But it is an example of the academic culture in its purest, most distilled form. The virulence of that culture's reaction to its Dartmouth critics indicates how close they came to the heart of the culture itself. And it provides a clue to the shape that any sort of meaningful reform must take.

---

[13]Ibid.

[14]Ibid.

[15]"The Joys of Hypocrisy," *Wall Street Journal,* April 4, 1988

[16]Interview with Debbie Stone, June 24, 1988

[17]"The Joys of Hypocrisy," op. cit.

Sociology and a Developing Administrative Tradition at Washington University: 1957–1971

Robert L. Hamblin

The recent decision of Washington University's dean to disband the sociology department is probably best understood in historical context of the administrative traditions at that institution. I have little and, of that, all second-hand information about developments during the last eighteen years, but from 1957 through 1971, when I left for Arizona, I was extensively involved with Washington University's administration, first as a member of the sociology faculty and, then, as chairman of the department. My purpose here is to recount the history of my and the department's dealings with the administration during that period, as frankly and honestly as I can, mainly to provide a background for judging the more recent events detailed by others in this issue.

When I was hired at Washington University in 1957, as a small groups experimenter, Nicholas Demerath was chairman and director of the newly established Social Science Institute. Sociology seemed to be on the move. Joseph Kahl had been hired as an assistant professor in stratification the year before, and the following year Albert Wesson and David Pittman joined the department as assistant professors in medical sociology.

By that time a split had developed in the department, between an old guard who had stopped publishing, on the one hand, and Nick Demerath and the assistant professors he had recruited, on the other. After a year or so of struggling for an accommodation, Dean Tom Eliot agreed to allow Sociology to recruit a new chairman from the outside.

Several prominent sociologists were on the list. I nominated Alvin Gouldner, whom I had met the previous year at the Midwestern Sociological Meetings. In my judgment, of the candidates, he was the most distinguished sociological re-

"Sociology and a Developing Administrative Tradition at Washington University: 1957–1971" by Robert L. Hamblin, *The American Sociologist*, 1989, pp. 324–329, New Brunswick, NJ: transaction. © 1989. Reprinted by permission.

The author expresses appreciation to Douglas McAdam, Albert Bergesen and Beverly Armstrong for reading and proofing the manuscript and for their helpful suggestions.

searcher, but he also had a reputation for abrasiveness. I suspected that reputation was not undeserved, but guessed that as chairman he would be more charming and persuasive than abrasive.

When the vote was taken to invite candidates to visit the department, Gouldner ranked fifth. However, when he visited, he charmed everyone—Dean Eliot, Demerath, the old guard, and the assistant professors. He was the unanimous choice, and came with a wife, Helen Pat Gouldner, a new Ph.D. in sociology, who also was voted a member of the department.

The next six or seven years were the golden ones for sociology at Washington University. Gouldner turned out to be a superb chairman, in almost everyone's view. As I anticipated, he used his charm and persuasiveness to keep conflict at a low level. He also recruited several new additions to the faculty—most notably, Lee Rainwater, to head up the Pruitt-Igo housing research, and Irving Louis Horowitz in political sociology. Everyone was busy with their research, publishing and teaching, and we began to hear that others in the discipline considered Washington University among the top ten departments nationally.

When Gouldner stepped down as chairman about 1964, things progressed smoothly for a time. He, Rainwater and Horowitz founded *Trans*-action magazine, which made a splash nationally and seemed to engross Gouldner intellectually. However, toward the end of his tenure as chairman, we began hearing reports that he was being abusive to graduate students. A year or two afterwards, the reports became more frequent and more serious.

Then, Gouldner got into a big verbal battle with the managing editor of *Trans*-action. Rainwater and Horowitz sided with Gouldner. The managing editor, who was not a sociologist, apologized at the threat of being fired. A few months later another blowup occurred. This time Rainwater and Horowitz sided with the editor. They felt Gouldner was being both unreasonable and abusive to a subordinate who had very little power, and that they could no longer support his behavior.

In the meantime, Tom Eliot had become chancellor and Al Wesson had served three years as chairman of the department. He and I had attempted to mediate the *Trans*-action conflicts, and he wisely opted against a second term. The department, including Gouldner, decided I should be the new chair.

To everyone's surprise, the administration, including Tom Eliot, upon receiving the department's nomination, asked for a meeting with the tenured members. In my presence, they asked for an alternative nomination. My inclination was to withdraw, but I kept quiet. My colleagues individually stood firm behind the nomination, explaining their reasons. The administration finally backed down, shaken by the department's resolve.

The administration's opposition to my becoming chair was never made clear in the meeting. However, we all surmised the reason, which is mentioned here only because it is probably germane to understanding the development of an administrative tradition at Washington University.

A year or so earlier, in a general faculty meeting, Tom Eliot had presented a linear extrapolation of the growth of tuition at Washington University, which forecasted an awesome budget deficit by 1970. Explicitly to prevent that deficit, he proposed eliminating three programs which he considered weak—including the

Graduate Institute of Education, whose faculty I knew well and whose research I generally respected.

In the next general faculty meeting which considered Eliot's proposal, I presented an exponential analysis which fit the data much better and which forecasted a substantial budget surplus (which later materialized). This temporarily saved the Graduate Institute of Education but, of course, did not earn me Eliot's friendship.

Shortly after I was appointed Chair, the *Trans*-action conflict—between Gouldner, on the one hand, and Rainwater and Horowitz on the other—heated up. Upon the advice of my colleagues, I attempted a resolution. With the help of Joe Kahl and Al Wesson, I persuaded Tom Eliot and the others in the administration to give *Trans*-action to Rainwater and Horowitz and, in recompense, to offer Al Gouldner, on the condition of no more conflict, a prestigious university professorship: he was to have the title of Max Weber Professor of Sociological Theory, to receive a generous salary, and was required to teach only two classes per year and to be in residence only one semester per year. I still admired Al as a scholar and did not want to lose him, a feeling evidently shared by the department and the administration since all bought the package, as did Al.

Things went splendidly for about two years. The peace was generally kept, and I negotiated a separate department for anthropology (something the social anthropologists wanted desperately, but had been unable to do for themselves), kept Jules Henry (a social anthropologist who late in his career published a prize-winning book, *Culture Against Man*) from deserting us for Berkeley, and recruited Phillips Cutright.

Then one day a poison pen letter attacking Al was posted on a bulletin board outside the departmental office. I retrieved it as soon as it was brought to my attention, and tried to track down its source, to no avail. Although I showed it to no one, a few people saw it. Within several days Al heard about it, possibly from its author, although no one thought of that at the time. Within a week or so, a second poison-pen letter attacking Al was posted. The writing was quite different; the composition was so gifted we all felt only Al could have written it.

The next day, I received a call from Laud Humphreys, an ex-minister and a fourth-year graduate student; he said Al Gouldner had just come to his office and had beaten him up. I was told later that on a previous weekend at a graduate student party, Laud had too much to drink and began criticizing Al. Al heard about it, and apparently surmised Laud was the poison-penman.

Laud had been pummelled on his temples, until he fell to the floor. When I arrived at his third-floor office, within a minute or so of the call, his temples were badly swollen. Al had also kicked and stomped Laud after he had fallen to the floor. Laud's back was gouged and bruised all over, but no bones were broken.

I had passed Al coming down the stairs as he reached the first floor. We said nothing, but his face was flushed and the skin on his knuckles was red and torn. On the other hand, Laud's hands gave no evidence of his having hit anyone. In retrospect, I should have encouraged Laud to call the police, to sign a complaint against Al for assault and battery. However, at the time, neither he nor anyone else suggested that. None of us knew what to do, having never experienced assault and battery before.

Rather, the tenured members of the department met, decided to report the matter to the administration, including the facts as we knew them, and asked them to take measures to protect us from such violence in the future. A letter was drafted and some one observed that it prejudged the issue and, therefore, might be counterproductive. In retrospect, because none of us had any doubts about what happened, we were not sensitive to that issue. All of us felt Al had finally stepped over a line, that it was him or us. If anyone ever needed expert legal advice, it was us, but we failed to seek it.

The dean, Merle Kling, appointed a committee of professors who were close to the administration, and they duly gathered testimony from professors and graduate students. Our faculty and most of the graduate students, including Laud, testified against Al. However, Al apparently used his silver tongue to persuade the committee that Laud had written the poison pen letters, something none of us in the department were ever able to verify. In their report, the committee did not present evidence as to who the poison penman was. However, incredibly, again without presenting any supporting evidence for the conclusion or even suggesting why, they found Al not guilty of any wrongdoing.

Instead, the administration had apparently decided before-hand they would use this incident as a pretext for getting rid of me, as chairman of the department. A few days later I was called into Dean Kling's office, and was told the committee had recommended a change in the chairmanship, with the suggestion I was responsible for the turmoil in the department. Like other departments in the early Viet Nam War era, we were experiencing graduate student unrest and were having meetings with the graduate students and their leaders. Some students apparently did not like the way I was responding, and so testified. In any event, Dean Kling and Tom Eliot asked for my resignation, and I resigned, having assessed the situation with Gouldner and the administration as being impossible.

My friends in the department were terribly upset, because the administration was being very irresponsible for not taking disciplinary action against Al and because they felt I had been doing an excellent job as chairman. They wanted to go to the wall again, but felt my resignation prevented them from doing so. I told them I was weary of trying and failing to mediate departmental disputes with Gouldner. I argued it was impossible to deal reasonably with the administration, whom I considered quixotic.

Without Al's interference, the sociology faculty had been doing quite well getting along with one another and with the vast majority of the graduate students, securing research grants, doing research, publishing, teaching and recruiting graduate students with fine undergraduate records. I suggested that if the administration could not recognize and appreciate the progress that was being made, if they could not correctly discern the source of the problems after receiving all the information that was provided, it was counterproductive to work for them any longer. I undoubtedly made mistakes, I always have, but they were not recognized as serious nor as ill-intentioned by the vast majority of the sociology faculty.

In retrospect, I feel the administration may not have anticipated the consequences of their actions. However, if they wanted to rid themselves of me and others in the sociology department, they succeeded. Most of us left as soon as we could: Rainwater to Harvard, Kahl to Cornell, Horowitz to Rutgers, Cutright to M.I.T. and then Indiana, Wesson to Brown, Helen Gouldner to Delaware, and myself to Arizona. Those were sad days. We had "grown up" with one another as sociologists, had been through so much together and were such good friends.

In the meantime, my resignation as chairman did not end the department's problems with the administration. Tom Eliot heard of Laud Humphreys' dissertation on homosexual activities in Forest Park toilets, which eventually was published as a prize-winning book—*The Tearoom Trade.* Tom, a lawyer, reasoned that homosexual acts were a felony in Missouri, and that Laud's failures to report observed felonies were themselves felonies. He, therefore instituted action to revoke Humphreys' Ph.D., and had a vice president report the matter to NIMH and request their withdrawal of a multi-hundred-thousand-dollar research grant to Rainwater, the principal investigator, and to myself, coprincipal investigator. In Eliot's view, Rainwater, as Laud's dissertation chairman, was irresponsible in this matter, as was I, as department chairman.

Rainwater and I met hours each day for about two weeks, trying to figure out a defense. Finally, it occurred to us that while homosexuality was on the Missouri statute books as a felony, it may not have been prosecuted as such for years. Rainwater checked with the prosecutor, who gave him a letter stating that homosexual acts had not been tried as felonies in St. Louis since 1926, only as misdemeanors. This meant that Laud had not committed felonies by failing to report to the police the homosexual acts he observed. The administration dropped its effort to revoke Laud's Ph.D. and apologized to NIMH.

The only other personal chapter worth reporting happened about three years later. As head of the sociology department at the University of Arizona, I found an administration that was both reasonable and interested in promoting excellence. With their and the department's support I recruited Jack Gibbs, Robert Nisbit, Dudley and Beverly Duncan and Stan Lieberson as professors and, among others, Michael Hout, Robert Wuthnow and Al Bergesen as assistant professors. At that juncture, Ira Hirsch—whom I had known well at Washington as a distinguished psychophysicist and who had succeeded Merle Kling as dean—called asking if I would consider returning to Washington as sociology chair. Politely, I thanked Ira but declined.

By then, Tom Eliot had left, and those who succeeded him and Merle Kling evidently were trying to undo the mistakes they had made. At least, their offering me the chairmanship seemed to be a belated apology for actions that had resulted only in the loss of a fine sociology faculty. Reportedly, when in residence, Gouldner still fought with those who had replaced us, and only two or three students were enrolling in his classes.

The above details may describe what may be an unusual administrative period at Washington University. However, it seems to have been an era in which an administrative tradition developed of plotting against departments with little consideration for academic or scientific excellence, a tradition continued by Merle Kling, who became vice chancellor to William Danforth. For example, the Graduate Institute of Education—whose faculty attracted huge amounts of grant money, generally did first class social science research and trained competent Ph.D.'s—was forced by a later administration to become an undergraduate Department of Education. This occurred without the history of conflict in the Graduate Institute of Education that had plagued Sociology. Thus, there appears to be more to Washington University's administrative fumbling than just the recent discontinuation of the sociology department in the guise of promoting academic excellence.

Business Group Uses Professors, Not Cash, To Influence Congress

Jeffrey H. Birnbaum

Coretech links universities, companies in seeking law on the R&D tax credit;
If the eyes glaze, back off

WASHINGTON—Senate Finance Committee Chairman Lloyd Bentsen is surrounded by special-interest pleaders pushing to extend a major corporate tax break. He is loving every minute of it. "You really know how to get to a guy," he says with a smile for the photographer they brought along. At the close of the April meeting in his high-ceilinged office, he utters the words that are music to every lobbyist's ears: "I'll do everything I can."

But what makes these lobbyists so successful is that most of them aren't really lobbyists at all. Most are soft-spoken professors from the University of Houston in Sen. Bentsen's home state of Texas. They are here to support the controversial research-and-development tax credit, a billion-dollar-a-year break that especially benefits a few dozen big-name corporations—corporations that, not coincidentally, are allied with the professors in an organization called the Council on Research and Technology, or Coretech.

NEW ALLIANCES

Unholy alliances between business and nonbusiness interests are the latest thing in Washington lobbying. "The difficulty of passing legislation has increased exponentially," says Coretech's top professional lobbyist, Stuart Eizenstat, who was President Carter's domestic-policy adviser. "To make common cause with people who would not be your traditional allies is important."

Money still talks in politics, but it may be about to talk a little more softly. Congress is moving, perhaps as early as this year, to reduce the import of campaign cash by overhauling the entire campaign-finance system. With such traditional avenues of influence as the political-action committee falling into increasing disrepute, lobbying stands at a crossroads. Corporate pleaders will have to rely less on political contributions to make their case, and more on subtler—some might say more insidious—means. The result is likely to be more lobbying, not less, and of an increasingly sophisticated kind.

Coretech represents the cutting edge of this new soft sell. It doesn't even have a PAC, and doesn't contribute to campaigns. Instead, it uses the services of a wide array of modern lobbying specialists, including a publicist, two scholars, a tax lawyer, video-production experts and, of course, dozens of researchers from both corporate and academic realms. "Lobbying is no longer somebody coming with a bag full of money and laying it on a member's desk or relying on personal contacts to have that member do you a favor," Mr. Eizenstat says.

SOMETHING FOR EVERYONE

Coretech includes 72 universities and 46 companies. For the universities, it lobbies to fatten the budget of the National Science Foundation to $3 billion by fiscal 1993, a $1 billion rise, and also to authorize an increase of millions of dollars in U.S. spending on research facilities.

But its biggest issues are clearly corporate, and the bulk of its $700,000 annual budget is bankrolled by businesses. Universities become members for $2,000 each; corporate dues run from $5,000 to $30,000, depending on the extent of research expenditures.

For the companies, those dues seem a worthwhile investment: Tax savings from the R&D credit for some of Coretech's biggest corporate members, such as Hewlett-Packard Co., Digital Equipment Corp., Merck & Co. and International Business Machines Corp., have run into the tens of millions of dollars a year. The average Coretech member saves at least a few million dollars from it, officials say.

CREDIT'S CRITICS

But critics say the tax credit—given to companies that raise their R&D spending by certain amounts—is basically a waste, a reward to big businesses for doing what they would have to do anyway. "It's used frankly more for tax avoidance than to spur research and development," says Rep. Brian Donnelly, Democrat of Massachusetts. "In a market-driven economy, these people are forced to invest by their desires to make profits."

Rep. Fortney Stark, a California Democrat who is on the tax-writing Ways and Means Committee, doesn't believe the tax credit spurs research at all. He thinks it's notable that at big pharmaceutical companies, for instance, budgets for research and for advertising have been growing at about the same rate, even though R&D carries a tax credit and advertising doesn't.

Even advocates of the credit concede that it hasn't been as effective as it could be. But that, they say, is because it has been allowed to lapse periodically since it was established in 1981. "I can't think of one discussion I've had internally or externally that said, 'What about the R&D credit?' because we don't know if it's going to be there," says Robert Gilbertson, chief executive of Data Switch Corp. "It's better than nothing, but you might as well forget it because it's not doing any good. It's just throwing money down a rat hole."

What Coretech really wants is a permanent extension of the credit. Its method was on full display during its recent Lobby Day. At Coretech's request, 108 scientists from 39 states had descended on Washington to meet with lawmakers and their aides to put the best face on the tax credit.

Those present include corporate representatives, too, but they tend to stay in the background. The lobby group's agenda is carefully structured to include an effort to increase federal funding for college research as well as extending the corporate tax break.

At an 8 a.m. breakfast briefing, Kenneth Kay, Coretech's executive director, gives his troops their marching orders. The college members are specifically instructed to speak on behalf of corporations, and vice versa. He also tells them to emphasize that they are scientists, not lobbyists.

"But let me warn you, please, not to spend 15 minutes doing that," he says. "One of the tests is to look at the other person's eyes, and as soon as they start to glaze over, back off."

Another test is to avoid overkill—which isn't met in the meeting with Democratic Rep. Thomas Downey: The delegation is so heavy with Cornell University professors from his home state of New York that the congressman is miffed. "It's not by coincidence that you decided to tap my natural inclination toward my alma mater," he says sarcastically. "I appreciate being appreciated."

But by the end of the day, the results are in, and they are good for Coretech. Its lobbyists have met with no fewer than 150 lawmakers and 100 congressional staffers. And for the most part, they report, they have gotten a sympathetic hearing.

In seeking to keep the credit going, Coretech faces one big problem. "There is no constituency for research," Mr. Eizenstat says. "Our job is to create one."

One way Coretech does this is by forming a network of home-state contacts in both the corporate and college communities. Last year, Coretech spent a day training a few dozen researchers in how to curry favor with lawmakers back home, and how to give them credit in the local press for their support. It was called an "adopt-a-member program." Now, at the drop of a fax or in response to a phone call, these people and others who care about research immediately know best how to ask their legislator for help.

In 1987, the group hired two Brookings Institution scholars to demonstrate that the R&D tax credit increases the amount of research corporations do.

Anticipating criticism of the credit from Congress's watchdog agency, the General Accounting Office, Coretech in 1989 retained a former staffer of the respected Congressional Joint Taxation Committee to negotiate changes in the credit. Thus, Coretech's alterations already were moving through Congress by the time the GAO published its report.

Coretech also works behind the scenes to develop what Mr. Kay calls "atmospherics" designed to improve the image of the group and its issue. To appeal to academics, it has published a pamphlet predicting a shortage of engineers and scientists. To bring its message to a wider audience, it has produced a videotape extolling increased federal subsidies for R&D, featuring the lawmakers who sponsor its bills. And to ingratiate itself with lawmakers, it sends the photographs it takes during Lobby Day to newspapers back home.

Coretech's assiduous work paid off handsomely last December when it learned that President Bush's budget proposal would drop a related $800 million-a-year R&D tax break having to do with how multinationals divide their research expenses between U.S. and foreign operations.

Mr. Kay immediately initiated "a fire drill." Using Coretech's network, he quickly drummed up letters and telephone calls to a variety of Bush administration officials to urge them to include the provision. Mr. Eizenstat and some congressional allies also made calls, and the tax break was eventually fully restored.

To try to prevent the episode from recurring, Coretech recently hired a Republican lobbyist, Craig Fuller, who as Mr. Bush's former vice presidential chief of staff has close ties to officials in the administration. The trouble with the allocation rules "clearly was a wake-up call," says Mr. Kay, a former aide to Sen. Max Baucus, Democrat of Montana.

Still, Coretech's lobbyists find that in an era of budgetary constraints, keeping the tax credit is a continuing struggle. Even its friends offer words of caution. "It's this overall deficit," Democratic Rep. Michael Andrews of Texas tells a delegation on Lobby Day. "All too often these issues are driven by revenue; the merits of the issue are secondary."

Last year, the House and the Senate Finance Committee both voted to make the R&D credit permanent. But only a week after the finance committee vote, the Senate stripped every revenue-losing provision from its tax bill, including R&D. Under pressure to reduce the budget deficit, Congress ultimately decided to extend the credit for only the equivalent of nine months. Mr. Eizenstat refers to the episode as creating "the shortest permanent tax credit in history."

This year Coretech is trying again for a permanent extension. President Bush, Sen. Bentsen and the House's top tax-writer, Ways and Means Chairman Dan Rostenkowski of Illinois, have all come out in favor of it. But while it has a decent chance, it is far from a done deal. For one thing, Mr. Rostenkowski's support is still shaky; he has had doubts about the credit's usefulness in the past, and this year is focusing his efforts on deficit-reduction, demanding that any tax cuts be fully paid for.

Coretech goes out of its way to soften up the chairman. Lobby Day participants stay in town an extra night to meet with the Chicagoan. At the session, Melvin L. Loeb, vice president for research and development of Chicago-based Wesley Jessen Corp., a unit of Schering-Plough Corp., thanks him profusely for his support, calls him a "champion" of the cause and hands him an award for his efforts to date.

Rep. Rostenkowski refuses to give a firm commitment. But, he allows, "I think I'm being boxed in."

Hero in Exposing Science Hoax Paid Dearly

Philip J. Hilts

WASHINGTON, March 21—When Dr. Margot O'Toole, a junior researcher in molecular biology, raised uncomfortable questions in 1986 about the validity of a senior colleague's work, she felt alone.

Dr. David A. Baltimore, a Nobel laureate who was a co-author of a research paper that used the disputed work, described her as a "disgruntled postdoctoral fellow." She lost her job and her house and feared that her husband's job was in jeopardy as well. She took work answering phones at her brother's moving company.

"It was very difficult," she said today. "There were times when I was really frantic."

"MAINTAINED HER COMMITMENT"

But Wednesday, in language rising above the scientific and bureaucratic jargon common in Government reports, the National Institutes of Health called her a hero. "Dr. O'Toole suffered substantially for the simple act of raising questions about a scientific paper," the agency said in a report on the case. "Notwithstanding the losses and costs she incurred, Dr. O'Toole maintained her commitment to scientific integrity."

In a draft report, the health institutes' Office of Scientific Integrity said in effect that Dr. O'Toole had been right all along: crucial data in the paper based on work by her superior, Dr. Thereza Imanishi-Kari, had been faked. The scientific paper described findings suggesting that transplanted genes could stimulate a recipient's immune system. The finding has not been confirmed by other researchers.

"One of the most surprising things to me is the way so many members of the scientific community and the scientific press were to denigrate Dr. O'Toole," said Dr. Mark Ptashne, a researcher at Harvard University who is an officer of Genetics Institute, where Dr. O'Toole was hired last year to do work in the immunology of breast cancer after years of being unable to obtain work in science.

"They were willing to go to battle with absolute certainty, without bothering to read the paper and think about the likelihood that the paper was wrong," Dr. Ptashne added.

"ALWAYS HAD A LEVEL GAZE"

The Cell paper was not the first time Dr. O'Toole had taken on powerful opponents in a celebrated incident, her mother, Elizabeth Ryan, said today.

"She's always had a level gaze, if you know what I mean," Mrs. Ryan said. "If she wanted an answer from you, you'd better give it or she'd challenge you. I wouldn't say it was an impractical honesty exactly, it was honesty whether it was practical or not."

Dr. O'Toole, 38 years old, came to the United States from Ireland at the age of 14 with her family, and still recalls summers on the banks of the Shannon River, where her grandfather raised thoroughbred horses. Before his death, her father taught at Boston University, but he was a man of several talents, being by training an engineer and by interest a literary man as well, who had one play produced in Ireland.

Mrs. Ryan, a teacher in Brookline, Mass., a Boston suburb, remembers one incident that occurred in 1985. In her County Clare Irish accent, Mrs. Ryan said her daughter "was rushing back from lunch" when she saw a slight man being beaten by a robust assailant. "She came trotting up sideways to the large man, and said, 'Well, what do you think you are doing?'"

"The man said: 'Go away, go away. I'm a detective making an arrest.' She said, 'Well, show me your badge.' Another man got out of a car and showed her something but it wasn't a badge, so she just didn't accept it. She said, 'I don't agree with what's going on here.'"

She collected the names of some people standing nearby and took the matter to the authorities. The matter eventually went to court, and the large man, who was a police officer, was suspended for a year.

The incident was well publicized in Boston and Mayor Raymond L. Flynn, delivered a bag of groceries to the victim, Long Guang Huang, as a sign of concern.

Dr. O'Toole was educated in Ireland, then in Brookline public schools, Brandeis University, and Tufts University, where she earned her doctorate in cellular immunology. She was a postdoctoral fellow at the Massachusetts Institute of Technology in 1985 and 1986 under Dr. Imanishi-Kari. It is Dr. Imanishi-Kari who was charged in the report of the National Institutes of Health with scientific misconduct.

Dr. O'Toole informally reported to her senior adviser, Dr. Henry Wortis at Tufts University, that she had found 17 pages of data, which she said clearly showed that information in a scientific paper published in the journal Cell that year was false. Dr. Wortis and two other researchers looked into the matter informally, but said he found no misconduct. M.I.T. later began its own investigation of the allegations.

After she reported the matter, Dr. O'Toole said she was told by Dr. Imanishi-Kari never to come back to the laboratory. Dr. Baltimore told her she could write a letter to Cell, she related, but he said he would write a rejoinder himself.

Dr. Baltimore, who is now president of Rockefeller University in New York, was a senior adviser on the paper who reviewed the research and the data for the paper, and though he did not do the scientific work himself, his signature on the paper signaled his acceptance of its claims.

He said Wednesday that he would ask that the paper be retracted, and the journal Cell, which published it, agreed today to do so. The Massachusetts Institute of Technology, where the work took place, said its procedures for investigating such matters would be reviewed. The chairman at Rockefeller University, Richard Furlaud, issued a statement reaffirming the university's total confidence in Dr. Baltimore.

The health institutes' draft report will lead to more steps in a process that could result in Dr. Imanishi-Kari being barred from receiving Federal money for research.

Dr. Baltimore said Wednesday that he did not believe at the time that Dr. Imanishi-Kari's data were faked. He publicly defended her, he said, because he believed in the principle that Congress and others outside science should not insert themselves in scientific disputes. In the process, he did not hide his dislike of Dr. O'Toole's actions and described her in one letter as a "disgruntled postdoctoral fellow."

Dr. O'Toole recalled hearing painful rumors about herself, everything from reports of incompetence to suggestions that, as a nursing mother, she was not acting rationally. That was one of the accusations that hurt the most, she said.

When she testified before Congress, Representative Norman Lent, Republican of Nassau, dismissed her, saying, "She had the attention and consideration of almost a score of eminent scientists from very high up in the ladder who have reviewed her complaint and found it wanting."

Describing her examination of laboratory records, Mr. Lent added, "If I had someone in my office who did that sort of thing with my notes, they'd be out of here in a flash, and they wouldn't be rehired by anybody I could call up."

The heat continued for five years, involving inquiries at universities, by the health institutes and in Congress. The dispute prompted a fear that her husband, Peter Brodeur, would be dismissed from his job in Dr. Imanishi-Kari's laboratory, but he continues to work there.

Dr. O'Toole found solace in the support of Dr. Linus Pauling, as well as that of Representative John Dingell, Democrat of Michigan, and his staff who continued the investigation of the matter. They were later joined by Dr. Ptashne.

They were among the few scientists who spoke out in her behalf as Dr. O'Toole's allegations were heard and reheard in investigations and hearings. Most scientists rallied around Dr. Baltimore and Dr. Imanishi-Kari, and were critical of Dr. O'Toole.

Dr. Ptashne said: "Scientists have a right to be wrong, and a right not to feel guilty for publishing things that are wrong. But they also have an obligation to find out if they are wrong and say so."

Deciphering Victorian Underwear and Other Seminars

Anne Matthews

Or how to be profane, profound and scholarly—all the while looking for a job—at the Modern Language Association's annual convention.

On the third morning of the Modern Language Association convention (known to members of the literary profession as the M.L.A.), a late-December fog veils Chicago's lakefront and visibility in the Loop falls to 0.0 miles. Near the entrance to the Hyatt Regency Hotel on East Wacker Drive, assistant professors in black leather pegged pants wade through icy slush. Andrew Ross watches them impassively. Under his mane of unruly hair he looks exhausted, but so do the hundreds of other literature scholars who eddy about in the hotel lobby, arguing.

"I haven't been outside in 72 hours," Ross murmurs in his throaty Edinburgh burr. Born in Scotland, Ross is a 34-year-old Marxist scholar of American popular culture who was recently recommended by Princeton's department of English for tenure. A former roustabout on North Sea oil platforms as well as the former butler of the great-grandson of Giuseppe Verdi in Berkeley, Calif., Ross has so far produced three books and 50 articles, his subjects ranging from Batman comics and computer hackers to new-age trance channeling and the semiotics of the Weather Channel.

For Ross, as for other rising stars in contemporary literary criticism, a good M.L.A. means hurtling between panel and symposium, publishing party and cash bar, seeing and being seen. Tall, lean, with saturnine good looks, Ross attracts attention wherever he goes. "That's him!" comes a reverent whisper from a group of graduate students nearby. "That's Andrew Ross!"

"M.L.A. is an anxious, exploitative, self-referential universe," Ross says, "but we do get a lot done at these bashes." He straightens his hand-painted Japanese tie, smooths his pale mango wool-and-silk Comme des Garçons blazer ("It's a sendup of the academic male convention of yellow polyester") and checks the wedge-heeled suede lace-ups recently acquired on West Eighth Street in Greenwich Village ("White boy's shoes, worn always with white socks"). Politely sidestepping a clutch of Dante experts, Ross disappears into an elevator, off to present a paper on censorship, Mapplethorpe and 2 Live Crew.

The Modern Language Association of America is about scholarly research and hiring, money, power and fashion—not always in that order. At the most recent convocation, members could choose among a dizzying 2,400 scholarly presentations, including the sedate ("Encyclopedias as a Literary Genre"), the arcane ("Aspects of Iconicity in Some Indiana Hydronyms") and the standing-room-only ("The Sodomitical Tourist"; "Victorian Underwear and Representations of the Female Body").

"Modern language" is a catchall term. Founded in 1883, the M.L.A. currently serves about 30,000 members. A few members are from overseas and rarely attend its meetings. Some join chiefly for the group health insurance. But the vast majority of the association's members teach and do research on literature and language at North America's colleges and universities.

"Managing M.L.A. gets more complicated all the time," says English Showalter, a professor of French literature at Rutgers University and former executive director of the association. "We recommend standards for the profession on academic freedom, on teaching loads and class sizes, on scholarly editions. There's a multimillion-dollar publishing program and a massive computerized bibliography. And the delegate assembly passes resolutions on everything from imprisoned scholars to fetal-tissue research." M.L.A. publications include bibliographies, teachers' guides and its perennial best seller, "The M.L.A. Handbook," which sets out rules for writing research papers and scholarly articles.

Two-thirds of the sessions at the annual M.L.A. concern the history, criticism and teaching of English. Similar panels are held on (and in) French, Italian, Spanish, Portuguese and German. Still other sessions feature what the association terms lesser-taught languages, like Tagalog, Xhosa, Pushtu and Ga.

As often happens at the M.L.A., this linguistic bounty spawns unending debate. Along the hallways, voices float out from packed meeting rooms expounding on sexual tourism, the pseudo-Jamesian use of allegory, the hermeneutics of suspicion. A session on "materializing culture" inspires a flood of purest critspeak: ". . . for the body commodified, in rap esthetics, the voyeuristic sampler self is a sound object, continuously metamorphosing, coded, re-tattooed, resignified into designer subjectivities prefiguring our own implosion, volatilizing culture to the point of hysteria and collapse."

The M.L.A. is the largest, wordiest, most angst-ridden gathering in American arts and letters. "Unlike sociologists, literary scholars don't throw each other in the swimming pool, and they're too politically correct to smoke or drink," one hotel manager explained at a previous convention. "M.L.A.-goers just talk, talk, talk—then sit in their rooms and cry."

Small wonder, then, that each year the M.L.A. insures ulcers, decides reputations, shatters and promptly reinvents definitions of literature, language and interpretation in just four frantic days. It also teaches academic combat skills. Tenure-hungry instructors learn to read convention ID badges in one flickering oblique

glance (always check the institutional name first) and to compose adroitly venom-
ous queries for the discussion periods that follow the presentation of papers
("What precisely do you mean by that?" can be very effective).

The arguments aired at the M.L.A. lie at the heart of the current furor in
American education over literary canons and social change. This is a heady (and
dangerous) moment for literary criticism. Just when many beyond the campus,
from uneasy parents to bewildered book lovers, want to know what the literate
person should read, and why, responses from the M.L.A. have never been more
divided. There are, in fact, so many differing opinions that the Chicago events
directory, at 350 pages, rivals the phone book for a fair-sized town.

Catharine R. Stimpson, an expert in women's studies and modern literature at
Rutgers University and the organization's 1990 president, is unruffled by the
heated arguments swirling everywhere. Commanding, tailored, Stimpson, who is
54, gives a calm, eloquent presidential address on difference and multiculturalism.
(At times, it would seem that multiculturalism—the drive to include non-Western
materials in every possible course—has superseded all other issues in American
higher education.) She speaks at panels on gender politics and women's publishing, as befits a self-defined mainstream feminist who fears oversimplified labeling.
And she leads a French philosopher, an African-American studies expert and an
Argentine novelist in a forum on how cultural values are defined.

"On taking office," Stimpson says, "I was startled both by the enormous variety
of M.L.A. activities—running literacy seminars attended by the A.F.L.-C.I.O.,
say—and by the ferocity with which we are misunderstood. We are not the Shri-
ners. We are not radical fat cats. M.L.A. is more like a bar association for the
literary profession. We try to provide a space for many vociferous opinions, but we
do not decree."

Whether the M.L.A. does or does not decree is, of course, fiercely contested.
And the last few M.L.A.'s have been so very vociferous that one can well ask: What
was all the shouting about? Why the bitter scenes in restaurants and hallways, the
colleagues not speaking to colleagues, the angry letters between teacher and pro-
tégé, friend and friend?

After attending almost two dozen M.L.A.'s, Alvin Kernan prefers the long
view. "Conservatives see the alteration of everything we once believed as the twi-
light of civilization," he says. "Radicals view it as the overdue fall of high culture's
Bastille." Blunt-featured, with a shock of silver-blond hair, Kernan, who is
67, looks like the Wyoming rancher he might have been had not a G.I. Bill scholarship to Yale led him into four decades as professor and administrator at Yale and
Princeton.

"Our convention used to be very stiff, a showcase for august senior men," he
notes. "Noisy debate is healthier for the profession. But underneath, M.L.A. remains a lot of insecure people in tweed jackets."

Tweed still abounds, but in Chicago it is sometimes transformed into downtown punk via glittery leggings, ripped Levi's and the Silence = Death buttons of
AIDS activists. At the M.L.A., you are what you wear: all-natural fibers for a University of Virginia job interview; power suits to meet a Northwestern committee;
hiking boots and hand-knit sweaters for Oregon State.

"It takes me all morning to get dressed," confides a male graduate student from California. "Everyone's so into subtexts and symbols and signifiers that the wrong earrings can destroy your credibility."

These shifts of fashion among M.L.A. participants mirror radical differences between schools of critical theory and practice, for the study of literature has in two generations changed more than any other academic field, including the sciences.

In the last 20 years, especially, ideas on how to approach a text have been turned utterly upside down ("unpacked" or "demystified" in the language of lit crit), a process that thrills some observers and alarms others.

Interpretive battles, rising from theories broadly known as post-structuralist, currently rage around these core assertions:

- Language itself is contradictory, if not empty.
- Meaning does not reside in a text or in an author's intent but in a reader's response.
- The reader is the equal of, and perhaps superior to, the author.
- The author is either dead or irrelevant. Literature is no longer a sacred calling, nor the writer a godlike creator.
- Literary influence—the accumulated insights of previous ages—can be harmful, not helpful.
- No form of discourse (folk tale, video, novel, sonnet) is superior to any other.
- The "classic books" approach to literary study is bankrupt. Multiculturalism is essential.
- All literary works must be viewed in a political context, as instruments of exclusion, oppression or liberation on the issues of race, class and gender.

An M.L.A. member without an opinion on these controversies is even rarer than one with no academic sub-sub-specialty. Some cultural commentators are making a career of resisting the new ways. Roger Kimball, author of "Tenured Radicals" and managing editor of *The New Criterion*, a monthly magazine of the arts, has the voice of an academician, all trans-Atlantic drawl and precise enunciation, but his animated face, like his button-down shirt, betrays him. Most M.L.A. attendees under 40 favor a deadpan hauteur, known as the Important Young Mind expression. Kimball, 37, fresh from a panel on "After Glasnost: Whither Marxist Criticism?" wears a look of frank exasperation.

"M.L.A.'s rank and file may murmur but refuse to speak out, through pusillanimity, against the Orwellian thought police who run these meetings," he fumes. "In four days, I have not heard a word of intelligent dissent." He frowns. "Liberalism's belief in meritocracy is being overwhelmed by a variety of florid radicalisms, all of which congregate under the term multiculturalism. People who care about education and freedom must challenge those who declare ideas and writers politically incorrect, and therefore nonexistent. That is intellectual tyranny."

Then there are those like Chauncey A. Ridley, 37, an assistant professor of English and an African-Americanist at California State University at Sacramento, who insist on quality over ideology.

"If you're a poor teacher, or a careless scholar, of course you stress politics, and not the Hispanic, black or Asian literary traditions," Ridley says, as he weaves his way from the "Representing Jazz" session toward a meeting on "Edith Wharton: Issues of Class, Race and Ethnicity." "Any lesser standard opens the way for opponents of multiculturalism. Maybe I'm a bourgeois intellectual, but I don't force-feed ethics or polemic. I teach the great ethnic literatures and their complex sources. Period."

A number of scholars watch the politicizing of literature with enthusiasm, seeing the natural evolution of a field that thrives on novelty and doubt.

"I teach in the Ivy League in order to have direct access to the minds of the children of the ruling classes," says Andrew Ross, unsmiling. "Whoever the politically correct are, it's about time some of them were in the universities."

Like Ross, many younger literary scholars aggressively seek change in the ways texts are read and taught, pressing for race or ethnic studies, feminism, Marxist analysis and textual deconstruction. Literature departments, these critics say, should become far looser entities and not insist on studying by historical period, author or genre.

A few centrist critics continue to define literature as "the best that has been thought or said" or as "the monuments of the European mind, showing who we were and what we might become." They view as a personal and intellectual affront all campaigns to reject Sophocles, Chaucer and Tolstoy as B.D.W.M.'s—Boring Dead White Males. But in revisionist circles, words like "taste," "hierarchy" and "tradition" bring an impatient roll of the eyes. "Judgmental" is a serious insult; "anti-exclusionist," a compliment.

Watching their elders do battle, many of the professors in training at the M.L.A. appear to suffer from intellectual whiplash (a record one-third of the registrants are graduate students). Richard Abowitz, 23, is a Hollins College graduate student in fiction, filling out applications to Ph.D. programs in English literature for fall 1991. In a battered leather jacket and Dead Milkmen T-shirt, Abowitz blends in nicely at the M.L.A., but although he looks avant-garde, he feels cheated.

"As an apprentice scholar, I've had to read Kate Chopin's 'The Awakening' three times," he says plaintively, "which was fine, but I never learned a thing about Dickens or T. S. Eliot. All I want is access to minds of any race or gender who will teach books like 'Moby-Dick.' Is that too much to ask?"

Well-trained in the new methodologies, Abowitz answers his own question: "Melville is profoundly suspect. There's not a woman in his book, the plot hinges on unkindness to animals and the black characters mostly drown by Chapter 29."

He watches the chattering crowds flow past: "This is my first M.L.A. I guess I expected more civility, less literature in the service of theory. These people eat their own." Abowitz sighs. "Maybe I'll go to law school."

Scholarship is thirsty work. Daily at 5:15 P.M., M.L.A. attendees pour out of meetings in search of the many cocktail receptions sponsored by allied organizations and specialized societies (political correctness sometimes lessens after hours). An observer may drop in on the Cervantes Society, the William Morris Society, the gay and lesbian literary group, then pause at the Marxist cash bar, liveliest of all.

Here, amid cigar smoke and the clink of Budweiser bottles, attendees sign one another's petitions "to reopen Palestinian universities," bemoan private-school tuitions and trade impressions of the M.L.A.: "My wallet was redistributed, right on Michigan Avenue!" "Half the people here have trust funds." "The bartender is probably C.I.A."

Between talks and parties, M.L.A.-goers prowl the exhibition area, a reader's nirvana of scholarly journals, glossy university-press catalogues and stacks of new books and other publications. Scholars bustle from booth to booth, seeking half-off discounts and free copies from publishers, or stare at computer programs designed to help students avoid plagiarism in their essays.

From lucrative contracts for college textbooks and instructional software to research grants sanctioned by peer-review panels at foundations and Federal endowments, millions of dollars can ride on the profession's instinct for trend.

"The pressure for fresh interpretations in literary study is enormous," explains Lindsay Waters, executive editor of Harvard University Press. "A Tennyson monograph may move 500 copies, but Terry Eagleton's guide to critical theory has sold over 120,000 so far. Scholars come in here like barracuda, searching for ideas." (Eagleton is a noted Marxist critic at Oxford University.)

Publish or perish, says the literary profession, teach or go under. At the nearby M.L.A. job headquarters, two blocks away, stern checklists of recruiting etiquette are heaped on chairs: "Candidate: do not be apologetic or arrogant, downgrade other institutions, chew gum, overstay your welcome. Interviewer: do not display boredom, doodle, produce stress intentionally, argue with candidate, do all the talking."

Nearly as much as scholarship, jobs are the real work of the M.L.A. Each year, the bedrooms and suites of convention hotels become hiring offices for hundreds of schools. Harried committees work four days straight, interviewing applicant after applicant for precious few college-teaching slots.

John C. Cobb, 37, completing his Ph.D. at Rutgers, knows the odds. "Even part-time adjunct placements are hard to find now, because of all the budget freezes," he says. Like many at the M.L.A., he is on a third or fourth life, an amiable South Carolinian turned blues-band guitarist, high-school English teacher and Restoration scholar.

"Late-17th-century criticism is not your most marketable specialty," Cobb adds, "but it interests me. Sure, I could be in business, but I do my best work with college kids. And I love to teach. These days, someone has to."

Cobb has four interview appointments. Although she sent out 33 applications, Sherry K. Young has none. At 45, having gained her Ph.D. in Romantic poetry from the University of Dallas in 1986, she is a visiting lecturer at the University of North Texas in Denton. Young has five children and she augments her yearly income of $16,000 from her college teaching by taking three other jobs. Each day, she rises at 5:15 A.M. and drives 100 miles to teach college literature, coach business writing at various corporations, manage an office for an exercise-equipment company and work as an A.T.&T. sales representative. "I can teach anything from Homer to James Joyce," she says, "but I'm also dying of exhaustion."

Like many graduates of the recessionary decade, 1975 to 1985, Young is traveling steerage in today's literary revolution. At every convention, graying hopefuls, some with several books and articles to their credit, wanly contemplate ads for one-semester posts at undistinguished schools—three sections of freshman composition, two of world mythology, no benefits, no hope of rehiring.

"I won't leave the field," Sherry Young says stubbornly. "I won't. Literature carries compensations that are not monetary. Great writing makes it all worthwhile."

Writers, great or otherwise, make infrequent appearances at the M.L.A. Because scholars must be ruthlessly honest, many prefer to work on poets and novelists who are safely dead. Too many convention panels on living authors have been marred by anguished cries from the back of the room: "But that's not what I meant at all!" That being the case, an evening reading by three young Midwestern Asian-American poets is surprisingly well-attended. Hundreds, in fact, are waiting in silence, eager and intent.

The last to read is Li-Young Lee, 33, an athletic young man with an angular face. He rises from his seat and lays five typed sheets of paper gently on the lectern.

"These are poems of memory and failure," he tells his audience. "As a refugee, poetry kept me sane." Following the political imprisonment of his father, a Chinese physician living with his wife and children in Indonesia, Lee's family fled to Hong Kong, arriving in the United States when Lee was 6. Lee attended the University of Pittsburgh and the University of Arizona, then worked for a number of years as a Chicago warehouseman and as a commercial artist. ("I read all I could in those early years in the warehouse—Homer, Shakespeare, everything," he says later. "It sounds ridiculous, but I would kiss the book when I began, a gesture of reverence for the page. I do that still.") Grants from the Guggenheim and Whiting foundations and the National Endowment for the Arts have bought him time for poetry.

He runs a hand through his shoulder-length shaggy hair. "My work is about the urge for ultimate things, for shapeliness, for destiny," he continues. Looking often at his wife in the audience, Lee begins to read, quietly, as though he were conversing:

Lie still now . . .
and recall this room and everything in it:
My body is estrangement.
This desire, perfection.
Your closed eyes my extinction . . .

When he sits down, many in the audience are weeping.

If arrogance and obscurity thrive at the M.L.A., so does a firm conviction in the power of words. Despite its splintered agendas and contrary voices, the meeting annually demonstrates the sheer fecundity of language, the life-giving richness that keeps Sherry Young on the road, Andrew Ross working for cultural and social change and Roger Kimball rising to proclaim the virtues of literary heritage.

If the M.L.A.'s of the last decade centered on literary theory, in the 1990's scholars in the humanities are more likely to focus on turf battles and budget crises. Many universities have begun to trim liberal-arts departments in order to support science research or to expand schools of medicine and business. Parents paying five-figure yearly tuitions are pressing for full-time faculty, not graduate students, in the classroom. Deans who in the mid-1980's bid lavishly for superstar theorists now want cost-efficient teaching, and lots of it.

In this new era of limits, dogmatic extremes can seem less appealing. "I am baffled as to why we cannot be students of Western culture and multiculturalism at the same time, why we cannot show the relationships among many cultures," observed Catharine Stimpson in her presidential speech.

"The great danger to all our elaborate M.L.A. fuss," Alvin Kernan says sadly, "is that in an impatient, postprint society, literature itself may dwindle away, becoming marginalized and pointless."

But not yet. As of December 1990, the M.L.A.'s defining quality is still movement—restless and unsettled, ideas in transit, theories in orbit, scholars in flight. On the last Sunday of 1990, beside the Hyatt escalators, the ritual farewells take place. See you in Berlin, at the computational linguistics meeting. In Nashville, for the Rabelais conference. At Dartmouth, for the esthetic fetishism course. In San Francisco, for M.L.A. '91.

Pedagogy, the profession's other most basic impulse, also remains vigorous. Posted on a convention announcement board is an agitated adolescent scrawl: "Did your parents force you to come to M.L.A.? Are you going stir-crazy, like me? Call if you are age 18 and just want someone normal to go sightseeing with!!"

Red-inked below, in a firm professorial hand: "Watch punctuation. Vary sentence structure. Try not to end sentences in prepositions."

Chapter
15

International Organizational Life

N o contemporary volume on organizational reality would be complete without at least some selections concerned with international organizational life. As Lester Therow, the noted economist, has observed so frequently, we live in a global economy where organizational lines and activities simply do not stop at national boundaries.

U.S. and foreign multinational firms have experienced an explosive growth in the past three decades and there is no sign of this trend abating. Further, an increasing proportion of domestic organizations obtain either their raw materials or their finished products from abroad. In many instances, organizations must either station North American managers and their families in foreign countries or, as a minimum, establish frequent and effective coordination with subsidiaries or suppliers. Yet, as the selections in this chapter illustrate, the reality of international organizational life presents a multitude of challenges for individuals and organizations and their countries.

While there are a number of excellent texts dealing with management and with international business, most neglect the impact on individuals and their families of moving to another country and culture. Americans, regretfully, are a distinctly insular people. Despite a love of foreign travel, Americans are historically loath to learn about cultures other than their own. Living successfully in a different culture requires a great deal of learning and North Americans have justly earned a bad reputation in this matter with natives of other countries: They often fail to study the local culture, observe the necessary courtesies, and otherwise adapt their behavior to the local situation. The piece by Frederick H. Katayama, "How to Act Once You Get There," offers some "basics" that can help the newcomer, at least initially. Of course, there is no substitute for learning as much as possible about the region, its history, politics, and, in particular, the local ways of doing business.

China offers formidable challenges to the North American who ventures there to do business of any sort. In "China, Inc.: How to Do Business with the Chinese," Roderick Macleod, a China veteran, illustrates how vastly the Chinese culture and business practices differ from those of the West. Macleod has written a book that is a useful primer on the topic.

The fall of the Berlin Wall and the reunification of West and East Germany took place with breathtaking swiftness. It now remains to be seen how East Germany will fare and in what ways Western management philosophies and practices will help or will hinder the transformation of business in that part of the world, as described in "It's Sink or Swim in East Germany."

Throughout this book, we have repeatedly focused on women, their problems and their achievements. In "Japan Discovers Women Power," Sally Solo acquaints us with the extent to which Japanese women are gaining entry into the managerial work force. In North America, women have made their gains in spite of resistance by older male managers. In Japan, however, the entry of women into management has been a matter of economic necessity, the necessity of dealing with a declining pool of male candidates. Since women are widely thought to be less prone to become workaholics, the author speculates that the growing numbers of female managers may, in time, have a significant impact on the Japanese work ethic. It is interesting to speculate whether the continued influx of American women into management will increase the erosion of the American work ethic.

"The Final Stretch" presents a true story that illustrates that we need not travel to distant countries to find examples of the difficulties that can arise in doing business internationally. Many people think of the border between Canada and the United States as open, yet this piece illustrates how trade laws can confound even this close relationship and make operating a business a very hazardous and frustrating experience.

The final selections of this chapter focus on organizational realities south of the U.S. border. In Mexico, businesses operate in a world of cheap labor and minimal laws regulating the environmental actions of corporations. Sonia Nazario chronicles some of the destructive consequences in "Boom and Despair." In "Managing Without Managers," Richard Semler describes efforts to harness the managerial potential of all employees at Semco, the Brazilian firm he heads.

How to Act Once You Get There

Frederick H. Katayama

Doing business in Asia *is* different. In Europe you are not going to blow a deal by slapping your new foreign partner on the back. But old hands in the Orient claim that happened once in Malaysia to a U.S. electronics executive who forgot—or never knew—that most Asians abhor physical contact.

Traveling to more than one country in Asia also means coping with the sharp differences in style and behavior that divide East from East, as well as West. Two things help. First, because the Chinese are so widely scattered throughout the region, a passing knowledge of the Middle Kingdom's history and customs usually gives you some common cultural ground. Second, everyone you meet will probably speak English. The mother tongue of Australia and New Zealand is also an official language in Hong Kong, Singapore, and the Philippines. In Japan, South Korea, and Taiwan, most businessmen can speak—though haltingly—the basic English they were forced to learn in school.

So relax. You can avoid serious blunders and make a good impression as long as you heed the following tips:

- **Dress conservatively.** "The biggest problem is the Texan with big boots and a big hat who wants to pat people on the back," says Thomas Sheldon, an American lawyer who spent two years in Seoul. Throughout most of Asia, the uniform is traditional business suits for men and plain dresses, not pantsuits, for women.

    In Japan clean socks without holes in the toes are crucial, since shoes come off whenever you visit someone's home or dine on tatami mats in a traditional restaurant. Your kit bag should also include a good supply of Kleenex and hankies. Many public restrooms and restaurants don't supply toilet paper or napkins.

- **Be punctual.** During a state visit last May, Vice President Dan Quayle scheduled a morning of deep-sea diving in Australia. Fair enough. His mistake was to ignore Secret Service warnings that he was running late, and insist on a second plunge and a round of tennis—a decision that made him almost two hours late for a meeting later that day in Indonesia. QUAYLE ARRIVES BEHIND SCHEDULE blared the front-page headline of the Jakarta *Post*.

"How to Act Once You Get There" by Frederick H. Katayama, *Fortune,* Pacific Rim 1989, pp. 87–88. Reprinted by permission of *Fortune* Magazine. © 1989 The Time Inc. Magazine Company. All rights reserved.

- **When greeting people,** a handshake and a simple nod will suffice. Extras—the full bow at the waist in Japan or the graceful, prayerlike folding of hands known as the *wai* in Thailand—are appreciated but not expected of foreigners. Stick to titles and surnames, unless you're in Thailand or Australia, where first names are the game.

  Naturally, no first encounter in Asia is complete without an exchange of business cards. Bring a full deck. If possible, have your name, company, and title printed in the local language as well as in English. Use both hands to present and receive cards, and be sure to show respect by reading them carefully. Diana Rowland, author of *Japanese Business Etiquette*, knows one U.S. businessman who lost a deal because he failed to examine the cards of his Japanese prospects thoroughly enough. Says she: "Even though they liked his product, the Japanese reasoned that such inattention was representative of what they could expect from him later."

- **Avoid physical contact.** You know about backslapping now, but don't pat heads either. Asians revere the head as the seat of the soul. They also consider the feet the lowliest part of the body, so don't cross your legs. You may disgrace yourself by waving the soles of your shiny new loafers in your host's face.

- **When making casual conversation,** leave the elaborate jokes at home. They almost never translate. And avoid politics at all cost. Once negotiations get serious, remember that most Asians will rarely turn you down flat, because they don't want you to lose face. If your prospect sucks in his breath during your sales pitch and says with a sigh, "It is difficult" or "We will consider it in a forward-looking manner," interpret that as a polite "no."

- **Though the region boasts** several outstanding cuisines, some Asian delicacies strike Westerners as, well, exotic. The sensitive of stomach should beware of such menu items as "fragrant meat" (dog meat) in Taiwan, "night duck" soup (bat soup) in China, and extremely raw sushi (the fish still writhes atop the rice) in Japan.

  When you have no choice, try to eat at least a tad of whatever is offered—even if it's sea slugs in Hong Kong or eggs in horse urine in Thailand. If you really feel shaky, though, decline politely. "That's certainly better than gagging at the table," says Scott Seligman, author of *Dealing with the Chinese*. Seligman suggests pushing the food around on your plate a bit so that it looks as if you have sampled something.

  But if you love the dish, forget what Mom said about cleaning your plate. Unless you leave a little, your host will think you are still hungry. Nor should happy eaters stick their chopsticks in the rice bowl. That connotes death. Place them on the chopstick rest, an indented eraser-size object made of porcelain or wood, or lay them across the side of your plate. When picking food off a communal dish, flip the sticks around and use the large end. That's not only polite, it's good hygiene.

- **Women executives** should prepare to put up with far more male chauvinism than they would back home. Warns etiquette expert Diana Rowland, who worked for six years in Kyoto: "Aggressiveness works against you in

Japan if you're a woman, because it makes the Japanese uncomfortable." That's also true in male-dominated Korea. Advises Robert Oxnam, president of the Asia Society: "Women have to be willing to overcome slights, some of which aren't intentional."

Ursula Gogel-Gordon, a director of product development at sportswear manufacturer Seattle-Pacific Industries, knows about that firsthand. When she was negotiating to buy yarn from a Japanese trading company, all questions were directed to her less senior male colleague. Says she: "Each time, he would say, 'You have to talk to her.' This happened ten times in a row." Gogel-Gordon kept her cool and closed the deal. But she does advise female managers to forestall such behavior by spelling out their responsibilities in writing and making sure their Asian contacts get the message before they arrive.

- **Gift giving is commonplace.** But outside Japan, where you should err on the side of expensive, don't give something too dear lest the recipient feel obliged to do likewise. If you think to stock up before the trip, local crafts and consumables—Shaker boxes, say, if you're from Pennsylvania, or maple syrup from Vermont—make good gifts.

  Avoid flowers, which can easily insult someone if they are the wrong color or type. White carnations, for example, suggest death or mourning in China. Don't present clocks to Chinese, either. The phrase "to give a clock" sounds like a Chinese expression that means "to care for a dying patient." It rattles the superstitious. As with name cards, use both hands to present and receive gifts. And don't open your gift in the giver's presence. It's the thought that counts.

- **Tipping is less common**—and tips are smaller—than in the U.S. or Europe. Most hotels and restaurants automatically assess a service charge, which will be noted on the bill. No further gratuity is expected. Where service isn't included, leave 10%.

- **With minor exceptions,** drinking is a national sport throughout Asia, and guests are expected to play. Whether the cry is *kanpai* (CON-pie) in Tokyo, *konbae* (GUHN-beh) in Seoul, or *ganbei* (GONE-bay) in Beijing, the message is the same: bottoms up. Kevin Chambers, author of *The Travelers' Guide to Asian Customs and Manners,* recalls that when he nonchalantly declined a business prospect's offer of a cup of *makkolli,* the Korean rice wine, the "frivolity suddenly came to a halt." So did Chambers's deal. If you really don't want to drink, tell your hosts that you are allergic to booze. Better yet, cite doctor's orders.

  In Tokyo and Seoul, and increasingly in Hong Kong and Taipei, you will likely be taken to a *karaoke* bar. In these joints, customers take turns crooning tunes to prerecorded background music, and for once, Asia's strait-laced businessmen shed their reserve and become as giddy as teenagers. Sure, it's silly. But if you feel self-conscious, consider practicing a verse or two of "My Way" or "Yesterday"—two ubiquitous Western classics—in the shower before you go out. This time, "doctor's orders" won't get you off the hook. You *will* be expected to sing for your sale.

China, Inc.: How to Do Business with the Chinese

Roderick Macleod

Ugly Americans and inscrutable Chinese: you can't do business with a
stereotype

China is getting to be a good place to do some business, in spite of—maybe because of—the strange things you've heard in the recent past. China isn't the dazzling array of enormously profitable opportunities once advertised—and we had to
get over that notion. It isn't the terrible swamp of delays, inefficiencies, and broken
promises that was subsequently portrayed by some disappointed venturers, and we
had to learn from those mistakes. It's just a good place to do some good business
that hasn't been done before.

Like any other business that you haven't done before, you have a lot to learn
when you are new to it, and it can cost you a lot to learn it if you aren't careful. In
that sense it isn't any different from going into franchising, or trying to get government contracts, or "going public." What is different is that the fundamentals of the
China business scene aren't even recognized, let alone well understood, by very
many people, and so good guidance is hard to get.

I found my way: let me offer some help.

If you are going to China for some serious business, working or negotiating,
you can do it the way most Westerners do: You can pay attention to chopstick
technique, banquet etiquette, and other exotic customs, and think you know all
you need to know. Then you can find out for yourself how much more there is to it,
and experience along the way all the betrayals, frustrations, and nightmares that go
with the discovery.

Or you can put a little effort into looking at *why they do things the way they
do*—and even more important, *why we do things the way we do*—and begin to
understand why we find each other so difficult. That way, you can skip a whole
generation of frustrating mistakes. You will be far ahead of where I was when I
started out, and far ahead of almost everybody else I know who has tried to do
business in China.

The emphasis throughout this book is on what Westerners might think about and perhaps do differently. This doesn't mean that the problems are all our fault, but rather that the actions available to *us* that can help us to succeed are the subjects of this book. If I wrote a book aimed at Chinese readers—and I've thought about it—the suggestions would be different, though the facts would be the same.

China is a huge country, vastly different from anything in the West, in addition to which it is Communist, which makes it even more different. Most people assume that nothing there works intelligibly, so they need never disappoint themselves. That's fun if you're a tourist, but it's no way to do business. For business purposes it is necessary to know how China works, that there is a system, and that it has an internal logic and pattern.

The way China is organized for administrative and economic purposes can be described in terms of Western corporate organization: every economic unit—factory, office, lab, school, hospital—belongs to and reports to a higher unit of the huge corporate conglomerate "China, Inc." This model of a Western-style corporation, like any model, necessarily simplifies and therefore leaves out some of the complexities of the real thing. But the concept of China, Inc., is nevertheless an accurate and very useful guide. It provides a familiar and orderly framework to help Westerners organize information about their Chinese counterparts—not only where they fit into their organizations, but what they are doing and why they do it. It helps to sort out and put into perspective the jumble of stereotypes and misconceptions that most people have about China. It also helps make sense of the extraordinary changes that have been going on there during the last few years—and are continuing apace.

As an example of the foreigners' misconceptions that can be corrected within the China, Inc., metaphor, it is widely believed that there is one central, all-knowing, all-controlling, decision-making structure in China. This belief manifests itself in many ways; one example is the common idea that every traveler to China (except tourists, and even some of them) goes "at the invitation of the Chinese government." The view is popular because it seems to confer high status. And it is true in a loose, poetic sense, because one Chinese organization or another has to authorize, or invite, every visitor.

In fact, the corporate analogy is more accurate. Presidents invite presidents in the names of their companies or countries, but for most of us getting the invitation is more akin to arranging an appointment with the maintenance engineer at the local IBM regional sales office to explain why your window-washing service is better than the one he uses now. That is hardly "at the invitation of IBM," but you could say it was, if you wanted to. And IBM wouldn't deny it. It's like that in China.

THE CASE OF THE MAGIC NUMBERS

The China-Schindler Elevator Company was one of the first joint ventures; its purpose was to manufacture elevators and control systems for high-rise buildings. It experienced the serious "growing pains" to be expected in such a new kind of enterprise. In this case the partners had budgeted enough time and money for such things, and one obstacle after another was overcome, until they came to the one that starts off this story.

The plan was to manufacture the systems in China for the domestic market and for export to the rest of Asia. The high-tech components would be imported, and Chinese materials would be used for parts such as housings and mounts, where anticipated uncertainties about quality could be accommodated. The forecast indicated that they would need to export about 40 percent of production to earn enough foreign exchange to buy the imported components and repay the foreign partners' investment and profit.

The start-up process took longer than anyone expected, but finally production began. Salesmen went out to the industrial centers of East and Southeast Asia and came back with orders. The domestic order book was filled differently: rather than making "sales" as we know them, they sent out negotiators to the units that had been designated to take their production under the National Plan, to negotiate quantities and delivery schedules.

The first several systems went off reasonably well, but then assembled motors started to stack up on the shop floor and in the warehouse. The steel for housings and mounts wasn't arriving. It had been ordered, the allotment had been built into the National Plan, the paperwork had been exchanged with the assigned supplier, everything that should have been done had been done. But the steel wasn't there.

There weren't any expatriate managers at the Chinese plant at the time, luckily for them. If they had been there they no doubt would have had a fine case of the fits. But that wouldn't have created any steel. The Chinese just built a shed to house the accumulating assemblies.

The domestic negotiators simply told the Chinese builders awaiting deliveries that there would be a delay, and that was all there was to that. Everybody in China is used to such things. The system doesn't work very well as a result, but it is loose enough to absorb all the thousands of delays along the way.

Not so in international markets. Orders have to be delivered on time or they are canceled and you don't get any more. So the export orders were canceled and the anticipated foreign exchange didn't materialize. The Chinese managers reported that event to the foreign partners as if it were routine and somewhat casually asked to be sent more foreign funds with which to buy parts.

The foreign partners of course reacted with alarm, and spent a lot of money on telexes of inquiry and even on phone calls and plane tickets. But that didn't produce any steel either. Finally, after a long delay, a whole year's allotment of steel came through in one shipment and the plant got going again, though without export orders to fill.

Meanwhile, the Chinese authorities kept announcing that the venture was a success and that profits equaled or exceeded the original plan. There were more telexes from the foreign partners, asking how that could be, with all the delays and canceled orders. Don't worry, was the reply, they would be able to ship more units and get higher prices from the Chinese builders of high-rises.

Things went on like that for some time, with problems and delays occurring but good reports coming from management, and the Chinese accountants turned out financial statements every six months that showed the joint venture on or ahead of its forecast. The foreign partners were mystified; they just didn't see how it could be so. But since the reports were good and the demands for more funds had stopped, and the time hadn't yet come for paying out profits and repaying the investment, they felt it better not to ask too many questions. . . .

The case illustrates two points: how plans can go awry, and how the Chinese can, if they want to, make it come out all right anyway.

The problem of unreliable sources of supply is so prevalent in China, and so much talked about, that everyone going into the joint venture undoubtedly knew that it could happen. Chinese managers have various ways of coping with it: wherever they can, they make their own supplies and components so that they aren't at the mercy of others; they order more and save up a "safety stock" wherever they can; they have "fixers" on their staffs who go around and wheedle, coax, and make deals to get scarce or delayed materials; they don't hesitate to pass on the delays to their customers.

While it's worthwhile to remind readers of the supply problem, and to illustrate what it can do to the best-laid plans, that isn't the reason for telling this story. The main reason is to show the way that the joint venture kept succeeding, and apparently making money, in spite of all the problems.

The Chinese authorities haven't confided their private thoughts to me or, as far as I know, to the foreigners involved in the venture, and I have no mind-reading powers. The pattern seems clear and logical enough to me, though, to venture an explanation for what was going on.

Everybody knew that Chinese managers had a lot to learn if they were to get into export markets. Foreign professors and businessmen were pouring into China to lecture to huge, attentive audiences on Western management techniques. But everybody who actually tried to do any of it knew that it was easier said than done. Foreign management doesn't work in China, but maybe it will work with some adaptation.

But what adaptation? Who knows? Nobody. But the managers of those ventures that must rely on exports will have to figure it out to make the ventures go. So what better way to get the techniques, whatever they are, discovered, adapted, and proven than to let the joint venture managers struggle with whatever faces them, such as the unreliable sources of supply of materials, and see what they come up with?

Meanwhile, the ventures can't be permitted to fail. They are, after all, China's method of buying what it needs from the West, and the method, and China's credit, must be seen to be good. Most of China's business is still controlled, and if necessary the Plan can be adjusted here and there to make sure the foreign investor gets paid according to the promises that induced him to come to China—for example, by directing a few enterprises to pay a premium price, even in foreign exchange, maybe, and compensate them for the added cost to them in the course of the annual planning process. Given the flexible Socialist concept of cost as a political decision, it would be seen as a simple enough thing to do.

So that is a possible explanation for why they didn't fix the supply problems, which they could have done, but they did fix the sales problems. As long as they regard the joint ventures as a device for long-term financing of purchases of technology and know-how, they will find ways to make the ventures come out as planned. A foreign joint venturer shouldn't take too much comfort in that thought, though, because what happens if they change their minds? Or if another policy conflicts, and seems to be more important?

I think that is what happened to the American Motors joint venture to build Jeeps that was much in the news in the first half of 1986. According to the newspaper, AMC suspended shipment of "kits" of Jeep parts, and the Chinese plant had to halt production for two months, because the Chinese wouldn't pay for them.

At first reading, that sounds pretty irresponsible of the Chinese, and that is the way many Westerners read it. But the Chinese just aren't that way: even their critics agree that they keep their promises. So take another reading: AMC should have known that those kits would have to be financed, and had it all in the agreement before they started. But AMC had one of the best helpmate-consultants available, Unison International, and I cannot believe they would have overlooked the matter. AMC must have known. We have to take a third reading.

I think AMC may have relied on the usually reliable Principle of Endless Possibilities—in this case, a subset of that principle that could be entitled "We'll Work Things Out Together As We Go Along." It was clear that that joint venture was a good thing for the Chinese: it gave them good experience in American automotive assembly technology and it substituted Jeeps for expensive imports of foreign cars. AMC was entitled to think that its partner would take care of it.

Then the 1985 foreign exchange clamp-down came. A lot of plans and even commitments had to be canceled, the way the Sun Microsystems deal fell through in "The Case of the Vanishing Contract." The AMC kit imports shouldn't have been affected, but that is what the papers said was happening. From the fact that payments were resumed after a couple of months, I infer that there must have been some big battle going on, possibly among units of China, Inc., rather than between AMC and China, to try to get AMC to invest more rather than use China's foreign exchange to buy the kits. The press releases were part of the campaign to shame the attackers into backing down. They did, but saved face by saying that it was only "temporary."

The Chinese at all levels are willing to make exceptions to any rule when the issue is important enough. In that they are like managers anywhere, and they regard the laws of China, Inc., as company policies designed to achieve corporate objectives, which can be overridden when they stand in the way of those objectives. I had a specific statement of that attitude once when we were having trouble getting the economics of a proposed venture to come out right. We were working late and under pressure and the minister himself dropped in to cheer on the troops; he said how important the project was, and that if we needed any special terms—a lower tax rate or customs duties, different prices, anything like that—just to let him know and he'd see to it. You can do that in China, Inc., as you can in any Western company, if you are important enough.

I don't mean that there is a Machiavellian master planner knowingly manipulating all the strings behind every venture. The whole system isn't tightly enough organized for that, and even if it were, it is changing too fast. What I mean is that the tendency to do what one can along those lines is sure to be operative.

It's Sink or Swim in East Germany

Steven Greenhouse

Workers and companies are facing the new order with hope and anxiety.

East Berlin—On July 2, Heinz Warzecha, the straight-talking, unflinching head of one of East Germany's most important industrial groups, will greet the new capitalist era by laying off 7,000 people, nearly a third of his work force.

That is the day when economic unification of the two Germanys takes effect, and Mr. Warzecha, who heads the October 7 Machine Tool Kombinat, is intent on taking whatever measures are needed to keep his empire of 16 factories afloat.

"The way I see it, there is one sure formula for survival," said Mr. Warzecha, a raspy-voiced, powerfully built man who has headed the 22,000-employee, state-owned kombinat, or business group, for six years. "You have to cut your work force by 30 to 40 percent, and you have to raise your sales by 50 percent."

East Germany's transition to capitalism will be far faster—and far more of a sink-or-swim proposition—than transitions elsewhere in Eastern Europe. That is because the melding of the two German economies means managers like Mr. Warzecha will suddenly have to follow Western business rules and pay wages in hard currency, following the swap of East German for West German marks.

The change will not be painless. Over the next two years, many economists here say, up to 2.5 million of the country's 9 million workers will lose their jobs and a third or more of East German enterprises will go under.

Yet Mr. Warzecha (pronounced vahr-TSEH-shah) said he was "absolutely sure" that his kombinat, which produces metal-cutting machinery, would survive. And thanks to aggressive managers like him—and to newly anxious and newly motivated workers like those at his kombinat—East German officials say the nation will double its economic output in 7 to 10 years, producing postwar Germany's second Wirtschaftswunder, or economic miracle.

Like many other East German managers, Mr. Warzecha hopes to secure the future of his kombinat through joint ventures with Western companies. He is negotiating alliances with a half-dozen West German and Italian companies that are attracted by his group's skilled labor and close links to Eastern European customers. These ventures, including one to develop a machine that uses lasers to cut metal, would bring sophisticated new technologies and much-needed research and development money to the kombinat, based in a gritty, 70-year-old building here.

"We have to accomplish this transition in a few months," said Mr. Warzecha, a 60-year-old engineer whose kombinat is named for the date in 1949 when the German Democratic Republic was established. "Where this transition isn't achieved, companies are going to die."

This hard reality has left workers deeply ambivalent—delighted about being paid in West German marks yet scared about their job prospects. In East Berlin, where West German chocolates, toys and televisions are already filling once-drab store shelves, there is much talk about an angst-filled autumn in which armies of the unemployed will take to the streets.

"THE IDEA OF GETTING FIRED"

"It's a new phenomenon, the idea of getting fired," said Jörg Lehmann, a technician at Planeta, an enterprise that produces printing presses outside Dresden. "There's a lot of uncertainty."

At the same time, fear of layoffs and the prospect of being paid in West marks has made workers more dedicated to their jobs. "There is more of a willingness to work hard nowadays," said Klaus-Dieter Nisch, a machine operator at October 7.

Although the German Democratic Republic is a small country, with just 16 million people, many economists view its unification with West Germany as a seminal event that will send huge and beneficial shockwaves throughout Europe and beyond. A unified Germany, with 78 million people, will have a gross national product about 45 percent larger than France's and almost 70 percent larger than Britain's.

What sets East Germany apart from other Eastern European countries is that that it is the only one that will benefit from a program remotely comparable to the Marshall Plan. Its sister republic is planning to pump in more than $70 billion over the next four years, while private investors may pour in another $80 billion or so.

"Other Eastern European countries will remain bogged down in slow growth," said Jean Le Dam, an economist with the Center for the Study of International Economic Prospects in Paris.

By contrast, East Germany hopes to quickly get past the bankruptcies and high unemployment that lie ahead. After that painful period is over, many economists say, East Germany will emerge with a far more efficient industrial base and an economy that will grow by a dazzling 8 to 10 percent a year, making it Eastern Europe's only economic tiger.

For its part, West Germany's $1.3 trillion economy will grow at a brisk 4 percent a year during the next few years, primed by all the demand tied to unification, according to many analysts. That would be more than double West Germany's growth rate in the early 1980's and, many economists say, a full percentage point more than it would be without unification. As West Germany, the locomotive of Europe, picks up speed, the European Community is expected to enjoy a unification-inspired extra half percentage point of growth a year. "Other countries will participate in the G.D.R.'s higher growth," said Manfred Melzer, an economist with the German Institute for Economics in West Berlin. "A lot of Western countries will be able to sell more products to the G.D.R."

In fact, unification will create opportunities for companies from Stuttgart to Seattle. The estimated $500 billion needed to rebuild East Germany's dilapidated infrastructure means a flood of orders for telecommunications equipment, computers and construction machinery. Since West German manufacturers are already operating at almost full capacity, with many supply bottlenecks, West German industry will not be able to handle all the orders. That leaves plenty of opportunity for non-German manufacturers.

The projected rapid increase in wealth for the East Germans will also create new vistas for banks and consumer-products companies. For starters, unification means that East Germans, who have an average of 10,000 East marks in savings, will receive one West mark for each of their first 4,000 East marks, and one West mark for every two East marks above that. That will leave the typical East German with 7,000 West marks, worth about $4,200.

Because they will be paid in West marks, East Germans—at least those still working—will earn double what they did before unification. Still, that remains much less than their counterparts in West Germany—a factor helping to attract Western investment.

THE WEST RUSHES IN

In the face of such sudden riches, West German titans like Volkswagen, Siemens, Deutsche Bank and Daimler-Benz are rushing in. Volkswagen is teaming up with the kombinat that produces the much-maligned Trabant automobile and plans to invest $2.9 billion to assemble 250,000 cars a year in East Germany. Deutsche Bank, West Germany's largest bank, plans to open 130 branches in East Germany next month as part of its joint venture with Deutsche Kreditbank A.G., a new commercial bank carved out of East Germany's central bank.

"East Germany was very underbanked," said Friedhelm Tuttlies, a board member of Deutsche Kreditbank. "We weren't allowed to buy stock or certificates of deposit. Our bank needed to enter a joint venture to gain modern technology and learn about Western banking services."

Swiss, British, French and American companies are also expanding in East Germany, though understandably in far smaller numbers than the West Germans. The American movers include General Motors, Honeywell, I.B.M., Coca-Cola, Citibank, Philip Morris and Eastman Kodak.

G.M.'s Opel division plans to invest more than $100 million in a plant in Eisenach to assemble 150,000 cars annually by 1993. And Coca-Cola has earmarked $140 million for trucks, bottling equipment and training.

"In the long term, it is a market with big chances," said Gert Leonhardt, Kodak's manager for East Germany. "It's a promising market of 16 million people where we start from zero."

AMERICANS TIPTOE IN

East Berlin—"East Berlin will replace Vienna as the center for all trade links between East and West," says Gerhard Baumgard, director of the Salomon Brothers office here. Maybe so, but American companies seem timid in approaching the presumed hub, acting as if it were West German industry's private preserve.

Most of the few dozen American companies expanding into East Germany so far are multinationals already well established in Europe and pursuing a pan-European strategy. They usually give their West German headquarters responsibility for East Germany. "We're thinking in all the steps we take that this will be one country," said Jean-Pierre Rosso, president of Honeywell Europe.

American companies see East Germany as a consumer market and a locale for skilled manufacturing. General Motors will assemble cars in East Germany, Philip Morris is seeking a tobacco partner, and International Business Machines has discussed cooperation with Robotron, East Germany's leading computer maker.

Coca-Cola is working with East German bottlers to set up a distribution system and with manufacturers to produce bottle caps and plastic shipment cartons. "There are 16 million people to consume soft drinks," said M. Douglas Ivester, president of Coke's European operations. "It is an underdeveloped cola market."

Citibank is expanding its West Berlin office to serve East Berlin, and plans to open offices in Dresden and Leipzig. Gunter Rexrodt, chairman of Citibank's West German subsidiary, said that consumer banking would be left to West Germany's giants while Citibank concentrated on specialty areas like foreign exchange and corporate finance.

"East Germans do not want to be completely dominated by West German banks," said Mr. Rexrodt. "They are keen to have contacts with international banks."

But for most East German companies, the one sure thing the market is promising is peril.

About 30 percent will go under quickly, many economists say, while another 40 percent might make it if they are given enough subsidies—and enough time—to shape up. Only 30 percent, including Mr. Warzecha's group, is clearly competitive enough to survive.

SPLITTING INTO PIECES

Actually, in the case of the October 7 kombinat, it is the group's components that will survive. That is because the Government is encouraging the breakup of kombinats into semi-independent parts as it seeks to end monopolization and centralization. October 7 is dividing into 30 operating companies, with Mr. Warzecha at the helm of the holding company.

The prognosis for October 7's many parts is good mainly because the Japanese and West Germans, the world leaders in machine tools, have concentrated on making highly computerized, top-of-the-line machines. This has left October 7 with a large market for affordable, less sophisticated machines. The company's East Berlin plant, a jumble of dark, high-ceilinged, grime-covered buildings, is the world leader in producing gear-grinding machines. October 7, which had $1 billion in revenues last year, holds 80 percent of the world market for these machines.

Mr. Warzecha explained that while the quality of many East German goods is acceptable, the big problem is producing them cheaply enough to compete on the world market. For decades, East German industry faced little pressure to be efficient because companies obtained materials at subsidized prices and were bailed out when they lost money.

"The main problem of enterprises in East Germany is costs," said Mr. Warzecha. "The best way to save right now is on the wage side, and reducing the work force is a result of that."

Mr. Warzecha, who is spending June rushing from urgent meeting to urgent meeting, never faced such tough business decisions while he was rising in the Communist hierarchy. He served as deputy minister in East Germany's machinery ministry before becoming director of October 7, one of the nation's three giant machine-tool kombinats. Today, however, he trumpets the free market more than Marxism, although his salary, just two-and-a-half times the 1,300 marks per month his workers earn (the national average), remains very uncapitalist.

On the wall above the 16-seat conference table where Mr. Warzecha was talking hangs a large photograph of the machine-tool executive with Soviet President Mikhail Gorbachev, who visited the plant here in 1987. Both men looked younger and more relaxed then.

WINNERS AND LOSERS

East German officials say that among the enterprises with the greatest chances of survival are machine-tool companies and specialized machinery makers. Another bright spot is the pharmaceutical industry, arguably the best in Eastern Europe.

The nation's pollution-spewing, energy-inefficient chemical industry will be one of the least likely survivors, economists say. Robotron, Eastern Europe's leading computer producer, may also see its manufacturing days numbered because it is considered at least 10 years behind Western competitors. Nevertheless, those competitors may save parts of Robotron from the scrap heap by forming joint ventures in which Robotron workers do assembly or servicing.

East Germany's car industry will also be hard hit. The waiting list for the tiny Trabants used to be years long, but now with the market opened to Western goods, no one wants to buy them. Still, the Trabant and Wartburg groups will survive, albeit in a different form, thanks to the joint ventures with Volkswagen and G.M.

The tendency is for plum enterprises to attract Western partners, while less promising companies seek bank loans and Government subsidies to tide them over until they are profitable or go under.

Mr. Warzecha said agreements he is negotiating with machine-tool companies like Trumpf GmbH outside Stuttgart are crucial to October 7's future. Since Trumpf already makes large laser-cutting machines and since October 7 is proficient in designing intricate machines, they are collaborating to develop a small machine for cutting metal by laser.

Ulrich Hermani, an assistant to Trumpf's president, said East Germany's skilled labor was a major reason for the venture. Trumpf was attracted by another factor enticing many Western companies to East Germany: it will be at once a springboard to Eastern Europe and a member of the European Community.

"We have very good relations with Western Europe," Mr. Hermani said. "They have very good relations with Eastern European customers."

Since East Germany opened its economy to foreign partners four months ago, its enterprises have agreed to more than 600 joint ventures and 1,000 cooperation pacts with Western companies.

Although West German companies account for the lion's share, East Germans are eager to attract investment from other countries. "East Germany would like to see other companies interested in investing so West German firms would face some competition in making deals," said Hans-Joachim Höhme, an economist with the Institute for International Politics and Economics in East Berlin.

At October 7, Hein Klare, an adviser to Mr. Warzecha, complains that Americans have shown little interest in his country and his company.

"The Americans have not awakened until recently," he said. "They have one chance to develop links with East German industry, and they are not taking advantage of it."

Japan Discovers Woman Power

Sally Solo

Remember that young woman who slipped into the room, deposited cups of green tea in front of everyone, then quietly backed out? Remember her, because on your next trip to Japan she may be sitting on the other side of the negotiating table. Gently, women are making their way into the *otoko no shakai,* the man's world, of corporate Japan.

For 13 straight years women have entered the Japanese labor market at a faster rate than men. In 1988 they made up more than 40% of the entire labor force. About half of all Japanese women hold jobs. Nor are these just singles waiting for the right man: Almost two-thirds of working women are married. Though they still are most visible as bank tellers and department store clerks, they are starting to appear in more than a token way in the paneled conference rooms where decisions are made.

The number of women with managerial titles increased 50% between 1982 and 1987. And there are many more coming up behind them. For years Japanese companies put new employees on two tracks, regardless of education. One led to management and was largely reserved for men. The other pretty much started and finished with clerical work and tea serving, and guess who ended up there. Now for the first time large numbers of college-educated women are being set on the management track. Since seniority still rules at most big Japanese companies, growing numbers of women managers are virtually guaranteed in the 1990s and beyond.

This is a revolution without marches or manifestoes. There is little confrontation, because of the nature of the change and the nature of those who are changing. For one thing, it is a revolution based on economic necessity, not ideology. For a year now, demand for labor in the booming Japanese economy has outstripped supply. According to Hajimu Hori, a senior official in the economic planning ministry, the shortage runs through the whole economy but is especially acute in the rapidly growing high-tech sector. Says he: "How to train and utilize woman power is one of the biggest issues for companies." Some 95% of Japanese women are high school graduates, and 36% have junior college or four-year college degrees.

Until recently most women did not want careers, and companies generally overlooked the few who did. Says Noriko Nakamura, president of the 300-strong (and growing) Japan Association for Female Executives, or JAFE: "In the past,

"Japan Discovers Woman Power" by Sally Solo, *Fortune,* June 19, 1989, p. 153. Reprinted by permission of *Fortune* Magazine. © 1989 The Time Inc. Magazine Company. Reprinted by permission.

companies lumped together the 80% of women who wanted to rush out at quitting time and the 20% who wanted to do the same work as men." As a result, she says, they shied away from putting *any* women on the managerial track.

Now personnel managers are realizing that a short interview can help them identify which women want to work like men. The rest will go the clerical route of the office lady, or OL for short. OLs come in a variety of outfits—black and white checkered uniforms at fibermaker Toray, jade green at Sanwa Bank. But most are of the same mind: Work ends at 5 P.M., and life begins at marriage. While men are trained in marketing and operations, OLs are trained in phone manner (soft and high voices preferred) and salutations (a 30-degree forward bow for most people; a 45-degree bow for special guests and executives).

For their part, the new fast-track women are treading softly. Says JAFE's Nakamura: "There are still a lot of conservative men out there. They haven't changed, even though the women have. These women must try to be easy for the men to accept." Nakamura quit a job as a television announcer in 1976 when she started her family. Three years later she was recruited by a group of politicians and businessmen to lead a series of seminars on political and economic issues. The job, which she has continued to do, brought her into contact with hundreds of people, mainly men. The experience made her realize that working women needed a network too. In 1985 she established JAFE, modeled after a similar American organization.

Nakamura's advice to young Japanese women would make Gloria Steinem and other U.S. feminists blanch: First, stick it out at an organization for at least ten years, no matter how routine your work is, because women must prove their loyalty. Second, when asked to serve tea, do it brilliantly, to show you can do anything.

It used to be that a career-minded woman had the choice of going into the government bureaucracy, joining a foreign firm, or establishing a business. Working for a big Japanese company was rarely an option. When Mariko Fujiwara returned from Stanford ten years ago with a degree in anthropology, employment agencies advised her to take a secretarial course. She ignored the advice, and with an act bold by Japanese standards—she presented her résumé—won a job at the Hakuhodo Institute of Life and Living, a research branch of the advertising agency Hakuhodo.

Fujiwara looks back on that period without anger. She points out that Japanese companies tended to hire employees fresh out of college, then train them for a lifetime career with the organization. Women who married and quit after a few years were not good investments. She adds, "We had a very bad track record, and men were not at all convinced by the exceptions."

When the rare woman did slip through, she ran into heavy prejudice. Miwako Doi pounded a lot of pavement ten years ago trying to find a company willing to hire her as an engineer, despite her master's degree from Tokyo University. She finally landed at Toshiba, but getting the job wasn't the only hard part. She recalls, "When I began, people said, 'What's this—a woman here?' " She stuck with it and eventually became a manager.

With companies now eager to hire them, women graduates can be choosy. The most popular employers among the management-minded are those known to treat men and women equally. The top five, according to a recent survey, are IBM Japan, NEC, Fujitsu, Nippon Telegraph & Telephone, and Suntory. By contrast, C. Itoh, the giant trading company, ranked 102. It failed to attract a single 1988 graduate from the prestigious Ochanomizu Women's College. Explains Eiichi Shimakura, who runs employment search efforts at the college: "There are lots of clerical women workers at C. Itoh, and one regular track female employee wouldn't have a chance."

Some women find themselves stuck in the middle between the men who have traditionally taken care of business and the office ladies who have taken care of the men. Yukari Yamaguchi, 25, who works in mergers and acquisitions at Nikko Securities, one of Japan's top four securities firms, feels as if she is balancing on a high wire. "I must be careful toward my supervisors," she says, "and I must be careful toward the assistant ladies." With supervisors, Yamaguchi brims—but does not overwhelm—with confidence. "Probably I will be a director of Nikko," she says casually. With the OLs, however, she is more cautious, to deflect any jealousy they might feel.

For Yamaguchi, nothing seems impossible. But her aspirations are shot full of realism: "Women are vulnerable. They must have qualifications or titles. A Tokyo University degree is very good protection." Now she will add another title. In September she will be Nikko's first woman to attend the Harvard business school. "An MBA," she says, "will also protect me well."

Yamaguchi has had her share of luck. Hideo Karino, the supervisor who supported her application to Harvard, finds nothing odd about encouraging a young woman to excel. Says Karino, who went to Vanderbilt University in Tennessee: "I have been educated in a foreign culture, not only in a business sense." Yamaguchi doesn't feel isolated: "I'm in the second generation. The true pioneers had to fight alone, but since the equal employment opportunity law [passed in 1986], we are hired in groups."

Unlike American women in the 1970s, Japanese women are not flocking to the banner of equal employment. One reason is that they don't see much to envy in the life of Japanese men. The average male white-collar worker regularly works well into the evening. From his office in Tokyo, he commutes 1½ hours to get home. He takes just one week's vacation a year. His wife is respected—no one apologizes for being "just a housewife." Better for her to hold a part-time job, if she works at all, so she can be home to fix dinner for her husband's eventual return in the evening.

A third of working women have settled for temporary jobs. Says Eiko Shinotsuka, an assistant professor of economics at Ochanomizu: "Women don't want to work the same way that men do. They want work that will not interrupt their marriage or raising their children. They can't give half of the 24-hour day to a company, which is what companies demand."

An equal opportunity clause was built into Japan's post–World War II constitution. No legislation backed it up, however, and the concept did not take hold during the country's rebuilding effort. The United Nations Decade of Women, observed from 1975 to 1985, was one impetus for change. Japan participated in a perfunctory way in the early years, sending delegations to various conventions. In

1985 representatives from countries around the world were to sign a treaty pledging elimination of discrimination against women. Politically, Japan had to sign. Practically, Japan couldn't do so without writing some kind of domestic law to back up the pledge. Corporations lobbied vigorously against it, but a statute finally took effect in April 1986, though without provisions for penalties.

It was a breakthrough of sorts. Says Ryoko Akamatsu, then director general of the women and young worker's bureau at the ministry of labor and chief architect of the law: "Companies stopped saying they wouldn't hire women." To implement the law, the ministry distributes a questionnaire, asking, for example, if companies give women the same training as men, or if they hire women older than 33. Answers are purely voluntary. "This is soft guidance," says Mari Watanobe, a planning manager in the women's bureau. "It helps companies establish goals."

Still, without the labor shortage the law might have gone the way of the constitutional provision. Says Akamatsu: "It's working. Of course, we cannot separate effects of the law and of the healthy economic climate. If the economic situation were very bad, the new law wouldn't work as well as it does." After the law's enactment, she was packed off to Uruguay with fanfare as Japan's second female ambassador.

Now some Japanese companies are slowly discovering that women workers can be more than a substitute for men. They can provide a new perspective. Dentsu, Japan's largest advertising firm, formed a mostly women subsidiary in 1984 with a mandate to do a better job of selling to female shoppers. Consider: Young OLs, whose income is 100% disposable because they live at home and pay no rent, are Japan's most conspicuous consumers. The post-school, premarriage set does so much shopping and traveling that no fewer than ten magazines aimed at this crowd began publication last year. After women marry, their spending ways continue since Japanese men hand over their entire salaries to their wives, who run the family budget. Says Naoe Wakita, president of the subsidiary: "To understand what the wife wants is to increase sales. How can a man know what she wants?"

An influx of working women may even help soften the blue-suited Japanese worker-bee stereotype. Japanese managers at every level cringe at the phrase "economic animal," a cliché used by critics to describe them. "We have no face, that's the problem," says an insurance company executive, in a heated discussion of what's wrong with Japan's international relations. Concurs Mariko Sugahara Bando, a counselor at the Prime Minister's office and author of books about women and the elderly: "Japanese businessmen are faces without names. They're organization men. Women tend to be more human. And more of them working can create a new image for Japan."

As they hire more women managers, Japanese companies face some of the same issues their counterparts confront in the West. Seibu Department Store, which employs 20,000 women, holds jobs open for mothers who take off a few years to raise children. The company also runs a small nursery for those who continue to work. Last November IBM Japan inaugurated a babysitter hotline for working mothers who need child care in an emergency situation. The service was modeled after one the company began in New York City. Toshiba is experimenting with flextime in its offices. The electronics maker has even organized seminars where women have told male colleagues to stop holding back their thoughts and start talking straight to them.

Japanese businessmen aren't about to throw their last geisha party, or stop making deals over a dozen bottles of cold beer and hot sake. But there could be less of that and more predusk negotiations as more women enter the work force. Wakita, for example, wants to get out of the office and back to her family in the evening. Says she: "Women do all their business in the daytime. It is said that Japanese businessmen have two tongues—one for the office and one for the pub afterward. Not women, because they don't have the time. They say what they mean at the office, and at night they go home." If Japanese business truly wants to present a more human face, that could be the most important trend yet.

The Final Stretch

Robert Fulford

One morning Mel Stein woke up to a costly ordeal. He was in a trade squabble with Uncle Sam that could turn his stretch-limo business to scrap

The bad news came to Melvyn Stein and his company, AHA Manufacturing, early on July 24. One minute it was an ordinary Monday morning at the plant in Brampton, Ont., and the next minute the fax machine was pumping out the most astonishing messages. They were all from Washington law firms with impressive letterheads, and they all said much the same thing: sorry about your problem, but we'd like the honor of representing you. Mel Stein, who at first didn't know he had a problem, counted five of these solicitations, then 10, eventually more than 20. By that time he understood that something he had been hearing about as a vague possibility for months was actually happening to him. One of his U.S. competitors in the business of building stretch limousines, Southampton Coachworks of Long Island, NY, had accused him of dumping underpriced limos on the United States market. Stein had to defend himself or accept a duty that would probably put him out of business.

It was an odd way to receive this information: it was like having the famous criminal lawyer Eddie Greenspan call to inform you of a crime you didn't know had been committed and then tell you that he's standing by to act as your counsel. Stein at first thought the lawyers were making a fuss over a little matter that surely would be settled in a hurry. "I had a clear conscience," he said later, "and I assumed that when it was known that we'd done nothing wrong, it would be all over. I thought it was like getting a ticket for parking at Portage and Main when you haven't been to Winnipeg—you settle it in a minute. But it's turned out to be a much more onerous thing than I imagined."

In fact, a vast machine had been set in motion, and those ambulance-chasing lawyers were on to a good thing. As Stein talked to Canadian government officials and interviewed five Washington lawyers who visited Toronto to seek his business in person, he discovered that before this commercial nightmare is over, his legal bills may well go to U.S.$200,000. For that price, he's getting a lesson in the politics of international commerce and a demonstration of how much tension over trade still exists in the first year of the Free Trade Agreement, the treaty that many people imagined would ease just this sort of conflict.

The paper filed in Washington was headed "Petition for the Imposition of Antidumping and Countervailing Duties," and was addressed to the U.S. Department of Commerce and the U.S. International Trade Commission. It made two charges against Stein. First, he was selling limos at a fifth or more below their fair market value, at a great loss to his company, in order to enlarge his share of the market—notice, the paper said, that AHA lost $3 million in 1988. That called for an antidumping duty. Second, he was receiving Canadian government subsidies, which enabled him to compete unfairly. Therefore, he should pay a tariff equal to the worth, per limo, of the subsidies.

The second charge was easier to deal with than the first, and the Canadian Embassy in Washington dealt with it immediately in a diplomatic note that said AHA had received no significant government help. In fact, the closest it had come to a subsidy was when it received $4.2 million as a subcontractor carrying out research projects under the controversial and now abandoned Scientific Research Tax Credit program in the mid-1980s. That wasn't a countervailable subsidy and wasn't mentioned in the petition filed by Southampton.

But the petition listed all the government help that *might* be available to Stein under certain circumstances—for instance, it said, he could get regional economic incentive grants, though how this would be done by a plant in southern Ontario wasn't specified. It even suggested that AHA benefits from the Quebec government's support of its electric system. "As a result of the ability to receive subsidized power from Hydro-Québec, Ontario Hydro is able to lower its own rates . . . the subsidized structure of the Canadian electric power industry confers a counteravailable benefit on the production of limousines."

That passage, presumably, was to be read quickly, without much thought— thinking about it could drive you crazy. (Southampton Coachworks is in New York state, which also buys power from Hydro-Québec, which is subsidized, and therefore. . . .) The purpose wasn't to draw up a serious bill of complaints; the idea was to make as many accusations as possible and shake the cages of those Americans who believe that foreign governments routinely subsidize their exports as part of a vicious plan to undercut U.S. business.

In a small way, it worked. In August, the Long Island edition of the New York *Daily News* carried a report headed "Limo maker: 'Road hog'—Canadian foe called unfair." It quoted John Gore, the head of Southampton. "These guys," he said, meaning AHA, "are selling cars for less than we can build them." Gore said—and this was almost the only point in the dispute where a couple of specific figures emerged—that AHA limos were going for US$35,000 wholesale while Gore's were selling for $50,000 retail. Later, in an interview with *Vista*, Gore said he was delighted with the early progress of his action. "I think it's going great," he said. "I think they're going to find dumping and I think they're going to put a duty on those cars."

By the time the story in the *Daily News* appeared, Mel Stein's education was well under way. He had discovered, for instance, that while *he* needed an expensive law firm, Gore didn't—the U.S. Department of Commerce drew up the brief that Gore and other American limo-builders signed. Stein had also discovered the curious fact that he would not be allowed to read all the details of the case against him. In the copy Stein received, many business statistics were blanked out, following standard practice. Stein learned that the U.S. International Trade Commission would get a copy with the numbers in, *and so would Stein's lawyers*—but they would be sworn not to tell him what the numbers were.

Stein was now involved in a Byzantine world of which most executives remain happily ignorant. It's a lawyer-infested world, where nationalism and political power play on economics, and where selling at the lowest possible price may be seen as something like a crime. Stein was informed that the government of Canada—while it could speak clearly on the subsidy question—really had nothing to say about whether Stein was dumping. He had to defend himself. The Free Trade Agreement, of course, has eliminated neither countervailing duties nor antidumping laws.

Stein had to think about the meaning of what trade lawyers call LTFV (less than fair value) and about dumping as an idea. Antidumping laws say that underselling your competitors, while commendable within any given country, becomes a matter for suspicion if the products cross a border—even a border as open as the U.S.-Canada is to auto products, and even if (as is the case with AHA) the products are 60 or 70 percent American in origin anyway.

Most economists regard antidumping regulations as obsolete and counterproductive, but they exist. Is there evidence that Stein violated them—and, if not, why do the Americans claim he did? To answer those questions, and because I've always wondered where limos come from, I went to Stein's plant on Chelsea Lane in Brampton. Naturally, I went by limo.

A white stretch limo, looking as if it could comfortably sleep four large adults, gently moored in my driveway one summer afternoon. It was an AHA product, as I'd determined before ordering it from a livery in Mississauga, Ont., so I shared the experience of those who ultimately benefit from Mel Stein's work: plenty of leg room, a smooth ride, and envious glances from the neighbors.

Stein's customers aren't rich people, for the most part, but people like the man who was driving me—Bernard Drag of Stars' Limousines Inc. It's true that Eddie Murphy has his own AHA limo, a Japanese businessman recently took one home to Tokyo, and two just went into service at palaces in the United Arab Emirates. These are exceptions, though. The real market is the livery business, which has expanded enormously in the 1980s—there are now about 7,000 livery operators in the U.S., where in 1980 there were about 1,000; in Canada, the total remains in the low hundreds, but the increase has been proportionately as great.

The typical livery operator is a man who summons up his courage, puts a second mortgage on his house, buys a limo, and thereby earns the right to get up at five o'clock in the morning to drive a stockbroker to the airport. When his business develops he may own four cars, which is average. Soon he'll discover that many others have had the same bright idea—if he doesn't see them on the road or at the garage he'll read about them in *Limousine & Chauffeur,* a trade magazine in which he can also read ads for handcrafted champagne buckets and news about crackdowns on illegal limos at the airports.

As anyone who walked the streets could tell, the livery business prospered through most of the 1980s. In New York particularly, there were stockbrokers and lawyers who never went anywhere except in a limo. They were imitated across the continent; it was the acceptance of the stretch limo as routine in certain business circles that enriched the livery companies. When that happened, AHA Manufacturing, which Mel Stein took over in 1975 from its founder, Andy Hotton (AHA: Andy Hotton Associates), also prospered. A Toronto chartered accountant who got into the auto-parts business in the 1960s, Stein recognized early that limousines were a promising niche.

At his plant on Chelsea Lane—which is, of course, not a lane at all but part of an industrial park—Stein told me a little about the stretch-limo business. Off and on, over the decades, the big car companies have produced their own limos. But the market—in a good year, around 7,000 limos—isn't really large enough for the major automakers. At the moment, limo-building is in the hands of half a dozen companies like AHA, which sell 400 or 500 limos each, and many smaller companies, some of which—"Tony-and-Joe shops," Stein calls them—produce no more than three or four a year, largely by hand.

To make a stretch limo, you buy, fresh from the plant, a good car—anything from a Cadillac to a Honda Accord. You cut it right down the middle, pull the two chunks of it apart, and in between them put 1.5 meters (5 feet) or so of floor, walls, windows, bracing, rug, seats, and so on. You install a bar, a TV, a phone, of course. You paint the whole thing and put it on sale.

People have been doing it like that for at least half a century, but when Stein took over AHA he decided to refine the process—and perhaps that's what led eventually to his trade-law troubles. He set out to bring the style of a big-car company to limo-building and limo-marketing. AHA developed a way to adapt one Lincoln after another on a version of the assembly line. Stein's people discovered, for instance, that by standardizing the wood panels they could eliminate the work of a skilled cabinetmaker and bring down the cost of interior woodwork from $3,000 to $200. This approach, with each worker assigned to learn limited tasks extremely well, required that the plant run all the time. So Stein set up—just like

GM—a system of dealers who would accept a stated number of cars a year, would handle only AHA, and would provide service.

All this worked beautifully, until the crash of 1987. Then limos, like many luxuries, quickly grew less popular. Many Wall Street firms cut off their limo accounts entirely. "Week by week," Stein said recently, "you could see the limo sales diminishing, in a ripple effect that moved outward from New York City." That was one factor that made 1988 a bad year for AHA. Another was the rise in the value of the Canadian dollar, which Stein, like most manufacturers, regards as calamitous. And that same year the division of AHA that makes ambulances lost a major contract with the Ontario Ministry of Health. The loss that Stein's U.S. competitor regards as part of a long-term plan for market dominance was, in Stein's recounting, both unintentional and unwelcome.

But 1989 was coming along well—limo sales in the U.S. were up and the ambulance business had turned around. There really wasn't a great deal to worry about, until the day the lawyers' faxes came in. Since then, after many conferences, much worrying, and much pondering of arcane trade laws, Stein remains confident he'll win his case—but at a high cost in money and time.

Recently he sat in his boardroom, looking at detailed legal papers that described issues and regulations he had barely heard about just a few weeks before. He had the original 145-page complaint, he had a 153-page transcript of the first, exploratory conference in Washington and he had another 100 pages of the first submission his lawyers had filed on his behalf. He looked around at the paper, he described legal wrangling that will likely last into the spring of 1990, and he summed up what he saw as the essence of the case. "We have a competitor in the United States," he said, "who has managed to crank up his government to go against a major competitor." For the moment at least, Mel Stein of Brampton, Ont., was in a battle with the U.S. government.

"I'm feeling a little battered by the process," he said as he showed me out to my limo. "But I'm constantly being reminded by the lawyers that they told me, all along, how hard it was going to be." I mentioned to him that I'd been telling his story to several of my friends and that every one of them had found it absolutely fascinating. "I'm glad they're enjoying it," he said.

Boom and Despair

Sonia Nazario

Mexican border towns are a magnet for foreign factories, workers and
abysmal living conditions

Nogales, Mexico—On a hillside here, 17 families have invaded a patch of land and
thrown up an instant shantytown they call Land & Liberty. There is no potable
water, raw sewage covers the ground, and the people fear an epidemic. They
are living in hovels pieced together from wood and cardboard smuggled out
of the places where they work, the gleaming factories on the horizon called
maquiladoras.

About 1,500 of these foreign-owned plants—most of them the property of
U.S. companies, including many blue-chip firms—now line the Mexican side of
the 2,000-mile border, and they have been of enormous economic benefit to struggling Mexico. But as the squatters of Land & Liberty can testify, it is a benefit that
carries a high price in other terms. And that price is being paid on both sides of the
border.

The *maquilas,* as the factories are usually called, assemble parts sent from
across the border into finished products and then ship them back. Duty is paid only
on the value added by the Mexican labor, which is dirt cheap; annual wage and
benefit costs per worker here are frequently $30,000 less than they would be in the
States. As for Mexico, the maquilas have helped drive a jobless rate of 40% in some
border points down to almost nothing and are earning more precious foreign exchange for one nation than anything else save oil.

But their very success is helping turn much of the border region into a sink-
hole of abysmal living conditions and environmental degradation. A huge, continuing migration of people looking for work has simply overwhelmed the already-
shaky infrastructure. Shantytowns spring up overnight around border cities where
there is little or no living space left; some of the 400,000 maquila workers pay more
than a third of their monthly income to share a bed in one room occupied by six
others.

GRIDLOCK AND CLOUDS OF DUST

Road building and repair can't keep up with the galloping population. Traffic is gridlocked in the cities. Old cars on dirt paths raise huge clouds of dust that mingle with exhaust fumes and industrial pollution to cast a poisonous pall of smog over the border towns—and their American neighbors. Aquifers shared by both Americans and Mexicans are being sucked dry at an alarming rate, and industrial toxics and untreated sewage are poisoning rivers, streams and other water sources.

The border has always attracted Mexicans seeking work, but since the maquila program began in 1965 the flow northward has become a torrent. The combined population of Juarez, Mexicali and Tijuana has multiplied almost fivefold, to about three million, since the pre-maquila days of 1960. And that figure doesn't include the people living in the belts of hovels that have been springing up around those and other cities.

This shadow population is unknown but large, and it is growing rapidly. Outside Tijuana, the wooden, cardboard and cinder-block huts that make up the shantytown of El Florido now seem to stretch endlessly, and it is only one of many such places here. In Nogales, where the population has increased sixfold, to about 300,000, since the first maquila opened in 1968, a recent survey found seven people for every room of living space. Rents have soared, and thus more and more people are living in hovels outside the city.

Sometimes they don't have even that much. On the hillside just above Land & Liberty, a fresh group of squatters is sleeping on the rocky ground, with families huddled together at night for warmth. A rooster serves as the communal alarm clock, and at his call most arise to get ready for work at a Kimberly-Clark Corp. maquila, where they sew hospital garments. Many maquilas offer clean and relatively pleasant working conditions, and those who toil in them also get some benefits. Though the base pay is low—most workers get only about $6.50 a day—almost any kind of regular job is a boon to people who otherwise wouldn't have one.

But even the best of the maquilas demand much more of workers, and give less incentive, than similar plants in the U.S. Maquilas are generally nonunion, set production quotas at rates at least 10% above those in similar factories north of the border, and grant little or no extra pay for seniority; a fresh recruit off the streets can make as much, or nearly as much, as someone who's been on the job for 10 years. Men don't have nearly the chance of getting jobs that women do, which creates social problems. (Factory managers say that women have more patience and manual dexterity.)

PASSING OUT FROM FUMES

Finally, some maquilas resemble sweatshops more than factories. They lack ventilation, and workers may pass out from the heat and fumes. Production demands can put them at risk; Edwviges Ramos Hernandez, a teacher in Juarez, worked at one factory where in a year three workers had fingers sliced off. The machines, she says, were set at a maddening pace.

In Tijuana, Zenaida Ochoa, one of six children in the same family who work at maquilas, wonders how long she can continue. She lives in the El Florido shantytown outside the city and must rise at 4 a.m. to get to work by 7. There she sews garments for nine hours straight in a tin-roofed enclosure that sizzles in the summer heat. She makes about $60 a week, which is higher than most—but a chicken costs a tenth of that. She is plagued by back pain from hunching over her sewing machine all day, and says, "My eyes burn from staring at the needle." A fellow worker, she relates, tried to organize a union to get better pay and working conditions—including toilet paper in the restroom—and was fired.

So it is perhaps unsurprising that the turnover at maquilas can exceed 180% a year. "Women only work at them because there is no other work," snaps Rosa Maria Palacio, sitting on a frayed red velveteen couch that is the only furniture in her cardboard hut at Land & Liberty. She left her own maquila job cleaning gun chambers to survive as she could: making tortillas, working as a maid, cooking for a church. She says she will never go back to work at a maquiladora.

These plants are also suspected of contributing mightily to toxic pollution. They are supposed to ship back across the border for disposal all toxic substances brought into them, less what was used in manufacture, but there is widespread doubt that they are uniformly doing so.

Mexican academics researching the shantytowns, and community workers who spend time in them, say that residents in places without water lines commonly eat and drink out of barrels, some of them labeled as previously holding toxic substances, that they've gotten at the maquilas where they work. If all these barrels are in use, the skeptics wonder, then what are the companies using to ship the leftover stuff back to the States?

Ana Maria Apolo, a chemical engineer who a year ago left her job at a Tijuana unit of San Diego-based Computer & Communication Technology Corp., says that although some of company's toxic waste was being recycled, much of it simply went down the drain. "The company wasn't concerned about it. They were concerned about production. If there was less to recycle, it meant less money spent," she says. (Proper disposal of toxic waste in the U.S. can cost $200 a barrel or more.)

'SCRUPULOUS EFFORTS'

Jerry Smith, a vice president of CCT, says the company "has made scrupulous efforts to deal with our toxic waste," and denies that such dumping occurs. On the whole, the toxics law is indeed being obeyed, insists William Mitchell, an American national who is vice president-marketing for Grupo Bermudez, the largest operator of maquila industrial parks in Juarez and a frequent spokesman on maquila doings in general. "It's being done, just very quietly," he says.

So quietly that the records don't show it. For example, the Texas Water Commission counts only 143 tons of such waste shipped north to Texas by the maquilas in 1987, but it estimates that Juarez-area plants alone produced perhaps 5,000 tons of it. The U.S. Environmental Protection Agency, which has tracked returning waste since 1985, can identify only 26 maquiladoras that have actually made such shipments.

Wherever they're coming from, it's clear that toxics are joining the general flow of pollution that is endangering water supplies and the environment generally. Water samples in Nogales have already revealed high levels of substances that can cause chronic damage to the liver or central nervous system. U.S. cities that share ground-water aquifers with their Mexican neighbors are worried. "Where is all this stuff?" asks Prof. Jeffery Brannon, a maquiladora expert at the University of Texas at El Paso. "We don't want to be the next Love Canal."

Raw sewage is already a major hazard, and its effects are not confined to Mexico. In San Elizario, Texas, where an aquifer shared with Mexico has already been contaminated, 35% of children contract hepatitis A by the age of eight and 90% of adults have had it by the age of 35. In Juarez, a torrent of lumpy sludge called the Black Water Ditch flows alongside the Rio Grande, a potential poisoner of joint water supplies. And in Imperial, Calif., county health officer Lee Cottrell helplessly watches over one of the world's most contaminated streams, the New River.

It flows 120 miles north of the border after passing by Mexicali, Mexico, and empties into the Salton Sea, a recreation spot where people have been known to frolic in waters untested by the health department. The New River's donation: more than 20 kinds of pathogenic viruses and bacteria, including three strains of polio. Mr. Cottrell, who has seen dead animals and even a few human corpses flow by, calls the stream "a time bomb waiting to blow."

Across the border from San Diego, the Tijuana River is an affront to both man and nature. This murky green ribbon of slime and stench flushes eight million to 12 million gallons of human waste per day from Mexico into the U.S. through the Tijuana Estuary, a 2,513-acre U.S. wildlife refuge that is turning into a biological desert.

KILLING PLANT AND ANIMAL LIFE

Decreasing salinity is killing plant and animal life that thrives on brackish water, and the smelly, poisoned goo entering the estuary has already done in more than half the fish species and almost all the bottom-dwelling invertebrates. "If this goes on, we could kill the estuary in 15 years," laments environmentalist Pat McCoy, who led the 1982 battle to make it a refuge.

In 1983, San Diego County had to close a stretch of beach where the estuary empties into the Pacific. Since then, two surfers who apparently defied the ban have almost died of an inner-ear infection that can infect the brain and that is caused by exposure to fecal matter.

The continuing rush of population to the border is affecting not only the quality but also the quantity of water, particularly in El Paso. Its main water supply is an aquifer that it shares with booming Juarez, and water levels in it have been dropping sharply. Due to run dry as early as 2010, El Paso is now re-injecting into the ground highly treated sewage in order to extend the supply.

As do other U.S. border cities, it also shares the air with Mexico, and that problem is proving well-nigh intractable. El Paso is out of compliance with federal air standards, and though it is spending millions to meet them, it has little chance of doing so.

The reason lies mainly across the border, where a great yellow-gray cloud rises over Juarez and enshrouds both cities; frequent temperature inversions seal it in place. There are 250,000 clunker autos on the Mexican side (average age: 15 years) spewing raw exhaust fumes into the air—they have no pollution-control devices— and raising plumes of dust on unpaved roads. Industry adds more poisons, some of them from plants of U.S. furniture makers who recently fled Los Angeles to escape new restrictions on solvents emissions. Still more is added to the mix by residents who burn tires and trash to keep warm, and by the Juarez city dump, which has a tendency to catch fire spontaneously.

STOPPING AIR AT THE BORDER

Glumly looking at dozens of smoke plumes rising above the Mexican side, Raul Munoz Jr., chief of environmental and community health services for El Paso, says: "Air doesn't stop at the border. We're just spinning our wheels over here."

Little is being done about the wholesale environmental destruction, health hazards and poor living conditions that the rush to the border has spawned. Though Mexico's environmental laws were stiffened last year, its fiscal crisis has left it with so few inspectors to enforce the laws that they can be evaded with ease; a 1988 survey of maquiladora plant managers in Agua Prieta, Mexico, disclosed that none had ever seen such an inspector. And there is no money for huge housing and infrastructure programs, either.

Maquila owners aren't doing much to help. A few have begun offering single-sex dormitories for workers, and in Agua Prieta they pitch in just over a dollar a month per worker to build roads, bridges and such. So far, the money has built one bridge. More significant measures are resisted; when the Mexican government last year proposed a 2% tax on the annual wages paid by maquilas, with the money to be used for such construction, the operators killed the idea.

Several say that they are in Mexico to make profits and that infrastructure is Mexico's problem, not theirs. They also fear that if they did pay extra for it, at least some of the money would wind up in some politician's pocket. They already refer to the one tax maquiladoras and all other Mexican industries pay, a 5% federal housing tax, as the "rip-off fund."

Mexican officials aren't eager to press the point. "We are not in a position to scare these companies away," says Leobardo Gil Torres, the mayor of Nogales. "We are in a crisis, you see. What do we do if these companies leave?"

Managing Without Managers

Ricardo Semler

How one unorthodox company makes money by avoiding decisions, rules, and executive authority.

In Brazil, where paternalism and the family business fiefdom still flourish, I am president of a manufacturing company that treats its 800 employees like responsible adults. Most of them—including factory workers—set their own working hours. All have access to the company books. The vast majority vote on many important corporate decisions. Everyone gets paid by the month, regardless of job description, and more than 150 of our management people set their own salaries and bonuses.

This may sound like an unconventional way to run a business, but it seems to work. Close to financial disaster in 1980, Semco is now one of Brazil's fastest growing companies, with a profit margin in 1988 of 10% on sales of $37 million. Our five factories produce a range of sophisticated products, including marine pumps, digital scanners, commercial dishwashers, truck filters, and mixing equipment for everything from bubble gum to rocket fuel. Our customers include Alcoa, Saab, and General Motors. We've built a number of cookie factories for Nabisco, Nestlé, and United Biscuits. Our multinational competitors include AMF, Worthington Industries, Mitsubishi Heavy Industries, and Carrier.

Management associations, labor unions, and the press have repeatedly named us the best company in Brazil to work for. In fact, we no longer advertise jobs. Word of mouth generates up to 300 applications for every available position. The top five managers—we call them counselors—include a former human resources director of Ford Brazil, a 15-year veteran Chrysler executive, and a man who left his job as president of a larger company to come to Semco.

When I joined the company in 1980, 27 years after my father founded it, Semco had about 100 employees, manufactured hydraulic pumps for ships, generated about $4 million in revenues, and teetered on the brink of catastrophe. All through 1981 and 1982, we ran from bank to bank looking for loans, and we fought persistent, well-founded rumors that the company was in danger of going under. We often stayed through the night reading files and searching the desk drawers of venerable executives for clues about contracts long since privately made and privately forgotten.

Most managers and outside board members agreed on two immediate needs: to professionalize and to diversify. In fact, both of these measures had been discussed for years but had never progressed beyond wishful thinking.

For two years, holding on by our fingertips, we sought licenses to manufacture other companies' products in Brazil. We traveled constantly. I remember one day being in Oslo for breakfast, New York for lunch, Cincinnati for dinner, and San Francisco for the night. The obstacles were great. Our company lacked an international reputation—and so did our country. Brazil's political eccentricities and draconian business regulations scared many companies away.

Still, good luck and a relentless program of beating the corporate bushes on four continents finally paid off. By 1982, we had signed seven license agreements. Our marine division—once the entire company—was now down to 60% of total sales. Moreover, the managers and directors were all professionals with no connection to the family.

With Semco back on its feet, we entered an acquisitions phase that cost millions of dollars in expenditures and millions more in losses over the next two or three years. All this growth was financed by banks at interest rates that were generally 30% above the rate of inflation, which ranged from 40% to 900% annually. There was no long-term money in Brazil at that time, so all those loans had maximum terms of 90 days. We didn't get one cent in government financing or from incentive agencies either, and we never paid out a dime in graft or bribes.

How did we do it and survive? Hard work, of course. And good luck—fundamental to all business success. But most important, I think, were the drastic changes we made in our concept of management. Without those changes, not even hard work and good luck could have pulled us through.

Semco has three fundamental values on which we base some 30 management programs. These values—democracy, profit sharing, and information—work in a complicated circle, each dependent on the other two. If we eliminated one, the others would be meaningless. Our corporate structure, employee freedoms, union relations, factory size limitations—all are products of our commitment to these principles.

It's never easy to transplant management programs from one company to another. In South America, it's axiomatic that our structure and style cannot be duplicated. Semco is either too small, too big, too far away, too young, too old, or too obnoxious.

We may also be too specialized. We do cellular manufacturing of technologically sophisticated products, and we work at the high end on quality and price. So our critics may be right. Perhaps nothing we've done can be a blueprint for anyone else. Still, in an industrial world whose methods show obvious signs of exhaustion, the merit of sharing experience is to encourage experiment and to plant the seeds of conceptual change. So what the hell.

PARTICIPATORY HOT AIR

The first of Semco's three values is democracy, or employee involvement. Clearly, workers who control their working conditions are going to be happier than workers who don't. Just as clearly, there is no contest between the company that buys the grudging compliance of its work force and the company that enjoys the enterprising participation of its employees.

But about 90% of the time, participatory management is just hot air. Not that intentions aren't good. It's just that implementing employee involvement is so complex, so difficult, and, not uncommonly, so frustrating that it is easier to talk about than to do.

We found four big obstacles to effective participatory management: size, hierarchy, lack of motivation, and ignorance. In an immense production unit, people feel tiny, nameless, and incapable of exerting influence on the way work is done or on the final profit made. This sense of helplessness is underlined by managers who, jealous of their power and prerogatives, refuse to let subordinates make any decisions for themselves—sometimes even about going to the bathroom. But even if size and hierarchy can be overcome, why should workers *care* about productivity and company profits? Moreover, even if you can get them to care, how can they tell when they're doing the right thing?

As Antony Jay pointed out back in the 1950s in *Corporation Man*, human beings weren't designed to work in big groups. Until recently, our ancestors were hunters and gatherers. For more than five million years, they refined their ability to work in groups of no more than about a dozen people. Then along comes the industrial revolution, and suddenly workers are trying to function efficiently in factories that employ hundreds and even thousands. Organizing those hundreds into teams of about ten members each may help some, but there's still a limit to how many small teams can work well together. At Semco, we've found the most effective production unit to consist of about 150 people. The exact number is open to argument, but it's clear that several thousand people in one facility makes individual involvement an illusion.

When we made the decision to keep our units small, we immediately focused on one facility that had more than 300 people. The unit manufactured commercial food-service equipment—slicers, scales, meat grinders, mixers—and used an MRP II system hooked up to an IBM mainframe with dozens of terminals all over the plant. Paperwork often took two days to make its way from one end of the factory to the other. Excess inventories, late delivery, and quality problems were common. We had tried various worker participation programs, quality circles, kanban systems, and motivation schemes, all of which got off to great starts but lost their momentum within months. The whole thing was just too damn big and complex; there were too many managers in too many layers holding too many meetings. So we decided to break up the facility into three separate plants.

To begin with, we kept all three in the same building but separated everything we could—entrances, receiving docks, inventories, telephones, as well as certain auxiliary functions like personnel, management information systems, and internal controls. We also scrapped the mainframe in favor of three independent, PC-based systems.

The first effect of the breakup was a rise in costs due to duplication of effort and a loss in economies of scale. Unfortunately, balance sheets chalk up items like these as liabilities, all with dollar figures attached, and there's nothing at first to list on the asset side but airy stuff like "heightened involvement" and "a sense of belonging." Yet the longer term results exceeded our expectations.

Within a year, sales doubled; inventories fell from 136 days to 46; we unveiled eight new products that had been stalled in R&D for two years; and overall quality improved to the point that a one-third rejection rate on federally inspected scales dropped to less than 1%. Increased productivity let us reduce the work force by 32% through attrition and retirement incentives.

I don't claim that size reduction alone accomplished all this, just that size reduction is essential for putting employees in touch with one another so they can coordinate their work. The kind of distance we want to eliminate comes from having too many people in one place, but it also comes from having a pyramidal hierarchy.

PYRAMIDS AND CIRCLES

The organizational pyramid is the cause of much corporate evil, because the tip is too far from the base. Pyramids emphasize power, promote insecurity, distort communications, hobble interaction, and make it very difficult for the people who plan and the people who execute to move in the same direction. So Semco designed an organizational *circle*. Its greatest advantage is to reduce management levels to three—one corporate level and two operating levels at the manufacturing units.

It consists of three concentric circles. One tiny, central circle contains the five people who integrate the company's movements. These are the counselors I mentioned before. I'm one of them, and except for a couple of legal documents that call me president, counselor is the only title I use. A second, larger circle contains the heads of the eight divisions—we call them partners. Finally, a third, huge circle holds all the other employees. Most of them are the people we call associates; they do the research, design, sales, and manufacturing work and have no one reporting to them on a regular basis. But some of them are the permanent and temporary team and task leaders we call coordinators. Counselors, partners, coordinators, and associates. Four titles. Three management layers.

The linchpins of the system are the coordinators, a group that includes everyone formerly called foreman, supervisor, manager, head, or chief. The only people who report to coordinators are associates. No coordinator reports to another coordinator—that feature of the system is what ensures the reduction in management layers.

Like anyone else, we value leadership, but it's not the only thing we value. In marine pumps, for example, we have an applications engineer who can look at the layout of a ship and then focus on one particular pump and say, "That pump will fail if you take this thing north of the Arctic Circle." He makes a lot more money than the person who manages his unit. We can change the manager, but this guy knows what kind of pump will work in the Arctic, and that's worth more. Associates often make higher salaries than coordinators and partners, and they can increase their status and compensation without entering the "management" line.

Managers and the status and money they enjoy—in a word, hierarchy—are the single biggest obstacle to participatory management. We had to get the managers out of the way of democratic decision making, and our circular system does that pretty well.

But we go further. We don't hire or promote people until they've been interviewed and accepted by all their future subordinates. Twice a year, subordinates evaluate managers. Also twice a year, everyone in the company anonymously fills out a questionnaire about company credibility and top management competence. Among other things, we ask our employees what it would take to make them quit or go on strike.

We insist on making important decisions collegially, and certain decisions are made by a company-wide vote. Several years ago, for example, we needed a bigger plant for our marine division, which makes pumps, compressors, and ship propellers. Real estate agents looked for months and found nothing. So we asked the employees themselves to help, and over the first weekend they found three factories for sale, all of them nearby. We closed up shop for a day, piled everyone into buses, and drove out to inspect the three buildings. Then the workers voted—and they chose a plant the counselors didn't really want. It was an interesting situation—one that tested our commitment to participatory management.

The building stands across the street from a Caterpillar plant that's one of the most frequently struck factories in Brazil. With two tough unions of our own, we weren't looking forward to front-row seats for every labor dispute that came along. But we accepted the employees' decision, because we believe that in the long run, letting people participate in the decisions that affect their lives will have a positive effect on employee motivation and morale.

We bought the building and moved in. The workers designed the layout for a flexible manufacturing system, and they hired one of Brazil's foremost artists to paint the whole thing, inside and out, including the machinery. That plant really belongs to its employees. I feel like a guest every time I walk in.

I don't mind. The division's productivity, in dollars per year per employee, has jumped from $14,200 in 1984—the year we moved—to $37,500 in 1988, and for 1989 the goal is $50,000. Over the same period, market share went from 54% to 62%.

Employees also outvoted me on the acquisition of a company that I'm still sure we should have bought. But they felt we weren't ready to digest it, and I lost the vote. In a case like that, the credibility of our management system is at stake. Employee involvement must be real, even when it makes management uneasy. Anyway, what is the future of an acquisition if the people who have to operate it don't believe it's workable?

HIRING ADULTS

We have other ways of combating hierarchy too. Most of our programs are based on the notion of giving employees control over their own lives. In a word, we hire adults, and then we treat them like adults.

Think about that. Outside the factory, workers are men and women who elect governments, serve in the army, lead community projects, raise and educate families, and make decisions every day about the future. Friends solicit their advice. Salespeople court them. Children and grandchildren look up to them for their wisdom and experience. But the moment they walk into the factory, the company transforms them into adolescents. They have to wear badges and name tags, arrive at a certain time, stand in line to punch the clock or eat their lunch, get permission to go to the bathroom, give lengthy explanations every time they're five minutes late, and follow instructions without asking a lot of questions.

One of my first moves when I took control of Semco was to abolish norms, manuals, rules, and regulations. Everyone knows you can't run a large organization without regulations, but everyone also knows that most regulations are poppycock. They rarely solve problems. On the contrary, there is usually some obscure corner of the rule book that justifies the worst silliness people can think up. Common sense is a riskier tactic because it requires personal responsibility.

It's also true that common sense requires just a touch of civil disobedience every time someone calls attention to something that's not working. We had to free the Thoreaus and the Tom Paines in the factory and come to terms with that fact that civil disobedience was not an early sign of revolution but a clear indication of common sense at work.

So we replaced all the nitpicking regulations with the rule of common sense and put our employees in the demanding position of using their own judgment.

We have no dress code, for example. The idea that personal appearance is important in a job—any job—is baloney. We've all heard that salespeople, receptionists, and service reps are the company's calling cards, but in fact how utterly silly that is. A company that needs business suits to prove its seriousness probably lacks more meaningful proof. And what customer has ever canceled an order because the receptionist was wearing jeans instead of a dress? Women and men look best when they feel good. IBM is not a great company because its salespeople dress to the special standard that Thomas Watson set. It's a great company that also happens to have this quirk.

We also scrapped the complex company rules about travel expenses—what sorts of accommodations people were entitled to, whether we'd pay for a theater ticket, whether a free call home meant five minutes or ten. We used to spend a lot of time discussing stuff like that. Now we base everything on common sense. Some people stay in four-star hotels and some live like spartans. Some people spend $200 a day while others get by on $125. Or so I suppose. No one checks expenses, so there is no way of knowing. The point is, we don't care. If we can't trust people with our money and their judgment, we sure as hell shouldn't be sending them overseas to do business in our name.

We have done away with security searches, storeroom padlocks, and audits of the petty-cash accounts of veteran employees. Not that we wouldn't prosecute a genuinely criminal violation of our trust. We just refuse to humiliate 97% of the work force to get our hands on the occasional thief or two-bit embezzler.

We encourage—we practically insist on—job rotation every two to five years to prevent boredom. We try hard to provide job security, and for people over 50 or who've been with the company for more than three years, dismissal procedures are extra complicated.

On the more experimental side, we have a program for entry-level management trainees called "Lost in Space," whereby we hire a couple of people every year who have no job description at all. A "godfather" looks after them, and for one year they can do anything they like, as long as they try at least 12 different areas or units.

By the same logic that governs our other employee programs, we have also eliminated time clocks. People come and go according to their own schedules—even on the factory floor. I admit this idea is hard to swallow; most manufacturers are not ready for factory-floor flextime. But our reasoning was simple.

First, we use cellular manufacturing systems. At our food-processing equipment plant, for example, one cell makes only slicers, another makes scales, another makes mixers, and so forth. Each cell is self-contained, so products—and their problems—are segregated from each other.

Second, we assumed that all our employees were trustworthy adults. We couldn't believe they would come to work day after day and sit on their hands because no one else was there. Pretty soon, we figured, they would start coordinating their work hours with their coworkers.

And that's exactly what happened, only more so. For example, one man wanted to start at 7 A.M., but because the forklift operator didn't come until 8, he couldn't get his parts. So a general discussion arose, and the upshot was that now everyone knows how to operate a forklift. In fact, most people can now do several jobs. The union has never objected because the initiative came from the workers themselves. It was their idea.

Moreover, the people on the factory floor set the schedule, and if they say that this month they will build 48 commercial dishwashers, then we can go play tennis, because 48 is what they'll build.

In one case, one group decided to make 220 meat slicers. By the end of the month, it had finished the slicers as scheduled—except that even after repeated phone calls, the supplier still hadn't produced the motors. So two employees drove over and talked to the supplier and managed to get delivery at the end of that day, the 31st. Then they stayed all night, the whole work force, and finished the lot at 4:45 the next morning.

When we introduced flexible hours, we decided to hold regular follow-up meetings to track problems and decide how to deal with abuses and production interruptions. That was years ago, and we haven't yet held the first meeting.

HUNTING THE WOOLLY MAMMOTH

What makes our people behave this way? As Antony Jay points out, corporate man is a very recent animal. At Semco, we try to respect the hunter that dominated the first 99.9% of the history of our species. If you had to kill a mammoth or do without supper, there was no time to draw up an organization chart, assign tasks, or delegate authority. Basically, the person who saw the mammoth from farthest away was the Official Sighter, the one who ran fastest was the Head Runner, whoever threw the most accurate spear was the Grand Marksman, and the person all others respected most and listened to was the Chief. That's all there was to it. Distributing

RICARDO SEMLER'S GUIDE TO STRESS MANAGEMENT

There are two things all managers have in common—the 24-hour day and the annoying need to sleep. Without the sleeping, 24 hours might be enough. With it, there is no way to get everything done. After years of trying to vanquish demon sleep and the temptation to relax, I tried an approach suggested by my doctor, who put it this way: "Slow down or kiss yourself good-bye."

Struck by this imagery, I learned to manage my time and cut my work load to less than 24 hours. The first step is to overcome five myths:

1. *Results are proportional to efforts.* The Brazilian flag expresses this myth in a slightly different form. "Order and Progress," it says. Of course, it ought to say, "Order *or* Progress," since the two never go together.

2. *Quantity of work is more important than quality.* Psychologically, this myth may hold water. The executive who puts in lots of hours can always say, "Well, they didn't promote me, but you can see how unfair that is. Everyone knows I get here at 8 A.M. and that my own children can't see me without an appointment."

3. *The present restructuring requires longer working hours temporarily.* We think of ourselves as corks on a mountain stream headed for Lake Placid. But the lake ahead is Loch Ness. The present, temporary emergency is actually permanent. Stop being a cork.

4. *No one else can do it right.* The truth is, you *are* replaceable, as everyone will discover within a week of your funeral.

5. This *problem is urgent.* Come on. The real difference between "important" and "urgent" is the difference between thoughtfulness and panic.

Those are the myths. The second step is to master my eight cures:

1. Set an hour to leave the office and obey it blindly. If you normally go home at 7:00, start leaving at 6:00. If you take work home on weekends, give yourself a month or two to put a stop to this pernicious practice.

2. Take half a day, maybe even an entire Saturday, to rummage through that mountain of paper in your office and put it in three piles.

    Pile A: Priority items that require your personal attention and represent matters of indisputable importance. If you put more than four or five documents in this category and are not currently the president of your country, start over.

    Pile B: Items that need your personal attention, but not right away. This pile is very tempting; everything fits. But don't fall into the trap. Load this stuff on your subordinates, using the 70% test to help you do it. Ask yourself: Is there someone on my staff who can do this task at least 70% as well as I can? Yes? Then farm it out. Whether or not your subordinates are overworked should not weigh in your decision. Remember, control of your time is an exercise in selfishness.

    Pile C: Items that fall under the dubious rubric "a good idea to look at." One of the most egregious executive fallacies is that you have to read a little of everything in order to stay well-informed. If you limit the number of newspapers, magazines, and internal communications that you read regularly, you'll have more time to do what's important—like think. And remember to keep your reading timely; information is a perishable commodity.

3. In dealing with Pile A, always start with the most difficult or the most time-consuming. It also helps to have a folder for the things that *must* be done before you go home that day and to make a list of the things that simply cannot go undone for more than a few days or a week. Everything else is just everything else.

4. Buy another wastepaper basket. I know you already have one. But if you invited me to go through that pile of papers on your desk, I could fill both in a tric э. To help you decide what to toss and what to save, ask yourself the question asked by the legendary Alfred P. Sloan, Jr.: "What is the worst that can happen if I throw this out?" If you don't tremble, sweat, or grow faint when you think of the consequences, toss it.

   This second wastebasket is a critical investment, even though you'll never be able to fill both on a regular basis. Keep it anyway. It has a symbolic value. It will babysit your in-basket and act like a governess every time you wonder why you bought it.

5. Ask yourself Sloan's question about every lunch and meeting invitation. Don't be timid. And practice these three RSVPs:
   "Thanks, but I just can't fit it in."
   "I can't go, but I think *X* can." (If you think someone should.)
   "I'm sorry I can't make it, but do let me know what happened."
   Transform meetings into telephone calls or quick conversations in the hall. When you hold a meeting in your office, sit on the edge of your desk, or when you want to end the discussion, stand up from behind your desk and say, "OK, then, that's settled." These tricks are rude but almost foolproof.

6. Give yourself time to think. Spend half a day every week away from your office. Take your work home, or try working somewhere else—a conference room in another office, a public library, an airport waiting room—any place you can concentrate, and the farther away from your office the better. The point is, a fresh environment can do wonders for productivity. Just make sure you bring along a healthy dose of discipline, especially if you're working at home.

7. About the telephone, my practical but subversive advice is: Don't return calls. Or rather, return calls only to people you want to talk to. The others will call back. Better yet, they'll write, and you can spend ten seconds with their letter and then give it to the governess.

   Two ancillary bits of phone advice: Ask your assistants to take detailed messages. Ask them always to say you cannot take the call at the moment. (Depending on who it is, your assistants can always undertake to see if you can't be interrupted.)

8. Close your door. Oh, I know you have an open-door policy, but don't be so literal.

little charts to produce an appearance of order would have been a waste of time. It still is.

What I'm saying is, put ten people together, don't appoint a leader, and you can be sure that one will emerge. So will a sighter, a runner, and whatever else the group needs. We form the groups, but they find their own leaders. That's not a lack of structure, that's just a lack of structure imposed from above.

But getting back to that mammoth, why was it that all the members of the group were so eager to do their share of the work—sighting, running, spearing, chiefing—and to stand aside when someone else could do it better? Because they all got to eat the thing once it was killed and cooked. What mattered was results, not status.

Corporate profit is today's mammoth meat. And though there is a widespread view that profit sharing is some kind of socialist infection, it seems to me that few motivational tools are more capitalist. Everyone agrees that profits should belong to those who risk their capital, that entrepreneurial behavior deserves reward, that the creation of wealth should enrich the creator. Well, depending on how you define capital and risk, all these truisms can apply as much to workers as to shareholders.

Still, many profit-sharing programs are failures, and we think we know why. Profit sharing won't motivate employees if they see it as just another management gimmick, if the company makes it difficult for them to see how their own work is related to profits and to understand how those profits are divided.

In Semco's case, each division has a separate profit-sharing program. Twice a year, we calculate 23% of after-tax profit on each division income statement and give a check to three employees who've been elected by the workers in their division. These three invest the money until the unit can meet and decide—by simple majority vote—what they want to do with it. In most units, that's turned out to be an equal distribution. If a unit has 150 workers, the total is divided by 150 and handed out. It's that simple. The guy who sweeps the floor gets just as much as the division partner.

One division chose to use the money as a fund to lend out for housing construction. It was a pretty close vote, and the workers may change their minds next year. In the meantime, some of them have already received loans and have begun to build themselves houses. In any case, the employees do what they want with the money. The counselors stay out of it.

Semco's experience has convinced me that profit sharing has an excellent chance of working when it crowns a broad program of employee participation, when the profit-sharing criteria are so clear and simple that the least gifted employee can understand them, and, perhaps most important, when employees have monthly access to the company's vital statistics—costs, overhead, sales, payroll, taxes, profits.

TRANSPARENCY

Lots of things contribute to a successful profit-sharing program: low employee turnover, competitive pay, absence of paternalism, refusal to give consolation prizes when profits are down, frequent (quarterly or semiannual) profit distribution, and plenty of opportunity for employees to question the management decisions that affect future profits. But nothing matters more than those vital statistics—short, frank, frequent reports on how the company is doing. Complete transparency. No hocus-pocus, no hanky-panky, no simplifications.

On the contrary, all Semco employees attend classes to learn how to read and understand the numbers, and it's one of their unions that teaches the course. Every month, each employee gets a balance sheet, a profit-and-loss analysis, and a cash-flow statement for his or her division. The reports contain about 70 line items (more, incidentally, than we use to run the company, but we don't want anyone to think we're withholding information).

Many of our executives were alarmed by the decision to share monthly financial results with all employees. They were afraid workers would want to know everything, like how much we pay executives. When we held the first large meeting to discuss these financial reports with the factory committees and the leaders of the metalworkers' union, the first question we got was, "How much do division managers make?" We told them. They gasped. Ever since, the factory workers have called them "maharaja."

But so what? If executives are embarrassed by their salaries, that probably means they aren't earning them. Confidential payrolls are for those who cannot look themselves in the mirror and say with conviction, "I live in a capitalist system that remunerates on a geometric scale. I spent years in school, I have years of experience, I am capable and dedicated and intelligent. I deserve what I get."

I believe that the courage to show the real numbers will always have positive consequences over the long term. On the other hand, we can show only the numbers we bother to put together, and there aren't as many as there used to be. In my view, only the big numbers matter. But Semco's accounting people keep telling me that since the only way to get the big numbers is to add up the small ones, producing a budget or report that includes every tiny detail would require no extra effort. This is an expensive fallacy, and a difficult one to eradicate.

A few years ago, the U.S. president of Allis-Chalmers paid Semco a visit. At the end of his factory tour, he leafed through our monthly reports and budgets. At that time, we had our numbers ready on the fifth working day of every month in super-organized folders, and were those numbers comprehensive! On page 67, chart 112.6, for example, you could see how much coffee the workers in Light Manufacturing III had consumed the month before. The man said he was surprised to find such efficiency in a Brazilian company. In fact, he was so impressed that he asked his Brazilian subsidiary, an organization many times our size, to install a similar system there.

For months, we strolled around like peacocks, telling anyone who cared to listen that our budget system was state-of-the-art and that the president of a Big American Company had ordered his people to copy it. But soon we began to realize two things. First, our expenses were always too high, and they never came down because the accounting department was full of overpaid clerks who did nothing but compile them. Second, there were so damn many numbers inside the folder that almost none of our managers read them. In fact, we knew less about the company then, with all that information, than we do now without it.

Today we have a simple accounting system providing limited but relevant in-

RICARDO SEMLER'S GUIDE TO COMPENSATION

Employers began hiring workers by the hour during the industrial revolution. Their reasons were simple and rapacious. Say you ran out of cotton thread at 11:30 in the morning. If you paid people by the hour, you could stop the looms, send everyone home, and pay only for hours actually worked.

You couldn't do such a thing today. The law probably wouldn't let you. The unions certainly wouldn't let you. Your own self-interest would argue strongly against it. Yet the system lives on. The distinction between wage-earning workers and salaried employees is alive but not well, nearly universal but perfectly silly. The new clerk who lives at home and doesn't know how to boil an egg starts on a monthly salary, but the chief lathe operator who's been with the company 38 years and is a master sergeant in the army reserve still gets paid by the hour.

At Semco, we eliminated Frederick Winslow Taylor's segmentation and specialization of work. We ended the wage analyst's hundred years of solitude. We did away with hourly pay and now give everyone a monthly salary. We set the salaries like this:

A lot of our people belong to unions, and they negotiate their salaries collectively. Everyone else's salary involves an element of self-determination.

Once or twice a year, we order salary market surveys and pass them out. We say to people, "Figure out where you stand on this thing. You know what you do; you know what everyone else in the company makes; you know what your friends in other companies make; you know what you need; you know what's fair. Come back on Monday and tell us what to pay you."

When people ask for too little, we give it to them. By and by, they figure it out and ask for more. When they ask for too much, we give that to them too—at least for the first year. Then, if we don't feel they're worth the money, we sit down with them and say, "Look, you make *x* amount of money, and we don't think you're making *x* amount of contribution. So either we find something else for you to do, or we don't have a job for you anymore." But with half a dozen exceptions, our people have always named salaries we could live with.

We do a similar thing with titles. Counselors are counselors, and partners are partners; these titles are always the same. But with coordinators, it's not quite so easy. Job titles still mean too much to many people. So we tell coordinators to make up their own titles. They know what signals they need to send inside and outside the company. If they want "Procurement Manager," that's fine. And if they want "Grand Panjandrum of Imperial Supplies," that's fine too.

---

formation that we can grasp and act on quickly. We pared 400 cost centers down to 50. We beheaded hundreds of classifications and dozens of accounting lines. Finally, we can see the company through the haze.

(As for Allis-Chalmers, I don't know whether it ever adopted our old system in all its terrible completeness, but I hope not. A few years later, it began to suffer severe financial difficulties and eventually lost so much market share and money that it was broken up and sold. I'd hate to think it was our fault.)

In preparing budgets, we believe that the flexibility to change the budget continually is much more important than the detailed consistency of the initial numbers. We also believe in the importance of comparing expectations with results. Naturally, we compare monthly reports with the budget. But we go one step further. At month's end, the coordinators in each area make guesses about unit receipts, profit margins, and expenses. When the official numbers come out a few days later, top managers compare them with the guesses to judge how well the coordinators understand their areas.

What matters in budgets as well as in reports is that the numbers be few and important and that people treat them with something approaching passion. The three monthly reports, with their 70 line items, tell us how to run the company, tell our managers how well they know their units, and tell our employees if there's going to be a profit. Everyone works on the basis of the same information, and everyone looks forward to its appearance with what I'd call fervent curiosity.

And that's all there is to it. Participation gives people control of their work, profit sharing gives them a reason to do it better, information tells them what's working and what isn't.

LETTING THEM DO WHATEVER THE HELL THEY WANT

So we don't have systems or staff functions or analysts or anything like that. What we have are people who either sell or make, and there's nothing in between. Is there a marketing department? Not on your life. Marketing is everybody's problem. Everybody knows the price of the product. Everybody knows the cost. Everybody has the monthly balance sheet that says exactly what each of them makes, how much bronze is costing us, how much overtime we paid, all of it. And the employees know that 23% of the aftertax profit is theirs.

We are very, very rigorous about the numbers. We want them in on the fourth day of the month so we can get them back out on the fifth. And because we're so strict with the financial controls, we can be extremely lax about everything else. Employees can paint the walls any color they like. They can come to work whenever they decide. They can wear whatever clothing makes them comfortable. They can do whatever the hell they want. It's up to them to see the connection between productivity and profit and to act on it.

Chapter
16

Environment

We have reached a period in the life of our planet where our actions, particularly the actions of our organizations have become sufficiently powerful to wreak havoc on the environment. This damage inevitably comes back to us, for we are very intimately tied to our environment. It is by no means certain that the problems we have created will be resolved by a new round of technological innovation. In fact, many of the technologies we have created and employed to solve problems facing humans have contributed significantly to the ecological disasters that occur with disturbing frequency these days. The disaster in Bhopal, the destruction of animal and plant life following the Exxon oil spill in Alaska, the nuclear reactor accidents at Three Mile Island in the United States and Chernobyl in the Soviet Union are all frightening examples of errors in the planning and execution of organizational decisions. The toxicity caused by pesticide overuse and by industrial waste dumped into the rivers and oceans makes clear the delicate interaction that exists between cumulative human and organizational actions and the environment. Environmental problems transcend national and economic boundaries. The accident at Chernobyl created nuclear fallout that spread to all parts of Europe and beyond. The sulphur emissions from industries in the United States and Canada produce acid rain that destroys forests and diminishes the quality of life on the entire continent. There is an increased awareness of environmental dangers throughout the world and the actions of individuals and groups from many walks of life are being directed at solving rather than creating problems. Nevertheless, much remains to be done.

In this chapter we have selected articles that address various aspects of this large and complex challenge. One major issue is that of attitude, of the orientation people have toward the world they live in. In her lyrics to the song "Why," Tracy Chapman expresses her anger at the amount of pain, fear, and destruction that exist in the modern world. Like many others, she warns that we need to act soon to deal responsibly and with a common will to tackle the various sources of human suffering. We recommend Robert Redford's "Search for the Common Ground" (published in *Harvard Business Review*, 1987) as an eloquent argument for bringing together interest groups such as business leaders and environmentalists, to solve rather than perpetuate current problems. He describes some of the positive experiences that have come from the joint efforts of industry, government, environmentalists and minority groups on such thorny issues as energy conservation, land use and so on. We see the emergence of new modes of collaboration as a major step toward helping to resolve environmental problems.

The struggle over uses of natural resources is not confined to North America, or only to the industrialized nations. It is a war being waged in many parts of the world. In "Trees 'Ordained' in Forest Fight," Philip Smucker describes tactics being used by Buddhists to save precious rain forests in Thailand.

"The 1990s will be the decade of the Environment." This statement, from the president of the Petroleum Marketers Association of America, is cited in "Environmentalism: The New Crusade" by David Kirkpatrick. The battle to deal with the human and technological excesses that have contributed to the environment problems we face in the years ahead has also created opportunities for change. People in general seem to be more aware of the problems accompanying environmental damage and to be more willing to demand and take action to try to undo the harm being done. In this climate many businesses have recognized that paying attention to the environment and delivering environmentally sound products can be profitable. Kirkpatrick chronicles the efforts of several companies, including Du Pont, McDonald's, 3M, and Proctor and Gamble. It remains to be seen which companies and which products are genuinely environmentally friendly.

In the next selection Robert Fulghum provides an amusing and provocative anecdote from his delightful book, *All I Really Need to Know I Learned in Kindergarten.* Fulghum's message in this anecdote about villagers felling trees in the Solomon Islands in the South Pacific is that words can do much harm when they are directed against people. Although this piece might logically have been included in Chapter 6, which deals with images, we think it belongs in a section on the environment. The names we give to people and to things can prove lethal. Language, words, and communication can pollute the atmosphere as do other outputs of human endeavor.

One of the truly disturbing facets of environmental balance centers on the way humans view and relate to other living species. As John Robbins points out again and again in his book *Diet for a New America* (Stillpoint Publishing, 1987), humans have increasingly adopted an orientation that is blind to the feelings, intelligence, and sensitivities of animals. They have become commodities that exist exclusively to serve human needs. In "The Most Unjustly Maligned of All Animals," Robbins chronicles the horrifying plight of pigs reared in factories across the United States, where they are treated like components on an assembly line, machines to be produced and marketed. There is no opportunity for any of these animals to live any kind of reasonable life. Robbins discusses the ethical, political, and health issues that stem from these kinds of human and organizational practices. He suggests that the consequences of the practices are disastrous for both humans and animals.

At times, the magnitude of the challenges we face when we try to turn things around seems so great, that the effect is one of paralysis. What can we as individuals do that might have a positive effect on environmental problems, or any other major societal problems for that matter? "The Child and the Starfish" suggests in a playful way that we can make a difference in significant ways. In our concluding article, therapist Terrance O'Connor recommends that we apply what we have learned from our understanding of solving problems of individuals and families to the dilemmas and illnesses facing the Family of Man. In "Therapy for a Dying Planet," he suggests that each of us is both victim and victimizer in the current breakdown of the health and well-being of the global family. He argues that as causal agents in this process, we can also therefore contribute to the rehabilitation of the planet. His statement is a passionate call to work together.

Why?

Tracy Chapman

Why do the babies starve
When there's enough food to feed the world
Why when there's so many of us
Are there people still alone

Why are the missiles called peace keepers
When they're aimed to kill
Why is a woman still not safe
When she's in her home .

Love is hate
War is peace
No is yes
And we're all free

But somebody's gonna have to answer
The time is coming soon
Amidst all these questions and contradictions
There're some who seek the truth

But somebody's gonna have to answer
The time is coming soon
When the blind remove their blinders
And the speechless speak the truth

Trees "Ordained" in Forest Fight

Philip Smucker

Battle tactic: Monks quietly clothing teak in sacred orange robes in hopes
strong Thai religious beliefs will spare them

In Thailand's impoverished northeast, where Buddhism thrives amid the pressures
to modernize, the country's monks are making a last-ditch effort to save precious
rain forests.

Rather than rage against the conduct of corrupt forestry officials, monks have
begun quietly ordaining trees, clothing them in the sacred orange robes previously
reserved for holy men.

Villagers, obsessed with the supernatural in their efforts to preserve, claim
that to cut a tree ordained with orange robes would be tantamount to killing a
monk, an unpardonable offence in Buddhist belief.

The tactic, though peaceful and still unproven, parallels other more militant
fights in the region waged by indigenous villagers determined to save East Asian
rain forests from commercial interests. Not all, but many of these villagers are
standing up to protect forests equal in size to 80 per cent of the much-heralded
rain forests of Brazil.

In Indonesia, the hunter-gatherer Penan tribesmen harass logging firms by
falling down before bulldozers, and in Myanmar, formerly Burma, ethnic guerril-
las fight a jungle war to protect mainland Asia's largest rain forest from the destructive intentions of the country's military.

"Trees 'Ordained' in Forest Fight" by Philip Smucker, *Toronto Globe & Mail*, July 13, 1990, p. A1, A7.
Reprinted by permission of the author.

Despite these efforts, the rate of destruction of tropical rain forests in Southeast Asia is an estimated 50 per cent faster than that in Brazil, according to United Nations research.

The forests of Southeast Asia are home to distinct Asian varieties of lions, tigers and elephants. In the jungle canopy swing gibbons and monkeys, and the moist decaying soil of the forest is home to thousands of tiny mammals and unknown species of insects.

For centuries the biological diversity of the forests has provided medicines for villagers and food. Throughout the world, at least 200 million people depend on tropical forests for their livelihood, according to the World Bank.

Each day at least 5,000 hectares of tropical East Asian forests are destroyed with less than 10 per cent of that replanted, according to officials at the United Nations Food and Agriculture Organization in Bangkok.

World wide, tropical forests generate $8-billion (U.S.) in export revenues yearly. In Thailand, home of the region's largest sawmills for decades, conservationists and a handful of concerned government officials have been unable to tame the relentless pursuit of hardwood by commercial loggers.

But East Asian officials are quick to point out to their Western critics that Westerners destroyed many of their own forests long ago. "They look at North Americans saying 'You shouldn't do this and that' and say, 'Who are you to tell us what we can and can't do?' " said Ron Livingston, a Canadian environmental analyst working in Southeast Asia. "I think in a lot of the cases they are right. They are just starting to get some of the benefits from development."

Having nearly exhausted their own reserves, Thai forest companies have sought out and found new contracts with the military junta in Myanmar, the Communist government in Laos and now the Khmer Rouge in Cambodia.

The Thai government, which assists those companies, has come under harsh criticism from international conservation groups for their policy of dealing with neighboring governments desperate for foreign exchange.

"Thailand is now engaging in crass hypocrisy by leading the charge to destroy the forests of neighboring Burma," said a recent report released by the U.S.-based Rainforest Action Network. Officials at the Food and Agriculture Organization say that the destruction of Myanmar's forests has jumped 500 per cent in recent years.

Bulldozers and elephants from Thailand work to extract teak trees from a virgin jungle even as the government battles ethnic insurgents.

The Myanmar military, which has shown reluctance to hand over power to a freely elected civilian government, is using money made from logging deals with Thailand to support a border war against minorities who have traditionally reforested as they cut.

The Rainforest group charges that Thai policy is decimating mainland Asia's largest intact rain forest. It contains an estimated 80 per cent of the world's remaining teak stands.

Environmental experts describe a pattern of abuse in East Asia beginning with big logging companies that clear roads, misuse concessions and create access for poor villagers who further clear the forests for farmland.

"When you get people taking individual trees, it is hard to talk to them about environmental issues," Mr. Livingston said. "They are using the wood just to stay alive. You've got to provide them with alternatives."

Environmentalism: The New Crusade

David Kirkpatrick

It may be the biggest business issue of the 1990s. Here's how some smart companies are tackling it.

Trend spotters and forward thinkers agree that the Nineties will be the Earth Decade and that environmentalism will be a movement of massive worldwide force. How massive? Listen to Gary Miller, a public policy expert at Washington University in St. Louis: "In the Nineties environmentalism will be the cutting edge of social reform and absolutely the most important issue for business." Futurist Edith Weiner of the Manhattan management consulting firm Weiner Edrich Brown concurs: "Environmentalism will be the next major political idea, just as conservatism and liberalism have been in the past."

The smartest companies are not just facing this thunderous music, they're singing along. Consider:

- Du Pont is pulling out of a $750-million-a-year business because it may—just may—harm the earth's atmosphere.
- McDonald's, which produces hundreds of millions of pounds of paper and plastic waste annually, has become a crusading proponent of recycling, and aims to become one of America's leading educators about environmental issues.
- 3M is investing in myriad pollution controls for its manufacturing facilities beyond what the law requires.

- Procter & Gamble and other smart marketers are moving to cast their products in an environmentally friendly light (see box on page 560).
- Pacific Gas & Electric teams up with environmental groups—some of them outfits it used to fight—to do joint projects, such as a $10 million study of energy efficiency.

"The 1990s will be the decade of the environment." That's not the chief druid of Greenpeace talking, but rather the new president of the Petroleum Marketers Association of America in a November speech. Mere corporate ecobabble intended to placate the latest group of special-interest loonies? Any company that thinks that way will probably regret it. Exxon provides the obvious if inadvertent example of the bitter costs of seeming unconcerned about the environment. Not long after the March accident in Valdez, Alaska, 41% of Americans were angry enough to say they'd seriously consider boycotting the company. Bill McInturff, senior researcher at the Wirthlin Group, a polling firm with close Republican ties, blames Exxon not for the accident but for its response: "It was a disservice to American industry the way the pullout last fall was handled. Exxon seemed satisfied with what they had accomplished. It hardened the notion that business is just interested in making a buck and doesn't give a damn. It flabbergasts me that a company that size doesn't get the drift." Even spending over $1 billion on cleanup hasn't salvaged the oil giant's reputation.

Such salvage won't get any easier. The New York Times/CBS News poll regularly asks the public if "protecting the environment is so important that requirements and standards cannot be too high, and continuing environmental improvements must be made regardless of cost." In September 1981, 45% agreed and 42% disagreed with that plainly intemperate statement. Last June, 79% agreed and only 18% disagreed. For the first time, liberals and conservatives, Democrats and Republicans, profess concern for the environment in roughly equal numbers.

Environmentalism is likely to continue as an issue at the forefront for several reasons. One is demographic. Says futurist Weiner: "The combination of baby-boomers having children and a significant part of the population moving into senior years means an enormous percentage of the population is taking the attitude of stewardship." The Gallup Organization reports that 49% of people over 50 feel strong identification with environmentalism, compared with 39% of those between 30 and 49 and 31% of those under 30. This reverses the pattern that prevailed during the country's last upsurge in environmentalism 20 years ago.

The new crusade will be different from the old in other ways as well. Miller of Washington University explains, "In the Sixties, environmentalism was the tail end of a period of social activism that was primarily based on civil rights and the antiwar movement," while now it's a movement of its own. The players are different. Far fewer activists of the 1990s will be embittered, scruffy, antibusiness street fighters.

As an example of the new breed, consider Allen Hershkowitz, who freely drops the names of his CEO acquaintances. As a solid-waste-disposal expert at the litigious Natural Resources Defense Council, Hershkowitz has won many legal battles with business. Now high-ranking executives of major companies regularly make the pilgrimage to his office in the elegant, airy, and amply funded New York

City headquarters of NRDC, coming to him lest he go after them. As he explains, "They come in here to see what they've got to cover their asses on." The cocky 34-year-old Ph.D., who serves as an adviser to banks and Shearson Lehman Hutton, among others, elaborates, "My primary motivation is environmental protection. And if it costs more, so be it. If Procter & Gamble can't live with that, somebody else will. But I'll tell you, Procter & Gamble is trying hard to live with it."

Still, for all his militancy, Hershkowitz is no fanatic or utopian. He understands that a perfect world can't be achieved and doesn't hesitate to talk of trade-offs: "Hey, civilization has its costs. We're trying to reduce them, but we can't eliminate them." Environmentalists of this stripe will increasingly show up even within companies. William Bishop, Procter & Gamble's top environmental scientist, was an organizer of Earth Day in 1970 and is a member of the Sierra Club. One of his chief deputies belongs to Greenpeace.

Eager to work with business, many environmentalists are moving from confrontation to the best kind of collaboration. In September an ad hoc combination of institutional investors controlling $150 billion of assets (including representatives of public pension funds) and environmental groups promulgated the Valdez Principles, named for the year's most catalytic environmental accident. The principles ask companies to reduce waste, use resources prudently, market safe products, and take responsibility for past harm. They also call for an environmentalist on each corporate board and an annual public audit of a company's environmental progress.

The group asked corporations to subscribe to the principles, with the implicit suggestion that investments could eventually be contingent on compliance. Companies already engaged in friendly discussions included Du Pont, specialty-chemical maker H.B. Fuller, and Polaroid, among others.

Earth Day 1990, scheduled for April 22, the 20th anniversary of the first such event, is becoming a veritable biz-fest. "We're really interested in working with companies that have a good record," says Earth Day Chairman Denis Hayes, who predicts that 100 million people will take part one way or another. Apple Computer and Hewlett-Packard have donated equipment. Shaklee, the personal and household products company, paid $50,000 to be the first official corporate sponsor. Even the Chemical Manufacturers Association is getting in on the act, preparing a list of 101 ways its members can participate. The more than 1,000 Earth Day affiliate groups in 120 countries propose to shake up politicians worldwide and launch a decade of activism.

The message that leading environmentalists are sending, and progressive companies are receiving, is that eco-responsibility will be good for business. Says Gray Davis, California's state controller, who helped draft the Valdez Principles and who sits on the boards of two public pension funds with total assets of $90 billion: "Given the increasing regulation and public concern, there's no question that companies will eventually have to change their ways. The first kid on the block to embrace these principles will increase market share and profit substantially."

While that's hard to prove, few dispute that farsightedness today will pay off tomorrow. Environmental regulations will continue to be tightened. Says Lester Lave, a professor of engineering and public policy at the Carnegie-Mellon business school: "If you build a plant that just squeaks past now, you'll have to pay much more money down the line."

That is partly why Minnesota Mining & Manufacturing is going beyond the call of duty and government deadlines. For example, new federal regulations require replacement or improvement by 1998 of underground storage tanks for liquids and gases. The company decided to comply by 1992 instead, and to have all tanks worldwide in compliance by 1993. Cost: more than $80 million. "Regulations are about to overwhelm us," says Robert Bringer, 3M staff vice president for environmental engineering and pollution control. "The only way we see to deal with that is to reduce the number of materials we emit that trigger regulation."

Chastened in part by Exxon's example, some corporate bosses don't see red when faced with green activists—they see themselves. One of Edgar Woolard's first acts after becoming CEO of Du Pont in April (just after the Valdez spill) was to deliver a speech in London entitled—and calling for—"Corporate Environmentalism." Said the top man of the chemical giant in remarks subsequently reprinted by the company on recycled paper: "Avoiding environmental incidents remains the single greatest imperative facing industry today." He bemoaned industry's lack of credibility on the issue and called for spending more money than "mere compliance" with laws would require.

Woolard now meets at least once a month with leading environmentalists, and his company is taking what seem dramatic steps demonstrating its concern. In March 1988, Du Pont announced that, based on new evidence that chlorofluorocarbons (CFCs) might be seriously depleting the Earth's ozone layer, it would voluntarily suspend all production of CFCs—a $750-million-a-year business in which it leads the industry—by 2000, or sooner if possible. The company has already spent $170 million developing safe compounds to replace CFCs in cleaning, refrigeration, and other uses. It is prepared to spend as much as $1 billion on the best replacements discovered so far, but since even these compounds may slightly deplete the ozone layer, Du Pont wants guarantees that new plants will be allowed to function long enough to recoup the investment. Says Woolard: "In my opinion it has not been proven that CFCs are harmful to the ozone, but there is a fairly good probability, and we have to deal with that."

Evidence of increased environmental sensitivity is everywhere in Du Pont, perhaps partly because that's now one of the criteria in determining managers' compensation. The company voluntarily spends an estimated $50 million each year on environmental projects beyond what the law requires, like the $15 million it spent at a Texas plant to reduce the risk of dangerous gases being released. Du Pont's ultimate goal is zero pollution in all activities. While Woolard is certain this new priority will strengthen the company, he admits profits will suffer from the effort over the next few years.

Du Pont also sees business opportunity in environmental concern. Building on expertise gained in cleaning up its own plants, the company announced in early December the formation of a safety and environmental resources division to help industrial customers clean up toxic wastes. Management forecasts potential annual revenues of $1 billion from the new business by 2000. Defensive actions sometimes pay off too. Faced with protests over the ocean dumping of acid iron salts off

LEADING THE CRUSADE INTO CONSUMER MARKETING

There's money to be made catering to the public's mounting concern for the environment, as astute consumer marketers are beginning to learn. A July 1989 survey conducted for the Michael Peters Group, which provides consulting on products and design, found that 77% of Americans say a company's environmental reputation affects what they buy. Observes Howard Marder of the Hill & Knowlton public relations firm: "For the past 20 years the environmental movement in the U.S. has focused on cleaning up damage. Almost overnight the focus is changing to prevention. Marketers had nothing to sell before, but now they can say, 'Be part of the solution by buying our product.' " Among those now making just that pitch in the U.S.: Arco, Colgate-Palmolive, Lever Brothers, 3M, Procter & Gamble, and Sunoco.

Marketers with experience abroad have seen France and Britain quickly catch up to West Germany and Sweden in the responsiveness of their populations to environmental marketing, and experts have little doubt the U.S. will soon follow. In mid-November, Procter & Gamble began test-marketing its first domestic product with an explicit environmental claim: Downy Refill comes in a 21½-ounce milk-carton-type container and is intended to be mixed with water in a used plastic Downy bottle to make 64 ounces of fabric softener. Prominently printed on the carton: "Better for the Environment . . . Less packaging to throw away." With a package 75% smaller, Downy Refill costs 10% less than regular Downy. It's too early to gauge the product's success.

For Wal-Mart, environmentalism is "a cause and not a marketing scheme," claims William Fields, the chain's executive vice president for merchandise. The giant discounter in July asked its 7,000 suppliers to provide it with more recycled or recyclable products. About 100 are already in stores, with labels (printed on recycled paper) explaining their supposedly beneficial features. K mart and at least a dozen small to medium-size grocery chains have announced similar programs. Experts suggest Wal-Mart and the others proceed slowly. Overeager green-marketing campaigns in Britain and Canada have been attacked by environmentalists for unsubstantiated or inappropriate claims.

The London-based Body Shop, with 14 outlets in the U.S., puts environmental concerns at its core and in the process finds its way to the green in customers' pockets. The skin- and hair-care stores display literature on ozone depletion next to sunscreens and fill their windows with information on issues like global warming. Every employee is assigned to spend half a day each week on activist work. Customers get discounts if they bring their old bottles back to the store for recycling. In 1988 the chain collected over a million signatures in Britain on a petition asking Brazil's President to save the rain forests. In 13 years the Body Shop has opened 420 stores in 38 countries. Sales for the year ended February 1989 were over $90 million with pretax profits of about 20%.

Make sure your green-marketing claims amount to more than a fig leaf. British Petroleum got flak recently for promoting a new brand of unleaded gasoline in Britain with the claim that it caused "no pollution." It later apologized for what it called an inadvertent error. A plastic grocery bag used by some New York supermarkets says: "This 'Earth Sack' will begin degrading within 3 days of exposure to ultraviolet light . . . and will continue the process until it turns into a nontoxic environmentally safe dust." Scientists believe the statement can be misleading, and in landfills light can be in short supply anyway. Some environmentalists have targeted "degradable plastics" for protest.

In general, the more you tell your customers, the better off you'll be. Procter & Gamble environmental chief Geoff Place visited his brother's family in England recently and found them no longer using several P&G products because of environmental concerns. Later a family member told Place they'd started using Fairy Dishwashing Liquid again because P&G had improved it. In fact the company had simply added a statement on the label saying "Only biodegradable surface active agents are used in this product." That has been true since 1963.

---

the coast of New Jersey, Du Pont halted a practice its scientists were convinced was harmless. It then discovered the salts could be sold to water-treatment plants.

At 3M, CEO Allen Jacobson directs that pollution-control installations be judged by their environmental benefit, not only by return on investment. But 3M too has learned that environmental controls often lead to cost savings. The company specializes in coated products (such as videotapes and pressure-sensitive tapes) whose manufacture has long emitted significant pollutants. It has saved well over $1 billion since 1975 through a program called Pollution Prevention Pays. The program spotlights projects that reduce pollution as well as save money. Solvents that were once emitted to the atmosphere may be recycled and reused, or a volatile solvent may be replaced by a water-based one, eliminating the need for costly air pollution control equipment.

If, as many predict, alliances between environmentalists and corporations are the wave of the future, Pacific Gas & Electric has already learned to surf. But it took practice. In the mid-1970s economists and lawyers from the Environmental Defense Fund started fighting the company's plan to build several giant coal and nuclear power plants. The environmentalists proposed instead a combination of smaller-scale generating facilities like windmills or cogeneration plants on the sites of regional businesses, combined with aggressive conservation measures.

The big plants were never built. A persistent EDF campaign of pressure at utility commission meetings and sophisticated television advertising came just as the price of fossil fuels started climbing dramatically. PG&E's resistance gradually melted. The company took several steps to conserve energy, and much of the rest of the electric industry eventually followed PG&E's lead. Says EDF attorney David Roe: "We spoke to them in their own language. We used their type of computer models, their financial analysis sheets. We weren't saying, do what's good for the environment and it will cripple you. We were saying, it will save you economically."

While the company says it would have eventually taken most of the actions EDF proposed anyway, it acknowledges that the give-and-take was beneficial. Says PG&E attorney Kermit Kubitz: "I think both sides may have been closer together than either side realized at the beginning." Echoes Roe: "The basic point is, there's usually a lot more common ground than either side realizes."

Today PG&E has a policy of aggressively seeking discussions and joint projects with any willing environmental group, even those that have opposed the company in the past. Its board includes Melvin Lane, a well-known West Coast environmentalist. In November, PG&E announced a $10 million study, conducted in conjunction with the Natural Resources Defense Council, among others, to improve efficiency in the use of electricity. And that computer model EDF developed to demonstrate the relationships between conservation and electricity costs—PG&E now rents it from EDF for about $18,000 a year.

PG&E chief Richard Clarke believes that on the rocky coast of Northern California, where quality of life has long been a paramount public issue, he has seen America's environmental mood foreshadowed. A few guiding principles Clarke has learned:

- "Make environmental considerations and concerns part of any decision you make, right from the beginning. Don't think of it as something extra you throw in the pot."
- "Develop an internal cadre of environmentalists. They have minds of their own and will advocate things. They may not get everything they want, but there certainly are occasions where they prevail."
- "Have a continuing dialogue with environmental groups."
- "Put someone on your board to help you factor in environmental issues."
- "Do these things because they are the right thing to do, not because somebody forces you to do them."

McDonald's might add another principle to the list: Educate customers incessantly. Faced with growing protests over the volume of waste it generates, especially the polystyrene foam packaging used for hot food, the restaurant giant has taken major steps to reduce waste at the source, to recycle what's left, and to explain what it is doing. Just by making its drinking straws 20% lighter, the chain eliminated one million pounds of waste per year. In October, McDonald's began collecting polystyrene waste in 100 New England outlets and recycling it; the company intends to include all 450 regional stores in the plan by March. Customers are asked to put polystyrene containers, such as those for Chicken McNuggets or Big Macs, in special bins. All napkins in U.S. stores are now made from recycled paper, as are carry-out drink trays and office paper at headquarters.

Shelby Yastrow, the company's general counsel and point man on environmental issues, says that since polystyrene is 100% recyclable, it is better for the environment than paper, which theoretically degrades but most commonly ends up in anaerobic landfills—virtually no oxygen gets through—which may instead preserve it for decades. Paper is also significantly bulkier than plastic in most uses, thus creating more waste. "Everything I look at tells me plastic is better," says Yastrow. "I have a little trouble convincing my children or my neighbors, but the scientific community isn't a problem."

To correct the misconceptions of those kids and neighbors and their peers nationwide, the company is embarking on a major educational campaign. McDonald's is describing its efforts and explaining recycling on the paper liners on customers' trays, in advertising, in brochures it hands out in stores, and in mailings to school teachers. That's a lot of describing and explaining: McDonald's serves 18 million customers in the U.S. each day, making its tray liners alone one of the largest of the nation's mass media.

Even if it improves public understanding of solid waste, McDonald's will continue to confront one of the nagging realities of the new environmentalism: Grass-roots local groups, many of them misinformed, wield increasing disruptive power. Says David Stephenson, a Boston public relations consultant who specializes in corporate environmental strategy: "The grass-roots groups are concerned about the value of their homes and the health of their children. That means they are relentless. In general, unlike the mainstream environmental groups, they are not interested in compromise or mediation." McDonald's successfully confronted antipolystyrene picketing at several of its Vermont stores with an aggressive local educational campaign. By the end, local activists were asking that the company convert its paper cold-drink cups to plastic.

One lesson from the company's experience: Don't ever assume you've solved an environmental problem. As knowledge evolves, attitudes change, and so do solutions. McDonald's switched from paper to polystyrene packaging for Big Macs and other sandwiches in 1976 largely because the public was worried about cutting trees and the energy that paper production consumed. As recently as the early Seventies, CFCs, one of today's leading environmental villains, were believed to be a harmless and inert triumph of modern chemistry.

You have to keep looking ahead—way ahead. For gutsy environmental farsightedness, few companies can top Applied Energy Services. The private, Virginia-based power-plant management firm donated $2 million in 1988 for tree planting in Guatemala to compensate for a coal-fired plant it was building in Connecticut. The trees, which of course consume carbon dioxide, are intended to offset the plant's emissions of the gas, which may lead to global warming. Says CEO Roger Sant: "We pride ourselves on being part of the solution, not part of the problem. We weren't trying to do any more than salve our own guilt, I guess." The company expects to couple tree-planting programs with all seven new plants on its drawing boards. Several large outfits have contacted Sant to ask his help in refining similar plans.

One recent weekday afternoon, three men walked out of the Environmental Defense Fund's midtown Manhattan office on their way to have lunch together. On the left was EDF's senior economist. On the right was an environmental expert in the Soviet government. Between them was a businessman, a trader in the nascent enterprise of buying and selling pollution rights. Together that trio forms a picture of how the new environmentalism is shaping up: global, more cooperative than confrontational—and with business at the center.

Logging in the Solomon Islands

Robert Fulghum

In the Solomon Islands in the South Pacific some villagers practice a unique form of logging. If a tree is too large to be felled with an ax, the natives cut it down by yelling at it. *(Can't lay my hands on the article, but I swear I read it.)* Woodsmen with special powers creep up on a tree just at dawn and suddenly scream at it at the top of their lungs. They continue this for thirty days. The tree dies and falls over. The theory is that the hollering kills the spirit of the tree. According to the villagers, it always works.

Ah, those poor naïve innocents. Such quaintly charming habits of the jungle. Screaming at trees, indeed. How primitive. Too bad they don't have the advantages of modern technology and the scientific mind.

Me? I yell at my wife. And yell at the telephone and the lawn mower. And yell at the TV and the newspaper and my children. I've even been known to shake my fist and yell at the sky at times.

Man next door yells at his car a lot. And this summer I heard him yell at a stepladder for most of an afternoon. We modern, urban, educated folks yell at traffic and umpires and bills and banks and machines—especially machines. Machines and relatives get most of the yelling.

Don't know what good it does. Machines and things just sit there. Even kicking doesn't always help. As for people, well, the Solomon Islanders may have a point. Yelling at living things does tend to kill the spirit in them. Sticks and stones may break our bones, but words will break our hearts. . . .

From *All I Really Need to Know I Learned in Kindergarten* by Robert Fulghum. Copyright © 1986, 1988 by Robert Fulghum. Reprinted by permission of Villand Books, a division of Random House, Inc.

The Most Unjustly Maligned of all Animals

John Robbins

*Whenever people say "we mustn't be sentimental," you can take it
they are about to do something cruel. And if they add, "we must be
realistic," they mean they are going to make money out of it.*

Brigid Brophy

*There is a single magic, a single power, a single salvation, and a single
happiness, and that is called loving.*

Herman Hesse

In our human blindness concerning the feelings, intelligence, and sensitivity of
animals, there is one in particular about whom we've been most wrong. If it were
possible to measure our misunderstanding about our fellow creatures on some
giant scale, our ignorance of this particular animal might well be the greatest of all.
This is an animal who has been abused and ridiculed by people for centuries, but
who is actually a friendly, forgiving, intelligent and good natured animal when he
isn't mistreated. I am talking, you may be surprised to find out, about the pig.

THE HIDDEN TRUTH ABOUT PIGS

To call a man a "pig," or a woman a "sow," is one of the worst insults in our common speech. This fact testifies not to the nature of pigs, but to our beliefs about
them, and only shows how far out of touch we are with these animals. The commonly held image of pigs as greedy, fat, and filthy creatures, gross beasts who eat
anything that isn't fastened down, and who selfishly indulge their basest instincts
without a trace of sensitivity, could hardly be further from the truth.

Pigs actually have one of the highest measured I. Q.'s of all animals, surpassing
even the dog. They are friendly, sociable, fun-loving beings as well. One person

"The Most Unjustly Maligned of All Animals" by John Robbins from *Diet For a New America*, 1987, pp.
73–96. Reprinted by permission of Stillpoint Publishing, Walpole, NH.

very familiar with pigs was naturalist W. H. Hudson. He wrote in his acclaimed *Book of a Naturalist:*

> I have a friendly feeling towards pigs generally, and consider them the most intelligent of beasts, not excepting the elephant and the anthropoid ape . . . I also like his attitude towards all other creatures, especially man. He is not suspicious, or shrinkingly submissive, like horses, cattle and sheep; not an impudent devil-may-care like the goat; nor hostile like the goose; nor condescending like the cat; nor a flattering parasite like the dog. He views us from a totally different, a sort of democratic standpoint as fellow-citizens and brothers, and takes it for granted, or grunted, that we understand his language, and without servility or insolence he has a natural, pleasant, camerados-all or hail-fellow-well-met air with us.[1]

In the common mind, pigs are disgusting creatures, but in fact the only thing disgusting about pigs is our attitude towards them. They are playful, sensitive, friendly animals, who like to roll around and rub on things, and consider the earth their home and not something with which to avoid contact. In a state of nature, pigs love to wallow in the mud, just as stags and buffaloes and many other animals do, especially in the hot days of summer when flies are most troublesome. But pigs don't love mud for its own sake. They use it to cool themselves off, and to gain relief from the flies. They enjoy themselves exuberantly because it is their way to enjoy what they do with robust good nature. People who have seen them in mud have accused them of being filthy animals, not understanding their simple love of the earth. However, when living in anything even remotely resembling their natural conditions, pigs are as naturally clean as any other forest creature. If at all possible, they will never soil their own bedding, eating, or living areas.

But for many years it was the belief in Europe that the filthier the state in which a pig was kept, the better tasting the pork would be. Hence it became commonplace for pigs to be kept in a fashion that made it impossible for them to stay clean. Even then, though, they would often go to great lengths to maintain as clean a living situation as they could manage.

THE FRAGRANCE OF THE FARM

Since I have found that pigs are such endearing and friendly chaps, I don't look at pork chops the way I once did. And there's something else I've learned that has forever changed the way I feel about such things as bacon and ham.

What I have learned is that the pork farmers have by and large followed the lead of the poultry industry in recent years. Instead of pig farms, today we have more and more pig factories.

The result is not a happy one for today's pigs.

Some of today's pig factories are huge industrial complexes, with over 100,000 pigs. You might think that would require an awful lot of pigpens. But the pigpen,

---

[1]Hudson, W.H., The Book of a Naturalist, George Duran Publishers, 1919, pgs 295–302.

like the chicken yard, is rapidly becoming a thing of the past. Every day, more and more of these robust creatures are placed in stalls so cramped that they can hardly move.

If you were to peek inside one of the buildings in which these stalls are kept, you'd see row upon row upon row upon row of pigs, each standing alone in his narrow steel stall, each facing in exactly the same direction, like cars in a parking lot.

But you would hardly notice what you saw, because you'd be so overwhelmed by the stench. The overpowering ammonia-saturated air of a modern pig factory is something no one ever forgets.

You see, many modern pig stalls are built on slatted floors over large pits, into which the urine and feces of the animals fall automatically. Thousands of this type of confinement systems are in operation, in spite of the fact that many serious diseases are caused by the toxic gases (ammonia, methane and hydrogen sulfide) that the excreta produce, and which rise from the pits and become trapped inside the building.[2]

Pigs have a highly developed sense of smell and their noses are, in a natural setting, capable of detecting the scents of many kinds of edible roots, even when those roots are still underground. In today's pig factories, however, they breathe night and day the stench of the excrement of the hundreds of pigs whose stalls are in the same building. No matter how much they might want to get away, no matter how hard they might try, there is no escape.

The pig factory I am describing is unfortunately not an isolated bad example. It's par for the course today. Just a couple of years ago, the owner of Lehman Farms of Strawn, Illinois, was chosen Illinois Pork All-American by the National Pork Producers Council and the Illinois Pork Producers Association. The Lehman farm is considered an industry model, and it is, in fact, one of the more enlightened swine management programs around today. But it seems to leave a little bit to be desired from the point of view of the pigs who call it home. When a "herdsman" at Lehman Farms, Bob Frase, was asked about the effect the ammonia saturated air had on the pigs, he replied:

> The ammonia really chews up the animals' lungs. They get listless and don't want to eat. They start losing weight, and the next thing you know you've got a real respiratory problem—pneumonia or something. Then you'll see them huddled down real low against one another trying to get warm, and you'll hear them coughing and gasping. The bad air's a problem. After I've been working in here awhile, I can feel it in my own lungs. But at least I get out of here at night. The pigs don't so we have to keep them on tetracycline . . .[3]

---

[2]Schell, O., Modern Meat, Vintage Books, 1985, pg 59.

[3]Ibid, pgs 61–62.

"FORGET THE PIG IS AN ANIMAL"

In my visits to modern pig factories, I keep thinking about pigs I have met, social critters . . . very capable of warm relationships with people. I remember their friendly grunts and their enjoyment of human contact. This is why I have such a hard time accepting the advice of contemporary pork producers:

> Forget the pig is an animal. Treat him just like a machine in a factory. Schedule treatments like you would lubrication. Breeding season like the first step in an assembly line. And marketing like the delivery of finished goods.
> (*HOG FARM MANAGEMENT*, SEPTEMBER, 1976)

Modern pig farmers, who like to be called "pork production engineers," pride themselves on having a clear purpose. The trade journal *Hog Farm Management* put it concisely:

> What we are really trying to do is modify the animal's environment for maximum profit.[4]

Even if an individual pig raiser feels an empathy with the animals in his charge and has a desire to do things in a more natural way, he is today practically forced to go along with the agribusiness momentum. The trend is set. Trade journals like *Hog Farm Management, National Hog Farmer, Successful Farming,* and *Farm Journal* are constantly telling farmers to "Raise Pork the Modern Way."

The trade journals tend to be downright hostile to anything but the most mechanized agribusiness ways of producing pork. Recently, *National Hog Farmer* became irate at the USDA, and editorialized, "Why don't we just turn the Department of Agriculture over to the do-gooders?"[5] What on earth had the USDA done to provoke such a terrifying thought? It had proposed spending two hundredths of one percent of its budget for two small projects that would have encouraged small-scale, local production of food, such as roadside markets and community gardens in urban areas.

The trade magazines, it must be remembered, derive their income from advertisers, and these are just the people who profit from the swing to total confinement systems of pork production—the huge commercial interests who sell equipment and drugs to the farmers. They're the ones who take out full page ads and pay for space in the journals which tell the farmers "How to Make $12,000 Sitting Down!"[6] That's quite a way to catch the attention of an exhausted farmer, who is only too glad to sit down at all after laboring on his feet all day.

So he reads on. And what does he find? The way to success in today's pork production world is through buying a "Bacon Bin."[7] This wonderful new doorway

---

[4]Brynes, J., "Raising Pigs by the Calendar at Maplewood Farm," *Hog Farm Management,* Sept., 1976, pg 30.

[5]Black, N., "Let's Give USDA to Do-Gooders, Gardeners," *National Hog Farmer,* Aug. 1976, pg 26.

[6]*Farm Journal,* Aug 1966, and elsewhere.

[7]Ibid.

to success, he is told, "is not just a confinement house . . . It is a profit producing pork production system."[8]

Actually, the Bacon Bin is a completely automated system whose designers clearly have overcome any vestiges of the anachronistic idea that pigs are sentient beings. In a typical Bacon Bin setup, 500 pigs are crammed into individual cages, each getting seven square feet of living space. It's difficult for us to conceive how confined this is. Every pig spends his entire life cramped into a space less than one-third the size of a twin bed.

The Bacon Bin system comes complete with slatted floors and automated feeding systems, so that it takes only one person to run the whole show. Another advantage of the system is that, with no room to move about, the pigs can't burn up calories doing "useless" things like walking, and that means faster and cheaper weight gain, and so more profit.

A typical example of Bacon Bin farming was happily described in *The Farm Journal* beneath the title: "Pork Factory Swings into Production."[9] The article begins proudly:

> Hogs never see daylight in this half-million dollar farrowing-to-finish complex near Worthington, Minnesota.[10]

This is something to brag about?

IMPROVING ON MOTHER NATURE

It may not be wise to tamper with nature. It may even be disastrous. But you can be sure that if it's profitable, someone is certain to give it a try. The leading edge in pork production these days is in getting more pigs per sow per year. The idea is to turn sows into living reproductive machines.

> The breeding sow should be thought of, treated as, a valuable piece of machinery, whose function is to pump out baby pigs like a sausage machine.
> (*NATIONAL HOG FARMER*, MARCH, 1978)[11]

In a barnyard setting, a sow will produce about six piglets a year. But modern interventions have cranked her up to over 20 a year now, and researchers predict the number to reach 45 within a short time.[12] Producers rave about the prospect of being able to force sows to give birth to over seven times the number of children nature designed them for.

They've got it down to a science. First of all, piglets are taken away from their

---

[8]Ibid.

[9]*Farm Journal*, Nov 1968.

[10]Ibid.

[11]Taylor, L., *National Hog Farmer*, March 1978, pg 27.

[12]*Farm Journal*, April 1970.

mothers much earlier than would ever occur in any natural situation. Without her babies to suck the milk from her breast, the sow will soon stop lactating, and then, with the help of hormone injections, she can be made fertile much sooner. Thus, more piglets can be extracted from her per year.

Unfortunately, the poor sow is not up-to-date enough in her thinking to appreciate the wonders of a system in which she will spend her whole life producing litter after litter, only to have her babies taken away from her as soon as possible after each birth. The sow calls and cries for them, though her distressed sounds always go unheeded. Not having gotten the hang of modern factory life, she only knows that her whole being is filled with an inexorable instinct to find her lost babies and care for them.

Most pork producers have found that they have to let the piglets suckle from their mother for a couple of weeks before taking them away, or else they die, which, of course, defeats the whole purpose. But at least one large manufacturer of farm equipment sees the waste in such an operation, and is now strongly promoting a device it calls "Pig Mama."[13] This is a mechanical teat that replaces the normal one altogether, and allows the factory manager to take the piglet away from his mother immediately, and get her back to the business of being pregnant, just a couple of hours after birth. Noting this development, *Farm Journal* said it was looking forward to "an end to the nursing phase of pig production."[14] The result, they predicted gleefully, would be a "tremendous jump in the number of pigs a sow could produce in a year."[15] For years now, pork breeders have also been hard at work developing fatter and fatter pigs. Unfortunately, the resulting products of contemporary porkbreeding are so top-heavy that their bones and joints are literally crumbling beneath them.[16] However, factory experts see nothing amiss in this because there is additional profit to be made from the extra weight.

There are, however, a few problems with the "new model pig" rolling across the assembly line in today's pork factories which do concern the factory experts. Singer and Mason point out a few of these problems in *Animal Factories*.

> The pig breeders' emphasis on large litters and heavier bodies, coupled with a lack of attention to reproductive traits, has produced . . . high birth mortality in these pigs. These new, improved females produce such large litters that they can't take care of each piglet. To cure this problem, producers began to select sows with a greater number of nipples—only to discover that the extra nipples don't work because there's not enough mammary tissue to go around.[17]

Not to be dismayed, however, the genetic manipulators are continuing their efforts to "improve" the pig, and convert this good-natured and robust creature into a more efficient piece of factory equipment.

---

[13]Singer, P., *Animal Liberation,* Avon Books, 1975, pg 118.

[14]cited in Singer, P., *Animal Liberation,* Avon Books, 1975, pg 118.

[15]Ibid.

[16]Mason J., and Singer P., *Animal Factories,* Crown Publishers, 1980, pg 30–31, 42.

[17]Mason J., and Singer P., *Animal Factories,* Crown Publishers, 1980, pg 42.

Breeding experts are trying to create pigs that have flat rumps, level backs, even toes, and other features that hold up better under factory conditions.[18]

HORMONE CITY

What they can't accomplish with genetics, today's pork producers shoot for with hormones. Hormones, as you may know, are incredibly potent substances which are naturally secreted, in minute amounts, by the glands of all animals, pigs and humans included. It takes minuscule amounts of these substances to control our entire endocrine and reproductive systems. If our taste buds were as sensitive to flavor as our target cells are to hormones, we could detect a single grain of sugar in a swimming pool of water.[19]

Given the immensely powerful effects hormones have on animals reproductive systems, even in concentrations so low they are discernible only by the most sophisticated laboratory technology, many scientists are extremely concerned about their use in animal farming, acknowledging that we know very little about many of the potentially dangerous effects of these substances. The factory experts, however, look through very different eyes. When they first realized the new drugs gave them the power to control a sow's estrus, and thus to induce or delay her fertility, they were overjoyed.

> Estrus control will open the doors to factory hog production. Control of female cycles is the missing link to the assembly line approach.
> (FARM JOURNAL)[20]

One pork producer was so taken with this new development that he called it the "greatest advance in hog production since the development of antibiotics."[21] Another new innovation which has the industry astir is called embryo transfer.[22] Here a specially chosen sow is dosed with hormones to cause her to produce huge numbers of eggs, rather than the usual one or two. These eggs are fertilized by artificial insemination, then surgically removed from the sow and implanted in other females. It is not uncommon for a breeder sow to go repeatedly through this unnatural violation until the stress kills her.

At the University of Missouri, work is being done in test tubes to combine sperm and eggs which have been taken from specially selected breeding animals.[23] The newly fertilized eggs are then implanted surgically in ordinary females.

Once a sow in today's pork factories is pregnant, she is injected with progestins or steroids to increase the number of piglets in her litter. She will also be given

---

[18]Ibid, pgs 43–44.

[19]Schell, O., *Modern Meat,* Vintage Books, 1985, pg 186.

[20]Ainsworth, E., "Revolution in Livestock Breeding On the Way," *Farm Journal,* Jan 1976, pg 36.

[21]Messersmith, J., personal communication to author.

[22]Mason, J., and Singer P., *Animal Factories,* Crown Publishers, 1980, pg 45.

[23]"Scientist Studies 'Test Tube Pig,' " *Hog Farm Management,* April 1975, pg 61.

products like the new feed additive from Shell Oil Company. Called XLP-30, it is designed to "boost pigs per litter,"[24] though it has a name that makes it sound like it should be added to motor oil instead of animal food. Incredibly, a Shell official acknowledges—"we don't know why it works."[25] Undeterred by such ignorance, however, the industry is not at all reluctant to tamper with the reproductive systems of the animals whose flesh is designed for human consumption. Anything that can speed up the assembly line and improve profits is considered fair practice.

The Child and the Starfish

"Anonymous"

The sun had just come out after a three-day storm had raged along the Florida coastline. The little child ran anxiously down to the seashore and watched as dozens and dozens of starfish were drying up along the beach, having been flung there by the advancing tide. As the rough seas continued to dump more and more starfish upon the sand, the child, hoping to save as many of them as she could, ran up and down the beach flinging them back into the ocean. Up and down the beach she ran, picking up a starfish, throwing it back in the ocean, turning around, picking up another, throwing it back.

The little girl's grandfather, who had been watching her carry on like this for 10 or 15 minutes, shook his head, walked down to the beach and approached his granddaughter. She was still running up and down the beach throwing one starfish after another as far as she could back into the life-granting waters of the Atlantic. "Jamie," he called, "Jamie, what are you doing?" Jamie threw another starfish into the ocean as she turned around to face her grandfather. "Jamie, what are you up to?" he asked again. She picked up another starfish and threw it back into the ocean as far as she could, picked up yet another one and threw it, and picked up another one. Her grandfather walked up to her, looked down at her and asked, "Jamie, what are you doing here?" The little child, her lifesaving ritual interrupted, looked up at her grandfather with a starfish in her hand and a sparkle in her eye and said, "I'm saving the starfish, Grandpa!"

---

[24]"New Treatment Boosts Pigs Per Litter," *Farm Journal,* March 1976, pg Hog-2.

[25]Ibid.

Used with permission of Mark Maier, SUNY, Binghampton.

"But Jamie," he replied, "There are thousands and thousands of starfish here along the beach. You'll never be able to save them all. What makes you possibly think that you can make a difference?" The little child looked stunned for a moment. She looked up at her grandfather, then down at the starfish in her hand. A twinkle came to her eye as she closed her hand gently around the starfish and heaved it as far as she could, far out into the ocean.

Beaming, she looked up at him and replied, "It sure made a difference to that one."

Therapy for a Dying Planet

Terrance O'Connor

We are the cause, we are the cure

There is a story, perhaps apocryphal, about an incident which occurred in Frieda Fromm-Reichmann's practice shortly before she left Germany for the United States. A young woman with numerous irrational fears came to her for help. During the course of the psychoanalysis, the patient gradually overcame her fears, and after three years the therapy was successfully ended. A few weeks later the young woman, who was Jewish, was picked up by the Gestapo and sent to a concentration camp.

By helping people adjust to a destructive society, are we doing more harm than good? Today, as desert sands advance across Africa like conquering armies, and life is on the retreat in every continent, it occurs to me that the sad tale of Frieda Fromm-Reichmann's client is more relevant than ever.

We sit in our offices helping parents raise children, divorcees get their bearings, couples find ways to deepen their relationships, while outside the air gets fouler and the oceans rise. In a year's time, if we are successful, the parents and children are doing well, the divorcee is enjoying her independence, the couple has

"Therapy for a Dying Planet" by Terrance O'Connor. Reprinted with permission from *Family Therapy Network*, September/October 1989. Subscription from Subscription Services, 9528 Bradford Road, Silver Spring, Maryland 20901.

developed a more satisfying relationship. Meanwhile the air is fouler, the oceans higher, and hundreds, perhaps thousands of species, have vanished forever from this earth. Each hour five square miles of rain forest are destroyed. By the end of a year, this area of destruction is the size of Pennsylvania.

We are facing an unparalleled global crisis, a disaster much greater than Hitler or Stalin or the Khmer Rouge could ever create. What is the meaning of therapy and what is the responsibility of the therapist in such a world?

A few years ago I was giving a talk on "The Mature and Healthy Intimate Relationship" to a group of divorced people. Midway through the talk a woman asked, "Last week we had a speaker who said that some people are satisfied with very limited relationships. So why should we want this mature relationship? Why should we bother?" The question caught me off guard. "I don't know," I admitted. "I would think that the benefits would speak for themselves. But obviously everyone has a choice."

I went on with my presentation, but her question kept nagging me until eventually I lost all concentration and came to a halt. "I need to stop here and go back to the question I was just asked," I finally said. "Let me say something about the status quo. Status quo is that the hole in the ozone layer is as big as the United States. Status quo is that some scientists are predicting that by the middle of the next century global warming will result in most of the coastal cities in the U.S. being below sea level and will make the grainbelt a wasteland. Status quo is that acid rain, besides destroying the lakes and forests, is now considered to be the leading cause of lung cancer after cigarette smoke. Status quo is that 35,000 people die of starvation every day. Also every day, two or more species become extinct, not due to natural selection but due to deforestation and pollution. By the year 2000— that's only 11 years from now—this is expected to accelerate to 100 species a day. In other words, mass extinction. What does this say to you? To me it says that the status quo is that the planet is dying! The planet is dying because we are satisfied with our limited relationships in which control, denial, and abuse are tolerated. The status quo is that we have these petty relationships with each other, between nations, with ourselves and the natural world. Why should we bother? Because healthy relationships are not an esoteric goal. It is a matter of our very survival and the survival of most of the life upon this earth."

After this outburst I stood silently facing an apparently stunned audience staring back at me. I was trying to remember where I had been in my presentation when a man in the back stood up and began talking about the destruction of the rain forests. The whole feeling in the room had shifted. The greater part of the audience had come in concerned with their own loneliness. As we began to look at all of our personal concerns from a global perspective, we could see that the patterns of control, denial, and projection which sabotage intimate relationships are the very patterns which endanger the world. To change these patterns is to change not just our social lives but our relationship to the planet.

In *The Unheard Cry for Meaning*, Viktor Frankl says that in finding meaning we are "perceiving a possibility embedded in reality," and that, "unless we use the opportunity to fulfill the meaning inherent and dormant in a situation, it will pass and be gone forever." Citing his own experience as an inmate in Auschwitz and

Dachau, and his work with POWs, he asserts that the will to meaning has survival value; that those most likely to survive were those who were oriented toward something outside themselves, a meaning to be fulfilled: "In a word, existence was dependent on 'self-transcendence.' " And so it is today. A transcendence of sorts is necessary if we are to meet the challenge of the global crisis, a transcendence of who we are in relationship with the human community and to the planet. Another way of saying this is that it is time for a shift in context. As Watzlawick et al. say in *Pragmatics of Human Communication,* ". . . a phenomenon remains unexplainable as long as the range of observation is not wide enough to include the context in which the phenomenon occurs."

We took a powerful leap when we widened our view of the individual's problems to include the family system in which they occurred. Perhaps it is time for another leap. It is time to begin to go beyond our individual families to attend to the Family of Man.

Of the 35,000 people who die of starvation each day, the large majority are children. Whose children are these? If we are the Family of Man, these are our children. Pure and simple. Tens of thousands of our children starve to death each day, not because there is not enough food to feed each and every one of them but because we are a dysfunctional family. Look at us! We are at once overcontrolling and dreadfully neglectful. And, like the alcoholic family, we ignore the bodies piling up in our living room; and we ignore them at our growing peril.

As the problems become more evident I am getting a more receptive response when I talk or write about the global crisis. Still, avoidance reactions are common. Most boil down to, "I don't want to hear about it," or "It's not my responsibility." Some people convince themselves that "It's not happening," and "It's not my planet." Some even mask their despair in a quasi-spiritual facade of nonattachment, "What the hell, it's only one planet. There are billions." More common are those who will admit to feeling a bit guilty about not doing anything. The equation here is, doing nothing plus feeling guilty about it equals doing something.

Action is called for, but action motivated by guilt may only compound the problem. We are in disharmony with the world because we are in disharmony with ourselves. Guilt is an indication of this. Guilt is a warning that there is an incongruity in our value system, a schism in our sense of self that needs to be investigated. If we act without introspection, we simply throw our weight to one side of the inner conflict, increasing the disharmony. Our actions will be incomplete and fragmented. We will make some token move and fall back into denial and minimization. To heal is to make whole.

A few years ago I spent some time alone in an isolated cabin far from a road, without water or electricity. I hiked in with a stack of books. For a week I sat on the porch of that cabin and watched the black snake lying in the rafters, the chipmunks scurrying between rocks, and listened to the song of the wind through the trees. I read about the state of the world. I cried. It was like reading the minute details of one's mother's cancer. When I had enough of reading and crying I went for long hikes. I followed a magnificent stream. The woods were lovely. I saw deer and grouse and wild turkey and once, I think, a coyote. I came back to the porch and read some more, and sometimes I cried, and sometimes I raged, and sometimes I looked up at the ancient stones and beautiful trees and the abundance of life around me and I loved it so fiercely I thought my heart would burst.

If this is not my planet, whose is it? If this is not my family, whose is it? If not my responsibility, whose? I am both the victim and the victimizer. I am the cause, and I am the cure. When I act out of this realization, I act not out of guilt but out of self-love, a love which includes my family, a self which includes my planet. When I look, I see. When I educate myself, I break through my denial and see that mankind is facing an absolutely unprecedented crisis. When I act from this knowledge, I act not out of obligation or idealism, but because I live in a straw house and I smell smoke. I realize the truth that, in Krishnamurti's words, "You are the world, and the world is on fire."

An awareness is dawning, and a shift is occurring. In the face of the darkening clouds there has been some very positive movement around the globe. The lessening of tensions between East and West is the absolutely necessary beginning to saving the world. We all know that if Mom and Dad can get together, the rest becomes workable. If the U.S.S.R. and the U.S. can continue to build trust, we can liberate enormous energies in the forms of money, natural resources, technology, intelligence, and manpower to meet the common threat. And in our own backyards a revolution is taking place, a powerful grass-roots movement. I am referring to the astounding proliferation of 12-step groups in the past few years.

While there are many healing aspects to the 12-step groups, two interest me here. The first is the philosophy of giving up the attempt to control that over which one has no control. Ultimately this seems to me to be blowing the whistle on our hubris, our worship of that will which has allowed us to gain dominion over the world. This is the will with which spouses try to dominate each other, and with which our clients struggle to get control over, rather than find harmony with, themselves and the world. This will is a useful tool, but it is a jealous and petty god. The second quality of these programs which gives me hope is their emphasis on responsibility for oneself and to each other. There is a recognition that we are all in this together.

As therapists we have learned some unforgettable lessons about our limits, but we have also witnessed the wondrous unfolding of human potential. We know better than most that reality is dependent upon our perception of it, and that a simple change in our point of view can yield a host of new possibilities. So how does an awareness of the global crisis translate to specific behaviors in our offices? In my waiting room I have a shelf stacked with literature from environmental organizations. Above the shelf is a photograph of the earth taken from space. Above the photograph is a sign which reads, "Mother Earth Needs You." Beside the photograph is a brief synopsis of the dangers and opportunities of the global crisis. Some of my clients are suffering from personal crises of such intensity that they are unable to focus on anything else. For them, my "Opportunity Corner" has little interest. But overshadowing many of my client's genuine issues is the general malaise which President Carter was so impolite to refer to a decade ago in a speech to a nation yearning to escape to the good old days. To these clients I mention the global crisis like I might tell an Ericksonian story or an incident from my own life. I bring it in intentionally when it is relevant and therapeutic.

Clients struggling with the purpose and meaning of their lives are often doing so in obsessive isolation from the movement of life around them. They are attempting to achieve a goal such as marriage without first being in relationship with themselves and the human community. Coming to grips with the global crisis offers both a deeper understanding of the human condition and a motivation to break down the psychological barriers which allow us to tolerate our starving children and rising oceans. I have even, upon occasion, interrupted a client's obsessive, self-absorbed soliloquy with, "Are you aware that the planet is dying?" I might interrupt a professional debate on the best therapeutic modality with the same question.

I am not suggesting that we drop our therapeutic tools, but that we use them with awareness of a rapidly and profoundly changing planet. Perhaps Frieda Fromm-Reichmann should have simply advised her patient to flee. We do not have that option. When I speak of global consciousness, I am taking a perspective in which the difference between client and therapist is only a difference of role. We are equally responsible for the state of the planet and equally affected by it. I must say that I do not see my colleagues being much more free of the malaise and denial than are my clients. Isn't it strange that we supposed experts and healers of human relations give but passing notice to our extraordinarily unhealthy relationship to the planet as a whole; a relationship which will ultimately undermine our work completely? We must become more aware and contribute that awareness rather than our denial to the stream of human consciousness. An active membership in just one environmental group puts one in the pipeline to receive all the information and direction one needs. We must become part of the solution rather than part of the problem. What is the responsibility of a therapist on a dying planet? Physician, heal thyself.

Epilogue

We call this an epilogue only because it comes at the end of the book. We intend it, however, as a prologue to the reader's own independent consideration of the realities of organizations.

In retrospect, the origins of this book and our decisions about what to include in it were guided by an underlying perspective or an unconscious spirit that the three of us shared initially and developed as we worked. This perspective or spirit continues to shape how we deal with organizations—both personally and professionally. Before concluding, we want to make this perspective or spirit explicit and invite our readers to make it an active part of the way they approach organizations.

Behavioral scientists view organizations as open social systems. Some emphasize that organizations are different from other social systems because they are deliberately constructed to achieve some purpose(s). Our perspective stresses an additional descriptor—that organizations are *human* systems.

While seemingly trite, the emphasis added by the label *human* is important because it stimulates us to expect and to take seriously the full range of human motives and experiences that exist in organizations. Recognition that organizations contain and express all aspects of humanness has several consequences.

First, we see how incomplete any one intellectual perspective will be as a guide to understanding organizations.

Second, we come to see the importance of the trivial. The contemporary state of any human system is the product of many small events—the failure to tell Sally Quinn what the red light on the TV camera meant and Anita Roddick's concern with words and spilled coffee are but two examples included in this book to show how important the seemingly trivial can be. Exactly how can we be sensitive to and manage the trivial without becoming obsessed and dominated by it? This is a key question for managers that is seldom accorded the attention it deserves either in business schools or elsewhere.

Third, the emphasis on fully human systems sensitizes us to the continuity between life in organizations and life. Just as life contains tragedy and comedy, love and hate, war and peace, and reason and emotion, so do most organizations. An adequate understanding of organizations means understanding this complexity. Further, to accomplish what we want to in and through organizations, we must be prepared to control and/or to navigate through or around these human processes.

Finally, and most important, recognition of the fully human nature of organizations makes learning about them a continuous process. In this light are formed additional chapters of *Organizational Reality:* from movies, plays, and other artistic expressions; from newspapers and magazine articles; from our contacts with other people; and, of course, from the daily experiences that all of us have as members of organizations.